Psychobiology of the
Human Newborn

WILEY SERIES IN DEVELOPMENTAL PSYCHOLOGY

Series Editor
Professor Kevin Connolly

The Development of Movement Control and Co-ordination
edited by J. A. Scott Kelso and Jane E. Clark

Psychobiology of the Human Newborn
edited by Peter Stratton

Further titles in preparation

Psychobiology of the Human Newborn

Edited by

Peter Stratton
Department of Psychology
University of Leeds

1807 1982

JOHN WILEY & SONS LTD

Chichester · New York · Brisbane · Toronto · Singapore

Library of Congress Cataloging in Publication Data:

Main entry under title:

Psychobiology of the human newborn.

  (Developmental psychology series)
  Includes Index.
  1. Infant psychology. 2. Infants (Newborn)
3. Psychobiology. I Stratton, Peter. II. Series:
Developmental psychology. [DNLM: 1. Infant,
Newborn—Psychology. 2. Neonatology. WS 420 P974]
BF719.P78 1982   618.92′01′019 81-14756

ISBN 0 471 10093 5 (U.S.)   AACR2

British Library Cataloguing in Publication Data:

Psychobiology of the human newborn.—(Developmental psychology series)
  1. Infants (New-born)—Psychological aspects
  2. Developmental psychobiology
  I. Stratton, Peter II. Series
  155.4′22   BF723.16

ISBN 0 471 10093 5

Photosetting by Thomson Press (India) Limited, New Delhi
Printed in the United States of America

Contributors

AMIEL-TISON, CLAUDINE, *Associate Professor at the University of Paris $\bar{V}$, Port-Royal Maternity Hospital, Paris 75674 Cedex 14, France.*

ATKINSON, JANETTE, *Senior Research Associate at the University of Cambridge, Kenneth Craik Laboratory, Downing Street, Cambridge, CB2 3EB, England.*

BARRETT, JOHN, *Lecturer in Psychology at the University of Bristol, Department of Psychology, Berkeley Square, Bristol, BS8 1HH, England.*

BRADDICK, OLIVER, *University Lecturer in Experimental Psychology at the University of Cambridge, Kenneth Craik Laboratory, Downing Street, Cambridge, CB2 3EB, England.*

BRONSON, GORDON, *Professor of Psychology at the Department of Psychology, Mills College, Oakland, California 94613, U.S.A.*

CHISWICK, MALCOLM, *Consultant-in-Charge, Special Care Baby Unit and Regional Neonatal Intensive Care Unit, St. Mary's Hospital, Whitworth Park, Manchester, M13 OJH, England.*

CROW, ROSEMARY, *Director, Northwick Park Nursing Research Unit, Harrow, Middlesex, England.*

LIPSITT, LEWIS, *Professor of Psychology and Medical Science and Director of Child Study Centre, Walter S. Hunter Laboratory of Psychology, Brown University, Providence, Rhode Island 02912, U.S.A.*

OAKLEY, ANN, *Wellcome Research Fellow, Neonatal Perinatal Epidemiology Unit, Radcliffe Infirmary, Oxford, OX2 6HE, England.*

O'BRIEN, MICHAEL JOHN, *Neonatal Pediatrician, Department of Developmental Neurology, University Hospital, Groningen, The Netherlands.*

PAPOUŠEK, HANUŠ, *Professor of Developmental Psychobiology, Max-Planck-Institute for Psychiatry, Kraeplinstrasse 10, 8000 Munchen 40, West Germany.*

PAPOUŠEK, MECHTHILD, *Professor Research Psychiatrist and Neurologist in Developmental Psychobiology, Max-Planck-Institute for Psychiatry, Kraeplinstrasse 10, 8000 Munchen 40, West Germany.*

PRECHTL, HEINZ, *Professor and Chairman of the Department of Developmental Neurology, University Hospital, Groningen, The Netherlands.*

ROVEE-COLLIER, CAROLYN, *Professor of Psychology at Rutgers University, New Brunswick, New Jersey 08903, U.S.A.*

STRATTON, PETER, *Senior Lecturer in Developmental Psychology at the University of Leeds, Department of Psychology, Leeds LS2 9JT, England.*

WRIGHT, PETER, *Lecturer in Psychology at the University of Edinburgh, Department of Psychology, 7, George Square, Edinburgh, Scotland.*

Contents

Foreward xiii

1. PETER STRATTON
Significance of the Psychobiology of the Human Newborn **1**
   Sources of significance of the neonatal period 4
   Adaptation and survival 5
   Continuity 5
   The Newborn as outcome 6
   Value of the Newborn 7
   Adaptation 8
   Transactions 11
   Perspectives needed for the study and treatment of newborns 12

SECTION 1   ASSESSMENT   17

2. HEINZ F. R. PRECHTL
Assessment Methods for the Newborn Infant, A Critical Evaluation . **21**
   The identification of risk factors. 22
   (a) Obstetrical complications. 22
   (b) The optimality concept. 24
   (c) Limitations of the at-risk concept 27
   The neurological assessment of the newborn infant. 28
   (a) The need for a concept of the nervous system. 28
   (b) The objective of neonatal neurological assessment 30
   (c) Essentials of design. 31
   (d) A comparison between the different methods 34
   The behavioural assessment 39
   Concluding remarks 46

3. HEINZ F. R. PRECHTL and MICHAEL JOHN O'BRIEN
Behavioural States of the Full-term Newborn
The Emergence of a Concept **53**

Why behavioural states?   53
What are behavioural states?   54
Essential characteristics of states   56
The systematic study of behavioural states   57
   (a) Naturalistic observations   57
   (b) Polygraphic investigations   58
   (c) Studies on the input-output-state relation   60
The choice of variables as state indicators   62
State classifications and their nomenclature.   66
Concluding remarks   69

4. C. AMIEL-TISON
   Neurological Signs, Aetiology, and Implications **75**
   Pathophysiologic considerations   76
   Cerebral symptoms   77
      Generalized hypotonia   78
      Hypertonia in neck extensors   78
   Diagnostic procedures   78
   Specific types of brain damage   80
   Follow-up studies: Methodological approach   84
   Follow-up studies: Results at school age   88
      (a) Preliminary remarks   88
      (b) Relative position of perinatal risk   88
      (c) Categories of perinatal risk   89
   Summary and practical conclusions ·   90
      (a) Who to include in follow-up studies?   90
      (b) Summary of perinatal risk according to gestational age and
        birth weight   92

SECTION II   CAPACITIES AND CHARACTERISTICS   95

5. GORDON W. BRONSON
   Structure, Status and Characteristics of the Nervous System at Birth   **99**
   The organization of the brain: An evolutionary perspective   100
   Indices of developmental status   101
      Patterns of myelinization   102
      Histological developments within the neocortex   104
      The growth of evoked potentials   105
      Summary of patterns of neural growth   108
   The mediational basis of infant behaviours   108
   The contribution of early sensory experience   112
   Summary   114

6. Peter Stratton

Rhythmic Functions in the Newborn **119**
When is a repetitive function a rhythm? 120
Pendulum versus relaxation 122
Brain rhythms. 125
Cardiac and respiratory function. 126
Vocal and oral rhythms. 127
    Crying 128
    Sucking. 128
Spontaneous behaviours 131
State cycles 133
Circadian rhythms 137
Rhythmic Input 140
Conclusions 141

7. Carolyn K. Rovee-Collier and Lewis P. Lipsitt

Learning, Adaptation and Memory in the Newborn **147**
The newborn as a biological organism. 148
Newborn learning. 149
    Habituation and conditionability 150
    Classical conditioning 152
    Hybrid conditioning procedures and instrumental learning. 164
Memory in the neonatal period 170
Clinical implications of reflexive transitions: Crib death 172
Final comment 177

8. Janette Atkinson and Oliver Braddick

Sensory and Perceptual Capacities of the Neonate **191**
Methods of studying sensory processes in the neonate 192
Visual acuity and contrast sensitivity of the neonate 194
The development of the visual pathway at birth. 196
Refraction and accommodation of the neonatal eye 197
Functional implications of infants' spatial vision 199
Eye movements. 199
Binocular function 200
Distance and depth perception. 201
Visual fields and the capture of visual attention 202
Colour vision. 203
Sensitivity to flicker and motion. 203
Pattern processing and preferences 204
The externality effect. 206
Visual development immediately following the neonatal period 207
Auditory sensitivity of the neonate. 208

Auditory localization 210
The chemical senses 210
Intermodel and sensory-motor correspondences. 212

9. PETER STRATTON
   Newborn Individuality **221**
   Criteria for significance of individual differences 223
   Group differences 226
   Oral and vocal 227
   Food intake 228
   Non-nutritive oral behaviour. 229
   Vocalization 230
   Cognitive processes 231
   Sensory function 231
   Perceptual functioning 234
   Learning and adaptation. 235
   Psychophysiology 237
   Autonomic nervous system functions 238
   Activation 240
   Spontaneous activity 241
   Irritability 242
   Soothability 243
   State 244
   Somatic 245
   Appearance. 246
   Size. 246
   Strength 247
   Maturity 248
   Higher order 250
   Psychobiological integrity. 250
   Interaction style 250
   Conclusion 251

SECTION III   INFLUENCES   263

10. JOHN H. W. BARRETT
    Prenatal Influences on Adaptation in the Newborn **267**
    An overview of the research 268
    Some problems of interpretation. 270
    Adaptation in fetus and newborn 272
    Some underlying processes. 277
    Interaction and nutrition. 280
    Preconception and transgenerational influences 284

11. ANN OAKLEY
   Obstetric Practice—Cross-Cultural comparisons **297**
   The social context and location of childbirth 299
   Delivery personnel 300
   The management of labour and delivery. 302
   The treatment of the baby after birth 304
   The social status of the neonate 307
   Conclusion 309

12. MALCOLM L. CHISWICK
   The Newborn Baby—Adaptation and Disease **315**
   Birth and adaptation 315
   Diseases of the newborn 317
   Low birthweight babies. 318
   Prematurity. 318
      Respiratory distress syndrome. 319
      Recurrent apnoeic attacks. 323
      Thermal homeostasis. 324
      Feeding problems 324
      Infection 325
      Jaundice 325
      Intracranial haemorrhage 327
   Light for dates babies 327
      Fetal hypoxia and delayed onset of breathing 330
      Other problems in LFD babies 331
   Congenital abnormalities. 332

13. PETER WRIGHT and ROSEMARY CROW
   Nutrition and Feeding **339**
   Development in the ability to recognise hunger and appetite 341
      Signals for hunger 343
      Hunger and crying. 346
      Expression of satiety. 347
   Patterns of milk intake in breast and bottle fed infants 349
      Introduction of solids 356
      Early infant feeding and rapid weight gain 358

   SECTION IV   IMPLICATIONS   365

14. HANUŠ PAPOUŠEK and MECHTHILD PAPOUŠEK
   Integration into the Social World: Survey of Research **367**
   Early integrative capacities: To know means almost everything 369
   Social integration: The neglected parent 374
   Didactic programmes for the newborn: intuitive parenting in
   dyadic interchanges. 379

15. PETER STRATTON
   Emerging Themes of Neonatal Psychobiology **391**
   Reflections from infancy 392
   Evolution 394
   Transition 396
   Early generality 397
   The fail-safe nature of neonatal adaptation 397
   The need for challenge 399
   Dismissive labelling 400
   Transactional adaptation revisited 402
   The flow of information and influence 404
      Newborn to mother 404
      Mother to newborn 407
      Newborn to institution 407
      Institution to newborn 409
      Mother to institution 409
      Institution to mother 411
   Conclusion 412

   Author Index **415**
   Subject Index **433**

Foreword

This series is aimed at treating issues in developmental psychology which have not already been adequately dealt with in book form in recent years. The newborn is a perfect example. Many psychologists and paediatricians have in the past perceived the newborn as a rather primitive creature; helpless and for the most part uninteresting, a mere reactor to the stimuli which impinge upon him. The newborn was not thought to possess any of the sensitive means available to his elders for effecting transaction with the environment and until relatively recently emphasis was placed upon cataloguing his limitations. But are these images correct? Do they accord with what we know of the competence of babies?

Beginning in the late 1950s there occurred what can only be described as an explosion of interest in the newborn and how his behavioural repertoire was employed in adapting to the marked discontinuities following birth. In what is perhaps the most famous quotation in developmental psychology, william James (1890) suggested, 'The baby, assailed by eyes, ears, nose, skin and entrails at once feels that all is one great blooming, buzzing confusion.' Over the last 20 years much has been learned about the capacities of the neonate and such a view is no longer tenable. Yet another dichotomy, that between a predetermined model of the child's development and the view of the child's mind as a *tabula rasa* has been shown to be seriously misleading. As the result of careful observations and ingenious experiments we now know that the newborn has extensive sensory and perceptual capabilities, that he can and does learn, that he is socially sensitive and active, and that far from being all alike babies show great individuality.

This book makes no pretence at a comprehensive review of the huge amount of material which has been published on the newborn. The ideas and material dealt with here provide what the editor describes as emerging themes, the beginnings of an organized and coherent body of knowledge. This knowledge is not yet a conclusive set of answers to sharply focussed questions, indeed what sometimes emerges is a clear realization that our implicit and explicit theories are inadequate, but we now have in outline form a framework within which to analyse and consider the newborn's behaviour. This book is likely to play an important role in shaping future work and ensuring that, as Browning put it, 'The best is yet to be.'

Kevin Connolly

Psychobiology of the Human Newborn
Edited by P. Stratton
© 1982, John Wiley & Sons, Ltd.

CHAPTER 1

Significance of the Psychobiology of the Human Newborn

PETER STRATTON

The last two decades have witnessed an explosion of research with the human newborn. Even halfway through this period Kessen *et al.* (1970) found that a review of early infancy with over 2000 references could not be comprehensive, but offered 'a strange mixture of false starts, wise guesses, tedious documentation, clever design, and a few insights that hold hope' (p. 360). Ten years on I believe that instead of being swamped by an unassimilable mass of data, we have reached a situation in which a much more productive use of the material is possible. The raw material derived from experimental studies in the sixties has become the basis for a much more coherent understanding of many aspects of the newborn which has in turn provided a context in which the knowledge can be evaluated. This book does not aspire to comprehensively review all that is known, believed, or suspected about the neonate. Rather it is intended to selectively encompass all of the most important areas of knowledge about the capabilities, characteristics and functioning of newborns, of the range of environments, influences and insults to which they may be exposed, and of the techniques currently available for studying these. The purpose of this introductory chapter is to formulate a general view of the newborn baby in relation to his/her world which will indicate the overall basis by which the different aspects of neonatal study were marked out as significant. A more detailed consideration of the criteria to be applied in particular areas is provided, where appropriate, in the individual chapters.

Early psychobiologists had low expectations of the newborn so that, for example, Gesell (1940) started his discussion of the first 5 years of life with the comment: 'Of all infants, the human infant is at birth the most helpless. In a sense, he is not fully born until he is about 4 weeks of age.' (p. 18). It is the first 4 weeks of life with which this book is concerned, but the newborn, although dependent, is far from helpless. An appreciation of the immaturity of the central

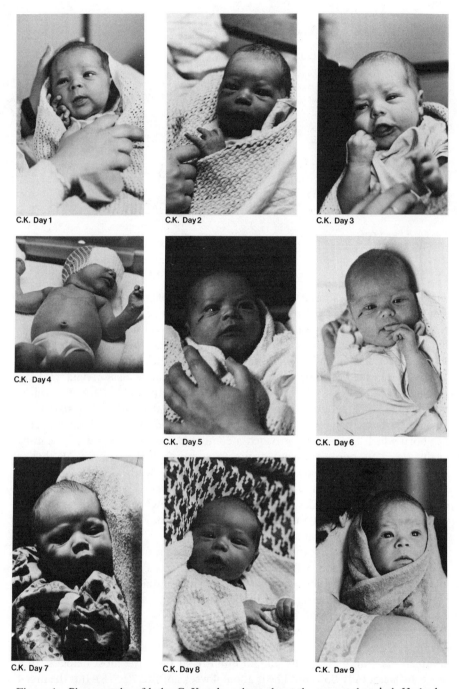

Figure 1 Photographs of baby C. K. taken throughout the neonatal period. He had a difficult birth and was treated for jaundice with phototherapy throughout his fourth day. The sequence of pictures gives a clear impression of individuality, of a rich variety of expression, and of substantial development over the 28 days

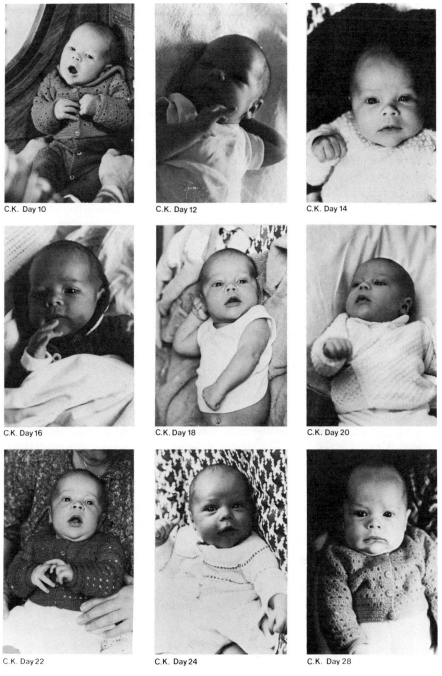

C.K. Day 10

C.K. Day 12

C.K. Day 14

C.K. Day 16

C.K. Day 18

C.K. Day 20

C.K. Day 22

C.K. Day 24

C.K. Day 28

I would like to thank Sue Kilroe and Mike Fisher for providing the photographs of Conor which are printed here and on the cover

nervous system at birth has frequently mislead researchers, medical workers, and even parents into not expecting, and therefore not perceiving, the sophistication of neonatal functioning.

This book contains plenty of examples of performance at a level which had previously been thought to be impossible. However, as a less formal exercise I would invite the reader to study the photographs of Figure 1. These show the same baby, usually in the state of alert-inactivity, over the period from the first to the twenty-eighth day. Bear in mind the cultural stereotypes which still see the newborn as relatively inert, unstructured and characterless, and the neonatal period as being marked more by settling down than by growth and development. Only 20 years ago Bridger (1961) could say 'all previous literature state rather unequivocably that babies do not show sensory discrimination in any modality'. (p. 991). Even one of the best of the current books for parents states that the newborn 'has no established patterns of behaviour . . . he is recovering from the birth experience, getting himself moving into life. So in these first weeks the mother cannot "know" him. He has not yet got himself into predictable, knowable shape.' (Leach, 1974; p. 24). The baby in Figure 1 had a difficult delivery, with high forceps, following a prolonged labour, induced over 22 h with syntocin. He is quite clearly a unique individual, engaged with his world, and undergoing significant development within the 4 weeks. The impressions that it is possible to gain from these pictures are very different from the expectations which have been derived from speculations about the limitations imposed by an immature nervous system. I would suggest that, adultopromorphic as such impressions undoubtedly are, they provide a more realistic set with which to approach the accumulating evidence of neonatal competence.

With growing evidence of the high level of functional adaptedness of the newborn, many of the optimistic claims of earlier workers have been vindicated. Neonatal research has proved not only to have been one of the most productive and stimulating areas of developmental psychobiology, it has also provided a basis for opening up previously intractable areas of infancy. This has come about partly through neonate researchers of the sixties extending their interests into infancy, and partly from an application of paradigms, techniques and insights derived from the intensive studies of newborns to older subjects. A reading of recent surveys of infancy (Osofsky, 1979; Shaffer and Dunn, 1979) indicates how dominant the neonatal work still is. However, not all of the early hopes were fulfilled and it is illuminating to review the major reasons for regarding neonatal studies as particularly worthwhile.

SOURCES OF SIGNIFICANCE OF THE NEONATAL PERIOD

The significance attributed to neonatal functioning can be examined under four headings, dealing with:

1. The immediate psychobiological demands of the period and the factors that influence the newborn's adaptation and survival.
2. The implications that recorded characteristics of the newborn, or events in the first month, may have for future functioning; the issue of continuity.
3. The extent to which the characteristics and deficits of newborns reflect previous influences. Although usually regarded as a beginning, the newborn also represents the outcome of a history which extends back through gestation to previous generations.
4. An interest in and concern for the newborn as such. I will suggest that the perspective which sees babies as merely potential adults is misleading and fails to recognize the intrinsic value of the newborn.

Adaptation and Survival

The neonatal period is one of immense biological vulnerability and, unlike the earlier phases of high risk, one in which a successful outcome depends largely on appropriate adaptive reactions on the part of the baby. Much of the content of this book testifies to the range of predispositions, structural and behavioural characteristics and adaptive capacities which come to fruition in time to maximize the individual's chances of survival. The converse is also important: any feature of the newborn must be studied in the context of its significance for survival and growth. The relationship is not always apparent as we do not yet understand all of the demands that are made on the newborn, and there is a further limitation in our knowledge. We have very inadequate models for predicting the effect on an individual's resources and resilience of having had to make particular adaptations. The study of 'transitions' has become a major concern of life-span developmental psychology. A transition is any change in the biosocial status of the individual, and we know that such changes invariably involve a cost in terms of increased vulnerability (Adams *et al.*, 1976). The changes required by birth and the first few days of extra-uterine existence must represent the most extreme transition in the life-cycle, so the precise forms of demands on the neonate for adaptation, and the consequences of the baby's reaction to these demands, are major concerns in every area of neonatal study.

Continuity

If there is an equivalent of the philosophers stone in developmental psychology it must be an early measure that will predict mature functioning. It has been shown (Kopp and Parmelee, 1979; Stratton, 1977) that even gross insults such as anoxia and pre-term birth have no consistent long-term consequences unless they are extreme enough to be incapacitating. The issue of continuity, particularly in mental performance, is discussed in detail by various authors in Osofsky's *Handbook of Infant Development* (1979, see Chapters 1, 2, 4, 5, 18–22), with the practically unanimous conclusion that there is almost no area in which worthwhile continuity from early infancy has been demonstrated. This cannot be explained simply in terms of the early instability of behaviour, as indicated by the growing realization of a lack of proven continuity throughout development. A very carefully designed prospective study of the relationship between childhood pathology and adult adjustment (Cass and Thomas, 1979) concluded that there was modest significance and minimal predictability. Meanwhile Clarke and Clarke (1976) have assembled an impressive case against the notion of consistency during development.

Despite all of this evidence the belief in consistency and continuity remains, with Lewis and Starr (1979) arguing that the continuous nature of development should be taken as a premise, not open to denial by fact. The argument concerning the absence of consistent long-terms effects of anoxia and pre-term birth was not that these are innocuous, but that if prediction from such gross influences is unreliable, then a failure of prediction cannot be taken as evidence against continuity in any area. Rather, it suggests that we are using models which do not have enough sophistication to match the complexities of the situation. Perhaps our mistake has been in hoping that once continuity had been established, it would tell us which aspects were most important. At an extreme this would entail an arbitrary selection of variables at two ages in the hope that some would correlate. We could then assume that the highest correlations picked out the measures which indicated the strongest influences. While the choice of variables has never been quite this arbitrary, neither has it usually been based in a detailed understanding of the ages concerned. In discussing the reasons for non-continuity in personality development. Freedman *et al.* (1967) point out that

each stage is usually negotiated by the organism in terms of the total situation, including a phylogenetically worked-out adaptation to that point in ontogeny, e.g. toddlerhood (etc.) . . . necessarily involve considerably different sets of evolved adaptations. (p. 475)

Rather than pursue continuity as the justification for developmental studies, this book accepts that a prior requirement is to achieve an adequate understanding of the adaptations and negotiations involved at each stage. The general features of adaptations and transactions which are basic to each of these 'sources of significance' are reviewed subsequently in this chapter while their detailed manifestations in the newborn form the underlying theme of the whole book. The issue of continuity will be deferred on the grounds that successful prediction must be based on detailed knowledge rather than hoping that we can assemble enough correlations across ages to eliminate the need for understanding.

The Newborn as Outcome

We are becoming increasingly (and in some cases, painfully) aware of the extent of prenatal and perinatal influence on the characteristics, functioning and viability of the newborn. This realization has been slow in coming and there are still many aspects of prenatal influence that are little understood. In part this must be attributed to the same difficulties that obscure continuities from the neonatal to later periods. Because we have such a limited appreciation of the more subtle aspects of the adaptations of the newborn, we are unlikely to identify all of the situations in which functioning is deficient. Nor are we in a position to identify and capitalize on particular strengths which individuals may have. In order to evaluate the effects of any but the grossest of influences, whether during gestation, birth, or arising from the ways we treat newborns, it is essential to have the most detailed understanding possible of neonatal functioning. In particular, because of the indirect paths that effects may take, this understanding must be as broad as current knowledge allows. The effects of phototherapy, for example, cannot be assessed purely in terms of bilirubin decomposition. The treatment involves separation from the mother, an abrupt change in the handling the baby receives, changes in feeding pattern (to replace fluid), and a disruption of visual sensation. There is also evidence that hormonal rhythms may be disturbed (Baum et al., 1977). This is not to suggest that phototherapy is unsafe, but that evaluation of even the most apparently benign of treatments requires an imaginative and informed consideration of the full range of neonatal functioning.

Value of the Newborn

When studying development there is a tendency to evaluate the immature organism entirely in terms of potential. On this view the characteristics of the newborn, and the effects of external influences, are significant in so far as they relate to later, ultimately adult, functioning. However, intensive study of the human neonate has generated another perspective. We now know that we are dealing with a highly complex being, superbly adapted to a very specific ecology and showing a range of sophisticated functioning that we may have only begun to explore. With such a realization comes a requirement that we should recognize the intrinsic value of the newborn and his/her right to appropriate treatment, a point made in some detail by Thoman (1978). The fact that the newborn is entitled to treatment appropriate to an independent, sensitive and cognitively aware being is easily forgotten from the adult perspective. Even Leboyer (1975) in considering obstetric procedures that could largely be described as simply treating the baby and mother nicely, felt it necessary to justify his proposals by claiming lifelong beneficial consequences.

The justification of studies of the newborn primarily by reference to their value in understanding, predicting and perhaps modifying the mature individual, not only undervalues the newborn, but may distort our understanding of neonatal processes. For a detailed review of such distortions the reader is referred to Oppenheim (1981). The general point he makes is that there are plenty of examples of ontogenetic adaptations which have no function outside of a brief stage of immaturity. An acceptance in practice that some functions serve their entire purpose at a particular time may save us from fruitless speculation. For example, there is no need to suppose that neonatal stepping and crawling reflexes must be the precursors of any future skills. They may exist purely to enable the fetus to adopt the vertex position before birth. From this perspective the first requirement is to account for the role that newborn characteristics and capabilities play in early adaptation. Only after this has been achieved is it worth trying to relate these adaptations to future functioning.

The problem in claiming rights for the newborn comes with the question 'rights to what?'. The answer depends on a judgement about how far the capacities and needs of the baby extend beyond basic physical requirements. Is it a positive experience for a baby at peace with his digestive system, to be securely and comfortably held while nuzzling into a warm breast? It may be the case that 'there are no emotions in the early weeks of life' (Sroufe, 1979; p. 471), but I believe there are experiences that can be valued in their own terms and without reference to any future consequences.

Whatever the source of interest in the newborn, it is confronted by the need to understand the adaptations demanded by the extra-uterine environment, how these demands are met, and how the longer-term implications of this dialectic are worked out. The chapters of this book all deal, from their different perspectives, with the issues of adaptation and of the significance of the neonatal period. To provide a common basis for these themes the next section considers the general characteristics of adaptation by the newborn. The subsequent section, 'Transactions', presents the theoretical framework which currently offers the best formulation of the process by which the characteristics of the individual newborn, and the characteristics of his/her environment mutually interact to produce a unique outcome.

ADAPTATION

All functioning in early infancy can be construed as an adaptation to the present conditions as they apply moment by moment. It is the psychobiological context that determines the future implications of the adaptation, while the history of the infant has had its effect in producing the individual's particular characteristics and tendencies which partake in the momentary adaptation. In considering the consequences of traumatic events, Stratton (1977) concluded that some kind of cost is always involved, but it may take the form of increased vulnerability and so will only appear as a deficit if the future environment makes demands of a kind that the infant is no longer capable of meeting. However, traumas are only one class of situations that demand an adaptation from the newborn and it is illuminating to consider the general principles involved.

An adaptation, by its nature, raises the probability of one class of events and therefore necessarily reduces the probability of others. This principle can be seen operating at various levels. A simple example is that a neonate experiencing a lowered body temperature, will metabolize brown fat to generate heat. The cost is in terms of an increased requirement for oxygen and calories (Chiswick, Chapter 12), which may normally be easily met, but which could reduce the viability of low weight or otherwise vulnerable babies. Crying increases the likelihood of an appropriate intervention by a caretaker but at the cost of energy expenditure. It seems likely that other functions, and possibly other costs, may be entailed by the sustained period of high activation involved in crying, but these have yet to be identified. Many adaptations clearly involve a balance between two or more costs. At the simple behavioural level, a strong nasal occlusion reflex reduces the risk of suffocation but if the threshold is too low it may be triggered by contact of the nose with the breast and so disrupt feeding (Gunther, 1961). A more complex case is the timing of birth which is subject to a variety of influences, each representing a potential risk or benefit.

It can be assumed that the natural timing of birth represents the optimal balance between the increasing risks and diminishing benefits of remaining in utero versus the changing dangers of birth and the demands of the extra-uterine environment. The system may not take perfectly accurate account of all of the relevant factors but more importantly, modern obstetric care has modified some of the risks in ways that are not yet represented in the biological system. Shortening of the gestation now carries very much less risk than during our past evolutionary history and so inducing an earlier birth may often be justified. However, it is important to remember that the procedures for inducing birth, and their consequences, are not fully understood, they do not clearly mimic the natural physiological processes (Chard, 1977), and we may be unaware of many factors which are taken into account in spontaneous parturition. This example makes it particularly clear that any intervention must take account of the widest possible definition of neonatal adaptation. It also indicates the value of investigating the adaptations made by newborns as an indicator of the demands made upon them in natural conditions, and as a means of identifying areas of potential risk particularly when significant changes are made in these conditions.

At the most abstract level is the degree of adaptability itself. A fixed genetic specification of any function has the advantage of a more or less guaranteed outcome with low variability, but with some corresponding loss of flexibility. The high degree of adaptability of the newborn, for which the contents of this book provide abundant evidence, is achieved by a dependence on an appropriate supportive environment. It may be supposed that environmental consistencies will have become exploited to foster particular outcomes with a minimum of genetic specification. Thus the characteristic position in which a baby must be held for breast feeding combines with a fixed focal length which corresponds with the distance from the mother's eyes, plus certain simple visual preferences, to give a high probability of sustained eye contact during feeding. The introduction of bottle feeding may have disrupted adaptations at all sorts of levels, but at present we are not even sure of all the consequences of differences in chemical composition between breast milk and formula. Weight gain and avoidance of infection are not the only criteria by which a feeding system should be judged, and before we introduce feeding by robots it would be desirable to try to ensure that all of the important functions of breast feeding (both for mother and baby) are known and can be substituted. This is not a fanciful assertion. The feeding of low-weight babies is being progressively improved by technological innovation but perhaps with an inadequate awareness of what the newborn normally gains by the process of adapting to the demands of breast feeding.

As a general principle it can be assumed that biologically specified adaptations operate in such a way as to optimize future functioning in the environment of evolutionary adaptedness. However, we have in many cases interfered either with the mechanisms of adaptation or with the contexts in which the consequences will be worked out. Also, for better or worse, we may interfere with processes because we evaluate outcomes according to criteria other than natural selection. This applies both when we save, through surgical intervention, a baby with congenital abnormalities that would otherwise have died; and when we artificially abort a deficient but viable fetus. The major consequence of our ability to modify the circumstances of fetus and newborn has been an enormous reduction in mortality and morbidity. In a slightly paradoxical sense it is the very improvements in outcome which have made an awareness of other consequences both possible and desirable.

When considering examples such as those described above it is apparent that any adaptation may have consequences which will depend not only on present, but also on future circumstances. In fact an adaptation which is damaging for a newborn entering one kind of environment may be harmless or even beneficial in other cases. Perhaps the clearest example in human development is the classic case of children who are subjected to multiple caretaking in infancy. Confronted with a situation in which the formation of attachments repeatedly leads to the trauma of having the bond abruptly broken, the child makes a highly adaptive adjustment of resisting any further deep relationships. The adjustment remains adaptive so long as the individual remains in an environment where the formation of attachment carries a high risk of traumatic disruption. Such children are called 'deprived' because they will in late adolescence be resistent to forming the deep attachment to a potential spouse which this society specifies as a universal norm. This example has been chosen because it exemplifies the important principles very clearly while comparable instances in the case of the newborn are less-well studied and are more appropriately illuminated by, rather than illuminating the principles of adaptation.

The implications of the 'maternal deprivation' example are, first, that the consequences of any trauma may not be identifiable as directly inflicted damage, but as the result of the attempts of the organism to adapt to the demands of the situation. Secondly, in the short term, the adaptation is likely to be the response best calculated to preserve the integrity of the individual. It is only with a longer term perspective, and often only with hindsight, that some adaptations can be seen to be maladaptive. The evaluation of any adaptation is dependent on a specification of the future environment in which the individual must function, and requires an understanding of the processes by which specific events may be related to later consequences.

TRANSACTIONS

From an analysis of the way that early influences are worked out during development it was concluded that the only model that could do justice to both the facts and the complexities was the transactional model (Stratton, 1977). This model, described in some detail by Sameroff and Chandler (1975), recognizes the extent to which the infant determines his/her own environment by modifying the behaviour of caregivers (Lewis and Rosenblum, 1974). The concept of adaptation is extended to include solutions which modify the environment and specific events are seen as having their major consequences when they set up self-perpetuating effects in the total infant-environment system. For example pre-term birth may produce a small weak newborn who, with adequate nutrition and an undemanding environment could develop comfortably within normal limits. However, while some mothers respond to weakly babies with excessive solicitude, others become impatient with the difficulties in feeding, provide less than adequate nutrition and so produce a miserable baby who will provide little rewarding social interaction. Even a single incident, like smothering at the breast during a feed, may set up a transactional chain as the baby will tend to fight the breast on subsequent feeds. If the mother responds with irritation and resentment her handling of the baby during feeding may be inappropriate, leading to further difficulties for the baby until both partners approach the feed with a tension which may interfere with the mother's milk production.

There is nothing inevitable about such chains and the sequence can be diverted at any point. It is therefore easy to see why a particular event may have no consistent predictable outcome and it is proposed that the transactional model applies very generally to all aspects of neonatal functioning. In some cases the chain may be somewhat obscure but the transactional process can still be seen operating. For example it is well known that the outcome from such insults as prematurity and obstetric toxaemia is closely related to social class. 'Children reared in a poor home environment will be the ones most likely to show significant long-term consequences of early birth trauma' (Stratton, 1977; p. 142). A refinement of this general statement is provided by Zeskind and Ramey (1978) who studied the mental development of full-term and full-birth-weight but fetally malnourished babies. All were in homes of low socio-economic status but one group was given intensive day care designed to support intellectual and social development. This group not only achieved normal mental development at 18 and 24 months, compared with depressed scores of the unstimulated control group. By 18 months they also received a significantly higher level of maternal involvement. It seems that fetal malnutrition results in early retardation (apparent in both groups at 3 months) which will be sustained in an unstimulating environment, eventually resulting in reduced maternal involvement which can be expected to reinforce the poor mental development. In a stimulating environment fetally malnourished infants do as well as equally stimulated normal infants and, apparently, significantly better than the normal but unstimulated group. For this to happen, the stimulation must have had a greater effect on the vulnerable group than on the intact babies.

The concept of transaction can also be usefully applied to the effect of an adaptation on different systems within the same individual. Re-working an example from the previous section in these terms: a lowered body temperature results metabolism of brown fat which means that subsequently, less of the food intake is available for building up body weight, which in turn leaves the baby more vulnerable to any future exposure to cold. From this example it can be seen that the idea of a transaction is a general statement of the mutual interdependence of different aspects of adaptation that is characteristic of any complex system, whether inter- or intra-individual.

PERSPECTIVES NEEDED FOR THE STUDY AND TREATMENT OF NEWBORNS

From the perspective outlined above it is possible to specify the background needed by anyone who wishes to understand any field of study of the human newborn within the whole context of the many, varied and interlocking aspects.

The first approach is to consider techniques for assessing newborns; the subject-matter of Section I. Standardized assessments represent the consolidation of considerable previous experience in the choice of items, the practicalities of testing and the findings from follow-up studies. Training in the administration of assessment scales is an effective means of gaining familiarity with the characteristic functioning of the newborn, and in many areas of study the refinements provided by detailed assessment are desirable in recruiting relatively homogeneous groups of subjects. Neurological assessments have a longer history than those dealing with behaviour, but both types must be regarded as being still at a relatively primitive stage. The major sources of complexity, arising from differences in functioning according to the changing state of the newborn (Chapter 3) and the variation in the effects of insult according to the stage of maturation of the nervous system (Chapter 4) are fully discussed. However, an intrinsic disadvantage of properly tested, standardized and validated assessment techniques is the time taken from inception to widespread availability. In a field advancing as rapidly as has the psychobiological study of the newborn over the past 10 years, the content of these scales is only a starting point for an appreciation of the range and complexity of postnatal functioning.

Our recognition of the sophistication of neonatal adaptation owes much to basic research which has demonstrated a surprising level of competence by the newborn. It would be dangerous to assume that all capacities develop in response to a demand for adaptation. However, it is a reasonable supposition, given the demonstrated economy and co-ordination of early maturational development, that the capabilities, characteristics and modes of functioning of the newborn result from a logic imposed by the requirements of human development within certain environmental constraints. Knowledge of the functioning of the normal newborn should provide useful clues to the demands to which our species has adapted though it is important to be aware that the use of a capacity will tend not to remain restricted to the function for which it was originally developed. So for example, our expanding (though far from complete), awareness of the learning capabilities of the newborn has made it possible to entertain the hypothesis that adaptive respiration is partly a learned skill (Chapter 7). Whatever were the original sources of this learning capacity, they can be presumed to have been operating early in our evolutionary history. The role of learning in such areas as infant-mother interaction might then be a consequence of the availability of the capacity rather than a source of it.

A general conclusion from our current knowledge of the newborn is the marked discrepancy between motor incompetence (excepting specialized systems such as sucking), and cognitive competence. Brazelton (1979) suggests that this frees the baby to acquire sensory and affective information and it certainly implies that adaptation to the physical and social environment is accomplished by a sophisticated cognitive system operating with minimal motor capability. Accordingly a major concern of Section II is to determine the range of cognitive capabilities of the newborn as a necessary first step towards understanding the adaptations to which they are disposed, and the roles they are capable of taking in transactions with the environment.

The influences to which newborns are subjected, and to which they must adapt, are surveyed in Section III. Demands to which the newborn must adapt fall under two headings. The first group are those which, by being clearly related to fundamental aspects of human structure or functioning, can be assumed to be part of our history as a species. Demands identified in this group will point to the existence of adaptations which are genetically based and universally available, though there is still likely to be individual variation in the effectiveness of adaptation. The second group of demands are those for which evolutionary adaptations have not been possible, due to their inconsistency or recency. Influences of this kind come from recently introduced practices (such as bottle feeding) and from the survival with modern obstetric care of babies that would in the past have certainly died. Such instances are particularly important because they include the possibility of adaptations which some babies may be unable to make, and of adaptations which leave the baby incapacitated or at least maladjusted for some future environment.

The final section considers the implications that emerge by combining the insights from the specific areas covered in the previous sections. The major area of current interest is the social context of neonatal functioning. Following a review of this topic, the final chapter attempts to survey the major themes which run through the varied subject matter and orientations of the chapters of this book. By making these themes explicit, a clearer conceptualization of neonatal psychobiology and its implications becomes possible.

The need for a clearer conception of neonatal adaptation can be illustrated by comparing two recent proposals for the care of low birth-weight babies. One suggestion has been that all babies below 2500 g should be kept in incubators and provided with minimal stimulation (Hughes-Davies, 1979). The regime, which is contrary to considerable evidence about the beneficial effects of early stimulation, was introduced on the basis of a clinical judgement that sick babies do not like being disturbed. The only outcome data quoted in support of the suggestion are favourable first-week mortality figures from a hospital in which this type of care was practised over a number of years. An alternative proposal (Davies et al., 1979) is that pre-term babies should be sent home as soon as they have passed the nadir of postnatal weight loss (provided they are clinically well and the home conditions are satisfactory). The criteria in this study were weight gain and readmission rates. Not surprisingly, with such insensitive measures applied to only twenty subjects in each group, no significant differences were found (readmission rates were zero for both groups). Despite their somewhat opposed recommendations, both of these studies exemplify the problems and requirements in using research to guide practice.

At its most concrete the point is that finding a measure on which the treated group does not differ from controls does not prove that the treatment had no effect. Nobody would expect reduced stimulation to prove fatal within a week, whereas it might be interesting to know the reactions of babies that had adjusted to this kind of regime, once they were confronted with a normal home environment. So outcome measures should be selected to be those which are most sensitive to the full range of possible effects. A prerequisite for identifying appropriate measures is an appreciation of all the various aspects of neonatal needs and functions. This book is an attempt to survey the many disparate areas of knowledge that are needed for such an appreciation and the use of 'Psychobiology' in the title is intended to indicate the wide range of content as well as the overall orientation.

Neither research nor practice is conducted on the basis of a random selection of variables for manipulation, but on an overall judgement of what is likely to be appropriate. Furthermore, individual research findings are markedly (and deservedly) ineffectual in persuading practitioners to modify their management of the newborn. The fact that the treatment of these most vulnerable and defenceless human beings is founded in an overall judgement of the likely consequences is entirely appropriate. However, it is my conviction that increasing specialization has narrowed the range of considerations within boundaries defined somewhat arbitrarily by the practitioner's particular basic discipline. Much of the content of this book pays tribute to the remarkable complexity and sophistication of the adaptations made by the newborn. In doing so it demonstrates how sensitive the adjustment to certain features of the postnatal environment has become and how interdependent are the different aspects of functioning. Returning to the examples of proposals for the management of low birth-weight babies, it is apparent that such changes in regime do not only affect the physical circumstances of the newborn. The demands made on caregivers, both professional and family, will be significantly altered and so will their attitudes towards the baby. These changes will in turn affect the treatment that the newborn receives, perhaps for a considerable time. The adaptations demanded of the newborn must be evaluated in all their aspects to ensure not only that they are within his or her capacity, but also to determine whether successful adaptation to the regime optimizes or disrupts functioning in subsequent environments.

In summary, any treatment of the newborn, whether applied for experimental or clinical purposes, should be evaluated in terms of the particular needs, characteristics and capacities of the baby, of the adaptations the treatment will elicit, and of the medical, biological, psychological and social environment in which the baby and the caregivers must function. I hope that this book will make it somewhat easier for the reader to take this broad perspective and, by putting our present knowledge into a coherent framework, will provide an improved foundation for future research and practice.

REFERENCES

Adams, J., Hayes, J., and Hopson, B. (1976). *Transition*. Robertson, London.

Baum, D., Macfarlane, A., and Tizard, P. (1977). The benefits and hazards of neonatology, in *Benefits and Hazards of the New Obstetrics* (Eds T. Chard and M. Richards), SIMP, London.

Brazelton, T. B. (1979). Behavioral competence of the newborn infant, *Seminars in Perinatology*, **3**, 35–44.

Bridger, W. H. (1961). Sensory habituation and discrimination in the human neonate, *American Journal of Psychiatry*, **117**, 991–996.

Cass, L. K. and Thomas, C. B. (1979). *Childhood Pathology and Later Adjustment: The Question of Prediction*. Wiley, New York.

Chard, T. (1977). The physiology of labour and its initiation, in *Benefits and Hazards of the New Obstetrics* (Eds T. Chard and M. Richards), SIMP, London.

Clarke, A. M. and Clarke, A. D. B. (1976). *Early Experience: Myth and Evidence*, Open Books, London.

Davies, D. P., Haxby, V., Herbert, T. S., and McNeish, A. S. (1979). When should pre-term babies be sent home from neonatal units? *Lancet*, **1**, 914–915.

Freedman, D. G., Loring, C. B., and Martin, R. M. (1967). Emotional behaviour and personality development, in *Infancy and Early Childhood* (Ed. Y. Brackbill), The Free Press, New York.

Gesell, A. L. (1940). *The First Five Years of Life*, Harper, New York.

Gunther, M. (1961). Infant behaviour at the breast, in *Determinants of Infant Behaviour*, Vol. 1 (Ed. B. M. Foss), Methuen, London.

Hughes-Davies, T. H. (1979). Conservative care of the newborn baby, *Archives of Disease in Childhood*, **54**, 59–61.

Kessen, W., Haith, M. M., and Salapatek, P. H. (1970). Human infancy: A bibliography and guide, in *Carmichael's Manual of Child Psychology* (Ed. P. H. Mussen), Wiley, New York.

Kopp, C. B. and Parmelee, A. H. (1979). Prenatal and perinatal influences on infant behavior, in *Handbook of Infant Development* (Ed. J. D. Osofsky), Wiley, New York.

Leach, P. (1974). *Babyhood: Infant Development from Birth to Two Years*, Penguin, London.

Leboyer, F. (1975). *Birth Without Violence*, Knopf, New York.

Lewis, M. and Rosenblum, L. A. (1974). *The Effect of the Infant on its Caregiver*, Wiley-Interscience, New York.

Lewis, M. and Starr, M. D. (1979). Developmental continuity, in *Handbook of Infant Development* (Ed. J. D. Osofsky), Wiley, New York.

Oppenheim, R. W. (1981). Ontogenetic adaptations and retrogressive processes in the development of the nervous system and behaviour: A neuroembryological perspective, in *Maturation and Development: Biological and Psychological Perspectives* (Eds K. J. Connolly and H. R. Prechtl), Heinemann, London.

Osofsky, J. D. (1979). *Handbook of Infant Development*. Wiley, New York.

Sameroff, A. J. and Chandler, M. (1975). Reproductive risk and the continuum of caretaking casualty, in *Review of Child Development Research*, Vol. 4 (Eds F. D. Horowitz, M. Hetherington, S. Scarr-Salapatek, and G. Siegel), University of Chicago Press, Chicago.

Shaffer, D. and Dunn, J. (1979). *The First Year of Life*. Wiley, Chichester.

Sroufe, L. A. (1979). Socioemotional development, in *Handbook of Infant Development*. (Ed. J. D. Osofsky), Wiley, New York.

Stratton, P. M. (1977). Criteria for assessing the influence of obstetric circumstances on later development, in *Benefits and Hazards of the New Obstetrics* (Eds T. Chard and M. Richards), SIMP, London.

Thoman, E. B. (1978). Changing views of the being and becoming of infants, in *Origins of the Infant's Social Responsiveness*. (Ed. E. B. Thoman), Lawrence Erlbaum Associates, Hillsdale, New Jersey.

Zeskind, P. S. and Ramey, C. T. (1978). Fetal malnutrition: an experimental study of its consequences on infant development in two caretaking environments, *Child Development*, **49**, 1155–1162.

SECTION I

Assessment

The newborn provides us with our first full opportunity to determine the extent of any damage which may have been incurred during gestation or birth, and to predict the potentials and special needs of the individual. Assessment has therefore been a primary concern for parents, clinicians and researchers. Much of our longest-established knowledge of the newborn derives from early attempts at assessment, which focussed on basic functions such as reflexes, and were concerned primarily with neurological dysfunction. The review provided in this section maintains an interest in dysfunction but, in accordance with the psychobiological approach, deficits are interpreted within a broader context, and more attention is directed towards higher forms of functioning.

The first chapter of this first section immediately encounters an issue which pervades the whole of this book. Research on the newborn has often been carried out without clear conceptualization of the significance of the functions being studied. The outcome has been a lack of the kind of criteria which could give practical meaning to the results, as well as providing a basis for deciding which findings should be taken seriously. We are at risk of generating a proliferating literature in which it is almost impossible to separate the significant from the trivial, and in which the lack of a clear conceptual basis allows fundamental methodological weaknesses to go unnoticed. This issue is tackled in all of the chapters in various ways as demanded by the subject matter. In reviewing assessment methods in Chapter 2, Heinz Prechtl establishes that each technique must be judged in relation to the task it is required to perform. One source of confusion has been that assessment procedures have been published without a straightforward and unequivocal rationale and so have been used inappropriately. Neurological assessments will differ according to whether they are directed to past damage, present dysfunction or future deficit, and whether the interest is in screening for major abnormalities or a comprehensive evaluation of neurological function. This latter distinction is partly based on a continuum in which the cost of false positives is traded off against the cost of false negatives and these will vary according to situation. Another essential factor in the choice of method is the model of the developing nervous system on which it is based. In some cases this will be an obsolete concept of reflex action while in others it is not articulated at all. After briefly reviewing our current understanding of neurological functioning, Prechtl compares the available techniques according to the criteria he has established. The final section deals with behavioural assessment. The situation here is rather different as there is only one major scale available, but the claims for what it can achieve are not at all consistent. An attempt is therefore made to determine what particular contribution a behavioural assessment is able to make, and what specific strengths and limitations are shown by the Brazelton Neonatal Behaviour Assessment Scale.

One of the unique features of working with human newborns is the attention which must be paid to their fluctuating behavioural states. In Chapter 3, Heinz Prechtl and John O'Brien use a survey of the remarkably short history of this concept to show why we have our present system of state classifications, and to point to deficiencies in its use. Again it becomes apparent that state criteria will be arbitrary unless they are selected in relationship to the use that is to be made of the classification. At our present stage of knowledge an appeal to the underlying (but unobservable) reality at the level of the nervous system, is not likely to be productive. Even less helpful are appeals to hypothetical processes like the continuum of arousal which is neither observable nor real. More useful criteria for the selection of variables can be derived from experience of the effects of incorporating them into the system in different forms, and of their relevance to the basic problem of detecting changes in the character of both sleep and wakefulness. Following a review of such considerations the chapter concludes with proposals for the most useful division of variables into criteria, which define the states, and concomitants which can be expected to accompany them. Although we cannot hope for a definitive formulation at this time it is a matter of some urgency that there should be a consensus over the definitions of the behavioural states. Almost every neonatal function discussed in this book is influenced in its form, strength and frequency, by the state during which it is examined. The use of idiosyncratic or undefined state ratings can only result in an uninterpretable and unusable literature.

With constantly improving medical care, the pattern of causes and consequences associated with neurological signs is rapidly changing. As Claudine Amiel-Tison clearly shows in Chapter 4, the incidence of incapacitating conditions has been substantially reduced, but the consequence is an inevitable increase in concern over minor abnormalities. This is partly a function of reductions in damage shifting more babies into the less severe categories, partly a change in attitude in which minor anomalies become more salient when there are fewer dramatic cases demanding attention. With the concentration on moderate and mild symptoms the problem of distinguishing the significant from the trivial or transitory becomes much greater. Amiel-Tison therefore comprehensively reviews the aetiological factors which can be identified in the history of the newborn, so that the conditions can be related to their probable causes. The descriptions of the forms of malfunction will also be useful to the psychobiologist in providing insight into the normal operation of the neonatal nervous system. The other criterion for interest in neurological symptoms of the newborn is the longer-term consequences. The methodological considerations in mounting longitudinal studies are reviewed, and major findings are evaluated. The major implications of the chapter are exemplified finally in the considerations which should guide the selection of newborns for inclusion in follow-up studies.

Psychobiology of the Human Newborn
Edited by P. Stratton
© 1982, John Wiley & Sons, Ltd.

CHAPTER 2

Assessment Methods for the Newborn Infant, A Critical Evaluation

HEINZ F. R. PRECHTL

Assessment techniques for newborn infants are only useful to the extent that they can provide answers to specific questions concerning the condition of the neonate. Circumstantial clinical evidence indicates that a host of pre- and perinatal risk factors converge in their effects on the nervous system of the fetus and infant. The threats to the structural and functional integrity of the nervous system during the pre- and perinatal period made it desirable to design methods which evaluate the condition of the infant's brain. The methodological arsenal ranges from *morphological methods* such as air study, angiography, ultrasound scan and, more recently, CT-scan technique, to *physiological measures* of bioelectric activity in polygraphic and evoked potential studies, both dealing with epiphenomena of functions and finally to more direct evaluation of *neural functions* by means of neurological and behavioural assessment techniques. They all may have their unique strengths within the frame of specific questions but can all fail outside this domain. Many debates in the literature concerning the significance and validity of certain techniques have been illusory because of the lack of a precise formulation of the problem to be solved by a particular method.

Since a universal technique for assessing the newborn infant is a fallacious construct, the aim of an assessment method must be expressed in terms of *what should be assessed* and *why this should be done*, two aspects which are too intimately related to be discussed separately. Because the nervous system of the fetus and newborn is particularly vulnerable during gestation and delivery to potentially damaging factors of biochemical and mechanical nature, it is the functional integrity of the developing nervous system which must be the focus of assessment techniques. The vulnerability of the developing brain and the decisive role of impaired brain functions for the fate of the affected individual corroborate this statement. Bearing this in mind the validity of the assessment will depend on how representative in fact the testing is in evaluating the

21

functional expression of the nervous system. Therefore, the third question arising concerns *the how of the assessment.*

In this chapter methods employing technical equipment will not be considered and I shall restrict myself to a discussion of the available neurological and behavioural assessment procedures. A distinction between these two procedures is not always clearcut because wide overlaps exist. It can be said, however, that neurological testing considers primarily those brain functions whose neural mechanisms are known while behavioural testing is concerned with brain functions whose neural mechanisms are less well understood or are simply not considered. The distinction is often arbitrary because the borders are blurred. Nevertheless the two approaches are based on different rationales and strategies. An attempt will be made to critically discuss the advantages and disadvantages of both these techniques and the indications for their use. Before discussing the assessment of the neonate it is important to be clear about risk conditions which form the rationale for the necessity of newborn assessment.

THE IDENTIFICATION OF RISK FACTORS

(a) Obstetrical Complications

There exists a considerable literature on the factors which determine whether a newborn infant is at risk of brain disorders or not. The descriptions range from single factors such as genetic metabolic errors or chromosome defects to cumulative registers of pre- and perinatal complications (Stembera *et al.*, 1975; Hobel *et al.*, 1973, 1979; Nesbitt and Aubry, 1969).

Describing maternal and fetal conditions and events as risk factors creates a series of methodological problems. First, definitions are often inexact, the criteria not being agreed upon unequivocally. Maternal toxaemia, fetal distress and asphyxia may serve as examples. ·Replacing the fuzzy connotation of complications is achieved by quantifying variables such as maternal blood pressure, fetal heart rate patterns and pH-values of umbilical blood. However, the distinction between normal and abnormal still creates problems. Secondly, it is difficult to incorporate quantitatively the varying intensity, duration and severity of many complications into at-risk registers. Thirdly, the various obstetrical complications differ in the degree to which they constitute potential risk for brain impairment. Since the external criterion 'brain impairment' is itself not clear cut, the only unequivocal criterion against which to estimate the level of dangerousness, is to evaluate the contribution of the various complications to perinatal mortality which in itself is the only strict criterion available. It is obvious that even with this criterion no more than a rough approximation can be achieved, because of the above-mentioned difficulties in providing adequate definitions of complications. Moreover, computed weights will depend on the peculiarities of particular populations and on the obstetrical techniques employed which change with time and place. Weights are, therefore, not generally applicable and once estimated their validity remains restricted to the study population.

Obstetrical complications are said to be multi-factorially structured, i.e. they aggregate in separate clusters. The occurrence of single complications is rare and their effects may be minor. If complications and their signs occur in combination, which they usually do, the diverse effects may be cumulative, sometimes simply additive, sometimes potentiating each other. This fact adds a new dimension of difficulties to the problems of estimating the weights of single complications. In many investigations on the detrimental effects of single complications, the risks are overestimated, because other accompanying factors with similar effects are not considered. One would need to cover for each individual case of the study group the whole spectrum of conditions which are relevant. On the other hand, a selection of cases with only one complication and comparable normality in all other respects can hardly be realized because of its rare occurrence. These cases, furthermore, would lack representativeness for this particular complication. Results will be erroneous or simply insufficient. But even if a small set of known, most dangerous complications is selected (e.g. prematurity, asphyxia, growth retardation) one deals only with the tip of the iceberg leading to a selection of a set of cases at-risk and leaving a large proportion of at-risk cases unidentified. This latter problem is a serious drawback for at-risk registers which attempt to select from the total population those infants who need special surveillance immediately after birth or later. If the list of items is too limited, an intolerably large number of at-risk cases will be missed. On the other hand, lists which attempt to cover all kinds of possible factors which may theoretically endanger the integrity of the developing nervous system are clinically impractical because they will cover the majority of newborn infants. By the same token, such comprehensive lists not only identify the majority of problem cases but simultaneously a very large number of cases are recruited which do not develop manifest clinical problems.

These insurmountable difficulties, inherent in this method, hampered the epidemiological use of at-risk registers for public health planning and public health services. This point is amply illustrated by Rogers (1968) in discussing the British use of at-risk registers during the sixties aimed at the detection of infants who will later develop handicapping conditions (see also Scott and Masi (1979) for a critical discussion of the effectiveness of registers to detect later mental retardation).

In clinical practice knowledge of obstetrical complications is indispensable for identifying the aetiology of certain conditions of the newborn infant. Nevertheless the cause-effect relation between pre- and perinatal complications and their suspected sequelae is often taken for granted on the basis of insufficient evidence. The rapid changes in methods of treatments in obstetrics and neonatology blur even previously accepted relationships in often unknown ways, including unpredicted iatrogenic effects. Notwithstanding all these pitfalls the clinician will have to continue to use diagnostic categories of complications in daily routine and research. Better standardization and sharper definitions remain as tasks for the future.

(b) The Optimality Concept

A method which can overcome some of the obstacles inherent to obstetrical complication-scales is the application of the optimality concept (Prechtl, 1967, 1968). The approach differs in essential ways from the traditional manner of dealing with pre- and perinatal complications. Instead of listing disease entities and pathological signs which may or may not have occurred in the history of individuals or groups of infants, optimality is evaluated by a set of strict criteria which must be met. It is undoubtedly easier to reach agreement about the optimal course of pregnancy and delivery than it is to obtain agreement about normalcy or pathology of these events. To be optimal is considered the best possible condition which carries consequently the least risk of mortality and morbidity. The definition of an optimal condition is more narrow and more precise than the definition of normality which is mostly based on the absence of pathology and disorders. With this in mind a list of criteria is designed which indicate optimal measurements of observed phenomena or reported events. A comprehensive list of optimality criteria is compiled which covers such items as maternal age, parity, maternal blood pressure, condition of the placenta, fetal position, fetal heart rate, spontaneous delivery, birth weight, onset of breathing after birth, gestational age, and course of postnatal adaptation. For each item which meets the predetermined criterion, a point is added to a total score which reaches a maximum if all items of the list are found to be optimal. For all those items which

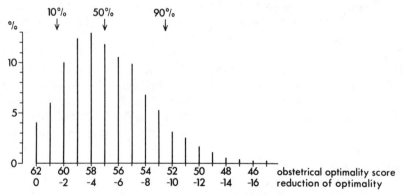

Figure 1   An example of a normalized distribution of obstetrical optimality scores consisting of sixty-two items. If points are lost, the individual score shifts to the right. The reduction of optimality can be read off on the scale of reduced optimality. The 10th, 50th and 90th percentiles are indicated by arrows

are not found to be in agreement with the respective optimality criteria, points are lost. Since only one point is given per item, a significant decrease of the total optimality is only possible if several items are not optimal. Michaelis *et al.* (1979a) have introduced the term 'reduced optimality' which is superior to the easily confusing term 'non-optimality', used previously. Figure 1 illustrates a possible distribution of obstetrical optimality scores.

This technique offers a series of advantages in comparison to the traditional complication scales:

1. Definitions are more precise and easier to agree upon
2. Different weights are not necessary for the separate items since there is no gradation of optimality within each item.
3. It has been empirically found that 'important items' when not found to be optimal, go together with a reduction of optimality in other items. Thus reduction in optimality in isolated items without substantial reduction of the total optimality score does not indicate a significant risk. The system is therefore selfweighting.
4. The optimality system is more easy to handle than complication scales. Through computation of percentiles of the distribution of scores in a population, an individual score can be located within the percentile areas and different populations can be easily compared, provided the same criteria and number of items are employed in the optimality scores.
5. The system is relatively robust against variables with little discriminating power between cases. Distributions are only shifted to the left if an item is optimal in all cases, or to the right if there is no case in the population fulfilling the criterion of optimality of an item. However, even under this condition the percentiles are not affected in their discriminating power between low-, intermediate-, and high-risk cases.
6. Since it has been demonstrated that reduction of the obstetrical optimality score is paralleled by a relative increase in the incidence of neurological problems in the newborn (Prechtl, 1968; Touwen *et al.*, 1980), it is relatively easy to set the cutting point in the known distribution from a population at a certain centile to provide special service for these cases. The location of such a cutting point will depend on the available number of expert personel and facilities in any given area.

Changes in the techniques of care and treatment do not invalidate the optimality system while they do invalidate weighted complication scales. These facts are of great help in solving epidemiological problems.

Naturally, like every other method, the application of the optimality principle has its limitations. The greatest drawback is that the gain in quantification of the risk is accompanied by a loss of qualitative information concerning the kind of risk factors. However, this shortcoming can easily be overcome by a combined use of complication and optimality score. For example, in assessing the effects drugs given to the mother have on the nervous system of the infant, the cases where drugs were given can be evaluated in their distribution over the optimality scores. In such a way, the advantages of both methods are preserved. Thus for the clinician who needs to relate morbidity to clinical diagnoses as etiological factors, this possibility remains, but the quantification of the risk is also not lost. This holds true for the individual patient as well as for groups under study. A striking illustration is given by Huisjes *et al.* (1975). Maternal hypertension was associated with an increasing risk of neurological abnormalities in the infant if it was combined with reduced optimality scores.

A quite different limitation lies not in the principle itself but derives from the difficulties people may have thinking in terms of optimality, an approach which is very unfamiliar for medical people. Being trained to search for abnormalities and pathology, it seems difficult to switch to thinking in terms of the most favourable and hence optimal conditions. In this light it is not perhaps surprising that the list of optimal criteria of the obstetrical history, published in 1968 by us, was mistaken by several authors as a 'non-optimal scale' (e.g. Forfar, 1968; Kittner and Lipsitt, 1976; Littman and Parmelee, 1978; Stennert *et al.*, 1978). The most confusing example of an 'obstetric complication scale' is given by Littman (1979). Most unfortunately, optimal items and plain complications are mixed, making the scale less than helpful. Failure to adhere strictly to the optimality criteria as exemplified by equating the absence of optimality with abnormality and complication, gives rise to all the difficulties which have been mentioned before in detail. The optimum is often more narrowly defined than the normal. Consequently, non-optimal conditions may fall within the limits of generally accepted normality, but they may also indicate severe pathology. The optimality concept is not merely a reversal of the complication concept, but is essentially different from it. The advantages of the optimality concept are lost to a large extent, if the clear distinction between optimality and complications becomes blurred. Most of the items of an obstetrical optimality list can be properly defined in terms of optimality. Unfortunately, a few create difficulties. For example, we have no short term to describe the course of a pregnancy during which no bleeding occurs. In such instances as this, the absence of an abnormal sign must be taken as the criterion for optimality, i.e. no bleedings during pregnancy—which is identical with a normal condition. This underlines the unfortunate fact that the traditional medical language often leaves us without an adequate terminology for the description of health; we call such conditions 'uneventful' and 'unconspicuous'.

The applications of the optimality scores are manifold in clinical practice and research. Different registers can be designed for different purposes. The selection of items will depend on systematically collected data, and as progress is made in diagnostic procedures, the lists can be updated. Since there is a change in the distribution and, therefore, in the percentiles of the scores from a population when the number of items in the register is altered, a recalibration of the percentiles is necessary. It should be kept in mind that distributions of optimality scores containing different numbers of items, can not be simply compared. For example, the 90th percentile in one distribution with 42 items may lie at a reduced optimality of -7 items, while in another distribution with 52 items the 90th percentiles are found at -10 items (Michaelis *et al.*, 1979b). Different populations can only be compared with the same register, because otherwise it is never clear which portion of the difference is due to differences in the scale, and which to different risks in the compared populations. As long as this aspect is taken care of the flexibility of optimality registers is a great advantage, not a limitation.

(c) Limitations of the At-Risk Concept

Neither a list of pre- and perinatal complications nor any optimality scale was ever successful in predicting all abnormal newborns in a population. Individual infants at high risk may turn out to be normal while others without complications in their history and a high optimality score may be unequivocally abnormal and damaged. This raises the question whether many of the identified risk factors are, except in their extreme form, more than conditional causes. Must there not be other conditions—as yet unknown—which determine that a low pH of a certain duration leads to neonatal convulsions and later to cerebral palsy in the one case, but not in another? This may be similar to kernicterus. It was discovered that hyperbilirubinaemia of a certain degree produces kernicterus, but not in all cases. Later it was found that hypoxia and hypoglycaemia which on their own never produce kernicterus, increase the susceptibility to kernicterus at levels of unconjugated bilirubin, which alone would not yet produce kernicterus. Such examples may be more common, as is certainly the case with psycho-social factors. Levels of education, poverty or affluence, the quality and status of parental relationships are conditional factors for the smoking and drinking habits of the mother and many other pre- and perinatal conditions. To speculate further, it seems at least highly plausible to assume that genetic factors may play a determinant role. A concept of a genetically determined vulnerability of the brain is not at all new, and it is questionable whether the well-known sex differences in vulnerability are only due to the early sex-typing of the brain by hormones. In the same line is the finding that many mothers of impaired infants have poor obstetrical histories.

It may very well be, that a better knowledge and understanding of genetical mechanisms as predisposing factors could help in coming to a more refined and reliable assignment of pre- and perinatal risk factors, and to better management. And perhaps the study of those infants who remain undamaged despite being at high risk may help us to learn what it is which the damaged ones are missing.

THE NEUROLOGICAL ASSESSMENT OF THE NEWBORN INFANT

(a) The Need for a Concept of the Nervous System

It is clear that the identification of risk factors is only meaningful if the risk can be expressed in terms of 'risks in respect to what'. Concerning the newborn period the 'what' may be perinatal death, malformations, genetic or chromosomal defects, and damage or dysfunction of the nervous system. But even within the latter category there exists a large variety of conditions. With the exception of the clinically well-known overt sign of dramatic neurological malfunctioning such as convulsions, jitteriness, severe apathy or immobility, and persistent deviations of head and eye position, dysfunctions of the nervous system only become manifest, if they are searched for in an examination. How such an examination should be designed and carried out crucially depends on the concept about the nervous system on which the examination is based. Those who expect to find explications of these theoretical concepts in the neurological literature on newborn examinations will be disappointed. Not only is a detailed description usually lacking, but the impression is often given that the authors have barely reflected on the traditional views they have obviously uncritically accepted. The differences between concept oriented approaches and those in which on purpose or by indifference a theoretical underpinning of the assessment method is neglected, have far reaching consequences. Not only will the strategy of the examination be different, but also the interpretations of the obtained results will vary. The consequences are very plain. Either a coherent system of design and interpretation can be achieved, or the method only will consist of a loose item collection of more or less relevant single tests.

Before turning to a description of the strategies of neurological assessment and a comparison of the various methods it seems necessary to discuss available concepts concerning the developing nervous system. Although such a discussion must inevitably remain superficial in the context of this chapter, the theoretical background of neurological assessment techniques for the neonate needs nevertheless to be made explicit before one can meaningfully deal with the strategies of examinations.

One of the most commonly employed concepts has been derived from classical neurophysiology and neurology. Explanations of neural functions are sought in activities of reflex arcs and chains of reflexes which are directly linked to peripheral sensory inflow. In this perspective tendon reflexes and other simple reflexes (e.g. skin reflexes) are treated as the most elementary functions, while increasing complexity of reflexive operation is reflected in muscle tonus, postural functions and co-ordination of voluntary acts, with the cranial nerves being seen as a special class. However, contemporary neuroscience has moved far away from such a view. The existing deep gap between traditional clinical methods and recent scientific concepts is too striking to be neglected. The nervous system is now seens as an information-processing apparatus in that it *generates* activity, receives, transmits, conducts, transforms, stores and compares messages. With the aid of these processes it *initiates* and keeps neural activity going, it *regulates* non-neural functions such as respiration, circulation, thermal balance, food intake and many others, it *adapts* the organism's posture and orientation in space, adapts social behaviour to the actual situation of interaction, and adapts behavioural states to the demands of the environment. Furthermore, it may *anticipate* events and may change responses according to previously *stored* experiences (habituation and learning). By no means is the nervous system an instrument which becomes only active by the grace of stimuli; on the contrary, it may seek for particular stimuli.

These various functional tasks can never be fulfilled by reflexes. The reflex concept has been developed in experiments in which the nervous system was brought into pathological conditions of relative inactivity (by decerebration, spinalization or anaesthesia), because only then does the intrinsic activity no longer interfere with consistent and stereotypic reflex responses to the applied and often unnatural stimuli. Reflexes do not appear as elementary building-blocks of neural functions in the intact organism under natural conditions. They are merely sub-parts of complex and centrally organized regulating circuitries in feed-back systems. As a conclusion it can be said that the traditional reflex concept is long since obsolete and has been replaced by concepts of systems analysis and control theory. The consequences for our problem, the neonatal neurological assessment, can not be ignored. The newborn's neural repertory is not a bundle of primitive reflexes, nor is it comparable to that of a decerebrated preparation of a cat. It is also incomparable to the nervous system of adult animals for reasons of species differences and the stage of maturation. Although this may seem trivial, it has not always been sufficiently appreciated. The other erroneous source of reference is the pathological brain of adult humans. Concepts of adult neurology are inapplicable for the normal as well as for the brain-damaged infant.

The differences between the developing and the adult nervous system have been extensively conceptualized by Anokhin (1964) within the perspective of evolution. During early development the brain does not mature simultaneously in all regions, but only in those parts and structures, which are necessary for performing vital functions. They mature selectively and with a higher speed. Such a specific early maturation differs across species, according to the specific ecological circumstances the young organisms are phylogenetically adapted to. Anokhin has called this process systemogenesis which is contrasted to organogenesis. The point is that the heterochronic maturation of different brain structures and functions can only be understood within the context of phylogeny. The effects of the selective pressure on the pre-programmed maturation of the nervous system should not be considered without the care-giver. There must be a process of matching between offspring and care-giver by mutual influences. Put differently, the young will only survive and grow and develop properly, if the mothering and nursing repertory of the care-giver is precisely adapted to the properties of the young and vice versa. This is an important point, because it helps to understand why it is possible that the nervous system of the young infant is so different from later. If the maturation of the nervous system should progress synchronously in all parts of the brain, the brain of an infant would be a miniature edition of the adult brain. Evidently, this is not the case. Seen in this context, it is not at all meaningful to speak of the 'immature' nervous system of the neonate. An appreciation of the rich repertory of highly adapted neural functions which are present at an early age, is not at all new. Comprehensive surveys of the literature have been compiled by Pratt 1954, Peiper, 1963, and Kessen *et al.*, 1970. While useful as traces to previous work, it is quite evident that these surveys were written from views on the nervous system which became outdated. A re-evaluation and re-integration of our knowledge on the developing nervous system is gradually emerging, but remains in many facets still a task for the future. On the other hand, our recent knowledge, based on modern approaches, seems developed enough to guarantee an appropriate basis for adequate methods of neurological assessment of the neonate.

(b) The Objective of Neonatal Neurological Assessment

The aim of a neonatal neurological examination has been most clearly expressed by Saint-Anne Dargassies (1979):

The purpose of a neurological examination of the neonate is to recognize any symptomatological impairment. Unfortunately, one cannot always ascertain the location or extent of a lesion, or even its pathology, by clinical examination. Thus the goal becomes one of recognizing CNS dysfunction, either transient or permanent. This can be minimal at first, yet indicate a deep-seated disorder which may manifest itself belatedly or appear as an acute insult. (p. 2)

In a less succinct description Parmelee and Michaelis (1971) proposed that

the neurological examination of the newborn must serve three major purposes, each requiring a slightly different technique and mode of analysis:
1) the immediate diagnosis of an evident neurological problem, such as extreme hypotonia, convulsions, coma or localized paralysis, to determine what therapy to institute.
2) the evaluation of the day to day changes of a known neurological problem to determine the evolution of a pathological process, such as an hypoxic episode, or to follow the evolution of the neurological signs of a systematic disease such as respiratory distress.
3) the long term prognosis of a newborn who is recovering from some neonatal neurological problem or is considered at risk due to abnormalities of the pregnancy, or delivery.

The requirements which the assessment method must satisfy are very rarely given. Prechtl (1965a) stated:

A neurological examination of a newborn infant must fulfil the following demands: (1) It must be reliable, that is, it should give the same results when carried out by different examiners. (2) It must be valid, that is, it must be sensitive enough not only to detect gross disturbances but minor abnormalities as well. (3) It should predict the risk of permanent damage.

The methodological considerations of the prerequisites for an adequate examination technique will be discussed in the following section.

(c) Essentials of Design

Many conflicting and confused statements in the literature on purpose, procedure and validity of the neonatal neurological examination may find their origin in the neglect of a clear concept of the developing nervous system, but equally often in a culpable disregard of the methodology employed in the design of the methods. There seem to be two exceptions. Prechtl has outlined some of the methodological essentials in a paper in 1960 and in several later remarks (Prechtl, 1970, 1977a). Parmelee and Michaelis (1971) have added suggestions on the rationale of employed strategies which are otherwise scarcely available in the literature. Recent views (St. Clair, 1978; Self and Horowitz, 1979) on newborn assessment techniques have not been written by experts in neurology and have understandably neglected this aspect. Such neglect justifies a detailed repetition of the previous attempt (Prechtl, 1972a) to formalize the general strategy of a neurological examination technique and the decision steps on which it is based (see Figure 2.).

The point of departure of this consideration is an imaginary set of all neural functions which have ever been present during a lifetime and are accessible to non-invasive testing. Only those tests which are specific for the age range of interest are selected. Therefore, this set must differ for example for preterm infants between 30 and 37 weeks from that for full-term infants to the extent that their repertoires of neural functions differ. As already mentioned, the term infant is equipped with a variety of transient neural mechanisms which are adaptations to the particular circumstances of early extra-uterine life. As they play a dominant role at this age, they are representative for the young nervous system, and the selection of items in the neurological examination technique will reflect this situation. In fact, there are few neural functions in the newborn infant which are not transformed at a later age, either in the sense that they disappear completely or become at least latent or modified (Prechtl, 1981). This very fact renders the neurology of the young infant unique and means that approaches and concepts of adult neurology are invalid and thus inapplicable in developmental neurology.

The next decision step involves the selection of those items to be incorporated in the examination. This step needs very careful consideration. It should contain a properly balanced selection to represent the important subsystems of the neural

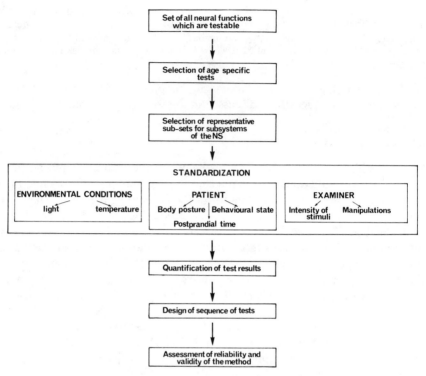

Figure 2   Flow diagram indicating the decision steps for the design of a neurological examination technique (From Prechtl, 1977a)

repertory. Only if this essential aspect is considered, will the examination be comprehensive and sufficiently sensitive. There is, however, a practical limit to the number of test items which are reasonable to handle, but here opinions differ. The complexity of the newborn's nervous system has not always been sufficiently appreciated. In order to save time, short versions of examinations are sometimes suggested. Nevertheless, the time spent on the examination cannot be reduced below a certain minimum without a serious loss of the crucial information a neurological examination must obtain. How good a compromise can be achieved between these two conflicting demands, namely being sufficiently comprehensive and at the same time not unreasonably time consuming in clinical use, is decisive for the efficiency of the method.

No less essential for the quality of a well-designed neurological examination technique is the degree of standardization of the procedure. There are three aspects which must be considered for standardization: (a) The environmental conditions; (b) the patient; and (c) the examiner. It is necessary to keep the temperature of the examination room warm enough (about 28 °C) to prevent thermal discomfort of the undressed baby. The light should be bright enough for the examination, but not so bright as to irritate the patient. The examination table should have a soft surface to reduce rolling movements of the baby. This is important for maintaining the posture of the infant as it has an influence on symmetry and intensity of many spontaneous activities and responses. Since food intake also has an effect, it is preferable to examine, as a rule, 2–3 h after the last feed.

One of the most crucial aspects to consider is the dependency of nervous functions on the various behavioural states. For a long time, the neural mechanisms of young infants have been perceived as being especially inconsistent, responses occurring at one moment, but not at another, or at least their intensity varying considerably. This variability was a reason for doubting whether a neurological examination of young infants was useful except for the detection of severe abnormalities. The critical break through came with the discovery that most infantile neural mechanisms are dependent on the behavioural states, (see Chapter 3), and with the application of this knowledge to the neurological examination. The occurrence and/or intensity of many responses is determined by the behavioural state in which they are examined, and it is therefore only meaningful to quantify the neurological findings when the state dependency is known. This latter problem has now been solved (for summary see Prechtl, 1972b, 1974). The optimal behavioural state for each test item is that one in which a response of medium intensity is consistently found, but, not the one in which a response is most intensive, 'best', or otherwise maximally expressed. There are good reasons for this procedure. Abnormally exaggerated responses as a sign of dysfunction would be missed in an examination intended to test the limits of the system. It is essential for an examination technique to indicate for each item the optimal state of the infant in which the examiner should carry out the testing, and for which states this is contra-indicated.

It is self-evident that the examiner should standardize the stimulus intensity when eliciting responses. Stimuli should be strong enough to elicit a clear response, but strong stimuli evoking maximal responses must be avoided. Finally, the standardization of the handling of the infant by the examiner during the test procedure reduces variations of the results between examiners and at repeated tests. A precise description of the maneouvres for each test is therefore indispensable.

The design of semiquantitative scales for the recording of each item needs special care. Usually, a four-point scale, comprising absence, weak, medium and exaggerated responses, is sufficiently discriminative. A finer grained scoring leads most often to overscoring and becomes accordingly unreliable as an operational definition and reproducible perception of the various response intensities is hardly possible. It should be kept in mind, however, that all attempts to quantify test items are in vain if the examination procedure is not subjected to a rigorous standardization.

It is not acceptable to carry out the examination in an arbitrary sequence.

Many responses affect the state or may have a carry-over effect on following responses. Hence, the sequence of the procedure, which should be strictly adhered to, needs careful design. Responses not influencing the state should be carried out in the beginning while those upsetting the infant must be delayed until the end. This increases the probability that those behavioural states which are optimal for the various test items occur one after the other. Such a sequence makes it impractical to follow a logic, based on the Bauplan of structure and function of the nervous system, and which has been so successfully followed in adult neurology.

The attempt to optimalize the strategy of the neurological examination technique must be supplemented by an assessment of the inter-observer agreement between different examiners and with some interpretative restrictions of the test-retest reliability. Only if they are satisfactory is it meaningful to evaluate the validity of the method. The test of validity will be a consistent relation between the neonatal neurological findings and the pre- and perinatal, and follow-up data. The stability of abnormal neurological signs and syndromes cannot be expected to be high because of the developmental changes the nervous system of the young infant undergoes. The clinical value is merely expressed in terms of short-term prognosis rather than in possible predictions over many years. Repeated examinations tell more about the course of an abnormal condition which may improve and disappear but may also re-appear with a different symptomatology, even after a long silent period. To judge the validity of the neonatal examination only on the criterion of long-term prediction of neurological impairment is misleading and was certainly overemphasized in the past. There are too many factors which influence the prognosis of early signs in an unpredictable way.

(d) A Comparison Between the Different Methods

In an attempt to compare different neurological examination techniques, the list of essential steps, mentioned above, may serve as a guide for this evaluation. The first criterion is the selection of age-specific test items, resulting in a collection which should be comprehensive in accounting for all important subsystems. How far a method is considered as being comprehensive and representative of the neural repertory depends largely on the concepts concerning the nervous system the examiner has accepted.

It may be apparent why an intimate knowledge of the specificities of the developing nervous system is a prerequisite for a responsible choice. There are only two extensive neurological methods for assessment of full-term neonates available, one described by André-Thomas et al. (1955, English version 1960) and later elaborated by Saint-Anne Dargassies (1974, English version 1977), and the other one by Prechtl and Beintema (1964, revised Prechtl, 1977a). All other techniques such as those by Joppich and Schulte (1968), Parmelee (1974),

O'Doherty (1977), and Amiel-Tison (1979) cover a more limited range of test items. Unfortunately, as the theoretical concepts upon which the selection of test items is based in these other techniques are hardly ever made explicit, we can only conjecture about their nature. On this basis a specific comparison between the different methods is not realistic and, therefore, only general comments are permissible.

Arbitrary collections of attractive reflexes and responses which instead of thoroughly evaluating only 'tap' the nervous system—an expression used by Brazelton (1973)—may not achieve their intended purpose. Eclectic collections, selected from different methods with different theoretical backgrounds, provide incoherent results, difficult to interpret. Another shortcoming may lie in a neglect of spontaneous activities such as postures, movements and behavioural states which reflect one of the most fundamental properties of the nervous system. If due time is not allotted for observation these properties can not be adequately evaluated. Parmelee's and O'Doherty's methods fall short in both these respects.

Such regrettable reductionistic approaches suffer from still another shortcoming. They lack the great advantage of extensive and comprehensive methods which make possible the diagnosis of neurological syndromes. Prechtl (1960) and Prechtl and Beintema (1964) have described a number of neonatal neurological syndromes such as hyperexcitability, apathy, hemisyndromes and hypo- and hypertonus, which all consist of specific clusters of symptoms and which are differential in respect to their sequelae.

An extensive method aiming at a comprehensive and representative assessment of the neonatal nervous system will be the only way to escape the pitfalls, previously mentioned in assessing babies who are not apparently sick but may nevertheless suffer from brain impairment. Such a method will of necessity take more than just ten minutes to administer if made sufficiently refined to evaluate an organ of the complexity of the newborn's brain. The notorious error of mistaking short examination techniques which are in reality at their best only screening instruments, as the only clinically usable method, carries the danger of bringing the whole of neonatal neurological assessment into disrepute.

It should not be forgotten, however, that a completely different approach is possible and necessary if the strategy deals pragmatically with acute situations in intensive care units. If patients are in vital or serious condition, no formalized and rigid neurological examination technique is adequate, and one should start from the overt signs of alarm. As crude as this may be, this strategy will insure that acute gross pathology is not missed. If the acute phase has passed, a comprehensive examination should be carried out to select those infants who suffer from more persisting dysfunctions, even if they may be of a minor degree.

Let us now turn to the aspect of standardization of the examination technique. There is uniform agreement concerning the timing and the environmental conditions during the examination. A precise description of the manipulations the examiner has to perform are only given in the manuals by Prechtl and

Beintema (1964) and Prechtl (1977a), and to some extent in Saint-Anne Dargassies' book (1977). Many test items are very sensitive to the way they are evaluated. If the manipulations are not made explicit, users will not achieve comparable findings, except after intensive individual training. This is even more important as far as the role of behavioural states is concerned. Prechtl and Beintema (1964) first introduced behavioural states into their neurological examination technique and since then most other techniques have used them. However, it should be understood that they used behavioural states in the connotation of 'distinct and qualitatively different modes of nervous activity' (see Prechtl, 1974), whilst rejecting the concept of a continuum of arousal, consciousness, or vigilance, for which evidence is lacking. Since even during different awake states, responses may vary considerably, it is not sufficient to postulate that the examination has to be performed during wakefulness of the infant, but needs to be specified in more detail. Certain parts of the examination can only be carried out properly in particular awake states and not in others, a point not made explicit by Saint-Anne Dargassies (1977; p. 7) and O'Doherty (1977; p. 27). Closely related to this aspect is the fixation of the sequence in carrying out the examination. A comparison of the different proformas for examinations reveals that disturbing items often precede those items which can only be assessed in a quiet infant. A violation of a consistent optimal sequence, which is consistently adhered to, implies also a loss of information concerning the profile of behavioural states over the length of the examination as an important neurological sign (Beintema, 1968; Michaelis et al., 1973).

The notation of the test results is obtained per item by use of semiquantitative scales in the method by Prechtl and Beintema (1964) and by Joppich and Schulte (1968), in a mixture of quantitative aspects and qualities by Saint-Anne Dargassies (1977) and Parmelee (1974), and on the basis of recording absent/present or normal/decreased/exaggerated by O'Doherty (1977) and Amiel-Tison (1979). The latter two mix descriptive and interpretative notations which is not advisable. Of course, the notation adopted influences how global or refined the assessment of the nervous system can be made. It will also influence the conclusion as to what is normal, pathological, or abnormal and the possibility to arrive at a diagnosis. If the quantitative scoring is refined enough the application of the optimality concept can be successfully applied to the results of the neurological assessment (Prechtl, 1968). Prechtl (1977a) has indicated in his manual the optimal finding for each test item. Neurological optimality scores are complementary to neurological diagnoses in a similar way as obstetrical optimality scores are complementary to the recording of obstetrical complications, and all that has been said previously about the latter is also valid for neurological optimality. It should be emphasized, however, that a neurological optimality score should never automatically replace the attempt to arrive at a diagnosis. It can add different information and can do this on a quantitative basis. Such a procedure is helpful in recruiting a group of optimal newborns which may serve as a control group in research, as well as clinically in those cases in which several symptoms do not form a recognizable syndrome.

The final aspect of our comparison concerns reliability and validity of the neurological assessment. A detailed study of the interobserver agreement does not exist for any of the neurological examination techniques. Sigman *et al.* (1973) have mentioned a correlation of $r = 0.92$ for a previous version of Parmelee's technique. Prechtl (1963) reports on agreements between three examiners varying between 0.80 and 0.96. An analysis per item indicated a complete agreement for the assessment of the behavioural states, but only a relatively low (70 per cent) agreement for the assessment of the resistance to passive movements, this being the most subjective evaluation. All other items vary within this range. Better documented is the test–retest reliability. Beintema (1968) examined daily a group of forty-nine full-term newborns from the first to the ninth day of life. Besides a very strong stability of nearly all of the items, a striking developmental course was evident in most of the items. Moreover, he confirmed the clinical impression from our previous study (Prechtl and Dijkstra, 1960) that during the first two or three days, the instability of states (and of many physiological variables) makes the standardization more difficult. This is primarily valid for healthy newborns. On the other hand, sick infants may improve or deteriorate over the newborn period, and this will appear as a change in the neurological findings. It is this information which concerns the clinician the most, because it reflects the severity and the course of the impairment. Unanimity exists that, in general, longer persisting abnormal signs (e.g. weeks) have a worse prognosis than most of the briefly transient signs (e.g. days). On the other hand, there are very few abnormal signs at newborn age which persist as such into later life. This is not surprising, if the profound transformations of the developing nervous system are considered.

There exists a vast literature on follow-up studies, relating pre- and perinatal conditions or neonatal symptoms with later findings. The varying and often contradictory results of such investigations are probably due to differences in methodological design but perhaps even more to the kind of sequelae to which the search was directed such as handicapping conditions (i.e. cerebral palsy, low IQ, sensory defects), or learning and related behaviour problems. Of similar importance for the estimation of sequelae is the age at which the follow-up assessment is carried out. In a developing organism abnormal signs are often age related, in that they not only appear, but also may endanger appropriate development at certain ages and not at others.

Dysfunctions of specific early neural mechanisms may be a sign of structural damage to the brain. They may or may not impair or influence later developing functions. However, structures in a pre-functional stage may become impaired which only much later manifest themselves in dysfunctions. Unspecific signs may be present for a short time after the acute insult, followed by a latent period of months or even years. And there is rapidly accumulating evidence for compensation and recovery of damaged structures which lead to nearly normal functions that may only fail in very specific life or test situations. On the basis of these arguments, one would not expect to find too close relationships between neurological findings at newborn age and long-term sequelae. Last but not least, studies on long-term prediction have been carried out on relatively large groups of cases in which correlations between early and late findings were found. The statistical correlations were generally low, albeit significant, and therefore explained only a small fraction of the variance. However, clinically the most important aspect is the prediction in the individual patient. The best we can achieve in this respect is to assign a certain degree of initial risk, expressed as a probability of the outcome. This is relatively easy if the neonatal findings were normal as then the prediction of later normality is very high but becomes more uncertain when abnormalities were found in the newborn period. Then a close short-term follow-up of repeated examinations can provide substantial predictions, a method which should be widely employed in the clinical care of such infants.

But do these critical arguments invalidate the clinical significance of neonatal neurology, as has been suggested? Several reasons plead for a negative answer to this question. Firstly these doubts are based on poorly documented evidence (or simply wrong arguments as indicated by Volpe, 1979). Secondly, the employed assessment techniques can easily be demonstrated as being deficient for reasons discussed above in detail. Thirdly, even transient neurological dysfunctions may have a deleterious effect on the development of the bond between infant and caregiver. Finally, there is indeed no other method as yet available which has such a high predictive value for later major or minor dysfunctions as the early neurological assessment. This method is by far superior to the prediction from pre- and perinatal risk scores of whatever kind. Of course, the grave mistake must be avoided, of taking the presence of risk factors as evidence for neural impairment which they never are. However, methods applied with insufficient competence and designed to evaluate the condition of the complex nervous system in a quick examination have a low predictive power. A carefully designed and standardized screening test, taking no more than 10 min, has been described by Prechtl and Beintema (1964). It is not possible to obtain a diagnosis with this method, but a successful selection of those infants who needed to be examined comprehensively has been demonstrated by Touwen et al. (1977) in a comparative study of 100 infants with Prechtl's screening test (10 min) and his comprehensive method (which takes 30–40 min). Hence the argument against a comprehensive method as being too time consuming cannot really be taken seriously as a valid excuse. The advantage of a validated screening method of ten-minute duration which is derived from the context of an extensive method, above non-validated short examination techniques, based on outdated concepts about the nervous system, can hardly be questioned. Those infants who need a careful neurological assessment for other than the most obvious reasons, can be reliably selected by a quick screening.

Concluding this section the following points should be made quite clear. There exist newborn neurological conditions to be detected and clinically evaluated which do not require a highly formalized and conceptually underpinned type of neurological examination, but others do. To decide about the design and the qualities of a neurological examination technique by considering only one of these two possibilities leads to wrong conclusions. What for the one is essential, is superfluous or insufficient for the other. It seems that much of the confusion in the opinions about techniques has its roots in an insufficient appreciation of the purpose and aim of a neurological examination technique as well as their application to particular types of problem cases.

THE BEHAVIOURAL ASSESSMENT

In addition to evaluating the neurological condition one may wish to know the behavioural make-up of an individual newborn. Although a comprehensive neurological examination technique such as the one by Prechtl (1977a) deals with spontaneous and reactive stability or lability of behavioural states (see Beintema, 1968), threshold and intensity of responses to standardized stimuli, readiness to respond to pacifying stimuli etc., the method is intended to be sufficiently insensitive so as not to reveal individual differences between normal infants. The instrument was designed to differentiate between normal and specific abnormalities, (or between optimal findings and reduced optimality), and it is directed to evaluating those items which can be readily interpreted in terms of distinct neural dysfunctions.

The renewed interest in the behavioural capacities of newborn infants during the last 20–30 years has brought to light many rediscoveries and confirmations of old observations, made at the beginning of this century, though they were at that time contradictory (see Peiper, 1963). A more recently added dimension is an awareness on the significance of the infant's behavioural repertoire for social interaction with the caregiver. Primarily, these behaviour patterns elicit interactive behaviour in the caregiver, while the number of social responses which can be elicited by the caregiver from the newborn seems to be rather limited. This behavioural system is rapidly developing during early infancy as many fine-grained observational investigations have demonstrated.

As the behavioural repertoire of newborns is rich and complex one would expect to find this reflected in a comprehensive test. Such a test should cover a wide collection of behaviour patterns which are important in the infant's daily life, rather than containing responses which, though possible to elicit, have no relevance under ordinary natural conditions. Hence, the selection of test items would be based empirically on an extensive ethogram of the infant-mother dyad and not on preconceptions about what newborns should do. There is no doubt that, such an instrument, if properly standardized, would be a most welcome complement to the neurological assessment, aiming as it would at aspects which are purposely not dealt with in such an assessment. If a representative selection could be made, it could evaluate what kind of partner the individual infant is, without the need of extremely time-consuming extensive *direct* observations. However, there needs to be a close relationship between the obtained test results and the actual behaviour of the individual baby in the natural situation.

Of the two existing formalized behavioural examination techniques which are specifically designed for the full-term newborn infant, the first, Graham's (1956) test was explicitly developed 'to provide a means of differentiating normal newborns from those who have been traumatized and possibly brain injured'. At a time when no standardized neurological examination method was available, Graham's pioneer work was a break-through, and some of her contributions can still be traced in recent techniques of others. She was in fact very close to a neurological assessment as she intended to discover brain dysfunctions by means of a number of rigorously standardized evaluations. These evaluations covered pain threshold, responses on a maturation scale, vision, elicited irritability, and posture. However, there was no intention to be comprehensive nor any attempt to detect and, if possible, localize specific nervous-system defects. She was in the tradition of Arnold Gesell who spoke of behaviour as an expression of neural functions. This may be the source of the still frequently uttered belief that assessment of behaviour is superior to neurological examination (e.g. Parmelee and Michaelis, 1971; Dubowitz, 1978; Als *et al.*, 1979; Hall, 1979). Although many neural dysfunctions may change the appearance of complex behaviour, they do so in a remote and unspecific way. However, the very information for which a neurological examination is searching, can not be obtained in this way, an obvious fact which cannot be sufficiently emphasized to make the fundamental differences between behavioural and neurological assessment clear. Rosenblith (1979), who has further developed and modified the Graham test, stated that 'the goal of developing the Graham/Rosenblith scales was to determine whether they might be useful in identifying groups of infants "at risk", but who were not considered medically suspect', and further, 'it was not assumed that individual predictions could result from neonatal testing'. The purpose is made clear, and the method to achieve the intended goal is straightforward. A recent description of the method and of the prognostic value of the results is well presented by Rosenblith (1979), making repetition here superfluous.

The second, more ambitious, method is the most comprehensive technique available for the assessment of newborn behaviour. This was introduced by Brazelton (1973) under the name Neonatal Behaviour Assessment Scale (NBAS). This method received wide popularity and often enthusiastic comment from psychologists and clinicians although admonitions for caution have also been raised. During the years since publication the method was subjected to several revisions and a number of refinements have been suggested, and in what follows, reference will be made mainly to the most recent publications. Despite such revisions, descriptions and terminology are not always clear cut, and are sometimes even contradictory. To begin with, there is a vagueness about the precise aim of the assessment scale. Brazelton stated that his 'scale is intended as a means of scoring interactive behaviour', and 'it is an attempt to score the infant's available responses to his environment, and so, indirectly, his effect on the environment' (1973; p. 4). It 'was originally designed as a clinical instrument'. 'Normal newborns are manipulated in such a way that over the course of the half-hour examination they exhibit motor, cognitive, social, and temperamental responses as well as observable psychophysiological reactions' (Brazelton, 1978; p. 3). The NBAS also 'attempts to capture the dimensions of the newborn's capacity to organize himself in the face of the physiological demands for recovery from labor, delivery, and exposure to the new extrauterine environment' (Als et al., 1979; p. 187). This last formulation is not very clear, but it seems to indicate an interest in the course of postnatal adaptation of the infant as reflected in neonatal behaviour.

The target group for the examination is given as normal neonates of not 'less than 37 weeks gestation' and not 'more than 30 days post partum'. Hence, it is clear that the detection of individual differences in full-term infants is the primary aim of the NBAS and the method is a powerful instrument with which to do this. On the other hand, the scale was employed in studies on a variety of at-risk groups such as low-birthweight infants (Scarr and Williams, 1971), small-for-date full-term infants (Als et al., 1976) and infants whose mothers received medication during delivery (Brackbill et al., 1974; Standley et al., 1974; Tronick et al., 1976). While these infants may have been neurologically normal, this can hardly be the case in NBAS studies on infants with high-pitched cries (Lester and Zeskind, 1978), infants suffering from hyperbilirubinaemia (Telzrow et al., 1976), and infants from heroin-addicted mothers (Soule et al., 1974; Kaplan et al., 1975).

Brazelton felt the need 'that a few basic neurological test items be included' in his method: 'The exam assesses the neonate's neurological intactness by 20 reflex items' (Als et al., 1979). 'Elicitation of reflex behaviour also reveals the baby's state control and the capacity to shut out disturbing stimuli' (idem). On the other hand, Brazelton wrote (1978; p. 8) that 'the neurological reflex items would be least likely to be influenced by stress of recovery or by extra-uterine events'. The extensive and careful study by Beintema (1968) has clearly indicated that the latter is not the case. Furthermore, these twenty items which 'are based on the descriptions of neurological assessment outlined by Prechtl and Beintema (1964)', are not tested and interpreted in the same way as was originally described. Brazelton uses a four-point scale and an additional possibility to record asymmetries. 'Most healthy fullterms will receive a score of 2 (medium) on these items, with the exception of the tonic neck reflex, ankle clonus, and visual nystagmus. In these three items 0, 1 and 2 are all normal scores' (Als et al., 1979). Here is an obvious fallacy. Ankle clonus during state 1 is normal, but during state

2 and wakefulness is highly abnormal. On the other hand, automatic walking, placing and crawling may very well be weak or absent in normal infants, especially if not tested in the appropriate state.

These mistakes become grave, when it is held that 'the reflex items will identify gross neurological abnormalities by deviant scores' (Als et al., 1979). Used with so little sophistication this can hardly be true, but it may be based on the belief that along with Apgar scores and 'pediatric examinations in present routine usage', Prechtl and Beintema's neurological examination

are successful in identifying gross abnormalities of central nervous system and psychophysiological function. They have not, however, been as effective in detecting milder dysfunction of the CNS during the neonatal period, nor do they capture the range of temperamental variations in normal infants which predict to differential effects on the caretaking they will elicit from their environments. (Als et al., 1979; p. 185)

In the last sentence the first part is simply wrong, and the second part while true is irrelevant, because it was never the task of any neurological method to achieve this goal. The selection of neurological items included in the 'reflex' scale, certainly does not include the most sensitive items for detection of neurological deviancy. A solution may be to replace this part of so-called 'neurological assessment' by a standardized neurological screening test, designed for this purpose and evaluated for its effectiveness (Touwen et al., 1977). The reflex items could be kept in the NBAS as a means of applying particular stimuli to the infant, but not as neurological items per se. In the present form the neurological part of the NBAS is inadequate for the assessment of neural intactness or impairment.

The importance of behavioural states in the assessment of behavioural functions of the infant is fully acknowledged in the NBAS. Great attention is paid to administering the various stimulations only when the infant is in the adequate state, and also to record the changes in states following the stimuli. The criteria for state identification are 'comparable with the descriptions given by Prechtl and Beintema (1964)', but a drowsy or semi-dozing state is introduced in addition to their five states. The difficulty with so-called drowsiness is the fact that it lacks consistency and stability which are essential characteristics of a condition accepted as a state. It is, therefore, not surprising that in Brazelton's state 3 (drowsiness) 'state change after stimulation is frequently noted'. In drowsiness, state changes also occur even without stimulation, and consequently drowsiness is considered only as a state transition. More important is Brazelton's misunderstanding of the theoretical concept of behavioural states which he calls 'states of consciousness' and describes as a continuum ranging from deep and light sleep to high arousal. As pointed out previously and discussed in detail in Chapter 3, such a view is obsolete and has been replaced by the notion of states as specific modes of neural activity. The consequences of this type of concept for the NBAS are by no means trivial. Furthermore, since states are 'involuntary' conditions, expressions such as infants 'manage their states' (Brazelton, 1978;

p. 8), or 'the baby's *use* of a state to maintain control of his reactions to environmental and internal stimuli is an important mechanism and reflects his potential for organization' (Brazelton, 1973; p. 2) are confusing and idiosyncratic.

The main part of the examination concerns the assessment of 'the newborn's interaction repertoire on 27 behaviour items, scored on a nine-point scale' (Brazelton, 1978). They consist of 'specific elicited behaviour patterns, and 16 general aspects to be observed during the examination'. These items have been grouped conceptually into four dimensions of newborn 'organization', namely (a) interactive capacities, (b) motoric capacities, (c) organizational capacities with respect to state control, and (d) organizational capacities—physiological responses to stress.

Without going into too much detail, a few comments concerning the test items can be made. For the first series of test items which deal with *response decrements* to light and auditory stimuli, appropriate states are given as state 2 or 3 (Brazelton, 1978) (and previously state 1, 2 or 3; Brazelton, 1973). However, it has already been shown for responses to light (Martinius and Papousek, 1970) and to auditory stimuli (Hutt *et al.*, 1968) that state 2 is inadequate because responses are absent or inconsistent even without stimulus repetition. In both studies, habituation was demonstrated during state 1 and Prechtl's state 3 (quiet wakefulness; Brazelton's state 4). One may argue that under the test conditions of the NBAS, habituation can not be achieved (Sameroff, 1978). Any other form of response decrement will be dependent on state changes, length of stimulus intervals and interference by other behaviour.

More clear cut are the tests on *orienting responses* to animate and inanimate visual and acoustic stimuli. These responses, including visual pursuit movement, should not be considered as cortical mechanisms, because the orientation of eyes and head to a lateral stimulus is performed by the tectum in the brain stem. No neurological examination technique for neonates has yet taken sufficient notice of these functions. Responses such as *'general-predominant tone'* (i.e. traction test), *'motor maturity'* (i.e. type of movements) are assessed in more detail and are better standardized in the extensive neurological examination techniques. *Cuddliness* and *defensive movements* are specific behavioural items not used in neurological methods. The measure of irritability may be better standardized, because it is certain that an infant in state 3 or 4 reacts less with crying to a mild stimulus such as 'prone' or 'uncover', than when he is in state 5. It should also be mentioned that the ambient temperature of the examination room will have a profound effect on *'irritability'* and state profiles in general. Standardization of temperature would be an important refinement of the NBAS, an aspect which is also relevant for the assessment of *'activity'* either spontaneous or reactive.

For the evaluation of *tremulousness*, it is important to take the frequency of the movements into account as is done in Prechtl and Beintema's examination. While tremors with a fast frequency of about 8–10 Hz are normal during the first few days and during or after vigorous crying, tremulous movements of 3–4 Hz and larger amplitude are neurophysiologically cloni (Schulte and Schwenzel, 1965) and are an abnormal sign forming part of the hyperexcitability syndrome (Prechtl, 1960). Without this distinction, essential information is lost. This holds true for the next item: *amount of startles.* Spontaneous startles and Moro-responses are explicitly lumped. Startles do occur only regularly in state 1 and more rarely in state 2. The Moro-response is an elicited movement and has a different electromyographic pattern (Prechtl, 1965b). If an infant has a low threshold for the Moro-response, handling, if not gentle enough, will elicit many Moro-responses. A low threshold for Moro-responses is a deviant neurological sign and is separately recorded in the neurological assessment. *Hand-to-mouth facility* and *smiles* are also specific behavioural items, not included in any neurological assessment. The NBAS manual gives all states as being adequate for these two items. This can hardly be correct, because hand-mouth contact does not occur in state 1 and 2 while an awake and active or crying newborn will never smile.

There are a number of items which deal with behavioural states as they occur and change during examination, an aspect not yet covered by any other technique. Taken on face value some of these items overlap or measure the same phenomena under different names[1]. These are overall *alertness* throughout the examination, *consolability with intervention, peak of excitement, repidity of build-up, irritability, lability of states and self quieting activity.* It should be stressed, however, that these aspects are the most important variables of the NBAS, which characterize the infant's temperament, or point to his deviancy. It should be stressed that abnormal state profiles during the neurological examination go together with similarly unstable profiles during polygraphic recordings without stimulation. It has been shown that these peculiarities are not a property of reactivity, but are spontaneously expressed signs of central regulation (Prechtl *et al.*, 1968, 1969; Prechtl, 1977b). On the other hand, individual differences in spontaneous activity and the readiness to react to all kinds of stimuli with specific responses and with shifts in behavioural states are long since known from neurological examinations of normal infants, but they have been purposely neglected in the scoring. It is clearly the merit of the NBAS to have systematically assessed these personal traits. Where the transitions to the exceptional and abnormal are, can only be clarified with accompanying proper neurological methods as an external criterion but can never be obtained from the behavioural assessment alone.

One may ask now, how representative the selection of behavioural test items is in respect to the behavioural repertoire the infant displays in his daily life. Undoubtedly, a lability of states with a strong tendency to cry in many situations, will not be restricted to the test session, nor will particular behavioural make-up of the placid or 'lazy' infant. Related to this aspect is the ability to generate and

[1] This has actually been demonstrated by G. Kestermann (1981). Assessment of individual differences among healthy newborns on the Brazelton scale, *Early Human Development*, **5**, 15–28.

maintain alertness in the social situation. Despite the fact that the occurrence and persistence of states is influenced by many internal and external conditions, to which due attention must be paid, they seem to be a relatively stable property of the individual. Ongoing research on intra-uterine activity and state cycles suggest a continuity between pre- and postnatal life, supporting the well-known anecdotal reports of many mothers.

Another dimension of the newborn's daily behaviour is his muscle power, especially postural control in various positions when carried around, and during nappy changing and feeding. Provided that neurological impairment can be ruled out, muscle power is closely related to birth weight and gestational age. It is highly unlikely that the neural mechanisms for postural control and antigravity responses are subjected to maturational changes around term age. They are present during late fetal life, but poorly expressed in movements because of weakness of the muscles. But small-for-dates infants have an even smaller muscle bulk and are consequently poor in all those responses which involve muscle power, as has been demonstrated by Michaelis et al. (1970) with neurological assessment, and by Als et al. (1976) with the NBAS. While this is rather trivial in terms of neurology, the behavioural performance may affect the care-giver during routine handling of the infant. This may be less true for neonatal locomotor activity such as crawling or stepping movements.

No attention is given in the NBAS to the behaviour involved in the feeding situation. This could be an important ommission, as rooting and sucking may very well have an effect on the care-giver in terms of their quality, intensity and patterning of these responses. Moreover, the rhythmicity of non-nutritive sucking is a very sensitive indicator of neural condition, even among apparently neurologically normal newborns (Dreier et al., 1979).

Another dimension of behaviour not specifically covered by the NBAS, is learning. While it is difficult to deal thoroughly with this aspect outside a rigorously controlled experimental situation, it may none the less be possible to make some form of assessment in relation to lying position in the crib. It has been shown by Casaer et al. (1973; see also Casaer, 1979) that normal newborns adapt to a particular lying position during the first few days of life and are easily discomforted if put in another position. It would be profitable to search for other such rapidly acquired habits which play a significant role in daily life.

Many other facets of the NBAS such as recording the modal versus the best performance (see Horowitz et al., 1978; Sameroff, 1978), the increase of prognostic value by repeating the examination, or the need for the examiner to test regularly normal infants when deviant infants are frequently seen, are similarly valid for the neurological examination and are not at all specific problems of behavioural assessment. A final remark concerns the stability of the test results over time. Obviously, influenced by psychometric considerations, psychologists seem often overconcerned with low test-retest reliability, while forgetting that in the developing organism this measure is inappropriate. One may successfully turn the question around and employ the NBAS as an assessment instrument for the developmental changes during the first weeks of life. Tracing the developmental course seems an important task for a behavioural assessment instrument.

The expectancy and claim of a higher prognostic value for the behavioural examination compared with the neurological assessment, has turned out to be wrong. The limitation—if considered as such—stems from insufficient appreciation of discontinuities in developmental processes (which have been clearly pointed out by Sameroff, 1978 and Emde, 1978). The ability to detect changes during development should not be seen as an artefact of the method, but can be of considerable clinical relevance.

Unfortunately, much has been made of a comparison of the long-term predictions of the NBAS and the rather crude neonatal neurological assessment employed in the Collaborative Study, showing that the NBAS has less 'false positives' by Tronick and Brazelton (1975). They arrived at far-reaching conclusions on the basis of follow-up data on only fifty-three children. The clinical importance of diagnosing significant but transient neurological conditions during early life has obviously completely escaped the authors. On the contrary, these results may rather indicate a worrying insensitivity of the NBAS to detect the presence of abnormal neurological conditions. The belief that in the NBAS: 'the 20 reflex items rule the neurological integrity in or out' (Als *et al.*, 1979; p. 212) is decidedly implausible.

CONCLUDING REMARKS

When trying to take an impartial look at the whole problem of neurological and behavioural assessment methods, one may easily agree that in this field encouraging advances have been achieved during the last 20 years. On the other hand the repeated *ad hoc* attempts to shorten or modify comprehensive and standardized methods have hampered rather than promoted progress, as they seem to have been made without careful reflection on the strategies of the approach, and without necessary expertise in examining the developing brain. One cannot escape the impression that item collections, which form a scale and produce a score, have a strong appeal despite the fact that what is to be quantified is often expressed only in vague terms.

Some of the disappointments with existing methods clearly originate from failures, which result from the use of techniques for problems, for which they were not designed and for which they are indeed inadequate. Uncritical application is often related to the fact that a particular method becomes fashionable. If it is fully appreciated what is examined by the different assessment methods, it is much easier to match the technique to the problem under study, and therefore, indiscriminate use can be avoided. This will also prevent false expectations, for instance that individual differences among newborns could be investigated with the aid of neurological assessment techniques, or that the neurological condition of a newborn infant could be evaluated by a behavioural assessment scale. This list of examples could be easily extended.

There are other neonatal assessment techniques which are, however, outside the scope of this chapter. The Apgar scoring system evaluates the acute condition of the infant in the first minutes after birth and nothing more. It does not really assess the condition of the nervous system as it has been clearly shown by Beintema (1968) that the items skin colour, tonus and reflex-excitability are closely correlated with the item respiration, provided the infants have a normal heart beat.

Neurological items have also been included in various techniques for the assessment of maturation of infants of unknown gestational age. As here neurological items are not used for the assessment of the condition of the nervous system but as indicators of neural maturation, together with external criteria of skin and cartilages, they have not been included in the present discussion.

A final point should not go unmentioned. Preterm infants can not be properly examine with techniques designed for full-term infants. Special neurological and behavioural assessment methods have to be employed but are only available to a limited extent. As these infants form clinically a most important group, future work will have to be directed to further development and to better standardization of these techniques. Since these infants more frequently suffer from neurological impairment than full-term newborns, special caution will be necessary in the design of behavioural assessment techniques to avoid the pitfalls already experienced with the methods for full-term infants.

It is to be hoped that with continuing refinement of present techniques and invention of new ones, newborn assessment will not only achieve the deserved recognition but will be even more actively used in the appropriate way.

ACKNOWLEDGEMENTS

For a thorough critique of the various versions of the manuscript I am deeply indepted to many friends and colleagues, especially to Dr O'Brien, Dr Touwen, Dr Hopkins, and Professor Huisjes. Without the inspiring and sometimes tough discussions, the manuscript would not have reached this final stage. For any shortcomings or inappropriate presentation of ideas of other authors I am exclusively at fault.

REFERENCES

Als, H., Tronick, E., Adamson, L., and Brazelton, T. B. (1976). The behavior of the full-term yet underweight newborn infant, *Develop. Med. Child Neurol.* **18**, 590–602.
Als, H., Tronick, E., Lester, B. M., and Brazelton, T. B. (1979). Specific neonatal

measures: the Brazelton Neonatal Behavioral Assessment Scale, in *Handbook of Infant Development* (Ed. J. D. Osofsky), pp. 185–215, Wiley, New York.

Amiel-Tison, C. (1979). Birth injury as a cause of brain dysfunction in full-term newborns, in *Advances in Perinatal Neurology*, Volume 1 (Eds R. Korobkin and Ch. Guilleminault), pp. 1–19, Sp. Medical & Scientific Books, New York.

André-Thomas, A., Chesni, Y., and Saint-Anne Dargassies, S. (1955). *Examen Neurologique du Nourrisson*, pp. 48, Vie médicale, Paris.

André-Thomas, A., Chesni, Y., and Saint-Anne Dargassies, S. (1960). *The Neurological Examination of the Infant*, Clinics in Developmental Medicine, no. 1, Heinemann, London.

Anokhin, P. K. (1964). Systemogenesis as a general regulator of brain development, in *The Developing Brain, Progress in Brain Research*, Volume 9 (Eds W. A. Himwich and H. E. Himwich), pp. 54–86, Elsevier, London.

Beintema, D. J. (1968). *A Neurological Study of Newborn Infants*, Clinics in Developmental Medicine, no. 28, pp. 178, Heinemann, London.

Brackbill, Y., Kane, J., Manniello, R. L., and Abramson, M. D. (1974). Obstetric meperidine usage and assessment of neonatal status, *Anaesthesiol.* **40**, 116.

Brazelton, T. B. (1973). *Neonatal Behavioral Assessment Scale*, Clinics in Developmental Medicine, no. 50, pp. 66, Heinemann, London.

Brazelton, T. B. (1978). Introduction, in *Monographs of the Society for Research in Child Development: Organization and Stability of Newborn Behavior Assessment Scale* (Ed. A. J. Sameroff), Serial no. 177, nos. 5–6, vol. 43, pp. 1–13, University of Chicago Press, Chicago.

Casaer, P. (1979). *Postural Behaviour in Newborn Infants*, Clinics in Developmental Medicine, no. 72, Heinemann, London.

Casaer, P., O'Brien, M. J., and Prechtl, H. F. R. (1973). Postural behaviour in human newborns, *Agressologie*, **14**, no. B, 49–56.

St. Clair, K. L. (1978). Neonatal assessment procedures: a historical review, *Child Develop.* **49**, 280–292.

Dreier, T., Wolff, P. H., Eager Cross, E., and Cochran, W. D. (1979). Patterns of breath intervals during non-nutritive sucking in full-term an 'at risk' preterm infants with normal neurological examinations, *Early Hum. Develop.* **3**, 187–199.

Dubowitz, V. (1978). Neurological assessment of small-for-dates and appropriate-for-dates full-term infants, *Asian Med. J.* **21**, 399–420.

Emde, R. N. (1978). Commentary, in *Monographs of the Society for Research in Child Development: Organization and Stability of Newborn Behavior Assessment Scale* (Ed. A. J. Sameroff), Serial no. 177, nos. 5–6, vol. 43, pp. 135–138, University of Chicago Press, Chicago.

Forfar, J. O. (1968). 'At risk' registers, *Develop. Med. Child Neurol.* **10**, 384–395.

Graham, F. K. (1956). Behavioral differences between normal and traumatized newborns. I. Test procedures. II. Standardization, reliability and validity, *Psychol. Monogr.* **70**, no. 20 and no. 21.

Hall, D. (1979). Neonatal neurology, in *Paediatric Neurology* (Ed. F. Clifford Rose), pp. 40–85, Blackwell Scientific Publications, Oxford.

Hobel, C. J., Hyvarinen, M. A., Okada, D. M., and Oh, W. (1973). Parenatal and intrapartum high-risk screening. I. Prediction of the high-risk neonate, *Amer. J. Obstet. Gynecol.* **117**, 1–9.

Hobel, C. J., Youkeles, L., and Forsythe, A. (1979). Prenatal and intrapartum high-risk screening. II. Risk factors reassessed, *Amer. J. Obstet. Gynecol.* **135**, 1051–1056.

Horowitz, F. D., Sullivan, J. W., and Linn, P. (1978). Stability and instability in the newborn infant: the quest for elusive threads, in *Monographs of the Society for research* in *Child Development: Organization and Stability of Newborn Behavior Assessment Scale* (Ed. A. J. Sameroff), Serial no. 177, nos. 5–6, vol. 43, pp. 29–45, University of Chicago Press, Chicago.

Huisjes, H. J., Oken, A., Prechtl, H. F. R., and Touwen, B. C. L. (1975), Neurological and pediatric findings in newborns of mothers with hypertensive disease in pregnancy, in: *Perinatal Medicine* (Eds Z. K. Stembera, K. Polacek, and V. Sabata), pp. 407–416, Thieme Verlag, Stuttgart.

Hutt, C., Bernuth, H. von, Lenard, H. G., Hutt, S. J., and Prechtl, H. F. R. (1968). Habituation in relation to state in the Human neonate, *Nature*, **220**, 618–620.

Joppich, G. and Schulte, F. J. (1968). *Neurologie des Neugeborenen*, Springer Verlag, Berlin.

Kaplan, S. L., Kron, R. E., Litt, M., Finnegan, L. P., and Phoenix, M. D. (1975). Correlations between scores on the Brazelton Neonatal Assessment Scale, measures of newborn sucking behavior, and birth-weight in infants born to narcotic addicted mothers, in *Aberrant Development in Infancy* (Ed. N. R. Ellis), pp. 139–148, Wiley, New York.

Kessen, W., Haith, M. M., and Salapatek, P. H. (1970). Human infancy: a bibliography and guide, in *Manual of Child Psychology* (Ed. P. H. Mussen), pp. 287–445, Wiley, New York.

Kittner, S. and Lipsitt, L. P. (1976). Obstetric history and the heart rate response of the newborn, *Develop. Med. Child Neurol.* **18**, 460–470.

Lester, B. M. and Zeskind, P. S. (1978). Brazelton scale and physical size correlates of neonatal cry features, *infant Behav. Develop.* **1**, 393–402.

Littman, B. (1979). The relationship of medical events to infant development, in *Infants Born at Risk* (Ed. T. Field), pp. 53–65, Sp. Medical & Scientific Books, New York.

Littman, B. and Parmelee, A. H. (1978). Medical correlates of infant development, *Pediat.* **61**, 470–474.

Martinius, J. and Papousek, H. (1970). Responses to optic and exteroceptive stimuli in relation to state in the human newborn: habituation of the blink reflex, *Neuropädiat.* **1**, 452–460.

Michaelis, R., Dopfer, R., Gerbig, W., Dopfer-Feller, P., and Rohr, M. (1979a). I. Die Erfassung obstetrischer und postnataler Risikofaktoren durch eine Liste optimaler Bedingungen, *Monatschr. Kinderheilk.* **127**, 149–155.

Michaelis, R., Dopfer-Feller, P., Dopfer, R., Gerbig, W., and Rohr, M. (1979b). II. Die Verteilung obstetrischer und postnataler Risikofaktoren bei 400 zufällig ausgewählten Neugeborenen, *Monatschr. Kinderheilk.* **127**, 196–200.

Michaelis, R., Parmelee, A. H., Stern, E., and Haber, A. (1973). Activity states in premature and term infants, *Develop. Psychobiol.* **6**, 209–216.

Michaelis, R., Schulte, F. J., and Nolte, R. (1970). Motor behavior of small for gestational age newborn infants, *J. Pediat.* **76**, 208–213.

Nesbitt, R. E. L. and Aubry, R. H. (1969). High-risk obstetrics. II. Value of semiobjective grading system in identifying the vulnerable group, *Obstet. Gynecol* **103**, 972–985.

O'Doherty, N. (1977). Neurological examination of the newborn, in *Neurodevelopmental Problems in Early Childhood* (Eds C. M. Drillien and M. B. Drummond), pp. 25–43, Blackwell Scientific Publications, Oxford.

Parmelee, A. H. (1974). Newborn neurological examination. Unpublished manuscript.

Parmelee, A. H. and Michaelis, R. (1971). Neurological examination of the newborn, in *Exceptional Infant*, vol. 2, *Studies in Abnormalities* (Ed. J. Hellmuth), pp. 3–23, Butterworths, London.

Peiper, A. (1963). *Cerebral Function of Infancy and Childhood*, Consultant Bureau, New York.

Pratt, K. C. (1954). The neonate, in *Manual of Child Psychology*, 2nd. edn (Ed. L. Carmichael), pp. 215–291, Wiley, New York.

Prechtl, H. F. R. (1960). Die neurologische Untersuchung des Neugeborenen, Voraussetzungen, Methode und Prognose, *Wiener Med. Wschr.* **110**, 1035–1039.

Prechtl, H. F. R. (1963). The mother–child interaction in babies with minimal brain damage (a follow-up study), in *Determinants of Infant Behaviour* II (Ed. J. M. Foss), pp. 53–66, Methuen, London.

Prechtl, H. F. R. (1965a). Prognostic value of neurological signs in the newborn infant, *Proc. Royal Soc. Med.* **58**, 3–4.

Prechtl, H. F. R. (1965b). Problems of behavioural studies in the newborn infant, in *Advances in the Study of Behavior* (Eds D. S. Lehrman, R. A. Hinde, and E. Shaw), pp. 75–96, Academic Press, New York.

Prechtl, H. F. R. (1967). Neurological sequelae of prenatal and perinatal complications, *Brit. Med. J.* **4**, 763–767.

Prechtl, H. F. R. (1968). Neurological findings in newborn infants after pre- and paranatal complications, in *Aspects of Praematurity and Dysmaturity. Nutricia Symposium.* (Eds J. H. P. Jonxis, H. K. A. Visser and J. A. Troelstra), pp. 303–321, Stenfer Kroese, Leiden.

Prechtl, H. F. R. (1970). Hazards of oversimplification, *Develop. Med. Child Neurol.* **12**, 522–524.

Prechtl, H. F. R. (1972a). Strategy and validity of early detection of neurological dysfunction, in *Mental Retardation: Prenatal Diagnosis and Infant Assessment* (Eds C. P. Douglas and K. S. Holt), pp. 41–46, Butterworths, London.

Prechtl, H. F. R. (1972b). Patterns of reflex behavior related to sleep in the human infant, in *Sleep and the Maturing Nervous System* (Eds C. D. Clemente, D. P. Purpura, and F. E. Mayer), pp. 287–301, Academic Press, New York.

Prechtl, H. F. R. (1974). The behavioural states of the newborn infant (a review), *Brain Res.* **76**, 1304–1311.

Prechtl, H. F. R. (1977a). *The Neurological Examination of the Full-term Newborn Infant.* Second revised and enlarged version. Clinics in Developmental Medicine, no. 63, pp. 65 Heinemann, London.

Prechtl, H. F. R. (1977b). Assessment and significance of behavioural states, in *Brain, Fetal and Infant* (Ed. S. R. Berenberg), pp. 79–90, Martinus Nijhoff, The Hague.

Prechtl, H. F. R. (1981). The study of neural development as a perspective of clinical problems, in *Maturation and Development* (Eds K. I. Connolly and H. F. R. Prechtl), pp. 198–215, Clinics in Developmental Medicine, Heinemann, London.

Prechtl, H. F. R., Akiyama, Y., Zinkin, P., and Kerr Grant, D. (1968). Polygraphic studies of the full-term newborn infants. I. Technical aspects and qualitative analysis, in *Studies in Infancy* (Eds M. C. O. Bax, and R. C. Mac Keith), pp. 1–25, Clinics in Developmental Medicine, no. 27, Heinemann, London.

Prechtl, H. F. R. and Beintema, D. J. (1964). *The Neurological Examination of the Full-term Newborn Infant.* Clinics in Developmental Medicine, no. 12, pp. 74, Heinmann, London.

Prechtl, H. F. R. and Dijkstra J. (1960). Neurological diagnosis of cerebral injury in the newborn, in *Prenatal Care*, pp. 222–231, Noordhoff, Groningen.

Prechtl, H. F. R., Weinmann, H., and Akiyama, Y. (1969). Organization of physiological parameters in normal and neurologically abnormal infants: comprehensive computer analysis of polygraphic data, *Neuropädiat.* **1**, 101–129.

Rogers, M. G. H. (1968). Risk registers and early detection of handicaps, *Develop. Med. Child Neurol.* **10**, 651–661.

Rosenblith, J. F. (1979). The Graham/Rosenblith behavioural examination for new-borns: prognostic value and procedural issues, in *Handbook of Infant Development* (Ed. J. D. Osofsky), pp. 216–249, Wiley, New York.

Saint-Anne Dargassies, S. (1974). *Le Développement Neurologique du Nouveau-né à Terme et Prématuré*, pp. 337, Masson, Paris.

Saint-Anne Dargassies, S. (1977). *Neurological Development in the Full-term and Premature Neonate*, Elsevier, Amsterdam.

Saint-Anne Dargassies, S. (1979). The normal and abnormal neurological examination of the neonate: silent neurological abnormalities, in *Advances in Perinatal Neurology*, Volume 1 (Eds R. Korobkin and Ch. Guilleminault), pp. 1–19, Sp. Medical & Scientific Books, New York.

Sameroff, A. J. (1978). Summary and conclusions: the future of newborn assessment, in *Monographs of the Society for Research in Child Development: Organization and Stability of Newborn Behaviour Assessment Scale* (Ed. A. J. Sameroff), Serial no. 177, nos. 5–6, vol. 43, pp. 102–123, University of Chicago Press, Chicago.

Scarr, S. and Williams, M. L. (1971). The assessment of neonatal and later status in low birthweight infants. Paper presented at biennial meeting of the Society for Research in Child Development, Minneapolis.

Schulte, F. J. and Schwenzel, W. (1965). Motor control and muscle tone in the newborn period. Electromyographic studies, *Biol. Neonat.* **8**, 198–215.

Scott, K. G. and Masic, W. (1979). The outcome from and utility of registers of risk, in *Infants Born at Risk* (Ed. T. M. Field), pp. 485–496, Sp. Medical & Scientific Books, New York.

Self, P. A. and Horowitz, F. D. (1979). The behavioral assessment of the neonate: an overview, in *Handbook of Infant Development* (Ed. J. D. Osofsky), pp. 126–164, Wiley, New York.

Sigman, M., Kopp, C. B., Parmelee, A. H., and Jeffrey, W. E., (1973). Visual attention and neurological organization in neonates, *Child Develop.* **44**, 461–466.

Soule, A. B., Standley, K., Copans, S. A., and Davis, M. (1974). Clinical uses of the Brazelton neonatal scale, *Pediat.* **54**, 583–586.

Standley, K., Soule, A. B., Copans, S. A., and Duchowny, M. S. (1974). Local-regional anesthesia during childbirth: effect on newborn behavior, *Science*, **186**, 634–635.

Stembera, Z. K., Zezulakova, J., Dittrichova, J., and Znamenacek, K. (1975). Identification and quantification of high-risk factors affecting fetus and newborn, in *Perinatal Medicine* (Eds Z. K. Stembera, K. Polacek, and V. Sabata), pp. 400–416, Thieme Publications, Stuttgart.

Stennert, E., Schulte, F. J., Vollrath, M., Brunner, E., and Frauenrath, C. (1978). The etiology of neurosensory hearing defects in preterm infants, *Arch. Otorhinolaryngol.* **221**, 171–182.

Telzrow, R., Snyder, D., Tronick, E., Als, H., and Brazelton, T. B. (1976). The effects of phototherapy on neonatal behavior. Presented at the Meeting of the American Pediatric Society, St. Louis.

Touwen, B. C. L., Bierman-Van Endenburg, M., and Jurgens-Van der Zee, A. (1977). The neurological screening of full-term newborn infants, *Develop. Med. Child Neurol.* **19**, 739–747.

Touwen, B. C. L., Huisjes, H. J. Jurgens-Van der Zee, A. D.. Bierman-Van Eendenburg, M. E. C., Smrkovsky, M., and Olinga, A. A. (1980). Obstetrical condition and neonatal neurological morbidity. An analysis with help of the optimality-concept, *Early Hum. Develop.* **4**, 207–228.

Tronick, E. and Brazelton, T. B. (1975). Clinical uses of the Brazelton Neonatal

Behavioral Assessment, in *Exceptional Infant* 3: *Assessment and Intervention* (Eds B. Z. Friedlander, G. M. Sterrit, and G. E. Kirk), pp. 137–156, Brunner/Mazel, New York.

Tronick, E., Wise, S., Als, H., Adamson, L., Scanlon, J., and Brazelton, T. B. (1976). Regional obstetric anesthesia and newborn behavior: effect over the first ten days of life, *Pediat.*, **58**, 94–100.

Volpe, J. J. (1979). Value of neonatal neurologic examination, *Pediat.* **64**, 547–548.

Psychobiology of the Human Newborn
Edited by P. Stratton
© 1982, John Wiley & Sons, Ltd.

CHAPTER 3

Behavioural States of the Full-term Newborn.
The Emergence of A Concept

HEINZ F. R. PRECHTL and MICHAEL JOHN O'BRIEN

WHY BEHAVIOURAL STATES?

It may be surprising that the concept of behavioural states in its contemporary connotations dates no further back than the end of the fifties of this century. What led 25 years ago to a gradual emergence of this concept in infant research? One of the main reasons was discontent with the large range of unexplained variations in many physiological and behavioural variables which had been measured in healthy neonates. This variability exists not only between but also within individuals, a fact clearly evident in tables appearing in Clement Smith's classic textbook *The Physiology of the Newborn Infant* (1959).

A similar inconsistency bedevilled early attempts to refine the technique of neurological examination of infants. For a long time the common opinion held was that refinement was not feasible because so many of the newborn's responses are inconsistent from one moment to another. Neurological responses showing unpredictable variance are unsuitable for inclusion in a neurological exam- ination. Therefore, this view held that one can do no better than look for consistent abnormal signs, all other findings being uninterpretable.

A further source of concern was the variability of EEG patterns in newborn infants. Not only are there differences between sleep and wakefulness but the EEG shows very different patterns throughout a single sleep epoch. The discovery of different distinct sleep states (Kleitman, 1963) helped to promote understanding of these variations and led to the realization of the necessity to complement EEG recordings with simultaneous polygraphic recordings of eye movements, respiration signals and ECG, in order to facilitate an interpretation of the EEG within the context of monitored sleep states.

In the domain of behavioural studies the well-known investigations of neonatal activity by Irwin (1932a,b) provide an excellent illustration of how indispensable a behavioural state concept is for a meaningful presentation and interpretation of such data. The large intra-individual variations in activity found in his study posed a puzzle which remained unsolved even when activity was measured in relation to sleep and wakefulness. Furthermore, Irwin's obvious reluctance to subject the raw data to a thorough visual analysis led him to overlook the cyclic waxing and waning of activity as well as the periodicity of gross movement bursts which are so characteristic for the young infant. A solution was delayed till later naturalistic observations of complex newborn behaviour led to a classification in terms of discrete states of ongoing sleep and wakefulness.

Although scientific interest in behavioural states such as sleep and wakefulness has been a recurring theme at least since Aristotle stated 'why we are asleep and awake and by which sense or senses, needs to be investigated' we still lack satisfactory answers concerning the causes of these phenomena, although the study of the quality and quantity of sleep states and to a lesser degree also of states of wakefulness has been more successful, not only in adults but also in newborn and young infants. It has become customary to open papers on newborn behaviour or psychophysiology with a statement about the importance of taking behavioural state into account. The existence of states is one of those phenomena which, once recognized, becomes so obvious as to make it difficult to understand why it was not appreciated earlier.

Those who expected to find clarification about states in the standard handbooks on infant development will be disappointed. In Carmichael's *Manual of Child Psychology* (1946) state is not yet mentioned. However, in Mussen's edition of 1970 there are a few short references to 'state of arousal' and in Osofsky's *Handbook of Infant Development* (1979) 'states of consciousness' are rather superficially dealt with without any theoretical discussion of the state concept. The discrepancy between the appreciation of the importance of states for infant research and the reluctance to arrive at a conceptual underpinning of the state concept is striking.

WHAT ARE BEHAVIOURAL STATES?

The connotation of the term state, which is derived from the Latin 'status', is: *condition* or *manner of existence*. It refers to 'a combination of circumstances or attributes belonging for the time being to a person or thing; a particular manner or way of existing, as defined by the presence of certain circumstances or attributes; a condition' (Oxford Dictionary).

The term state has been widely used in classical physics to describe the condition of matter, i.e. gaseous, fluid, solid, crystallized or amorphous. In quantum mechanics the condition of particles or subparticles is referred to as state. In systems theory a more general and ubiquitous connotation is given to the term state, applicable also to living matter in biological and psychological problems. The great advantage of a system's theoretical approach is the rigor of formalization which helps to overcome some of the uncertainty and fuzziness of living processes. There are good reasons to apply the concept of state developed in systems theory to the description of states in the infant, as a considerable gain in clarity can be obtained.

A very useful definition of state is given by Ashby (1956; p. 25) 'by a state of a system is meant any well-defined condition or property that can be recognized if it occurs again. Every system will naturally have many possible states.' If the definition is applied to describe and categorize the behaviour of newborns as revealed by prolonged observations, it is clear that many different types of states can be observed. The infant can be in a state of hunger or satiation, he can be in a state of quiescence or motor-activity, and there is also the dichotomy between the states of sleep and wakefulness. The term 'state' was used with a diversity of meanings in a number of early papers on infant behaviour (e.g. Prechtl, 1958; Escalona, 1962). Such an all-embracing connotation of 'states of the organism' is not very useful because one simply ends up with a minute listing of all possible behaviours and physiological conditions. It seems more fruitful, therefore, to restrict the connotation of state to the various classes of wakefulness and sleep.

A keen interest in sleep in young infants was already present before the turn of the last century. The amount of sleep was and has remained a matter of intensive research for 100 years. The percentage of sleep and its distribution over 24 h was intensively studied (Bühler and Hetzer, 1927; Gesell and Amatruda, 1945; Parmelee, 1961).

The investigation of the depth of sleep was another matter of concern. The idea of 'level of arousal' or 'level of vigilance or consciousness' with their notions of a continuum progressing from deep sleep to extreme alertness probably derived from this interest. This concept has more or less been given up, although the terms still linger. One reason which led to a shift away from this concept was the discovery, or rather the rediscovery, of motor phenomena such as eye movements under closed eye lids, irregularities in the rhythm of breathing, grimaces and twitching movements during sleep. These phenomena had been observed in infants, for instance by Preyer (1880), Czerny (1892), and Zipperling (1913) but their significance as indicators of a particular sleep stage was not appreciated until Aserinsky and Kleitman (1955) described their cyclic appearance during sleep. When a relationship between eye-movement sleep periods and dreaming came to be suspected, a new boom in sleep research began, which included the young infant as an object for study. There were other contributing reasons for this also. Electrophysiological recordings in laboratory animals and sleeping humans revealed two different EEG patterns during sleep, the slow-high amplitude-EEG and the fast-low amplitude-EEG. The latter gave rise to the term 'paradoxical sleep' because the EEG pattern resembled that during the awake condition. Furthermore the concept of an unspecific regulatory system localized in the reticular formation of the brain stem (Moruzzi and Magoun, 1949) became a theoretical framework for studies on sleep and arousal. The impact these approaches had on the investigation of the infant's behavioural states was to lead to the designing of 'EEG states', 'eye movement states' and, as a result of both combined, 'polygraphic states'. The latter was especially necessary in the light of awareness that the EEG alone could not be interpreted in its relation to state if other variables (EOG and respiration) were not also recorded.

Taking a different approach, and one which had important consequences, Wolff (1959) made naturalistic observations of newborns. These led him to a more comprehensive inventory of states, as there were now no technical restraints prohibiting the inclusion of awake behaviour in the investigation—the frequent movements during wakefulness made artefact-free EEG recording impossible and wakefulness was therefore more or less neglected in EEG studies, although Kleitman, back in 1929, had suggested moving away from exclusive sleep research in order to pay due attention to wakefulness.

ESSENTIAL CHARACTERISTICS OF STATES

Naturally one does not want to call every condition in which a newborn infant can be found a state. Many are transitory events, such as gross movements or apnoea and therefore lack the main characteristic of states—the stability of the condition over time (in the order of minutes rather than of seconds). It is also desirable to exclude from the state classification specific activities such as sucking and feeding. What is left are spontaneous conditions of sleep and wakefulness which are in themselves stable but during which many events or special activities may occur which may or may not be exclusively restricted to particular states.

The consequence of this concept is obvious. The assessment of states can only meaningfully be carried out if the window of the observed or monitored signals is sufficiently large. Seen in the light of this consideration, state assessment in consecutive 10 or 20 s epochs is an inadequate method. The method of choice is a moving window of at least one, often preferably three, minutes. (for details see below).

Another characteristic of states is that they refer to complex conditions. Only if a set of variables displays a particular property in concert, can a state be identified. Hence, states are complex conditions which by definition can never be recognized and described by the analysis of only one variable. In the past this became patently clear through the failure of state assessment based on fetal heart-rate patterns alone or on the recording of only the EEG in the young infant. In both cases, the proper interpretation of these signals turned out to be impossible without the simultaneous recording of other signals.

The mutually exclusive conditions, called states, are characterized by their *quality* which is determined by particular parameters (statistical properties) of an *ensemble* of variables. Therefore, states have qualitative rather than quantitative properties and are properly assessed by pattern-recognition.

A further characteristic of states is their cyclic organization. This means that under normal conditions, states tend to follow each other in an ordered, non-random sequence.

THE SYSTEMATIC STUDY OF BEHAVIOURAL STATES

(a) Naturalistic Observations

A human newborn infant when closely watched in his usual environment over a long time reveals an amazingly wide variety of specific behaviour patterns. They seem to be spontaneously generated although they are not entirely unrelated to environmental stimuli. This may be one of the important reasons why they received no attention within the behaviouristic paradigm and were only discovered during systematic observations of unstimulated infants. After about 100 years of anecdotal reports on the behavioural expressions of sleep and wakefulness in the neonate a systematic and descriptive categorization was provided by Wolff (1959). His scale of behavioural state—although not yet called such—was arrived at from naturalistic observations on four newborn infants who were watched for 16–18 h a day during their first 5 days of life. During this study the author saw recurrent behaviour patterns of similar morphology in all infants which he described empirically as (a) regular sleep, (b) irregular sleep, (c) drowsiness, with in addition (d) alert inactivity, (e) alert activity and (f) crying, which were mentioned but not defined until a later publication (Wolff, 1966) based on similar observations of a larger group of infants. Such a convenient classification of easily observable behavioural phenomena was a break-through in infant research for which Wolff deserves full credit. Strange to say, Wolff never mentioned exactly how this categorization was achieved but his motivation to carry out such observations was that they had 'many implications for Piaget's theory of intelligence and for the psychoanalytic theory of development' (Wolff, 1959).

Many later observational studies on neonatal behavioural states took as their starting point this early description and classification by Wolff. Although the emphasis and the purpose of these later studies was different, they all aimed at a better understanding of the phenomena of behavioural states. The newly discovered high degree of organization in the behaviour of newborn infants was the attraction which motivated these investigations. Korner and her coworkers (Korner, 1969; see Korner, 1972) extended Wolff's observations, focussing on individual and sex differences in concomitants of states such as startles, smiles, erections and oral activity. Thoman originally working with Korner, continued her work on states and developed methods of state monitoring (by observing the unstimulated infant) as an instrument for assessing the infant's condition (Thoman, 1975; Thoman and Tynan, 1979; Thoman et al., 1981). In Denver, Emde and coworkers (1969) paid special attention to smiling in REM sleep, and to wakefulness in relation to the feeding regime during the first 3 days of life

(Gaensbauer and Emde, 1973). It is clear that observational studies are greatly facilitated by the use of film (Korner, 1972) and video techniques (including time lapse recording, (Anders and Miller Sostek, 1976).

(b) Polygraphic Investigations

Substantial contributions to a better understanding and quantification of behavioural states came from polygraphic recordings of a varying number of physiological signals. When during the 1950s recording equipment for elec-troencephalography became more widely available, systematic studies of the EEG in infants began. Before this the only information available was derived from the early work of Lindsley (1936, 1939) on his own child, using home-made amplifiers.

After 1950 Paris became a centre of newborn research. Interest was concentrated firstly on finding out about the age-related changes of EEG patterns during development of the preterm and term infant as an approach to the estimation of the conceptional age, and secondly on detecting cerebral abnormalities on the basis of characteristic pathological changes of the EEG tracings. Very soon, however, it became clear that the states of sleep and wakefulness are strong determinants of the EEG-patterns and must be taken into account when a proper evaluation of the EEG is attempted. Arising from the need to monitor other variables in addition to the EEG as state-indicators (e.g. Delange et al., 1962) polygraphic techniques came to be recognized as a powerful tool with which to study the phenomena of behavioural states in their own right, even though such studies were mainly restricted to sleep. In a series of studies the quantitative inter-relationship between EEG, respiration, eye movements and tonic activity in the chin muscles were investigated (Monod and Pajot, 1965; Eliet-Flescher and Dreyfus-Brisac, 1966). Under abnormal neurological con-ditions these relationships were found to be distorted, (Monod et al., 1967) indicating that the analysis of behavioural states might provide a diagnostic tool to complement the clinical neurological examination (Prechtl et al., 1969; Prechtl, 1977, 1978).

Parmelee and his coworkers continued this kind of investigation in Los Angeles in order to objectify behavioural observations by means of polygraphic recordings. His main interest was in the maturation of EEG patterns (Parmelee et al., 1968, 1969) and in comparing sleep states in preterm infants recorded when they reached 40 weeks conceptional age with those found in normal full-term babies (see Parmelee and Stern, 1972).

While this first-mentioned line of research developed from EEG studies, another line of investigation was directed to the ontogeny of rapid eye movement sleep. To a considerable extent, this interest was stimulated by the description of two sleep states, namely rapid eye movement sleep (REM) with bodily motility and non-rapid eye movement sleep (NREM) without gross motility in infants of

1–7 months of age (Aserinsky and Kleitman, 1955). These authors have not reported on newborns although they are often wrongly cited as having done so. There was some ambiguity in the beginning of this new wave of sleep research between sleep states on the one hand and motility cycles with interspersed quiescence periods (the so-called Basic-Rest-Activity cycles, abbreviated as BRAC) on the other hand. Roffwarg *et al.* (1966) discussed their findings on active and quiescent phases in newborns as well as up to middle and old ages but concluded that 'there can be no certainty as to whether infants have actual sensory hallucinations ("dreams") during REM sleep'. Moreover, the phenomenon of rapid eye movements had been studied in detail by Petre-Quadens (1967; Petre-Quadens *et al.*, 1971) who showed age-related changes in the amount of REM sleep between 28 weeks gestation and the first month post-term. Prechtl and Lenard (1967) analysed the statistical characteristics of eye movements from recordings with long time constants which permitted proper evaluation of slow as well as rapid eye movements. The REMs have non-sequential interval distributions which are not Poisson distributions and have a tail with longer intervals. These interval distributions also differ from those of saccadic eye movements during wakefulness (investigated in the same babies).

A third line of polygraphic investigations in full-term neonates had still another background and purpose. Prechtl and his coworkers were interested in a more thorough understanding of the quality of the neural mechanisms underlying behavioural states, including awake states. This question arose from Prechtl's neurological examinations of newborn infants. Although behavioural states were originally introduced in his method (Prechtl and Beintema, 1964) for standardization of the examination procedure, it soon became apparent that some babies with neurological problems showed odd sequences of their behavioural states throughout the examination. It was not clear, however, whether these deviations in the 'state profile' were due to alterations of the baby's reactivity to the stimulations, which were applied during the examination, or whether these infants had suffered from a disturbance of those neural functions responsible for the organization of the sequence and quality of behavioural states. In order to find an answer to this question a series of polygraphic studies was carried out on healthy and neurologically deviant newborn infants, during which no stimuli were applied. In contrast to the normal infants, abnormal babies in this unstimulated condition often showed unstable state sequences and dissociated states similar to those seen during the neurological examination. It can be concluded that abnormal states are a sign of neural dysfunction and are not induced by, nor do they only become manifest during, stimulation.

A critical point in the assessment of long polygraphic recordings is the way in which the signals are analysed. The most common technique is the subjective judgement of states per consecutive short epoch (per page of 20 or 30 s) on the basis of visual inspection (e.g. Monod, Parmelee). Anders (1974) has suggested computer processing techniques for these subjective evaluations once they are transferred to punch cards. A more convenient and objective way is the direct computer processing of the recorded analog signals, as has been introduced by Prechtl (1968; Prechtl et al., 1969; Theorell et al., 1974). These authors computed the parameters of the following variables per consecutive 3 min epoch: EEG power, medians and quartiles of respiration and of heart beat, and number of rapid eye movements. The computer plots provided compiled state profiles from which the cycling, state transitions, state durations and state sequences can be easily derived.

More recently the method of consecutive epoch analysis has been replaced by continuous moving window analysis (Prechtl, 1978; Scholten and Vos, 1981, and in press) which provides better statistical descriptors of the recorded signals which can also be subjected to cross-correlation analysis. This enables identification of significant relationships between variables which cannot be achieved by epoch analysis because of the serial correlation of the data, a problem also present in Anders's (1974) technique. A crucial point is, however, that the window for the state identification be sufficiently long. It is not helpful, to diagnose states per short epoch of 20 s or so, as behavioural states are by definition relatively stable conditions which do not change after such short durations.

As a final point, it should be mentioned that for a proper evaluation of the state expressions per recording, the recording needs to be sufficiently long. To record one sleep cycle is usually insufficient because even the intra-individual variations are large from cycle to cycle. Prechtl has therefore stated that a 6 h recording time, including wakefulness is advisable (Theorell et al., 1973; Prechtl et al., 1973; Prechtl, 1974).

(c) Studies on the Input-Output-State-Relation

The notion that certain reflexes in the newborn cannot be examined if the infant is not in an appropriate behavioural state, has a long tradition of anecdotal observations. Systematic studies of this phenomenon were not carried out before the sixties. If behavioural states represent not only a merely convenient categorization of observable behaviours, but are an expression of particular conditions of neural functioning, it can be expected that the stimulus-response patterns of different modalities vary with states. The concept of states as a continuum of vigilance or arousal ranging from deep sleep to high alertness, would predict an absence of responses in deep sleep and an increase in responsivity with increasing arousal. Such a gradient of responsivity which parallels the supposed continuum of states, has not been found in any stimulus-response pattern. On the contrary, it became evident that response patterns to stimuli of different modalities show striking differences in their input–output relation. This fact is a strong plea for the assumption that behavioural states do not represent a continuum of internal, neural conditions, but are expressions of discontinuous and distinct modes of neural activity and reactivity.

It is clear that for an investigation of the input-output-state-relation only those state classifications are valid which are not based on or influenced by the observed changes in reactivity, but which are derived from observations of the unstimulated organism. To the first category belong for instance the Pavlovian 'state of optimal excitability of the CNS' which he considered a fundamental prerequisite for conditioning. Such a class of state, however, is derived from the very property which it is the investigators intention to explain. Papoušek (see for review of his previous work 1967, 1969, 1974) tried to escape this pitfall by introducing a classification of 'state of alertness' which he used in his experiments on conditioned head turning in young infants. The design of his scale seemed not to have fully excluded a bias in the direction of responsiveness, but he clearly indicated that the stimulation and/or the execution of the response may have an effect on the ongoing state. Such an awareness was also crucial for Prechtl's standardized neurological examination. Only a carefully designed sequence of the tests could prevent a baby from being in inappropriate states in the beginning of the examination. Items interfering with the infant's state must only be tested at the end of the procedure.

Wolff (1959) reported on state related changes in responsiveness to tactile, auditory and vibration stimuli. His scale of states (called 'stages', 'conditions' or 'states of responsiveness') was obtained from observations of unstimulated infants, and was therefore independently designed. He (Wolff, 1966) also drew attention to the possible change of the existing state by stimulation '. . . the infant's response was not exclusively a function of state, and modality (of stimuli) had something to do with the direction of change (response)'.

A different design was adopted in a series of studies on the input-output-state-relation, carried out in Groningen by Prechtl's group (Prechtl, 1972). States were monitored polygraphically over several hours. The infant remained unstimulated for about half of the time, while during the other half one type of stimulus of constant intensity was presented at regular intervals, avoiding too close a spacing of the stimuli. The state-related waxing and waning of the response intensities was monitored and measured from either the EMG or EOG, depending on whether the response consisted of a limb-muscle contraction (e.g. knee-jerk) or eye movement (e.g. vestibulo-ocular response). For the assessment of a possible influence of the stimulation on the distribution of the states each infant acted as his own control.

As could be expected, striking differences in the response intensities were found in different states. However, the state dependent input–output relations were similar in various responses when the modality of the eliciting stimuli were the same. The group of proprioceptive responses such as tendon jerk reflexes or the Moro-reaction to vibration of the labyrinth, are all maximally strong during state 1 (quiet sleep, NREM sleep). It is also the only condition in which an ankle clonus can be observed in normal infants (Lenard *et al.*, 1968). Proprioceptive responses are weak or absent during state 2 (active sleep, REM sleep). There is a close negative correlation between the density of rapid eye movements and the size of the response (Prechtl and Lenard, 1967; Prechtl *et al.*, 1967a). These types of responses are of medium intensity during state 3 (quiet wakefulness), but cannot be examined in strongly moving and crying infants (Lenard *et al.*, 1968; Prechtl *et al.*, 1967a, b).

Exteroceptive skin responses show a state-dependent pattern different from that of proprioceptive responses. Whether the stimulus is tactile or mild pressure on the skin, responses are virtually absent during state 2, and reliably obtainable during state 3, (Vlach *et al.*, 1969; Prechtl *et al.*, 1967b; Lenard *et al.*, 1968).

A peculiar group of responses are nociceptive responses. Of all responses studied so far, they are the least state dependent. The stimulus does not necessarily have to be painful, tickling also being effective. Nociceptive responses to scratch of the skin, such as the Babinski and abdominal reflex, are present and only slightly weaker during state 1 than during state 2 and 3 (Lenard *et al.*, 1968).

Auditory orienting responses to well-defined artificial and natural stimuli have usually been found to be absent during state 1, consistently present in state 2 although slightly weaker in this state than during state 3 (Hutt *et al.*, 1968).

Responses elicited from the semicircular canal such as the vestibulo-ocular response are clearly absent during state 1, but present during state 2 when REMs are superimposed on the slow oscillating eye movements elicited in response to the stimulus. During state 3 the amplitude of the response is larger still and the phase angle between stimulus and response is different from that found during state 2 (v. Bernuth and Prechtl, 1969).

THE CHOICE OF VARIABLES AS STATE INDICATORS

According to the behavioural state concept, recurrent cyclical changes occur in the state of the nervous system. These system states are recognizable through their effect on both spontaneous behavioural output and on input–output relations. The existence of a small number of mutually exclusive sleep and wakefulness states in newborn infants has been confirmed at a variety of levels of analysis varying from the behavioural through the electrophysiological. Differences in background led those interested in categorizing states to adopt varying criteria and nomenclature for states. Despite some differences, there is a rather high level of agreement about the classification of states. This is important in strengthening the view that states are *a priori* patterns of activity and not simply constructs of the observer's mind (Schleidt and Crawley, 1980). This is not to say that a considerable element of arbitrary choice does not exist in the categorization of states. For instance, state scales designed by an investigator interested in the extent to which states represent patterns of activity shared by all normal newborns, are likely to exclude variables subject to considerable inter-individual differences, whereas scales intended to be sensitive to just this aspect will include such variables. To the extent that such differences in purpose result in different methods of identifying and quantifying states, states have an arbitrary quality.

There are some limiting factors, however, in the choice and handling of variables intended as state criteria. Those variables chosen, whether they be behavioural or electrophysiological or both, must be relevant to the basic problem, namely that of detecting changes in the character of sleep and wakefulness. As Arbib says:

There is essentially no limit to how many variables one could include in the analysis—the art of good theory is to select the variables that really matter. A theory of human cognition might take into account wind gusts and the temperature of the left armpit, but one has no reason to expect the inclusion of such whimsical variables to yield a better theory. A crucial task in any theory-building is to pick the right variables (1972; p. 58).

The variables that have been found in the past to show state-like changes in pattern and have therefore been incorporated in state scales include the regularity or irregularity of the breathing and heart beat rhythms, the presence or absence of eye movements under closed eyelids, sustained openness or closedness of the eyelids, the presence or absence of motility and its quality, the presence or absence of crying, the presence of a high- or a low-voltage EEG pattern, and the presence or absence of tonic chin muscle electromyographic activity.

Certain considerations should influence the drafting of a set of state criteria. States should preferably be identified on the basis of no more than three or four essential criteria. Use of a small but representative group of either visually observable or technically recordable items maximizes the probability of identifying stable states of the central nervous system. It avoids on the one hand the risks of error deriving from the use of only single variables to indicate state, and on the other hand the fragmentary state profiles that result when states are defined according to rigid criteria using many variables which differ widely in their properties and in their consistency as state indicators. This latter type of scoring leads to dubious state categories such as indeterminate sleep or ambiguous sleep. A further practical argument in favour of a small number of straightforward criteria is that this increases the ease and reliability with which state can be scored by relatively naive or inexperienced investigators.

Good criteria have a continuous quality as opposed to an episodic one. Thus respiration pattern which can be scored from visual observation or from recorded signals as regular or irregular has proven to be a good criterion for the full-term infant. It distinguishes clearly between two mutually exclusive eye-closed states ('sleep' states) under all but the most pathological conditions such as coma or sedative overdose. This was recognized by Wolff (1959) in his original state classification.

Absolute respiratory rate and heart rate on the other hand are poor criteria, being easily influenced by incidental gross movements and exhibiting inconsistent discrimination between states. Rates are usually higher after a feed, irrespective of the state (Prechtl *et al.*, 1968; Ashton and Connolly, 1971; Ashton, 1973).

The condition of the eyelids, tonically open or closed, which can either be observed directly or scored from appropriate film or video recordings, is generally very useful in distinguishing between sleep and awake states. In the preterm infant, however (Prechtl *et al.*, 1979), and occasionally also in the full-term infant, periods of frequent eye opening and closing may occur during which this criterion can no longer be applied. This phenomenon led Wolff (1959) and Brazelton (1973) to invent a state of drowsiness. It seems highly dubious whether the unstable conditon they refer to meets the criterion of a separate state. It has more the character of either a transition, between state 3 and state 2, or of transient behaviour within an ongoing state 2. Frequent eyelid opening and closing is not uncommonly associated with intense eyeball movements and appreciation of the condition of other variables often permits confident inclusion of such periods in an ongoing state 2.

The value of eyeball movements under closed eyelids as an essential criterion of one of the two distinct sleep states has been rather uncritically accepted. Though fairly easy to observe and to record, they have the disadvantage of being episodic and of being subject to specific reduction in number under certain abnormal conditions.

Another widely but uncritically used state criterion is the presence or absence of chin muscle tonic EMG activity. Polygraphic studies show that the presence of tonic EMG activity is unsuitable as an *essential* criterion for quiet sleep because its expression is too variable (Eliet-Flescher and Dreyfus-Brisac, 1966, Schloon *et al.*, 1976). This type of parameter is thus better viewed as a state concomitant, whose presence is confirmatory but whose absence should not preclude recognition of quiet sleep if other, more robust, criteria are met. Interestingly, the tonic activity of respiratory muscles, especially the diaphragm is very consistent during state 1 (Prechtl *et al.*, 1977).

The last commonly employed state criterion is the EEG pattern. If it can be reliably recorded this is, under normal circumstances, quite a good sleep-state criterion being continuously scoreable and showing good state specificity. Mainly because of the difficulties many laboratories experience in recording artefact-free signals during movement, its usefulness as an indicator of discrete awake states has not been evaluated. Even as a sleep-state indicator it is susceptible to changes not related to state, changes so dramatic as to nullify the value of the EEG pattern as a state criterion. Thus in neurological illnesses such as during the acute stages of severe birth asphyxia and in severe brain malformations, states may still be recognizable on the basis of respiration and eye condition while the EEG may be so grossly abnormal as to show no cyclic changes (Monod and Guidasci, 1976; Theorell, 1974). This raises the important point that in clinical situations where the EEG is abnormal, the use of non-EEG measures to indicate the state may make it possible to diagnose the state dependency of paroxysmal or frankly convulsive EEG activity.

A further problem in state categorization concerns the minimum acceptable duration of states. Since states reflect complex modes of nervous system operation and since stability, to the eye of the observer, is a defining characteristic of states, the minimum duration of states and of the corresponding moving time window to be used in assessing state changes must be in the order of minutes and not seconds, a point which becomes evident on reviewing time-compressed polygraphic records. The characteristics of the fluctuations in the parameters, thought to have relevance as state indicators, must determine the choice of a minimum duration of states. Once this minimum duration has been decided, changes in state can be evaluated by applying a moving-window analysis technique. This method of analysis contains the idea that a state change is only accepted if the new state lasts for at least the necessary minimum duration. A willingness to retain a certain intelligent flexibility is desirable as a general principle of state categorization, and a too rigid formalistic approach is to be eschewed.

This raises the crucial question as to whether the observer is interested in studying the neural mechanisms of state in the sense of conditions of the nervous system or is simply devoted to the strict application of the algorithm of chosen state criteria. If the latter is the case he will easily become a victim of the fact, that practically all variables which can be employed as state criteria, display signs of noise. When the criterion is 'open eyes' all blinks are noise whereas when the eyes are closed, strong rapid eye movement in the upward direction may be accompanied by shortlasting opening of the eyelids. During state 1, the respiration is regular and there are no gross movements except short startles. But even in perfectly healthy newborns, incidental stretches or other general movements may occur and they do disrupt the regular breathing briefly. This should be considered as noise and not as a different state. To give a final example: The number of eye movements does fluctuate even during normal REM sleep and there may be short epochs with very few or even without any eye movement (see Prechtl and Lenard, 1967), followed later by an increase again in their rate of occurrence. If the presence of eye movements is used as an obligatory state criterion, the ongoing state would have to be scored as being interrupted.

What the consequences are of including these noise phenomena in the scoring of state sequences can be most impressively demonstrated when the time course of states is graphically displayed in a state profile (Figure 1). The need for a smoothing procedure with a moving window (e.g. of 3 min length) is obvious, to filter out rapid fluctuations. Superimposed on the ongoing stable states, these fluctuations obscure the very information one is searching for. This illustrates again the fact that states, whatever criteria are used, are abstractions, derived

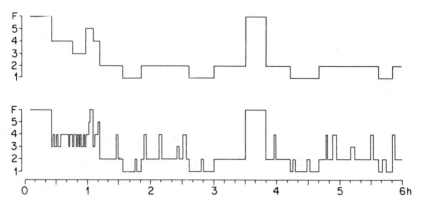

Figure 1   Above: Smoothed state profile with a 3 min moving window. Five day old neonate. Below: The same as above, with a 1 min moving window. F = feeding and handling

from noisy indicators. Each variable has some degree of instability in the parameters which can be used as state indicators and it is a matter of proper data processing and often of common sense to distinguish between 'real' state changes and artefacts produced by too rigid a scoring system.

Each episode of a stable state is separated from the one before and after it by a state transition. During these transitions the various variables change their parameters. These changes in the regularity of the breathing, the pattern of the EEG, onset or cessation of slow and rapid eye movements are somewhat spread over a period of a few minutes. It was tempting to study the precise 'morphology' of these state transitions, because of the possibility that changes in the different variables might shed light on the nature of the underlying switching mechanisms of state sequences and cycles. In two studies (Monod and Curzi-Dascalova, 1973; Shirataki and Prechtl, 1977) it has been shown that only a very loose and inconsistent relationship exists between the changes in the different parameters when several transitions are compared within the same recording. There are no 'leading variables' which could help in understanding the physiological processes underlying the changes of states.

STATE CLASSIFICATIONS AND THEIR NOMENCLATURE

Although there is wide agreement that different behavioural states do exist in newborn infants, researchers have made different selections of state criteria on the basis of their own preference and scientific background. It is therefore understandable that scales differ as does the terminology. This is regrettable because easy comparison of the results of different studies is hampered. On the other hand as long as precise operational definitions are provided by the authors, the damage should not be dramatized.

As has been previously said, the number of variables should be limited to a few and the discriminating parameters of these variables should be continual and clearly distinguishable, either from direct observation of the infant, or from the polygraphic paper write-out. What the consequences are if too many and inconsistent criteria are included in the state criteria can be seen in Anders (1974). He found that for identification of the two sleep states of the newborn infant only, all of their five criteria were rather rarely simultaneously met, but 'flexible' scoring with four and, especially, three out of the five items respectively improved the state identification and reduced the 'waste bag' of indeterminate sleep which was scored when state parameters were discrepant. It seems preferable to designate parameters with an inconsistent relationship with other parameters as state concomitants and not as state criteria. Moreover, it is an advantage if state criteria are consistently applicable over all state categories and are not restricted to particular states only. In the newborn, the presence or absence of REMs only has relevance for distinguishing between the two sleep states and not for awake states. REMs should not be included when scales for behavioural states are intended to cover all possible sleep and awake states. To achieve this latter aim, states can be defined as vectors, and all vectors together form a discrete and finite vector space (Prechtl, 1974). What is gained is a lucidly formalized scale of behavioural states of the full-term infant (Table 1). If the statement concerning a specific variable is 'true', a sign of $+1$ is used; if the statement is 'false', a -1 is used; and if the statement can be 'true' or 'false', a 0 is given. The last condition, for instance, occurs in state 5, when the eyes can be either closed or open during crying. It is easy to see that no single variable can be excluded, if all five states are to be reliably distinguished from each other. On the other hand, additional criteria would not improve the definition of these states but would rather lead to other state categories or to conditions, which would not be covered by all criteria, consequently one would have to accept long state transitions. However, to call them 'undefined' or 'transitional states' is illogical.

There are a number of variables which change their parameters in relation to states defined by the above-mentioned state indicators. For various reasons such as inconsistency, easy disruption in pathological conditions, or because they

Table 1   Vectors of behavioural states

	Eyes open	Respiration regular	Gross movements	Vocalization
State 1	-1	$+1$	-1	-1
State 2	-1	-1	0	-1
State 3	$+1$	$+1$	-1	-1
State 4	$+1$	-1	$+1$	-1
State 5	0	-1	$+1$	$+1$

Signs: $+1 =$ true; $-1 =$ false; $0 =$ true or false

Table 2   Vectors of state concomitants

States	1	2	3	4	5
Tracé alternant EEG	+ +	−	−	−	−
Low-voltage EEG	−	+ +	+	+ +	+ +
Startles	+ +	+	−	−	−
Rhythmical mouthing	+ +	−	−	−	−
Smiles, grimaces	−	+ +	+	−	−
Gross movements	−	+ +	−	c	+ +
Stretch movement	−	+ +	−	±	−
Antigravity posture	+	−	+ +	+	+
Slow eye movements	−	+ +	−	−	−
Rapid eye movements	−	+ +	+ +	+	+
Stable heart rate	+ +	−	+	−	−

− absent, ± rarely present, + and + + present, 0 not applicable, C is a state criterion

consist of incidental events, they can only be considered as state concomitants. When they are arranged as vectors, it appears that their discriminant function between states is less clear (Table 2).

Over the years the terminology employed in investigations on state became more and more diverse. Wolff's (1959) scale was a descriptive categorization of overt behaviour. Prechtl and Beintema (1964), Prechtl (1965 and later) followed this line, but preferred to number states from one to five, deliberately avoiding any suggestion as to the physiological or behavioural qualities of the various states. Others (Dittrichova, 1962; Greenberg *et al.*, 1963; Brown, 1964; Weller and Bell, 1965; Crowell, 1967) related their terminology to the concept of depth of sleep, and distinguished states of deep and light sleep and various degrees of wakefulness, implying an arousal continuum. More descriptive but restricted to sleep is the French classification of quiet (sommeil calme) and active (sommeil agité) sleep (Delange *et al.*, 1962; Monod and Pajot, 1965) studied by polygraphic techniques. This terminology is still widely used among poly-graphists, but the criterion which gives these states the name, the motility of the infant, is never measured except perhaps through the impression that during quiet sleep there are less movement artefacts in the recording then during active sleep.

Sleep researchers who use the REM sleep–NREM sleep dichotomy also apply this terminology in infant studies but it is less-widely accepted in newborn studies.

It should be noted that an exclusive attention to sleep states neglecting wakefulness is found to produce errors when the relative percentages of states are quantified. As soon as one sleep state changes (e.g. under abnormal conditions, such as the decrease of state 2 in Down's syndrome) the amount of the other sleep state does not necessarily increase but an increase may be found in the awake states instead (see Prechtl *et al.*, 1973).

A manual for a standardized assessment of states from polygraphic recordings has been produced by Anders *et al.* (1971). Even this attempt has unfortunately not solved the problem that diverse state scales and terminologies still exist.

While such scales for polygraphic assessment are restricted in their usefulness to technically recorded signals, scales based on observable indicators have the great advantage of being applicable in both observational and polygraphic studies as Prechtl has suggested. A further advantage of such indicators is that they can be applied as vectors for all sleep and awake states.

As a final point we want to warn against the practice of dividing states into substates just because quantitative fluctuations exist in a single state parameter. It is more informative to measure and report on these particular fluctuations than to hide them in new state classes.

CONCLUDING REMARKS

Scales for classifying behavioural states are of an arbitrary nature as they depend on the selection of the variables and parameters which are used as state indicators. They nevertheless aim to capture and describe some distinct conditions of the nervous system and are *not only* a mere convenient categorization of behaviours which emerge 'on the surface of the organism'. That states are no mystical nuisance can be experimentally verified by distinct state-related changes in stimulus-response patterns (input–output relation). These changes occur rather abruptly at the step-wise transitions between states, but response intensities remain relatively stable during the ongoing states.

A certain vagueness of the state concept inevitably remains because many kinds of state classifications are approximations of conditions of the nervous system which cannot be measured directly. The nervous system can be thought of as a 'black box' whose complex conditions are evaluated by a set of outputs as indicators. The last 25 years of research have helped to make the box more grey but we are still far from understanding the basic neural mechanisms of states. Nevertheless many investigations have furthered our knowledge of the appearance and organization of states in the infant. In this chapter we have deliberately abstained from a discussion of the developmental aspects of states in the fetus—a topic of considerable importance in obstetrics—or in the preterm infant or of the postnatal development of states in the growing infant. The limited space has it made impossible to deal with more than the full-term infant.

Inevitably this essay reflects a personal view of the history of the state concept seen through the eyes of an actively engaged participant in its emergence.

ACKNOWLEDGMENT

We thank Dr Brian Hopkins for his helpful suggestions.

REFERENCES

Anders, T. F. (1974). The infant sleep profile, *Neuropädiat.* **5**, 425–442.

Anders, T., Emde, R. and Parmelee A. (1971). *A Manual of Standardized Terminology, Techniques and Criteria for Scoring States of Sleep and Wakefulness in Newborn Infants*, Brain Information Service, UCLA School of Health Serv., Los Angeles.

Anders, T. F. and Miller Sostek, A. (1976). The use of time lapse video recording of sleep-wake behaviour in human infants, *Psychophysiol.* **13**, 155–158.

Arbib, M. A. (1972). *The Metaphorical Brain*, Wiley, New York.

Aserinsky, E. and Kleitman, N. (1955). A motility cycle in sleeping infants as manifested by ocular and gross bodily activity, *J. Appl. Physiol.* **8**, 11–18.

Ashby, W. R. (1956). *An Introduction to Cybernetics*, 295pp., Chapman and Hall, London.

Ashton, R. (1973). The state variable in neonatal research: a review. *Merrill Palmer Quart.* no. 1, 3–20.

Ashton, R. and Connolly, K. (1971). The relation of respiration rate and heart rate to sleep states in the human newborn, *Develop. Med. Child Neurol.* **13**, 180–187.

Bernuth, H. von and Prechtl, H. F. R. (1969). Vestibulo-ocular response and its state dependency in newborn infants, *Neuropädiat.* **1**, 11–24.

Brazelton, T. B. (1973). *Neonatal Behavioral Assessment scale.* Clinics in Developmental Medicine, no. 50. 66 pp., Heinemann, London.

Brown, J. L. (1964). States in newborn infants, *Merrill Palmer Quart. Behav. Develop.*, **10**, 313–327.

Bühler, Ch. and Hetzer, H. (1927). *Inventar der Verhaltensweisen des ersten Lebensjahres*, Verlag G. Fischer, Jena.

Carmichael, L. (1946). *Manual of Child Psychology*, 1st edn Wiley, New York.

Crowell, D. H. (1967). Infant motor development, in *Infancy and Early Childhood* (Ed. Y. Brackbill), pp. 125–207, The Free Press, New York.

Czerny, A. (1892). Beobachtungen über den Schlaf im Kindesalter unter physiologischen Verhältnissen, *Jahrbuch f. Kinderheilkunde*, **33**, 1–28.

Delange, M., Castan, Ph., Cadilhac, J., and Passquant, P. (1962). Les divers stades du sommeil chez le nouveau-né et le nourisson, *Revue Neurologique*, **107**, 271–276.

Dittrichova, J. (1962). Nature of sleep in young infants, *J. Appl. Physiol.* **17**, 543–546.

Eliet-Flescher, J. and Dreyfus-Brisac, C. (1966). Le sommeil du nouveau-né et du prématuré. II. Relations entre l'électroencéphalogramme et l'électromyogramme mentonnier au cours de la maturation, *Biol. Neonat.* **10**, 316–339.

Emde, R. N. and Koenig, K. L. (1969). Neonatal smiling and rapid eye movement states, *J. Am. Acad. Child Psychiat.* **8**, 57–67.

Escalona, S. K. (1962). The study of individual differences and the problem of state, *J. Child Psychiatry*, **1**, 11–37.

Gaensbauer, T. and Emde, R. N. (1973). Wakefulness and feeding in human newborns, *Arch. Gen. Psychiat.* **28**, 894–897.

Gesell, A. and Amatruda, C. S. (1945). *The Embryology of Behavior. The Beginnings of the Human Mind*, Harper & Brothers, New York.

Greenberg, N., Cekan, P., and Loesch, J. (1963). Some cardiac rate and behavioural characteristics of sucking in the neonate, *Psychosom. Med.* **25**, 492.

Hutt, S. J., Hutt, C., Lenard, H. G., Bernuth, H. von, and Muntjewerff, W. J. (1968). Auditory responsivity in the human neonate, *Nature (Lond.)*, **218**, 888–890.

Irwin, O. C. (1932a). The amount of motility of seventy-three newborn infants, *J. Comp. Psychol.* **14**, 415–428.

Irwin, O. C. (1932b). The distribution of the amount of motility in young infants between two nursing periods, *J. Comp. Psychol.* **14**, 429–445.

Kleitman, N. (1963). *Sleep and Wakefulness*, 2nd edn, The University Press, Chicago.

Korner, A. F. (1969). Neonatal startles, smiles, erections and reflex sucks as related to state, sex and individuality, *Child Develop.* **40**, 1040–1052.

Korner, A. F. (1972). State as variable, as obstacle, and as mediator of stimulation in infant research, *Merrill Palmer Quart. Behav. Develop.* **18**, 77–94.

Lenard, H. G., Bernuth, H. von, and Prechtl, H. F. R. (1968). Reflexes and their relationships to behavioural state in the newborn, *Acta Paediat. Scand.* **3**, 177–185.

Lindsley, D. B. (1936). Brain potentials in children and adults, *Science*, **84**, 354.

Lindsley, D. B. (1939). A longitudinal study of the occipital alpha rhythm in normal children. Frequency and amplitude standards, *J. Gen. Psychol.* **55**, 197–213.

Monod, N. and Pajot, N. (1965). Le sommeil du nouveau-né et du prématuré, *Biol. Neonat.* **8**, 281–307.

Monod, N. and Curzi-Dascalova, L. (1973). Les états transitionnels de sommeil chez le nouveau-né à terme, *Rev. EEG Neurophysiol.* **3**, 87–96.

Monod, N., Eliet-Flescher, J., and Dreyfus-Brisac, C. (1967). Le sommeil du nouveau-né et du prématuré. III. Les troubles de l'organisation du sommell chez le nouveau-né pathologique: Analyse des études polygraphiques, *Biol. Neonat.* **11**, 216–247.

Monod, N. and Guidasci, S. (1976). Sleep and brain malformation in the neonatal period, *Neuropädiat.* **7**, 229–249.

Moruzzi, G. and Magoun, H. W. (1949). Brain stem reticular formation and activation of the EEG, *Electroecenphal. Clin. Neurophysiol.* **1**, 455–473.

Mussen, P. H. (ed.) (1970). *Carmichael's Manual of Child Psychology*, 3rd edn, Wiley, New York.

Osofsky, J. D. (ed.) (1979). *Handbook of Infant Development*, Wiley, New York.

Papousek, H. (1967). Conditioning during early postnatal development, in *Behavior in Infancy and Early Childhood* (Eds Y. Brackbill and G. G. Thompson), pp. 259–274, The Free Press, New York.

Papousek, H. (1969). Individual variability in learned responses in human infants, in *Brain and Early Behaviour* (Ed. R. J. Robinson), pp. 251–266, Academic Press, London.

Papousek, H. (1974). Early human ontogeny of the regulation of behavioral states in relation to information processing and adaptation organizing, *Sleep Res. Rome*, **1974**, 384–387.

Parmelee, A. H. (1961). Sleep patterns in infancy. A study of one infant from birth to eight months of age, *Acta Paediat.* **50**, 160–170.

Parmelee, A. H., Akiyama, Y., Stern, E., and Harris, M. A. (1969). A periodic cerebral rhythm in newborn infants, *Exp. Neurol.* **25**, 575–584.

Parmelee, A. H., Schulte, F. J., Akiyama, Y., Wenner, W. H., Schultz, M. A., and Stern, E. (1968). Maturation of EEG activity during sleep in premature infants, *Electroenceph. Clin. Neurophysiol.* **24**, 319–329.

Parmelee, A. H. and Stern, E. (1972). Development of states in infants, in *Sleep and the Maturing Nervous System* (Eds C. Clemente, D. Purpura and F. Meyer), pp. 199–228, Academic Press, New York.

Petre-Quadens, O. (1967). Ontogenesis of paradoxical sleep in the human newborn, *J. Neurol. Sci.* **4**, 153–157.

Petre-Quadens, O., De Lee, C. and Remy, M. (1971). Eye movement density during sleep and brain maturation, *Brain Res.* **26**, 49–56.

Prechtl, H. F. R. (1958). The directed head turning response and allied movements of the human baby, *Behaviour*, **13**, 212–242.

Prechtl, H. F. R. (1965). Problems of behavioural studies in the newborn infant. In *Advances in the Study of Behavior* (Eds D. S. Lehrman, R. A. Hinde, and E. Shaw), pp. 75–96. Academic Press, New York.

Prechtl, H. F. R. (1968). Polygraphic studies of the full-term newborn infant. II. Computer analysis of recorded data, in *Studies in Infancy* (Eds M. C. O. Bax and R. C. Mac Keith), pp. 26–40, Clinics in Developmental Medicine, no. 27, Heinemann, London.

Prechtl, H. F. R. (1972). Patterns of reflex behavior related to sleep in the human infant, in *Sleep and the Maturing Nervous System* (Eds C. D. Clemente, D. P. Purpura, and F. E. Meyer), pp. 287–301, Academic Press, New York.

Prechtl, H. F. R. (1974). The behavioural states of the newborn infant (a review), *Brain Res.* **76**, 1304–1311.

Prechtl, H. F. R. (1977). Assessment and significance of behavioural states, in *Brain, Fetal and Infant* (Ed. S. R. Berenberg), pp. 79–90, Martinus Nijhoff, The Hague.

Prechtl, H. F. R. (1978). Clinical neurophysiology of early life, in *Contemporary Clinical Neurophysiology* (Eds W. A. Cobb and H. van Duijn), EEG suppl. no. **34**, pp. 57–66. Elsevier. Amsterdam.

Prechtl, H. F. R., Akiyama, Y., Zinkin, P., and Kerr Grant, D. (1968). Polygraphic studies of the fullterm newborn infants. I. Technical aspects and qualitative analysis, in *Studies in Infancy* (Eds M. C. O. Bax and R. C. MacKeith), pp. 1–25, Clinics in Developmental Medicine, no. 27, Heinemann, London.

Prechtl, H. F. R. and Beintema, D. J. (1964). *The Neurological Examination of the Full-term Newborn Infant*, Clinics in Developmental Medicine, no. 12, Heinemann, London.

Prechtl, H. F. R., Eykern, L. A. van and O'Brien, M. J. (1977). Respiratory muscle EMG in newborns: a non-intrusive method, *Early Hum. Develop.* **1**, 265–283.

Prechtl, H. F. R., Fargel, J. W., Weinmann, H. M., and Bakker, H. H. (1979). Posture, motility and respiration in low-risk preterm infants, *Develop. Med. Child Neurol.* **21**, 3–27.

Prechtl, H. F. R. and Lenard, H. G. (1967). A study of eye movements in sleeping newborn infants, *Brain Res.* **5**, 477–493.

Prechtl, H. F. R., Kerr Grant, D., Lenard, H. G., and Hrbek, A. (1967). The lip-tap-reflex in the awake and sleeping newborn infant, *Exp. Brain Res.* **3**, 184–194.

Prechtl, H. F. R., Theorell, K., and Blair, A. W. (1973). Behavioural state cycles in abnormal infants, *Develop, Med. Child Neurol.* **15**, 606–615.

Prechtl, H. F. R., Vlach, V., Lenard, H. G., and Kerr Grant, D. (1967). Exteroceptive and tendon reflexes in various behavioural states in the newborn infant, *Biol. Neonat.* **11**, 159–175.

Prechtl, H. F. R., Weinmann, H. M., and Akiyama, Y. (1969). Organization of physiological parameters in normal and neurologically abnormal infants: comprehensive computer analysis of polygraphic data, *Neuropädiat.* **1**, 101–129.

Preyer, W. (1880). *Die Seele des Kindes*. Grieber's Verlag, Leipzig.

Roffwarg, H. P., Muzio, J. N., and Dement, W. C. (1966). Ontogenetic development of the human sleep-dream cycle, *Science*, **152**, 604–618.

Schleidt, W. M. and Crawley, J. N. (1980). Patterns in the bahaviour of organisms, *J. Social. Biol. Struct.* **3**, 1–15.

Schloon, H., O'Brien, M. J., Scholten, C. A., and Prechtl, H. F. R. (1976). Muscle activity and postural behaviour in newborn infants, *Neuropädiat.* **7**, 384–415.

Scholten, C. A. and Vos, J. E. (1981). Descriptors of the rhythmicity in respiration and heart beat of newborn infants, *Med. & Biol. Eng. & Comput.* **19**, 83–90.

Scholten, C. A. and Vos, J. E. (1982). A comparative investigation of the mathematical properties of some descriptors for biological point processes: examples from the human newborn, *Med. & Biol. Eng. & Comput.* **20**, 89–93.

Shirataki, S. and Prechtl, H. F. R. (1977). Sleep state transitions in newborn infants: preliminary study, *Develop. Med. Child Neurol.* **19**, 316–325.

Smith, C. A. (1959). *The Physiology of the Newborn Infant*, 3rd edn, Blackwell Scientific Publications, Oxford.

Theorell, K. (1974). Clinical value of prolonged polygraphic recordings in high-risk newborn infants, *Neuropädiat.* **5**, 383–401.

Theorell, K., Prechtl, H. F. R., Blair, A. W., and Lind, J. (1973). Behavioural state cycles of normal newborn infants, *Develop. Med. Child Neurol.* **15**, 597–605.

Theorell, K., Prechtl, H. F. R., and Vos, J. E. (1974). A polygraphic study of normal and abnormal newborn infants, *Neuropädiat.* **5**, 279–317.

Thoman, E. B. (1975). Sleep and wake behaviors in neonates: consistencies and consequences, *Merrill Palmer Quart.* **21**, 293–313.

Thoman, E. B., Denenberg, V. H., Sievel, J., Zeidner, L. P., and Becker, P. (1981). State organization in neonates: developmental inconsistency indicates risk for developmental dysfunction, *Neuropediatrics*, **12**, 45–54.

Thoman, E. B. and Tynan, W. D. (1979). Sleep states and wakefulness in human infants: profiles from motility monitoring, *Physiol. Behav.* **23**, 519–526.

Vlach, V., Bernuth, H. von, and Prechtl, H. F. R. (1969). State dependency of exteroceptive skin reflexes in newborn infants, *Develop. Med. Child Neurol.* **11**, 353–362.

Weller, G. M. and Bell, R. Q. (1965). Basal skin conductions and neonatal state. *Child Develop.* **36**, 647–657.

Wolff, P. H. (1959). Observations on newborn infants, *Psychosom. Med.* **221**, 110–118.

Wolff, P. H. (1966). The causes, controls and organization of behaviour in the neonate, in *Psychological Issues,* vol. 5, no. 1, monogr. 17, International University Press, New York.

Zipperling, W. (1913). Über eine besondere Form motorischer Reizzustände bei Neugeborenen (sog. 'Stäupchen'), *Ztschr. Kinderheilk.* **5**, 31–40.

Psychobiology of the Human Newborn
Edited by P. Stratton
© 1982, John Wiley & Sons, Ltd.

CHAPTER 4

Neurologic Signs, Aetiology, and Implications

C. AMIEL-TISON

Any group of newborns is likely to include some who have suffered nervous system damage, and it is important that researchers, as well as medical practitioners, should be aware of the symptoms, causes and consequences of the different neurological conditions. This chapter will deal with brain damage, cell loss, lesions and organicity. From the anatomical point of view, brain damage can be described as a 'continuum of casualty'. The severe damage linked with perinatal asphyxia is identified long since, main causes are well known, as well as neonatal symptoms and later outcome. In these cases, which are now the exception, the amount of warmth provided by the mother or the amount of skill provided by the medical team will not help much to reduce the resulting incapacity.

The problem, which as yet remains unsolved, is how to identify moderate and mild lesions and how to follow the track of these lesions until school age, as their clinical expression varies according to development. With the progress of perinatal medicine, these mild lesions are much more frequent than the severe ones, therefore it appears more and more necessary to identify them in order to evaluate the results of care. Transitory motor abnormalities within the first year of life will be described as a possible clue to minimal deficit at school age.

In this chapter, when chronic fetal distress is mentioned, it will not be in terms of maternal frustration or culpability but of early detection of fetal asphyxia or fetal hypotrophy and their implications on the timing and type of delivery advisable. When modern obstetrics is mentioned, it will not be in terms of warm water, music and generous feelings but of prevention of prematurity, prediction of mechanical difficulties, early detection of fetal asphyxia during labour, and decision of caesarean section. When neonatal intensive care is mentioned it will not be in terms of impairment of maternal bonding and later consequences but of prevention of apnoeic spells and cardiac arrest, optimal management of respiratory distress syndrome, maintenance of cerebral blood flow and oxygenation, the aim being to preserve brain integrity. The delineation of this chapter does not mean ignoring or neglecting all these aspects of care which will be described in other sections of this book. It means that the reader not interested in organicity can omit this particular chapter.

PATHOPHYSIOLOGIC CONSIDERATIONS

The nervous system of the newborn is very immature, even in the full-term newborn; cell differentiation, synaptic connections, myelination are showing rapid changes in the last trimester of pregnancy. As the infant progresses from 28 to 40 weeks gestational age the location and histopathology of the lesions change: lesions are directly related to the degree of maturation. This relation of maturation-lesion exists for other viscera but is even more close in brain pathology.

Gestational age, therefore, must always be considered before speculating on the probable lesions in a given child. A pre-term newborn is born before 37 weeks of gestation; a full-term newborn is born between 37 and 41 weeks, a post-term newborn at 42 weeks or more. Birth weight does not interfere with these chronological definitions.

Fetal hypotrophy or growth retardation is defined by a birth weight under the tenth percentile for a given gestational age, using intrauterine growth curves. The detection of hypotrophy is now done before birth in most cases, fetal hypotrophy being defined by echographic criteria. The clinical definition of hypotrophy in the newborn implies that the gestational age is known with a reasonable accuracy. Fetal hypertrophy is defined by a birth weight above the 90th percentile of the same curves. These definitions are now considered as essential to the understanding of neonatal problems. The birthweight alone does not allow one or the other type of classification.

The history of labour has to be known in great detail to allow any conclusion on the aetiology of neonatal problems: presentation, progress of labour, drugs, fetal monitoring, etc.

The neonatal status is usually evaluated in the first few minutes by the Apgar score, and the rescucitation described precisely when vital functions were depressed. When subacute or acute fetal distress has been observed at any stage of labour, the duration of the insult is extremely important for the occurrence of lesions, *the chronology of events* with precise timing is therefore very important for the understanding of obstetrical difficulties.

As a conclusion, gestational age, intrauterine growth, history of pregnancy and labour, and neonatal status in the delivery room are good clues to an aetiological diagnosis in the newborn. Correlation of these data usually yields a reasonably accurate aetiology and compensates for the lack of specificity of the symptoms.

Where mechanism of CNS dysfunction is concerned, anatomical and experimental data have recently brought some light. However, it remains difficult to separate hypoxia from ischaemia (Volpe, 1976). In acute fetal distress, both factors are usually present. In subacute distress, when these two factors have more chance to be separated, neonatal death is now less frequent and anatomical data very scattered. Experimental data, particularly the studies of partial asphyxia in monkeys (Myers *et al.*, 1969; Myers, 1972; Myers, 1975) have provided a lot of data, and help to emphasize the role of brain oedema.

CEREBRAL SYMPTOMS

Symptoms have to be recognized and collected very carefully all through the neonatal period. They are more easy to recognize in full-term newborns than in premature newborns. Monitoring devices, catheters, respirator, infusions, etc. often make a detailed evaluation impossible during the first days or weeks. This means that most of the evaluation will be the result of inspection.

The main symptoms are listed in Table 1, they will not be described in detail here.

The physiologically and morphologically immature neonatal cerebrum is capable of producing *seizure discharges*, but the clinical appearance of the seizures is considerably different from that manifested in older infants. The correlating of clinical and EEG findings is still a matter of discussion, so that the identification and classification may vary widely on clinical grounds as well as on EEG grounds.

Status epilepticus is defined by the repetition of seizures in short intervals.

Table 1 Clinical features of nervous system dysfunction in the neonate

Coma	Areactivity, absence of corneal and sucking reflexes
Lethargy	Hyporeactivity, no crying
Status epilepticus	Repeated seizures and coma
Isolated seizure	With rapid recovery of consciousness after seizure
Hyperexcitability	Jitteriness, tremor, clonic movements, burst of agitation, poor sleep, high-pitched cry, sustained clonus
Hypertonia	Generalized, limited to neck extensors, opisthotonus
Hypotonia	Generalized, upper part of the body, one side of the body (hemi-syndrome)
Primary reflexes abolished	No primary reflexes, in particular Moro reflex and sucking
Primary reflexes diminished	Poor responses, not reproducible
Ocular signs	Conjugated deviation, setting-sun sign, sustained nystagmus
Intracranial hypertension	Tense fontanelle, distended sutures, particularly the squamous, neck extensors hypertonia
Abnormal respiration	Irregular, apnoea

Seizures are more often 'subtle' and difficult to recognize in a comatose child. The EEG patterns associated with status epilepticus have been described (Harris and Tizard, 1960; Rose and Lombroso, 1970; Dreyfus-Brisac and Monod, 1972) in many texts. The prognosis is more dependent upon the intercritic tracing, inactive or paroxystic (Dreyfus-Brisac and Monod, 1972) and upon the aetiology.

Generalized Hypotonia

The evaluation of tone in the newborn infant requires considerable experience, practice, and patience on the part of the physician. Although much has been written about the hypotonic or floppy infant, establishing the cause of hypotonia is difficult and fraught with many pitfalls. The reader is referred to the monograph by Dubowitz (1969) for detailed study of this important group of disorders.

Hypertonia in Neck Extensors

Testing active tone in the neck is an important part of neurologic assessment. Two manoeuvers which involve the straightening reactions of the head can be performed (Amiel-Tison, 1974). When the infant, lying supine is moved slowly to the sitting position, the active straightening of the head is observed. This manoeuver enables assessment of tone in the flexor muscles.

When the infant, sitting and leaning forward, is slowly moved backward, the acting straightening of the head is observed. This enables the assessment of tone in neck extensors. Permanent hypertonia in the neck extensors is an abnormality found in cases with intracranial hypertension (Amiel-Tison et al., 1977).

DIAGNOSTIC PROCEDURES

(1) Repeated Evaluation of Sutures, Fontanels and Head Circumference Measurement

This simple approach is extremely helpful and reliable. Normal values are well established (Nellhaus, 1968). Daily measurements are essential. Excessively rapid growth is always to be regarded with suspicion. Gestational age and health of the infant were found to be significant factors in determining the pattern of head growth in the preterm infant (Sher and Brown, 1975). Difficulty is that of separating hydrocephalus from 'Catchup' growth (Sher and Brown, 1975; Korobkin, 1975).

(2) The Cerebrospinal Fluid (CSF)

This often is yellowish. Up to a few hundred red blood cells per mm^3 is a frequent normal finding. The presence of leucocytes, if less than 30–40 per mm^3 can be considered normal. The CSF protein normally is between 50 and 130 mg 100 ml^{-1} and may be higher in premature newborns (Bauer *et al.*, 1965, Escobedo *et al.*, 1975). Intracranial haemorrhage is defined by the presence of more than 3000 red cells in the cerebrospinal fluid. Non-invasive monitoring of intracranial pressure is now routinely performed (Philip, 1979).

(3) Examination of the Optic Fundus

Retinal haemorrhages in the first days of life are very frequent and usually are not indicative of subdural of subarachnoid haemorrhage. Papilloedema does not appear with cerebral oedema because distention of the sutures occurs when intracranial pressure increases.

However, the optic fundus has to be examined routinely and may be of invaluable help for the diagnosis of certain diseases (e.g., toxoplasmosis, phacoma, and vascular malformation).

(4) Transillumination

This simple procedure may provide information about the existence and location of abnormal fluid spaces in the brain. In a darkened room, a cuffed flash-light is held against the skull. Normally, one sees only a small halo (about 1 cm) around the light, expecially prominent in the premature. Asymmetrical transillumination or distal illumination is abnormal. This procedure should be done routinely, especially if hydrocephalus or malformation is suspected.

(5) X-Ray of the Skull

X-Ray of the skull can be valuable, showing the size of the sutures and the digital impressions. The films should be examined carefully for evidence of fracture of the skull or periventricular calcifications.

(6) Electrophysiological Studies

The EEG is helpful in the perinatal period. It provides the main data in neonatal seizures, confirming the clinical dignosis, evaluating treatment and providing reliable information concerning long-term prognosis (Tharp, 1981). Auditory brain stem potentials are extensively studied, as providing objective parameters of neurological status (Starr and Amlie, 1981).

(7) Computed Axial Tomography Scan (CAT)

An increasing number of units will be equiped to utilize this technique for sick newborns (Gomez and Reese, 1976). It has been demonstrated to be an extremely reliable and elegant way to evaluate the ventricular intracranial haemorrhage and ventricular size (Fitz, 1981). Recently echoencephalography has been widely used, at bedside, and repeated safely (Pape *et al.*, 1979).

SPECIFIC TYPES OF BRAIN DAMAGE

In the last 10 years, the increasing knowledge of the probable pathophysiology of perinatal brain damage and in some cases the possibility of prevention or cure made a more analytic approach necessary. As it appears possible to separate the clinical pictures that correspond to particular damage, schematic guidelines to establish a diagnosis with reasonable accuracy will be given. The data of Larroche (1976) has been mostly used in establishing these correlations.

Three situations will be studied in some detail, being common and usually schematic in their particular perinatal circumstances, clinical signs and outcome, i.e. intraventricular haemorrhage in the premature newborn, hypoxic-ischaemic brain injury in the full-term newborn, and periventricular leucomalacia.

(1) Intraventricular haemorrhage (IVH)

A major cause of death in the preterm newborn, is described in Table 2. The veinous distension in the galenic system is a very constant finding for anatomists (Larroche, 1964), explaining that IVH is often associated with IRDS and very likely results from circulatory trouble in immature newborns. This pathogenic

Table 2   Intraventricular haemorrhage (IVH)

GA	Less than 34 weeks
Gestation and delivery	Nothing specific
Timing	Post natal
Clinical course (frequent association with HMD)	Secondary deterioration: with coma, apnoeic spells, seizures, absence of tone and reflexes When IRDS associated: sudden and unexplained drop of PaO_2
Investigations	CSF: presence of blood drop of hematocric EEG: positive rolandic spikes CAT or echo: blood in lateral ventricles
Outcome	Neonatal death Survival rate higher with artificial ventilation High incidence of hydrocephalus in survivors
Treatment	Prevention: early correction of hypoxia, acidosis, hypothermia Treatment: follow head circumference, shunt when evidence of significant ventricular enlargement
Mechanism and anatomical findings	Brain immaturity + anoxia, acidosis, dic? → venous stasis, over distension. Rupture of the veins of the matrix. Rupture of the ependyma; haemorrhage into the lateral ventricles—spreading to III and IV Ventricles and posterior fossa Various associated brain lesions

conception possibly will contribute to prevention, avoiding all kind of stress in the premature newborn.

Hydrocephaly is a very threatening complication in infants who survive after intracranial haemorrhage (Larroche, 1972). The early diagnosis is one of the most difficult, ventricular dilatation often preceding clinical signs (Korobkin, 1975). Early shunting has to be performed, repeated lumbar punctures can be curative in transient cases (Goldstein et al., 1976).

In massive intraventricular haemorrhages, the diagnosis is easy, the outcome very poor: neonatal death or hydrocephaly. But when the bleeding is in moderate or minimal amount, there is difficulty in determining the site of the bleeding. When the presence of blood in the CSF is a finding associated with mild neurological signs, subarachnoïdal haemorrhage can be proposed as a presumptive diagnosis, after eliminating mild intraventricular haemorrhage, by CATscan. For the clinician, the subarachnoïdal haemorrhage is the most frequent intracranial haemorrhage, with the rare pathological correlations since survival is the usual outcome. The symptoms, mainly irritability and hypertonia, are transitory and the outcome excellent. It is therefore legitimate, in these cases, not to alarm the family, which means avoiding emphasis on the presence of blood. The diagnosis of haemorrhage is unnecessarily threatening. The diagnosis of subdural haemorrhage is rarely made; in this site, bleeding results from a real mechanical trauma; the symptoms are immediate and severe, the diagnosis should be evoked and the subdural tap should be done. Neonatal death is the usual outcome.

(2) Perinatal Hypoxic-ischemic Brain Injury

Under the term of perinatal hypoxic-ischemic brain injury, all the varieties of cellular damage are included. The most severe degree in full-term newborns is cerebral necrosis involving all cortical areas (but preferentially hippocampal cerebral cortex), basal ganglia, brain stem, cerebellum, with severe brain oedema (Larroche, 1968, 1976). The cerebral necrosis is massive, status epilepticus is the clinical expression, neonatal death or severe sequelae are the usual outcome (Table 3).

This severe type of anoxic lesion is now rare, the incidence is around 2 per 1000 births. But milder degrees of brain damage can be observed if the obstetrical circumstances are less unfavourable, the fetal distress less acute or less prolonged.

A moderate degree, with moderate cell damage and brain oedema is individualized on clinical data and animal experiments (Myers, 1972), but no anatomical correlations have been established in humans. Hypotonia, hyporeactivity and hyporeflectivity are the usual clinical findings, with specific signs of brain oedema in 70 per cent of the cases (Amiel-Tison et al., 1977); sequelae, if detectable, are usually moderate or mild (Amiel-Tison, 1969, 1972).

Table 3   Cerebral necrosis: severe degree

GA	Full term mostly
Gestation and delivery	Acute fetal distress: cord strangulation or prolapse
	Abruptio placentae
	Mechanical or functional dystocia, hypercontractibility
Timing	Antepartum, or more often first or second stage of labour
Clinical course	Status epilepticus: with repeated convulsions, coma, apnoea
Investigations	CSF: usually clear
	EEG: Status epilepticus
	Inactive or paroxysmal interictal tracing
Outcome	Neonatal death about 50 per cent
	Major CNS lesions in about 50 per cent of survivors
Treatment	Prevention: fetal monitoring
	Treatment: anticonvulsant drugs, artificial ventilation, treatment of cerebral oedema
Mechanism and anatomical findings	Reduction of cerebral blood flow: anoxia, acidosis (hypoxic-ischaemic brain injury) → oedema + massive cerebral necrosis

A mild degree is defined clinically by transitory abnormalities of tone and activity, without consciousness or reflectivity trouble. It correlates in animal experiments with mild brain oedema without cell damage. The obstetrical circumstances are of the same sort but with milder and shorter abnormalities of labour. Compression of the head in mild cases of cephalopelvic disproportion is the usual cause. No sequelae are observed in this group (Amiel-Tison, 1969, 1972) when complete normalization is obtained at the end of the first week of life.

This three-grades classification is helpful for the clinician, according to probable anatomical data and therefore to prognostic implications (Amiel-Tison, 1979). The quantification of clinical and EEG data in term of duration of transitory findings within the first weeks of life defines the severity of the insult to the brain and increases the accuracy of early prognosis in asphyxiated neonates (Sarnat and Sarnat, 1976). Modern obstetrics has nearly eliminated the severe degree and considerably decreased the incidence of moderate and mild degree.

Fetal heart-rate monitoring and acid base sampling during labour are fundamental for prevention. The main problem of modern obstetrics is one of eradicating this type of brain damage without reaching an excessive incidence of caesarean section (Amiel-Tison, 1978). Within the last 10 years, fetal intensive care has decreased the incidence of severe brain damage and has changed the relative frequencies of its various aetiologies. In effect, clear cases of cephalopelvic disproportion and breech presentation in primiparas are now rarely the cause of severe brain damage, when related to the total number of births.

In placenta praevia, abruptio placentae, umbilical cord prolapse, and cord strangulation, the rapidity with which the situation is handled will reduced the morbidity and mortality.

Table 4 Leucomalacia

GA	Preterm mostly
Gestation and delivery	Not contributive
Timing	Post natal mostly
Clinical course	No specific neurologic abnormalities: lethargy, hypotonia in *sick* newborns (IRDS, meningitis or septicaemia, apnoetic spells, cardiac arrest, congenital heart disease)
Investigations	None
Outcome	Cerebral palsy: mainly spastic diplegia or spastic hemiplegia
Treatment	Prevention: alarm on apnoea or bradycardia
	Maintenance of a normal blood pressure and oxygenation
Mechanism and anatomical findings	Reduction of cerebral blood flow, anoxia: → necrosis in the periventricular white matter ± neuronal loss in gray matter

Table 5 Main causes of central nervous system malfunction in the neonatal period

Prenatal	Chronical fetal distress: toxemia, maternal diabetes
	Chromosomal abnormalities
	Congenital malformations
	Infections: cytomegalic inclusion disease, rubella, toxoplasmosis, herpes
	Neurocutaneous syndromes: neurofibromatosis, tuberous sclerosis
	Drugs: narcotics, barbiturates, general anaesthetic agents, local anaesthetics, anticonvulsants, tranquilizers, alcohol, nicotine
During birth process (mainly in full-term)	Mechanical birth injury, in case of breech, high forceps, cephalopelvic disproportion: tearing of dural sinuses and bridging veins, subdural, subarachnoid haemorrhage, depressed skull fracture, spinal cord injury (breech delivery)
	Subacute or acute fetal distress with hypoxia and ischaemia, in any type of mechanical or functional dystocia: oedema, and neuronal damage
Postnatal (mainly in low birth weight)	Acute distress with hypoxia and ischaemia, in apnoeic spells, bradycardia, cardial arrest, neuronal damage, particularly leucomalacia in premature newborns
	Immaturity + IRDS: intraventricular haemorrhage
	Infections: bacterial or viral meningoencephalitis
	Metabolic: hypoglycaemia, hypocalcaemia, hypomagnesaemia, hyponatraemia, hypernatraemia, hyperbilirubinaemia, inborn errors

(3) Periventricular Leucomalacia

Periventricular leucomalacia is characterized by areas of necrosis of periventricular white matter in a border-zone distribution suggesting ischaemia as the primary mechanism (Banker and Larroche, 1962). Leucomalacia (Table 4) is clinically silent in the neonatal period. Nevertheless it is probably the most common lesion (Towbin, 1971; Larroche *et al.*, 1975) associated with cerebral palsy in the premature newborn.

(4) Other Causes of CNS Problems in the Neonatal Period

Perinatal damage described above, mostly due to brain immaturity, ischaemia and anoxia before, during or after birth explain only a fraction of the CNS problems. Infection transmitted by the mother in the early stage of pregnancy, maternal drug intake, acute perinatal infection, metabolic toxic or genetic disorders are frequent causes of neonatal difficulties and poor outcome. These causes are not available for intervention, but can be identified from a detailed history and should always be taken into account. They are listed chronologically in Table 5.

FOLLOW-UP STUDIES: METHODOLOGICAL APPROACH

Perinatal injury can result in all kinds of brain damage or dysfunction, from cerebral palsy to low IQ, sensorial deficit or behavioural problems. All the recent reports of follow-up studies clearly show that the incidence of brain damage in high-risk newborns is continuously decreasing with the progressive improvement in intensive care. Different groups have been studied: newborn with IRDS treated with artificial ventilation, low birth-weight infants, small for dates, children who had received intrauterine transfusions, infants of diabetic mothers and those with unfavourable obstetrical circumstances. For each intensive care unit follow-up studies are obviously important for the sake of the team itself. The criteria of selection of high-risk newborns and the methods of survey are usually unique to each individual group. The variability of the published data from different institutions reflects the lack of a uniform approach to patient selection and methods of follow-up. When one looks over this literature, it is difficult to compare individual studies, discount local biases or draw firm general conclusions on the overall outcome of infants treated in newborn intensive care units.

One of the multiple reasons for the failure of these studies is the lack of agreement on a satisfactory and reproducible method of neurological assessment. Only major defects are given a precise definition. In the majority of these studies mild or transitory abnormalities are not taken into account or are described by such a variety of terminology that comparisons between different studies are impossible. As there is a 'continuum of reproductive casualty' as well as progressive improvement in the results of newborn intensive care, the neurologist will deal more and more with mild deviations from normal development and less with major defects. This lack of methodology has therefore become unacceptable. Because the neurological examination is often considered impractical and non-quantifiable, developmental scales, with the appealing precision carried by numbers, have very often been the only tests utilized in these studies.

The number of infants studied is often too small to evaluate the influence of socioeconomical and cultural factors upon development. These factors, which clearly have an impact on the acquisition of learning abilities, increase the problems of establishing a clear causal relationship between perinatal injury and subsequent development. Moreover, socio-economic factors are not just alternative sources of influence but interact with neurological damage so that the amount of impairment from a given level of insult will vary considerably according to the life circumstances of the child.

Three periods of neurologic development can be roughly isolated from birth to 7 years of age. During the first year, passive tone, active tone, and reflexes manifest rapid changes with a fairly precise pattern, such that deviations from the normal can be evaluated. This neurologic evaluation, since it is not influenced by the socio-economic background, should not be omitted from a systematic assessment of the infant. Between 1 and 6 years, the development of normal motor ability is usually observed even in children who previously showed moderate abnormalities during the first year. The development of language, fine motor skills, and behaviour give better guide lines than the neurologic evaluation alone. After 6 years the end result can be most usefully assessed from learning abilities, behaviour, and fine motor skills together with the loose concept of minimal brain dysfunction; by this time, however, a poor home environment has often become more deleterious than the minimal brain lesions.

Is there a way for the neonatologist to obtain a rapid answer concerning the presence and the degree of brain damage after a perinatal insult? It seems reasonable to expect that, in addition to the major sequelae easily recognizable shortly after birth, neurologic abnormalities observed during the first year of life offer the best clues to establishing a relationship between perinatal insult and an unfavourable late outcome (Amiel-Tison, 1978). The data of Drillien (1972, 1978) and Drillien et al. (1980) already suggest this link in low birth-weight infants, with data on the long-term significance of transitory abnormal neurological signs seen in the first year of life in children of low birth weight who are now of school age. Table 6 refers to children attending schools. All the children had a full battery of tests; IQ, educational progress, motor impairment, perceptual impairment, etc. An overall impairment score was assigned. Roughly speaking, children with a score of 0–1 are getting on quite well in school, those with a score of 2 have some problems, and those with scores of 3 or over are having

Table 6 (Drillien). Overall impairment score on a test battery applied in primary schools at age 6 years 8 months to controls and to children of low birth weight who did or did not show early transient neurological abnormality

Impairment score	Low birth weight (LBW)		Controls %
	Neuro. abnormal %	Neuro. normal %	
0	31	55	68
1	33	28	16
2	13	8	12
3	23	9	4
Total	100	100	100
No. of cases	103	131	111

Source: Major Mental Handicap Ciba symposium 59.
≤ 1500 g, 60 per cent transient neurological abnormality
1501–2000 g, 37 per cent transient neurological abnormality
Six children with cerebral palsy excluded

considerable problems. The control children were matched for social class; there is no statistical difference between the neurologically normal LBW group and the control group. However, of the LBW children who were neurologically abnormal (excluding all children with cerebral palsy) 23 per cent are in considerable difficulty at 6 years 8 months of age. These transient abnormal neurological signs are therefore very important and may be a good measure of what is going on in the intensive care unit. However, one can see that 64 per cent of the infants having had neurological abnormalities within the first year are in the normal range at school age, which means a high percentage of possible compensation without detectable deficit.

It is clear that a cohort of infants born between 1966 and 1970 is not representative of the effects of current practices in intensive care units in 1980. These data then give an inflated idea of the percentage of the deficit to expect nowadays. However, this study remains essential to demonstrate the link between early motor symptoms and outcome at school age.

The data of Wallace (1975) show another aspect of the association between perinatal abnormality and future disorder. Wallace found, when studying factors predisposing infants to an initial complicated febrile convulsion, a significantly large number of cases of perinatal abnormality. However, between birth and the first febrile convulsion, these children were either mildly affected or had never required medical attention for any neurological symptoms. It is therefore very probable that the cellular lesion which was the predisposing factor is of perinatal origin and was mild enough to have been ignored before the febrile convulsion supervened.

The data from the collaborative project analysed by Friedman et al. (1977)

with developmental studies at 3 and 4 years of age demonstrate the long-term effect of dysfunctional labour or abnormal delivery. A significant adverse effect is seen among offspring delivered by midforceps procedures or born after complicated labour characterized by prolonged deceleration, secondary arrest of dilatation, or arrest of descent. There were no such correlations in that group with tests of motor development at 1 year of age. This suggests that 1 year of age is a silent period, probably preceded by motor signs within the first few months of life, and possibly followed much later by statistical differences in IQ score and behavioural testing.

The collection of data of this sort will provide a reliable means of evaluating new methods of intensive care, which can determine not only the decreasing number of severely handicapped children but also the number of mild lesions. Until this link between lesions of perinatal origin and minimal brain dysfunction has been more clearly established, the neonatologist who wants a rapid answer concerning the presence and degree of brain damage after a perinatal insult has to regard all children with transitory abnormalities during the first year of life as belonging to a high-risk group for minimal brain damage.

We have developed a neurologic examination for the first year, that does not duplicate standard mental and motor scales of infant development. Before

Table 7   Most common patterns of transitory abnormalities
observed within the first year of life

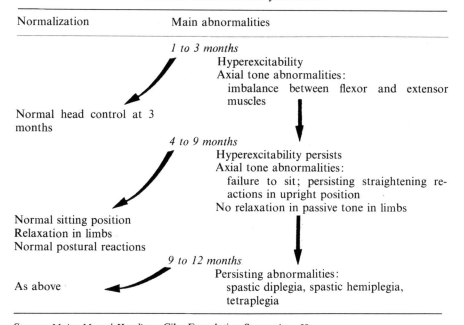

Normalization	Main abnormalities

	1 to 3 months
	Hyperexcitability
	Axial tone abnormalities:
	  imbalance between flexor and extensor
	  muscles

Normal head control at 3 months	
	4 to 9 months Hyperexcitability persists Axial tone abnormalities: failure to sit; persisting straightening reactions in upright position No relaxation in passive tone in limbs
Normal sitting position Relaxation in limbs Normal postural reactions	

As above	*9 to 12 months*
	Persisting abnormalities:
	  spastic diplegia, spastic hemiplegia,
	  tetraplegia

Source: Major Mental Handicap. Ciba Foundation Symposium 59

correlations between the first- and seventh-year data are possible, a provisional classification can be reached at 1 year of age and categorized into the following three groups: no abnormalities, transitory abnormalities, and persisting abnormalities (Amiel-Tison, 1976, 1977).

The most common patterns of transitory abnormalities observed within the first year of life are summarized in Table 7. In severe cases, it is of course not necessary to wait until the end of the first year for the diagnosis of cerebral palsy, whereas it is in mild cases of diplegia or hemiplegia. The association of generalized hypotonia and lethargy is not shown in Table 7, since it is rarely transitory but rather a severe sign observed after status epilepticus.

FOLLOW-UP STUDIES: RESULTS AT SCHOOL AGE

(a) Preliminary Remarks

Different stages of technical improvement of neonatal care have been observed in the last 10 years (Reynolds, 1978). Before the advent of intensive care, morbidity and mortality was very high. As soon as intensive care methods are instituted, mortality decreases: morbidity, however, increases until overall care is improved. Only after this unfavourable transitory period does morbidity decrease in the same proportion as mortality.

The ethical position has an important, though not measurable influence on the results in this area. To keep a child alive without discrimination until the last heartbeat leads to a high percentage of sequelae. On the other hand, a certain selection based on a high presumption of severe cerebral damage, (particularly in case of IVH of the premature and ischaemic necrosis of the term newborn) would have little effect on the overall mortality but a large one on the resulting percentage of serious sequelae. Most of these comments are applicable to obstetrical supervision and displaying a certain amount of audacity in rescuing a fetus in distress before an extreme degree of brain damage has occurred, will be essential factors of fetal survival with an intact brain.

Other difficulties can be added, making the generalization of the results extremely difficult; many factors cloud the results, e.g., varying proportions of cases that cannot be followed up, the lumping in the same groups of children of widely varying ages, the varying definition of an acceptable IQ (from 70 to 85), and different methodologies of evaluation. However, disregarding these innumerable biases, the recent results can be summarized as follows, in various groups at risk.

(b) Relative Position of Perinatal Risk

A recent Ciba symposium focussed on the main causes and possible prevention of major mental handicap, one of the aims being to delineate the relative position of perinatal risks as opposed to other aetiologies as a cause of mental and motor handicap.

A Swedish team (Gustavson *et al.*, 1977) studied a random group of 122 children from the County of Uppsala, born between 1959 and 1970, afflicted with severe mental retardation, to determine the magnitude and distribution of the various aetiologies and pathogenic factors that caused the sequelae.

Five main categories were identified and distinguished according to the presumed major causative factors. The proportion of cases falling within the several categories are as follows:

1. Prenatal (before delivery): 73 per cent (of which 36 per cent were attributable to chromosomal abnormalities).
2. Perinatal (during delivery or within 7 days after): 10 per cent
3. Post natal (from 7 days to 18 days): 3 per cent
4. Infantile psychosis: 3 per cent
5. Untraceable: 11 per cent

It is clearly apparent that the category of cases related to a natal or post-natal aetiology is small as compared to that of the prenatal one; There are, unfortunately, no such data for children of moderate mental handicap (IQ between 50 and 70). It would appear, however, that the etiology for this group is to a greater extent of natal or post-natal origin.

(c) Categories in Perinatal Risk

(1) Infants with a Birth Weight of Less than 1500 g

The best recent results are described at University College Hospital from 1966 to 1975. There is less than 10 per cent of infants with severe handicaps. There is no difference in percentage of handicaps between SGA and AGA, or birth weight less than 1000 grams and birth weight of 1000 g to 1500 g (Stewart *et al.*, 1978).

Less favourable results have been found by the Toronto group in 1974. They found 30 per cent of severely handicapped children in infants weighing less than 1500 g. Fetal hypotrophy, IVH and birth-weight less than 1000 g were additional risk factors (Fitzhardinge and Pape, 1978; Commey and Fitzhardinge, 1979). At Port-Royal, a decreased incidence of severe sequelae was observed: while there were 17 per cent handicapped infants in a group treated from 1967 to 1970, there were only 10 per cent in a group treated with Continuous Positive Airway Pressure (CPAP) from 1973 to 1974. The value of the neonatal neurological signs appears quite clearly in the study of Port-Royal (Cukier *et al.*, 1978) as well as in the Canadian (Fitzhardinge and Pape, 1978) and the English studies (Stewart *et al.*, 1978). The results of intensive-care therapy for neonates with Respiratory Distress Syndrome (RDS) have been recently analysed from published data (Thompson and Reynolds, 1977).

The increasing survival rate in infants under 1000 g certainly generates anxiety about their outcome, as seen in two recent reviews in the *New England Journal of Medicine* and in *Lancet* (Hack *et al.*, 1979; *Lancet*, 1980).

(3) Small-for-date Term Infants

Fitzhardinge, in 1972, showed that for small-for-date infants born at 37 weeks or later, major neurological defects were uncommon (Fitzhardinge and Steven, 1972). The incidence of cerebral palsy was 1 per cent, of convulsions 6 per cent, and of 'minimal brain dysfunction' 25 per cent.

(4) Obstetrical Risk Factors in the Term Newborn

Severe brain damage of obstetrical cause is now so exceptional that combining intra-partum death with severe handicap in infants is no longer statistically meaningful for evaluating obstetrical results. The comparison between 1974 and 1976 data shows a decreased percentage of cerebral symptoms as fetal care improves (Amiel-Tison, 1978).

SUMMARY AND PRACTICAL CONCLUSIONS

(a) Who to Include in Follow-up Studies?

All Premature Newborns or Small-for-dates, Even if
Symptomless within the Neonatal Period

This means all the low birth-weight population, weighing less than 2500 g at birth. This appears reasonable as the lesions in this group may be completely silent during the neonatal period. However, this means following about 8 per cent of the neonatal population, including a lot of healthy twins. If the technical possibilities of a follow-up clinic are overwhelmed, it is reasonable to focus on newborns weighing less than 1800 g or having had a very stormy neonatal course. This means a selection on birth weight and/or unfavourable circumstances, keeping in mind that it is not possible in low birth weight to base a selection on neurological symptoms. As a consequence, a high proportion of these infants selected, even if their birth weight is less than 1000 g, will be ultimately perfectly normal.

Full-term Newborns with Cerebral Symptoms Persisting after 7 days

When neonatal signs have been classified as moderate or severe, the neurological examination is never normal at 7 days. In the group with mild signs, the normalization within the first week is observed in about half of the cases; these

Table 8 Summary of lesions and late outcome linked with perinatal risk, according to gestational age and birth weight

GA and birth weight	Mechanism	Timing	Anatomical findings in the neonatal period	Possible sequelae
Premature newborns GA < 37 weeks	Brain immatury Anoxia and acidosis Systemic hypotension Veinous stasis Ischaemia	Mostly *post-natal* risk increased by respiratory distress	Intracranial haemorrhages Secondary hydrocephaly Periventricular leucomalacia.	Cerebral palsy (spastic diplegia) Hydrocephaly Intellectual or sensorial impairment Frequency of minimal brain dysfunction Frequency of epilepsy Rarity of cerebral palsy
Small for dates (birth weight below 10 percentile on growth curve)	Prolonged undernutrition Chronic fetal distress Poor tolerance to the stress of labour	Mostly *prenatal* but perinatal too	Very few data on the lesions	
Full term with normal birth weight	Frequency of ischaemia and anoxia during labour Rarity of real birth trauma	*Perinatal*	Cerebral necrosis, cortex and brain stem Brain oedema	Cerebral palsy in very severe cases All kind of intellectual, sensorial, behavourial problems Epilepsy

infants with rapid normalization need not be followed any longer; previous work indicates that the late outcome for them will be normal. Based on the reliability of neurological signs in the full term neonate, this selection reduces to less than 1 per cent of birth the number of full-term newborns to be followed. Conversely all studies based on unfavourable circumstances in full-term newborns are not really contributive, the majority of the infants being and remaining normal. Finally, 4–6 per cent of the general population (genetic problems excepted) will be followed in specialized clinics, with repeated neurologic evaluation, developmental scales, and assessment of sensorial development and behaviour.

(b) Summary of Perinatal Risk According to Gestational Age and Birth Weight

So far as perinatal risk is concerned, the anatomical and aetiological data related to late outcome could be very grossly summarized as in Table 8.

For continuous evaluation of the adequacy of obstetrics, a neurological assessment of every newborn infant is required whatever the Apgar score may be. The neonatal neurological evaluation should be added to the perinatal data for the full-term newborn, so that the high-risk group for abnormal neurological outcome could be more closely identified.

For continuous evaluation of the adequacy of neonatal intensive care, repeated neurological evaluation within the first year is required in low birth weight infants, whatever the neonatal period has been. The high risk group can be identified on transitory motor abnormalities, even if the normalization appears satisfactory. The long-term follow-up, therefore, will focus on a small group of infants, concentrating the medical and educational possibilities on the real risk population, trying to minimize as much as possible the final deficit, if any.

REFERENCES

Amiel-Tison, C. (1969). Cerebral damage in full-term newborn. Aetiological factors, neonatal status and long term follow-up *Biol. Neonat.*, **14**, 234.

Amiel-Tison, C. (1972). Follow-up of infants presenting neurological abnormalities in the first day of life, *Third European Meeting of Perinatal Medicine*, Hans Huber, Bern.

Amiel-Tison, C. (1974). Neurological evaluation of the small neonate: the importance of the head straightening reactions, in *Modern Perinatal Medicine* (Ed. L. Gluck) Year Book Medical Publisher, New York.

Amiel-Tison, C., Korobkin, R., and Esque-Vaucouloux, M. T. (1977). Neck extensor hypertonia: a clinical sign of insult to the central nervous system of the newborn, *Early Human Development*, **1/2**, 181.

Amiel-Tison, C. (1976). A method for neurologic evaluation within the, first year of life, in *Current Problems in Pediatrics* (Ed. L. Gluck), pp. 1–50, Year Book Publisher, New York.

Amiel-Tison, C. (1977). *The Neurological Evaluation within the First Year of Life*. Video Cassette. Health Sciences. Case Western Reserve University. Cleveland.

Amiel-Tison, C. (1978). A method for neurological evaluation within the first year of life: experience with full-term newborn infants with birth injury, in *Major Mental Handicap* Ciba Symposium no. 59, Elsevier/North-Holland, Amsterdam.

Amiel-Tison, C. (1979). Birth injury as a cause of brain dysfunction in full-term newborns in *Advances in Perinatal Neurology* (Ed. R. Korobkin and C. Guilleminault), Spectrum Publications.

Banker, B. Q. and Larroche, J.Cl. (1962). Periventricular leukomalacia of infancy. A. M. A., *Arch. Neurol. and Psychiat.* 7, 386.

Bauer, C., New, M., and Miller, J. (1965). Cerebro-spinal fluid protein values of premature infants, *J. Pediat.*, 66, 1017.

Commey, J. O. O. and Fitzhardinge, P. M. (1979). Handicap in the preterm small for gestational age infant, *J. Pediatr.*, 94, 779–786.

Cukier, F., de Bethmann, O., Moriette, G., Relier, J. P., and Minkoswski, A. (1978). Le devenir de l'enfant prématuré. *Rev. Neuropsychiatr. Infant*, 26, 435–438.

Dreyfus-Brisac, C. and Monod, N. (1972). Neonatal status epilepticus. in *Handbook of EEG and Clinical Neurophysiology*, XVB, 38.

Drillien, C. M. (1972). Abnormal neurologic signs in the first year of life in low weight infants. Possible pronostic significance, *Dev. Med. Child. Neurol.*, 14, 575.

Drillien, C. M. (1978). Discussion, in *Major Mental Handicap*. Ciba Symposium no. 59, p. 120. Elsevier/North-Holland, Amsterdam.

Drillien, C. M., Thomson, A. J. M., and Burgoyne, K. (1980). Low birth weight children at early school age: A longitudinal study. *Develop. Med. Child. Neurol.*, 22, 26–47.

Dubowitz, V. (1969). *The Floppy Infant*. Spastics International Medical Publications, Lavenham.

Escobedo, M., Barton, L. L., and Volpe, J. (1975). Cerebro-spinal fluid studies in an intensive care nursery, *J. Perinat. Med.*, 3, 204.

Fitz, C. R. (1981). Computed tomography in the newborn. In *"Progress in perinatal neurology"* (Ed. Korobkin and Guilleminault) Williams & Wilkins (vol. I) London: pp. 85–120.

Fitzhardinge, P. and Steven, E. M. (1972). The small for date infant. II: Neurological and intellectual sequelae, *Pediatrics*, 50, 50.

Fitzhardinge, P. and Pape, K. E. (1978). Present status of the very low birth weight infant treated in a referral neonatal intensive care unit in 1974, in *The Cost of Preventing Major Mental Handicap*. Ciba Symposium, Elsevier, Amsterdam.

Friedman, E. A., Sachtleben, M. S., and Bresky, P. A. (1977). Dysfunctional labor. XII. Longterm effects on infant, *Am. J. Obstet. Gynecol.*, 127, 779.

Goldstein, G. W., Chaplin, E. R., Maitland, J., and Norman, D. (1976). Transient hydrocephalus in premature infants: treatment by lumbar punctures, *Lancet*, March 6, 512.

Gustavson, K. H., Hagberg, B., Hagberg, G., and Sars, K. (1977). Severe mental retardation in Swedish country. II: etiologic and pathogenetic aspects of children born 1959–1970, *Neuropädiatrie*, 8, 293.

Hack, M., Fanaroff, A. A., and Merkatz, I. R. (1979). The low-birth-weight infant. Evolution of a changing outlook *N. England J. Med.*, 30, 1162–1165.

Harris, R. and Tizard, J. P. M. (1960). EEG in neonatal convulsions, *J. Pediat.*, 57, 501.

Korobkin, R. (1975). The relationship between head circumference and development of communicating hydrocephalus following intraventricular hemorrhage, *Pediatrics*, 56, 74.

Lancet (1980). The fate of the baby under 1501 g at birth (Editorial), 461–463.

Larroche, J. Cl. (1964). Hemorragies cérébrales intraventriculaires chez le prématuré. I. Anatomie et physiologie, *Biol. Neonat.*, 7, 26.

Larroche, J. Cl. (1968). Nécrose cérébrale massive chez le nouveau-né. *Biol. Neonat.*, 13, 340.

Larroche, J. Cl. (1972). Post-hemorrhage hydrocephalus in infancy. Anatomical study. *Biol. Neonat.*, **20**, 287.

Larroche, J. Cl. (1976). *Developmental Pathology of the Neonate*, pp. 545, Elsevier Excerpta Medica. North-Holland, Amsterdam.

Larroche, J. Cl., Amiel-Tison, C., Relier, J. P., and Korn, G. (1975). Leucomalacies et avenir cérébral en relation avec les soins intensifs néonataux, *Ann. Anesth. Franç.* Spécial 1, 171.

Myers, R. E., Beard, R., and Adamsons, K. J. (1969). Brain swelling in the newborn rhesus monkey following prolonged partial asphyxia. *Neurology*, **19**, 1012.

Myers, R. (1972). Two patterns of perinatal brain damage and their conditions of occurrence, *Amer. J. Obstet. Gynec.*, **112**, 246.

Myers, R. E. (1975). Four patterns of perinatal brain damage and their conditions of occurrence in primates, *Adv. Neurol.*, **10**, 223.

Nellhaus, G. (1968). Composite international and interracial graphs, *Pediatrics*, **41**, 106.

Pape, K. E., Cusik, G., Houang, M. T. W *et al.* (1979). Ultrasound detection of brain damage in preterm infants. Lancet I: 1261.

Pape, K. E. and Fitzhardinge, P. M. (1981). Perinatal damage to the developing brain. In: "*Advances in perinatal medicine*". (Vol. I), pp. 45–85. (Ed. Milunsky, Friedman and Gluck), Plenum medical, New York.

Philip, A. G. S. (1979). Non invasive monitoring of intracranial pressure. Clin. Perinatal. **6**, 123.

Reynolds, E. O. R. (1978). Neonatal intensive care and the prevention of major handicap, in *The Cost of Preventing Major Mental Handicap*. Ciba Symposium, Elsevier, Amsterdam.

Rose, A. L. and Lombroso, C. T. (1970). Neonatal seizure states, *Pediatrics*, **45**, 404.

Sarnat, H. B. and Sarnat, M. S. (1976). Neonatal encephalopathy following fetal distress, *Arch. Neurol.*, **33**, 696.

Sher, P. K. and Brown, S. B. (1975). A longitudinal study of head growth in preterm infants. I. Normal rates of head growth *Develop. Med. and Child Neurology* **17**, 705.

Sher, P. K. and Brown, S. B. (1975). A longitudinal study of head growth in preterm infants. II. Differentiation between 'catchup' head growth and early infantile hydrocephalus, *Develop. Med. Child Neurology*, **17**, 711.

Starr, A. and Amlie, R. (1981). The evaluation of newborn brainstem and cochlear functions by auditory brainstem potentials. In: "*Progress in Perinatal Neurology*", pp. 65–83. (Eds Korobkin & Guilleminault), (Vol. I) Williams & Wilkins (Publs). London.

Stewart, A., Turcan, D., Rawlings, G., Hart, S., and Gregory, S. (1978). Outcome for infants at high risk of major handicap, in *The Cost of Preventing* Major Mental Handicap. Ciba Symposium, Elsevier, Amsterdam.

Tharp, B. R. (1981). Neonatal electroencephalography. In: "*Progress in Perinatal Neurology*", (Ed. Korobkin and Guilleminault). Williams & Wilkins (publs) (Vol. I). London: pp. 31–83.

Thompson, T. and Reynold, J. (1977). The results of intensive care therapy for neonates with respiratory distress syndrome, *J. Perinat. Med.*, **5**, 149.

Towbin, A. (1971). Organic Causes of minimal brain dysfunction. *J. Amer. Med. Assoc.*, **217**, 1207–1214.

Volpe, J. J. (1976). Perinatal hypoxic-ischemic brain injury. *Pediatrics Clinics of North. Am.*, **23**, 383.

Wallace, S. J. (1975). Factors predisposing to a complicated initial febrile convulsion. *Arch. Dis. Childh.*, **50**, 943.

SECTION II

Capacities and Characteristics

The key to any understanding of newborns is an appreciation of the range and limitations of their capacities, of the characteristics they share, and of the inter-individual variation in those capacities and characteristics. Research over the last two decades has concentrated particularly on cognitive capacities and has resulted in a substantial shift in perspective. Earlier statements about what newborns could or could not do were derived from assumptions about their total dependency and malleability and the immaturity of their nervous systems. Once substantial experimentation with newborns was under way it became clear that their capacities had been significantly underestimated. This section does not attempt to comprehensively review the specific experimental work but to present the understanding which is now possible of how the particular forms that neonatal capacities and characteristics take are related to the status of the physiological substrate, and to the requirements for adaptation which have been relatively consistent in our evolutionary history.

The shift in perspective is very clear in Gordon Bronson's survey of the nervous system at birth (Chapter 5). A consideration of the relationship between the evolutionary development of our nervous system and the relative maturity of different systems at birth points to the likelihood that newborn functions will be performed by the most phylogenetically primitive system capable of such performance. The conclusion that functions such as learning and perception may be mediated by different parts of the nervous system, and therefore may be quite different from adult forms, returns us firmly to the need to study newborn functioning in its own right. Assumptions imported from research with adults will be misleading, as are arguments from the existence of a capacity to a claim that the part of the nervous system responsible for the capacity in the adult must therefore be functional at birth. Similarly fallacious is the claim, which still appears from time to time, that immaturity of the system responsible for a function in the adult proves that the newborn must be incapable of that function. What can legitimately be concluded is that the function is likely to take a unique form in the newborn. The analysis of the maturity of different parts of the

95

nervous system leads finally to a consideration of which systems are developing most rapidly during the neonatal period and will therefore be most sensitive to the quality of stimulation provided at this time.

Rhythmic variation in function and behaviour (Chapter 6) has long been assumed to make a significant contribution to neonatal adaptation but the nature of this contribution has never been coherently worked out. Instead it is argued that a somewhat intuitive appreciation of the wide variety of apparent rhythmicities has led to premature speculations about underlying mechanisms and functional significance. In this chapter an attempt is made to provide a descriptive model which will allow clear judgements about whether a rhythm is actually present and which will be a basis for determining the contribution that rhythmicity makes to adaptation in specific cases. A description of oscillations as tending towards either a relaxation (build-up and discharge) or a pendulum mode of functioning leads to the hypothesis that neonatal rhythms are likely to operate more in a relaxation mode but will tend towards the pendulum type as development proceeds. This model is used to co-ordinate what is known about rhythmic tendencies in functions whose periodicities range from fractions of a second up to twenty-four hours. There appear to be several aspects of neonatal behaviour which are more easily understood when their detailed rhythmic properties are considered in conjunction with their other aspects.

A clue to the general significance of rhythms may come from the increase in predictability they provide, and the biological advantage which Carolyn Rovee-Collier and Lewis Lipsitt (Chapter 7) point out comes from knowing 'what to expect and when to expect it' (p. 150). Their chapter shows clearly how valuable has been the shift away from applying learning paradigms derived from adults and towards a consideration of the unique demands for adaptation of the neonatal period. The overriding requirement for the newborn is to maximize caloric intake and minimize caloric expenditure. The review of adaptive learning suggests that this principle should be a starting point for explaining any newborn characteristic. The principle is readily applied in contexts of caloric intake such as oral functioning, while understanding caloric expenditure in these terms is more complex but very fruitful. The balance reached by the newborn by a level of responsiveness which maximizes the chances of eliciting appropriate caretaking at minimal cost in energy is an example of the payoffs between different aspects of adaptation discussed in Chapter 1. In this case it leads to a consideration of the particular kinds of learning capacities, and perhaps of limitations in learning and memory, which ensure that, at least in an environment consistent with our evolutionary past, adaptations will be closely related to their biological significance. The implications for research findings and methodology are extensive and fully discussed, while the potential practical significance is indicated by applying these conclusions to the explanation of crib death.

While learning is closely related to adaptation and survival, perception has more obvious implications for the kinds of cognitive function which underly social interaction. The full implications of the newborn's cognitive capacities are explored in Section 4, while in Chapter 8, Janette Atkinson and Oliver Braddick provide a detailed account of the sensory and perceptual tendencies that newborns bring to these transactions. This is an area in which the depth of knowledge is closely correlated with the techniques available. Although the significance of other senses is stressed, it is the visual modality which has been most intensively studied and about which we have the fullest information. While the relative maturity of ocular control, providing an accessible and sensitive response measure, must be partly responsible, the account of visual functioning that emerges from this chapter suggests a further factor. As Bronson's analysis in Chapter 5 would lead one to expect, the visual system is developing very rapidly during the period under review, so that studies of this modality have been particularly rewarding. Furthermore, while it may be the more mature (and more primitive) senses, processing such factors as taste and temperature, which have the most significance for immediate adaptation, the development of vision, by being more open to environmental influence, will play a major role in the transactions between the baby and his/her care-givers.

Given the value placed on individuality in this culture it is not surprising that the move to direct study of the newborn should have been quickly followed by claims for the range and significance of individual differences. The ease with which subjective impressions of newborn individuals may be formed can be appreciated by studying Figure 1 of Chapter 1. It would be difficult to view these pictures without a feeling that this is a unique individual with well-defined and persisting characteristics (compare days 1, 5, and 9; 3 and 18; and 8, 14, and 24). While not necessarily misleading, such impressions may have seduced us into accepting that stable and meaningful individual differences exist without any close examination of the evidence. Chapter 9 sets out to make explicit the (six) different reasons for regarding individual variation as significant, so that it becomes possible to estimate for each function whether the differences between babies are sufficiently marked and persistent to have implications for any of the criteria. The comprehensive review of newborn individuality according to these criteria reveals rather little evidence for differences which are related to fundamental characteristics or significant later functions. What does emerge is that babies differ from each other in ways that are likely to affect the quality of their immediate adaptations and their relationships with care-givers.

Each of the areas reviewed in this Section makes its contribution to our understanding of newborn adaptation and in each case the refinement of our knowledge which the review is able to provide leads to a stronger appreciation of the subtlety and complexity of this adaptation and of how much more we have to find out.

Psychobiology of the Human Newborn
Edited by P. Stratton
© 1982, John Wiley & Sons, Ltd.

CHAPTER 5

Structure, Status, and Characteristics of the Nervous System at Birth

GORDON W. BRONSON

Conceptual models of psychological phenomena that are developed purely in the light of the behavioural evidence are not likely to be homologous with the underlying neural process. The human brain is the product of a long sequence of evolutionary refinements and elaborations of structure, each of which was constrained by the form of previous adaptations and was selected without regard to future requirements. The resulting convoluted network of complexly interacting systems will not be accurately reflected in formulations guided in large part by considerations of parsimony and logical order.

Whether psychologists should, in general, be concerned over probable major discrepancies between the formal characteristics of the behaviourally conceived models and the actual organization of the mediating networks raises issues outside the scope of this chapter. However, at least in the present instance where the focus is on an age marked by rapid neural growth, models which treat the growth of functional capacities conceived without reference to the changing form of the mediating networks are likely to prove less than satisfactory. This assertion will be documented by offering a model of early functional development which recognizes the transitional status of the neonatal nervous system.

Aspects of the evolution and current organization of the human brain will briefly be reviewed, followed by rather more detailed analyses of the developmental status of the brain during the initial postnatal months; throughout the exposition a series of inferences will be offered linking these neurological data to evidence on early behavioural development. It should be noted that in interrelating findings drawn from a variety of scientific fields the inferential leaps will at times span areas where the data are thin or of uncertain quality—and therefore the notion of 'plausibility' often must stand as a provisional substitute for hard data. Counterbalancing such uncertainties, however, is the broader perspective on the functional status of the newborn infant to be gained from juxtaposing relevant findings from a variety of related fields.

THE ORGANIZATION OF THE BRAIN:
AN EVOLUTIONARY PERSPECTIVE

The sequence of ancestral forms that preceded the present mammalian brain has been reconstructed in considerable detail by Sarnat and Netsky (1974); for present purposes a brief résumé highlighting selected aspects of their analysis will suffice. Our very remote ancestor presumably was in essence a spinal animal, capable only of responding reflexively to various kinds of discrete stimuli. At a much later stage, organisms with the added capacity provided by networks roughly similar to the brain stem of contemporary mammals gained the potential for a more complex within-modality analysis of sensory signals, an ability to assess between-mode contingencies, and some primitive forms of learning capacity. Finally, the recent evolution of the primitive forebrain, and particularly developments within the neocortex, has led to a further refinement of within-mode pattern analyses, an enhanced ability to synthesize information across modalities, and a capacity for the symbolic representation of prior experience. In contemporary species this hierarchy of neural structures seems to mature in the general order in which it evolved (see below), moving the fetus and then the infant from a reflexive status, through a stage marked by more complex yet still immediate and stimulus-bound automatic reactions, to the point where responses begin to have the character of volitional decisions based upon appraisals of symbolic significance.

On the evidence to be reviewed, it appears that at about the time of birth the human infant is in a transitional period in which effective mediation by neocortical networks is either just marginally present or about to emerge. Therefore, in conceiving a model of the human brain appropriate to the present age period it is useful to focus on the gross distinction between subcortical and neocortical systems. (At other ages other distinctions would become more appropriate—for example during fetal development the relevant discrimination might be between spinal and brain-stem functions; at rather older postnatal ages finer distinctions would be drawn between levels of functioning within the neocortex itself.) Of particular relevance here are the series of developments that emerged out of the rudimentary telencephalon of premammalian species: first the further evolution of cortical sensory and motor areas, and then the development of adjacent neocortical association areas. Accompanying the evolution of the neocortex, the primary sensory and motor tracts developed as the major afferent and efferent pathways for the transmission of sophisticated forms of information. The previously dominant pathways connecting subcortical systems with the periphery of the organism have remained functional in higher animals, however, and hence in very gross terms one can conceptualize the present organization as a set of parallel information processing networks (see Figure 1). The subcortical components of interest here include the superior and inferior colliculi, the several intrinsic thalamic nuclei, and the brain stem reticular

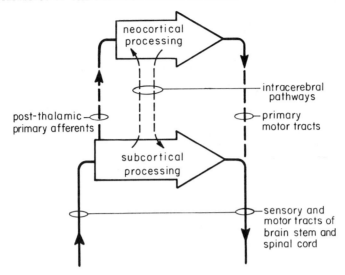

Figure 1 A schematic representation of selected aspects of the nervous system. Density of lines reflects relative degrees of myelinization at around the time of birth. For details see text

system. Apart from the reticular system (which in part evolved along with the neocortex), these various subcortical systems are similar to the most sophisticated mediational networks that existed in the brains of our precorticate ancestors. In consequence, at least in some domains the networks within the two levels appear to serve analogous adaptive functions, but at different degrees of sophistication (see Bronson, 1965).

On the evidence reviewed below it appears that the behavioural reactions of the newborn infant may in large part be mediated by the initially more developed subcortical systems. This possibility, together with evidence of the rapid postnatal growth of neocortical systems, suggests that early changes in behavioural capacity often may reflect the dawning participation of the more complexly organized neocortical components. In such cases seemingly similar behavioural effects may in fact be processed quite differently at different postnatal ages.

Evidence bearing upon the developmental status of the brain at birth and over the following postnatal months is reviewed in some detail in the following section. Readers less concerned with the specifics of such materials may wish to turn directly to the section summary.

INDICES OF DEVELOPMENTAL STATUS

The materials to be reviewed are limited largely to studies of the human circumstance. Data regarding the neonatal status of other mammalian species cannot properly be extended to humans, and even evidence regarding *sequences* of development must be considered of uncertain validity for humans (although in general the order in which various components of the nervous system mature appears to be rather similar across mammalian species; see Gibson (1977); Gottlieb (1974); Himwich (1970))).

At birth the human brain weighs only 300–400 g—about one quarter of the adult weight. Roughly half of this difference is made up during the course of the first year. The major source of this rapid increase in bulk lies in the development of new glial cells; the emergence of additional neurones, if it occurs at all in humans, would presumably be a minor phenomenon (see Altman, 1970). The migration of neurones to their final location within the cortex, a major process in prenatal development, has essentially been completed by the time of birth and the major neocortical areas already show their characteristic six-layer structure. The most marked function-related changes during the paranatal period are to be found in the growth and myelinization of axons, the multiplication and extension of dendrites, and synaptic development.

Patterns of Myelinization

Probably because the assessments here are relatively less time-consuming, the course of myelinization has been the most extensively examined index of early neural growth. Prior to their myelinization neurones generally are marked by slower transmission rates, are limited in the rate of repetitive firing, and are prone to fatigue effects. Therefore, although the myelin sheath is not necessary for conduction of action potentials, relative rates of myelinization in different areas of the brain can serve as a rough measure of the sequence in which various components of the nervous system approach adult levels of functional effectiveness. The following generalizations are based upon the extensive findings reported by Yakovlev and Lecours (1967).

The most peripheral components of the system, the sensory and motor roots within the spinal column (and head), are the first to show myelinization. Both sensory and motor pathways begin the process some 5–6 months prior to birth. The motor roots are essentially completed in the neonate, while sensory components mature less rapidly and in some cases the process of myelinization continues into the middle of the first year. Segments of the afferent pathways extending into the various subcortical networks are somewhat slower to myelinate, and there are marked differences among the several modalities. Components of the vestibular system are the most advanced, completing the course of myelinization by the time of birth. Pathways serving subcortical visual networks (retina to the Edinger–Westphal nucleus, and to the superior colliculus), begin the process about 2 months prenatally and are completed about 3 months after birth. (These several subcortical systems mediate, respectively, the neonatal eye movements induced by passive turning of the head, pupillary responses to changing illumination, and simple visual pursuit reactions—see bleow.) Pathways connecting midbrain components of the auditory system (the brachia of the inferior colliculus) similarly show a relatively early myelinization, beginning some 4 months before birth and completing at about 3 months after birth. Somatosensory afferents into midbrain areas also begin myelinization about 4 months prenatally, although here minor increases can be found through childhood. In sum, while not in all cases completed, myelinization of the various sensory pathways feeding into subcortical networks appears to be fairly well advanced by the time of birth; see Figure 1.

In contrast to the relatively advanced condition of subcortical afferents, sensory pathways into the neocortex only begin the process of myelinization at or shortly before birth. Somatosensory tracts are the most advanced, beginning the process about a month pre-term and being completed by the end of the first year. The auditory afferents begin myelinization only at birth, and continue into the preschool ages. Development of the neocortical branch of the visual afferent system differs from both of these patterns: although only beginning myelinization at birth, here the process proceeds very rapidly and is completed by around age 4 months.

To summarize: if one were to use the myelinization patterns of sensory afferents as an index of the relative growth of function, it would be expected that subcortically mediated sensory functions would be most advanced at birth, whereas neocortically mediated abilities would show the greatest degree of postnatal change. Among the latter developments, visual reactions should show the most rapid functional growth in the initial postnatal months.

Within the motor system sequences roughly parallel the course of sensory development. The pyramidal tract, the major efferent pathway from the motor cortex, begins the process about a month before birth and myelinization is completed by the end of the first year. Supporting the postnatal growth of increasingly refined motor control, the myelinization of pathways to and from the cerebellum, and of various components within the cerebellum, begins around birth and continues into the second and third years. (An exception is the inner division of the cerebellum; intimately connected with the vestibular system, this area is fully myelinated some 2 months before birth. Presumably this early development contributes to the various motion-elicited reflexes found in the newborn infant.)

The multiple feedback networks integrating activity between cortical and subcortical components of the nervous system are the least advanced at birth and show the most protracted development. For example, the diffusely projecting connections between non-specific thalamic nuclei and association areas of the neocortex only begin to show myelinization about 4 months after birth, and reach adult levels only in midchildhood. Paralleling these delayed developments, myelinization of the various short-axon interneurones within the cortex, and within those components of the reticular system that evolved along with the mammalian neocortex, also begin at or somewhat after birth, and similarly continue into midchildhood or beyond. The delayed onset and protracted development of the various cortical–subcortical pathways, and of the short-axon interneurones within the more recently evolved neural structures, presumably is related to the gradual emergence of more refined cognitive and motor capabilities during later infancy and midchildhood (see below). The overall pattern of myelinization sequences is indicated in Figure 1.

Histological Developments within the Neocortex

The most extensive data on human cortical development are provided by Conel's (1939–1967) multiple volumes detailing the characteristics of neocortical neurones at various postnatal ages. The following generalizations are drawn from Conel's summaries comparing the relative degrees of development across cortical areas and between ages. (The various criteria cited by Conel appear to be in good agreement; included are the development of cortical axons and dendrites and exogenous fibres, degree of myelinization, development of bulbs, and growth of chromophil and neurofibrils within cell bodies. Notice, however, that Conel's comparisons are not made with respect to the condition of the adult brain. While the latter might provide a better index of relative maturity, and Conel provides tables of quantitative data which might seem to permit such comparisons, the values obtained on many of these measures are highly sensitive to procedural details (Purpura and Reaser, 1974) and hence any 'percent of maturity' indices derived by introducing adult data collected by other investigators would be subject to an indeterminate degree of error. For present purposes it therefore seems best to rely on Conel's interpretations.)

Conel found the neocortex to be markedly undeveloped in newborn infants, and during the first month overall development seemed relatively slow in comparison to progress shown at 3 months and beyond. At birth and throughout the first year the primary sensory and motor areas were found to be the most advanced. Adjacent sensory elaboration areas were next in development, followed finally by the more remotely located parietal and temporal association areas for the intermodal synthesis of refined sensory information. The order here seems to parallel the general sequence in which information is processed in the adult neocortex—a point to be returned to below. (Least developed at birth, and beginning to show marked advances only after the second year, were the prefrontal lobes. Basic to the planning of a sequence of goal-oriented actions, such networks presumably only become functional at ages beyond the scope of the present chapter.)

Among primary sensory areas the somatosensory area was found to be most advanced at birth, followed by auditory and then visual areas. Postnatally, however, development proceeds most rapidly in the visual cortex, which approximates the status of the auditory area by 3 months and becomes the most advanced of the sensory systems by the end of the year. At birth and throughout the first year the primary motor area is more developed than the sensory areas.

All of these patterns fit well with the earlier discussion of myelinization sequences. Finding that the course of postnatal development within the neocortex roughly follows the order in which information is processed suggests that in later-maturing areas the form of neural growth may be guided in part by patterns of neural activation elicited by sensory experiences. Evidence that this is indeed the case will be presented below. Notice that no clear inferences have yet been drawn regarding the exact ages at which various neocortical systems might first begin to contribute to infant behaviour. While adequate for specifying developmental sequences, the various indices of structural growth cannot be used to predict the onset of effective functioning with any precision.

The Growth of Evoked Potentials

The pattern of electrical activity recorded from the surface of the head which is elicited by the single stimulus often is masked by the background of ongoing neural activity. However, by using contemporary techniques for averaging patterns across repeated stimulations the latent form of the evoked potential can be determined with considerable accuracy. Typically, the average evoked potential consists of a series of positive and negative peaks lasting for about one-half second. The interpretations offered for the various components of the evoked potential are in many regards far from certain. Not only is the pattern dependent upon the form of stimulation within the given modality, but the recorded wave-form typically includes the effects of activities within subcortical as well as cortical networks and the various sources may summate or cancel in varying degrees depending upon their polarity and amplitude and their relative latencies following stimulation. Adult studies recently have introduced a variety of complex experimental and analytical techniques for sorting out the latent significance of various aspect of the evoked potentials (e.g. in the visual area see Spekreijse et al., 1977), but in general such procedures have not yet been extended to work with infants. Although the neonatal wave forms are usually less complex, the analysis of infant data may additionally be confounded by the marked age-related changes that occur at around the time of birth: often it is difficult to determine whether a given developmental change represents merely a shift in the latency or amplitude of some previously observed peak, or is due to the emergence of a new form of activity occurring in some different neural locus. Nevertheless, the forms of the infant evoked potentials reported from different laboratories are in fairly good agreement, and in some limited domains of interpretation the consensus among authorities seems sufficient to make the findings useful in appraising the growth of neocortical function.

Neglecting for the moment some intermodality differences, the general position taken in many of the more recent articles is that the medium-latency components of the evoked potential (typically, in newborn infants, those with a latency of roughly 100 msec) probably represent activity within the given primary sensory system, while later positive or negative peaks (typically of latencies around 200 msec and beyond) appear to be due to activities in non-specific or extraprimary sensory systems. In addition, a number of current studies have rather clearly linked short latency (under 10 msec) aspects of the auditory evoked potential with activity in brainstem components of the auditory pathway (see Hecox, 1975). For present purposes it is the medium-latency components—those which might be indicative of the growth of function within the various primary sensory areas of the cortex—that are of greatest interest.

The evoked potential elicited by somatosensory stimulation appears to be relatively mature at birth, and indeed it has been described as comparable in form to that found in adults (Hrbek et al. 1973). The pattern is similar whether elicited by low-voltage electrical stimulation (Desmedt and Manil, 1970; Hrbek et al., 1973) or by tapping a muscle tendon (Hrbek et al., 1968). In either case it probably represents the effects of proprioceptor activity due to the stimulus-induced motor reflex, rather than activation of a tactile sensation (Hrbek et al., 1968)—a point that should not be overlooked. Of particular interest is the observation that the medium-latency components are far stronger over the appropriate somatosensory area, and are found primarily on the contralateral side. Given this specific and limited locus, at least in this instance it seems clear that the latent source of activity is indeed in the primary sensory area. Such effects can be found in premature infants born as early as 2 months before term (Hrbek et al., 1973). This degree of maturity in newborn infants is not clearly found in other sensory modes, and is congruent with the various structural indices reviewed above that similarly indicate an early development within this modality. In contrast to the limited locus of these medium-latency components, later peaks occurring at around 200 msec and beyond can be found both in the primary sensory area and at the vertex of the head, and are stronger in the latter area (Desmedt and Manil, 1970; Hrbek et al., 1973). On such evidence these components usually are described as reflecting 'non-specific' activity, although their exact anatomical locus remains uncertain.

Studies of auditory evoked potentials in infants are fewer, and their interpretation is in some regards less certain. The long latency components seem similar to those of the somatosensory potentials—both in form and in appearing most clearly at the vertex of the head (Hrbek et al., 1969; Schulte et al., 1977). The form here is similar in infants born up to six weeks before term (Schulte et al., 1977). The short-latency components, indicative of activity in the subcortical stages of the auditory system, also can be found as much as 6 weeks before term (Schulman-Golambos and Golambos, 1975). Curiously, in adults as well as in infants the mid-latency components that might indicate activity in the primary sensory area have proved difficult to identify in the auditory mode, apparently being confounded with thalamic activity or with artefacts from associated muscle activity (Picton *et al.*, 1974; also see Schulte *et al.*, 1977). The evidence in this modality therefore provides no clear basis for inferring the onset of primary-system cortical activity. It is relevant to note, however, that the major differences found between preterm and full-term responses lie primarily in the latencies of the various components, not in the *form* of the evoked pattern (Schulte *et al.*, 1977).

In marked contrast to the preceding findings, the form of the evoked potential in the visual mode is found to be notably different between premature and full-term infants. Although preterm infants show the long-latency spacially dispersed pattern of activity (Hrbek *et al.*, 1973; Schulte *et al.*, 1977), only in infants born at around 40 weeks is there a small complex of activity at around 100 msec latency (Ellingson, 1967; Schulte *et al.*, 1977). Hrbek *et al.* (1969), and Ferriss *et al.* (1967), also report such medium-latency activity in full-term infants, but found it to be present only marginally, and not in all infants. Although the evidence is hardly conclusive, it is suggested that these emerging medium-latency effects reflect the beginnings, at around term, of activity induced in the occipital cortex via the primary afferent system (see Lindsley, 1969). If so, neonatal development within this modality is relatively retarded—an interpretation that is in accord with previously discussed evidence of initially retarded structural development within the primary visual system. However, this medium-latency complex develops very rapidly in the postnatal interval, and becomes a stable attribute of the evoked potential within a few months following birth (Ferris *et al.*, 1967). Ellingson (1967) reports that although at birth this medium-latency component quickly wanes with stimulation rates of as little as once per second, this limitation on effective functioning rapidly decreases in succeeding postnatal months. Both of these latter findings are in accord with the preceding evidence of rapid postnatal histological developments within the primary visual system.

White *et al.* (1977) have offered provisional evidence from the study of a few infants of a medium-latency component indicative of some degree of colour-specific activity at birth. However, comparisons with the more complete sets of adult data lead them to suggest that the locus of the observed activity may be in a subcortical stage of the primary visual system—perhaps at the level of the lateral geniculate. It was noted earlier that the final stages of the primary afferent systems are generally the last to myelinate, which is congruent with the notion that at the time of birth such colour-specific activity within the primary visual system may not yet extend as far as the neocortex.

To summarize: if it is assumed that the medium-latency components of the infant evoked wave-form are indeed indices of emerging primary system activity, then:

1. it seems that considerably prior to birth proprioceptive components of the somatosensory system can induce stimulus-related activity within the primary sensory area;

2. present data on developments within the auditory system can provide no direct evidence regarding the age of onset of induced primary system activity;
3. in the visual system it appears that the primary sensory area of the neocortex is just beginning to be marginally responsive to peripheral input in full-term infants.

In this latter modality, however, there is evidence of particularly rapid postnatal development. The repeated finding, here and in the preceding sections, of apparently differential rates of development among the several modalities may perhaps be related to corresponding differences in the amounts of modality-specific stimulation provided during normal fetal development—a thesis that will be returned to in a later section.

Summary of Patterns of Neural Growth

Two major generalizations emerge from the various materials reviewed in the preceding sections. First, the sequence of neural development appears to roughly parallel our evolutionary history, with the more recently evolved components of the nervous system being relatively less mature at birth. Since there is reason to believe that the phylogenetically older and initially more mature subcortical systems still carry residual capacities for the direct mediation of sensory, motor, and learning phenomena (see below), it seems possible that many of the behaviours observed in the newborn infant may be processed largely by networks at this level. This raises the question as to just when, and in what domains, components of the neocortex first begin to play a significant role in contributing to infant behaviour. Second, the most recently evolved association areas within the neocortex together with the various pathways interlinking these areas with subcortical components of the nervous system are least mature at birth, and in most instances show a rather protracted course of postnatal development. One might therefore anticipate that postnatal experience may play a significant role in programming the final organization of such networks. These two issues are considered in the remaining sections of the chapter.

THE MEDIATIONAL BASIS OF INFANT BEHAVIOURS

Given repeated evidence of the relative immaturity of neocortical networks at birth, one must entertain the possibility that the behavioural repertoire of the newborn infant is mediated in large degree by subcortical networks, with neocortical mediation becoming progressively more important during the initial postnatal months. Consider the evidence bearing upon this issue.

The classic formulation of this position is that of McGraw (1943), in which she attributed the postnatal growth in motor capacities to progressive developments within the infant neocortex. The core of her argument rested on her detailed analyses of the development of motor control: in a variety of different behavioural areas she identified an initial interval marked largely by the strengthening of reflexive reactions, then a transitional period of waning reflexive effectiveness, followed closely by the progressive emergence of various more sophisticated 'voluntary' reactions. McGraw's argument linking such developmental progressions to the emergence of neocortical mediation rested on the then available evidence of relative neocortical immaturity at birth, together with reports of an essentially normal repertoire of reflexive behaviours being present in some anencephalitic infants. More recent data support her general conclusions.

The mediational bases for various types of automatic sensory-motor reactions have now been well documented by lesion studies conducted on non-human primates and from analyses of the non-volitional responses of human adults suffering from various types of neural damage. If it is granted that reactions which can be elicited without neocortical mediation in adults are likely to be similarly processed in the newborn infant, then on the evidence below it appears that most of the motor reactions found at birth can indeed be attributed to subcortically mediated processes. The following summary of findings in this area is drawn from Curtis *et al.* (1972).

At the spinal level, adult primates are capable of a variety of flexion reflexes in response to tactile stimulation, extensor thrust reactions in response to activation of proprioceptive (stretch) receptors, and the crossed extensor reflex. The latter, in combination with the ipsilateral flexion reflex, can provide the rudiments for alternate stepping reactions. When various midbrain components also are functional a number of complex postural responses are added, including a variety of head and body adjustments in response to vestibular stimulation, to a passive turning of the head, or to the pattern of stimulation produced by lying on one side. Also found at this level is the traction response, an integrated flexion of elbow, wrist, and fingers in response to pulling on a hand. Addition of components at the level of the thalamus contributes the grasp reflex in response to palmar stimulation. Although the automatic placing response—a lifting of the foot when stimulated on the top side—appears to require some degree of neocortical mediation in adults, it can be argued that during the first months of life this reaction also falls within the domain of subcortically mediated reactions (Zapella, 1967). In sum, it appears that many (and indeed perhaps all) of the automatic motor reactions found in the newborn infant can be mediated by subcortical mechanisms, and, following McGraw, their subsequent waning during the succeeding postnatal months can plausibly be attributed to the overriding effects of dawning neocortical processes. Acceptance of this general pattern, however, does not preclude the possibility of some limited forms of neocortically mediated sensory-motor reactions in newborn infants, and a final position on this issue must await a close analysis of the entire range of automatic motor reactions found in the newborn infant. Also, it must be recognized that the possible presence of some form of neocortical mediation at birth need not imply volitional control. For instance, the complex sequence consisting of an orienting of the hand to tactile contact on the side in order to facilitate subsequent grasping (a neocortically mediated response which typically appears some months after birth) may reappear as an involuntary reaction in adults suffering from lesions around cortical areas 6 and 8 (Curtis *et al.*, 1972).

To summarize: with regard to the hierarchy of automatic motor responses, while it remains possible that there may be some limited degree of neocortical participation at birth, the majority of the neonatal motor responses can plausibly be attributed to subcortical processes. If the motor areas of the neocortex are indeed characterized by this transitional status at birth, then one might anticipate that during the early postnetal period, (a) reactions requiring only subcortical mediation should be more readily elicited, (b) a wider range of individual differences should be found in reactions which indeed depend upon some degree of neocortical participation, and (c) one should find a rapid postnatal advance in motor abilities. Although the full array of neonatal motor reactions has yet to be analysed from this perspective, it is relevant to note that most of the responses found at birth can be elicited at least 1 month before term (see Schulte, 1974), while subsequent developments occurring over the initial postnatal months show marked individual differences in age of onset (Touwen, 1976).

The degree to which neocortical networks contribute to the processing of complex forms of sensory information at birth is far from clear. However, given that neural developments seem less advanced in primary sensory than in primary motor areas, and that the various sensory elaboration areas of the neocortex lag still further behind, one might suggest that, in general, the neocortical processing of sensory information is at best minimal at birth. One might also anticipate—both from the data on relative structural developments and from the quality of evoked potentials—that the various sensory modes may perhaps differ considerably in this regard. Furthermore, it should be noted that at least in some modalities there appear to be efferent motor pathways coming from areas directly adjacent to primary sensory areas of the cortex that can produce behavioural reactions (e.g. in the visual system, see Bronson, 1974). Therefore, findings indicative of some limited form of neocortical sensory processing at birth do not constitute evidence that subsequent neocortical stages for the analysis and encoding of complex patterns are as yet functional. Given the complexities involved, and the often uncertain implications of the available evidence, the present chapter concentrates primarily on data regarding the growth of visual capacities. Here the development of behavioural function has been closely analysed with respect to patterns of postnatal neural growth (Bronson, 1974, 1978).

Evidence from neurologically damaged (human and non-human) primates shows that the capacities of subcortical components of the visual system are sufficient for the mediation of the several types of visual reaction typically found at birth, including the smooth tracking of a moving visual field, an orienting toward a peripheral stimulus, and giving differential attention to different types of visual stimuli. Congruent with evidence of particularly rapid postnatal developments within the primary visual system, early in the second month there is behavioural evidence indicative of the dawning participation of neocortical systems in promoting the perception of complex patterns and in the emergence of visual pattern encoding. Volitional control over the direction of gaze seems to follow a month or so afterward, presumably under the guidance of an accruing store of visual memory images. If this analysis of the growth of visual capacity is correct (and it has not gone uncontested, see Haith and Campos, 1977, and a reply by Bronson, 1978), then the earliest visually elicited reactions—like most or all of the neonatal vestibular and somatosensory motor responses—do not depend upon the effective participation of neocortical networks. It need not follow, however, that the neocortical components of the visual system initially remain unaffected by visual input. Indeed, being at a transitional status at the time of birth, and entering into a period of rapid neural development, may be attributes which make the system particularly sensitive to the quality of the early environment—a theme that is pursued in the following section.

The behaviours of newborn infants elicited by auditory and somatosensory stimulation have yet to be closely analysed with regard to their mediational bases, and it would be a mistake to extrapolate into these areas from evidence on patterns of visual development. Both the data on structural growth within the neocortex and the tentative conclusions drawn from studies of evoked potentials indicate a perhaps relatively more advanced status in these modalities at the time of birth. Moreover, the different sensory systems have followed different paths of evolutionary development (see Sarnat and Netsky, 1974), and in consequence are organized differently in contemporary mammals (for example, the peripheral bifurcation of sensory afferents found within the visual system, one pathway going to subcortical visual networks and the other to the neocortex, is not replicated in the auditory system). Given their different evolutionary histories, and the differences in current organization, one might expect that the various sensory modes also may differ in both the nature and scope of preprogrammed automatic reactions and in the loci of the neural structures supporting such reactions. Until the characteristics of early somatosensory and auditory responses are specifically analysed with regard to the functional organization and postnatal growth of the related networks the neonatal status of these sensory systems will remain unclear. On present evidence, however, one might anticipate finding an initially greater degree of neocortical mediation in one or both of these latter modalities.

With regard to the nature of the mediational processes underlying neonatal learning capacities, one can at present only comment on the inherent difficulty of the issue and our current ignorance. Granting that learning capacities of various sorts must have been present in many of the ancestral forms through which we evolved, it seems plausible to expect that there may be a number of encoding systems mediating various kinds of learning effects distributed among several levels within the human nervous system. Unlike the case for sensory and motor processes, however, the nature of the neural systems underlying various types of learning effects remain largely unidentified (see Rosenzweig and Bennett, 1976). Indeed, the delineation of appropriate categories of learning is in itself an unresolved issue. Current practice often classifies early learning effects largely on the basis of the type of procedure used—a classification format which may in fact prove to bear little relation to the nature of the neural processes involved. (It has recently been argued, for example, that visual 'habituation' phenomena may be subcortically mediated in newborn infants, whereas a few months later seemingly identical effects elicited by the same procedure may be processed neocortically (Bronson, 1974).) When the term 'memory' is introduced the situation becomes even more confused. Sometimes used simply as a synonym for the enduring effects of learning, the term also may carry an implication that the event is stored in a form (or in a neural structure) that in principle is open to conscious retrieval. From evidence that association areas of the neocortex are basic to this latter attribute of memory in adults, and given that these are among the least developed cortical areas at birth, it would be hazardous to assume that such learning effects as have been demonstrated in newborn infants actually constitute the nucleus of an accruing memory system.

THE CONTRIBUTION OF EARLY SENSORY EXPERIENCE

For the purposes of the preceding section the human brain was conceived as a hierarchy of networks processing information of differing degrees of complexity at different levels within the central nervous system. Here the focus is on the integration of processes between the different levels, and on the progressive refinement of function within the neocortex. This requires a rather different model of neural organization. In contrast to the organization of the primary sensory and motor pathways, networks interlinking cortical and subcortical structures are notable for the numerous reciprocal pathways providing multiple feedback loops (Brodal, 1975). On the evidence from myelinization patterns, these internal pathways are the least mature at birth and show a protracted development extending into midchildhood. On a finer scale, the short axon interneurones within the neocortex similarly provide an expanded capacity for multiple feedback loops, and similarly show a delayed postnatal development (Bodian, 1970). As a gross generalization, therefore, it is suggested that postnatal development proceeds along two general dimensions:

1. along the already noted progression from predominantly subcortical processing toward the simultaneous processing of information at both cortical and subcortical levels;

2. from an earlier, predominantly linear processing of automatic reactions, towards an organizational status characterised by multiple feedback networks, thereby supporting an increasingly refined modulation of neural activity both within the neocortex and between the various levels.

This latter functional mode presumably is basic to the synthesis and subsequent symbolic interpretation of the multiple levels of information that typically are carried by the sensory signal. A review of our current understanding of the various sorts of feedback processes—as they function both within neocortical networks, and in feedback loops linking analogous neocortical and subcortical systems—is beyond the scope of this chapter. However, some consideration must be given to evidence which indicates that an optimal final structuring of these highly sophisticated feedback networks requires a 'fine tuning' under the guidance of organized patterns of sensory input.

The major neural pathways that delineate the species-characteristic structures of the human brain are largely laid down before birth. On evidence drawn mainly from studies of other species, such gross prenatal developments appear to be guided by a combination of chemical affinities and physical constraints (Lund, 1978). Later stages of neural growth, however, and particularly those occurring postnatally, seem to be in part shaped by the quality of modality-specific sensory input. Here again the evidence is largely from studies of non-human mammals—but since the effects of variations in early experience seem generally stronger in more complexly organized species it seems plausible to also assume the presence of such phenomena in human development. The exact nature of the processes is far from clear, but in reviewing evidence from a variety of studies across a number of species Gottlieb (1976) has suggested that the effects of sensory-induced activation on neural growth may include, (a) the maintenance of synaptic connections already present in the infant organism, (b) the selective enhancement of the more functionally appropriate connections, and (c) the inducing of additional dendritic growth, thereby enhancing the probability of additional synaptic connections. It seems likely that the nature of the effects may differ depending on the stage of neural development and the modality involved.

The bulk of the evidence for the existence of such effects comes from studies of visual development—either following total visual deprivation or after rearing in some form of visually biased environment. Depending on age and the form of the deprivation, the receptive fields of neurones in the visual cortex show various types of limitations or anomalies. Similar types of deprivation in adult animals fail to produce such effects, indicating that they are particular to some 'sensitive period' of neural development (for reviews see Blakemore, 1974; Daniels and Pettigrew, 1976; and Grobstein and Chow, 1976). In some limited domains the enduring effects of an early visually biased environment also have been demonstrated in humans (Banks *et al.,* 1975; Freeman *et al.,* 1972).

The relatively less advanced status of the (primary) visual system at the time of birth has been noted repeatedly in previous sections—a delay that may be related to the inevitable absence of prenatal sensory stimulation in this modality. In contrast, the vestibular system, the somatosensory system, and perhaps the auditory system, may begin to be affected by organized patterns of sensory input during later stages of fetal development. Some support for this generalization can be found in studies of the development of evoked potentials in preterm infants. Within the visual domain, the wave form of (otherwise normal) infants born about 2 months before term appears at 40 weeks conception age to be distinctly different from that of full-term infants (Schulte *et al.* (1977): curiously, the authors report the effect to be one of 'retarded development' in infants prematurely exposed to visual stimulation; 'anomalous development' might be a preferable term since Parmelee and Sigman (1976) have found such infants to be less visually attentive at age 4 months.) In contrast to these visual effects, in the auditory domain the same pre-exposure to the external environment produced no observable differences between the 40-week evoked wave forms of premature and full-term infants (Schulte *et al.*, 1977). Therefore, perhaps in this latter modality the act of birth produces a less dramatic change in the available sensory stimulation. A study of somatosensory evoked potentials in preterm infants (Hrbek *et al.*, 1973), while offering no direct comparisons at 40 weeks with the patterns of full-term infants, stresses the generally precocious development of this type of evoked pattern—a finding which might similarly be attributed to the presence of prebirth sensory activation. Finally, the markedly early myelinization of various components of the vestibular system noted in an earlier section also seems a plausible consequence of the early availability of the corresponding form of sensory input. In sum, reflecting perhaps some degree of evolutionary adaptation within the various sensory systems to the qualities of the normally expected fetal environment, it appears that the role of early sensory stimulation may differ considerably as a function of the modality involved and the developmental status of the infant—a possibility to be recognized in considering the optimal environment for infants born prematurely (see Korner *et al.*, 1978; Schulte *et al.*, 1977).

SUMMARY

Evidence drawn from a variety of fields has been combined to delineate a model of the neonatal condition. Emphasizing the transitional status of the neocortex at around the time of birth, the model posits major changes in the nature of underlying mediational processes over the initial postnatal months. This carries a number of implications regarding the kinds of inferences which might plausibly be drawn from observations of early behavioural reactions.

A brief consideration of our evolutionary past provided the context for an interpretation of data on early neural growth. Evolving through a long series of successive refinements and elaborations of structure, the human brain can be viewed as an hierarchy of interconnecting networks in which analogous components at different levels of the nervous system often serve roughly similar adaptive functions at different degrees of sophistication. Briefly, reactions mediated at the spinal level are essentially reflexive adjustments to the single stimulus event, brain stem components add the capacity for an analysis of intermodal contingencies and some learning capabilities, while the neocortex, and particularly the recent elaborations within association areas, provides the basis for complex pattern analysis and for the symbolic representation of accrued experience. In general, the sequence of neural maturation in human infancy roughly follows the order in which the various components evolved in our evolutionary past—with neocortical networks being generally the least developed at birth, and with association areas within the cortex being particularly slow to mature. From a juxtapostion of data on the developmental status of the neocortex at birth, the probable functional capacities of the various subcortical systems, and the behavioural repertoire of the newborn infant, it appears plausible to suggest that subcortical processes play the dominant role in the mediation of neonatal behaviours. Components of the neocortex develop rapidly in the postnatal interval, however, presumably contributing to rapid developments in a variety of behavioural areas—including sensory, motor, and learning effects. In consequence, in some instances seemingly similar behavioural phenomena may in fact be processed quite differently at different postnatal ages.

When viewed more closely, data on the order of developments within the infant neocortex indicate that the various sensory modalities differ both in their status at birth and in their rates of subsequent postnatal development. At birth the somatosensory and auditory networks appear more advanced than those of the primary visual system. Postnatally, however, developments in the latter domain proceed most rapidly, supporting a marked advance in visual capabilities during the first few months of life. Given such intermodal differences in both initial status and rates of subsequent development, the sensitivity of infants to the quality of the sensory environment at birth should vary across modalities, and subsequent developments should show age by modality interactions. Such differences carry implications not only with regard to just what an infant might be learning from sensory exposures at different ages, but also with respect to the kinds of environments that might be optimal to support appropriate forms of sensory development in infants of varying degrees of maturity.

One unfortunate limitation of the data on early neural growth is that while passing reference often is made to an extensive range of individual variation, this rarely is offered in quantified form. Nevertheless such comments, together with the frequent observation of marked individual differences in behavioural indices of initial status, indicate that infants must differ considerably in relative maturity at birth. When viewed in the context of the present developmental model this carries implications regarding the potential predictive power of various measures of early individual differences. In general, assessments tapping emerging neocortical functions in the recently born infant should be of limited value in predicting future psychological attributes, since here variation in infant performance often may reflect mainly relative maturity at birth. Measures indicative of abnormal functioning within subcortical networks, however, should be less confounded in this regard, and hence may carry greater diagnostic power. Similarly, it is suggested that at older ages various more sophisticated functions can most meaningfully be assessed after the related neocortical processes have passed beyond the period of transitional status.

A second aspect of the proposed model of infant development focused on the multiple feedback processes that modulate activity within the neocortex and integrate the processing of analogous forms of information within the different levels of the nervous system. The major neural structures which support such complex feedback effects—the short axon interneurones of the neocortex, and the (often diffusely projecting) cortical—subcortical pathways—are the least mature at birth, and typically show continued developments into midchildhood. An analysis of such delayed developments would extend into ages beyond the province of this book, but some reference to the behavioural capacities which presumably are associated with this type of complex modulation of neural activity can illuminate the limited functional status of the newborn infant. Briefly, these types of neural activity seem to underly the capacity to comprehend the overall quality of a stimulus event and to encode the pattern in a manner that can contribute to an accruing store of memory images. This involves the integration of analytic processes that are conducted simultaneously at several levels within the nervous system; the synthesis, at a high level of abstraction, of the information carried by the several sensory modes; and the capacity to attribute symbolic significance to this multifaceted array of information. Since these various functions require mediation by those components within the neocortex that are the least developed at birth, and even the initially most advanced of the cortical areas appear to be at best only marginally effective at this time, it is doubtful that this complex of sophisticated functions is within the capacity of the newborn infant. From behavioural evidence (e.g. Sroufe and Waters, 1976), such capacities seem to first begin to appear some several months after birth.

REFERENCES

Altman, J. (1970). Postnatal neurogensis and the problem of neural plasticity, in *Developmental Neurobiology* (Ed. W. Himwich), pp. 197–240, Charles C. Thomas, Springfield.

Banks, M. S., Aslin, R. N., and Letson, R. D. (1975). Sensitive period for the development of human binocular vision, *Science*, **190**, 675–677.

Blakemore, C. (1974). Environmental factors in the development of features extracting neurons, in *The Neurosciences: Third Study Program* (Eds. F. O. Schmitt and F. G. Worden), pp. 105–115, MIT Press, Cambridge.

Bodian, D. (1970). A model of synaptic and behavioral ontogeny, in *The Neurosciences:*

Second Study Program (Ed. F. O. Schmitt), pp. 129–140, MIT Press, Cambridge.

Brodal, A. (1975). The 'wiring patterns' of the brain: neuroanatomical experiences and their implications for general views of the organization of the brain, in *The Neurosciences: Paths of Discovery* (Eds. F. G. Worden, J. P. Swazey, and G. Adelman), pp. 123–142, MIT Press, Cambridge.

Bronson, G. W. (1965). The hierarchical organization of the central nervous system: implications for learning processes and critical periods in early development, *Behavioral Science*, **10**, 7–25.

Bronson, G. W. (1974). The postnatal growth of visual capacity, *Child Development*, **45**, 873–890.

Bronson, G. W. (1978). 'The postnatal growth of visual capacity': considerations and clarifications, paper presented at the International Conference on Infant Studies, Providence, Rhode Island.

Conel, J. L. (1939–1967). *The Postnatal Development of the Human Cerebral Cortex*, Vols. I–VIII, Harvard University Press, Cambridge.

Curtis, B. A., Jacobson, S., and Marcus, E. M. (1972). *An Introduction to the Neurosciences*, Saunders, Philadelphia.

Daniels, J. D., and Pettigrew, J. D. (1976). Development of neuronal responses in the visual system of cats, in *Neural and Behavioral Specificity* (Ed. G. Gottlieb), pp. 196–227, Academic Press, New York.

Desmedt, J. E., and Manil, J. (1970). Somatosensory evoked potentials of the normal human neonate in REM sleep, in slow wave sleep and in waking, *Electroencephalography and Clinical Neurophysiology*, **29**, 113–126.

Ellingson, R. J. (1967). The study of brain activity in infants, in *Advances in Child Development and Behavior*, Vol. III. (Eds. L. P. Lipsitt and C. C. Spiker), pp. 53–91, Academic Press, New York.

Ferriss, G. S., Davis, G. D., Dorsen, M. M., and Hackett, E. R. (1967). Changes in latency and form of the photically induced average evoked response in human infants, *Electroencephalography and Clinical Neurophysiology*, **22**, 305–312.

Freeman, R. D., Mitchell, D. E., and Millodot, M. (1972). A neural effect of partial visual deprivation in human, *Science*, **175**, 1384–1386.

Gibson, K. R. (1977). Brain structure and intelligence in macaques and human infants from a Piagetian perspective, in *Primate Bio-social Development: Biological, Social and Ecological Determinants* (Eds. S. Chevalier-Skolnikoff and F. E. Poirer), pp. 113–157, Garland, New York.

Gottlieb, G. (1974). *Aspects of Neurogenesis*, Academic Press, New York.

Gottlieb, G. (1976). The roles of experience in the development of behavior and the nervous system, in *Neural and Behavioral Specificity* (Ed. G. Gottlieb), pp. 25–56, Academic Press, New York.

Grobstein, P. and Chow, K. L. (1976). Receptive field organization in the mammalian visual cortex: the role of individual experience in development, in *Neural and Behavioral Specificity* (Ed. G. Gottlieb), pp. 155–195, Academic Press, New York.

Haith, M. M. and Campos, J. J. (1977). Human infancy, in *The Annual Review of Psychology*, Vol. 28 (Eds. M. Rosenzweig and L. W. Porter), pp. 251–294, Annual Reviews, Inc., Palo Alto.

Hecox, K. (1975). Electrophysiological correlates of human auditory development, in *Infant Perceptions: From Sensation to Cognition* Vol. II. (Eds. L. B. Cohen and P. Salapatek), pp. 151–192, Academic Press, New York.

Himwich, W. (1970). *Developmental Neurobiology*, Charles C. Thomas, Springfield.

Hrbek, A., Hrbkova, M., and Lenard, H. (1968). Somato-sensory evoked responses in newborn infants, *Electroencephalography and Clinical Neurophysiology*, **25**, 443–448.

Hrbek, A., Hrbkova, M., and Lenard, H. (1969). Somato-sensory, auditory, and visual evoked responses in newborn infants during sleep and wakefulness, *Electroencephalography and Clinical Neurophysiology*, **26**, 597–603.

Hrbek, A., Karlberg, P., and Olsson, T. (1973). Development of visual and somatosensory evoked responses in pre-term newborn infants, *Electroencephalography and Clinical Neurophysiology*, **34**, 225–232.

Korner, A. F., Guilleminault, C., Van den Hoed, J., and Baldwin, R. B. (1978). Reduction of sleep apnea and bradycardia in pre-term infants on oscillating waterbeds: A controlled polygraphic study, *Pediatrics*, **61**, 528–533.

Lindsley, D. B. (1969). Average evoked potentials—achievements, failures and prospects, in *Average Evoked Potentials* (Eds. E. Donchin and D. B. Lindsley), pp. 1–44, National Aeronautics and Space Administration, Washington, DC.

Lund, R. D. (1978). *Development and the Plasticity of the Brain*, Oxford Press, New York.

McGraw, M. B. (1943). *The Neuromuscular Maturation of the Human Infant*, Columbia University Press, New York.

Parmelee, A. H. Jr., and Sigman, M. (1976). Development of visual behavior and neurological organization in pre-term and full-term infants, in *Minnesota Symposia on Child Psychology*, Vol. 10 (Ed. A. D. Pick), pp. 119–155, University of Minnesota Press, Minneapolis.

Picton, T. W., Hillyard, S. A., Krausz, H. I., and Golambos, R. (1974). Human auditory evoked potentials. I. Evaluation of components, *Electroencephalography and Clinical Neurophysiology*, **36**, 179–190.

Purpura, D. P., and Reaser, G. P. (1974). *Methodological Approaches to the Study of Brain Maturation and its Abnormalities*, University Park Press, Baltimore.

Rosenzweig, M. R. and Bennett, E. L. (1976). *Neural Mechanisms of Learning and Memory*, MIT Press, Cambridge.

Sarnat, H. B. and Netsky, M. G. (1974). *Evolution of the Nervous System*, Oxford University Press, New York.

Schulman-Golambos, C. and Golambos, R. (1975). Brain stem auditory evoked responses in premature infants, *Journal of Speech and Hearing Research*, **18**, 456–465.

Schulte, F. J. (1974). The neurological development of the neonate, in *Scientific Foundations of Pediatrics* (Eds. F. A. Davis and J. Dobbing), pp. 587–615, Saunders, Philadelphia.

Schulte, F. J., Stennert, E., Wulbrand, H., Eichorn, W., and Lenard, H. G. (1977). The ontogeny of sensory perception in preterm infants, *European Journal of Pediatrics*, **126**, 211–224.

Spekreijse, H., Estevez, O., and Reits, D. (1977). Visual evoked potentials and the physiological analysis of visual processes in man, in *Visual Evoked Potentials in Man: New Developments* (Ed. J. E. Desmedt), pp. 19–89, Clarendon Press, Oxford.

Sroufe, L. A. and Waters, E. (1976). The ontogenesis of smiling and laughter: A perspective on the organization of development in infancy, *Psychological Review*, **83**, 173–189.

Touwen, B. (1976). *Neurological development in infancy*, Spastics International, London.

White, C. T., White, C. L., Fawcett, W., and Socks, J. (1977). Color evoked potentials in adults and infants, paper presented at the meeting of the Society for Research in Child Development, New Orleans.

Yakovlev, P. I. and Lecours, A. (1967). The myelogenetic cycles of regional maturation of the brain, in *Regional Development of the Brain in Early Life* (Ed. A. Minkowski), pp. 3–70, Davis, Philadelphia.

Zapella, M. (1967). Placing and grasping of the feet at various temperatures in early infancy, *Pediatrics*, **39**, 93–96.

Psychobiology of the Human Newborn
Edited by P. Stratton
© 1982, John Wiley & Sons, Ltd.

CHAPTER 6

Rhythmic Functions in the Newborn

PETER STRATTON

At a time in neonatal studies when the concepts of biological rhythms were being applied almost exclusively to circadian (approximately 24 h) and state fluctuations, Wolff (1966, 1967) pointed to the advances in understanding that might come from considering rhythmic aspects of functions with higher frequencies. His analysis derived from proposals by Piaget (1942) and Lashley (1951) but was the first to explore the quantitative characteristics of neonatal micro-rhythms as a basis for determining their significance. Since this time there has been much interesting speculation on the role of rhythms in early life, but in only a few areas has there been any substantive advance beyond Wolff's preliminary statements.

There are a number of quite fundamental reasons for supposing that biological rhythms could play a significant part in the adaptation of the newborn. Sollberger (1965) and Winfree (1980) have pointed out the biological advantages of control systems which oscillate around a mean rather than trying to maintain a fixed level. In particular, the existence of a rhythm makes it easier for the organism to capitalize on regular environmental occurrences which have comparable periodicities. Endogenous pacemakers would seem to offer considerable advantages in the control of repetitive functions such as respiration until the immature organism has acquired sufficient learning experiences and maturation of the neural substrate to take over more sophisticated and adaptive control. Regular occurrence of significant behaviours makes the individual more predictable which may be useful both to the care-giver and for the integration of different functions within the newborn. Finally, if externally provided rhythmic stimuli can influence neonatal state it is at least possible that endogenous rhythms of comparable frequency serve the same function.

Wolff (1967) compared neonatal rhythmic behaviours of crying and sucking with stereotypic mannerisms of older children. From a consideration of the course of mannerisms such as rhythmic rocking and kicking in normal, deprived, and mongoloid children, Wolff concluded that neonatal and subsequent rhythms are preludes to the acquisition of new motor patterns or postures. However, spontaneous behaviours such as startles, smiles and erections were interpreted as discharging 'neural energy' which builds up continuously and so reaches a critical value after a constant interval thereby explaining the regular occurrences of these behaviours (Wolff, 1966). As is often the case the sophistication of the explanation goes far beyond the evidence for the supposed phenomenon. The risk then is that we are so impressed with the explanation that we take the phenomenon for granted. This has been particularly true of neonatal rhythms in which the most tenuous evidence of cyclic tendencies has been accepted as a good enough basis for elaborate speculations about innately determined rhythms controlling large areas of neonatal adaptation and interaction with caretakers. I would suggest that such speculations are likely to be much more productive if they arise from a detailed understanding of the ways that rhythms are actually manifested by the newborn. This chapter therefore concentrates on reviewing the available evidence about the forms of rhythmic fluctuations in various systems. In most cases it will be apparent that detailed claims concerning the nature of the functional significance of the rhythms are premature. This is not to deny that such speculation can be a stimulating source of ideas for the direction of future work. For example the analysis by Kaye (1977) relating sucking rhythms to early mother-infant dialogue is both plausible and enlightening. However in the absence of any consensus about the most basic issues such as what it means to say that a function is rhythmic, it is very difficult to evaluate such suggestions.

In the other direction, speculation about underlying mechanisms is likely to be even less productive in our present state of knowledge. Even in the study of single-celled organisms a full account of the mechanisms of biological rhythms is beyond us at present. What is required is a descriptive account of the forms, consistency and response to changing conditions, of the rhythms which appear at different levels of neonatal functioning. Before embarking on this account it is necessary to establish the criteria by which repetitive functions can usefully to called rhythmic, and to introduce the major descriptive dimension of rhythmic manifestations.

WHEN IS A REPETITIVE FUNCTION A RHYTHM?

The general considerations offered at the beginning of this chapter as a basis for belief in the significance of biological rhythms would each imply a degree of consistency in the timing of relevant behaviour. Until now there has been little explicit consideration of what kind of consistency must be demonstrated to justify labelling a function as rhythmic. A very loose definition, which has often been employed in practice, accepts any repetitive function for which a mean period between occurrences can be computed. On such a criterion the rainfall during a British Spring would count as rhythmic, and adding a requirement that the mean period between occurrences should be constant does not exclude some obviously non-rhythmic events. The occurrence of the number nine in a set of random digits would be an extreme example. The disadvantage of attributing rhythmicity on such grounds is that it adds nothing to what we know about the function. For example Emde *et al.* (1975) found that the rest-activity cycle during the 10 h after birth had a mean period of 39 min. To call the cycle rhythmic on this basis alone deprives the term of any connotations of regularity of occurrence and certainly does not justify speculation about control by 'endogenous rhythms'.

While a loose criterion may deprive the term of significance a strict criterion can have the effect of excluding cases which could profitably have been considered in the context of their rhythmic qualities. Many writers would count as biological rhythms only those functions which are tied to environmental time cues (Brady, 1979; Kleitman, 1963; Palmer, 1976). This would exclude such functions as respiration, sucking and, in the newborn at least, sleep. It is the contention of this chapter that a consideration of the temporal regularities in the operation of many of the newborn's systems provides a useful complement to other approaches. At our present state of knowledge it is appropriate to require evidence of a consistent periodicity at a level related to the imputed significance. Ideally, statistical proof in the form of autocorrelation or power spectrum analysis will provide an unequivocal basis for determining whether or not a constant periodicity is present in the data. Such criteria may, however, be too stringent for our present state of knowledge. There are many reasons why an observable fluctuation which is controlled by a stable underlying rhythm may show departures from a completely regular occurrence, and often it is the departures from regularity which are the most informative. A variety of quite ingenious ways of presenting cyclic data has been developed and in the review that follows the next section, the judgement about whether a rhythm is present is often quite intuitive. For example Wolff (1967) claims stability of non-nutritive sucking on the grounds that the variations in intervals between sucks were 'extremely small'. What he reported was the range of the standard deviations of the mean frequency per second of sucks in a burst, calculated for each individual. The standard deviations certainly seem quite small but I find it impossible to guess what they might have been if the sucking were not rhythmic.

Winfree (1980) has attempted a detailed account of 'temporal morphology' which may in due course come to provide a mathematical basis for a description, or even a descriptive taxonomy, of rhythmic phenomena. However, as he points out, not only may one mechanism produce different behavioural manifestations, it is also likely that similar manifestations, arising as solutions to common evolutionary problems, may have totally different underlying mechanisms. At present, particularly in the case of the newborn, the appropriate approach would seem to require descriptions of the observable manifestations in sufficient detail to allow a judgement about possible rhythmicity. This judgement, based as it is on the 'hands' rather than the 'clockwork' (Richter 1965), will need to pay as much attention to the characteristic changes in temporal parameters brought about by external influence, as to regularities under stable conditions. A major mathematical distinction which is fundamental in understanding the effects of load on the rhythmic functions and which may have particular relevance in early human development, is that between pendulum and relaxation oscillations.

PENDULUM VERSUS RELAXATION

While the swinging pendulum provides a compelling image of oscillation, it can be seen as separated by a continuum from the other extreme of relaxation oscillation (Wever, 1965). The basic distinction is in terms of energy loss to the environment. When minimal energy is exchanged, the oscillation is pendulum type with a sinusoidal shape. When maximum energy is transferred to the environment at each cycle the shape of the oscillation becomes jagged (saw-tooth or square wave), representing the phases of build-up and discharge, or relaxation. Readers unfamiliar with this distinction may find it helpful to think in terms of a concrete example. A simple case of a relaxation oscillation is provided by a ball being blown up a ramp by a jet of air. Once it goes over the top it drops to ground level, releasing the potential energy it had acquired during the first phase of the cycle. It then rolls to the bottom of the ramp and the cycle starts again. Under stable conditions both the amplitude (measured, say, by kinetic energy on impact) and the frequency will be constant. Changing the conditions, for example, increasing the pressure of air or the friction of the surface will change the frequency but the amplitude will not be affected. The only way to change the amplitude of a relaxation oscillation, is to modify the structure of the system; in our example this could be achieved by making the ramp longer. Correspondingly, a pendulum can readily be made to swing at different amplitudes but will always have the same frequency unless, for example, the length of the string is altered. Note that the character of a rhythm—whether it approximates more to a relaxation or a pendulum mode of functioning, will only be revealed by conditions of changing input or load. In stable conditions both relaxation and pendulum oscillations generate constant amplitude and frequency and may be indistinguishable.

No real system can either conserve or discharge all of its energy and therefore all oscillations will fall between the extremes of the continuum. A consideration of the characteristics of the two extremes (Table 1) shows that a tendency towards one type or the other depends on the function of the rhythm and the conditions in which it is operating. A rhythm whose main function is to transfer energy will tend towards a relaxation oscillation. The firing of neurones is an example and shows the expected characteristics quite clearly, in particular a constant amplitude with readily variable frequency. Wever (1965) proposes that biological rhythms tend towards relaxation when the frequency is high (as in

Table 1 Characteristics and functioning of relaxation and pendulum oscillations. (Based largely on Wever, 1965)

Relaxation	Pendulum
General characteristics	
Constant frequency and amplitude in stable conditions	Constant frequency and amplitude in stable conditions
Loss of energy to environment	Energy conserved
Damps out if energy input too low	Maintains oscillation with minimal energy input
Change in conditions produces change in frequency	Change in conditions produces change in amplitude
Amplitude stays constant	Frequency stays constant
Rapid build up to full amplitude	Slow build up of amplitude
Readily entrained by wide range of external synchronizers including approximate multiples and submultiples of the basic frequency	Entrained slowly to external synchronizers with closely similar frequency
Oscillates around a mean energy level close to zero	Oscillates around an extreme mean energy level
Triggering close to time of firing will precipitate function. At other times may have no effect on the cycle	Triggering has same effect whatever stage of the cycle it is applied
Probable uses	
Energy transduction and conversion of constant energy supply to pulses	Accurate timing when buffered from feedback
Examples	
Nerve impulses	Circadian rhythms
Heart beat	Menstrual cycle
Speculations	
Wever: Characteristic of higher biological frequencies	Characteristic of lower. frequencies
Stratton: Predominates early in ontogenesis	Emerges as organs mature and in functions characteristic of the mature organism

nerve impulses) and towards pendulum when the frequency is low. Thus at intermediate frequencies both amplitude and frequency will vary, as in respiration, while circadian rhythms maintain their frequency within narrow limits.

    When considering rhythms with low frequencies, such as the menstrual cycle, or cyclic psychoses which may be measured in years (Richter, 1965), it becomes difficult to specify exactly what is meant by amplitude and so to determine whether a perturbation changes the amplitude or the frequency most. This is what would be expected from pendulum oscillations which are well suited to timing functions but are not effective energy transducers. Wever's suggestion has never been pursued in detail, probably because of the difficulty in ordering particular manifestations with respect to a mathematically defined criterion. For example it is very difficult to determine whether respiration has more pendulum tendencies than has heart rate, even though we have considerable information on both amplitude and frequency variations under various conditions. Although the proposal that lower biological frequencies tend towards pendulum oscillations remains an untested but plausible hypothesis, a further speculation, which may be easier to test, does seem justified.

There are grounds for proposing that ontogenesis is marked by a shift from a relaxation mode towards a pendulum mode, both in the order of appearance of different functions and in the operation of individual systems. The former aspect is more obvious but perhaps less interesting: the first rhythmic functions to appear are, so far as we know, the high-frequency relaxation oscillations of neuronal discharge, and no low-frequency rhythms have been identified early in gestation (Sollberger, 1965). This might be expected as rhythmic functions will be initiated in the service of specific requirements which, early in development, will tend to be dominated by energy transduction. Postnatally, the 4-h sleep rhythm appears before the 24-h rhythm (Meier-Koll et al., 1978) while longer perio-dicities tend to be found in functions associated with maturity such as menstruation and manic-depressive psychosis (Richter, 1965). It is possible that the failure to identify low frequency rhythms early in life is misleading. If the suggestion of a tendency to the relaxation mode in early life is valid, the frequency of fluctuations will be variable and so the function is less likely to be seen as rhythmic. There is also a practical consideration, that identification of a rhythm requires observations over a time that is at least several multiples of the periodicity. Sustained monitoring of the fetus is difficult and, by definition, no periodicity much greater than 48 h can be identified during the 28 days of the neonatal stage.

The second aspect of our speculation is that individual systems will tend towards relaxation oscillations at the start but will shift towards pendulum type with development. There are several reasons for expecting this to happen. The most obvious is that, with the growth in the size of organs, frequencies decrease and so on Wever's original hypothesis, some shift towards pendulum type would be anticipated. There are, however, other considerations which suggest that the shift should be greater than is predicted by this fact alone. In accordance with the tendency for the cyclic functions concerned with energy exchange to be required earlier in development, there may also be a similar tendency within given functions. For example, respiration serves many purposes other than supplying oxygen and eliminating CO_2 (Purves, 1979), but most of them are irrelevant to the newborn. Differential emotional response, helping maintain the upright posture, and the fine control needed for talking, singing and playing the oboe come into play later in development. The factor which makes such uses possible is the ability of the mature organism to sustain deficit without undue risk or discomfort. This ability allows basic functions to be controlled by a fixed frequency which is relatively unresponsive to fluctuating demand, a solution which is not available to the newborn operating with extremely limited reserves. There are some other functions to which early respiration must adapt itself, particularly crying, sucking and swallowing. These functions are themselves rhythmic and the necessary adaptation will be aided by another feature of relaxation oscillations—the ability to synchronize with a wide range of frequencies including approximate multiples and submultiples of the basic periodicity. Early in development, when frequencies are more likely to be unpredictable and variable, there would be a considerable advantage in the type of oscillation that could show this adaptability. A further possibility is a general tendency for organs to be functioning nearer to their capacity early in development. Considering respiration again as a convenient example, the neonatal tidal volume constitutes a higher proportion (18 per cent, versus 13 per cent for adults) of the available vital capacity (Strang, 1977). There is therefore less scope for adjusting to demand by altering the amplitude and so relaxation oscillations, which facilitate frequency changes, would be desirable.

A final general point is that pendulum oscillations, with their minimal energy exchange, must require a more efficient mechanism than relaxation oscillations. We have learned how easy it is to make the mistake of under-rating the newborn but it still seems likely that earlier in maturation any system may function less efficiently and so will benefit from the relative robustness of relaxation oscillations. It should be clear that while there are several reasons for suggesting an early tendency towards relaxation oscillations, we do not yet have adequate grounds for claiming it to be a universal tendency. I would propose that there is sufficient support to justify investigation of the relevant evidence in more detail and to explore the possible implications. At present we lack the kind of detailed quantitative information that is necessary for a full account of this (or indeed any) general aspect of neonatal rhythmic functioning. The survey that follows is therefore only intended to suggest the kinds of advantages that may come from viewing repetitive functions in terms of their rhythmic tendencies. Anything like a comprehensive account of neonatal rhythms must await the acquisition of a considerable amount of data at an appropriate level of quantification.

BRAIN RHYTHMS

Electroencephalographic (EEG) studies of the newborn have proved difficult to interpret. Prechtl (1968) reported significant power only in low-frequency components (< 2 cps). Eichorn (1970) reviewing the development of EEG concluded that from the eighth month of gestation, through the neonatal period, the pattern is apparently less mature then previously. Although it is difficult to label neonatal EEG patterns, as any analogues to adult rhythms are likely to operate within different frequency bands, it seems that theta waves dominate until the end of the first month of life. It is tempting to relate this tentative conclusion to recent speculation about the function of the theta rhythm. Komisaruk (1977) proposes that theta arises from a fluctuating mobilization of the mechanisms for adapting to environmental contingencies. The frequency (4–7 cps) allows the process from stimulus accumulation through to the initiation of a response to occur within the cycle. The advantage is to maximize the available processing capacity at the crucial stage of the cycle, an advantage particularly to lower and immature organisms with limited functional capacity. In the human newborn Komisaruk suggests that theta, arising in lower brain centers, also synchronizes sucking–swallowing–respiratory–facial grimace linkages until this control can be taken over by cortical mechanisms.

The sophistication of neonatal cognitive functioning and the impressive co-ordination of functions such as sucking and respiration have been difficult to explain in view of the known immaturity of the newborn's brain. Komisaruk's hypothesis, arising from an analysis of the functional significance of theta in other species, gives an intriguing foretaste of the exciting possibilities in the study of the early brain rhythms. It is, though, the beginning not the end of the story.

CARDIAC AND RESPIRATORY FUNCTION

The heart is the first organ to show rhythmic functioning, and until about 27 weeks conceptional age, operates as a free-running rhythm with a fixed frequency (Berg and Berg, 1979). After this time central control mechanisms develop and rate becomes progressively less regular, reflecting an increased adaptability to varying demand. Through the last eight weeks of pregnancy the average rate stays constant around 140 bpm, while variability increases (Lewis et al., 1970). Just before birth mean variability was found to be 12 beats per minute (bpm) while at two and four weeks postnatally it was 17 bpm, and the mean rate had risen to 152 bpm. This change presumably corresponds to the increased and more variable demands of extra-uterine life. Lewis et al. (1970) found overall variability and rate to decrease steadily through the first year of postnatal life though Harper et al. (1976) report differences according to state, with variability during waking increasing for the first 3 months.

Cyclic variability in heart rate has also been reported. De Haan, et al. (1977) using power spectrum analysis found peaks around 1, 4 and 8 cycles per minute for an individual subject during active sleep while Sollberger (1965) reports rhythms of 1, 2 and 4 cycles per minute. Similar frequencies have been found in respiratory rhythms and De Haan et al. (1977) suggest a common source. The basic cycle of respiration first appears in fetal breathing movements by 20 weeks conceptual age. The movements are rapid (30 to 100 per minute), irregular and episodic (Dawes, 1979). As yet there is too little information to allow their significance to be assessed but they may well come to provide useful information about the endogenous oscillations which influence neonatal respiration. Extra-uterine respiratory movements are first seen at 17 weeks gestation with the first regular respiration appearing at 32 weeks (Parmelee and Stern, 1972). Periods during which respiration stops completely (apnoea) are very common at this age though they can be eliminated by increasing the oxygen concentration in the inspired air (Lagercrantz et al., 1979). These episodes become progressively less common but can still be seen in full-term newborns, particularly during active (REM) sleep (Thoman et al., 1977). Apnoea is arousing much current interest because of a possible correlation with subsequent 'sudden infant death', (Steinschneider, 1975). However Thoman et al. (1977) suggest that it is the newborns who have abnormally few apnoeic episodes, and so fail to develop an ability to adapt to unusual respiratory demands, that are most at risk. This issue is discussed in more detail by Rovee-Collier and Lipsitt (Chapter 7) but leaves us with the question of why the respiratory cycle should be interrupted in this way.

Although apnoea may be regarded as an extreme of irregular respiration, apnoeic spells also occur in the clearly rhythmic context of periodic (Cheyne-Stokes) breathing. During a few cycles, breathing increases in both amplitude and frequency and then decreases to be followed by an apnoeic period of approximately equal duration. The whole cycle lasts between 12 and 18 s and may be repeated with considerable regularity. In a study of cyclic variability in respiration, Hathorn (1979) found periodicities averaging 8–10 s in both frequency and amplitude. In term neonates constant ventilation seems to be maintained by keeping these oscillations fairly consistently out of phase, so that maximum frequency tends to coincide with minimum amplitude and vice versa. This effect was less consistent during active sleep but only in preterm babies were there times when frequency and amplitude were consistently in phase, and these were episodes of periodic breathing. On this analysis it would appear that stable functioning is maintained by preventing the supramedullary oscillator (which is hypothesized as controlling both heart rate and respiratory rhythms) from locking the amplitude and frequency components into phase. As with the earlier suggestion concerning the role of theta rhythms, the function of the rhythm seems to be superseded as more mature systems take over control.

VOCAL AND ORAL RHYTHMS

The major consummatory and communicative functions of the newborn are necessarily temporally integrated with respiration and so might be expected to share the same underlying rhythms. They must also operate in conjunction with the care given and so may be constrained by some characteristics of human adults.

Crying

The cry of the newborn sometimes adopts an apparently rhythmical pattern with a frequency around one cycle per second. Wolff (1967) called the pattern 'remarkably stable' and labelled it the basic cry, though it is also called the hunger cry. The precise temporal structure of crying would seem to be significant as Wolff found differences in reactions of mothers when the timing of the pain cry was altered. However, no detailed normative data on rhythmic aspects of crying have been published. The claims for stable rhythms in the individual cry burst have been supported only with sample data and means (but not variances) from small groups of subjects (Truby and Lind, 1965; Wolff, 1967). Prechtl et al. (1969) did find individual consistency in the duration of cries over the first 9 days, while Cullen et al. (1968) reported that delayed auditory feedback (with the cry reaching the newborn's ears 0.2 s late) reduced the length of the expiratory burst by 0.1 s. It would seem that the newborn can cry to a regular rhythm which has, through its temporal characteristics, a compelling effect on the care-giver and which is modifiable by external influence. At present we lack even the most basic information about the incidence of such crying and the variations in its properties, so that questions concerning the possible influence of central pacemakers must be deferred. Similarly the possibility of an 8-s periodicity corresponding to that found in respiration and heart rate seems not to have been explored.

Sucking

Sucking has been one of the most intensively studied of neonatal functions. Although the rhythmic properties of sucking patterns are frequently mentioned, most of the detailed quantitative data were provided in the classic studies of Balint and Wolff. While these data are extensively reviewed in this section, other aspects of sucking are only mentioned where they have a bearing on rhythmic tendencies. More comprehensive reviews of sucking are provided by Crook (1979), Kaye (1977) and Wright (Chapter 13, this volume).

The first detailed analysis of sucking rhythms was reported by Balint (1948). Of ten babies in their first week, nine sucked at a characteristic individual frequency between 0.8 and 1.2 cps while one had a higher, unstable rate of sucking. At two weeks, six of the eight babies sucked in the 1.0 to 1.4 cps range. Subsequently frequency increased with age but the older infants in his sample were suffering from a variety of medical conditions so the effects of age and illness are confounded. Of his 200 infants, irregular frequencies were shown by twelve, half of whom were suffering from respiratory illnesses. Balint also identified a high frequency rhythmical clonus of the tongue. Frequencies ranged between 4 and 10 cps, but were extremely stable for each individual. This 'quivering' was found in 50 per cent of his sample at all ages but was twice as common in female as in male infants.

Wolff (1968) reported a similar frequency of nutritive sucking with a range of 0.8 to 1.2 cps at 4–6 days rising to 1.3 to 1.6 cps at 7–9 months. He also reported that non-nutritive sucking, which can be elicited by a pacifier or blind nipple, occurs at twice the rate of nutritive sucking and has a characteristic pattern of alternating bursts of sucking and pauses. Both authors claimed the rate of sucking to be remarkably stable for individual babies and an interesting comparison was provided by Wolff who asked young adults to mimic the neonatal sucking pattern. The most stable adult performance was five times as variable as any of the newborn's and the adults became tired within 2 min. Balint also found higher rates of sucking that sometimes initiated bursts (lasting for 1–2 s before settling to the normal rate) and occasionally were sustained for the whole burst. The frequency range (1.2–3.5 cps), and the fact that sustained high rates occurred under conditions which would reduce or stop the flow of milk, such as a stiff teat or empty bottle, indicate that he was describing non-nutritive sucking. Wolff (1967) claimed that the inter-burst interval in non-nutritive sucking was 'a stable value' but gave no figures. Subsequently Wolff (1968) reported data for 40 newborns in which the mean rest period was 6.61 s with a mean standard deviation of 1.5 s, but also stated that both burst and pause length changed considerably with slight changes in state.

The detailed studies of Balint and Wolff suggest four rhythms with frequencies of approximately 7, 1, 0.5 and 0.1 cps. The highest frequency (quivering) has not been shown to have either diagnostic or functional significance and will not be considered further. Wolff (1968) regarded nutritive and non-nutritive sucking as controlled by separate central oscillators but this would not seem to be the most efficient solution. Far more likely is a basic centrally generated frequency at 1 cps which is adjusted to the first sub-harmonic under 'load' conditions. It is possible that it is the nutritive sucking rate which is basic, but this seems less likely in view of the finding by Balint (1948) that nutritive bursts are sometimes initiated by a few rapid sucks before settling to the slower rhythm. Although a distinctive pattern of non-nutritive sucking is unique to humans, the source of the oscillator would seem to be in the primitive brain. Peiper (1963) and Wolff (1968) found that the rhythm was only disrupted by clinical conditions involving gross brain damage. Balint (1948) gives no details of the 'respiratory illnesses' that were associated with unstable sucking rhythms but in view of the capacity for nutritive sucking and breathing to become synchronized (Peiper 1963), such cases could be particularly interesting. Dreier et al. (1979) found changes in respiration rate during non-nutritive sucking while Lipsitt et al. (1974) reported increases in heart rate. In neither case do the data allow a claim of synchronization and much more detailed studies would be needed to support the suggestion of the first authors of 'co-ordination by a central sequencing mechanism'. A final intriguing claim is that if a pacifier is removed during a sucking burst, rhythmic mouthing will continue for the expected duration of the burst (Wolff, 1967). This would imply considerable independence of the oscillator but as yet no data have been published so the extent of independence from feedback cannot be assessed.

The burst-pause pattern has a mean periodicity in the ubiquitous 8–12 s range but is much less stable than other rhythmic aspects of sucking. Recent work, which has concentrated on influences that may modify sucking patterns, has been comprehensively reviewed by Crook (1979). On the basis of this review, and of his own extensive research, Crook concludes that there is a continuum from nutritive to non-nutritive sucking. Increases in nutrient flow and palatability produce a progressive reduction in rate and a prolongation of the length of sucking bursts until, with normal milk in the early part of a feed, sucking is continuous. Apparent complications are introduced by the fact that a single delivery of nutrient during non-nutritive sucking triggers a burst of slower sucks, and that sucking for a (presumed) highly palatable glucose solution is slower than for milk (Crook, 1977). This latter finding has been discussed in terms of hedonic properties of sweet taste (Crook and Lipsitt, 1976) but taste qualities should perhaps be seen as influencing the choice of sucking mechanism rather than as direct determinants of parameters of sucking. A related finding is that when babies were bottle fed with breast milk (from another mother) rather than formula, the sucking pattern became more like that of non-nutritive sucking (Johnson and Salisbury, 1975). This discovery raises an intriguing possibility that much of what we know about nutrient sucking concerns the response of the system to chemical constituents of formula which have been added to increase palatability. Commercial formula may, in some sense, be a superoptimal stimulus and by concentrating on bottle feeding for ease of instrumentation we may be studying only one extreme of the possible range of functioning of the system. Although Johnson and Salisbury felt that it was the nature of the milk rather than the characteristics of the bottle which modified the feeding rhythm, Wright (Chapter 13) reports a rather different pattern when comparing bottle feeding with true breast feeding. In Wright's study it was the bottle which produced more of a burst–pause pattern. It must be concluded that there is no simple determinant of the choice of sucking pattern and that an understanding of behaviour during feeding will require an understanding of the available rhythms as well as a consideration of all of the factors which may influence their operation.

Viewed as a rhythm, sucking is a system with high energy exchange but having no environmental pacemaker. The most plausible system would seem to be a relaxation oscillator triggered from a central pacemaker which is relatively buffered from feedback. As increases in palatability, which could be presumed to provoke an increase in overall output (more concretely, input), are associated with a reduced rate, a corresponding increase in amplitude (pressure) would seem to be required. It is easy to see how taste in the mouth could slow the priming of the relaxation cycle so that the next pulse from the pacemaker is ineffective, and so the suck is initiated on every second (or later) pulse. In this case there is no paradox in finding that a single injection of nutrient, which would leave a taste in the mouth for several seconds, will trigger a burst of slower sucking. What is more difficult to explain is a substantial change in amplitude of what is presumed to be a relaxation oscillator. This could only be achieved by altering the physical structure of the system, as in the increase in the length of the ramp in our earlier example. An investigation by Burke (1977) of the relationship between sucking and swallowing suggests that this might be precisely what is happening. Analysing the intervals between individual sucks in relation to swallowing, Burke found that sucrose concentration had no direct effect on sucking rate. During and after a swallow the rate of sucking was significantly reduced but at all other times the rate was very close to that of non-nutritive sucking during periods of zero fluid delivery. The effect of sucrose solution was to increase the number of swallows thereby depressing the mean suck rate. Swallowing uses many of the muscles involved in sucking in ways that may well increase intraoral pressure, and so allow changes in amplitude which are compatible with the assumption of a relaxation oscillator.

Unfortunately, amplitude measures are not normally reported (Crook 1979) and so we do not know what changes occur under different sucking conditions. It is at least possible that non-nutritive sucking generates the same pressure as does nutritive sucking, and that intake is controlled entirely by a reduction in pauses so that sucking becomes more continuous. Presumably the high frequency and burst-pause character of non-nutritive sucking are optimally suited to stimulate milk flow from the breast and perhaps to stimulate erection of the nipple. In this case we can only expect to understand sucking patterns when we know more about the effects of these rhythms on the mother. A detailed comparison with the temporal characteristics of crying which are most effective in inducing the milk let-down reflex would be particularly interesting. It should also be possible to relate the changes in burst–pause pattern which can be produced by changes in external stimulation, state and time since the last feed (Crook, 1979), to the probability of eliciting milk in the normal breast-feeding situation.

SPONTANEOUS BEHAVIOURS

During sleep, various movements can be observed ranging from sudden gross movements of the upper body resembling the Moro reflex (called spontaneous startles) through sobbing inspirations, erections, and rhythmical mouthing to reflex smiling and twitches of the face and extremities. Wolff (1966) described these behaviours as 'spontaneous' because they occur in the absence of specific external or visceral stimulation. In reporting their frequency of occurrence in different states Wolff claimed that in phases when only one type of spontaneous behaviour is occurring, the timing approximates a rhythm, and that different behaviours have different frequencies. The only group data offered to support the claim are means and standard deviations for spontaneous mouthing and the distribution of intervals between startles and erections. Following the discussion in the previous sections it is not surprising that Wolff found the clearest evidence for rhythmicity in oral behaviours and this cannot be taken as support for rhythmicity in other spontaneous behaviours. The finding that 42 per cent of startles followed one another 'at 60-second intervals' (Wolff, 1966; p. 28), i.e. between 30 and 60 s, is not strong evidence for a stable rhythm and may be largely attributable to the selection of data only from periods during which startles predominated.

During unselected periods of deep sleep Ashton (1971) found spontaneous startles to be randomly distributed, though this does not contradict Wolff's rather limited claim. Wolff also described in detail the timing and sequences of spontaneous behaviours during selected episodes for individual subjects. On the basis of all of his data he concluded that these behaviours are alternative means of discharging 'neural energy' which progressively accumulates over time. An implication of this view is that the different behaviours substitute for each other and this was supported by descriptions of cases in which a sequence of one type of spontaneous behaviour ceased when a different behaviour began. In a more detailed analysis of the spontaneous behaviours of 209 infants Myers (1977) showed that these different behaviours do indeed substitute for each other within a complex temporal pattern. However they may be substitutes only in the sense that rain is a substitute for sunshine; the claim that they may serve the same function derives from the theory (which is discussed below) not from the data.

Another observation by Wolff (1966) was that near to the time at which a spontaneous behaviour would be expected, external stimulation was effective in eliciting the behaviour. Thus a small jolt to the crib which would have no observable effect if applied soon after a spontaneous startle has occurred will, if applied near the time that the next startle is due, be very likely to elicit the reaction. A similar effect would be seen in our original example of a relaxation oscillation. Jolting the ramp when the ball is near the top may tip it over, but a jolt when it is half way up will leave the cycle length unaffected. This finding, combined with others such as the tendency to a regular frequency only under very stable conditions strongly suggests a relaxation oscillation. It is furthermore possible that despite the different frequencies of different functions, there is a single underlying pacemaker, as it would be expected that different manifestations, by imposing a different load, would each tend towards their own characteristic frequency. Myers (1977) provides a more detailed analysis of temporal contingencies in the records of a large number of subjects, and found that following a short interval between behaviours the next interval was most likely to be longer whereas longer intervals were most likely to be followed by a reduction. This does not, as Myers claims, conflict with Wolff's neural discharge hypothesis. Early triggering of a relaxation oscillation, giving a short interval, and delayed firing due to inertia giving a longer interval will both tend to be followed by a period of average length unless the triggering stimulus or the inertial force are repeated. This would account for the finding by Myers that short intervals are followed by an increase and long intervals by a decrease. There is a difficulty in interpreting Myers' results arising from the fact that only alternate 10-s periods were observed. Consequently only 50 per cent of behaviours will have been recorded and so half of the times reported cover two or more intervals.

From the evidence so far neonatal spontaneous behaviours clearly show the characteristics of a relaxation oscillation. Wolff's neural discharge hypothesis amounts to a speculation concerning the mechanism of such an oscillation. The image of neural (and/or psychic) energy building up until it overflows has a long history in psychobiology, (Ashton (1973) described it as 'antediluvian'). While it undeniably provides a vivid example of a relaxation cycle there has never been much reason to suppose that it describes how the central nervous system functions. If there was any point in discussing ways that relaxation oscillations might be implemented in the nervous system it would no doubt be possible to describe a number of plausible mechanisms. Unfortunately we do not have sufficient information about the rhythmic manifestations to provide any basis for choosing between alternative possibilities. Until we have extensive data on the temporal consistencies and contingencies, speculations about mechanisms are unlikely to be productive.

STATE CYCLES

The alternation of states in the newborn is obviously cyclic, but this does not in itself justify claims of endogenously organized rhythms. As discussed earlier in this chapter, evidence of consistency in the timing of a function is required before it is worth invoking the concept of a rhythm. Anders (1978) has pointed out that most researchers have concentrated on the spatial or structural aspects of state. He suggests that a focus on the temporal sequencing of states would resolve some of the difficulties over state definitions. Unfortunately Anders provides no evidence that states occur with any regular periodicity during infancy. The literature is in fact devoid of any analysis which would indicate a rhythmic character of states as described by Prechtl (Chapter 3). What we do have is evidence of rhythms at the grosser levels of periods of rapid eye movements (or activity) and of the wakefulness or feeding cycle.

Kleitman (1963) proposed that the basic alternation is between rest and activity and that this cycle should be distinguished from the sleep-wakefulness cycle. Sterman (1972) accepted the identification of the activity phase with rapid eye movement (REM) sleep but argued that neonatal states fulfil different functions which cannot be mapped onto adult sleep and waking states, from which he concluded that it is not meaningful to speak of infant sleep. Such a view is not really extreme as it only proposes avoiding use of a label with inappropriate implications, leaving one free instead to objectively describe the states and analyse their time course. However, it seems unlikely that the use of the term 'sleep' for grouping certain infant states will be fact be abandoned. For present purposes the term 'basic rest-activity cycle' (BRAC) will be applied to the alternation of quiet and active phases which has frequently been reported with a periodicity of around 40–60 min, and sleep-wakefulness for the periodicity of around 4 h which corresponds to the feeding cycle. Both of these periodicities were described by Aserinsky and Kleitman (1955) on the basis of their own results and from analyses of other published data. The BRAC (motility cycle) was found to be normally of 60–70 min in their own infants (aged 1–7 months and 55 min in data provided by Gesell on one neonate from 8–15 days. Sterman and Hoppenbrouwers (1971) found a cycle of fetal activity of 40 min which was stable enough to be identified by power-spectrum analysis and appeared to be independent of any maternal rhythms. Stern et al. (1973) found similar periodicities postnatally and Roffwarg et al. (1966) found a 50 min REM cycle in 2–5-day-old newborns. Their technique involved synchronizing subjects at sleep onset and plotting a histogram of percentage of babies asleep at each 4-min interval over the next 2.8-h. Group means are an unreliable guide to the shape of individual functions (Estes, 1956), while an observation period that allows only two or three occurrences of the periodicity does not lend itself to statistical evaluation.

Long periods uninterrupted by feeding are rare during the neonatal period but an opportunity for extended recording is provided by the period of prolonged sleep which occurs soon after birth. This period is particularly important as it makes possible the identification of a rest-activity cycle before the operation of other influences. One such possible influence is the 4-h sleep–wakefulness cycle. An early suggestion was that feeding intervals may be integer multiples of the BRAC with the implication that time of feeding is determined by a specific phase of the individual's characteristic BRAC (Aserinsky and Kleitman, 1955). Given the ages of the subjects in their study (1–7 months) it is equally possible that the BRAC had become established as a sub-multiple of a more fundamental feeding cycle. It would therefore be interesting to compare the stability of the two cycles from the first day of life.

A study of both the BRAC and of sleep-wakefulness during the 10 h following birth was reported by Emde et al. (1975). Unfortunately, their claim of endogenous rhythms was based entirely on group means for the two cycles. No evidence for the stability of the periodicities was given, so although their mean periodicity for the BRAC (39 min) corresponds to that found with older babies, this study cannot be taken as evidence for stable rhythms on the first day. Theorell et al. (1973) have shown that the duration of episodes of all states is much less stable on the first than on the fifth day, but their data do not allow any

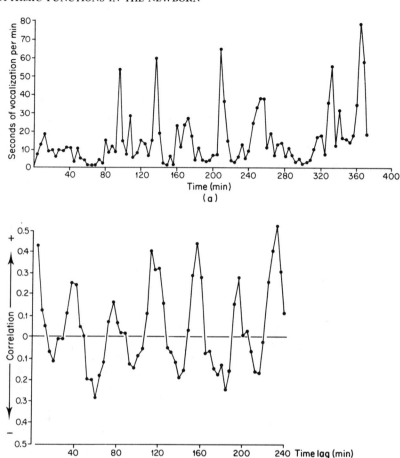

Figure 1 (a) Frequency of vocalizations in successive 4-min periods during sleep on first day of life. (b) Autocorrelogram indicating stability of the 40 min cycle

conclusion about possible rhythmic tendencies in the alternation of states.

In an unpublished study the present author recorded vocal activity throughout the first extended sleep of eight healthy full-term newborns. Vocalization was chosen because it is one of the most highly developed response systems available, and on the basis of the (then) current finding of a cycle of adult waking oral behaviour (Friedman and Fisher, 1967) in the frequency range believed by Kleitman (1963) to correspond to the infant BRAC. Vocal activity was recorded as the number of seconds during which there was a sound, accumulated over successive 4-min intervals. The signal was passed through a band-pass filter centred at 1000 cps to reduce environmental noise, so some squeaks and grunts would also have been lost.

The first subject to be recorded had a clear 40 min cycle of vocal activity (Fig. 1a) which is shown to be significant by autocorrelation (Fig. 1b). There were no periods of sustained crying. Variation in the auto-correllogram is due to the absence of peaks (at 52 and 292 min) rather than the presence of activity during troughs. Missing a cycle does not seem to affect the timing or amplitude of the next peak, and the stability of the periodicity is indicated by the undiminished correlations when the first 2 h are matched with the last 2 h of the record. This very stable rhythm did not appear in any subsequent recordings taken over the period 2–14 days from the same baby, nor were any significant periodicities found in first day recordings of the other seven newborns. It must be concluded that while a BRAC of great stability may be expressed through vocalization, this will only occur in unknown, and perhaps quite uncommon, circumstances.

While the very early operation of the BRAC is somewhat unclear, a more detailed analysis of the sleep-wake rhythm is available. Meier-Koll et al. (1978) applied a combination of power-spectrum analysis and sophisticated graphing to the wake density data of a single subject from birth to 17 weeks of age. Their analyses suggest a periodicity of approximately 4 h present from birth, which is free-running during the first 4 weeks. After 5 weeks, as the circadian rhythm became established, the waking period extended during the night while remaining around 4 h during the day until, after 11 weeks the night consisted of a single 12-h cycle. These results are very similar to those reported by Morath (1974) who analysed the feeding cycles of a single subject over a similar period. The only disagreement is over the lengthening period during the night which Morath felt was attributable to the omission of one or two feeds, leaving the basic 4-h frequency undisturbed, whereas Meier-Koll et al. (1978) found evidence of a gradual lengthening of the sleep period. Of more concern in the present context is the conclusion of both authors that the 4-h rhythm is present on the first day of life. Again it is unfortunate that the methods used do not allow a statistical evaluation of this claim. Meier-Koll et al. (1978) provide a computerized simulation which generated an impressive match to the real data, particularly after the neonatal period. It would be interesting to see whether alternative models would produce equally convincing pictures.

The study of ultradian rhythms in the newborn is complicated by the requirements of feeding, but this is not accidental. The pattern of wakefulness is intimately involved in preparing the newborn for feeding at appropriate times, and it should be no surprise that Morath (1974) studying feeding rhythms found exactly the same pattern as did Meier-Koll et al. (1978) studying sleep-wake behaviour. It would be reasonable at this stage to conclude that both waking and feeding are controlled by an endogenous rhythm with a period of approximately 4 h. The relationship with the BRAC is still unclear. Even in adults Kleitman (1973) believes the 90 min BRAC to be related to hunger, but an understanding of the relationship between the two rhythms during the period when feeding is becoming established requires more detailed study of babies free from external temporal constraints during the first days of life.

Although the feeding cycle is subject to considerable external interference, the fact that a clear measure of amplitude is available should facilitate an analysis of the kind of rhythm which drives the cycle. The best available data on amplitude changes in early infancy are presented by Wright in Chapter 13. From that study it would appear that in the neonatal period, input is determined by current stimuli. These may derive either from internal signals (perhaps relating to the diurnal cycle or the state of the digestive system deriving from the time since the previous feed) or from external signals in the form of the composition of the milk. The fact that the diurnal variation is only apparent in breast-fed babies suggests the latter. Subseqently circadian variation is shown by dropping out night feeds. As can be seen from Chapter 13, Figures 1–3 (pages 350–353) bottle-fed babies lose more feeds earlier so that from 4 months they are normally receiving only three feeds per day compared with five feeds for breast-fed babies. This seems to result in breast-fed babies having the latitude to adjust the amplitude of their intake to compensate for the loss of a night feed. By 6 months they are taking their largest feeds in the evening, anticipating the gap, whereas earlier the largest feed had followed the longest interval. In contrast the bottle fed infants have to maintain a high intake for all of their three feeds.

The data presented by Wright indicate that the feeding rhythm already has pendulum characteristics by being able to adapt through changes in amplitude during the first week. However, as might be anticipated from our hypothesis, this tendency becomes more marked as development proceeds. A full analysis of the rhythm, which would explore the autonomous interaction of amplitude and frequency, requires data from babies fed entirely on demand. Peter Wright has acquired complete feeding records of two such babies (personal communication) and it will be fascinating to see an analysis of the detailed relationships between time and amplitude in these data.

CIRCADIAN RHYTHMS

Periodicities approximating 24 h have dominated the study of biological rhythms, in some cases to the exclusion of any other (Brady, 1979). The human newborn shows remarkably little evidence of any circadian rhythms: remarkably because the current environment and the previous intra-uterine experience are powerfully structured to provide 24-h variation in stimulation. It is possible to produce circadian variation in the first week as shown by Irwin (1930). Babies who are not fed throughout the night will be more active than during the day and so could be said to have a 24-h activity cycle. Such purely exogenous control, which is believed to account also for fetal circadian rhythms (Mills, 1974), is of little interest to the chronobiologist. Much of the experimental work with adults and other species has been directed towards determining whether circadian rhythms are controlled by some kind of internal clock or can be accounted for entirely by environmental (mostly geophysical) variation. While some techniques, such as transplanting brain tissue, are not applicable to the newborn for ethical reasons there are a few reports from workers who have found it acceptable to subject newborns to constant conditions (see below). The continuation of a rhythm after environmental cues have been eliminated is regarded as good evidence of the operation of an endogenous clock. A common finding in such free-running conditions is that the 24-h rhythm shifts to a close but not identical periodicity. This suggests an internal source with a fixed frequency (usually assumed to be genetically determined) which can be modified by environmental fluctuations to be brought into precise synchrony with the 24-h variation.

The classic study of the development of the circadian sleep–wakefulness rhythm provided a complete record of the sleep of a single subject over the first 6 months (Kleitman and Engelmann, 1953). No circadian variation is apparent in the neonatal period but from about 8 weeks sleep periods tend to consolidate at 25-h intervals. The resulting drift of sleep onset across the day is very similar to that found under free-running conditions in organisms with already established 24-h rhythms (Pittendrigh 1960). By about 16 weeks, sleep onset settled to a precise 24-h period and so became synchronized to the environment. Similar patterns have been identified by a number of subsequent studies, in one case (Parmelee, 1961) the initial periodicity being 23 h. Additional evidence that the circadian sleep rhythm is endogenous has come from French studies in which babies were kept in relatively constant conditions (Mills, 1974). Two infants, kept in constant light from 8 to 80 days developed a circadian sleep rhythm after 8 weeks, in one case sleeping for 8 h during the period 0500–1300 hours. The fact that the sleep started out of phase with any possible environmental cues, strongly supports the claim of endogenous determination.

In another study, also discussed by Mills (1974) a circadian rhythm in urinary flow was established by 6 weeks but was lost when the infant was kept in continuous darkness. It would seem that the early appearance of urinary rhythms, which Hellbrügge et al. (1964) found to be significant at two weeks, may be largely, if not entirely, exogenous. Hellbrügge (1960) recorded a number of physiological functions from birth and found the earliest significant circadian variation was in skin resistance during the first week. Rhythms in other functions appeared later: temperature at 4 weeks, pulse rate from 6 weeks and sodium and potassium excretion from 8 weeks. All of these variations could be environmentally determined and at present we have no basis for deciding whether, or at what stage, they are under endogenous control. Hellbrügge felt that a certain maturity was necessary before any system could control a circadian periodicity, so there is no contradiction in suggesting that a rhythm may appear first under environmental influence and only later be controlled by an internal clock.

One other very early circadian rhythm was identified in an ingenious experiment by Cooper (1939). Mitosis was recorded in preputial skin which had been removed at routine circumcision of 6–11-day olds. A clear circadian rhythm was found which, in the absence of any plausible external influence, must be assumed to be endogenous. It is now fairly certain that there are a number of independent sources of endogenous circadian rhythms (Winfree, 1980), so it can be anticipated that different systems will come under control at different times. If, as Hellbrügge suggests, the maturity of the particular system is crucial, it is not surprising that the first clearly endogenous rhythm should be at the cellular level.

Circadian periodicities are the longest that have been identified in the neonatal period and they have little scope for adaptation by changing frequency. It is therefore to be expected that they will approximate a pendulum oscillation. Even so they must initially be capable of some variation in frequency to bring that innate circadian timing into synchrony with the exact 24 h of the environment. Attempts to entrain the circadian rhythm onto different frequencies indicate that the range over which this can be done is, for man, extremely narrow (Lobban, 1960). Another pendulum characteristic is that the amplitude of the variation builds up very slowly (Wever, 1965). Hellbrügge (1960) found that all of the functions he studied showed a steady increase in the amplitude of their oscillation which continued in some cases for a considerable time. Temperature swings in particular attain their maximum only by the age of 5 years (Abe *et al.*, 1978).

Circadian rhythms would seem to be potentially available from birth and yet in many cases do not appear until some time later. To attribute this to immaturity of the systems is surely teleological reasoning; the neonate provides countless examples of what Anokhin (1964) called systemogenesis. Systems become adequately mature in advance of the time that they will be needed. With this orientation the time of first appearance of a function leads to a search for an explanation not of a previous incapacity but of the advantage of that particular timing. The most obvious circadian rhythm, in sleep and wakefulness, is also the simplest to explain. As discussed in the previous section the pattern of sleep is intrinsically related to the pattern of feeding. The neonate cannot afford a long period without food to digest and has insufficient capacity to take in enough food to last for 8 h. At such a time any daily period of prolonged sleep would be extremely disadvantageous. Presumably at some time between 8 and 16 weeks the balance shifts in favour of providing the infant and care-taker with regular periods of extended rest. It would be interesting to know whether the onset of the circadian sleep rhythm can be delayed in response to a different balance of advantage as in the case of delays in weight gain. If so, then as we come to understand the reasons for the normal timing of onset of circadian fluctuations in various functions, we may find that departures from these timings tell us a lot about the suboptimal adaptation of the individuals concerned.

RHYTHMIC INPUT

Although the newborn may benefit from an insensitivity to circadian environmental cues, the same does not apply to shorter durations. Salk (1962) provoked a number of studies with his claim that playing a recorded maternal heart beat to newborns for 4 days accelerated weight gain and reduced crying. Furthermore the heart beat was more effective than another rhythmic stimulus (a metronome) in inducing sleep. However other workers failed to replicate this finding. For example Brackbill *et al.* (1966) found a metronome and a lullaby not to be significantly less effective than a heartbeat. Smith and Steinschneider (1975) compared the effects of fast and slow heartbeats on babies born to mothers with high and low heart rates. They failed to find a significant effect but it is worth noting that, as with the Brackbill *et al.* (1966) study, all of the findings are in the direction that would be predicted by Salk (1962). Ambrose (1969) found that rocking at once per second was more effective than other frequencies and this seems to be a natural frequency for parents to adopt when attempting to soothe a baby. Some doubt about the primacy of rhythmic stimuli is raised by the finding of Birns *et al.* (1966) that rocking was no more effective than non-rhythmic stimuli. An important factor may have been the frequency of rocking which was not reported and may not have been precisely controlled.

The effectiveness of a 1 cps rocking frequency, and the finding of a similar rhythm in heart rate and sucking suggests that it may be fruitful to look for particular effectiveness of rhythmic stimuli at frequencies shown spontaneously by the neonate. It has been shown that newborns respond to time intervals in the range of 5–30 s (Stratton and Connolly, 1973), which incorporates some of the periodicities discussed in this chapter. However, there have been no attempts to explore rhythmic stimulation with periodicities between 2 s and 24 h.

A more complex situation arises in the case of cyclic interactions between two active partners. Minute analyses of film of mothers with their babies have revealed patterns of turn-taking behaviour which Stern (1977) and others have described as a 'dance'. Such a term implies two partners coordinating their behaviour according to a shared rhythm, and this is certainly quite a common interpretation of these interactions. An alternative possibility is that the cyclicity as achieved entirely by the mother fitting in to the infant's ongoing behaviour (Schaffer *et al.*, 1977), and Newson (1979) has pointed out that if that behaviour is rhythmic then the interaction will appear to be rhythmic as well. There would appear to be a genuine question as to whether mother and infant interact on the basis of a shared rhythm or whether consistencies arise from one partner co-ordinating his/her behaviour to a rhythmic output from the other. Even the very precise timings reported by Condon and Sander (1974) leaves this issue unresolved. Their research found that neonates' body movements were apparently synchronized with the speech sounds of an adult who was talking to the baby. It may be that this synchrony depends on a shared rhythm corresponding to the rhythmic structure of language, but there are other possibilities. The adult could have been sensitively timing his speech to correspond to the neonate's behaviour. Alternatively the baby could have been responding either to an underlying rhythm in the adult's speech or simply reacting to speech cues which indicated an imminent change in the speech element currently being produced. Condon and Sander mention similar results obtained with tape-recorded speech which would suggest that responsibility for the synchrony rests with the newborn.

While the findings of Condon and Sander (1974) seem to require surprising capabilites on the part of the newborn, it is not yet clear just what these capabilities are, or whether they depend on a rhythmic process.

CONCLUSIONS

In some respects the foregoing survey has been a chronicle of loose ends. In a few areas such as sucking and sleep we have sufficient information to show how an analysis from the perspective of rhythmic qualities provides a useful complement to other approaches. For most areas a similar exercise must await the acquisition of much more data, specified at an appropriate level of quantification and hopefully presented with an ingenuity equivalent to that shown in several of the more recent studies. Even so there are enough hints in all of the areas reviewed to suggest that the exercise would be very worthwhile.

One reason for the lack of substantial advance since Wolff's (1967) formulation has been the absence of any discussion or consensus over what it means to say that a function is rhythmic. The present analysis suggests that any variation that is worth calling a rhythm will have a stable frequency and amplitude under constant conditions. However, it will be the changes in these parameters in response to changes in endogenous or exogenous conditions which will be most informative about the particular form taken by the control of the rhythm. Statistical requirements for stability cannot be defined too rigidly at present. One reason is that stable conditions may be quite difficult to define and identify in many systems and so the occurrence of very constant frequencies and amplitudes may be quite elusive. On the other hand, as Sackett (1979) has pointed out, with temporal data it is very easy to find a null hypothesis which can be statistically rejected. What is of far more use is the formulation of models which may give insight into the practical significance of rhythmic tendencies.

The hypothesis of an ontogenetic shift from relaxation towards pendulum-type oscillations has succeeded in giving coherence to what might otherwise seem to be disjointed facts. The cases for which suitable information is available have tended to be compatible with the hypothesis and I would suggest that it has been sufficiently well supported by this review to justify its use as a starting point for further work. I would also reaffirm the claim made at the end of the preliminary section of this chapter: at our present state of knowledge a concentration on possible underlying mechanisms would be misplaced as would elaborate speculation about the more esoteric implications. We have much to find out about the actual functioning of the different rhythmic processes of the newborn and this information is not only essential before any speculations about mechanisms are likely to be productive, it is also likely to be of much more use in the attempt to understand specific aspects of neonatal psychobiology.

REFERENCES

Abe, K., Sasaki, H., Takebayashi, K., Fukui, S., and Nambu, H. (1978). The development of circadian rhythm of human body temperature, *Journal of Interdisciplinary Cycle Research*, **9**, 211–216.

Ambrose, A. (1969). *Stimulation in Early Infancy*, Academic Press, London.

Anders, T. F. (1978). State and rhythmic processes, *Journal of American Academy of Child Psychiatry*, **17**, 401–420.

Anokhin, P. K. (1964). Systemogenesis as a general regulator of brain development, in *Progress in Brain Research*, vol. 9 (Eds W. A. Himwich and H. E. Himwich), Elsevier, London.

Aserinsky, E. and Kleitman, N. (1955). A motility cycle in sleeping infants as manifested by ocular and gross bodily activity, *Journal of Applied Physiology*, **8**, 11–18.

Ashton, R. (1971). State and the auditory reactivity of the human neonate, *Experimental Child Psychology*, **12**, 339–346.

Ashton, R. (1973). The state variable in neonatal research, *Merrill Palmer Quarterly*, **19**, 3–20.

Balint, M. (1948). Individual differences of behaviour in early infancy and an objective method of recording them, *Journal of Genetic Psychology*, **73**, 57–117.

Berg, W. K. and Berg, K. M. (1979). Psychophysiological development in infancy: state, sensory function and attention, in *Handbook of Infant Development* (Ed. J. D. Osofsky), Wiley, New York.

Birns, B., Blank, M. and Bridger, W. H. (1966). The effectiveness of various soothing techniques on human neonates, *Psychosomatic Medicine*, **28**, 316–322.

Brackbill, Y., Adams, G., Crowell, D. H. and Gray, M. L. (1966). Arousal level in neonates and preschool children under continuous auditory stimulation, *Journal of Experimental Child Psychology*, **4**, 178–188.

Brady, J. (1979). *Biological Clocks*, Edward Arnold, London.

Burke, P. M. (1977). Swallowing and the organisation of sucking in the human newborn, *Child Development*, **48**, 523–531.

Condon, W. S. and Sander, L. W. (1974). Synchrony demonstrated between movements of the neonate and adult speech, *Child Development*, **45**, 456–462.

Cooper, Z. K. (1939). Mitotic variation in human epidermis, *Journal of Investigative Dermatology*, **2**, 289–300.

Crook, C. K. (1977). Taste and the temporal organization of neonatal sucking, in *Taste and Development. The Ontogeny of Sweet Preference* (Ed. J. M. Weiffenbach), US Government Printing Office, Maryland.

Crook, C. K. (1979). The organization and control of infant sucking, in *Advances in Child Development and Behavior*, Vol. 14 (Eds H. W. Reese and L. P. Lipsitt), Academic Press, New York.

Crook, C. K., and Lipsitt, L. P. (1976). Neonatal nutritive sucking: effects of taste stimulation upon sucking rhythm and heart rate. *Child Development*, **47**, 518–522.

Cullen, J. K., Fargo, N., Chase, R. A., and Baker, P. (1968). The development of auditory feedback monitoring: I. delayed auditory feedback studies on infant cry, *Journal of Speech and Hearing Research*, **11**, 85–93.

Dawes, G. S. (1979). *Fetal Breathing* in *Central Nervous Control Mechanisms in Breathing* (Eds C. von Euler and H. Lagerantz), Pergamon, Oxford.

De Haan, R., Patrick, J., Chess, G. F., and Jaco, N. T. (1977). Definition of sleep state in the newborn infant by heart rate analysis, *American Journal of Obstetrics and Gynecology*, **127**, 753–758.

Dreier, T., Wolff, P. H., Cross, E. E., and Cochran, W. D. (1979). Patterns of breath intervals during non-nutritive sucking in full-term and 'at risk' pre term infants with normal neurological examinations, *Early Human Development*, **3**, 187–199.

Eichorn, D. (1970). Physiological development, in *Carmichael's Manual of Child Psychology*, Vol 1. (Ed. P. H. Mussen) Wiley, New York.

Emde, R., Swedberg, J., and Suzuki, B. (1975). Human wakefulness and biological rhythms after birth, *Archives of General Psychiatry*, **32**, 780–787.

Estes, W. K. (1956). The problem of inference from curves based on group data, *Psychological Bulletin*, **53**, 134–140.

Friedman, S. and Fisher, C. (1967). On the presence of a rhythmic diurnal, oral instinctual drive cycle in man: A preliminary report, *Journal of the American Psychoanalytic Association*, **15**, 317–343.

Harper, R. M., Hoppenbrouwers, T., Sterman, M. B., McGinty, D. J., and Hodgman, J. E. (1976). Polygraphic studies of normal infants during the first six months of life. I. Heart rate and variability as a function of state, *Pediatric Research*, **10**, 945–951.

Hathorn, M. K. S. (1979). Analysis of the depth and timing of infant breathing, in *Central Nervous Control Mechanisms in Breathing* (Eds C. von Euler and H. Lagercrantz) Pergamon, Oxford.

Hellbrügge, T. (1960). The development of circadian rhythms in infants, *Cold Spring Harbour Symposia on Quantitative Biology*, **25**, 311–323.

Hellbrügge, T., Lange, J. E., Rutenfranz, J., and Stehr, K. (1964). Circadian periodicity of physiological functions in different stages of infancy and childhood, *Annals of the New York Academy of Sciences*, **117**, 361–373.

Irwin, O. C. (1930). The amount and nature of activities of newborn infants under constant external stimulating conditions during the first ten days of life, *Genetic Psychology Monographs*, **8**, 1–92.

Johnson, P. and Salisbury, D. (1975). Breathing and sucking during feeding in the newborn, in *Parent-infant interaction* Ciba Foundation Symposium, Vol. 33, (Ed. M. O'Connor) Elsevier, Amsterdam.

Kaye, K. (1977). Toward the origin of dialogue, in *Studies in Mother–Infant Interaction* (Ed. H. R. Schaffer) Academic Press, London.

Kleitman, N. (1963). *Sleep and Wakefulness*, University of Chicago Press, Chicago.

Kleitman, N. (1973). The basic rest–activity cycle in sleep and wakefulness, in *The Nature of Sleep* (Ed. U. Juranovich), Verlag, Stuttgart.

Kleitman, N. and Engelmann, T. G. (1953). Sleep characteristics of infants, *Journal of Applied Physiology*, **6**, 269–282.

Komisaruk, B. R. (1977). The role of rhythmical brain activity in sensorimotor integration, in *Progress in psychobiology and Physiological Psychology*, Vol. 7 (Eds J. M. Sprague and A. N. Epstein) Academic Press, New York.

Lagercrantz, H., Ahlstrom, M., Jonson, B., Lindroth, M., and Svenningsen, N. (1979). A critical oxygen level below which irregular breathing occurs in preterm infants, in *Central Nervous Control Mechanisms in Breathing* (Eds C. von Euler and H. Lagercrantz) Pergamon, Oxford.

Lashley, K. S. (1951). The problem of serial order in behaviour, in *Cerebral Mechanisms in Behaviour* (Ed. L. A. Jeffries) Wiley, New York.

Lewis, M., Wilson C. D., Ban, P., and Baumel, M. H. (1970). An exploratory study of resting cardiac rate and variability from the last trimester of prenatal life through the first year of postnatal life, *Child Development*, **41**, 799–811.

Lipsitt, L. P., Reilly, B. M., Butcher, M. J., and Greenwood, M. H. (1974). The stability and interrelationships of newborn sucking and heart rate, *Developmental Psychobiology*, **9**, 305–310.

Lobban, M. C. (1960). The entrainment of circadian rhythms in man. *Cold Spring Harbor Symposia on Quantitative Biology*, **25**, 325–332.

Meier-Koll, A., Hall V., Hellwig, U., Kott, G., and Meier-Koll, V. (1978), A biological oscillator system and the development of sleep–waking behaviour during early infancy, *Chronobiologia*, **5**, 425–440.

Mills, J. N. (1974). Development of circadian rhythms in infancy, in *Scientific Foundations of Paediatrics* (Eds J. A. Davis and J. Dobbing) Heinemann, London.

Morath, M. (1974). The four-hour feeding rhythm of the baby as a free running endogenously regulated rhythm. *International Journal of Chronobiology*, **2**, 39–45.

Myers, A. (1977). Organization of spontaneous behaviours of sleeping neonates, *Perceptual & Motor Skills*, **45**, 791–794.

Newson, J. (1979). Intentional behaviour in the young infant, in *The First Year of Life*. (Eds D. Shaffer and J. Dunn) Wiley, Chichester.

Palmer, J. D. (1976). *An Introduction to Biological Rhythms*, Academic Press, London.

Parmelee, A. H. (1961). A study of one infant from birth to eight months of age, *Acta Paediatrica*, **50**, 160–170.

Parmelee, A. H. and Stern, E. (1972). Development of states in infants in *Sleep and the Maturing Nervous System* (Eds C. B. Clemente, D. P. Purpura, and F. E. Mayer) Academic Press, New York.

Peiper, A. (1963). *Cerebral Function in Infancy and Childhood*. Consultants Bureau, New York.

Piaget, J. (1942). Les trois structures fondamentales de la vie physique: rhythme, regulation et groupement, *Revue Suisse de Psychologie*, **1**, 9–21.

Pittendrigh, C. S. (1960). Circadian rhythms and the circadian organization of living systems, *Cold Spring Harbor Symposia on Quantitative Biology*, **25**, 159–182.

Prechtl, H. F. R. (1968). Polygraphic studies of the full-term newborn: II Computer analysis of recorded data, in *Studies in Infancy* (Eds M. Bax and R. MacKeith) Clinic in Developmental Medicine, no. 27, Heinemann, London.

Prechtl, H. F. R., Theorell, K., Gransbergen, A., and Lind, J. (1969). A statistical analysis of cry patterns in normal and abnormal newborn infants, *Developmental Medicine and Child Neurology*, **11**, 142–152.

Purves, M. J. (1979). What do we breathe for?, in *Central Nervous Control Mechanisms in Breathing* (Eds C. von Euler and H. Lagercrantz) Pergamon, Oxford.

Richter, C. P. (1965). *Biological Clocks in Medicine and Psychiatry*, C. C. Thomas, Illinois.

Roffwarg, H. P., Muzio, J. N., and Dement, W. C. (1966). Ontogenetic Development of the human sleep-dream cycle, *Science*, **152**, 604–619.

Sackett, G. P. (1979). The lag sequential analysis of contingency and cyclicity in behavioural interaction research, in *Handbook of Infant Development* (Ed. J. D. Osofsky) Wiley, New York.

Salk, L. (1962). Mother's heartbeat as an imprinting stimulus, *Transactions of the New York Academy of Sciences*, **24**, 753–763.

Schaffer, H. R., Collis, G. M., and Parsons, G. (1977). Vocal interchange and visual regard in verbal and pre-verbal children, in *Studies in Mother–Infant Interaction*. (Ed. H. R. Schaffer) Academic Press, London.

Smith, C. R. and Steinschneider, A. (1975). Differential effects of prenatal rhythmic stimulation on neonatal arousal states, *Child Development*, **46**, 574–78.

Sollberger, A. (1965). *Biological Rhythm Research*, Elsevier, Amsterdam.

Steinschneider, A. (1975). Implications of the sudden infant death syndrome for the study of sleep in infancy, in *Minnesota Symposia on Child Psychology*, Vol. 9 (Ed. A. D. Pick) University of Minnesota Press, Minneapolis.

Sterman, M. B. (1972). The basic rest-activity cycle and sleep: developmental considerations in man and cats, in *Sleep and the Maturing Nervous System* (Eds C. B. Clemente, D. P. Purpura, and F. E. Mayer) Academic Press, New York.

Sterman, M. B. and Hoppenbrouwers, T. (1971). The development of sleep–waking and rest-activity patterns from fetus to adult in man, in *Brain Development and Behavior* (Eds M. B. Sterman, D. J. McGinty, and A. M. Adinolfi) Academic Press, New York.

Stern, D. (1977). *The First Relationship: Infant and Mother*. Fontana/Open Books, London.

Stern, E., Parmelee, A. H., and Harris, M. (1973). Sleep state periodicity in prematures and young infants, *Developmental Psychobiology*, **6**, 357–365.

Strang, L. B. (1977). *Neonatal Respiration*, Blackwell Scientific Publications, Oxford.

Stratton, P. M. and Connolly, K. J. (1973), Discrimination by newborns of the intensity, frequency and temporal characteristics of auditory stimuli, *British Journal of Psychology*, **64**, 219–232.

Theorell, K., Prechtl, M. F. R., Blair, A. W., and Lind, J. (1973). Behavioral state cycles of normal newborn infants, *Developmental Medicine and Child Neurology*, **15**, 597–615.

Thoman, E. B., Miano, V. N., and Freese, M. P. (1977). The role of respiratory instability in the sudden infant death syndrome, *Developmental Medicine and Child Neurology*, **19**, 729–738.

Truby, H. M. and Lind, J. (1965). Cry sounds of the newborn infant, *Acta Paediatrica Scandinavica, Supplement*, **163**, 7–59.

Wever, R. (1965). Pendulum versus relaxation oscillations, in *Circadian Clocks* (Ed. J. Aschoff), North-Holland, Amsterdam.

Winfree, A. T. (1980). *The Geometry of Biological Time*, Springer-Verlag, New York.

Wolff, P. H. (1966). The causes, controls and organization of behavior in the neonate, *Psychological Issues*, **5**, 1 (Monograph 17).

Wolff, P. H. (1967). The role of biological rhythms in early psychological development, *Bulletin of the Menninger Clinic*, **31**, 197–218.

Wolff, P. H. (1968). The serial organization of sucking in the young infant, *Pediatrics*, **42**, 943–956.

Psychobiology of the Human Newborn
Edited by P. Stratton
© 1982, John Wiley & Sons, Ltd.

CHAPTER 7

Learning, Adaptation, and Memory in the Newborn

CAROLYN K. ROVEE-COLLIER and LEWIS P. LIPSITT

Although newborn behaviours have long fascinated parents, grandparents, and psychologists, reports of their behaviours were for many years simply catalogues of the responses of which infants were capable (Dennis, 1934; Watson, 1919; Weiss, 1929) and of the stimuli to which they were responsive (for review, see Peiper, 1963). These descriptions still form the basis of many widely-used infant developmental scales (Cattell, 1940; Gesell, 1928) and manuals for parents (Gesell and Ilg, 1943; Spock, 1957; Spock and Lowenberg, 1955). Investigations of infant learning were undertaken to document the origins of adult behaviour in the expansion of infant reflexes (e.g., Watson and Rayner, 1920) and the generality of the laws of learning, rather than the nature of infant learning *per se*. Because the experimental designs and methods were patterned after traditional models of adult and animal research without regard for the special problems of the newborn, it is not surprising that these initial studies provided a disappointing view of newborn learning ability (for review, see Lipsitt, 1963). Only recently have researchers begun to view the newborn within the broader context of his evolutionary history. The perspective of the newborn as a biological organism has led us to pose different and more suitable experimental questions and, as a result, has enabled us to increase dramatically our estimates of newborn competence.

In this chapter, we will emphasize the biological origins and adaptive significance of newborn behaviour. We assume that newborn humans, like the young of all species, display behaviours which have been maximized by selection. To the extent that infants of many species, and mammalian newborns in particular, share common survival-related problems, we expect them to share also common physiological and behavioural solutions. For this reason, we will consider relevant research on non-human mammalian newborns as a means of confirming and supplementing our understanding of the abilities of the human neonate. In doing so, however, we recognize and caution with Hinde (in press) that the utility of this approach does not derive from direct comparisons of specific human and non-human behaviours but from the common principles of behaviour which may be extracted.

THE NEWBORN AS A BIOLOGICAL ORGANISM

The biological requirements for survival dominate the earliest interactions of all newborns with their environment. Most if not all of their responses are manifestations of either physiological or behavioural regulations. The younger the organism the fewer the number of physiological regulations which are operative hence the greater the dependence upon behavioural regulations (Adolph, 1968). In fact, Adolph (1968) has characterized the newborn's regulatory arrangements and their interactions as the major constraints on infant behaviour and on the environmental conditions which the newborn can tolerate.

Physiologists are in general agreement that the major problem of all newborns is to grow (Kennedy, 1967). This requires the conversion of as many calories as possible into tissue which, in turn, requires maximizing caloric intake while minimizing all other forms of caloric expenditure. While the significance of behaviours such as rooting, sucking, swallowing, etc., bear obvious relation to caloric intake, the behaviours related to caloric expenditure are less obvious and are intimately associated with thermal homeostasis. Newborn mammals acquire reflexive control of body temperature only gradually (Adolph, 1957, 1968) but nevertheless demonstrate considerable competence in maintaining body temperature behaviourally, given the opportunity (for review, see Satinoff and Hendersen, 1977). The extended sleep/inactivity states of the newborn, which are associated with lower metabolic rates and generally slowed rates of physiological functions, comprise the infant's major energy conservation strategy (Horne, 1977), while clinging and orienting toward warm stimuli (Harlow, 1958; Jeddi, 1970) or huddling with conspecifics (Alberts, 1978; Ewer, 1968) are simultaneous behavioural solutions to the problems of thermal homeostasis and caloric conservation. Conversely, activity and crying or even inopportune or unnecessary wakefulness increases metabolism and is energetically costly, thereby increasing survival risk, particularly in small or premature organisms (Brackbill and Fitzgerald, 1969).

Michael Leon and his associates (Leon et al., 1978; Woodside and Leon, 1980; Woodside et al., 1980) have described a complex but highly efficient pattern of thermal-caloric relations in the mother–infant interactions of rodents. The duration of a given feeding is limited by the mother, who leaves the nest in response to the elevation of her body temperature. This increase is the result of huddling with the pups, reduced heat dissipation from her ventrum during suckling, and an endocrine secretion stimulated by suckling which increases heat production. Thus the newborn rat pup produces both milk and heat by sucking, and the latter indirectly regulates the size of his meal. Thus the rat pup requires (and apparently has) no 'satiety' shut-off mechanism (Hull, 1973). (The return of the mother to the nest for the next feeding is stimulated, in turn, by a decrease in her body temperature.) Other infant behaviours such as crying, smiling, eye-contact, and gaze aversion do not contribute directly to body temperature regulation or milk provision but are effective indirectly through their effects on parental care-taking behaviour. The rat pup, when cooled, emits ultrasounds and is retrieved to the nest (Hofer and Shair, 1977), as is the vocalizing kitten who has strayed from the litter (Haskins, 1977). Similarly, the cry of the human newborn is highly effective in eliciting nurturance and bodily contact (Bernal, 1972), and it induces anticipatory milk let-down and increased breast temperature in the lactating mother (Vuorenskoski *et al.*, 1969), probably as a result of classical conditioning. Thus mother–infant reciprocity (Brazelton *et al.*, 1974) must also be viewed in terms of its contribution to newborn regulation (cf. Hull, 1973).

We wish to emphasize four points at the outset:

1. newborn behaviours cannot be interpreted independent of their regulatory functions;
2. there are multiple regulations, each of which is multiply determined and each potentially having a unique ontogenetic course;
3. procedures which alter one relation of the newborn with his environment may also alter countless others, thereby affecting a number of response probabilities in different directions; and
4. the behavioural regulations of the newborn will severely constrain the types of experimental problems he will solve as well as the nature of his solutions.

As we will see, conditioning procedures which have produced evidence of newborn learning have not competed with behavioural thermal homeostasis or energy conservation, have exploited behaviours associated with caloric intake, and/or have provided other adaptive benefits, even if they have not always been immediately obvious.

NEWBORN LEARNING

Tinbergen (1951) has suggested that it might be useful to 'approach learning phenomena from a more naturalistic standpoint than is usually done and to ask, not what can an animal learn, but what does it actually learn under natural conditions?' (p. 142). If all organisms, including the newborn, are equally and completely adapted to their environments at all stages of development (Von Uexküll, 1934; Lehrman, 1953), then it becomes clear that we must consider the structure of the newborn's environment as well as his sensory and response capabilities in both the design and interpretation of newborn research. Unfortunately, the analysis of newborn behaviour in terms of its adaptive significance is made difficult by the rapidity with which the structure of the newborn environment has changed in recent times. Thus, while the newborn is the product of his evolutionary history, the environmental pressures which once operated and resulted in the evolution of behaviours sufficient to see a newborn through the most stringent of conditions (Wilson, 1975; pp. 42–43) may no longer exist. In addition, recent advances in public health and medicine, which have led to high survival rates of infants in recent times, preclude the operation of selection pressures which were once effective. As a result, newborn behaviours that we witness today must be assessed in terms of their historical success, even though their current adaptive value may be obscure.

Learning is the process by which infants determine lawful relations between environmental events and between their own behaviours and succeeding environmental events (Bolles, 1972), thereby establishing order in an environment which otherwise would appear semi-chaotic (see Brunswick, 1952; p. 28). A common way in which members of all species determine environmental regularities is through the accumulation of frequency and temporal information (Jerison, 1973). This is well-documented in the habituation literature (Peeke and Herz, 1973a, 1973b) and has received substantiation by the discovery of 'counting cells' in the cat's associative cortex which code the ordinal position of stimuli, irrespective of modality (Thompson et al., 1970). Temporal information is closely related to biological rhythms which buffer the organism against environmental irregularities. This is complemented by frequency-of-occurrence information, which facilitates the recognition and tracking of recurrent events. The 'automatic' processing of both types of information has been described as a primary process in human cognitive development (Hasher and Zacks, 1979) and may play a significant role in linguistic development (e.g., Ungerer et al., 1978). The role of such information in conditioning is clear: once an organism knows what to expect and when to expect it, he can respond anticipatorily, thereby gaining a biological advantage (Skinner, 1953; p. 38).

In the following sections, we will consider the evidence of newborn learning ability which has been obtained from habituation procedures, classical and instrumental conditioning paradigms, and 'hybrid' procedures which are combinations of the other paradigms.

Habituation and Conditionability

Habituation is a 'stimulus specific response decrement resulting from repeated or constant exposures to the response eliciting stimulus' (Wyers et al., 1973; p. 12;) as in definitions of learning, the definition of habituation excludes decrements reflecting diurnal changes, aging, maturation, sensory adaptation, illness, injury, drugs, etc. The defining characteristics of habituation have been detailed elsewhere (Thompson and Spencer, 1966). Functionally, habituation has been viewed as a means by which the organism eliminates non-essential responses to biologically irrevelant stimuli, thereby permitting energy conservation and fitness (Lorenz, 1965; Thorpe, 1963).

Most of the infant habituation research has been based on Sokolov's (1963) postulation of a brain-comparator process. This presumes that the infant stores internal representations of the characteristics of an external stimulus. Response to subsequent stimuli is an inverse function of the extent to which new input matches that which has been stored. An alternative model which has inspired considerable animal research but which has been neglected by infancy researchers was proposed by Groves and Thompson (1970). They view habituation as only one of two processes that result from environmental change, sensitization being the other. Repetitious events which lack strong consequences presumably alter a unique population of interneurones in S–R pathways (type H neurones) and result in habituation; events with strong consequences alter a population of 'state' (type S) neurones and result in response enhancement. The balance between these two processes determines response to stimulus change. The frequent finding of an increase rather than a decrease in response to repeated stimulations in newborn infants (Graham *et al.*, 1968) is consistent with this model.

Because a number of reviews of habituation research with a wide variety of species (Peeke and Herz, 1973a, 1973b) and with human infants (Clifton and Nelson, 1976; Jeffrey and Cohen, 1971; Tighe and Leaton, 1976) have recently appeared, our discussion will focus on the relation between habituation, conditioning, and the conditionability of the newborn.

Although many investigators regard habituation as a primitive form of learning (e.g. Clifton and Nelson, 1976), this view is by no means universal (Jeffrey and Cohen, 1971). Historically, recovery from habituation after an extended interval has distinguished habituation from conditioning, the latter being considered a more durable change. However, Kimmel and Goldstein (1967) found evidence of retention of an habituated galvanic skin response in college students after a 2-week interval, and Bishop and Kimmel (1969) reported savings in the rehabituation to an auditory stimulus after 6 months. Similarly, Davis (1972) found evidence of retention of an habituated startle response after 6 days in adult rats, and Keen *et al.* (1965) observed residual habituation of a heart-rate change in human infants after a 24-h interval. Thus a distinction between habituation and conditioning which is based on relative permanence is tentative, at best.

A number of investigators have theoretically linked habituation and conditioning (Petrinovich, 1973; Stein, 1966). An analysis which has particular relevance for infant research designs was proposed by Kimmel (1973). He defined two classes of reflexes, positive and negative feedback reflexes, which differ with respect to habituability and in their efficacy as reinforcers in classical or instrumental conditioning. Positive feedback reflexes (e.g. orienting, searching) are plastic and non-reinforcing and increase afferent input to the CNS; negative feedback reflexes reduce afferent input (e.g. nocioceptive, righting, withdrawal, or ingestion reflexes), do not habituate (or do so only slowly), and are effective reinforcers. The pairing of positive and negative feedback reflexes will produce classical conditioning when the first member of the pair is readily habituable. The replacement of this reflex by some semblance of the homeostatic (negative feedback) reflex permits the homeostatic reflex to operate more rapidly and more efficiently. When the first member of the pair is not habituable, however, it may gain in strength or frequency and instrumental conditioning will be observed. In the latter situation, the second reflex would enhance (reinforce) the first one. The implications of the Kimmel model for infant conditioning research are clear. Moreover, the model implies that a major factor which will determine conditioning 'success' in a classical conditioning paradigm is the habituation of reflexes to the conditional stimulus (CS) in the interstimulus interval. As we shall see, this looms as a major determinant of infant conditioning. More generally, the familiar S-shaped learning curve also reflects the fact that competing responses to the test context, etc., must habituate before learning can proceed. Similarly, Papousek (1967; pp. 260–272) has reported that the initial appearance of a CR typically follows habituation of non-specific orienting responses to the CS, and Kling (1972) cited the habituability of the response to the CS as a criterion for CS selection.

Although current evidence shows the newborn to be capable of habituation (Engen and Lipsitt, 1965; Engen *et al.*, 1963; Friedman, 1972; Friedman, *et al.*, 1974; Friedman and Carpenter, 1971; Keen *et al.*, 1965), the ease with which this is achieved experimentally increases with age (e.g. Stern, 1968). Notably, habituation in laboratory experiments may be abnormally fast (Curio, 1969; Lorenz, 1965); in nature, stimuli are more complex and rarely occur in the same way twice. The latter point leads us to speculate that habituation in the newborn may actually mimic natural habituation functions. In spite of the care taken by experimenters to exert precise control over the parameters of stimulation which they present to the newborn, the rapid state transitions of the newborn preclude a constant *subjective* stimulus over (and perhaps within) trials, thereby retarding habituation. When stimulus presentations are restricted to a single infant state, habituation proceeds more efficiently (Engen and Lipsitt, 1965; Engen *et al.*, 1963).

The functional significance of habituation to non-critical stimuli may also be greater for a sleeping than an awake newborn. If sleep is an energy conservation strategy (Horne, 1977), repeated unnecessary arousals would be energetically costly and could pose a risk to survival. In this light, it is not surprising that Brackbill (1977) observed more rapid habituation of 45-h-old infants to an auditory stimulus, as well as a greater probability of classical heart rate conditioning, in quiet than in active sleep.

Classical Conditioning

The problems associated with the use of adult conditioning parameters in infant conditioning research is nowhere better illustrated than in the early classical conditioning literature. Krasnogorskii (1913), after a number of failures, concluded that classical conditioning was precluded by cortical immaturity during the first six postnatal months. As other researchers either failed to demonstrate newborn classical conditioning (Morgan and Morgan, 1944; Rendle-Short, 1961) or obtained relatively unstable increases in conditioned response (CR) frequency (Wenger, 1936), the notion of a classical conditioning deficit in the newborn became generally accepted and is still occasionally espoused (Sameroff, 1971, 1972; Sameroff and Cavanagh, 1979). Much of this initial work has been reviewed in detail, as has more recent research with infants (Brackbill and Fitzgerald, 1969; Brackbill and Koltsova, 1967; Fitzgerald and Brackbill, 1976; Fitzgerald and Porges, 1971; Lipsitt, 1963; Peiper, 1963; Sameroff, 1971, 1972; Sameroff and Cavanagh, 1979; Siqueland, 1970).

As a result of selecting conditioning parameters more carefully, researchers have now demonstrated classical conditioning of the Babkin reflex (Connolly and Stratton, 1969; Kaye, 1965), heart rate (Brackbill, 1977; Clifton, 1974; Stamps and Porges, 1975), pupillary dilation and constriction (Brackbill et al., 1967), eyeblinks (Fitzgerald and Brackbill, 1971; Janos, 1968; Kasatkin, 1969; Little, 1970, 1973; Naito and Lipsitt, 1969) and sucking (Lipsitt and Kaye, 1964; Marquis, 1931). In an extensive review, Fitzgerald and Brackbill (1976) were unable to find evidence of the systematic effects of 'traditional' conditioning parameters such as the intensity, duration, or modality of the unconditioned stimulus (US). They concluded that somatic or skeletal responses appear to be more readily associated with auditory, tactile, and visual CSs, whereas autonomic responses were more likely to become associated with temporal CSs. Finally, they found no empirical support for the hypothesis that differential rates of maturation in the sensory analysers (hence of CS sensitivity) mediate developmental differences in classical conditioning (see Brackbill and Koltsova, 1967).

The strong proclivity of newborns to exhibit temporal conditioning and to manifest other evidence of temporal precision is one of the most striking aspects of newborn behaviour. In 1941, Marquis had reported that newborns switched to a 4-h feeding schedule following 8 days on a 3-h feeding schedule exhibited activity increases anticipatory to the time at which feeding had previously occurred. Infants shifted from a 4-h schedule had to be aroused for their 3-h feeding. Although recent findings of 4-h endogenous sleep/waking cycles in newborns which are independent of feeding (Emde et al., 1975; Morath, 1974) have raised questions concerning the conditioned aspects of the Marquis finding, subsequent studies of different responses and with different temporal parameters have verified the phenomenon of infant temporal conditioning.

Temporal conditioning of respiration, heart rate, and motility within a single session was observed by Lipsitt and Ambrose (1967) following eight presentations each of a vestibular, olfactory, and auditory stimulus at 30-s intervals. Although the effect was not large, it was consistent with the findings of Brackbill and her associates (Brackbill and Fitzgerald, 1969, 1972; Brackbill et al., 1967) that infants can discriminate temporal regularities in events and will respond on the occasion of their omission. Similar effects have been reported on other classical conditioning paradigms by Clifton (1974) and Stamps and Porges (1975): infants exhibit heart rate deceleration to US omission but no evidence of anticipatory responding to the US. Brackbill and Fitzgerald (1972) also demonstrated that 38- to 44-day-old infants can discriminate temporal patterns. Using an illumination change as a US, they presented thirty infants with multiple trials of light onset or light offset after alternating intervals of 20 s and 30 s (i.e., 20-s interstimulus interval or ISI, 4-s US, 30-s ISI, 4-s US, 20-s ISI, etc.) in a stereotype temporal conditioning paradigm. On interspersed test trials, as many USs were omitted as there were interstimulus intervals (i.e., two). Significant pupillary conditioning was obtained at both intervals in the light-off (dilation) condition, but none was seen in the light-on (constriction) condition. Differential conditionability of dilation and constriction is not characteristic of simple temporal conditioning paradigms (Brackbill and Fitzgerald, 1972; Fitzgerald *et al.*, 1967); rather, both reflexes appear as CRs in these paradigms.

The relative ease with which temporal conditioning is achieved may reflect a number of factors. First, the CS (time passage) does not elicit orienting or other reflexes which must be habituated prior to the development of a CR (cf. Kimmel, 1973). Secondly, the lengthy intervals involved in successful demonstrations of temporal conditioning (from 20 s to several hours) relative to those of other classical conditioning procedures (expressed in msec) permit the dissipation of any refractory, inhibitory, or otherwise disruptive effects of the US prior to its subsequent recurrence. Thirdly, environmental changes may become temporally linked to circadian or ultradian rhythms (Hellbrügge, 1974; Morath, 1974), feeding rhythms (Nelson *et al.*, 1975), or sleep/waking cycles (Meier-Koll *et al.*, 1978). An extraordinary demonstration of the synergistic effects of the feeding cycle and the sleep/waking cycle on conditioned orienting responses of 4-month-olds has been reported by Koch (1968). These effects should have an even greater impact on newborn conditionability. And, finally, the close relation between habituation at constant ISIs and temporal conditioning, as well as the widespread incidence of temporal conditioning among higher vertebrates, suggests that this represents a phylogenetically primitive form of conditioning which permits greater plasticity in short-term behavioural adaptations than can be achieved through biological rhythms.

The functional utility of temporal conditioning is seen in the feeding patterns of many species and is particularly clear-cut for animals whose food supply is available at certain times of the day and/or in certain locations only. By remaining relatively quiescent except when a meal is likely to be forthcoming, a very young organism is maximizing the efficiency of its caloric regulation. For example, the rabbit mother enters the burrow for only a few minutes once every 24 h (Ewer, 1968; Venge, 1963; Zarrow *et al.*, 1965), at which time each newborn typically consumes approximately a fifth of its body weight (Hull, 1973). The tree shrew returns to the brood nest only once every 48 h to feed young (Martin, 1966). Newborn of these species who do not learn to anticipate this event and either remain active throughout the mother's absence or remain lethargic in her presence clearly risk survival. Similarly, McFarland (1977) has described the considerable precision of herring gulls in anticipating each of a series of food resources which are briefly available at different times throughout the day (e.g., worms in the farmer's field at dawn and dusk, the mussels along the beach at low tide, the arrival of the garbage trucks at the garbage tips at 11 am and 3 pm, etc.). Clearly, complex (stereotype) temporal conditioning of this type cannot reflect prewired associations; the availability of prey will vary seasonally and annually in each location, depending upon environmental catastrophies, new predator species, trade union strikes, etc. However, the gulls that learn to track these events and anticipate them with regularity must surely gain an advantage in terms of fitness. Because natural selection operates on populations rather than at an individual level, however, variability among individuals in temporal conditioning would be both expected and essential.

Lengthy temporal intervals between stimuli also appear to facilitate infant responding within other classical conditioning procedures. Caldwell and Werboff (1962) conditioned 1-day-old rat pups to produce leg movements to a vibrotactile CS prior to the onset of a forelimb shock. Not only did the neonates achieve a lower level of conditioning than adults but also groups receiving longer ISIs (1200 and 2300 msec) than those optimal for adults exhibited the best conditioning. The improvement in level of conditioning as a function of age as well as the ISI effect was subsequently verified by Gray et al. (1967). Similarly, Cornwell and Fuller (1961) obtained conditioning in newborn puppies at ages younger than had previously been reported (e.g. Fuller et al., 1952) when they increased the ISI from 2 to 9 s, although the nature of the tactile CS was also changed. In young children (Braun and Geiselhart, 1959; Ohlrich and Ross, 1968) and newborn infants (Little, 1970, 1973), better classical eyelid conditioning has been obtained with ISIs lengthier than those typical of adult paradigms.

The work of Little (1970) stands as the only systematic research on the effects of the ISI on human newborn conditioning. In an initial study, she subjected thirteen infants ranging in age from 37 to 59 days to fifty presentations of a CS (1000-cps, 70 db tone) which overlapped and terminated with a US (400 msec air puff) and to twenty randomly interspersed CS-alone test trials. Independent groups received ISIs of 500, 1000, 1500, or 2000 msec, and conditioning was assessed both within the CS–US interval and during test trials. Conditioned eyeblinks were defined as those which blended with the US (i.e., occurred within 170 msec of the US), hence could be considered 'defensive' reactions. Both response measures yielded the same conclusions: Conditioning was achieved only at the two lengthiest ISIs. In a second study, she investigated age effects more systematically, testing infants at 10, 20, or 30 days of age and administering a second session 10 days after the first. Infants were assigned to ISI groups of 500

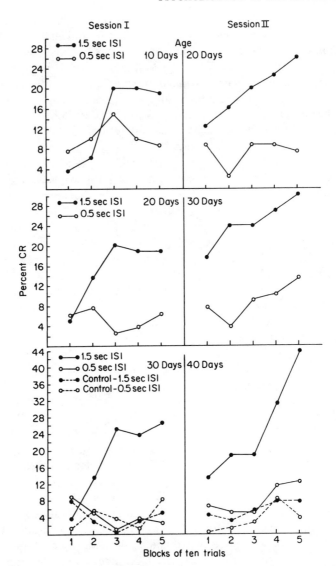

Figure 1 Percentage of conditioned responses on CS–US trials by infants trained at 10, 20, or 30 days age (left side of each panel) and retrained in a second session 10 days later (right side). Infants received either a 1500-msec or 500-msec ISI. Performance of a Random Control group is shown in the bottom panel. (From Little, 1970)

or 1500 msec, and a random control group (Rescorla, 1967) was formed for 30-day-olds. Again, all measures indicated superior performance on the part of infants in the 1500 msec ISI group, irrespective of the age at which training began (see Figure 1).

Although conditioning rate was not age-differentiated, the level of terminal conditioning performance increased with age (see also Gekoski, 1977). The performance of the 1500-msec ISI group trained initially at 30 days significantly exceeded that of the same-age random control group, but performance of the 500-msec ISI group did not. Finally, significant savings were exhibited by infants trained at all but 10 days of age. In fact, performance of the 20-day-olds during their retention test at 30 days of age was superior to that of 30-day-olds being tested for the first time. Notably, the Little procedure included controls for infant state; infants were tested immediately after a nap and following receipt of a portion of their typical postnap ration. A pacifier was used to maintain alertness (see Macfarlane et al. 1976), and no trial began until at least 8 s had elapsed since the preceding US and the infant's eyes were open.

The greater efficacy of longer ISIs with younger organisms has typically been attributed to the relative lack of neural development or low degree of myelinization present at earlier stages of maturation, or the relatively slower processing of stimuli by young organisms for whom most stimuli are relatively novel. However, an alternative interpretation consistent with our earlier emphasis on habituation and conditionability is based on evidence from the animal literature that habituation of startle behaviour is greater after longer and more regular intervals between training stimuli (Davis, 1970). Thus the longer ISIs simply permit the habituation of competing responses within the ISI.

Hoffman et al. (1979) obtained conditioning of eyeblinks in infants 7 weeks to 14 months of age which was highly similar to that obtained by Little (1970) in spite of major differences in procedure and infant age. Compared with adults, infants acquired CRs more slowly, were more variable in responding, and did not achieve as high a final level of conditioning. However, the infants' CR latencies were longer than those of adults, and they anticipated the US onset more efficiently. The long-latency CRs were not merely a reflection of general long-latency responding in infants because their UR latencies were shorter than those of adults. The preceding studies demonstrate the excellent temporal discrimination of the newborn.

Unfortunately, it is all too common to read of the newborn's lack of capacity, which has been inferred from an unsuccessful attempt to demonstrate a particular competence. Such inferences are perpetuated, almost without questioning, because they are consistent with various theoretical biases. When the experimental questions are posed differently, however, we frequently see that the deficit resides in our methods, not in the infant. For example, trace conditioning procedures typically yield poor acquisition relative to delay conditioning procedures when animal or adult subjects are used. Given the previous controversy about infant conditionability (Sameroff, 1971, 1972), few researchers would be willing to commit time and subjects to a conditioning study involving trace procedures with young infants. In addition, it is commonly assumed that young infants are incapable of inhibiting or suppressing active responding. These two capacities were investigated in an unpublished dissertation by Little (1973) in the Brown University infant laboratories. In an initial experiment, Little determined the relative efficacy of trace and delay procedures in establishing infant classical conditioning. She administered fifty CS (800 cps, 72 db tone)–US (300 msec air puff) pairings and ten interspersed test trials daily to two age-matched groups (Delay, Trace) of eight infants each. Training continued until infants in one of the groups had attained a 70 per cent CR criterion in a single session. This criterion was met by the Delay group after six sessions, at which time the duration of their CS was progressively decreased in each succeeding session, resulting in a corresponding increase in the size of the trace interval (i.e. the interval between CS offset and US onset). In addition, because the 50 msec CS was virtually indistinguishable from a room noise and produced few CRs, a 100 msec CS was also presented with the same (1450 msec)

Table 1   CS–US temporal relations, experiment 1

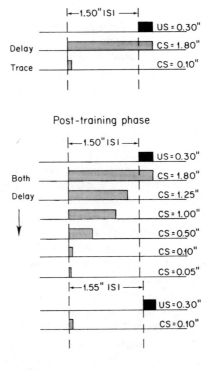

trace interval. These conditions are summarized in Table 1. At the same point in time that the Delay group was shifted to an ascending series of trace intervals, the Trace group was shifted to the original Delay condition (Table 1).

Although no infant in the Trace group reached the 70 per cent criterion, both groups significantly increased anticipatory responding over paired CS–US trials. On CS-alone trials, however, and in Session 1 paired trials, the Trace group did not exhibit evidence of conditioning. Performance of the Delay group significantly exceeded that of the Trace group (see Figure 2) and was maintained after the shift to trace procedures. An analysis of CR latencies indicated that significantly more of the conditioned blinks in the Delay group (89 per cent) overlapped the US than in the Trace group (52 per cent). The ineffectiveness of the defensive CRs in the Trace group was substantial: most of their CRs were produced early in the ISI with the peak frequency occurring 625 msec after CS onset. In contrast, most of the CRs of the Delay group were within 125 msec of US onset. Similarly, conditional probabilities (the probability of a CR given that one has not already occurred) indicated that only the Delay group distributed responses in such a way as to maximize response efficiency in relation to the US (see Figure 3).

Little attributed the inefficacy of the trace procedure to a failure of infants in that group to discriminate the ISI (Ebel and Prokasy, 1963). Because those infants had increased conditioned responding over sessions, she hypothesized that they may have learned the CS–US relationship but that their response timing may have been disrupted by the offset of the CS within the ISI. If CS offset

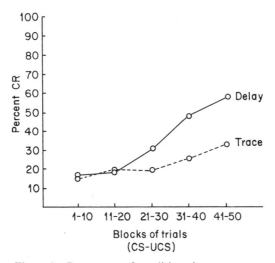

Figure 2 Percentage of conditioned responses on CS–US trials during the first acquisition session for infants in either Trace (dotted lines) or Delay (solid lines) groups. (From Little, 1973)

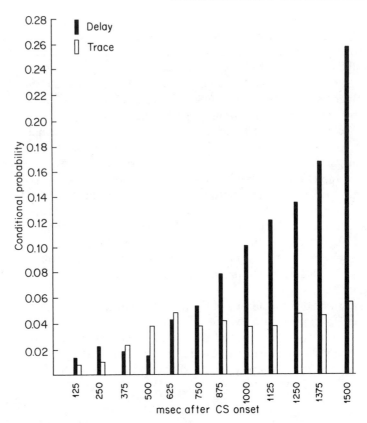

Figure 3   Conditional probability distribution of conditioned responses occurring throughout the ISI in Delay and Trace groups throughout all acquisition sessions. (From Little, 1973)

did elicit an orienting response, when it ultimately habituated the conditioning performance of the Trace group should improve. To assess this possibility, Little used a CER (conditioned emotional response) paradigm in which conditioning could be assessed early in the ISI, prior to CS offset. The CER paradigm involves the imposition of a classical conditioning procedure on stable operant responding. Introduction of a CS which signals a noxious US produces a suppression of the ongoing operant responding, presumably by introducing competing responses (CERs) in the ISI, and the extent of the suppression indexes the extent of classical conditioning.

The operant task consisted of sucking to produce rotation of a doll mounted on a disk over the crib. Each criterion suck (individually determined) rotated the doll through 22.5° of arc, with sixteen sucks producing a complete rotation (see Figure 4). Twelve 6-week-olds were initially trained on a continuous reinforce-

Figure 4   A 6-week-old infant performing the operant phase of the CER task used by Little (1973). Each criterion suck produced a 22.5° rotation of the doll.

ment schedule and subsequently shifted to a mixed schedule until single-session response rates were high and stable. Thereafter, infants in the two experimental groups (Trace, Delay) received six CS–US pairings at a minimum of 1 min apart in each session. The CS and US were the same as in the previous studies, but the ISI was 15 s and the duration of the US was 5 s. For the Delay group, the CS was 20 s, overlapping and terminating with the US. For the Trace group, CS duration was 13.6 s and the trace interval was 1.4 s, as before. Infants in a random CS–US control group received a different schedule of randomly ordered stimuli in each session. Infants in the experimental groups were trained to a suppression criterion, whereas infants in the control group were maintained for as many sessions as were required for all infants in the other groups to meet criterion. Suppression ratios of the form $B/A + B$ ($A =$ total sucks in the pre-CS minute; $B =$ total sucks during the CS) were comparable for the three groups at the outset of conditioning, but by the conclusion of training, the two experimental groups had both reached criterion and exhibited significant and equivalent suppression (see Figure 5). Moreover, both Trace and Delay groups attained criterion with equal rapidity and the establishment of the CER was gradual.

The findings indicate that the relatively poor performance of infants in trace conditioning procedures may be attributable to non-associative factors rather than to a learning deficit. Further, they emphasize the relation between habituation and conditionability and demonstrate the impact upon conditioning performance of competing responses. We concur with Little (1973) that developmental differences in the habituation of orienting may comprise a major source of demonstrated age differences in conditioning. More generally, the findings illustrate that the experimenter's ingenuity and persistence may be the limiting factors in our understanding of infant capacity.

The defensive reflexes are among the most primitive unconditional responses of phylogeny and ontogeny; it is paradoxical that evidence of their conditionability in young infants is so difficult to obtain. Similarly, from an energy

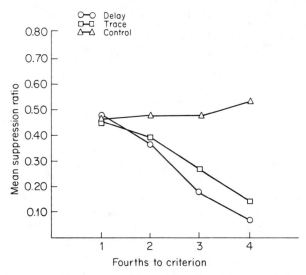

Figure 5   Mean suppression ratios of infants in Trace, Delay, or Random Control groups at comparable points in acquisition of a CER. (From Little, 1973).

cost-benefit perspective, it would seem to be advantageous for the newborn to stop producing active and costly responses which do not produce important consequences. Why is it so difficult to demonstrate this in the young infant? First, in altricial species, it is the function of the parent to protect the offspring against environmental danger. The very young typically remain in the nest or in close proximity to the parent. As the infant matures, this protective function is gradually shifted, and by the time sexual maturity has been attained, the transfer from parent to offspring is complete. Therefore, while the infant possesses emergency defensive responses as a 'margin of safety' (Cannon, 1932), noxious stimulation is not a regularly recurring event of infancy and its anticipation does not constitute a problem which, in natural circumstances, infants must solve. Secondly, response persistence is not always maladaptive. The infant who stops crying without achieving either caretaking or the assurance of caretaking, or who 'gives up' rooting or sucking prior to encountering or obtaining a meal is clearly the 'loser' in terms of reproductive fitness. We have alluded previously to the lack of an apparent satiety mechanism in the newborn rat pup; recall that the mother terminated the feeding behaviour (Leon *et al.*, 1978). Whether a particular response will be inhibited or not, therefore, must depend upon the evolutionary history of the organism, the energetic costs versus the potential benefits of the response, and the ontogenetic opportunities to discriminate the occasions in which the response is most likely to be successful. Early in infancy, it would appear than an optimal strategy is perseverance.

Additional evidence of the interactions between habituation and conditioning and of the specificity of learning is contained in the animal literature. Rudy and Cheatle (1977) placed groups of 2-day-old rat pups into a container bearing a lemon odour and, after 5 min, injected them with either an illness-inducing US (lithium chloride) or saline. Pups were replaced in the container and those who became ill there exhibited conditioned odour aversions in subsequent tests. Their avoidance of lemon-scented pine shavings persisted for at least 6 days. Smith and Spear (1978) hypothesized that the conditioning observed by Rudy and Cheatle might have been facilitated by the presence of littermates during the conditioning. They had previously found that familiar cues (e.g. home shavings) facilitated passive avoidance conditioning and spontaneous alternation behaviour in infant rat pups. They repeated the Rudy and Cheatle procedure but trained half of the pups in each injection condition in isolation. Pups injected with lithium chloride in isolation exhibited neither classical conditioning nor retention. Subsequently it has been found that neonatal rat pups do not readily acquire taste aversions in an environment which has been associated with the nursing context (Martin and Alberts, 1979; Spear, 1979), where they typically learn the characteristics of their adult diets. Thus one must question what it is that the infant typically learns and where he typically learns it before attributing negative evidence to a learning deficit. Except in the instance of conditioned taste or odour aversions, most often a familiar training environment enhances conditioning of newborns and infants but has less of an effect on adult conditioning; conversely, the familiarity of the test environment affects adults performance more severely.

The preceding studies demonstrate that inhibitory and conditioning deficiencies which have previously been attributed to immaturity may simply reflect the nature of the conditioning task in relation to the organism's capabilities, the evolutionary significance of the experimental problem, and the extent to which the context within which the task is presented acts as a 'setting event' (Lipsitt, 1972) for conditioning. Familiar cues in a novel setting may minimize orienting reactions which compete with the development of the CR and which distract from effective conditioning cues. Adults, for whom the habituation of orienting is relatively rapid, would not be expected to benefit from procedures which further hasten habituation. Given the proper circumstances, conditioning will be exhibited in the neonate; in other circumstances it will not or it will occur only slowly. Thus the development of conditioned responding appears to depend upon non-associative environmental factors and does not reflect prewired or 'prepared' stimulus-response associations.

Hybrid Conditioning Procedures and Instrumental Learning

The distinctions between classical and instrumental conditioning are far from clear-cut, with both paradigms yielding behaviours containing components of each. In classical eyelid conditioning, for example, the CR is timed to anticipate the US in such a manner that the noxious effects of the US are avoided (Little, 1973). Sameroff (1971, 1972) has contended that demonstrations of neonatal classical conditioning are, in fact, instances of instrumental conditioning. Although this argument is contradicted by recent research (Little, 1973; Rudy and Cheatle, 1977; Smith and Spear, 1978), it is also true that much of the newborn's learning does not readily fit either of the two paradigms. The most critical question appears to be how the newborn uses certain general characteristics of his environment and develops specific behaviours appropriate to it.

To answer this, we must recall that the newborn differs little in the first few days and weeks of life from other newborn mammals, only later beginning the transition to a unique cultural organism (cf. Hinde, in press). The newborn monkey, once it has been pulled from the birth canal by its mother, must climb her ventrum and locate her nipples without assistance. This is accomplished through a combination of negative geotaxis and thermotaxis (Rosenblum, in press; Rosenblum and Youngstein, 1973). The human newborn receives assistance but also must locate the breast. The probability of doing this is increased by a propensity to root towards stimuli that touch the cheek or oral area, the rooting being more intense before (but not following) a feed if the stimulus is warm (Peiper, 1963). Experimental procedures which have exploited this adaptation have demonstrated the adeptness with which the newborn solves this highly specific but critical problem.

Papousek (1961, 1967, 1970) tested infants daily from birth at the time of their regular feedings and measured the rapidity with which their rooting behaviours (head-turning) were modified by experimenter-arranged contingencies. He sounded an acoustic stimulus (CS), and if the infant's head rotated to the left, the infant received milk from a bottle at the end of the arc of rotation. If an infant's head did not turn within 10 s of the CS, his left cheek was stroked with a nipple (US); if this failed to elicit ipsilateral rooting (UR), the infant's head was physically rotated through the arc. The biological significance of the behavioural sequence is clear; not only does rooting in the cued direction produce access to milk, but a shorter latency results in a faster encounter. Papousek (1970) reported that newborns receiving 10 trials/day attained a criterion of conditioning within 28 days, although some infants did so within 7–12 days. Relative to infants initially trained at 12 weeks, newborns were more variable, learned more slowly, and attained a lower conditioning asymptote (see also Gekoski, 1977; Little, 1970).

Using a similar procedure but with a dextrose solution as the reinforcer, Siqueland and Lipsitt (1966) demonstrated that infants as young as 48–96 h could maximize their encounter rate with a nutrient within less than an hour in a single session. In the last of three studies, they presented 16 newborns with

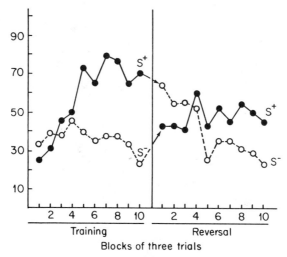

Figure 6   Percent head-turns to positive and negative stimuli during original training and reversal trials with newborn infants. Response to S + was reinforced with a dextrose solution, and S + and S − were a tone and buzzer, respectively, counterbalanced over subjects. (Reproduced by permission of Academic Press. From E. R. Siqueland and L. P. Lipsitt (1966). *Journal of Experimental Child Psychology*, **3**, 356–376.)

pairings of either a buzzer or a tone and tactile stimulation of the right cheek. Only one of the acoustic stimuli was correlated with dextrose (S +), which was presented following a right head-turn. As seen in Figure 6, responding to S + increased while that to S − (the other acoustic stimulus) did not change. When the stimuli defining S + and S − were reversed, the newborn's response pattern also shifted. These findings illustrate the speed and precision with which the newborn acquires and uses information which signals not only 'where' but also 'when' to seek food.

The generality of this type of conditioning is demonstrated in a recent study of appetitive conditioning in newborn rat pups (Johanson and Hall, 1979). They

Figure 7 A newborn rat pup performing an operant response of probing upward on a terrycloth-covered paddle. An upward force of approximately 3 g closed a microswitch and produced a brief milk infusion via the intra-oral cannula. (Photograph courtesy of Ingrid Johanson and W. G. Hall; photographed by A. Johnson)

placed newborn pups in a styrofoam cup containing a terry-cloth paddle which, when probed upward, resulted in the infusion of 3–4 ml of milk into the oral cavity via a cannula which had been implanted 30 min earlier (see Figure 7). Pups had been allowed 6–8 h of postnatal sucking access prior to testing. Relative to littermate yolked controls (paddle and infusion but no contingency) and deprived controls (paddle but no infusion), experimental pups probed the paddle significantly more often during acquisition and persisted responding significantly longer during extinction. In a second study, Johanson and Hall placed two paddles in the container and saturated a terry-cloth triangle (see Figure 8) beneath each with a different odour (S + , S −). Within 12 h, six of eight pups in the experimental group had acquired the discrimination, some doing so in an hour or two. In contrast, yoked controls not only failed to respond differentially but also showed an overall lower rate of paddle pushing. When S + and S − were reversed for five pups, four achieved the reversal within 10 h (one doing so within 2 h), while the fifth increased responding on the previous S − (now S +) but

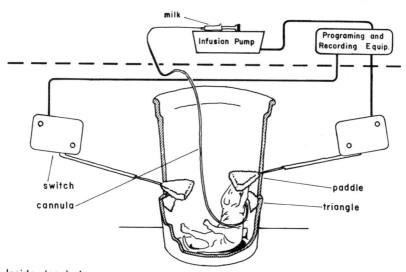

Outside Incubator

milk

Infusion Pump

Programing and Recording Equip.

switch

cannula

paddle

triangle

Inside Incubator

Figure 8   The two-paddle apparatus used in the discrimination conditioning of an operant paddle-probe response of newborn rat pups. Odourants used as discriminative stimuli were placed on terrycloth triangles beneath the paddles. Each correct response resulted in a brief intra-oral milk infusion. The styrofoam cup was housed in an incubator maintained at 33°C. (Copyright 1979 by the American Association for the Advancement of Science. Reproduced with permission of the authors and copyright holder from I. B. Johanson and W. G. Hall (1979). *Science*, **205**, 419–421.)

persisted in responding to the previously reinforced paddle as well. These findings closely parallel those of Siqueland and Lipsitt (1966) and demonstrate that paradigms which do not interfere with normal neonatal regulatory behaviours but, in fact, capitalize on them offer considerable possibilities for the assessment of newborn learning and memory (see also Thoman *et al.*, 1968).

Other hybrid procedures have focused on the efficacy of novel reinforcers in maintaining elicited (Koch, 1967) or free-operant (Siqueland, 1968, 1969a) responding. Investigators using aversive stimulation commonly must prevent the infant's adaptation to it by gradually increasing US intensity over repeated presentations (e.g., Brackbill, 1977). Koch (1967) reinforced infant headturns (UR) elicited by calling to the infant from one side of the crib (US) with visual access to either the mother, a stranger, a succession of novel toys over trials, etc. An acoustic CS sounded at the outset of each trial, and CRs were measured within the ISI. Although infants initially turned towards the mother when called, they did not exhibit anticipatory head-turning toward her; moreover, after eight sessions, infants began to behave negatively to both the CS and US (crying, turning away), refusing even to let their heads be turned in the direction of the mother. In contrast, the other stimuli were effective in establishing anticipatory CRs, with the novel toys being the most efficacious. On the one hand, it could be argued that the infants had learned to expect that one or more social consequences (e.g., being picked up, talked to, smiled at, etc.) typically follow when they orient towards a familiar figure (the mother) and, when these consequences did not occur, the infants responded negatively and exhibited avoidance responses. (Such consequences would not be expected from strangers or toys!) An alternative account, consistent with animal conditioning studies involving acoustic USs, is in terms of habituation to the US (Rescorla, 1973). That is, the more novel the visual consequences of an orienting response (UR), the greater the potency of the US which, in turn, influences CR production. Both the Papousek (1970) and Koch (1967) studies illustrate the value of incorporating natural behavioural sequences into research paradigms. Just as rooting typically leads to milk provision, orienting toward a sound source typically results in visual access to the source.

While Koch (1967) minimized US habituation by means of novel UR consequences, Siqueland and his associates (Eimas *et al.*, 1971; Milewski, 1976; Milewski and Siqueland, 1975; Siqueland, 1968, 1969a, 1969b; Werner and Siqueland, 1978) exploited the declining efficacy of reinforcers as a means of assessing the dimensions of stimulation which infants could discriminate (high-amplitude sucking/recovery paradigm) and the effects of prior stimulus exposure on reinforcer efficacy (high-amplitude sucking satiation paradigm). They made presentation of a visual or auditory conjugate reinforcer (cf. Rovee-Collier and Gekoski, 1979) contingent upon the emission of a 'high-amplitude' suck (e.g., exceeding 18 mm Hg) on a non-nutritive nipple. Response persistence reflected the duration of familiarization experience, and 4-week-old infants took longer to satiate than 16-week-olds (Siqueland, 1968, 1969a, 1969b). Following partial satiation of the reinforcer, they altered one or more dimensions of the response-contingent stimulus and observed the extent to which high-amplitude sucking was reinstated. This work has provided extensive and detailed descriptions of neonatal perceptual abilities.

A number of reviews have focussed on instrumental conditioning in infants and have included reference to research within the neonatal period (Fitzgerald and Porges, 1971; Hulsebus, 1973; Rovee-Collier and Gekoski, 1979; Siqueland, 1969a, 1969b; Williemsen, 1979). Without exception, these have depicted the newborn as particularly competent in modifying and controlling his environment. Notably, all of the instrumental responses which have been conditioned in infants less than 4 weeks of age have been low-energy responses which can be produced for relatively lengthy periods at little cost to the organism. These include eye opening (Siqueland, 1969b), sucking (Cairns and Butterfield, 1975; DeCasper and Fifer, 1980; Kobre and Lipsitt, 1972; Kron, 1966; Lipsitt and Kaye, 1964; Mills and Melhuish, 1974; Sameroff, 1968; Siqueland, 1969a, 1969b), and perhaps, head-turning (Papousek, 1961), although this frequently requires an eliciting stimulus in newborn paradigms. Little or no success has been achieved in attempts to condition high-energy responses such as footkicking (Solkoff and Cotton, 1975) prior to the time that the infant achieves physiological control over body temperature (4–9 weeks). As reflexive thermo-regulation becomes more efficient over the first 6–8 weeks infants emit increasing numbers of varied and energetic responses, and attain increasingly high asymptotes of conditioning (e.g., Gekoski, 1977). Even in the performance of low-energy responses which do not challenge growth or disrupt behavioural thermal homeostasis, however, the newborn is highly sensitive to response cost and behaves in a manner which maximizes the benefits of a given activity in relation to its energetic cost (Rovee-Collier and Gekoski, 1979). Sameroff (1968), for example, observed that most infants occasionally omitted an irrelevant suction component of sucking when milk provision was made contingent upon the expression component only. Further, when high and low amplitudes of each component were differentially reinforced in succeeding studies, infants exhibited response amplitudes which approached the minimum requirement for milk provision. In other words, infants did not work harder than necessary to obtain milk, even though it would have been forthcoming had response amplitudes been maintained at higher levels. Skinner (1938) described the tendency of organisms to adopt easy and efficient response forms in the absence of specific external contingencies for doing so as 'spontaneous topographical differentiation'. This has also been demonstrated in the free-operant mobile conjugate reinforcement paradigm with infants as young as 8 weeks (Rovee-Collier et al., 1978) and probably characterizes the behaviour of newborns of all species during learning, although the concentration of researchers on the simple presence or absence (or rate) of a global response instead of on the changing behavioural components which define the response in a given situation (cf. Bindra, 1961) precludes detection of shifts in response form.

Other findings, such as the rapidity with which newborns alter suck rate as a function of the nature of quantity of an ingestant (Crook, 1976; Crook and Lipsitt, 1976; Kobre and Lipsitt, 1972) or the tactile characteristics of an intraoral stimulus in relation to the nutritional consequences of the stimulus (Lipsitt and Kaye, 1964; Lipsitt et al., 1966) testify to the facility with which the newborn can extract and use environmental information in developing efficient response forms which optimize growth.

MEMORY IN THE NEONATAL PERIOD

To the extent that tests of learning are, in fact, tests of memory (Bolles, 1976), we have reviewed much of the evidence of newborn memorial abilities already. In spite of the importance which has been accorded early experiences for subsequent development, however, there has been almost no documentation of long-term (i.e., between-session) memory in very young infants. With three exceptions (Little, 1970, 1973; Papousek, 1970), the research reviewed above has focussed on behavioural changes within a single session or has not permitted analysis of response carry-over from one session to the next (but see Keen et al., 1965, and Sameroff, 1968, 1972).

In older infants, retention is typically assessed by means of habituation-discrimination paradigms (e.g. Cohen and Gelber, 1975, paired-comparison paradigms (e.g. Fagan, 1970) or conditioning paradigms (Little. 1970; Rovee and Fagen, 1976). The first two of these have been used to assess recognition memory and are based on the Sokolovian (1963) model which presumes that greater attention to a novel stimulus indexes the extent to which the familiarized stimulus is remembered. If attention is non-differentially distributed between familiarized and novel stimuli, or if response renewal occurs equally to both stimulus types following habituation, a memory failure is generally inferred from the negative evidence. Conditioning analyses are modelled after animal memory studies in which a distinctive response is trained in a given context and, at a later point in time, the experimenter returns the organism to the context and observes whether or not the response is still produced. Retention is measured directly, in terms of responding during cued-recall tests prior to the reintroduction of reinforcement (Davis and Rovee-Collier, 1979; Sullivan et al., 1979) or during reacquisition, in terms of savings (Little, 1973; for review, see Rovee-Collier and Fagen, 1981).

Kaplan (1967) found no evidence of differential fixation of pre-exposed and novel stimuli in infants tested longitudinally prior to 84 days of age, although all had received daily stimulus exposures beginning at 42 days of age. Weizmann et al. (1971) modified her design, initiating the familiarization routine at 28 days of age and testing groups at 42 and 56 days (or only at 56 days) in a novel or familiar bassinet. They reported that 42-day-old infants fixated familiar stimuli for a significantly longer period than novel stimuli and that 56-day-old females who had been tested 2 weeks earlier fixated all test stimuli less than infants tested for the first time at 56 days. However, the inconsistencies in the infancy literature regarding sex differences in visual attention measures, the complexity of their statistical interactions, and the discrepancy between their findings and those of Kaplan (1967) make interpretations of long-term memory difficult.

In contrast, Werner and Siqueland (1978) tested premature infants in two sessions (counterbalanced within-subjects for order of experimental and control conditions) and retested almost half of the original group during a partial replication in two additional sessions. In the original sessions, the newborns exhibited a significant increase in high-amplitude sucking following a shift in the colour and pattern of a visual reinforcer relative to their own no-shift performance. In the partial replication, they exhibited even greater differences in post-shift relative to no-shift performance. This could have resulted from either a greater decline during continued familiarization in the no-shift condition, from a sharpening of post-shift discrimination, or both. Given the care with which state factors were controlled, however, these data strongly implicate long-term retention for at least 24 h (cf. Keen et al., 1965).

Retention of speech stimuli over extended periods was reported by Ungerer et al., (1978) using a modified retention paradigm in which infant facial expressions and eye and head movements indexed stimulus recognition. Mothers repeated one of two words ('tinder', 'beguile') 60 times daily beginning when their infants were 14 days old. Recognition tests of the familiarized and novel word as well as of the infant's own name were conducted 7, 10, 13, and 14 days later. The average retention interval averaged 14 h for the first three tests and 42 h for the final test when infants were 28 days old. Relative to a control group which received no repetitions, the experimental group exhibited differential responsiveness to the two words in the final two tests. Because of the exposure to stimulus words in the third test, however, performance in the final test must be viewed as evidence of 28-h rather than 42-h retention.

Conditioning analyses have provided evidence of lengthier retention at earlier ages than has been obtained with other techniques. In the Little (1970) study, for example, 20-day-old infants demonstrated significant savings during reacquisition 10 days following initial training, outperforming 30-day-olds being trained for the first time. No evidence of savings was seen, however, in the reacquisition performance of 20-day-olds whose first session had occurred at 10 days of age. Davis and Rovee-Collier (1979) found that many 8-week-olds were superior to 12-week-olds during cued-recall tests of instrumental responding after a 14-day interval, in spite of their poorer initial conditioning performance. This finding raises questions regarding the nature of ontogenetic changes in memory. Campbell and his associates (Campbell and Coulter, 1976; Campbell and Spear, 1972) have attributed the poorer retention of immature organisms to neurological and perceptual changes which alter either the nature of stored memory attributes or subsequent access to them. Recently, Spear (1979) has suggested that younger organisms may store either qualitatively different memory attributes or simply fewer of them. Most animal research on infantile amnesia, however, has involved relatively simple tasks which do not produce initial acquisition differences. In the Little (1970) study, poor initial conditioning performance may have resulted in the poor retention by the youngest group. On the other hand, this interpretation would be challenged by the Davis and Rovee-Collier (1979) report. Since information regarding infant memory is sparse, it is probably more appropriate to reserve the concept of infantile amnesia to developmental differences observed in retention tests which span intervals sufficiently lengthy as to permit relatively large-scale changes in neurological and psychological development.

Alternatively, the 8-week-olds in the Davis and Rovee-Collier study (see also Gekoski, 1977) may have *learned* the contingency between footkicks and mobile movement (the reinforcer) quite readily, as one would infer from their retention performance, but were constrained from performing the energetically costly response at a high level during acquisition at the younger age. Thus the level of conditioning attained by infants of different ages must be viewed not solely as an index of their learning ability but also as a manifestation of the infant's solution to the more general problem of energy conservation.

Recent findings in the animal infant literature suggest that some associations may be retained more readily and over longer periods than others. Odour aversions conditioned in 2-day-old rat pups are still exhibited 6 days later (Rudy and Cheatle, 1977), but shock escape (Misanin et al., 1971; Nagy and Murphy, 1974) or avoidance (Spear and Smith, 1978) is poorly retained by 7-day-old rodents for 24 h. Finally, recent procedures developed with animals (Campbell and Jaynes, 1966; Spear, 1973, 1976; Spear and Parsons, 1976) which involve the presentation of reminders have been shown to alleviate forgetting in infant rats (Hamberg and Spear, 1978) as well as in children (Hoving et al., 1972) and, after periods as long as 4 weeks, in 3-month-old infants (Rovee-Collier et al., 1980). The latter finding strongly supports the hypothesis that reinstatement is a major means by which early experiences influence later behaviour (Campbell and Jaynes, 1966). It appears that conditioning analyses of newborn and infant long-term memory hold considerable promise.

CLINICAL IMPLICATIONS OF REFLEXIVE TRANSITIONS: CRIB DEATH

With increasing physiological regulation of body temperature, the neonate is freer to engage the environment and to manipulate it more actively. The period between 2 and 4 months, roughly, seems to represent a major transitional phase for the embellishment and voluntary expression of many reflexes which had been previously elicited only under highly circumscribed conditions (Lipsitt, 1976; McGraw, 1943). The classic work of McGraw on the swimming reflex in young infants, and its waning over time, suggests that primitive reflex patterns are supplanted eventually by more deliberative, probably learned, patterns of behaviour with organizations of their own. The transitional period described by McGraw seems to lie within the aforementioned age period. Interestingly, this is precisely the period of greatest risk of crib death and, although McGraw did not allude to the sudden infant-death phenomenon, she did in fact describe the transitional period as one involving neurobehavioural disorganization and disarray. Figure 9 shows the three distinct phases of reflex development and transition: the waning of the basic reflex, the onset of a transitional period of response confusion, and the eventual predominance of a more 'mature' learned response. McGraw supposed that the transition is one essentially from sub-cortical to cortical responding.

There have been few studies of the role of practice in facilitating the transition from obligatory reflexive responding to what might be regarded as operant

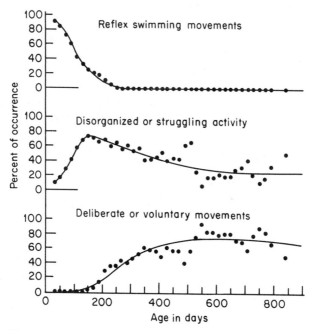

Figure 9   The three phases of infant reflex development as described by McGraw (1943). The example is that of the swimming reflex. Note that as the reflex component wanes, the voluntary or learned component increases in frequency, and that an intermediary period of 'confusion' peaks at about 150 days of age

responding. In the case of ambulatory behaviour, the facility with which the transition is ultimately accomplished appears to be related to the extent to which the reflexive components of the eventual voluntary behaviours were previously exercised (Konner, 1973; Zelazo, 1976; Zelazo et al., 1972). The adaptive value of practicing motor skills, particularly those involving extensive coordination or split-second timing, has in fact been extensively documented in the animal literature (e.g. Kavanau, 1967). Variability in environmental opportunities to exercise these skills as well as normal individual variation in reflex characteristics, however, leads to the culling of some infants during developmental transitional periods whose behaviour patterns are inadequate at moments critical to survival.

It is reasonable to presume that variation in environmental opportunity to exercise reflexes, and the emerging skills which capitalize upon the prior presence of those congenital reflexes, will have some bearing on how smoothly the infant will traverse the transitional period of confusion or disarray. By the same token, to the extent that the quality of the initial reflex upon which later behaviour will ultimately be based is compromised by birth defect, perinatal hazards, or environmental insufficiencies, one might presume that the practice apparently required for the transition through the period of confusion and into a period of adaptive, cortically mediated learning might be less effective. An ineffective transition may well lead to some condition of developmental jeopardy and perhaps even a life crisis in the first year. It is an exciting developmental and clinical prospect that, for purposes of implementing 'experiential prostheses', the *process of maturation* may be more important than the *achievement of maturation*. Experiences endured in the course of maturation may be precisely those responsible for the kinds of learning that endure most profoundly. Similarly, infants born at risk or presenting signs of developmental jeopardy within the first year of life might be just the infants who require special experiential interventions to enable them to surmount the developmental obstacles inherent in the periods of neuro-behavioural transition.

About 8000 babies each year in the United States alone die, most of them between 2 and 4 months of age, without having manifested any diagnosable problem prior to their deaths. While some of these infants seem, on close examination of perinatal history or through an incisive autopsy, to have had predisposing deficits, most die of as yet undiscovered causes. Recent indications, however, suggest that congenital or constitutional factors may conspire with environmental insufficiencies in some cases (Lipsitt, 1971, 1976).

The most common 'cause' of death in the first year of life, excluding the especially hazardous first few days of life, crib death shows some seasonal variation, with peaks in the winter or spring for the United States. More cases of sudden infant death syndrome (SIDS) occur during a sleep period, and the infants are usually found in the morning after no apparent sign of struggle. Babies who succumb to crib death simply stop breathing, as least as far as most later inquiries can determine. There is usually no evidence of any agonal experience, no sign of pain or struggle. Perhaps significantly, a mild upper respiratory infection is found in 40–50 per cent of the cases, with parents reporting a runny nose or raspy breathing. There is seldom any fever. The baby has been regarded in the few days immediately preceding the death as essentially normal (Valdes-Dapena, 1978).

Several recent publications (e.g. Anderson and Rosenblith, 1971; Lipsitt, 1976, 1978; Lipsitt et al., 1979; Naeye et al., 1976; Protestos et al., 1973; Steinschneider, 1975; Thoman et al., 1977) have provided evidence suggesting strongly that babies who succumb to crib death are as a group (but there are, of course, many exceptions) the products of difficult gestation and birth, and that a number of indices of physiological and behavioural insufficiency are present in the earliest days and weeks of life. Crib death infants are more frequently premature or small for their gestational age, more often require delivery of oxygen at birth, and more frequently show indications of respiratory distress in the few days immediately following birth. While most infants who eventually become cases of crib death are discharged from hospital as essentially normal, and most have been considered asymptomatic right up to the moment of their death, statistical examination of the birth and developmental records reveals that, contrasted with appropriate control cases, they have often harboured signs each of which while not alarming, taken as a constellation might constitute a pattern of jeopardy. In brief, it appears that the histories of SIDS cases often reveal hazardous signs of respiratory instability, behavioural lethargy, and inability to engage in appropriate defensive manoeuvers in response to aversive or annoying stimulation (Lipsitt, 1976). As a result of perinatal adversities or early developmental lethargy, often involving periodic apnoeic spells and associated anoxia, eventual SIDS victims often seem to have generally subdued activity. Consequently, they suck weakly, they move less, they respond with higher thresholds to noxious events, and in general engage their environment less. It is not unlikely that such infants subject themselves to fewer opportunities for learning than 'normal' infants do.

Although considerable medical attention has been devoted to the problem of crib death, only recently have the infant's behavioural contributions to his own fitness (Lipsitt, 1976, 1978) been considered seriously. Both Naeye (Naeye et al., 1976) and Valdes-Dapena (1980), two prominent American pathologists studying crib death, have recently documented or acknowledged behavioural insufficiencies or idiosyncrasies as relevant and worthy of further research.

Lest it seem unusual to suggest that a stimulation and learning aberration may contribute to infantile death, it should be remembered that both Spitz (1946) and Goldfarb (1945) have spoken convincingly of the debilitating effects, including death, of certain types of adverse environments that have been implemented for human infants. Psychobiological researchers have for some time (e.g., Cannon, 1932; Richter, 1957; Seligman, 1975), moreover, called attention to the phenomenon of death in adults and animals from psychological causes—e.g.

soldiers giving up and dying on the battlefield without apparent cause, spouses dying shortly after the deaths of their partners, and animals giving up and dying in apparent desperation and despondency when confronted with life stresses that seem inescapable. Seligman (1975) has described the conditioning paradigms that seem to promote helplessness and hopelessness which can lead to stupor and death.

Some congenital responses of the newborn have much adaptive significance. They promote survival and adaptation to the biological condition of the species (Emde and Robinson, 1976). When the infant is touched on one side of the mouth or the other, for example, the head turns ipsilaterally, whereupon mouth opening occurs and is further promoted by continuing contact with the touch stimulus. When a nipple is placed in the infant's mouth, as is usual under such circumstances, the lips close around it, a pressure seal is created, and sucking ensues in regular rhythm depending in part on the shape of the oral stimulus and on the quality or 'incentive value' of the fluid which the infant receives. The sucking response is in fact modulated in several of its dimensions by the sweetness of the fluid. The 'incentives' for sucking are operative from the earliest moments after birth (Lipsitt, 1976).

Innate response systems which are strikingly apparent at birth and soon after (e.g. the grasping reflex, the Babkin response, primitive reaching responses, and obligatory visual attention) diminish in their frequency and intensity with time, up to around two or three months of age (McGraw, 1943; Paine, 1976). The firm grasp reflex, for instance, becomes a slow exploratory mode of behaviour in response to sudden pressure of an object on the palm of the hand. At least some of these response propensities are later displaced or complemented by learned responses mediated by higher cortical centres. Such 'voluntary' responses stand in contrast to the brain-stem control that existed before experience could superimpose itself upon the lower-brain function. Much brain tissue maturation occurs shortly after birth, and particularly in the first 2 months of human life (Bronson, Chapter 5, this volume; Dobbing, 1975; Purpura, 1975). This period of rapid development of neural function is in some respects critical for the experiential accretion of certain learned responses; some behavioural patterns apparently *must* be learned during this time. The relevant age may be the time by which the unlearned protective reflexes have diminished to an ineffective level. Otherwise, the organism might not have been prepared adequately for survival.

The response of the normal neonate to respiratory occlusion, or even to the *threat* of occlusion as imposed by the presence of a covering over a part of the baby's face, is for a series of defensive actions to be taken (Brazelton, 1973; Graham, 1956). The pediatrician Gunther (1955, 1961) observed such struggling of newborns as they suckled at the breast. The response pattern is rather like an enraged response which escalates as the stimulus is prolonged. At birth and in the intact organism, the behaviour pattern is essentially fail-safe, culminating in crying and ultimately freeing the respiratory passages. If the newborn does not have a strong head-and-hand defensive response to threats to respiration or to head restraint, however, it is possible that the appropriate voluntary operant behaviours which must ultimately supplant this congenital response by 2–4 months of age will not become learned.

This supposition seems to have validity as a hypothesis, both in terms of the circumstances usually surrounding crib death and in consideration of data already available. SIDS cases have as a group begun life with some organismic deficits associated with perinatal stresses. Infants who succumb in the first year of life without any obvious fatal disease are demonstrably, as a group, mildly deficient in their responses to respiratory occlusion at birth or were in some other respect behaviourally lethargic (Anderson and Rosenblith, 1971; Lipsitt, 1976; Purves, 1974). Moreover, the data of Steinschneider (1975), Thoman et al. (1976), and others, point to respiratory anomalies in many histories of crib death and near-miss cases. Respiratory occlusion, failure of appropriate defensive behaviour, and inadequate compensatory mouth-breathing when the nostrils are clogged could conceivably lead to anoxia and a comatose state, and ultimately to the infant's death, particularly when all of these conditions converge (as in sleeping infants with a cold and a history of insufficient response to threatening stimulation). Such a pathway to death might involve no agonal responses whatever, as the eventual death might well have occurred in a comatose child.

A hypothesis worthy of serious investigation, then, is that infants who have not learned to engage in responses necessary for clearing of the respiratory passages, or clearing the way *to* those passages when threatened with occlusion, will be those in particular jeopardy at the vulnerable age range for crib death. The plausibility of the proposition derives presently from circumstantial evidence, arguing for crib death as a consequence of the interaction of minimal congenital deficiencies with environmental conditions that fail to ameliorate the basically organic deficit. Through the implementation of intervention studies, the hypothesis can be subjected to experimental scrutiny.

FINAL COMMENT

There is considerable evidence that the major impact of birth on mammalian young is the abrupt transition from a water-living to a land-living existence (Adolph, 1968; Hull, 1973). This transition requires a number of physiological and behavioural solutions to the problems associated with maintenance of the *internal milieu* (Cannon, 1932) in a dry, dessicating and thermally variable environment and one in which food and water resources are discontinuous. Although a number of physiological regulations are triggered at birth (e.g., use of the lungs), a large number of them develop only gradually after birth. The behavioural solutions upon which the newborn must depend must necessarily vary as a function of the momentary conditions of a variable and unique environment. In fact, the variability of the environment virtually precludes the possibility that *specific* stimulus-response associations are preprogrammed. Rather, information about the structure of the environment is more efficiently stored directly in the environment (e.g. Jeffrey, 1976; p. 284) than in the brain, and even the youngest organism must be able to extract and use this environmental information rapidly. Because the number of critical problems unique to the newborn are relatively small, the newborn's behaviours can be focussed, and solutions can be acquired with rapidity.

It is this rapidity, however, which has led critics of infant learning research (Sameroff, 1971, 1972; Sameroff and Cavanagh, 1979) to argue that newborns do not learn to use environmental information but simply exhibit prewired stimulus-response associations which have special biological significance. Sameroff and Cavanagh (1979) view the appearance of differences in experimental and control performance within an initial block of learning trials (Clifton, Meyers, and Solomon, 1972; Clifton, Siqueland, and Lipsitt, 1972; Lipsitt *et al.*, 1966) as too rapid to reflect learning processes.

Paradoxically, were the infant less competent (i.e. were conditioning curves more gradual), this would satisfy Sameroff's criterion for the implication of learning. Given his emphasis on the newborn as a biological organism, the question of newborn conditionability must be applied equally to the behaviours of all species. Recent findings with animal young (Martin and Alberts, 1979; Smith *et al.*, 1979; Smith and Spear, 1978; Spear, 1979), showing that the familiarity of the training and testing context is a major determinant of the acquisition and expression of conditioning, challenge the speed-of-learning criterion as a basis for distinguishing between prepared and learned associations (Sameroff and Cavanagh, 1979; p. 363). For example, neonatal rat pups learn conditioned taste aversions in novel but not in familiar settings; this is understandable in view of the fact that they learn what to eat 'at home' (Martin and Alberts, 1979). If acquisition were slowed by the addition of novel cues to the training context, would this constitute a stronger demonstration of learning than if fewer were present and acquisition of the very same stimulus-response association were then achieved in only one or two trials? Obviously, some associations (e.g., conditioned taste or odour aversions) are so critical that multiple trials could be fatal. Associations which are critical to survival and which can only be learned *ex utero*, with reference to a particular environmental context, are learned rapidly whether the stimuli are highly artificial or not (Thoman *et al.*, 1968), attesting to the behavioural plasticity of the newborn. Finally, it should be noted that the Sameroff-Cavanagh distinction between *prepared* and *learned* associations is not universally recognized, although the concept of preparedness (Seligman, 1970) is. Most learning psychologists agree that some associations are more readily acquired than others, but few argue that those which are acquired readily, even in a single trial, are not learned.

Unquestionably, successful demonstrations of learning in the newborn capitalize upon the biological response systems (e.g. sucking, rooting) which directly affect survival. However, these responses are not used exclusively in association with biologically correlated consequences. For example, newborn sucking bursts increase in duration when synchronously reinforced with music (i.e., when duration of the music is determined by the duration of a burst) and decrease in duration when interburst pauses are synchronously reinforced (Cairns and Butterfield, 1975); similarly, eye-opening by premature infants increases when reinforced by contingent (but not non-contingent) auditory stimulation (Siqueland, 1969b). In short, it appears that infants are equipped with a repertoire of phylogenetically successful responses which they apply in a variety of situations. In natural settings, there is a high probability that these responses will produce environmental consequences of value to the organism, either immediate or long-term. The consequences can shape responses and sustain them or eliminate irrelevant or costly responses from the behaviours applied to a particular problem. At the same time, the infant rapidly learns the stimulus occasions which signal those consequences, thus eliminating energetic waste. In these ways, the range of situations which the newborn can effectively anticipate and control are rapidly and efficiently expanded. In fact, it is the generality and not the specificity of early stimulus-response associations which permits the newborn such considerable flexibility in solving survival-related problems (cf. Thoman et al., 1968). That infants can be bottle-reared or aunt-reared demonstrates the advantages of such a plastic arrangement for fitness. Thus the newborn who turns toward warmth and roots, or who sucks on any object, will be most likely to encounter milk; newly hatched chicks or ducklings, by following the first moving object, are most likely (although not certain) to follow their mothers or conspecifics. Lamb (1977) has offered a similar account of the manner in which infants acquire caretaking. Instead of possessing precise genetic definitions of 'breast', 'milk', 'mother', etc., the newborn can possess only the essential, key elements of these important environmental objects (e.g. warmth, fluid, movement, texture) and the phylogenetically successful behaviours likely to procure them. The newborn must learn 'when' and 'where' to make a given response and, because any energetic expenditure affects the entire metabolic economy (Rovee-Collier and Gekoski, 1979), he or she must achieve an optimal response form.

Challenging the empirical facts of learning in the newborn because his accomplishments do not readily fit one or another arbitrary experimental paradigm is raising a false issue which detracts from the critical questions of what the infant must accomplish and how he does it. Simply labelling accomplishments as 'prepared' does not and cannot provide new insights into the processes or mechanisms underlying newborn behavioural change. By exploring the adaptive value of a given accomplishment, as it may have existed historically, we can begin to achieve some of these insights.

Finally, what conclusions can be drawn concerning the extent to which laboratory demonstrations of newborn conditioning actually reflect every-day learning? Sluckin (1970; p. 32) has implied that laboratory studies overestimate the learning competence of the newborn. We conclude, on the contrary, that they grossly *underestimate* newborn competence. This underestimation has resulted from the unquestioning commitment of researchers to the traditions of experimental physics and, in particular, to the Galilean refinement experiment. (As scientists we have regarded the control or elimination of all sources of experimental variation except the independent variable as a worthy methodological goal and have applauded those who have attained it.) These methods have to an extent compromised our conclusions and diminished the apparent behavioural and learning capabilities of the baby under study. The newborn is not a physical object but a complex biological system, shaped by its evolutionary history to solve problems in a complex environment. The attempt to gain precise experimental control has interfered in many instances with the very processes which researchers have sought to measure. The varied sources of environmental stimulation which, to an experimenter, may seem extraneous may constitute the critical parameters of conditioning for the newborn or older infant (cf. Spear, 1979). It is a credit to the flexibility of the newborn that we have been able to obtain so much evidence of learning competence in the midst of so many experimental constraints.

ACKNOWLEDGMENTS

Preparation of this chapter was facilitated by Grants MH 32307 and a James McKeen Cattell Sabbatical Award to Carolyn K. Rovee-Collier and by grants from the Harris Foundation, the W. T. Grant Foundation, and the March of Dimes Birth Defects Foundation to Lewis P. Lipsitt. We thank Jeffrey Alberts, Ingrid Johanson, W. G. Hall, Lynn Hasher, Howard Hoffman, Kenneth Hoving, Arlene Little, Louise Martin, Evelyn Satinoff, and Norman Spear for their generosity in making available unpublished materials used in the preparation of the manuscript. Finally, we thank George H. Collier and Charles F. Flaherty of Rutgers University for critical comments and suggestions which led to the final manuscript.

REFERENCES

Adolph, E. F. (1975). Ontogeny of physiological regulations in the rat, *Quarterly Review of Biology*, **32**, 89–137.
Adolph, E. F. (1968). *Origins of Physiological Regulations*, Academic Press, New York.
Alberts, J. R. (1978). Huddling by rat pups: Group behavioural mechanisms of temperature regulation and energy conservation, *Journal of Comparative and Physiological Psychology*, **92**, 231–245.
Anderson, R. B. and Rosenblith, J. F. (1971). Sudden unexpected death syndrome: Early indicators, *Biologia Neonatorum*, **18**, 395–406.
Bernal, J. (1972). Crying during the first ten days of life, and maternal responses, *Developmental Medicine and Child Neurology*, **14**, 362–372.

Bindra, D. (1961). Components of general activity and the analysis of behavior, *Psychological Review*, **68**, 205–215.

Bishop, P. D. and Kimmel, H. D. (1969). Retention of habituation and conditioning, *Journal of Experimental Psychology*, **81**, 317–321.

Bolles, R. C. (1972). Reinforcement, expectancy, and learning, *Psychological Review*, **79**, 394–409.

Bolles, R. C. (1976). Some relationships between learning and memory, in *Processes of Animal Memory* (Eds. D. L. Medin, W. A. Roberts, and R. T. Davis), pp. 21 – 48, Lawrence Erlbaum, Hillsdale, N. J.

Brackbill, Y. (1977). Behavioral state and temporal conditioning of heart rate in infants, in *New Developments in the Behavioral Research: Theory, Method, and Application* (Eds B. C. Etzel, J. M. LeBlanc, and D. M. Baer). In honor of Sidney W. Bijou. Lawrence Erlbaum, Hillsdale, N. J.

Brackbill, Y. and Fitzgerald, H. E. (1969). Development of the sensory analyzers during infancy, in *Advances in Child Development and Behavior*, Vol. 4 (Eds. L. P. Lipsitt and H. W. Reese), pp. 173–208, Academic Press, New York.

Brackbill, Y. and Fitzgerald, H. E. (1972). Stereotype temporal conditioning in infants, *Psychophysiology*, **9**, 569–577.

Brackbill, Y., Fitzgerald, H. E., and Lintz, L. M. (1967). A developmental study of classical conditioning. *Monographs of the Society for Research in Child Development*, **32** (whole no. 8).

Brackbill, Y. and Koltsova, M. M. (1967). Conditioning and learning, in *Infancy and Early Childhood* (Ed. Y. Brackbill), pp. 205–286, Free Press, New York.

Braun, H. W. and Geiselhart, R. (1959). Age differences in the acquisition and extinction of the conditioned eyelid response, *Journal of Experimental Psychology*, **57**, 386–388.

Brazelton, T. B. (1973). *Neonatal Behavioral Assessment Scale*, J. B. Lippincott, Philadelphia.

Brazelton, T. B., Koslowski, B., and Main, M. (1973). The origins of reciprocity: The early mother-infant interaction, in *The Effect of the Infant on its Caregiver* (Eds M. Lewis and L. A. Rosenblum), pp. 49–75, Wiley, New York.

Brunswick, E. (1952). *The Conceptual Framework of Psychology*, University of Chicago Press, Chicago.

Cairns, G. F. and Butterfield, E. C. (1975). Assessing infants' auditory functioning, in *Exceptional Infant*, Vol. 3 *Assessment and intervention*, (Ed. B. Z. Friedlander), pp. 84–108, Brunner/Mazel, New York.

Caldwell, D. F. and Werboff, J. (1962). Classical conditioning in newborn rats, *Science*, **136**, 1118–1119.

Campbell, B. A. and Coulter, X. (1976). Neural and psychological processes underlying the development of learning and memory, in *Habituation* (Eds T. J. Tighe and R. N. Leaton), pp. 129–157, Lawrence Erlbaum, Hillsdale, N. J.

Campbell, B. A. and Jaynes, J. (1966). Reinstatement, *Psychological Review*, **73**, 478–480.

Campbell, B. A. and Spear, N. E. (1972). Ontogeny of memory, *Psychological Review*, **79**, 215–236.

Cannon, W. B. (1932). *The Wisdom of the Body*, W. W. Norton, New York.

Cattell, P. (1940). *The Measurement of Intelligence of Infants and Young Children*, Psychological Corporation, New York.

Clifton, R. K. (1974). Heart rate conditioning in the newborn infant, *Journal of Experimental Child Psychology*, **18**, 9–21.

Clifton, R. K., Meyers, W. J., and Solomon, G. (1972). Methodological problems in conditioning the head turning response of newborn infants, *Journal of Experimental Child Psychology*, **13**, 29–42.

Clifton, R. K. and Nelson, M. N. (1976). Developmental study of habituation in infants: The importance of paradigm, response system, and state, in *Habituation* (Eds T. J. Tighe and R. N. Leaton), pp. 159–205, Lawrence Erlbaum, Hillsdale, N. J.

Clifton, R. K., Siqueland, E. R., and Lipsitt, L. P. (1972). Conditioned head turning in human newborns as a function of conditioned response requirements and states of wakefulness, *Journal of Experimental Child Psychology*, **13**, 43–57.

Cohen, L. B. and Gelber, E. R. (1975). Infant visual memory, in *Infant Perception: From Sensation to Cognition*. Vol. 1 *Basic visual processes* (Eds L. B. Cohen and P. Salapatek), pp. 347–403, Academic Press, New York.

Connolly, K. and Stratton, P. (1969). An exploration of some parameters affecting classical conditioning in the neonate, *Child Development*, **40**, 431–441.

Cornwell, A. C. and Fuller, J. L. (1961). Conditioned responses in young puppies, *Journal of Comparative and Physiological Psychology*, **54**, 13–15.

Crook, C. K. (1976). Neonatal sucking: Effects of quantity of the response-contingent fluid upon sucking rhythm and heart rate, *Journal of Experimental Child Psychology*, **21**, 539–548.

Crook, C. K. and Lipsitt, L. P. (1976). Neonatal nutritive sucking: Effects of taste stimulation upon sucking rhythm and heart rate, *Child Development*, **47**, 518–522.

Curio, V. E. (1969). Funktionsweise und stammesgeschichte des flugfeinderkennens einiger Darwinfinken *(Goespizinae)*, *Zeitschrift für Tierpsychologie*, **20**, 394–487.

Davis, M. (1970). Interstimulus interval and startle response habituation with a 'control' for total time during training, *Psychonomic Science*, **20**, 39–41.

Davis, M. (1972). Differential retention of sensitization and habituation of the startle response in the rat, *Journal of Comparative and Physiological Psychology*, **78**, 260–267.

Davis, J. and Rovee-Collier, C. K. (1979). A conditioning analysis of long-term memory in 8-week-old infants. Paper presented at the meeting of the Eastern Psychological Association, Philadelphia, Pa.

DeCasper, A. J. and Fifer, W. P. (1980). Of human bonding: Newborns prefer their mothers voices, *Science*, **208**, 1174–1176.

Dennis, W. A. (1934). A description and classification of the response of the newborn infant, *Psychological Bulletin*, **31**, 5–22.

Dobbing, J. (1975). Human brain development and its vulnerability, in *Mead Johnson Symposium on Perinatal and Developmental Medicine,* No. 6, *Biologic and clinical aspects of brain development*, pp. 3–12.

Ebel, H. C. and Prokasy, W. F. (1963). Classical eyelid conditioning as a function of sustained and shifted interstimulus intervals, *Journal of Experimental Psychology*, **65**, 52–58.

Eimas, P. D., Siqueland, E. R., Jusczyk, and Vigorito, J (1971). Speech perception in infants, *Science*, **171**, 303–306.

Emde, R. N. and Robinson, J. (1976). The first two months: Recent research in developmental psychobiology and the changing view of the newborn, in *Basic Handbook of Child Psychiatry* (Eds J. Noshpitz and J. Call), Basic Books, New York.

Emde, R., Swedberg, J., and Suzuki, B. (1975). Human wakefulness and biological rhythms after birth, *Archives of General Psychiatry*, **32**, 780–783.

Engen, T. and Lipsitt, L. P. (1965). Decrement and recovery of responses to olfactory stimuli in the human neonate, *Jounal of Comparative and Physiological Psychology*, **59**, 312–316.

Engen, T., Lipsitt, L. P., and Kaye, H. (1963). Olfactory responses and adaptation in the human neonate, *Journal of Comparative and Physiological Psychology*, **56**, 73–77.

Ewer, R. F. (1968). *Ethology of mammals*, Logos Press, Great Britain.

Fagan, J. F. (1970). Memory in the infant. *Journal of Experimental Child Psychology*, **9**, 217–226.

Fitzgerald, H. E. and Brackbill, Y. (1971). Tactile conditioning of an autonomic and somatic response in young infants, *Conditional Reflex*, **6**, 41–51.

Fitzgerald, H. E. and Brackbill, Y. (1976), Classical conditioning in infancy: Development and constraints, *Psychological Bulletin*, **83**, 353–376.

Fitzgerald, H. E. and Porges, S. W. (1971). A decade of infant conditioning and learning research, *Merrill-Palmer Quarterly*, **17**, 79–117.

Fowler, S. J. and Kellog, C. (1975). Ontogeny of thermoregulatory mechanisms in the rat, Journal of comparitive and Physiological Psychology, **89**, 738–746.

Friedman, S. (1972). Habituation and recovery of visual response in the alert human newborn, *Journal of Experimental Child Psychology*, **13**, 339–349.

Friedman, S., Bruno, L. A. and Vietze, P. (1974). Newborn habituation to visual stimuli: A sex difference in novelty detection, *Journal of Experimental Child Psychology*, **18**, 242–251.

Friedman, S. and Carpenter, G. C. (1971). Visual response decrement as a function of the age of human newborn, *Child Development*, **42**, 1967–1973.

Fuller, J. L., Easler, C. A., and Banks, E. M. (1952). Formation of conditioned avoidance responses in young puppies, *American Journal of Physiology*, **160**, 462–466.

Gekoski, M. J. (1977). Visual attention and operant conditioning in infancy: A second look (Doctoral dissertation, Rutgers University, 1977). *Dissertation Abstracts International,* **38**, 875B. (University Microfilms No. 77–17, 533).

Gesell, A. (1928). *Infancy and Human Growth*, Macmillan, New York.

Gesell, A. L. and Ilg, F. (1943). *Infant and Child in Culture of Today*, Harpers, New York.

Goldfarb, W.(1945). Psychological privation in infancy and subsequent adjustment, *American Journal of Orthopsychiatry*, **15**, 247–255.

Graham, F. K. (1956). Behavioral differences between normal and traumatized newborns. I. The test procedures, *Psychological Monographs*, **70** (whole number 427).

Graham, F. K., Clifton, R. K., and Hatton, H. M. (1968). Habituation of heart rate response to repeated auditory stimulation during the first five days of life, *Child Development*, **39**, 35–52.

Gray, P. H., Yates, A. E., and McNeal, K. (1967). The ontogeny of classical conditioning in the neonatal rat with varied CS-UCS intervals, *Psychonomic Science,* **9**, 587–588.

Groves, P. M. and Thompson, R. F. (1970). Habituation: A dual-process theory, *Psychological Review*, **77**, 419–450.

Gunther, M. (1955). Instinct and the nursing couple, *Lancet*, **1**, 575.

Gunther, M. (1961). Infant behavior at the breast, in *Determinants of Infant Behavior* (Ed. B. M. Foss), Wiley, New York.

Hamberg, J. M. and Spear, N. E. (1978). Alleviation of forgetting of discrimination learning, *Learning and Motivation*, **9**, 466–476.

Harlow, H. F. (1958). The nature of love, *American Psychologist*, **13**, 673–685.

Hasher, L. and Zacks, R. T. (1979). Automatic and effortful processes in memory, *Journal of Experimental Psychology: General*, **108**, 356–388.

Haskins, R. (1977). Effect of kitten vocalizations on maternal behavior, *Journal of Comparative and Physiological Psychology*, **91**, 830–838.

Hellbrügge, T. (1974). The development of circadian and untradian rhythms of premature and full-term infants, in *Chronobiology* Eds L. E. Scheving, F. Halberg, and J. E. Pauly), pp. 339–341, Igaku Shoin, Tokyo.

Hinde, R. (in press) The uses and limitations of studies of non-human primates for understanding human social development, in *Parental Behavior: Its Causes and consequences* (Eds R. Gandelman and L. W. Hoffman), Lawrence Erlbaum, Hillsdale, N. J.

Hofer, M. A. and Shair, H. (1977). The social context of ultrasound production by infant rats. Paper presented at the meeting of The Psychonomic Society, Washington, DC.

Hoffman, H. S., DeVido, C. J., and Shaak, M. E. (1979). A comparison of eyelid conditioning in adults and infants. Unpublished ms., Bryn Mawr College, Bryn Mawr, Pa.

Horne, J. A. (1977). Factors relating to energy conservation during sleep in mammals, *Physiological Psychology*, 5, 403–408.

Hoving, K. L., Coates, L., Bertucci, M., and Riccio, D. C. (1972). Reinstatement effects in children, *Developmental Psychology*, 6, 426–429.

Hull, D. (1973). Thermoregulation in young mammals, in *Comparative Physiology of Thermoregulation*, Vol. III, *Special Aspects of Thermoregulation*, (Ed. G. Causey Whittow), pp. 167–200, Academic Press, New York.

Hulsebus, R. C. (1973). Operant conditioning of infant behavior: A review, in *Advances in Child Development and Behavior*, Vol. 8 (Ed. H. W. Reese), pp. 111–158, Academic Press, New York.

Janos, O. (1968). The influence of individually differing intensity of the unconditioned stimulus (UCS) on the elaboration of the conditioned response (CR), *Activitas Nervosa Superior*, 10, 219–220.

Jeddi, E. (1970). Confort du contact et thermoregulation comportementale, *Physiology and Behavior*, 5, 1487–1493.

Jeffrey, W. E. (1976). Habituation as a mechanism for perceptual development, in *Habituation* (Eds T. J. Tighe and R. N. Leaton), pp. 279–296. Lawrence Erlbaum, Hillsadale, N. J.

Jeffrey, W. E. and Cohen, L. B. (1971). Habituation in the human infant, in *Advances in Child Development and Behavior*, Vol. 6 (Ed. H. W. Reese), pp. 63–97, Academic Press, New York.

Jerison, H. J. (1973). *Evolution of the brain and intelligence*, Academic Press, New York.

Johanson, I. B. and Hall, W. G. (1979). Appetitive learning in 1-day old rat pups, *Science*, 205, 419–421.

Kaplan, M. G. (1967). Infant visual preferences: The role of familiarity and responsiveness. Unpublished master's thesis, University of Illinois.

Kasatkin, N. L. (1969). The origin and development of conditioned reflexes in early childhood, in *A Handbook of Contemporary Soviet Psychology* (Eds M. Cole and I. Maltzman), Basic Books, New York.

Kavanau, J. L. (1967). Behavior of captive white-footed mice, *Science*, 155, 1623–1639.

Kaye, H. (1965). The conditioned Babkin reflex in human newborns, *Psychonomic Science*, 2, 287–288.

Keen, R., Chase, H., and Graham, F. K. (1965). Twenty-four hour retention by neonates of habituated heart rate response, *Psychonomic Science*, 2, 287–288.

Kennedy, G. C. (1967). Ontogeny of mechanisms controlling food and water intake, in *Handbook of Physiology. Section 6: Alimentary Canal* Vol. 1, *Control of Food and Water Intake* (Ed. C. F. Code), pp. 337–351, American Physiological Society, Washington, DC.

Kimmel, H. D. (1973). Habituation, habituability, and conditioning, in *Habituation*, Vol. 1 (Eds H. V. S. Peeke and M. J. Herz), pp. 219–238, Academic Press, New York.

Kimmel, H. D. and Goldstein, A. J. (1967). Retention of habituation of the GSR to visual and auditory stimulation, *Journal of Experimental Psychology*, 73, 401–404.

Kling, J. W. (1972). Learning: Introductory survey, in *Woodworth and Schlosberg's Experimental Psychology*, Vol. II, *Learning, Motivation, and Memory*, 3rd Ed (Eds J. W. Kling and L. A. Riggs), pp. 551–613, Holt, Rinehart and Winston, New York.

Kobre, K. R. and Lipsitt, L. P. (1972). A negative contrast effect in newborns, *Journal of Experimental Child Psychology*, 14, 81–91.

Koch, J. (1967). Conditioned orienting reactions in two-month-old infants, *British Journal of Psychology*, **58**, 105–110.

Koch, J. (1968). The change of conditional orienting reactions in 5 month old infants through phase shift of partial biorhythms, *Human Development*, **11**, 124–137.

Konner, M. (1973). Newborn walking: Additional data, *Science*, **178**, 307.

Krasnogorskii, N. I. (1913). Über die grundmechanismen der arbeit der grosshernrunde bei Kindern, *Jahrbuch für Kinderheilkunde*, **78**, 373–389.

Kron, R. E. (1966). Instrumental conditioning of nutritive sucking behavior in the newborn, *Recent Advances in Biological Psychiatry*, **9**, 295–300.

Lamb, M. E. (1977). A re-examination of the infant social world, *Human Development*, **20**, 65–85.

Lehrman, D. S. (1953). A critique of Konrad Lorenz's theory of instinctive behavior, *Quarterly Review of Biology*, **28**, 337–363.

Leon, M., Croskerry, P. G., and Smith, G. K. (1978). Thermal control of mother-young contact in rats, *Physiology and Behavior*, **21**, 793–811.

Lipsitt, L. P. (1963). Learning in the first year of life, in *Advances in Child Development and Behavior*, Vol. I (Eds L. P. Lipsitt and C. C. Spiker), pp. 147–195, Academic Press, New York.

Lipsitt, L. P. (1971). Infant anger: Toward an understanding of the ontogenesis of human aggression. Unpublished paper presented at the Department of Psychiatry, The Center for the Health Sciences, University of California at Los Angeles, March 4.

Lipsitt, L. P. (1972). The experiential origins of human behavior, in *Life-span developmental psychology: Research and theory* (Eds L. Goulet and P. Baltes), pp. 285–303, Academic Press, New York.

Lipsitt, L. P. (1976). Developmental psychobiology comes of age: A discussion, in *Developmental psychobiology* (Ed. L. P. Lipsitt), pp. 109–127, Lawrence Erlbaum, Hillsdale, N. J.

Lipsitt, L. P. (1978). Perinatal indicators and psychophysiological precursors of crib death, in *Early Developmental Hazards: Predictors and Precautions* (Ed. F. D. Horowitz), Westview Press, USA.

Lipsitt, L. P. and Ambrose, J. A. (1967). A preliminary report of temporal conditioning to three types of neonatal stimulation. Paper presented at the meeting of the Society for Research in Child Development, New York City.

Lipsitt, L. P. and Kaye, H. (1964). Conditioned sucking in the human newborn, *Psychonomic Science*, **1**, 29–30.

Lipsitt, L. P., Kaye, H., and Bosack, T. N. (1966). Enhancement of neonatal sucking through reinforcement, *Journal of Experimental Child Psychology*, **4**, 163–168.

Lipsitt, L. P., Sturner, W. Q., and Burke, P. (1979). Perinatal indicators and subsequent crib death, *Infant Behavior and Development*, **2**, 325–328.

Little, A. H. (1970). Eyelid conditioning in the human infant as a function of the interstimulus interval, Unpublished master's thesis, Brown University.

Little, A. H. (1973). A comparative study of trace and delay conditioning in the human infant (Doctoral dissertation, Brown University, 1973). *Dissertation Abstracts International*, **34** (University Microfilms No. 74–3046).

Lorenz, K. Z. (1965). Evolution and modification of behavior, University of Chicago Press, Chicago.

Macfarlane, A., Harris, P., and Barnes, I. (1976). Central and peripheral vision in early infancy, *Journal of Experimental Child Psychology*, **21**, 532–538.

Martin, R. D. (1966). Tree shrews: Unique reproductive mechanisms of systematic importance, *Science*, **152**, 1402–1404.

Martin, L. T., and Alberts, J. R. (1979). Taste aversions to mother's milk: The age related role of nursing in acquisition and expression of a learned association, *Journal of Comparative and Physiological Psychology*, **93**, 430–445.

Marquis, D. P. (1931). Can conditioned responses be established in the newborn infant? *Journal of Genetic Psychology*, **39**, 479–492.

Marquis, D. P. (1941). Learning in the neonate: The modification of behavior under three feeding schedules, *Journal of Experimental Psychology*, **29**, 263–282.

McFarland, D. J. (1977). Decision making in animals, *Nature (Lond.)*, **269**, 15–21.

McGraw, M. B. (1943). *Neuromuscular maturation of the human infant*, Columbia University Press, New York.

McGraw, M. B. (1945). *Neuromuscular maturation of the human infant*, Hafner, New York.

Meier-Koll, A., Hall, V., Hellwig, U., Kott, G., and Meier-Koll, V. (1978). A biological oscillator system and the development of sleep-waking behavior during early infancy, *Chronobiologia*, **5**, 425–440.

Milewski, A. E. (1976). Infants' discrimination of internal and external pattern elements, *Journal of Experimental Child Psychology*, **22**, 229–246.

Milewski, A. E., and Siqueland, E. R. (1975). Discrimination of color and pattern novelty in one-month human infants, *Journal of Experimental Child Psychology*, **19**, 122–136.

Mills, M. and Melhuish, E. (1974). Recognition of mother's voice in early infancy, *Nature (Lond.)*, **252**, 123–124.

Misanin, J. R., Nagy, Z. M., Keiser, E. F., and Bowen, W. (1971). Emergence of long-term memory in the neonatal rat, *Journal of Comparative and Physiological Psychology*, **77**, 188–189.

Morath, M. A. (1974). The four-hour feeding rhythm of the baby as a free running endogeneously regulated rhythm, *International Journal of Chronobiology*, **2**, 39–45.

Morgan, J. J. B. and Morgan, S. S. (1944). Infant learning as a developmental index, *Journal of Genetic Psychology*, **65**, 281–289.

Naeye, R., Ladis. B. and Drage, J. S. (1976). SIDS: A prospective study, *American Journal of Diseases of Children*, **130**, 1207–1210.

Naeye, R. L., Messmer, J., Specht, T. and Merritt, T. A. (1976). Sudden infant death syndrome temperament before death, *The Journal of Pediatrics*, **88**, 511–515.

Nagy, Z. M. and Murphy, J. M. (1974). Learning and retention of a discriminated escape response in infant mice, *Developmental Psychobiology*, **7**, 185–192.

Naito, T. and Lipsitt, L. P. (1969). Two attempts to condition eyelid responses in human infants, *Journal of Experimental Child Psychology*, **8**, 263–270.

Nelson, W., Scheving, L. and Halberg, F. (1975). Circadian rhythms in mice fed a single daily meal at different stages of lighting regimen, *Journal of Nutrition*, **105**, 171–184.

Ohlrich, E. S. and Ross, L. E. (1968). Acquisition and differential conditioning of the eyelid response in normal and retarded children, *Journal of Experimental Child Psychology*, **6**, 181–193.

Paine, R. S. (1976). The contribution of developmental neurology to child psychiatry, in *Infant Psychiatry: A New Synthesis* (Eds. E. N. Rexford, L. W. Sander, and T. Shapiro), Yale University Press, New Haven.

Papousek, H. (1961). Conditioned head rotation reflexes in the first six months of life, *Acta Pediatrica*, **50**, 565–576.

Papousek, H. (1967). Conditioning during early postnatal development, in *Behavior in Infancy and Early Childhood*, (Eds. Y. Brackbill and G. G. Thompson), pp. 259–274, Free Press, New York.

Papousek, H. (1970). The development of higher nervous activity in children in the first half-year of life, in *Cognitive Development in Children: European Research in Cognitive Development*, Society for Research in Child Development, pp. 667–676, University of Chicago Press, Chicago.

Peeke, H. V. S. and Herz, M. J. (Eds) (1973a). *Habituation*, Vol. 1, *Behavioral Studies*, Academic Press, New York.

Peeke, H. V. S. and Herz, M. J. (Eds)(1973b). *Habituation*, Vol. 2, *Physiological Substrates*, Academic Press, New York.

Peiper, A. (1963). *Cerebral Function in Infancy and Childhood*, Consultants Bureau, New York.

Petrinovich, L. (1973). A species-meaningful analysis of habituation, in *Habituation*, Vol. 1 (Eds H. V. S. Peeke and M. J. Herz), pp. 141–162, Academic Press, New York.

Protestos, C., Carpenter, R., McWeeny, P., and Emery, J. (1973). Obstetric and perinatal histories of children who died unexpectedly (cot death), *Archives of Disease in Childhood*, **48**, 835–841.

Purpura, D. P. (1975). Neuronal migration and dendritic differentiation: Normal and aberrant development of human cerebral cortex, in *Biologic and clinical aspects of brain development*, pp. 13–27, Mead Johnson Symposium on Perinatal and Developmental Medicine, No. 6.

Purves, M. J. (1974). Onset of respiration at birth, *Archives of Disease in Childhood*, **49**, 333.

Rendle-Short, J. (1961). The puff test, *Archives of Diseases of Childhood*, **36**, 50–57.

Rescorla, R. A. (1967). Pavlovian conditioning and its proper control procedures, *Psychological Review*, **74**, 71–80.

Rescorla, R. A. (1973). Effect of US habituation following conditioning, *Journal of Comparative and Physiological Psychology*, **82**, 137–143.

Richter, C. (1957). On the phenomenon of sudden death in animals and man, *Psychosomatic Medicine*, **19**, 191–198.

Rosenblum, L. (in press). Monkeys, mothers, peers and others, in *Parental Behavior: Its Causes and Consequences*. (Eds R. Gandelman and L. W. Hoffman), Lawrence Erlbaum, Hillsdale, N. J.

Rosenblum, L. A. and Youngstein, K. P. (1973). Developmental changes in compensatory dyadic response in mother and infant monkeys, in *The Effect of the Infant on its Caregiver* (Eds M. Lewis and L. A. Rosenblum), pp. 141–161, Wiley, New York.

Rovee, C. K. and Fagen, J. W. (1976). Extended conditioning and 24-hour retention in infants, *Journal of Experimental Child Psychology*, **21**, 1–11.

Rovee-Collier, C. K. and Fagen, J. W. (1981). The retrieval of memory in early infancy, in *Advances in Infancy Research*, Vol. 1 (Ed. L. P. Lipsitt), Ablex Publishing Co., Norwood, N. J.

Rovee-Collier, C. K. and Gekoski, M. J. (1979). The economics of infancy: A review of conjugate reinforcement, in *Advances in Child Development and Behavior*, Vol. 13 (Eds H. W. Reese and L. P. Lipsitt), pp. 195–225, Academic Press, New York.

Rovee-Collier, C. K., Morrongiello, B. A., Aron, M. and Kupersmidt, J. (1978). Topographical response differentiation and reversal in 3-month-old infants, *Infant Behavior and Development*, **1**, 323–333.

Rovee-Collier, C. K., Sullivan, M. W., Enright, M., Lucas, D., and Fagen, J. W. (1980). Reactivation of infant memory, *Science*, **208**, 1159–1161.

Rudy, J. W. and Cheatle, M. D. (1977). Odor-aversion learning in neonatal rats, *Science*, **198**, 845–846.

Sameroff, A. J. (1968). The components of sucking in the human newborn, *Journal of Experimental Psychology*, **6**, 607–623.

Sameroff, A. J. (1971). Can conditioned responses be established in the newborn infant?, *Developmental Psychology*, **5**, 1–12.

Sameroff, A. J. (1972). Learning and adaptation in infancy: A comparison of models, in *Advances in Child Development and Behavior*, Vol. 7 (Ed. H. W. Reese), pp. 169–214, Academic Press, New York.

Sameroff, A. J. and Cavanagh, P. J. (1979). Learning in infancy: A developmental perspective, in *Handbook of Infant Development* (Ed. J. D. Osofsky), pp. 344–392, Wiley, New York.

Satinoff, E. and Hendersen, R. (1977). Thermoregulatory behavior, in *Handbook of Operant Behavior* (Eds W. K. Honig and J. E. R. Staddon), pp. 153–173, Prentice-Hall, Englewood Cliffs.

Seligman, M. E. P. (1970). On the generality of the laws of learning, *Psychological Review*, **77**, 406–418.

Seligman, M. E. P. (1975). *Helplessness*, W. H. Freeman, San Francisco.

Siqueland, E. R. (1968). Visual reinforcement and exploratory behavior in infants. Paper presented at the meetings of the Society for Research in Child Development, Worcester, Mass.

Siqueland, E. R. (1969a). The development of instrumental exploratory behaviour during the first year of human life. Paper presented at the meeting of the Society for Research in Child Development, Santa Monica, California.

Siqueland, E. R. (1969b). Further developments in infant learning. Symposium paper presented at the meeting of the XIXth International Congress of Psychology, London, England.

Siqueland, E. R. (1970). Basic learning processes. I. Classical conditioning, in *Experimental Child Psychology*, (Eds H. W. Reese and L. P. Lipsitt), pp. 67–89, Academic Press, New York.

Siqueland, E. R. and Lipsitt, L. P. (1966). Conditioned head-turning in human newborns, *Journal of Experimental Child Psychology*, **3**, 356–376.

Skinner, B. F. (1938). *The Behavior of Organisms*, Appleton-Century, New York.

Skinner, B. F. (1953). *Science and Human Behavior*, Macmillan, New York.

Sluckin, W. (1970). *Early Learning in Man and Animal*, George Allen & Unwin, London.

Smith, G. J., Greenfield, R. J., and Spear, N. E. (1979). Effects of home environmental cues on learning a shock-escape spatial discrimination in neonatal rats. Paper presented at the meeting of the Midwestern Psychological Association, Chicago.

Smith, G. J. and Spear, N. E. (1978). Effects of the home environment on withholding behaviors and conditioning in infant and neonatal rats, *Science*, **202**, 327–329.

Sokolov, E. N. (1963). *Perception and the Conditioned Reflex*, Macmillan, New York.

Solkoff, N. and Cotton, C. (1975). Contingency awareness in premature infants, *Perceptual and Motor Skills*, **41**, 709–710.

Spear, N. E. (1973). Retrieval of memory in animals, *Psychological Review*, **80**, 163–194.

Spear, N. E. (1976). Retrieval of memories: A psychobiological approach, in *Handbook of Learning and Cognitive Processes*, Vol. 4, *Attention and Memory* (Ed. W. K. Estes), pp. 17–90, Lawrence Erlbaum, Hillsdale, N. J.

Spear, N. E. (1979). Memory storage factors leading to infantile amnesia, in *The Psychology of Learning and Motivation*, Vol. 13 (Ed. G. H. Bower), Academic Press, New York.

Spear, N. E. and Parsons, P. (1976). Alleviation of forgetting by reactivation treatment: A preliminary analysis of the ontogeny of memory processing, in *Processes in Animal Memory* (Eds D. Medin, W. Roberts, and R. Davis), pp. 135–165, Lawrence Erlbaum, Hillsdale, N. J.

Spear, N. E. and Smith G. J. (1978). Alleviation of forgetting in preweanling rats, *Developmental Psychobiology*, **11**, 513–529.

Spitz, R. (1946). Hospitalism: A follow-up report, *The Psychoanalytic Study of the Child*, **2**, 113–117.

Spock, B. (1957). *Baby and Child Care*, Pocket Books, Inc., New York.

Spock, B. and Lowenberg, M. E. (1955). *Feeding Your Baby and Child*, Duell, Sloan, and Pearce, New York.

Stamps, L. E. and Porges, S. W. (1975). Heart rate conditioning in newborn infants: Relationships among conditionability, heart rate variability, and sex, *Developmental Psychology*, **11**, 424–431.

Stein, L. (1966). Habituation and stimulus novelty: A model based on classical conditioning, *Psychological Review*, **73**, 352–356.

Steinschneider, A. (1975). Implications of the sudden infant death syndrome for the study of sleep in infancy, in *Minnesota Symposium on Child Psychology*, Vol. 9 (Ed. A. D. Pick), University of Minnesota Press, Minneapolis.

Stern, J. A. (1968). Toward a developmental psychophysiology: My look into the crystal ball, *Psychophysiology*, **4**, 403–420.

Sullivan, M. W., Rovee-Collier, C. K., and Tynes, D. M. (1979). A conditioning analysis of infant long-term memory, *Child Development*, **50**, 152–162.

Thoman, E., Miano, V. N., and Freese, M. P. (1977). The role of respiratory instability, in Sudden Infant Death Syndrome, *Developmental Medicine and Child Neurology*, **19**, 729–738.

Thoman, E., Wetzel, A., and Levine, S. (1968). Learning in the neonatal rat, *Animal Behavior*, **16**, 54–57.

Thompson, R. F., Mayers, K.S., Robertson, R. T., and Patterson, C. J. (1970). Number coding in association cortex of the cat, *Science*, **168**, 271–273.

Thompson, R. F. and Spencer, W. A. (1966). Habituation: A model phenomenon for the study of neuronal substrates of behavior, *Psychological Review*, **73**, 16–43.

Thorpe, W. H. (1963). *Learning and instinct in animals*, Methuen, London.

Tighe, T. J. and Leaton, R. N. (1976). *Habituation*, Lawrence Erlbaum, Hillsdale, N. J.

Tinbergen, N. (1951). *The study of instinct*, Oxford University Press, Oxford.

Ungerer, J. A., Brody, L. R., and Zelazo, P. R. (1978). Long-term memory for speech in 2 to 4-week-old infants, *Infant Behavior and Development*, **1**, 177–186.

Valdes-Dapena, M. A. (1978). *Sudden Unexpected Infant Death 1970 Through 1975: An Evolution in Understanding*, Department of HEW Publication No. (HSA) 78–5255, Bethesda, Maryland.

Valdes-Dapena, M. (1980). Sudden infant death syndrome: A review of the medical literature 1974–1979, *Pediatrics*, **66**, 597–614.

Venge, O. (1963). The influence of nursing behaviour and milk production on early growth in rabbits, *Animal Behavior*, **11**, 500–506.

Von Uexküll, J. (1934). A stroll through the worlds of animals and men, in *Instinctive Behavior* (Ed. C. H. Schiller), (1957), pp. 5–80, International Universities Press, New York.

Vuorenskoski, V., Wasz-Höckert, O., Koivisto, E., and Lind, J. (1969). The effect of cry stimulus on the temperature of the lactating breast of primipara: A thermographic study, *Experientia*, **25**, 1286–1287.

Watson, J. B. (1919). *Psychology from the Standpoint of a Behaviorist*, Lippincott, Philadelphia.

Watson, J. B. and Rayner, R. (1920). Conditioned emotional reactions, *Journal of Experimental Psychology*, **3**, 1–14.

Weiss, A. P. (1929). The measurement of infant behavior, *Psychological Review*, **36**, 453–471.

Weizmann, F., Cohen, L. B., and Pratt, J. (1971). Novelty, familiarity, and development of infant attention, *Developmental Psychology*, **4**, 149–154.

Wenger, M. A. (1936). An investigation of conditioned responses in human infants, in *Studies in Infant Behavior III* (Eds M. A. Wenger, J. M. Smith, C. Hazard, and O. C. Irwin), *University of Iowa Studies in Child Welfare*, **12**: 7–90.

Werner, J. S., and Siqueland, E. R. (1978). Visual recognition memory in the preterm infant, *Infant Behavior and Development*, **1**, 79–84.

Williemsen, E. (1979). *Understanding Infancy*, W. H. Freeman, San Francisco.

Wilson, E. O. (1975). *Sociobiology*, Harvard University Press, Cambridge, Mass.

Woodside, B., and Leon, M. (1980). Thermoendocrine influences on maternal nesting behavior in rats, *Journal of Comparative and Physiological Psychology*, **94**, 41–60.

Woodside, B., Pelchat, R., and Leon, M. (1980). Acute elevating of the heat load of mother rats curtails mother nest bouts, *Journal of Comparative and Physiological Psychology*, **94**, 61–68.

Wyers, E. M., Peeke, H. V. S., and Herz, M. J. (1973). Behavioral habituation in invertebrates, in *Habituation*, Vol. 1 (Eds H. V. S. Peeke and M. J. Herz), pp. 1–57, Academic Press, New York.

Zarrow, M. X., Denenberg, V. H., & Anderson, C. O. (1965). Rabbit: Frequency of suckling in the pup, *Science*, **150**, 1835–1836.

Zelazo, P. R. (1976). From reflexive to instrumental behavior, in *Developmental Psychobiology* (Ed. L. P. Lipsitt), pp. 87–104, Lawrence Erlbaum, Hillsdale, N.J.

Zelazo, P., Zelazo, N., and Kolb, S. (1972). 'Walking' in the newborn. *Science*, **177**, 1058–1059.

Psychobiology of the Human Newborn
Edited by P. Stratton
© 1982, John Wiley & Sons, Ltd.

CHAPTER 8

Sensory and Perceptual Capacities of the Neonate

JANETTE ATKINSON and OLIVER BRADDICK

Modern studies of the neonatal period have greatly increased our awareness of the 'competence' of the infant. The evidence for a wealth of adaptive behaviour in neonates should not, however, be allowed to obscure an important asymmetry in their competence. Much of the motor behaviour displayed by neonates is rudimentary, both in terms of the differentiation of its basic units and in how these are organized. In contrast, the neonate's senses are functioning and appear to be capable of differentiating stimuli on most of the basic dimensions which will be used in mature perception. At a very early age these elementary discriminations can be used as components in performances as complex as voice and face discrimination. It is clear that in the early months infants have an ability to take in information from the material and social world around them which far outstrips their limited capability to intervene in that world: an asymmetry which suggests that the primary modes of learning in this period may be rather different from those of later infancy when manipulation is so prominent in the child's interaction with the world.

The very limited repertoire of motor behaviour in neonates makes it difficult to determine just how far advanced their sensory abilities may be. In fact, one of the main behavioural routes into the neonate's sensory discrimination has been the use of those responses, such as eye movements, which can be regarded as elements in the active process of perception. In line with the idea that perception has a flying start over action, these responses appear to approximate their mature organization much more closely than is the case with motor behaviour in general.

Sensory psychology, in adults and infants, has been dominated by the study of vision and hearing, and this is reflected in the balance of the work reviewed here. Presumably the justification for this dominance is that these modalities can convey complex patterning in time and space. They therefore provide the richness of structured information which is required and exploited by human cognitive activities and motor skills, both in acquisition and in mature execution.

However, the chemical senses of taste and smell are important for different reasons, since they are so intimately connected with eliciting, sustaining and regulating the vital intake of food and fluids (olfaction also plays a part in identifying individuals). Neonates have rather little capacity or responsibility for the kinds of behaviour which are controlled by vision and hearing in the adult, but they do carry a considerable part of the responsibility for regulating their own feeding and drinking. It might, therefore, be expected that these senses would be relatively advanced at birth both in their intrinsic powers of discrimination and in their links to motivational and response systems. Some data related to this issue will be reviewed.

Information about the distribution of temperature and pressure over the body surface is presumably also of very great significance for the newborn infant's well-being and for the establishment of emotional bonds with caregivers. Also, the various neonatal reflexes elicited by pressure around and inside the mouth, on the palms and on the feet, are well known. However, the limited amount of work on the sensitivity of the skin senses does not seem to advance our understanding very much of the important part these senses must play in the life and development of the neonate, and so this work is not considered further here.

Similarly, the absence of any discussion of vestibular, muscle and joint senses is due to the paucity of our knowledge rather than to any judgment that these are not significant for the neonate. Advances in posture and motor control are among the most dramatic changes during infancy. To achieve these advances, infants must possess, or start to develop, a representation of the posture and movement of their own body parts, and the relationship of these to external frames of reference. Such a representation surely requires information to be obtained through the proprioceptive senses, and correlated with that from other senses (notably vision and skin pressure).

For the purpose of this chapter we have taken the neonatal period to cover approximately the first month of life. In some cases, however, the special features of the neonate's sensory processes are best brought out by contrast with later developments, so some data from later stages of infancy are introduced for comparison.

METHODS OF STUDYING SENSORY PROCESSES IN THE NEONATE

Infants' ability to detect a stimulus can be demonstrated if that stimulus elicits a reflex response. The reflexes used generally play the role of optimizing the adjustment of the sensory system itself. For example, if a large part of the visual field is occupied by uniformly moving pattern, reflex repetitive following eye movements known as optokinetic nystagmus (OKN) serve to stabilize the patterned image on the retina. The occurrence of OKN in an infant is evidence that the moving pattern used can be detected at some level in the visual pathway.

In audition, the 'acoustic reflex'—a muscular adjustment of transmission through the middle ear serving to protect the inner ear from intense sound levels—has been used as an indicator of the relative sensitivity of neonate and adult.

The general class of responses which orient the infant to a stimulus have been the most important indicators of neonates' sensory abilities. It is doubtful whether these can be classed as reflex responses, especially when one of the main examples, the preferential looking procedure, often involves the infant orienting selectively to one of two stimuli each of which would produce the response if presented alone. Directed orienting responses have been used in audition to investigate the ability of neonates to localize sound stimuli, rather than the more basic ability to detect them. However, as well as directed responses, acoustic stimuli can produce diffuse arousing or orienting effects which are observable in heart and respiration rates and in the general level of motor activity, and these have been used to investigate neonates' absolute and relative sensitivities to sounds.

It is also possible to establish a learned connection between a sensory event and a response with no intrinsic relation to it. The conjugate reinforcement of high-amplitude sucking by visual and auditory stimuli (Siqueland and Delucia, 1969) has been an effective means of investigating infants' responsiveness to these stimuli in the first months of life.

The methods outlined so far test detection or discrimination simply by the ability of a stimulus to elicit a response. It is also possible to investigate discriminations by using a habituation/recovery paradigm. In this method a single stimulus is presented repetitively until the infant gives a measurable decline in response. At this point a different stimulus is presented and any recovery of responsiveness produced by the change is measured. While behavioural habituation is harder to demonstrate in neonates than in older infants, the technique has been effectively used to study capabilities of infants around 5–6 weeks of age, and these studies have demonstrated some of the special characteristics of neonatal perception.

Some part of our knowledge of neonates' sensory systems comes not from behaviour but from measures of electrical activity in the nervous system produced by a stimulus. Evoked potentials (EPs) are electrical brain responses recorded from electrodes on the scalp, which can be identified as stimulus-related because they occur in a fixed time relationship to the stimulus. Although the detailed site of origin of EPs and their relation to neural information transmission are in many cases uncertain, the occurrence of an EP provides evidence that a stimulus is effectively getting through to the infant's central nervous system. However, many EPs that are studied have complex waveforms, and clear criteria for the occurrence of an EP are required if arguments of this kind are to be of any value.

Electrical activity from the sense organs themselves can also be recorded, and in the case of the electroretinogram (ERG) has provided some information on the maturity of the neonate's sensory pathway.

In some cases physical measurements of the infant's sense organs, made using the stimulus energy which they are transducing for the nervous system, can tell us something about the stimulus information available and can detect active adjustments made by the infant. For example, optical measurements can indicate how well the infant's eye forms a focussed image, and this is a function not only of the static structure of the eye but also of the infant's accommodative response, which must depend on an ability to discriminate image defocus. Similarly, acoustic impedance measurements as well as indicating transmission through the middle ear provide a means of detecting the action of the neonate's acoustic reflex which is evidence of an active response to sound.

Any of the methods discussed may give positive evidence that the newborn's sensory systems can detect or differentiate stimuli, but of course the absence of such evidence does not show a failure to discriminate. Estimates of the neonate's capabilities, when well-founded, are therefore necessarily conservative and may quite possibly be revised upwards as techniques are refined. However, the demonstration of discrimination does not tell us whether the sensory information concerned is available to the infant for behavioural or cognitive uses other than that directly observed, and we should certainly not suppose that any stimulus dimension necessarily has the same significance to the infant that it does for the adult. These cautions apply at least as strongly to electrophysiological measures of sensory performance as to behavioural ones.

VISUAL ACUITY AND CONTRAST SENSITIVITY OF THE NEONATE

All important uses of vision require the detection and interpretation of information about spatial pattern. To understand the visual capabilities of neonates, therefore, we must have some measure of the pattern information that they can extract. The commonest measure is visual acuity, that is a measure of the finest detail that can be resolved: in infant work this has almost always been tested as the discrimination of a fine black/white stripe pattern (grating) from a uniform field of the same average luminance.[1] However, the pattern information available in vision is not completely characterized by knowing the finest detail detected. Some recent studies of infant vision have used the more general measure of contrast sensitivity. This is tested by the lowest contrast at which a grating can be discriminated from a uniform field.[2] This contrast varies with spatial frequency, the relation being expressed as the *contrast sensitivity function*. Acuity corresponds to one point on this function: the high spatial frequency at which a grating contrast of 100 per cent is required for detection, and above which no finer grating is visible however high its contrast. Many visual tasks depend on contrast sensitivity at spatial frequencies below the acuity limit, as much as on acuity *per se*. For instance, a single, very small object is detectable as a low-contrast, low-spatial-frequency blur even when poor acuity leads to the visual loss of high spatial frequencies: it follows that detection of a fine dot is not a particularly appropriate test of acuity. Besides describing visual performance more completely than acuity, the contrast sensitivity function has proved to yield a wealth of information about normal and abnormal visual mechanisms that is not revealed by acuity measures alone.

The acuity and contrast sensitivity of the newborn has been assessed by three methods: optokinetic nystagmus (OKN), preferential looking (PL), and visual-evoked potentials (VEP). The comparison of these techniques and their results are reviewed in some detail by Dobson and Teller (1978) and Atkinson and Braddick (1981a).

Optokinetic nystagmus is the oculomotor response to continuous uniform motion of a large part of the field of view. It consists of a 'slow phase' which smoothly follows the stimulus motion and a 'fast phase' in which the eyes jump back in the opposite direction. These two phases follow each other in rapid alternation. Gorman *et al.* (1957) showed that OKN could be elicited in infants under 6 days of age by placing them under a cylindrical canopy of moving stripes. Ninety-three per cent of their subjects showed the response with stripes 34 min arc wide. These authors (Gorman *et al.*, 1959) later reported that all of 100 newborns tested responded to 20 min arc stripes. Fantz *et al.* (1962) also found that all seven infants they tested under 1 month of age showed OKN to 20 min arc stripes but none to 10 min arc. Dayton *et al.* (1964) tested 0–8-day infants using a range of stripe widths. Only 56 per cent of their subjects showed OKN with any of their patterns, but of these half responded to stripes as fine as 7.5 min arc. (However, it has been pointed out by Dobson and Teller (1978) and Banks and Salapatek (1981) that there are likely to have been imperfections in these stimuli which could have elicited eye tracking without the need for acuity high enough to resolve the nominal stripe width.)

Preferential looking assesses acuity from the infant's orientation of head and eyes towards a pattern in preference to a uniform field of matched average luminance. Miranda (1970) has used this method to demonstrate that infants in the first days of life can resolve 70 min arc stripes. Fantz *et al.* (1962), with their group aged 0–1 month, found an acuity of 20 min arc. More recent studies have used the 'FPL' technique introduced by Teller (see Teller, 1979), in which an observer, 'blind' to the position of the stripes, has to make a forced-choice judgment of which side they are on from observation of the infant's behaviour. FPL studies have led to estimates of the acuity of 2-week infants of 27 min arc (Allen, 1978) and at 4–5 weeks of 15–40 min arc (Atkinson *et al.*, 1977a; Banks and Salapatek, 1978; Allen, 1978). Variations of luminance, screen size, and eccentricity must be borne in mind when comparing different experiments (Dobson and Teller, 1978; Atkinson and Braddick, 1981a): it should also be emphasized that the methods show the existence of reliable differences in acuity between individual infants which can be as large as a factor of 2—3 at a given age (Allen, 1978; Atkinson and Braddick, 1981a).

Visual evoked potentials can be generated by an unpatterned flash of light. Most studies of neonates have been of this type, which demonstrate that the visual pathway is functioning and show a sharply decreasing latency of response with increasing age in the neonatal period (Ferriss *et al.*, 1967), but do not indicate anything about pattern vision. Comparison of patterned with un-patterned flashes (Harter *et al.*, 1977) demonstrates the effect of pattern but leads to complex response functions that are difficult to interpret. The most direct evidence of pattern vision comes from VEPs that are generated by an appearance or reversal of pattern contrast which does not produce any change in the total amount of light entering the eye. Using rapid (10 Hz) pattern reversal, Atkinson *et al.* (1979) showed a limiting stripe width of 35 min arc in a group of infants aged 1–10 days, and 25 min arc in two infants aged 3 weeks. The only other data on the neonatal period come from Marg *et al.* (1976) who report VEPs from appearance of 25 min arc stripes, in three infants aged 1 month.

In this age range, the various techniques converge on quite similar estimates of acuity, with strong support for an estimate around 30 min arc at birth and somewhat better acuity (15–20 min arc) at 1 month. This is the beginning of a steady improvement over at least the first 6 months of life (see Dobson and Teller, 1978). Studies of premature infants (Fantz *et al.*, 1975; Dobson *et al.*, 1980) indicate that performance on PL acuity tests is a function of gestational rather than postnatal age, suggesting that at least the early stages of this improvement are due to a determinate process of maturation.

The infant contrast sensitivity function has been the subject of a single study in newborns using pattern reversal VEPs (Atkinson *et al.*, 1979) and two PL studies in 1-month-olds (Atkinson *et al.*, 1977a; Banks and Salapatek, 1978, 1981). In so far as the two techniques can be compared (and comparisons by Atkinson *et al.* (1979) on a single infant suggest that they can) there appears to be a rather gradual improvement in contrast sensitivity over the first month. Between 1 and 2 months there is a striking qualitative change. The contrast sensitivity function of the 2-month-olds, like that of the adult, shows lower sensitivity to very low spatial frequencies than for intermediate frequencies. Atkinson *et al.* (1977a) and Banks and Salapatek (1978) both found that 1-month-olds did not show this 'low-frequency cut'. The low-frequency cut in the adult's contrast sensitivity function is generally ascribed to the operation of lateral inhibition in the retina, so its appearance between 1 and 2 months of age presumably marks the functional emergence of this important feature of retinal organization.

THE DEVELOPMENT OF THE VISUAL PATHWAY AT BIRTH

Acuity and contrast sensitivity are determined by two types of factor: the quality of the optical image on the retina, and the fidelity with which that image is represented by neural signals in the visual pathway. Potentially, therefore, infant acuity and contrast sensitivity reflect the maturity of both the optical and the neural components of the visual system.

Evidence on the optical properties of the neonate's eye will be considered shortly. Neurally, anatomical and physiological studies make it clear that considerable postnatal development occurs, although it is not easy to know what any particular neural change implies in terms of visual function and behaviour.

The various cell types of the retina, and so far as has been studied their interconnections, are present and adult-like in their morphology at birth. However, Mann (1964) states that the fovea is poorly differentiated before 4 months, with fewer and stumpier cone receptors than in the adult and without the characteristic thinning of the ganglion cell layer. Since these factors are associated with the high acuity provided by the foveal region in adults, they are important. This widely cited statement rests on a single nineteenth-century paper and it would be very valuable to have it confirmed by a modern histological study. More central neural structures also develop visibly in early infancy. Myelination of the optic nerve is still proceeding for some time after birth: it is likely that the changing latency of the VEP is partly due to this process, but how much effect it has on the quality of information transmission up the optic nerve is unknown. In the visual cortex, the adult number of cells has been reached some time before birth (Rakic, 1977) but there is a striking increase in their size and connectivity between birth and three months (Conel, 1939, 1947).

Animal studies give some picture of visual neural development (Blakemore, 1978) although the analogy to human infants should be applied with caution. Experiments on kittens and young monkeys show that the receptive fields of retinal ganglion cells become more sharply defined over the early weeks of life (Rusoff, 1979) and the acuity reflected in responses of retinal and geniculate cells improves considerably (Ikeda and Tremain, 1978; Blakemore and Vital-Durand, 1979). In the kitten's visual cortex only 1 per cent of the adult number of synapses are present at the time of eye opening (around 9 days). These few synapses allow many cortical neurones to show qualitatively the general properties of directional and orientation selectivity, and binocular organization, that are found in the adult cat, but it is rare to find a cell that is adult-like in all these respects, and cell responses are relatively sluggish and uncertain.

REFRACTION AND ACCOMMODATION OF THE NEONATAL EYE

The quality of the retinal image is determined first, by the physical parameters of the optics of the infant eye, and second, by how well those optics are behaviourally adjusted—i.e. by the accuracy of accommodation.

Ophthalmoscopic examination of the newborn eye shows that the media are clear and the general optical quality is good. The refraction (that is, the focus determined by the dimensions and optical power of the eye when accommodation is relaxed) is on average somewhat hypermetropic (Duke-Elder, 1949). However, the potential amplitude of accommodation is at its maximum in early childhood and is undoubtedly adequate to overcome this long-sightedness and focus the eye on nearby objects, if accommodation can be properly controlled. It is therefore the accuracy of accommodation rather than the relaxed refraction which is most obviously relevant to the quality of infant vision.

Haynes *et al.* (1965) made retinoscopic measurements on freely accommodating infants which led them to conclude that infants of 1 month and under kept their accommodation fixed at a focussing distance of about 20 cm, regardless of target distance. More recent studies, using either a photographic method of assessing instantaneous refractive state (Braddick *et al.*, 1979) or retinoscopy (Banks, 1980; Brookman, 1980) find that this under-represents the performance of 0–1-month olds, who are capable of adjusting their accommodation in the appropriate direction for the target distance. Their most accurate and consistent adjustment, however, is for relatively near distances (20–75 cm); if the stimulus is more distant their position of focus tends to be too close on average (Banks, 1980; Brookman, 1980) and shows large fluctuations (Braddick *et al.*, 1979). These fluctuations led to a number of newborns and 1-month-olds being occasionally but not consistently focused on the target at 1.5 metres, implying that failures to accommodate accurately are due to failures of control rather than to a muscular incapacity to adjust accommodation to some particular range of values.

The above studies indicate that the accuracy of accommodation improves rapidly over the first 3–4 months of life, a period when acuity is also showing a rapid improvement. However, it does not follow that the improving focus is the cause of the improving acuity. In fact, most measurements of neonatal or 1-month acuity have been done with the infants viewing at distances (20–50 cm) at which best focussing has been found, and calculations show that even the largest errors of focus to be expected would not degrade the image sufficiently to restrict infant acuity to the values of 20–30 min arc typical of the first month (Braddick *et al.*, 1979; Banks, 1980). The conclusion is that neonatal acuity is limited by the ability of the immature nervous system to transmit spatial information, not by any optical blurring of the retinal image. It is not known which of the neural changes discussed above is responsible for the increase of acuity in infancy, if any single one is.

If poor optical focus is not the cause of the infant's acuity limit, it may be that instead, any errors of focus are a *consequence* of neurally limited acuity. If information about fine detail is not transmitted by the visual pathway, the infant will not be able to distinguish in-focus from out-of-focus images, since fine detail information will be absent from both. With the visual information needed to adjust the accommodative system appropriately missing, poor or inaccurate control of accommodation is to be expected.

FUNCTIONAL IMPLICATIONS OF INFANTS' SPATIAL VISION

The levels of acuity reported in the first month of life are about twenty to thirty times lower than normal adult acuity. This might at first sight appear so poor as to be functionally ineffective. However, the tasks which demand high acuity in an adult involve either great distances, or resolution of fractions of a millimetre at near distances (e.g. in reading or delicate manipulative tasks). These tasks are not relevant to the neonate, who cannot direct effective action towards objects a few metres away, and to whom objects of concern, such as the face of a parent interacting with them, are normally presented at very close range. At near distances, resolution of 30 min arc will correspond to a useful level of object detail; for instance, at half a metre 5 mm would be resolved, which would allow not just detection of major facial features, but extraction of some information about their shape and expression. This is, as we have seen, the order of distance at which the neonate is usually best accommodated, and at which visual attention is most readily captured (McKenzie and Day, 1972, 1976).

Contrast sensitivity is also relevant to the visual information available to the infant, and like acuity is a small fraction of its adult value. However, as Banks and Salapatek (1981) point out, features such as the hairline of the face normally have a contrast well above the infant's threshold. Further, care should be taken to avoid the fallacy that, because the infant's contrast threshold may be high, targets of contrasts above threshold 'look much fainter to the infant than to an adult'. Apart from the difficulty in principle of making statements about infants' perceptual experience, it should also be realized that in adults, a drop in contrast sensitivity does not necessarily imply a drop in apparent contrast for supra-threshold stimuli (Georgeson and Sullivan, 1975; Hess and Bradley, 1980).

EYE MOVEMENTS

The movements of the eyes are an integral part of the processes of spatial vision. They serve to sample significant parts of the visual world with the high-resolution foveal region of the retina (saccadic eye movements of fixation) and to maintain a stable and foveated image of a steadily moving target (smooth pursuit and optokinetic eye movements).

Saccadic eye movements are present from birth. Individual saccades appear basically similar to those of the adult in their dynamics, and the success of the preferential looking method shows that they are directed towards significant visual targets. However, the programming of these directed saccades is not adult-like. The initial saccade is normally in the required direction but may cover only a fraction of the distance to the target. Fixation is attained by a succession of saccades which appear to be of standard amplitude rather than matched to the target distance (Aslin and Salapatek, 1975).

Newborn infants are often spoken of as 'tracking' a steadily moving object. It must be realized, however, that this is not the same as the adult response, which would be a smooth pursuit movement whose velocity was well matched to the stimulus motion. Instead, the infant refixates along the object's path by a series of abrupt saccades. Smooth pursuit of a discrete target is not observed before about 2 months of age (Dayton and Jones, 1964; Aslin, 1981). However, as we have seen in the discussion of acuity, a moving stimulus that fills a large part of the field of view can elicit OKN in newborns. The dissociation between OKN and pursuit can be demonstrated in the same individual infants with stimuli that are identical except that multiple copies of the ineffective pursuit target are moved to elicit OKN (Atkinson and Braddick, 1981b). The slow phase of OKN follows stimulus motion in a very similar way to smooth pursuit. Thus a response mechanism similar, if not identical, to that producing smooth pursuit must exist in newborns. Perhaps the newborn cannot activate it selectively to follow a moving object when there are competing stationary contours in the rest of the field. (The alternative hypothesis would be that competition is not the factor, but simply that the summated action of a large stimulus field is needed to elicit the response.)

An asymmetry of the OKN response in newborns (and infants under approximately 3 months of age) is revealed when the infant views monocularly. OKN can only be elicited when the stimulus motion is in a temporal-to-nasal direction (Atkinson, 1979). Animal studies, (see Hoffman, 1979) suggest that this direction of OKN is controlled by a pathway that is entirely subcortical, while the opposite direction requires a relay from binocular neurones in the visual cortex to a subcortical centre, the nucleus of the optic tract (NOT). It seems likely, therefore, that the route involving binocular cortex is not functioning in the newborn infant, though we do not yet know whether what is lacking is visual cortex function in general, binocular interaction in cortex in particular, or a functioning pathway from the cortex to the NOT.

BINOCULAR FUNCTION

Most of the eye movements of newborns are conjugate, that is the two eyes execute similar movements together. Binocular vision, however, requires not only that the eyes move together but that their axes are aligned. A number of studies have reported the newborn's eyes to be divergent, but this is probably the result of a systematic error in the corneal reflex method (Slater and Findlay, 1975a). Slater and Findlay (1975b) with newborns, and Aslin (1977) with one-month-olds, have found that convergence changes systematically with target distance, in the direction appropriate for maintaining binocular fixation, but the quantitative precision of these changes improves up to at least 3 months.

The ability to maintain binocular fixation is a requirement for binocular vision, and in adults is specifically controlled by the detection of binocular disparity (Rashbass and Westheimer, 1961). However, it is possible that the newborn's binocular fixation is the result of independent fixation control for each eye. There is not yet any positive evidence of functioning binocular interaction in the newborn. At least some infants of 5–8 weeks show evoked potentials that originate in binocular interaction (Braddick *et al.*, 1980) and behavioural evidence of the detection of stereoscopic disparities has been obtained from infants by 2–4 months (Atkinson and Braddick, 1976; Appel and Campos, 1977; Fox *et al.*, 1980) but none of these techniques has yet been applied to infants in the first month. As mentioned in the previous section, one interpretation of the asymmetry of monocular OKN in neonates is that cortical binocular interaction is not functioning.

Binocular interaction is of particular interest in relation to the course of neural development because it has been extensively studied in animals as an example of neural plasticity (Blakemore, 1978), leading to the idea of a 'critical period' when connections to the cortex may be modified by imbalance or asynchrony of the two eyes' inputs. In monkeys it is believed that this critical period begins at birth (Blakemore *et al.*, 1978). Retrospective studies of strabismic individuals (Banks *et al.*, 1975) have given some information about the time course of plasticity in the human but have not yet been able to answer whether the onset of the critical period for binocularity is at birth or later.[3]

DISTANCE AND DEPTH PERCEPTION

Depth perception in adults is usually discussed in terms of various 'cues', i.e. distinct properties of the stimulus which convey depth information. In principle, there are two distinct questions which can be asked about depth perception in infancy: first, are infants sensitive to the various cue dimensions, and second, if they are sensitive, do they interpret differences in these dimensions as differences in depth? For instance, the preceding section referred to studies which showed that infants (beyond the neonatal period) could detect an area which was differentiated from its background by a difference of binocular disparity. It does not necessarily follow that the infants treated this difference as a depth difference. A similar argument arises from the finding by Fantz (1961) that 1-month infants preferentially fixated a textured sphere when it was paired with a disk of the same diameter. The two stimuli differed in properties such as shading and texture gradients which serve as depth cues for the adult. However, there is no reason to suppose that the preference shown by Fantz's infants depended on a depth interpretation, or even on any organization of the pattern along the cue dimensions which correlate with depth; the fact that the pattern of contrast differed between sphere and disk could be enough to determine a preference.

To demonstrate depth perception as distinct from a sensitivity to properties of the image which serve as depth cues for adults, it is necessary to demonstrate either 'stimulus convergence'—i.e. an equivalence is recognized between similar depth arrangements even when signalled by different cues—or 'response convergence'—a stimulus elicits a response that implies localization in three-dimensional space (Yonas and Pick, 1975). Studies of neonates have so far been restricted to the second of these. Bower *et al.* (1970a) and Ball and Tronick (1971) used 'virtual objects', optical projections whose motion and stereoscopic effects simulated an object approaching the infant. They reported avoidance or defensive responses, such as head withdrawal implying that the change of distance was registered as such. It has proved difficult to distinguish between the supposed withdrawal response and a head movement following the upper moving contour of the moving object, but other defensive response elements such as blinking have been found in further experiments using this technique (Yonas *et al.*, 1979).

As discussed in the next section, McKenzie and Day (1972, 1976) found that the probability that a visual target elicited a change of fixation by infants in the neonatal period was a function of target distance. (The visual angle subtended by the target was constant in these experiments). This implies that infants are sensitive to some property of the stimulus that varies with distance, but gives no indication of what the relevant cue might be.

VISUAL FIELDS AND THE CAPTURE OF VISUAL ATTENTION

The only way in which the extent of the infant's visual field has been studied is by determining the range of positions in the field where the appearance of a target can elicit a shift of fixation. In these terms, the effective visual field of infants appears to be rather restricted: the target has to be within about 25° of the initial fixation point to cause refixation in a newborn, this range increasing to about 35° at age seven weeks[4] (Harris and MacFarlane, 1974). These figures are for the case when the initial central target disappears at the time the peripheral target appears. If the central target remains visible, the newborn's attention can only be attracted by a peripheral target appearing within 15°, and this figure is no greater in the 7-week olds. Moving or flashing stimuli will attract attention at greater peripheral angles (McKenzie and Day, 1976). However, the apparent visual field of young infants contracts in the face of competition from other activities such as sucking.

The effectiveness of a stimulus in capturing a young infant's attention depends not only on its visual angle from the fixation point but also on its distance. Even for an object subtending a constant angular size at the eye, the probability of fixation decreases with increasing distance (McKenzie and Day, 1972, 1976; De Schonen *et al.*, 1978). This finding reinforces the view, discussed above, that the neonate's acuity performance should be considered in relation to nearby targets. It also probably explains, at least in part, the finding that young infants' accommodation is most accurately matched to target distances less than 75 cm:

more distant targets simply do not capture infants' attention effectively enough to serve as the controlling stimuli for accommodation.

COLOUR VISION

The electroretinogram of newborn infants shows responses which are character-istic of the cones, the receptors which subserve colour vision in adults (see reviews by Maurer, 1975; Werner and Wooten, 1979). Beyond this, there is little information on colour vision in neonates. At age 2 months, it is established that spectral sensitivity is similar to the adult (with greater sensitivity in the blue probably as a consequence of less absorption by the macula and ocular media), implying that the three cone types are contributing to overall sensitivity. It is also established that colour discriminations are possible which must depend on the infant's visual system making a comparison of the signals from at least two of these cone types (see Werner and Wooten (1979) who critically review many of the methodological problems of infant colour work). How far these statements are also true of the newborn, and hence how far the newborn is capable of distinguishing different hues, is at present an open question.

SENSITIVITY TO FLICKER AND MOTION

Stimulus motion is effective in attracting the attention both of newborn (see Haith, 1978) and older infants (Volkmann and Dobson, 1976). It might be supposed from this that infants show a differential sensitivity to moving patterns. However, Atkinson *et al.* (1977b) compared contrast sensitivity functions obtained using moving and static gratings with the same infants. They found, both in 1-month-old and older infants, that sensitivity for moving gratings was only higher for those spatial frequencies where adults are also more sensitive to moving gratings, and the difference for infants was no greater than that for adults. This study gave no support, therefore, to any view that systems detecting static and changing stimuli (Kulikowski and Tolhurst, 1973) develop differen-tially in early infancy.

However, there is one respect in which infants show a remarkably high sensitivity to temporal change. Regal (1981), using the preferential looking method, has shown that 1-month infants can detect the flicker of a spatially uniform field at rates up to about 75 per cent of the adult flicker fusion frequency. This may be compared with the detection of *spatial* modulation (i.e. acuity) which at the same age shows less than 10 per cent of adult performance. This result suggests the near-maturity of some mechanism in the infant visual system that is sensitive to rapid temporal modulation; what contribution this me-chanism can make to infants' processing of *spatial* pattern will only be understood when the range of possible stimuli combining spatial and temporal modulation of light has been more fully explored.

PATTERN PROCESSING AND PREFERENCES

The marked preference shown by neonates for fixating a patterned rather than an unpatterned field has encouraged investigators to look for preferences among quantitatively and qualitatively different patterns.

A common theoretical speculation has been that, in the neonatal period at least, infants' pattern preferences could be predicted by ordering the patterns along in a single dimension. 'Complexity' has often been proposed as such a dimension, although it has been difficult to find any satisfactory definition of it. Most attempts to vary complexity, such as varying the check size in a checkerboard, have completely confounded the manipulation with variations of more simply specified physical parameters such as contour length or area (discussed by Haith, 1978). Karmel and Maisel (1975) have argued for contour density (i.e. contour length per unit area) as a predictor of infants' preference, with preference following inverted U-shaped function of contour density that peaks at higher density values with increasing age. (The evidence for this form of function, however, is weaker for neonates than at later ages.). High contour density necessarily implies close contour spacing, and hence it seems inevitable that any decreasing preference for denser contour must be reflecting the limited acuity of the infant. A model which explicitly includes the infant's differential sensitivity to different spatial frequencies might therefore express the underlying sources of the preference better than one which simply incorporates some function of contour density. Banks and Salapatek (1981) have suggested that this could be achieved by taking the summated amplitude of the spatial frequency components of the pattern weighted by their transmission through the infant's visual system as expressed in the contrast sensitivity function. They also suggest some alternative possible determinants of fixation preference that can be expressed in terms of spatial frequency analysis, but do not find that presently available data differentiates among these various possible rules for preference. In summary, although it is plausible that some measure of 'amount of pattern' will prove to be a useful predictor of infants' preferences, we are not yet in a position to express such a rule quantitatively.

Karmel and Maisel (1975) and Haith (1978) go beyond the devising of empirical rules to express pattern preferences, to propose that what underlies such rules is the infant's attempt to maximize the total activity of neurones in the visual cortex. This is an interesting speculation and may have some heuristic value in expressing a number of aspects of neonates' visual behaviour (Haith, 1978). However, in view of the fact that the best quantitative rule of pattern preference is still undecided, and that the properties of the infant's visual cortex must themselves in large part be an inference from visual behaviour, it cannot be regarded as a principle that can be empirically supported or used as a basis for prediction. In considering how complete a theory of preference could be provided along these lines, it should be remembered that one of the most basic preferences shown by neonates is for orienting to moderate light intensities and away from high intensities. Neurones in the cat's visual cortex show rather little dependence of activity on overall level of illumination (Hubel and Wiesel, 1959), so it is possible that infant preference behaviour may depend heavily on the level of neural activity elsewhere in the visual system, e.g. in retinal ganglion cells. Another possibility is that the properties of infant visual cortex are rather different from those that have so far emerged from neurophysiological research on other species.

The attempt to predict visual preferences from some single variable that reflects 'amount of pattern' implies that the form or configuration of that pattern is not being considered as a determinant of visual behaviour in the neonatal period. Indeed, a widespread generalization has been that 'before approximately 1 to 2 months of age there is little evidence that the arrangement or pattern of figural elements plays any role in visual selection or memory' (Salapatek, 1975). Two possible exceptions to this generalization deserve discussion: the effect of curvature and the case of face-like stimuli.

Early in the study of infant visual preferences it was found that a target of concentric circles was a potent stimulus, an important contributing factor to this being general preference for stimuli containing curves over straight edges, in patterns that are matched for area, luminance, and total contour length (Fantz et al., 1975). The specific preference for concentric circles is not found until about 2 months. However, a preference for curved over straight edges in other patterns, matched for total contour, area and luminous flux, has been demonstrated in infants under 7 days of age (Fantz and Miranda, 1975). This preference occurs only when the outermost contour of the figure is curved, an example of the 'externality effect' to which we shall return. Curvature, therefore, seems to be a form variable that is significant even for the youngest infants. No satisfactory ecological or physiological basis for this significance has yet been proposed.

The early work of Fantz (1963) led to the suggestion that a schematic face was a configuration highly preferred by neonates. However, the consensus from more recent work is that any preference for face-like over non-face patterns in infants under 2 months can be accounted for in terms of simpler variables such as contour density and contrast, and possibly symmetry (Haith, 1978; Maurer and Barrera, 1981). Maurer and Barrera used a habituation method to test infants' discrimination of a natural face pattern from symmetrical and asymmetrical scrambled versions of the same elements. This might be expected to show discriminative abilities that were not revealed by preference studies, but while these authors found evidence that 2-month-olds could discriminate among all three patterns, their 1-month-old subjects gave no evidence of discrimination.

However, Goren et al. (1975) tested infants a few minutes after birth for extent of head and eye turns following moving face-like and scrambled-face configurations. Observers who were 'blind' as to the stimulus being presented reported following of the face-like pattern over significantly greater angles than for either scrambled pattern, implying an innate differentiation of these stimuli. Maurer and Hutchison (personal communication) have attempted to replicate this result (with some differences from Goren *et al.*'s rather complex scoring procedure and with the infants seated rather than held), but found weaker effects, with a significant difference in following only when the face-like stimulus was compared with the more grossly scrambled face.

It is therefore still equivocal whether infants have any innate sensitivity to the configuration of the face as such, or indeed whether they acquire it in the first month. However, there are studies showing that, by 5–7 weeks, infants can visually differentiate between the real (Carpenter, 1974) or photographed (Bushnell, 1980) faces of different individuals. The contrast between these results on the one hand, and the difficulty of showing discrimination of face-like from scrambled configurations on the other, is not as striking as it may seem. Bushnell (1980) showed that 5–7-week-olds required differences in the external outline of the face area (i.e. hairline) to perform this discrimination, although older infants could discriminate on the basis of internal features alone. In the face versus scrambled face studies, the features were presented within a standardized outline. The 'externality effect' (see below) appears to be playing an important role here. Maurer and Barrera (personal communication) found that, when there was no outer limiting contour, 1-month infants could differentiate the face-like and scrambled configurations that had not been differentiated in these authors' earlier habituation study. It may be that the discriminations of internal detail shown in Goren *et al.*'s experiment and in Maurer's attempted replication were possible because the use of a moving stimulus overcame the externality effect (Bushnell, 1979).

THE EXTERNALITY EFFECT

We have already described a number of lines of evidence that the visual discriminations of infants in the first month of life depend on the outermost contour of figures and are not sensitive to internal detail. This has been explicitly demonstrated by Milewski (1976) who tested recovery from habituation to visual patterns which were presented contingent on high-amplitude sucking. His patterns consisted of one geometrical figure enclosed within another: response recovery occurred in 5-week-olds if there was a change in the outer figure but not with an equivalent change in the inner figure. Older infants demonstrated response recovery with changes of either the internal or external figure. Milewski's result does not appear to be a consequence of acuity limitations. Nor is it due to a capacity limit that restricts visual attention to one element at a time, since Bushnell (1979) has shown that motion of the internal figure allows it to be discriminated but does not divert the infant from being able to discriminate the outer figure also.

These findings on discrimination are consistent with the results of eye-movement recordings (Salapatek, 1975; Maurer and Salapatek, 1976; Hainline, 1978) which have shown that infants in the first month concentrate their fixations on the outer boundaries of faces and geometric figures, while 2-month-olds scan internal features also.

VISUAL DEVELOPMENT IMMEDIATELY FOLLOWING THE NEONATAL PERIOD

In many of the aspects of visual behaviour that have been discussed, radical changes occur between the first and third month of life, implying that the vision of the neonate is qualitatively different from that of an infant only a few months older. These differences may be summarized: (i) the low-spatial-frequency cut appears in the contrast sensitivity function; (ii) smooth pursuit eye movements become possible; (iii) the cortical-to-subcortical route that controls monocular OKN in response to nasal-to-temporal stimulus motion becomes effective; (iv) infants come to fixate internal pattern details as well as the external boundary, and becomes able to make pattern discriminations based on internal details; (v) various pattern preferences, e.g. for a concentric bullseye pattern and for irregular over regular arrangements of elements, become manifest (Fantz et al., 1975).

We do not know what underlying development might be responsible for this set of changes, or indeed to what extent they have a common cause. One proposal is that the changes around 2 months of age mark the onset of cortical visual function, and that the visual behaviour of the neonate is controlled by subcortical pathways, particularly that to the superior colliculus (Bronson, 1974). Difference (iii) above is obviously in accord with this suggestion, and the externality effect (iv) bears a suggestive resemblance to behaviour reported for a monkey with bilateral striate cortex lesions (Humphrey, 1974). Maurer and Lewis (1979) point out that the pattern discriminations that can be demonstrated in newborns and 1-month-olds go beyond those that are believed possible for primates lacking striate cortex. They propose instead that while the X-cell pathway to cortex is functional at birth, until about 2 months the retinal Y-cells project effectively to the colliculus but not to the cortex. (See Stone et al. (1979) and Lennie (1980) for discussion of these two pathways.) This proposal is in line with neurophysiological evidence on the relative development of these two classes of cell within the geniculo-striate pathway (Daniels et al., 1978; Rusoff, 1979). However, it is a difficult proposal to evaluate, since if both X- and Y-cells are functional in the newborn's visual system, albeit projecting to different central structures, no simple predictions can be made concerning whether particular types of visual behaviour will show sensitivity characteristic of X- or Y-cells. It is also not clear, if one major route to striate cortex is effective in the newborn, that visual behaviour should show the resemblances that it does to what would be expected in the absence of cortical function. At present, therefore, both the suggestion that neonatal vision reflects subcortical processing only, and the suggestion that it reflects a partial function of the cortical pathways must be regarded as speculative.

AUDITORY SENSITIVITY OF THE NEONATE

Since the complex structures of the ear have to transmit mechanical vibration to the neural transducers in the cochlea, auditory function depends heavily on the dimensions and mechanical properties of these structures. However, these are in an advanced state of development at birth (Hecox, 1975). The external ear is still a long way short of its adult dimensions but this is of little acoustic importance. The middle ear cavity also continues to grow during early childhood but the chain of ossicles whose properties principally determine transmission to the inner ear have reached adult dimensions and rigidity by birth. The dimensions of the cochlea, which are a major factor in determining the frequency response of the ear, attain adult values by the fifth month of gestation. Within the cochlea, all the main anatomical features are essentially adult-like at birth, except that development of the outermost row of hair cells (the sensory receptors) continues after birth. The auditory nerve is said to be well myelinated at birth.

Measurements of acoustic impedance ('tympanograms') in the neonate can give some information on the mechanical properties of the middle ear (Bennett, 1975; Weir, 1979). They do not support the view that the neonate's middle ear is filled with fluid or tissue, which if true would be expected to produce considerable transmission loss. This technique also allows the acoustic reflex or stapedial response to be detected (Robertson et al., 1968; Bennett, 1975). Robertson et al. found that the threshold sound level to elicit this response was only 5-10 dB higher than in the adult. This is taken as evidence that any conductive loss in the neonatal ear, relative to the adult, is no greater than this figure. It must be realized, however, that these observations do not tell us anything directly about auditory thresholds, since in both adult and infant the sound levels eliciting the reflex are well above those which are known to be detected. The argument therefore has to suppose that the reflex is not more sensitive in the neonate than in the adult.

Auditory 'thresholds' have been determined in neonates as the lowest sound intensities which will elicit changes in cardiac, respiratory, or general motor activity (Weir, 1979; Schneider et al., 1979). A number of studies find that these responses can be produced by pure tones 40-60 dB above adult thresholds for the same sounds. Similar relationships between neonate and adult sensitivities have been found for the intensity of clicks needed to produce cortical evoked potentials (Hecox, 1975; Schneider et al., 1979). However, there are components of the auditory evoked potential which have shorter latency than those ascribed to the cortex, known as 'brainstem evoked potentials' and believed to reflect activity in the auditory nerve and brainstem nuclei. Hecox (1975) reports that brainstem EPs could be detected in newborns from click stimuli 17 dB louder than the minimum intensity required in adults. It seems likely, therefore, that the neonate's peripheral auditory apparatus has a sensitivity at most 10–20 dB lower than the adult's. We do not know how far the lower sensitivity shown by behavioural and cortical EP measures reflects immaturity of the central auditory pathway and how far it is due to the insensitivity of these measures.

Auditory sensitivity is, of course, a function of sound frequency. Neonatal behavioural studies have generally found either an approximately constant sensitivity (in terms of sound pressure level) in the range 100–4000 Hz (Weir, 1979; Crowell et al., 1971) or a decline in sensitivity with increasing frequency over this range (Hutt et al., 1968; Eisele et al., 1975). Either result implies a greater effectiveness of low-frequency relative to high-frequency sounds for infants compared to adults, who show maximum sensitivity for frequencies between 2000–4000 Hz.

It must be kept in mind, however, that 'effectiveness' here means 'effectiveness in eliciting the behaviour under study'. Eisele et al.'s measure, for instance, can be argued to reflect the aversive effect of the various sounds, which could well depend on other factors besides sensory sensitivity.

Most evoked potential studies have not been suitable for analysing neonatal frequency sensitivity, since the click stimuli most commonly used contain a broad band of frequencies. However, Hecox (1975) has investigated how effectively the brainstem EP from clicks is suppressed by masking noise in various frequency bands. He found that masking frequencies of 4000 Hz and above, which had quite marked effects on adult EPs, made little difference to the neonates' EPs, implying that the latter were generated primarily by mechanisms responding to low frequencies.

The physiological explanation of any differential development of low- and high-frequency sensitivity is uncertain. Functionally, Hutt et al. (1968) suggest that the neonate's frequency response 'ensures that the voice at normal intensities is non-aversive and prepotent'. While we might be sceptical of the implied teleology, or argue that the low-frequency band is rich in informative environmental sounds besides voices, it is at least clear that neonates' auditory apparatus is quite capable of detecting many of the significant sounds surrounding them at ordinary levels, including the information-bearing frequency components of human speech.

The capability to discriminate sounds is perhaps of more functional interest than the simple ability to detect them, but is also more difficult to study in neonates. There have been studies aimed at neonatal frequency discrimination, but without either firm knowledge of infants' equal-loudness functions, or experimental designs that randomize intensity, it is difficult to separate frequency and loudness discrimination in the interpretation. However, it is clear that soon after the neonatal period infants are capable of some very subtle auditory discriminations. For example, at three weeks, the ability to detect differences between different individuals' voices has been indicated (Mills and Melhuish, 1974; Mehler and Bertoncini, 1979), and there is a large body of work on discrimination of speech sounds from 1 month onwards (Eimas, 1975; Kuhl, 1978). Nor are the phenomena studied limited to speech sounds (Jusczyk *et al.*, 1977). These performances depend on detecting complex invariants of temporal and spectral patterning, and it seems likely that the foundations of the ability to differentiate these dimensions should be present very soon after birth, which is only a few weeks earlier.

AUDITORY LOCALIZATION

Wertheimer's (1961) observation that a single neonate made head turns towards a clicking stimulus within minutes after birth has stimulated a good deal of research and controversy on the neonate's ability to localize sounds (reviewed by Muir *et al.*, 1979). Although some studies have failed to find any evidence of neonates orienting to sound sources (e.g. Butterworth and Castillo, 1976) it now seems established that such orientation does occur when the conditions of testing are optimized. Optimal conditions may include: the use of prolonged stimuli rather than stimuli which terminate before the response is initiated; an experimental design which allows the detection of responses with latencies which may be as long as 20 s; the use of voice stimuli rather than pure tones; an upright rather than a lying posture for the infant; the absence of any competing central visual stimulus. Muir *et al.* (1979) report that, when these conditions are met, head turns are not simply in the appropriate direction but are also graded in extent according to how far the sound source is from the midline. It is likely that the use of prolonged stimuli is especially important here, since if the stimulus continues while the infant is making the turn, accurate orientation could be achieved even if the only discrimination possible was a crude left/right one *relative to the head.*

Muir *et al.* (1979) also present evidence that it actually becomes more difficult to elicit orientation to sound sources as infants grow older, up to about 3 months. By 4 months a brisk and accurate response has appeared. There is not yet any established explanation of the decline from the neonate's responsiveness, although Muir *et al.* (1979) suggest that it is associated with a developing co-ordination of auditory and visual space.

THE CHEMICAL SENSES

Neonates' ability to make discriminations of odour is demonstrated by the fact that they show odour aversions and preferences. Rieser *et al.* (1976) found a significant tendency for 1–6-day-olds to turn away from a drop of ammonium hydroxide presented on a cotton swab, and Steiner (1979) reports that neonates produced 'accepting' facial expressions (assessed by observers 'blind' to the odour) when presented with fruit odours and 'rejecting' expressions for fishy and rotten-egg odours! Much more subtle discriminative ability is shown by Macfarlane's (1975) finding that 6–10-day infants oriented to the odour of their own mothers' breast pads not only in preference to an unused breast pad but also to one taken from an unfamiliar nursing mother. (The preference was not found in 2-day infants, possibly implying that it was learned.) It is striking how readily infants make the complex sensory discriminations between human individuals, not only in olfaction but also only a few weeks later in the visual (Carpenter, 1974; Bushnell, 1980) and auditory (Mills and Melhuish, 1974) modalities.

Habituation studies (Engen *et al.*, 1963; Engen and Lipsitt, 1965) give further evidence of neonates' powers of odour discrimination. In these tests respiratory and activity changes decrease with repeated presentation of one odorant, but reappear when a new odorant is introduced. Discrimination has been shown in this way between anise oil and asafoetida, and between amyl acetate/heptanol mixtures and solutions of the separate components which adults judge to be of equal odorous intensity. However, it is difficult to take studies of this kind much further in the absence of a satisfactory theory of the dimensions of odour sensation in adults.

Presumably, infants' odour discriminations play a part in food preferences and the avoidance of noxious substances. These appear more directly in studies of taste, which have generally depended on infants' sucking responses when solutions are introduced into the mouth. An increase in sucking rate induced by sweet tastes has been quite widely found. In the data of Crook (1978) this effect increases with sucrose concentrations up to 0.4 molar but declines for stronger solutions, a U-shaped function which is in accord with some data on adult preferences. Desor *et al.* (1973) found that adult preferences were also reflected in neonates' greater ingestion of sucrose and fructose compared with glucose and lactose.

Maller and Desor (1973) could not demonstrate any discrimination of salt, sour, or bitter solutions from water on the basis of quantity ingested. However, Crook (1978) suggests that this measure is influenced by sucking induced by the simple presence of fluid in the mouth. He measured changes in sucking induced by the delivery of very small volumes of solution, and found that salt solutions decreased non-nutritive sucking below baseline rates by an amount which increased with concentration. Steiner (1979) has reported distinctive facial expressions from newborns ingesting sweet, sour (citric acid) and bitter (quinine sulphate) solutions, similar to those of adults tasting the same substances.

In summary, the chemical senses are clearly capable of a variety of qualitative and quantitative discriminations in the neonate, some quite subtle. Most of these discriminations seem to be coupled with marked appetitive or aversive effects, and in general these reflect a similar structure of preference to that found in the adult, a structure whose links to the sensory mechanisms appear to be innate.

INTERMODAL AND SENSORY-MOTOR CORRESPONDENCES

We have seen that newborn infants are capable of a wide variety of discriminations in different sensory modalities. The fact that some behaviour reflects a sensory discrimination, however, does not necessarily tell us what the sensory patterns concerned signify for the infant. Indeed, it may be difficult to attach a clear meaning to the 'significance' of a stimulus to an infant, so long as we are only considering its relationship to other stimuli in the same modality. We can say more, however, if the infant shows evidence that differences in one sensory modality bear some relation of correspondence to differences in another. For example, Spelke (1976) showed infants (who were beyond the neonatal stage) a pair of films while playing a soundtrack appropriate to one of them: the infants preferentially looked at the film corresponding to the sound. At the least this indicates that the infants possessed a structure of associations linking classes of stimulus sequence in the two modalities. Such a structure can be considered to be the foundation of a representation of external events which goes beyond the simple registration of particular sensory properties. One of the most fundamental examples is the idea of a representation of space around the infant's body, and of the body itself, which couples the various sensory modalities which give spatially localized information. Space has to be psychologically represented not only as a framework for perceived objects and events, but also as the framework within which actions are planned and executed. Therefore, evidence of spatially organized sensory-motor links, as well as that of correspondences between sensory modalities, can tell us about the development of representations which make it meaningful to think of sensory events as having a 'significance' for the infant. We have already presented arguments of this kind in our discussion of depth perception.

While there has been quite extensive study of auditory-visual correspondences, both spatial and otherwise, in older infants (see review by Mendelson, 1979) there seems to be almost no evidence on whether infants in the first month can respond to correspondences and mismatches between these modalities. Experiments on auditory localization, especially when eye rather than head turning has been the dependent measure, have sometimes been cited as evidence for auditory-visual correspondence. The occurrence of an orienting response, even one involving the eyes, shows that there is a mapping of an auditory sensory dimension onto a response dimension in a spatially organized way. The occurrence of orientation to visual stimuli establishes the existence of an analogous visuomotor relationship. Each of these mappings can be regarded as an internal representation of space, but it does not strictly follow that they involve a unified representation that is common to auditory and visual modalities. However, this is plausible, especially given neurophysiological evidence that the superior colliculus, which is known to play an important part in eye and head orientation (Wurtz and Albano, 1980), has a neural representation of space which is common to visual, auditory, and tactile modalities (Dräger and Hubel, 1975).

The richer the repertory of spatially directed responses, the more compelling is the idea of a central representation of space which interlinks different sensory modalities and different motor acts, since it would be absurdly cumbersome for each class of actions to depend on an independent set of sensory-motor links. From later infancy to adulthood, such a representation is most strikingly evident in the variety, precision and flexibility of eye-hand co-ordination. The prototype of this co-ordination is visually directed reaching. Hence the reports that neonates will make frequent and quite accurate reaches for a seen object (Bower *et al.*, 1970b) and even adjust the form of the hand appropriately to object size (Bower, 1972) have excited a great deal of interest and controversy. A number of studies (reviewed by McDonnell, 1979) have failed to replicate these findings in terms of the frequency and precision of the reaches. However, it appears from these studies that the presence of a nearby visual object does elicit occasional (1–5 per min) arm movements in neonates, and that the direction of these movements bears a statistically significant relationship to the position of the object (McDonnell, 1979). It would be valuable to know how far these results can be accounted for by orientation of the trunk towards the stimulus, coupled with a range of arm movements which is non-random with respect to the trunk.

It should be pointed out that investigators agree that these neonatal responses, while initiated visually, are not visually guided. That is, they are ballistic in nature and are not corrected during execution by means of visual information. Visually *guided* reaching, in which the seen position of the hand is related to the seen position of the target, and used to control the reach during the course of execution, does not develop until around 5 months.

Spatially directed responses are not the only possible type of actions that are linked to sensory input via a shared representation. Imitation provides another instance. Meltzoff and Moore (1977) report that 12–21-day infants will imitate gestures presented to them by an adult, sufficiently reliably that scorers who did not know the gesture being presented could significantly differentiate the different gestures by watching videotapes of the infants. (Some other workers[5] have not been able to obtain this result, however.) The occurrence of imitative behaviour indicates that the infants possess a representation which links the initiation of their own motor actions to the visual appearance of the same actions performed by others. In the case of manual gestures these links could be mediated by infants' visual observation of the appearance of their own actions. However, several of the gestures used by Meltzoff and Moore were facial gestures (mouth opening, tongue protrusion) for which it is very unlikely that the infants had experienced the visual appearance of the gestures when performed by themselves. Meltzoff and Moore therefore suggest that newborn infants possess an intrinsic 'supramodal representation' (Bower, 1974) in which visual, proprioceptive and motor control information are unified. This idea seems to carry the implication that infants do not differentiate between the different modalities contributing to this representation, i.e. in imitation the visually perceived actions performed by others are not represented as distinct from the proprioceptively perceived actions performed by the infants themselves. Moore and Meltzoff (1978) contrast this neonatal imitation with the better-known imitation of the 12-month-old which they believe is based on the infant's knowledge that 'he looks like the other and the other looks like him'. On this view perceptual development does not involve the formation of correspondences between initially unconnected modalities, but rather the recognition of distinct modalities within a system in which they are initially undifferentiated. While the imitation experiments support the idea of a representation that combines modalities, it is challenging to think of an experiment which could provide persuasive evidence that these modalities are undifferentiated for the infant. Whatever its nature, a representation which incorporates correspondences between the infant's own body and that of other human beings (what Trevarthen has called 'primary intersubjectivity') is clearly of great importance in the development of social cognition. The act of imitation itself (and also the imitation of children by parents) may well serve as one of the prototypes for reciprocal social behaviour.

REFERENCES

Allen, J. L. (1978). *The development of visual acuity in human infants during the early postnatal weeks.* Unpublished PhD thesis, University of Washington.

Appel, M. A. and Campos, J. J. (1977). Binocular disparity as a discriminable stimulus parameter for young infants, *J. exp. Child Psychol.*, **23**, 47–56.

Aslin, R. N. (1977). Development of binocular fixation in human infants, *J. exp. Child Psychol.*, **23**, 133–150.

Aslin, R. N. (1981). The development of smooth pursuit in human infants, in *Eye Movements: Cognition and Visual Perception*, (Eds D. F. Fisher, R. A. Monty, and J. W. Senders), Lawrence Erlbaum, Hillsdale, N. J.

Aslin, R. N. and Salapatek, P. (1975). Saccadic localization of peripheral targets by the very young human infant, *Percept. Psychophys.*, **17**, 293–302.

Atkinson, J. (1979). Development of optokinetic nystagmus in the human infant and monkey infant: an analogue to development in kittens, in *Developmental Neurobiology of Vision* (Ed. R. D. Freeman), Plenum Press, New York.

Atkinson, J. and Braddick, O. (1976). Stereoscopic discrimination in infants, *Perception*, **5**, 29–38.

Atkinson, J. and Braddick, O. (1981a). Acuity, contrast sensitivity and accommodation in infancy, in *The Development of Perception: Psychobiological Perspectives*, Vol. II (Eds R. N. Aslin, J. R. Alberts, and M. R. Peterson) Academic Press, New York.

Atkinson, J. and Braddick, O. (1981b). Development of optokinetic nystagmus in infants: an indicator of cortical binocularity? In *Eye Movements: Cognition and Visual Perception*,(Eds D. F. Fisher, R. A. Monty, and J. W. Senders), Lawrence Erlbaum, Hillsdale, N. J.

Atkinson, J., Braddick, O., and French, J. (1979). Contrast sensitivity of the human neonate measured by the visual evoked potential, *Invest. Ophthal. vis. Sci.*, **18**, 210–213.

Atkinson, J., Braddick, O., and Moar, K. (1977a). Development of contrast sensitivity over the first 3 months of life in the human infant, *Vision Res.*, **17**, 1037–1044.

Atkinson, J. Braddick, O., and Moar, K. (1977b). Contrast sensitivity of the human infant for moving and static patterns, *Vision Res.*, **17**, 1045–1047.

Ball, W. and Tronick, E. (1971). Infant responses to impending collision: optical and real, *Science*, **171**, 818–820.

Banks, M. S. (1980). The development of visual accommodation during early infancy, *Child Devel.*, **51**, 646–666.

Banks, M. S., Aslin, R. N., and Letson, R. D. (1975). Sensitive period for the development of human binocular vision, *Science*, **190**, 765–767.

Banks, M. S. and Salapatek, P. (1978). Acuity and contrast sensitivity in 1-, 2- and 3-month-old human infants, *Invest. Ophthal. vis. Sci.*, **17**, 361–365.

Banks, M. S. and Salapatek, P. (1981). Infant pattern vision: a new approach based on the contrast sensitivity function, *J. exp. Child Psychol.*, **31**, 1–45.

Bennett, M. (1975). Acoustic impedance bridge measurements with the neonate, *Brit. J. Audiol.* **9**, 117–124.

Blakemore, C. (1978). Maturation and modification in the developing visual pathway, in *Handbook of Sensory Physiology*, Vol. VIII, *Perception* (Eds R. Held, H. W. Leibowitz, and H. L. Teuber), Springer-Verlag, Berlin.

Blakemore, C., Garey, L. J., and Vital-Durand, F. (1978). The physiological effects of monocular deprivation and their reversal in the monkey's visual cortex, *J. Physiol.*, **283**, 223–262.

Blakemore, C., and Vital-Durand, F. (1979). Development of the neural basis of visual acuity in monkeys. *Trans. Ophthal. Soc. U.K.*, **99**, 363–368.

Bower, T. G. R. (1972). Object perception in infants, *Perception*, **1**, 15–30.

Bower, T. G. R. (1974). *Development in Infancy*, W. H. Freeman, San Francisco.

Bower, T. G. R., Broughton, J. M., and Moore, M. K. (1970a). Infant responses to approaching objects, *Percept. Psychophys.*, **9**, 193–196.

Bower, T. G. R., Broughton, J. M., and Moore, M. K. (1970b). The co-ordination of visual and tactual input in infants, *Percept. Psychophys.*, **8**, 51–53.

Braddick, O. J., Atkinson, J., French, J., and Howland, H. C. (1979). A photorefractive study of infant accommodation, *Vision Res.*, **19**, 1319–1330.

Braddick, O., Atkinson, J., Julesz, B., Kropfl, W., Bodis-Wollner, I., and Raab, E. (1980) Cortical binocularity in infants. *Nature, (Lond.)*, **288**, 363–365.

Bronson, G. (1974). The postnatal growth of visual capacity, *Child Devel.*, **45**, 873–890.

Brookman, K. E. (1980). *Ocular accommodation in the human infant*, Unpublished doctoral dissertation, Indiana University.

Bushnell, I. W. R. (1979). Modification of the externality effect in young infants, *J. exp. Child Psychol.*, **28**, 211–229.

Bushnell, I. W. R. (1980). *Face perception in early infancy*, Unpublished PhD thesis, University of Cambridge.

Butterworth, G. and Castillo, M. (1976). Co-ordination of auditory and visual space in newborn human infants, *Perception*, **5**, 155–160.

Carpenter, G. C. (1974). Visual regard of moving and stationary faces in early infancy, *Merrill-Palmer Quarterly*, **20**, 181–184.

Crook, C. K. (1978). Taste perception in the newborn infant, *Infant Behav. and Devel.* **1**, 52–69.

Conel, J. L. (1939, 1947). *The Postnatal Development of the Human Cerebral Cortex*, Vols 1, 3. Harvard University Press, Cambridge, Mass.

Crowell, D. H., Jones, R. H., Nakgawa, J. K., and Kapuniai, L. E. (1971). Heart rate responses of human newborns to modulated pure tones, *Proc. roy. Soc. Med.*, **64**, 472–474.

Daniels, J. D., Pettigrew, J. D., and Norman, J. L. (1978). Development of single unit responses in the kitten's lateral geniculate nucleus, *J. Neurophysiol.* **41**, 1373–1393.

Dayton, G. O. and Jones, M. H. (1964). Analysis of characteristics of fixation reflexes in infants by use of DC electrooculography, *Neurology*, **14**, 1152–1156.

Dayton, G. O., Jones, M. H., Aiu, P., Rawson, R. A., Steele, B., and Rose, M. (1964). Developmental study of co-ordinated eye movements in the human infant. I, *Arch. Ophthalmol.*, **71**, 865–870.

De Schonen, S., McKenzie, B., Maury, L., and Bresson, F. (1978). Central and peripheral object distances as determinants of the effective visual field in early infancy, *Perception*, **7**, 499–506.

Desor, J. A., Maller, O., and Turner, R. E. (1973). Taste acceptance of sugars by human infants, *J. comp. physiol. Psychol.*, **84**, 496–501.

Dobson, V., Mayer, D. L., and Lee, C. P. (1980). Assessment of visual acuity in pre-term infants. *Invest. Ophthal. vis. Sci.*, **19**, 1498–1505.

Dobson, V. and Teller, D. Y. (1978). Visual acuity in human infants: a review and comparison of behavioural and electrophysiological studies, *Vision Res.*, **18**, 1469–1483.

Dräger, U. C. and Hubel, D. H. (1975). Responses to visual stimulation and relationship between visual, auditory, and somatosensory inputs in mouse superior colliculus, *J. Neurophysiol.*, **38**, 690–713.

Duke-Elder, W. S. (1949). *Textbook of Ophthalmology*, Vol. IV, Henry Kimpton, London.

Eimas, P. D. (1975). Auditory and phonetic coding of the cues for speech discrimination of the /r/-/l/ distinction by young infants, *Percept. Psychophys.*, **18**, 341–343.

Eisele, W. A., Berry, R. C., and Shriner, T. H. (1975). Infant sucking response patterns as a conjugate function of changes in the sound pressure level of auditory stimuli, *J. Speech. Hear. Res.*, **18**, 296–307.

Engen, T. and Lipsitt, L. P. (1965). Decrement and recovery of responses to olfactory stimuli in the human neonate, *J. comp. physiol. Psychol.*, **59**, 312–316.

Engen, T., Lipsitt, L. P., and Kaye, H. (1963). Olfactory responses and adaptation in the human neonate, *J. comp. physiol. Psychol.*, **56**, 73–77.

Fantz, R. L. (1961). A method for studying depth perception in infants under 6 months, *Psychol. Record*, **11**, 27–33.

Fantz, R. L. (1963). Pattern vision in newborn infants, *Science*, **140**, 296–297.

Fantz, R. L. and Miranda, S. (1975). Newborn infant attention to form and contour, *Child Devel.*, **46**, 224–228.

Fantz, R. L., Fagan, J. F., and Miranda, S. B. (1975). Early visual selectivity. In *Infant Perception: From Sensation to Cognition*, Vol. 1 (Eds L. B. Cohen, and P. Salapatek), Academic Press, New York.

Fantz, R. L., Ordy, J. M., and Udelf, M. C. (1962). Maturation of pattern vision in infants during the first 6 months, *J. comp. physiol. Psychol.*, **55**, 907–917.

Ferriss, G. S., Davis, G. D., Dorsen, M. M., and Hackett, E. R. (1967). Changes in latency and form of the photically induced average evoked response in human infants, *Electroenceph. clin. Neurophysiol.*, **22**, 305–312.

Fox, R., Aslin, R. N., Shea, S. L., and Dumais, S. T. (1980). Stereopsis in human infants, *Science*, **207**, 323–324.

Georgeson, M. A. and Sullivan, G. D. (1975). Contrast constancy: deblurring in human vision by spatial frequency channels, *J. Physiol.*, **187**, 517–552.

Goren, G. C., Sarty, M., and Wu, P. Y. K. (1975). Visual following and pattern discrimination of face-like stimuli by newborn infants, *Pediatrics*, **56**, 544–549.

Gorman, J. J., Cogan, D. G., and Gellis, S. S. (1957). An apparatus for grading the visual acuity of infants on the basis of optokinetic nystagmus, *Pediatrics*, **19**, 1088–1092.

Gorman, J., Cogan, D., and Gellis, S. (1959). A device for testing visual acuity in infants, *Sight-saving Rev.*, **29**, 80–84.

Hainline, L. D. (1978). Developmental changes in the scanning of face and non-face patterns by infants, *J. exp. Child Psychol.*, **25**, 90–115.

Haith, M. M. (1978). Visual competence in early infancy, in *Handbook of Sensory Physiology*, Vol. VIII, *Perception* (Eds R. Held. H. Leibo witz, and H. L. Teuber), Springer-Verlag, Berlin.

Harris, P. and MacFarlane, A. (1974). The growth of the effective visual field from birth to seven weeks, *J. exp. Child. Psychol.*, **18**, 340–348.

Harter, M. R., Deaton, F. K., and Odom, J. V. (1977). Visual evoked potentials to checkerboard flashes in infants from six days to six months, in *New Developments in Visual Evoked Potentials of the Human Brain* (Ed. J. E. Desmedt), Oxford University Press, Oxford.

Haynes, H., White, B. L., and Held, R. (1965). Visual accommodation in human infants, *Science*, **148**, 528–530.

Hecox, K. (1975). Electrophysiological correlates of human auditory development, in *Infant Perception: From Sensation to Cognition.* Vol. II (Eds L. B. Cohen and P. Salapatek), Academic Press, New York.

Hess, R. F. and Bradley, A. (1980). Contrast perception above threshold is only minimally impaired in human amblyopia, *Nature (Lond.)*, **287**, 463–464.

Hoffman, K. P. (1979). Optokinetic nystagmus and single-cell responses in the nucleus tractus opticus after early monocular deprivation in the cat, in *Developmental Neurobiology of Vision* (Ed. R. D. Freeman), Plenum Press, New York.

Hubel, D. H. and Wiesel, T. N. (1959). Receptive fields of single neurones in the cat's striate cortex, *J. Physiol.*, **148**, 574–591.

Humphrey, N. K. (1974). Vision in a monkey without striate cortex: a case study, *Perception*, **3**, 241–256.

Hutt, S. J., Hutt, C., Lenard, H. G., Bernuth, H., and Muntjerweff, W. J. (1968). Auditory responsivity in the human neonate, *Nature (Lond.)*, **218**, 888–890.

Ikeda, H. and Tremain, K. E. (1978). Development of spatial resolving power of lateral geniculate neurones in kittens, *Exp. Brain Res.*, **31**, 193–206.

Jusczyk, P. W., Rosner, B. S., Cutting, J. E., Foard, C. F., and Smith, L. B. (1977). Categorical perception of nonspeech sounds by 2-month-old infants, *Percept. Psychophys.*, **21**, 50–54.

Karmel, B. Z., and Maisel, E. B., (1975). A neuronal activity model for infant visual attention, in *Infant Perception: From Sensation to Cognition*, Vol. 1 (Eds L. B. Cohen and P. Salapatek), Academic Press, New York.

Kulikowski, J. J. and Tolhurst, D. J. (1973). Psychophysical evidence for sustained and transient detectors in human vision, *J. Physiol.*, **322**, 149–162.

Kuhl, P. K. (1978). Predispositions for the perception of speech-sound categories: a species-specific phenomenon? In *Communicative and Cognitive Abilities—Early Behavioural Assessment*, (Eds F. D. Minifie and L. L. Lioyd), University Park Press, Baltimore.

Lennie, P. (1980). Parallel visual pathways: a review, *Vision Res.*, **20**, 561–594.

McDonnell, P. M. (1979). Patterns of eye-hand co-ordination in the first year of life, *Canad, J. Psychol.*, **33**, 253–267.

Macfarlane, A. (1975). Olfaction in the development of social preferences in the human neonate, in *Parent-Infant Interaction. CIBA Symposium*, Vol. **33**, pp. 103–113, Ciba Foundation, Amsterdam.

McKenzie, B. and Day, R. H. (1972). Object distance as a determinant of visual fixation in early infancy, *Science*, **178**, 1108–1110.

McKenzie, B. and Day, R. H. (1976). Infants' attention to stationary and moving objects at different distances, *Austral. J. Psychol.*, **28**, 45–51.

Maller, O. and Desor, J. A. (1973). Effect of taste on ingestion by human newborns, in *Fourth Symposium on Oral Sensation and Perception* (Ed. J. F. Bosma) U.S. Government Printing Office, Washington DC.

Mann, I. C. (1964). *The Development of the Human Eye*, British Medical Association, London.

Marg, E., Freeman, D. N., Peltzman, P., and Goldstein, P. J. (1976). Visual acuity development in human infants: evoked potential measurements. *Invest. Ophthalmol.*, **15**, 150–153.

Maurer, D. (1975). Infant visual perception: Methods of study. In *Infant perception: From Sensation to Cognition*, Vol. I (Eds L. B. Cohen and P. Salapatek), Academic Press, New York.

Maurer, D. and Barrera, M. (1981). Infants' perception of natural and distorted arrangement of a schematic face, *Child Devel.* **52**, 196–202.

Maurer, D. and Lewis, T. L. (1979). A physiological explanation of infants' early visual development, *Canad. J. Psychol.*, **33**, 232–252.

Maurer, D. and Salapatek, P. (1976). Developmental changes in the scanning of faces by young infants, *Child Devel.*, **47**, 523–527.

Mehler, J. and Bertoncini, J. (1979). Infants' perception of speech and other acoustic stimuli, in *Psycholinguistics Series—2: Structures and Processes*. (Eds J. Morton and J. C. Marshall), Paul Elek, London.

Meltzoff, A. N. and Moore, M. K. (1977). Imitation of facial and manual gestures by human neonates, *Science*, **198**, 75–78.

Mendelson, M. (1979). Acoustic-optical correspondences and auditory-visual co-ordination in infancy, *Canad. J. Psychol.*, **33**, 334–345.

Milewski, A. (1976). Infants' discrimination of internal and external pattern elements, *J. exp. Child Psychol.*, **22**, 229–246.

Mills, M. and Melhuish, E. (1974). Recognition of mother's voice in early infancy, *Nature (Lond.)*, **252**, 123–124.

Miranda, S. (1970). Visual abilities and pattern preferences of premature infants and full-term neonates, *J. exp. Child Psychol.*, **10**, 189–205.

Moore, M. K. and Meltzoff, A. N. (1978). Object permanence, imitation and language development, in *Communicative and Cognitive Abilities—Early Behavioural Assessment* (Eds F. D. Minifie and L. L. Lloyd), University Park Press, Baltimore.

Muir, D., Abraham, W., Forbes, B., and Harris, L. (1979). The ontogenesis of an auditory localization response from birth to four months of age, *Canad. J. Psychol.*, **33**, 320–334.

Rakic, P. (1977). Prenatal development of the visual system in the rhesus monkey, *Phil. Trans. Roy. Soc. Lond. B.*, **278**, 245–260.

Rashbass, C. and Westheimer, G. (1961). Disjunctive eye movements, *J. Physiol.*, **159**, 339–360.

Regal, D. M. (1981). Development of critical flicker frequency in human infants, *Vision Res.*, **21**, 549–555.

Rieser, J., Yonas, A., and Wikner, K. (1976). Radial localization of odours by human newborns, *Child. Devel.*, **47**, 856–859.

Robertson, E., Peterson, J., and Lamb, L. (1968). Relative impedance measurements in young children, *Arch. Otolaryngol.*, **88**, 162–168.

Rusoff, A. C. (1979). Development of ganglion cells in the retina of the cat, in *Developmental Neurobiology of Vision* (Ed. R. D. Freeman), Plenum Press, New York.

Salapatek, P. (1975). Pattern perception in early infancy, in *Infant Perception: From Sensation to Cognition*, Vol. I (Eds L. B. Cohen and P. Salapatek), Academic Press, New York.

Schneider, B. A., Trehub, S. E., and Bull, D. (1979). The development of basic auditory processes in infants, *Canad. J. Psychol.*, **33**, 306–319.

Siqueland, E. R. and DeLucia, C. A. (1969). Visual reinforcement of non-nutritive sucking in human infants, *Science*, **165**, 1144–1146.

Slater, A. M. and Findlay, J. M. (1975a). The corneal reflection technique and the visual preference method: sources of error, *J. exp. Child Psychol.*, **20**, 240–247.

Slater, A. M. and Findlay, J. M. (1975b). Binocular fixation in the newborn baby, *J. exp. Child. Psychol.*, **20**, 248–273.

Spelke, E. S. (1976). Infants' intermodal perception of events, *Cognitive Psychol.*, **8**, 553–560.

Steiner, J. E. (1979). Human facial expressions in response to taste and smell stimulation, in *Advances in Child Development and Behaviour*, Vol. 13 (Eds H. W. Reese and L. P. Lipsitt), Academic Press, New York.

Stone, J., Dreher, B., and Leventhal, A. (1979). Hierarchical and parallel mechanisms in the organization of visual cortex, *Brain Res. Rev.*, **1**, 345–394.

Teller, D. Y. (1979). The forced-choice preferential looking procedure: a psychophysical technique for use with human infants, *Infant Behav. and Devel.*, **2**, 135–153.

Volkmann, F. C., and Dobson, M. V. (1976). Infant responses of ocular fixation to moving visual stimuli. *J. exp. Child Psychol.*, **22**, 86–99.

Weir, C. (1979). Auditory frequency sensitivity of human newborns: Some data with improved acoustic and behavioural controls, *Percept. Psychophys.*, **26**, 287–294.

Werner, J. S. and Wooten, B. R. (1979). Human infant colour vision and colour perception, *Infant Behav. & Devel.*, **2**, 241–273.

Wertheimer, M. (1961). Psychomotor coordination of auditory and visual space at birth, *Science*, **134**, 1692.

Wurtz, R. H. and Albano, J. E. (1980). Visual-motor function of the primate superior colliculus. *Ann. Rev. Neurosci.*, **3**, 189–226.

Yonas, A., Peterson, L., and Lockman, J. J. (1979). Young infants' sensitivity to optical information for collision, *Canad. J. Psychol.*, **33**, 268–276.

Yonas, A. and Pick, H. (1975). An approach to the study of infant space perception, in *Infant Perception: From Sensation to Cognition*, Vol. II (Eds L. B. Cohen and P. Salapatek), Academic Press, New York.

NOTES

1. Acuity can be expressed in several ways: (i) the maximum spatial frequency discriminated, that is the number of cycles (black/white pairs of stripes) in a unit of visual angle, e.g. 3 cycles per degree; (ii) the minimum stripe width detected, expressed as a visual angle, e.g. 10 min arc; (iii) the fractional measures commonly used in clinical sight testing, e.g. 6/60 (British), 20/200 (USA), 0.1 (European). 6/6 or 20/20 is the criterion of normal adult vision, and is conventionally taken to be equivalent to detection of 1 min arc stripes or 30 cycles per degree. It follows that the examples given above for the three measures are all equivalent and correspond to one-tenth of conventional adult acuity. All these measures are related to the angle subtended at the eye, and therefore the physical target sizes to which they correspond will increase in proportion to viewing distance. In this chapter we shall express all results on acuity in terms of stripe width, in minutes of arc.

2. For a meaningful measure of contrast sensitivity the test grating has to have a sinusodial profile, i.e. the variation of luminance from bright bar to dark bar follows a sine curve. High spatial frequency gratings have fine stripes, while the detection of a low spatial-frequency grating requires sensitivity to the gradual gradients of light intensity in a pattern of broad, fuzzy stripes. If the brightest point of the bright bars has

luminance L_{max}, and the darkest point of the dark bars L_{min}, then contrast is defined as $(L_{max} - L_{min})/(L_{max} + L_{min})$: this measure ranges from 1.0 or 100 per cent when the dark bars are completely dark down to zero for a uniform field.

3. The initial period of non-plasticity shown in Banks *et al.*'s published function is purely a consequence of the class of curve they chose to fit to their data: none of their data actually speak to the question of plasticity in different periods of the first year of life.

4. To give some scale for comparison, if you look at the centre of the open pages of a book from a reading distance of 30 cm and each page is 14 cm wide, the outer edges of the pages will be at a position equivalent to the 25° limit of the newborn's effective field.

5. Contributions by M. Lewis and B. McKenzie to discussion session on early imitation, Society for Research in Child Development, San Francisco, March 1979.

Psychobiology of the Human Newborn
Edited by P. Stratton
© 1982, John Wiley & Sons, Ltd.

CHAPTER 9

Newborn Individuality

PETER STRATTON

Comparing any two neonates it is possible to discover innumerable differences between them. Many of these differences will disappear having had no lasting impact on the life of the baby. Recent studies of newborn individual differences which have listed existing findings (e.g. Falender and Mehrabian, 1978; Osofsky, 1976) have not discussed their significance beyond referring to the possibility of relationships with the later personality. The only extensive reviews (Dunn, 1979; Korner, 1979) have been written in the context of infant development and have justified their interest by reference to continuity with later functioning and, in the case of Korner, influence on the care-taker. However, these have not been applied as criteria by which particular findings were evaluated. For example Korner (1979) and Osofsky and Connors (1979) refer to individual differences in soothability as a characteristic which will affect the care-taker. There can be little doubt that a care-taker's behaviour would be influenced by a baby who, over a long period, was consistently either resistant or responsive to soothing. However, as shown in the review that follows, consistency in soothability has only been demonstrated over very short periods. The general point is that the particular reason for supposing a difference to be significant imposes its own requirement for the magnitude and stability of the relevant measure of individuality. Empirical evidence of individual differences cannot be meaningfully evaluated outside the context of the particular reason for supposing them to be significant.

This chapter attempts to make explicit the criteria by which the practical significance of individual differences between newborns can be determined, then to review our existing knowledge in these terms. It is proposed that there are six headings under which the reasons for being concerned about individual differences can be grouped. One of the headings, for example, is 'exerts a differential influence on care-taker behaviour'. A difference is significant if it fulfills any of the criteria but each criterion will impose its own requirements. So if soothability is being considered because it might be expected to influence the care-taker, it can only be regarded as important if the differences between babies are sufficiently marked and persistent to reliably modify the care-taking to which they are subjected. The failure to relate claims of individual differences to a clear statement of why the differences would matter has deprived the literature of any clear criteria for such claims. In consequence, we now have a long list of characteristics which are in some sense individual differences but which are not tied to stated criteria. The temptation then is to use the characteristic as if all potential claims of significance were in fact justified. In this way it is possible to produce impressive but misleading claims for the range and importance of neonatal individuality.

Studies of individual differences between newborns have usually started with a general, if sometimes implicit, assumption about their potential significance. The major early empirical study of individuality (Shirley, 1933) was viewed as an investigation of early manifestations of personality and concluded that 'personality differences are apparent from birth' (p. 216). Subsequently Neilon (1948) wrote current character sketches of the same children (now 17-years old) and found that in a significant number of cases, independent judges could match the descriptions with Shirley's account of the same child during the first 2 years of life. Apart from the interest in early manifestations and precursors of personality the primary impetus for the more recent research has been provided by the prospect of predicting future disturbance (Bridger and Reiser, 1959; Richmond and Lustman, 1955).

With these sources of interest it is not surprising that there has been a general assumption that newborn individuality would be expressed in a relationship with later comparable characteristics; a criterion of continuity of function. However, the discussion in Chapter 1 made it clear that continuity of function from the neonatal period to any later age is very difficult to prove and such a criterion, rigorously applied, would exclude most of the measurable characteristics of newborns. Furthermore continuity is not, in itself, sufficient evidence that a potential difference is worth studying. There may well be characteristics which persist throughout the life of the individual and yet have no relationship with any significant aspect of his or her functioning. Of course an enduring characteristic, apparent from birth, is likely to reflect an important aspect of the individual's structure and may well influence the treatment that person will receive, but in this case it is the latter considerations that confer the significance. Continuity as such is not a sufficient condition to ensure the importance of a difference, and there are grounds for questioning whether it is a necessary condition. Bell *et al.* (1971) demanded that individual differences should show at least short-term reliability because 'if a measure cannot correlate with a replication under comparable conditions after an interval of a few hours or days, it has little chance of correlating with a measure obtained from another period weeks or years later' (p. 12). However, given the findings of Kennell *et al.* (1975) it becomes difficult confidently to reject the possibility that differences in responsivity and alertness during the few minutes in which a mother holds her baby immediately after birth, may have lasting consequences. On this basis the issue of continuity reduces to a requirement that the characteristic should be sustained for long enough to meet a more fundamental criterion for significance.

There would appear to be six criteria by which the existence or strength of a particular characteristic may be judged to be significant. Once described, these criteria will be used to structure the available information about neonatal individuality and to indicate the value in investigating particular classes of variables. It is proposed that characteristics which discriminate between individuals through their presence or strength should be regarded as significant if, and only if, they fit at least one of the following criteria.

CRITERIA FOR SIGNIFICANCE OF INDIVIDUAL DIFFERENCES

The criteria are presented in order of an increasing requirement for the length of time that the characteristic must be demonstrated. So, for example, any feature which is sustained for long enough to influence the care-taker's behaviour (5) is likely to be sufficiently stable to potentially affect adaptation (4) etc. The criteria proposed here are:

1. Indicates a fundamental characteristic (Fundamental).
2. Clusters meaningfully with other measures (Clustering).
3. Affects research or diagnostic findings (Research).
4. Relates to the success of adaptation to the extra-uterine environment (Adaptation).
5. Exerts a differential influence on caretaker behaviour (Influence).
6. Predicts future significant function or characteristic (Predictive).

The single-word titles, while not fully explanatory, are to simplify reference to the criteria in the survey of findings that follows.

Fundamental

Any measure of an individual difference becomes of interest if it is believed to be related to a fundamental characteristic of clear significance. Of particular interest are measures which are potential indicators of stable aspects of nervous system functioning, which can be presumed to have a sustained and significant impact on the development of the individual. A simple example would be a measure of the proportion of muscle in the total body weight. Such fundamental characteristics will be relatively stable and so, in principle, need only be recorded on a single occasion. However, in practice repeated testing will provide a check on the reliability of the measuring instrument and, when an indirect indicator is being used, will show how much it is affected by less stable influences. In some cases the significance of the fundamental characteristic is obvious, but it should not be assumed that a structural basis necessarily confers significance. For example the ability to roll one's tongue is a persisting characteristic of genetic origin, but has no known function beyond providing text-book writers with an example of a genetically determined characteristic with no known function. However, in most cases such a characteristic would predict an enduring cluster of tendencies which will influence important aspects of functioning, i.e. it would qualify as significant under the following criteria, as well.

Clustering

When several characteristics are found to co-vary, at the lowest it becomes possible to use one to predict the others, but it can further be supposed that there may be some fundamental relationship which accounts for the clustering. Factor analyses of scores on neonatal assessment scales (e.g. Osofsky and O'Connell 1977) are presumably based on this supposition. The discovery that neonatal functioning is precisely co-ordinated according to such principles as systemogenesis (Anokhin, 1964; Prechtl, Chapter 2) gives confidence that significance can be attributed to clusters of characteristics but, as with all such purely statistically generated relationships, it is necessary to formulate a conceptually defensible account and to ensure that the correlations are not an artefact of similar test procedures or of a transient condition that affected only some of the subjects.

Research

The possibility of stable individual differences in characteristics that would influence the behaviour of the newborn in an experimental situation or clinical evaluation is being taken increasingly seriously. The common procedure, in many cases inevitable, of excluding the more active and responsive babies from a sample places severe limits on the generalizability of many findings, while in other cases the recognition of a relevant individual difference might have allowed the removal of a significant source of noise in the data. Relevant to this heading is the practice in some aspects of neonatal assessment, of using parental characteristics to determine norms for the newborn. Simple examples would be taking account of the parents' height or skin pigmentation when evaluating the size and skin tone of their baby.

Adaptation

In view of the biological vulnerability of the newborn, and of his needs for finely tuned adaptation to his environment (Rovee-Collier and Lipsitt, Chapter 7), differences which have a relationship to the individual's current viability or success in adaptation are clearly significant. This question is complicated by the fact that differences of significance in one environment, or in conjunction with another characteristic may be unimportant in other contexts. Activity level, for example, may be of particular significance in an unstimulating environment (Schaffer, 1966), or when 'generally subdued activity' is combined with a learning deficit to make the infant vulnerable to respiratory failure (Lipsitt, 1978).

Influence

A characteristic may have no intrinsic biological significance but still exert a major influence on the neonate's environment. For example Bennet (1971) reports how the frequent appearance of a wry facial expression affected nurses' treatment of a newborn with a consequent effect on several aspects of the baby's behaviour.

The recently increased awareness of the extent to which the infant influences the behaviour of caretakers (Korner, 1979; Lewis and Rosenblum, 1974) allows a meaningful evaluation of characteristics of which the significance might otherwise have been obscure. It should be noted, however, that the availability of a sign to the caretaker does not necessarily mean that it will have any influence. External circumstances such as hospital procedures will affect access to the baby while attitudes and expectations of the care-takers will determine which characteristics they will regard as significant and others will be disregarded or not even perceived (Stratton, in preparation). Unless a characteristic is very obvious it is therefore desirable to have some evidence that differences between babies are in fact related to differential treatment.

Predictive

A relationship with measures of individual functioning at some later age. The relationship may be merely correlational, which would allow for prediction; or causal which potentially permits modification of the future functioning. The significance is clear when the later measure has obvious importance (intelligence for example, or emotional disturbance) but there is some justification for exploring *any* long-term relationship when it can be regarded as indicating a persisting characteristic. A complication arises from the tendency for environmental influences to remain stable. An early difference between babies might be entirely due to differences in external influence. If the influence is sustained (e.g. mothers who minimize or maximize tactile stimulation) then long-term consequences might be identifiable. The error would come in assuming that a relationship with later significant functions proves that the earlier measure tapped a congenital characteristic of the baby.

The above criteria are proposed as minimal conditions for a difference between newborns to be regarded as worthy of attention. Meeting one or more of the criteria does not ensure that the characteristic is a basic aspect of individuality.

For example a baby might cry a lot because of cerebral irritation consequent on brain damage, because of discomfort from a transient problem with digestion, from hunger due to underfeeding, or thirst from a too concentrated bottle formula, through discomfort because the father smacks him when he cries or for any number of other reasons. Whatever the cause, a sustained high frequency of crying will have an effect on energy expenditure (adaptation), the attitudes and behaviour of the care-takers (influence) and the probability of being included in a research sample (research). Therefore a simple measure of how much a baby cries is of interest in its own right. However, in order to predict beyond the period of observation, or to relate the measure to stable tendencies, it would be necessary to determine the cause.

GROUP DIFFERENCES

A difference between two groups of newborns will often be taken as an indication that the measure concerned reflects some aspect of individuality. This would not always be the case, although it may be assumed that the difference is attributable to one of the features which differentiates the groups. For example, if boys vocalize more than girls at 4 weeks (Klein and Jennings, 1979) this must be caused by some feature in which the sexes differ, such as morphological differences, hormonal function, or differential treatment. The effect of establishing a group difference is thus to narrow the range of possible causes. The sources of differences between the sexes are quite well defined in general terms and most of them would qualify for significance under the above criteria. Possible exceptions are maturity and differential treatment. Female newborns are on average more mature than males of the same gestational age. When interpreting sex differences, but in other areas too, it is important to determine whether they arise from temporary discrepancies in maturation which might be very transient at a time of such rapid change (Bronson, Chapter 5). Alternatively it is possible to regard differences in maturation as a significant aspect of individuality (see discussion below). Similarly, differential treatment may not be an arbitrary influence. While some aspects may derive from an inappropriate transfer of adult constructs to the newborn, it is at least possible that differences in treatment may reflect cultural expectations which have developed out of practical experience. In such cases the differential treatment of the sexes is likely to reinforce an existing biological tendency.

The usefulness of a group difference as a pointer to individuality depends on the extent to which it limits the range of possible explanations. Sex differences offer a comparatively small choice of clear alternatives. The same is not true of all group differences and class differences in particular are difficult to interpret. The list of differentiating characteristics between social classes is extensive, poorly defined and not generally agreed upon. The discovery of a difference between newborns of different classes does not significantly limit the range of possible explanations, nor does it give great confidence that the cause of the difference is of any real significance. Studies of group differences become meaningless unless the groups are clearly defined and many studies of racial differences are even more deficient in this respect than studies of social class. A further difficulty arises when the groups are also differentiated by complex and subtle cultural patterns. Kagan (1979) has pointed out how this undermines studies of racial differences but the same limitation applies to much simpler groupings such as whether or not the mother smokes during pregnancy. Quantifiable correlates such as maternal age and economic status can be dealt with but differences in life style etc. are not entirely subsumed under such measures, and can bring about differences through both antecedent and concurrent influence.

Group differences may therefore be a helpful pointer to the source of individual differences but they do not necessarily confer significance and each case must be evaluated on its merits.

The review that follows groups individual differences under six broad headings of: Oral and Vocal; Cognitive; Psychophysiological; Activation; Somatic; and Higher Order. The stated criteria are used not only to evaluate the significance of individual differences, but also to determine the requirements for the stability of the measures. For example, a low sensory threshold need only be shown to be stable over a short test–retest interval to justify an interpretation of its relationship with other measures (clustering), but would probably need to be sustained over a number of days to have much impact on the treatment provided by care-takers (influence). Magnitude of a difference may be equally important in determining whether the criterion is met, but this information is not generally available in published results. The review, therefore, concentrates on the temporal stability of individual tendencies, leaving the proof that they are substantial enough to have the presumed effect as a refinement for future research. The findings of this survey are summarised in Table 2 in the Conclusion.

ORAL AND VOCAL

Oral functioning is so intrinsic to survival that it is highly developed well before birth (Anokhin, 1964). Differences in oral behaviour are therefore likely to reflect fundamental tendencies of the newborn rather than short-lived maturational differences, and to significantly influence adaptation. As sucking and crying are basic to many of the interactions between mother and baby these interactions are likely to be significantly affected by individual variation in such functions. Finally the belief that oral behaviour represents the highest level of co-ordinated functioning of the newborn has resulted in widespread experimental interest and to an expectation of continuity with later function which dates back to Freud. Variation in oral functioning, if demonstrated, may therefore be regarded as significant under any of the criteria stated above.

Food Intake

Dubignon *et al.* (1969) found consistency in food intake scores across days 1–4, but individual intake was much affected by perinatal factors. However, inspection of their data suggests that the effects of sedation, apgar rating and parity weakened over days while the consistency of food intake increased, implying at least some independent determinant of consumption. Ounsted and Simons (1976) found food intake at 2 and 12 months to be related to birth weight in relation to gestation. This implies, but does not prove, individual stability over a considerable length of time. Bell *et al.* (1971) found the amount of feed taken (as a proportion of body weight) had the highest stability of all of their measures on a relatively homogeneous sample, so amount consumed at each feed would seem to be a fairly stable measure at least in the early neonatal period. They also found that this feed/weight ratio loaded on a factor which included measures of non-nutritive sucking, crying in response to nipple removal, and prone head reaction, but only the measures of sucking (and only for males) produced significant individual correlations. The evidence that amount of feed clusters with other, not closely related functions, must therefore be regarded as rather weak. On follow-up at 2 years they found that food intake correlated with intensity, friendliness and vigour. This predictive relationship applied only for females, was based on a very small sample, and is difficult to interpret (the authors describe it as 'tenuous'). It should perhaps not be treated as evidence of prediction but be used to inspire a search for a third factor, not recorded by Bell *et al.* (1971), which would provide a causal explanation for the correlation. Kron *et al.* (1968) found the greatest individual stability in sucking pressure, with consumption being a function of pressure and rate. This would suggest that at least part of the consistency in consumption may be attributable to individual differences in such characteristics as muscular strength or fatiguability. Bell *et al.* (1971) make the same suggestion on the grounds that prone head reaction correlated significantly with feed/weight ratio (for bottle-fed females). However their Table 2 shows a non-significant correlation of 0.38, df < 13 for this relationship.

Significant stability of individual sucking rate and a tendency towards characteristic burst-pause patterns were reported by Balint (1948). These findings were replicated for 2-day-old babies on consecutive feeds by Pollitt *et al.* (1978) who also found stability in sucking pressure. They also reported stability of measures of sucking strength from day 2 to 1 month. As Crook (1979) has pointed out, by the time the newborn is old enough for the confounding effects of obstetric medication to have worn off, sucking patterns may have been affected by accumulating maternal influence. Even so, the evidence for consistency in individual style of nutritive sucking is very strong. Less clear is the significance of these differences and in particular, the direction of any causal relationship between sucking patterns and food intake. The issue of which are the fundamental factors determining amount consumed at each feed is extremely complex and is discussed in detail by Wright (Chapter 13). However, even if some more basic factor is found to be causally responsible, the characteristic food intake of an individual remains of interest in its own right in the contexts of the effect the neonate has on the mother and of the neonate's adaptation to the demands of the environment.

Non-nutritive oral behaviour

The potential significance of oral behaviour outside the feeding situation is less obvious. It has no clear biological significance, the relationship with nutritive sucking is unclear (cf. Stratton, Chapter 6), and it does not appear to be influenced by perinatal factors (Dubignon et al., 1969). It has however been extensively studied and is regarded as a sensitive indicator of arousal (Korner, 1973), readily influenced by changes in stimulation (Bronshtein et al., 1958), and showing discrimination between different stimuli (Dubignon et al., 1969). Furthermore if mothers do use some aspects of spontaneous oral behaviour to judge their baby's hunger (Wright, Chapter 13), the differences in the 'readability' of such signals could be quite important. It has also been suggested (Kaye, 1977) that the burst-pause pattern, which is clearest in non-nutritive sucking, is the basis for the earliest mother–infant dialogue.

Measures of oral behaviour have been found to show short-term stability. Kessen et al. (1961) and Korner (1973) found significant stability in hand–mouth contact over the first few days of life, while six of the twelve measures that Bell et al. (1971) reported as showing adequate stability, related to non-nutritive oral behaviour. The test-retest interval was normally 8 h. The measures have also been found to cluster together. The factor analysis of these twelve measures generated a first factor incorporating the five aspects of sucking, mouth movements, and the feed/weight ratio. Yang et al. (1976), factor analysing twenty-six measures of neonatal behaviour identified 'reflexive and discriminative sucking' as their third factor. However, the stability of the measures is unknown as they report that only eight of their measures showed a test–retest reliability above 0.5 and they do not specify which these were.

Despite the prominence of oral measures in the neonatal phase of the Bell et al. (1971) study, relationships with behaviour 2 years later were less clear. Response to nipple removal was related to active participation in teacher-initiated activities at preschool for boys only, while there was a suggestion that girls showing few mouth movements had less-advanced speech. Similarly the variables in the sucking factor of Yang et al. (1976) failed to correlate with any measures at 90 days (Yang and Moss, 1978), while in a partial replication of the Bell et al. (1971) study, Yang and Halverson (1976) failed to find any relationship between neonatal sucking and preschool-age behaviour. Dunn (1975) found a relationship between sucking on day 8 and maternal behaviour at 14 and 20 weeks. Dunn and Richards (1977) report that sucking rate correlates with measures of maternal affection in the neonatal period, but it is not clear which was causally influencing the other or whether some third factor was responsible for both. Dunn (1977) also found a relationship of neonatal sucking with the percentage of baby's utterances that were demands at 14 months, as well as with three maternal measures at this time. As she points out it is more appropriate to speak of continuity between aspects of mother-baby interaction at the two ages than to try to justify a claim of continuity in baby behaviour.

It can be concluded that there are individual differences in non-nutritive oral behaviours as indicated by their short-term stability, tendency to intercorrelate, and relationships with other significant measures. Such evidence as we have suggested that these behaviours may well prove to have some of the significance that earlier, particularly psychoanalytically oriented, theorists attributed to them. However, continuity remains a tantalizing possibility rather than an established fact, and it is difficult to share the confidence of Dunn (1979) that 'newborn differences in sucking . . . are related to differences in reaction patterns that continue into the third or fourth year'. (p. 78). The only criterion of significance that is met by the data so far is that of clustering, and we do not yet have a conceptually defensible interpretation of the patterns of relationships that are known to exist.

Vocalization

The neonate's cry has a clear biological significance and a compelling effect on the parents. Furthermore, it has been established that mothers respond differently to different cries (Wolff, 1969) and that the kind of response made by the mother has an effect on the infant's later crying (Bell and Ainsworth, 1972).

The simplest measure of crying, and the one to which parents most consistently refer, is quantity. Korner (1971) found significant individual consistency in frequency and duration of crying over days 2–3. The first factor identified by Yang et al. (1976) was labelled reactivity-irritability, but all of the contributing variables related to amount of crying. Ainsworth et al. (1972) point out that individual differences in amount of crying may be attributed to differences in infant conditions such as colic or hunger. This does not necessarily deprive measures of crying of significance, but if they have a close association with simple and measurable conditions of the infant which convey further useful information, for example about how long the crying will persist and how it might be reduced, there is little justification for ignoring the causes of the crying. In particular it seems quite likely that the same gross behaviour may have quite disparate causes and this may account for the fact that Yang and Moss (1978) failed to find any relationship between their first factor and measures of behaviour at 90 days. However Karelitz et al. (1964) found that the amount of crying in response to a painful stimulus at 4–10 days correlated with Stanford-Binet intelligence scores at 3 years. This finding supports the suggestion that continuity from early crying will only be demonstrated when the eliciting conditions are defined.

Bell (1974) reviews the evidence that crying is a major determinant of the quality of some parent–infant relationships. Subsequently Frodi *et al.* (1978) have shown that the cry of the premature infant is more aversive than that of the term infant but their premature babies were several weeks old and it is possible that the cry becomes more aversive with age. However, in an unpublished study, Hanks (1979) found that the neonatal cry was judged to be more irritating than the cry at 10 weeks for both term and premature babies. All of these authors concluded that the characteristics of the cry could be a significant factor in child abuse. In this context the quality of the cry may be at least as important as the quantity. Presumptive evidence that neonates have characteristic cries comes from the fact that mothers can usually identify the cry of their own baby as early as three days after the birth (Morsbach and Bunting, 1979). If this was attributable merely to differences in structure of the vocal cavity the finding would have limited interest. However, Prechtl *et al.* (1969) demonstrated different patterns of cry between neonates, and certain patterns of cry can be used to identify specific CNS abnormalities (Wasz-Höckert *et al.*, 1968). Zeskind and Lester (1978) found that the pain cry differentiated healthy term newborns with complications from those without. They, and Michelsson *et al.* (1977) concluded that such differences are not attributable to peripheral mechanisms or mechanical defects, but reflect structural differences in the CNS.

It can be concluded that newborns express some basic aspect of their individuality in their crying and that a detailed knowledge of the causes and structural features of the cry might prove informative about fundamental characteristics of the individual and allow prediction of future functioning.

COGNITIVE PROCESSES

This section covers those processes by which the neonate responds differentially to the environment. Psychology has not usually classed learning as an aspect of cognition but the grouping with sensory and perceptual processes appears meaningful in the present context at least. The substantial cognitive capacities of the newborn are well documented in this book, and their significance for survival and quality of functioning is unquestionable. Individual differences would be particularly significant in having practical implications for the optimal treatment of different babies.

Sensory function

Most of the work on individual differences in sensory functioning has concentrated on the visual and tactile modalities. An early interest was in infants who are abnormally sensitive to stimulation (Anderson and Rosenblith, 1964;

Bergman and Escalona, 1949). However this group of infants tends to show a variety of abnormalities and it is not possible to draw reliable conclusions about variation within the normal range from the characteristics of an extreme or aberrant group. Escalona (1968) reported that inactive babies were more visually responsive but very little of the data in her study came from the neonatal period. Korner (1970) found significant differences over four observation periods, in frequency of visual alertness ($p < 0.05$) though duration of alertness (with which it correlated highly) failed to reach significance. Both measures correlated with visual pursuit, though there was no direct evidence of a stable individual tendency on this measure. However Barten et al. (1971) demonstrated consistency over days in amount of visual pursuit while Korner and Thoman (1970) found highly significant differences in the tendency to alert when stimulated. Salapatek and Kessen (1973) report consistent individual differences in the style of scanning a triangle which Falender and Mehrabian (1978) regard as a difference in the seeking of stimulation. However, Salapatek and Kessen suggest that it is most likely to be attributable to differences in maturation. In the specific context of the 'en face' position Hittelman and Dickes (1979) found that female neonates maintained eye contact for longer than males though the frequency of contacts did not differ. Of the possible source of sex differences, they propose that differential maturation is the most likely explanation, but whatever the cause, differences in maintaining eye contact are likely to influence the care-taker's beliefs about the baby's capacity for a social relationship.

Tactile sensitivity has been studied by traditional psychophysical methods of threshold determination. Lipsitt and Levy (1959) using limb withdrawal to ascending electrical stimulation found consistency over the first 4 days with males apparently less sensitive than females. Birns (1965) studied individual differences in responsiveness to four stimuli of which one was a cold disc applied to the thigh, and stated that there was day-to-day constancy for all stimuli, though separate analyses for each type of stimulus were not reported. Bell and Costello (1964) reported a sex difference in tactile threshold and it was one of the most stable measures reported by Bell et al. (1971). It also provided some of the clearest relationships with behaviour 2 years later with the relatively insensitive babies becoming assertive and (in the case of females) co-ordinated and skilful, with opposite characteristics from the more sensitive (lower threshold) babies. In their replication Yang and Halverson (1976), using a different method, did not find tactile threshold to be reliable in the neonatal period and so did not include it in their follow-up. It is tempting to relate the Bell et al. (1971) finding to the suggestions by Schaffer (1964) that some babies are 'non-cuddlers' because they consistently avoid tactile stimulation and by Als et al. (1976) that parent–infant interactions with underweight term babies might be impeded because they give an appearance of being stressed when handled. However, the effect is not straightforward: none of the relationships with tactile sensitivity derived from social behaviour in pre-school.

Birns (1965) found consistent individual differences in the strength of response to both loud and soft tones. Korner (1974) attempted to determine auditory threshold and found several infants who consistently responded to a 53 db signal, but she has now abandoned the attempt because of the difficulty of obtaining sufficient reliable threshold determinations (Korner, 1979). Turkewitz *et al.* (1971) found that the auditory threshold varied according to the response indicator used, which suggests that apparent individual differences in auditory threshold may be attributed to individual-response specificity (Engel, 1960). Escalona (1968) has discussed the 'impossibility' of differentiating threshold from response by behavioural methods, and certainly when a single measure of response is used with a specific kind of stimulus the distinction would seem to be unproductive. Many of the studies using auditory stimuli have recorded psychophysiological responses and these are reviewed in a later section. However, the relationships between different measures of sensory sensitivity may be quite informative.

Although Birns (1965) did not report comparisons between stimuli an analysis of her data shows that the measures of responsiveness to different stimuli are positively correlated (Table 1). A factor analysis indicated that all of the stimuli loaded onto a single factor which accounted for 51 per cent of the total variance. Korner (1970) found very significant intercorrelations between her three visual measures (frequency and duration of visual alertness and visual pursuit) but they differed in their other relationships. The measures of alertness were strongly associated with a number of measures which seem to index arousal while visual pursuit correlated only with auditory responsiveness. These findings suggest that alertness may be more a matter of state than of visual functioning while visual pursuit relates to other measures of responsivity. Bell *et al.* (1971) did find that tactile threshold loaded onto the factor labelled 'sleep', but the significant correlations were with the measures of maximal and basal respiration rates. Bell and Costello (1964) also report that low-sensitivity infants (using three different tactile stimuli) showed a lower level of activation and responsiveness. There is an apparent contradiction between the favourable outcome of high thresholds

Table 1   Correlations between responses to different stimuli reported by Birns (1965)

| | Tones | | | |
	Soft	Loud	Cold disc	Pacifier
Loud Tone	0.62**			
Cold disc	0.26	0.34*		
Pacifier	0.31*	0.17	0.32*	
Factor loading	0.809	0.800	0.640	0.563

*$p < 0.05$ **$p < 0.001$ (one-tailed).

reported by Bell *et al.* (1971) and the finding by Graham (1956) that traumatized infants had higher tactile thresholds. One possibility is that, as suggested by Bell, high thresholds have a protective function in the perinatal period. It may be that babies under stress maintain a high stimulus barrier in order to conserve resources for the exceptional demands being made upon them. A high threshold could therefore be diagnostic of a stressed baby (and therefore a potentially poor prognosis) but within a homogeneous group, those babies capable of excluding stimuli may be demonstrating a basic capacity for regulating input which is a favourable sign.

A number of items on the Brazelton Neonatal Behavioural Assessment Scale (BNBAS; Brazelton, 1973) relate to sensory functioning, and these consistently emerged as the major factors in the factor analytic studies reviewed by Standley *et al.* (1978). As Als *et al.* (1979) point out, many of these studies employed subject numbers that statisticians would reject as totally unreliable. It is therefore of interest that the smallest study, (Chisholm *et. al.*, 1978), with twenty-seven variables and thirty-three subjects obtained the same first two factors as the larger studies, and Aleksandrowicz and Aleksandrowicz (1974), employing forty-four subjects to factor analyse twenty-seven variables identified almost precisely the same five factors (with a slight change of order) as did Osofsky and O'Connell (1977) who used 328 subjects and 25 variables. From these studies it is quite clear that the measures of orienting to auditory and visual stimuli, and alertness, are consistently related in many different kinds of samples. As already discussed such clustering may well indicate a significant underlying function and these items would seem to indicate a willingness to engage the environment that amounts to a higher level of functioning than that tapped by sensory thresholds.

Perceptual Functioning

The debate as to whether newborns can be said to orient has a long history but the evidence, reviewed by Berg and Berg (1979) suggests that under optimal conditions, orienting does occur in the neonatal period. This is significant because the orienting reflex implies an active response which has the effect of making the organism receptive to environmental information with the function of building up neuronal models or schemas (Sokolov, 1963). There are some indications of individual differences in the extent to which neonates display such sophisticated behaviour. The clustering of orientation items and alertness on the BNBAS, referred to above suggests a coherence in these functions, and Osofsky (1976) not only found stability in these characteristics (responsiveness) across situations, but also found that responsive babies had sensitive and stimulating mothers. These findings are intriguing but need further exploration before the causal sequences can be determined. However, the fact that responsive infants (and sensitive mothers) maintained more eye contact indicates the potential significance of this particular neonatal characteristic, whatever its source.

A negative way of conceptualizing these tendencies is in terms of the relative inefficiency of the neonate's perceptual filter. Thus Mehrabian (1977) regards activity level as determined by the individual's inability to screen out irrelevant stimuli and Falender and Mehrabian (1978) state that 'Activity level or alertness are of course prime indices of infant arousability' (p. 24). In this view individual differences in the operation of a rejective filter (of the kind proposed by Broadbent, 1958), expressed as a distinction between screeners and non-screeners, are the source of differences in responsiveness, alertness, and spontaneous activity. It should be noted that none of the empirical work by these authors had involved infants, and there is little reason to suppose that the three characteristics are intercorrelated in the way that their hypothesis would require. Rovee-Collier and Lipsitt (Chapter 7) have indicated the significance of neonatal learning, and it would seem that a more fruitful conceptualization, arising from the proposals of Lewis and Goldberg (1969) is in terms of the facility with which schemas can be acquired. Responses are elicited by the discrepancy between a stimulus and an existing schema, and habituation is the reduction in response as this discrepancy is reduced through repeated exposure. An example of research in this framework is the finding by Friedman *et al.* (1974) that after habituation to a stimulus, females (at 2 weeks) were more likely than males to respond with recovery of attention when a moderate discrepancy was introduced. The response to discrepancy (or novelty) is fundamental to the infant's interaction with the environment and Lewis and Goldberg (1969) found that by 12 weeks there were differences in the efficiency of acquisition of new schemata that could be related to the responsiveness of the mother. Differences in learning in the neonatal period may not only affect the relationship with care-takers, they may determine whether or not the baby survives (Lipsitt, 1978), and might also be expected to indicate fundamental aspects of the individual's CNS.

Learning and Adaptation

Research on neonatal learning has been conducted primarily in the American tradition of behaviourist learning theory, in which the universal features and developmental sequence are the primary interest and individual differences have been almost completely ignored. Habituation might be expected to yield the best evidence of individuality as it is the most fundamental form of learning and has been used extensively by psychophysiologists who are likely to be concerned with individual differences. However, even when such a concern has been most likely, individual differences have been ignored. For example, Graham *et al.* (1968) studied habituation of heart-rate responses in the same subjects during each of the first five days of life, but did not report any tests for individual consistency in parameters of habituation, while from the same experiment Clifton and Graham (1968) report an analysis of individual differences in fourteen measures of heart-rate response over the same period but did not include measures of habituation even though they state that habituation occurred. This is particularly unfortunate since individual differences in habituation would result in some subjects giving consistently smaller responses to later stimuli, thereby giving a spurious impression of differential response magnitude or variability when responses are pooled. In other words, findings of individual differences in parameters of responses which are based on repeated stimulation may be artefactual unless the effects of habituation are taken into account.

Work with older subjects strongly suggests that parameters of habituation may index individuality. O'Gorman (1977) concluded that habituation of physiological responses was consistently related to certain personality characteristics of normal adults. In infancy habituation has been related to broader aspects of cognitive function both concurrently (Lewis and Goldberg, 1969) and predictively (Miller et al., 1977). The most direct evidence that the differences in habituation seen in any group of neonates reflect some basic aspects of nervous-system functioning would seem to come from the four 'habituation' items of the Brazelton scale. If these show test-retest reliability (Brazelton, 1973) and also cluster together on a factor analysis (Osofsky and O'Connell, 1977) there would seem to be some stable individual characteristic underlying them. Unfortunately we cannot be sure that the scores on these items are entirely based on habituation. While it is unlikely that habituation plays no part, it is entirely possible that the consistency derives from some other aspect of adaptation or responsiveness.

This area has suffered from a lack of clear consensus about the criteria by which a response decrement can be said to be habituation, so that there is still disagreement about when habituation has occurred. In fact, while pointing to the potential significance of individual differences in habituation, Korner (1979) doubts whether habituation in the neonate has been demonstrated at all although in the same volume Berg and Berg (1979) conclude an extensive review with the statement that 'habituation appears to be readily elicited in active or REM sleep in neonates' (p. 330).

In a discussion of the essential criteria for habituation, Stratton (1970) concluded that it was necessary to demonstrate, (a) an initial response, tested against prestimulus controls, (b) a decrement over trials, and (c) an increase in response to an adequate change in the stimulus. This final criterion of dishabituation was also seen as central by Berg and Berg (1979). Adopting these criteria, several studies have shown group differences in neonatal habituation.

Eisenberg et al. (1966) found differences between neonates in different risk categories and Vander Maelen et al. (1975) found differences related to obstetric medication. Rate of habituation in the experiment reported by Stratton (1970) was also found to correlate negatively with obstetric medication but there was a somewhat stronger relationship with head circumference. Upon further investigation it was discovered that early measurements of head circumference as recorded in that particular hospital primarily indicated the amount of deformation of the skull during birth. The more direct causal factor in both cases is likely to be the after effects of a difficult birth (and not, for example, that neonates with larger brains learn faster). Such studies do not therefore support the suggestion that individual differences in habituation within a single session necessarily reflect structural characteristics of the nervous system.

Friedman *et al.* (1974) found that female neonates produced larger dishabituation responses, while a possible link with other cognitive functions is suggested by Stratton and Connolly (1973). In two independent experiments, those neonates who did not habituate to stimuli presented at fixed intervals were the ones to respond when the stimulus was omitted. Finally in the only direct study, Sostek and Brackbill (1976) report significant stability in rate of habituation of a motor response on consecutive days at 1, 2, and 3 weeks of age. However by the fourth week the correlation was no longer significant although there seemed to be significant stability from the third to the fourth week. Stratton (1970) has pointed out that measures of rate of habituation will be affected by magnitude of initial response, and it was shown earlier in this section that there are individual differences in responsiveness. It therefore remains to be determined whether the consistency found by Sostek and Brackbill derives from differences in fundamental processes of habituation or merely reflects differences in responsiveness. A further possibility since they did not include checks for dishabituation, is that they have discovered individual differences in adaptation or fatiguability.

It must be concluded that while there is support for the supposition that there are individual differences in habituation which reflect important underlying functions, as yet there is no reliable direct evidence. In the case of higher forms of learning, no evidence at all is available. This may have been unavoidable in that the capability of the newborn for such learning has only recently been unequivocally established, and we have only begun to explore the implications (Rovee-Collier and Lipsitt, Chapter 7). Individual differences in parameters of learning and adaptation during the neonatal period would have immense significance. We now have sufficiently well-established methods for studying the traditional forms of learning in the neonate for this much needed research to be begun.

PSYCHOPHYSIOLOGY

Differences in structural characteristics of the nervous system, and functional differences which are of a kind to indicate a structural basis, could be expected to have major implications for the development of the individual. Anatomical variation in the nervous system has not been available for study in the intact newborn and so the significance of such variation cannot be assessed. For the future the advent of brain scanners (computed axial tomography) opens up an exciting prospect of relating individual differences in brain structure to differences in overt functioning. The next most direct measures are provided by

EEG studies, but these have been entirely concerned with developmental function rather than individual differences (cf. McCall, 1979 for a discussion of the distinction). Butler and Engel (1969) found that newborns with short photic latencies had higher scores on mental and motor development at eight months, independently of birth weight and gestational age. Photic latency is closely related to maturity and this would be a possible explanation of the effect, but Turkewitz and Birch (1971) have pointed out the difficulty of relating individual differences in such measures to particular underlying functions. The major research effort has been in the area of autonomic functions, particularly heart rate.

Autonomic Nervous System (ANS) Functions

Towards 1960 instrumentation became available to quantify manifestations of ANS functioning. There had already been considerable speculation about the role of autonomic specificity in the determination of personality (e.g. Lacey, 1956), and the possibility of identifying stable individual differences in the neonate aroused both practical and theoretical interest.

The first major study (Lipton et al., 1961) was an analysis of the heart rate (HR) responses of sixteen female neonates from 2–5 days. The stimulus was a $2\frac{1}{2}$ lb puff of nitrogen to the abdomen lasting 5 s, and sixteen parameters of the HR responses were recorded. Although extensively and uncritically quoted, these studies do have limitations. The first is that the analyses were based on a restricted sample of the trials, those on which the response was not a monophasic acceleration being eliminated, as were trials on which the baby was whimpering or crying, and those on which no behavioural response was observed. On this final criterion alone Lipton et al. (1965) excluded approximately 50 per cent of trials in a different study but using a similar stimulus. Individual differences in responsiveness, tactile threshold, state, and habituability may account for the fact that the number of trials analysed ranged from 24–93 for different subjects (Lipton et al., 1961), and may have had a considerable influence on the findings.

Individual differences were claimed when the mean for any subject lay outside the 95 per cent confidence interval of scores on that measure for any other subject. With 120 possible comparisons between subjects on each of 16 measures, this is not a conservative procedure. Some differences were also tested using Duncan's Multiple Range Test which is also known to be subject to type I errors (Petrinovich and Hardyck, 1969; Scheffé 1959). It is difficult to draw detailed comparisons between different measures of HR responses from these results, although a pervasive tendency was for the magnitude measures to show greater consistency than the latencies, as was later reported by Clifton and Graham (1968).

Bridger et al. (1965) pointed out that in both the Lipton et al. (1961) study and Bridger and Reiser's (1959) report of individual differences in HR responses, interpretation in terms of autonomic functioning was unjustified because no account had been taken of behavioural state. In a study of the responses of 20 neonates to sound and cold disc, state (called over-all excitation) was continuously recorded. Consistent individual differences were found in HR responses both within and across the three common states. However it appears that all recordings took place within a period of 25 min of a single session. Even with the behavioural ratings it is not possible to be certain that consistency over such a short period reflects structural differences. Lipton et al. (1966) recorded fifteen measures of the HR responses of neonates and again at $2\frac{1}{2}$ and 5 months. There were no correlations between newborn and $2\frac{1}{2}$-month measures and little consistency from newborn to 5 months. In contrast most measures gave significant correlations between $2\frac{1}{2}$ and 5 months. The authors conclude the HR responses are unstable in the newborn, but their data merely exclude a homotypic relationship. It is quite possible that some aspects of response would be sufficiently stable over a short period to be meaningfully related to some different aspect of later functioning i.e. a heterotypic relationship as defined by Kagan (1971).

The most detailed investigation of HR was the analysis by Clifton and Graham (1968) of the stability across days of fourteen different measures. All but one of the measures showed some degree of consistency, with the temporal measures being least reliable, and magnitude of response where resting HR was at a minimal level being the most effective in discriminating between individuals. While the writers do not consider the consistency to be adequate for a 'test' of individual characteristics, there is no question that they have demonstrated that the HR response has significant individual tendencies over the period from the second to the fifth day. A further measure of HR response which has shown stability is the deceleratory response which Lipsitt and Jacklin (1971) showed could be elicited by a non-aversive odour. The frequency of decelerations correlated over 24 h. Lewis et al. (1970) reported correlations of mean resting neonatal HR with the same measure earlier (fetal) and later (up to 56 weeks). HR variability showed only short-term consistency but was most stable in the neonatal period (2–4 weeks). Lipsitt and Jacklin (1971) also found that the basal rate (lowest mean prestimulus rate) was stable over 24 h.

The evidence for stable individual differences in HR functioning of the neonate is very strong but the significance of these findings is not so obvious. The sensitivity of HR changes as an indicator of response to a wide variety of influence from structural characteristics of the individual to small differences between stimuli, has resulted in most of the research on neonatal psychophysiology concentrating on this measure. However, the very sensitivity precludes any simple interpretation of the data. Individual differences in HR response may indicate structural differences in ANS functioning which have implications for adaptation and potential psychopathology, as proposed at the outset of this research (Bridger and Reiser, 1959; Richmond and Lustman,

1955). However, they may equally indicate differences in aspects of cognitive functioning described above or, in many cases, be an artefact of individuality in state, or in responsiveness in terms of motor movement, change in respiration etc. In terms of the criteria proposed above, there would seem to be two possible routes towards further progress. One would be to explore the relationships between individual tendencies in manifesting aspects of HR responses. Once the relationships between the various parameters have been determined it might be possible to interpret them in terms of what is known about the mechanisms controlling the HR response. Schachter *et al.* (1971) have indicated that this is likely to be a very complex task. The second route would be to identify, by means of longitudinal study, significant later correlates of neonatal HR functioning. So far this approach has been marked by considerable speculation but no empirical data.

A number of studies have recorded respiratory responses of newborns. Bell *et al.* (1971) found stability in both the highest and lowest respiration rates recorded during sleep. On follow-up at age 2 years there was a negative correlation between respiration rate and attentiveness, while slow respiration also predicted advanced speech, communication and modeling of adults. These findings were significant for both sexes, but were not replicated by Yang and Halverson (1976), although they did also find the measures to be stable on day 3. Thoman *et al.* (1977) found consistency in frequency and length of apnoea during sleep over the first 5 weeks of life, and Thoman *et al.* (1978) found consistency from the first 5 weeks to 6 and 12 months for females but not for males, and in quiet but not in active sleep. They suggest that the lack of predictability in male sleep apnoea may account for the higher incidence of SIDs among males but it does seem that the opposite argument would be equally valid. That is, if some babies are vulnerable to SIDs because of the occurrence of apnoea, then the group in which some showed consistently frequent and prolonged apnoeic spells (i.e. females), should be at greater risk. Even so, anomalies of respiratory function do seem to be implicated in SIDs (cf. Rovee-Collier and Lipsitt, Chapter 7) and this is the most convincing instance of the possible significance of the individual variation in respiratory function. A further consideration is the probability of a relationship between styles of respiration and crying which has not yet been explored. For the present we must conclude that, like heart rate, respiration is an essential function showing consistent individual variation, but the implications of this variation have yet to be determined.

ACTIVATION

One of the most salient behavioural characteristics of the newborn is the activity level, and it is natural for parents to ascribe temperamental tendencies of restlessness, laziness, etc. according to their perception of how active their baby is. Psychologists too have postulated fundamental qualities of the nervous system on the basis of responsivity and spontaneous activity, as well as hypothesizing constructs such as 'level of arousal'. It was however already clear, before most of the empirical studies were undertaken, that the concept of activity level as a unitary phenomenon indexing a continuum of arousal was untenable. The analysis by Lacey (1959, 1967) should have been an adequate warning but, in common with other areas of psychobiology, neonatal researchers found the implications too difficult to accept. It is, therefore, not surprising that there are many apparent contradictions in a literature which attempts to treat different measures of activity and arousal as indices of the same characteristic, despite the fact that even the same measure of activity can reflect the operation of totally different genetic mechanisms (in two strains of the same species of rat; Hirsch, 1963). In discussions of activity and arousal levels it is therefore essential to remember constantly that findings with one measure of activity or arousal cannot be generalized to other measures or, necessarily, to other samples.

Spontaneous Activity

Kessen et al. (1961) made an early claim for individuality in amount of movement (spontaneous and reactive combined). The measure, based on only 30 s of film each day, showed significant stability over 5 days. McGrade et al. (1965) attributed the individual differences to fatigue arising from delivery difficulty. However, this conclusion was based on a single significant correlation out of twenty-five relationships examined and so cannot be regarded as reliable. McGrade (1968) reported that less active neonates were, at 8 months, more active, happier and less tense. This favourable outcome from lower activity is in accordance with the findings on responsivity discussed under 'sensory function' above, and may similarly relate to birth trauma in a heterogeneous sample, but indicate a good functional adaptation within a homogeneously healthy group. Escalona (1968) found that low activity infants (4–12 weeks) showed more oral and visual attentive behaviour, and responded more to social and other 'interesting' stimulation, while more active babies were better co-ordinated during spontaneous activity or mild stimulation. Although the entire study was based on the distinction between active and inactive infants, no information is given on the stability of the measures over the one-week period during which each baby was studied. Bell (1966) found greater arousal during wakefulness among breast-fed babies, which he attributed to greater hunger but he did not report on individual stability, and Bell et al. (1971) did not find stability in gross motor activity.

Using automated recording, Campbell et al. (1971) were able to obtain measures of overall motor activity over 8 h each day. They found significant stability over the first 4 days, which also correlated with scores up to 5 weeks, but not beyond. Korner (1979) also reports significant stability over 3 days in the total of motor output (when not crying) for a complete interfeed interval. Such measures confound amount of movement within and between states, so that we do not know whether the more active babies had more of the states involving movement or were just more active during all (or some) of the states. How much this matters depends on what significance the measure is expected to have. The belief that activity level is an enduring individual characteristic led to speculation about its role in personality (Fries and Wolff, 1953) and in mediating environmental influence (Schaffer, 1966). However Partington *et al.* (1971) failed to find a relationship between neonatal activity and later characteristics, though they did suspect that this may have been due to their sampling period being too short. Using rather varied measures of activity with slightly older infants, Thomas *et al.* (1963) also failed to find long-term consistency, although other longitudinal studies (reviewed by Yarrow, 1964) did find continuity in activity level through later childhood.

The frequency and intensity of a baby's movements are a compelling feature which appear to show something very characteristic of the individual. While there is some positive evidence to suggest that some measures of activity are stable in the neonatal period, we are very far from understanding the relationships between measures, and even further from being able to relate specific measures to any stable underlying function. In this situation speculations about the effects of some aspect of activity on the newborn's adaptation or environment are likely to be unproductive. There are, however, two characteristics related to activation which appear to be less problematic. These are irritability (or reactivity) and soothability.

Irritability

The simplest definition of irritability is the ease with which a baby will cry, and on this basis Korner (1979) reports a strong relationship between irritability (i.e. time spent crying) and an overall measure of activity. However, irritability on the Brazelton scale contributes to the factor including peak of excitement, rapidity of build-up and lability of states, but which does not include activity (Osofsky & O'Connell, 1977; Standley *et al.*, 1978). The factor is labelled reactivity by the former, and irritability by the latter and others. Chisholm *et al.* (1978) found that this factor correlated with maternal blood pressure, especially in the second trimester of pregnancy, in different racial samples. They suggest that the irritability may result from reduced placental blood flow, possibly related to subjective stress. They also suggest a possible link with later hyperactivity, and while this remains speculative, the finding of higher levels of irritability among males (Osofsky and O'Connell, 1977; Phillips *et al.*, 1978) could point to a relationship with vulnerability. Standley *et al.* (1978) found no sex difference but did report a relationship with amount of medication during labour. Yang *et al.* (1976) also using factor analysis, but not on Brazelton scores, identified reactivity-irritability as their first factor. The factor identified babies who responded to aversive stimuli quickly, vigorously, and with crying. As all of the measures involved crying this finding is discussed under *vocalization* (above) but the authors point to similarities with the irritability factor from the Brazelton studies, and they too found arousal items to load onto a different factor. As already mentioned, the neonatal reactivity-irritability factor did not correlate significantly with any of the factors at 90 days.

It would seem that irritability, as defined by the clustering of items on the Brazelton scale and independently of amount of time spent crying, is a measurable characteristic of the neonate which relates to significant aspects of vulnerability. We do not know how long the characteristics remain a stable feature of the individual's functioning, but it would not have to be for very long in order to have a significant impact on the behaviour and attitudes of the care-takers. It is also worth noting that irritable neonates are likely to be excluded from much research, particularly if a specific state must be sustained for a given time. This could be an advantage in many cases if it results in exclusion of babies who have been subjected to more stress during gestation or birth, but it may also result in findings based only on less reactive individuals. If neonatal irritability within the normal range proves to have longer term implications, it would become worth speculating about CNS features which could account for this pattern of characteristics (e.g. Sontag, 1941).

Soothability

The ease with which a distressed neonate can be soothed is of obvious practical significance to the care-taker. Prechtl (1963) reported on a small group of stressed babies who showed an extreme from of the characteristics of irritable babies and were very difficult to pacify. Birns *et al.* (1966) found individual levels of behavioural and heart-rate response to four different soothing conditions. The consistency applied across conditions within a single session and across successive days, but was based on scores during the soothing stimulus rather than on a difference from the control condition. It could, therefore, be accounted for equally well by individual differences in basal levels on the various measures. Individuality in soothability would require a demonstration of characteristic differences in change from a common level, or a consistent proportional change from the individual's basal condition. Korner and Thoman (1972) found consistency in the amount that crying was reduced by six different stimuli, but the interventions all took place within a single session and could, therefore, have been confounded by individual differences in lability of state, persistence in crying, or by differences in state during the experiment. Thoman *et al.* (1977) reported that 60–70-h-old babies who had substantial earlier experience of being held while talked to, were more likely to decrease crying when given auditory stimulation (mother talking). Some caution is necessary in deriving implications (either theoretical or practical) from these findings as the effect seems to be attributable not so much to less crying during stimulation, as to the higher incidence of crying during no stimulus trials, of the group that had received earlier holding. The true lesson would seem to be that frequent holding will result in a baby who cries more persistently unless stimulated.

The importance of distinguishing between level and change in behaviour when soothed arises also in the results of Smith and Steinschneider (1975). They reported differences in soothability between newborns according to whether maternal heart rate was high (100–110 bpm) or low (70–80 bpm). Babies of low HR mothers fell asleep sooner when subjected to rhythmic stimulation, but the most effective stimulation reduced this time by 28 per cent compared with a 35 per cent reduction for high maternal HR babies. Similarly the effect of stimulation on changing state differed depending on whether the proportional change or the final level is considered. The optimal stimulation produced a 256 per cent increase in sleep for the high HR group (compared to 120 per cent for the low) but a 24 per cent reduction in crying (compared with 49 per cent for the lows). The conclusion that babies of high HR mothers are less soothable and will provide less reinforcement for the parents ministering efforts does not seem to be justified. Although the research quoted leaves individual differences in sooth-ability as a plausible supposition, it cannot be said that such differences have been proved. Individuality has certainly been demonstrated but the design of the research does not allow this to be attributed unequivocally to stable differences in the amount that distress is reduced by the application of soothing stimuli.

State

The concept of state occupies a unique position in the study of the newborn. The original supposition of an underlying continuum of arousal or activation has been decisively rejected (Ashton, 1973; Prechtl, 1974), but conceptual confusion remains. The problems are discussed in detail by Prechtl (Chapter 3), but the specific issue that complicates any evaluation of the significance of individual differences is the ease with which state can be modified by external influence. Reviews such as that by Berg and Berg (1979) make apparent the range of factors which can influence the states that will be manifested at a particular time, as well as the range of functions which will be affected by the state prevalent at the time of recording. The pervasiveness of state gives it an obvious potential significance but its sensitivity to influence makes it difficult to justify any assumptions that individual tendencies will be sustained beyond the period of observation.

Individual differences in state would be manifested by different proportions of different states; by different patterns of state sequence; or by the same state having different characteristics in different newborns. A strong claim for all three forms of individuality is made by Thoman (1975a) on the basis of observations of forty-one infants on the day following birth. Each newborn was observed for 1-h midway between feeds in the morning and the afternoon. Correlations for the amount of time spent in different states of sleep demonstrated significant consistency across the two sessions. Waking and transitional states failed to show the same consistency, though amount of crying was significant. Ratings were made of 'state organization', that is how stable the states were and how clearly manifested. The five best organized and the five most poorly organized babies were followed up at 8 months. The descriptions provided by the mothers at that time of their infants' current behaviour, and of how they remembered the neonatal period tended to agree with the original classification. While not conclusive, this finding is supported by the fact that lability of states loads onto the *irritability* dimension of the Brazelton scale, as discussed above. Thoman also reports one baby whose state changes increased in frequency over the first 5 weeks and who subsequently died (Sudden Infant Death Syndrome). No firm conclusions can be drawn from such an isolated case but it does suggest that differences in state organization should be taken seriously.

Finally, Thoman claimed consistent differences in the behaviours that accompanied particular states. Although no statistical proof is offered, the description of the baby who consistently slept with open eyes provides a compelling example and a clear demonstration of the possible effect on the transactional relationship with the mother.

The study by Thoman has been presented as a good, representative example, since a comprehensive review of the state literature is beyond the scope of this section. The general conclusion that can be drawn is that consistent individual differences in the organization of neonatal states have been demonstrated over short periods, but the significance of these differences is unclear. In the Thoman study, for example, a low level of quiet sleep in both sessions could be attributable to obstetric medication, amount of feed provided by the mother, amount of stimulation on the ward before being brought to the observation room, birth difficulty (which must vary even though subjects were carefully screened for lack of complications), digestive problems resulting in continual crying, through more subtle factors such as variations in temperature on the ward which would require a different adaptation to the 36.1 °C of the observation room. Such a list could be extended almost indefinitely, but even if it is assumed that a fundamental aspect of individual state organization is responsible, many possibilities remain. The baby with a low level of quiet sleep may have a shorter sleep–wake cycle, an order of states in which quiet sleep is minimal midway between feeds, a high proportion of undefinable states or just a consistently low occurrence of quiet sleep. While there can be no question about the potential of individual differences in state to have a significant effect under any of the six headings, the short-term stability that has been demonstrated leaves too many other possibilities open for any firm conclusions to be drawn.

SOMATIC

Psychologists rarely mention bodily characteristics when reviewing individual differences, yet physical appearance, weight, strength and functional maturity are regarded as being of primary importance by parents. Physical measures such as length are not subject to rapid fluctuation and so, in this area, the range or standard deviation is an acceptable indication of individual differences. The significance of such differences is, however, still subject to the same criteria as are the other, possibly more ephemeral, characteristics considered in this chapter.

Appearance

Lorenz (in Hess, 1970) has described the appearance that a baby should have in order to be regarded as 'cute', and it can be assumed that newborns vary in their conformity to this ideal (as parents may vary in their susceptibility). Objectively, newborns certainly differ in physical attractiveness, but this may not affect their treatment. A not uncharacteristic comment from a mother in one of our samples at 6 months was 'I thought she was beautiful. I went round the ward looking at the other babies and feeling awfully sorry for their mothers. Now I realise she was just as ugly as all the others.' Abusing parents do sometimes attribute their rejection of the child to his or her early appearance, but we do not at present have any direct evidence that abused children were likely to have been less-attractive babies. A kind of exception arises in the case of newborns who were subjected to alcohol during gestation. These babies may have a characteristic and unattractive facial profile (Rosett and Sander, 1979), though even here individuality prevails as the features may be shown by only one of a pair of dizygotic twins. Low-weight-for-dates babies may also be less attractive than the term newborn, but it is not know whether this is a factor in their greater vulnerability to abuse.

The persistence of facial features does not seem to have been systematically studied though English folklore (at least) contains a belief in an inversion of attractiveness between babyhood and adulthood.

Size

Variations in newborn weight and length have been reviewed by Tanner (1974, 1978) who points out that the percentage variation at birth is very similar to that at age five and at adulthood. Size at birth does not relate closely to genetic tendencies of the infant, but is determined almost entirely by the intrauterine environment. Thus parity, nutrition, habits (such as smoking) and constitution of the mother are the major influences, though sex accounts for an average difference of 4 per cent in weight and 1.25 per cent in length. The size of a newborn in relation to gestation cannot therefore be used as an index of any fundamental tendency. 'Only after birth can the genes of the fetus controlling adult size express themselves' (Tanner, 1974, p. 88). It is, therefore, not surprising that adult size is not predictable from neonatal dimensions. However, the maternal characteristics and circumstances responsible for determining neonatal size may have significant consequences, and the overriding need of the lighter babies to gain weight must have corresponding costs compare with heavier babies. Ounsted and Simons (1976) suggest that large-for-dates babies have more 'latitude' in their early development which allows them to 'turn more of their energy into the processes concerned with adaptation to extra-uterine life' (p. 69). Thus large neonates have less weight gain per unit of food intake than do normal or small neonates, they lose more weight during the first 5 days, and they gain less, in proportion to length, throughout the first year. The pattern of weight gain, even in the first few weeks, may therefore be highly indicative of the kind of adaptation the newborn is making.

Strength

The Prone Head Reaction (PHR) was proposed by Bell and Darling (1965) as the optimal measure of neonatal muscular strength. While strength itself is not likely to change rapidly, a particular measure in a given set of conditions may do so. They did not report on stability of the measure but found differences in relationship to sex and feeding between test (74-h average age) and retest (87 h). Bell et al. (1971) using a mean for three trials at test and retest (8 h apart) found the measure to be stable, with males scoring significantly higher than females. PHR for females correlated with negative emotional expression at age 2 years and the authors propose that this relationship may be attributed to the role of tonus rather than muscular strength, in the PHR. It is difficult to see why this should make the relationship more comprehensible. Yang et al. (1976) found PHR to load onto a factor of arousal, with respiration and heart rates, and number of startles which suggests that the measure may not be as independent of general activity as Bell and Darling (1965) suggest. In their factor analysis of Brazelton scores Osofsky and O'Connell (1977) found muscle tonus loading with activity, defensive movements and pull-to-sit. There were no sex differences in any of these measures. Given that on average boys have considerably more muscle than girls at birth (Tanner 1974) it would seem that sex differences in PHR and its correlates are more likely to be due to differences in strength than in tone. Muscle tone influences the amount of strength that will be shown with a given level of musculature, but it is subject to more transient influences. For example Scanlon et al. (1974) found reductions in four separate measures of tonus between 2 and 8 h after birth when the mothers had received epidural block.

Whilst extreme cases of high or low tone may have diagnostic significance (Prechtl, 1963) variations within the normal range do not have clear implications. Tanner (1974) has proposed that musculature may be important to the parents particularly as an indication of masculinity for boys, but there is no evidence to support this suggestion. The clearest grounds for possible significance come from the likelihood (discussed under Food Intake) that overall strength is a major determinant of the amount of milk consumed at each feed.

Maturity

Newborns, even of the same gestational age, differ in their maturity, with girls averaging 1–2 weeks in advance of boys on most measures (Tanner, 1974). Racial differences have also been reported, and although many of the differences could be due to differential stimulation (as proposed by Kagan, 1979) it is unlikely that this would account, for example, for differences between races in photic latency (Butler and Engel, 1969). In the study of individuality, differences in maturity can be a contaminating factor by causing substantial differences between individuals which are stable over a short period, but which will disappear, having had no lasting effect. However, it is also possible that differences in maturity may themselves reflect fundamental characteristics of the individual, or may bring about a lasting change in his/her functioning through the differential availability of environmental resources at a particular period of life. For example the less mature baby may be less able to acquire responses to particular maternal ministrations during the first few days, and so may be unable to influence the mother during what may be a period of particular concentration and receptivity. We should also be aware of the risk that a more mature newborn may be less protected against the wide variety and intensity of stimulation which is characteristic of much hospital care.

Any function which follows a monotonic developmental course can be used as an index of maturity. As Tanner (1974) points out, different measures give different results, partly because of differential sensitivity to external influences. Of the measures reviewed by Tanner, conduction velocity of the peripheral nerves seems to be the least influenced by experience and to give large and reliable differences between newborns of the same conceptual age, relatively independent of the age at birth. The choice of maturity measure will depend on the reasons for wanting to use it whether theoretical or practical. These can range right through the given criteria so that if the interest is in an index of the working out of genetic tendencies that determine basic aspects of nervous-system function, measures like photic latency or conduction velocity will be used. If the concern is with the effect of differences in maturity in increasing error variance in an experimental study, then a measure of maturity must be selected to have a close relationship with the experimental measures for use either as a covariate to partial out the effect statistically or for selection of a more homogeneous group of subjects. This would require knowing the relationship between measures of maturity and other functions. Factor analytic studies have repeatedly identified clusters of measures relating to maturity. Brazelton Motor Maturity related to a low level of tremulousness (Osofsky and O'Connell, 1977; Standley et al., 1978) and to fewer startles only in the latter. Yang et al. (1976) found gestational age to relate to low autonomic variability, respiration rate and body size. Yang and Moss (1978) found a correlation between newborn maturity and a factor of 'tonic-active' at 90 days. This was the only correlation significant out of

21 so must be interpreted with caution, but the breakdown of components of the factor appeared to give a meaningful pattern of individual relationships. Standley *et al.* (1978) found their motor maturity factor to correlate significantly with parental characteristics and pregnancy orientation and (negatively) with drug dosages though this effect was confounded with parental characteristics. Such findings must be regarded as just a sample of the full range of relationships that could fruitfully be studied and which might eventually permit a resolution of the many issues raised particularly by the Standley *et al.* (1978) work.

It has already been suggested that differences in maturity might affect the adaptability of the newborn. Basic functions such as sucking mature well in advance of the time that they are needed (Anokhin 1964) and individual differences in maturity of babies born within the normal range of gestation will not be significant in such cases. Conversely, functions that become established after 40 weeks gestation can be assumed to make their major contribution to adaptation after that time. It is only through a detailed understanding of the demands made on the newborn that the significance of the differential maturity in specific functions can be evaluated, but the most likely context is provided by practices which are comparatively recent in terms of our evolutionary history. Although systemogenesis seems to allow for a large margin of error in the time of appearance of essential functions, it is possible that we have introduced new demands which only the faster (or slower) developers are equipped to meet.

Tanner (1974) points out that variations in size, shape and maturity are unlikely to have a negligible effect on the attitude of the care-taker. The aspects of maturity that would be most relevant here are those that are most salient to the care-taker, which will partly be determined by culturally prescribed expectations. Parents vary considerably in their expectations of which characteristics a newborn is mature enough to display (Stratton, in preparation) and thereby in the characteristics that they are prepared to perceive. As these are in fact most likely to be tendencies of the kind recorded by Standley *et al.* (1978), which are in turn affected by prior parental attitudes, the process will inevitably involve a complex transaction in which a search for neonatal characteristics which exert a unidirectional effect would be quite inappropriate. Some evidence of continuity to other functions has been cited above but given the diversity in determinants of different aspects of maturity, it would be unrealistic to attempt any general statement. Indeed, some neonatal differences may be subject to specific compensatory mechanisms. For example babies born with relatively large heads will show little increase in head circumference throughout the first year of life (Ounsted and Simons, 1976) so that their proportions will tend back towards the norm.

There would seem to be little advantage in a concept of overall maturity. In fact it may well be that an important aspect of individuality is the pattern of differential maturity of different functions and characteristics, analogous to autonomic specificity (Lacey, 1956). However the paucity of relevant data at present precludes any fruitful exploration of this issue. An alternative strategy would be to use criteria such as those listed here to identify specific aspects of maturity which would have clear implications. The present survey suggests that there are many areas in which this could be extremely productive.

HIGHER ORDER

A number of writers have proposed dimensions of individuality which cannot be indexed by a single type of measure. Some of these have already been discussed as they related closely to one of the earlier headings. Thus orality, cuddliness, screener/non-screener, irritability and maturity all represent hypothesized clusterings of characteristics, although in some cases it has been shown that the evidence does not support the necessary assumptions. There remain two groups of concepts, which relate closely to the criteria of adaptation and influence respectively and which naturally imply a clustering of lower-level characteristics.

Psychobiological Integrity

In attempting to account for correlations between mental test scores in infancy, Crano (1977) proposes a general factor or psychobiological well-being. The idea of an overall measure of 'intactness' is at the basis of neonatal assessment scales and the effectiveness of these in predicting later functioning is well documented in Osofsky (1979). Kopp and Parmelee (1979) discuss individual differences in vulnerability attributable to prenatal influences and it may be worth distinguishing measures of deficit from measures of particular strengths. That is, instead of a unipolar dimension in which the newborn is characterized by how far he/she falls short of some hypothesized ideal biological state, it may be more productive to think in terms of combinations of characteristics which may confer special potentials or vulnerabilities.

A limit on the usefulness of such general concepts is set by the relationship with the environment. What is a source of vulnerability in one setting may be innocuous or even advantageous in another (see Chapter 1). General measures of psychobiological integrity may be a useful interim expedient, but it is to be hoped that they will be superceded eventually be a coherent understanding of the relationship between particular patterns of neonatal characteristics and the environments in which their development will be worked out.

Interaction Style

The division of babies into cuddlers and non-cuddlers has been one of the most quoted aspects of individuality although the original finding was based only on mothers' reports at monthly interviews (Schaffer, 1964). Osofsky (1976) found that cuddliness correlated significantly between a stimulation situation and

Brazelton assessment. It also correlated negatively with the Brazelton factor of irritability (reactivity). Ainsworth *et al.* (1972) reported that babies who enjoy contact with the mother are less likely to cry when put down. These authors concluded that 'There are conspicuous individual differences in the way an infant organises his attachment behaviour . . .' (p. 142). Most of their data come from after the neonatal period, as did those of Field (1977), who found that both infant and mother's interactions could be predicted from Brazelton neonatal interactive process scores. On this basis Field proposes that each baby has an interaction style which is stable from birth. The data do not fully support this claim and the idea that a baby can have an interaction style independent of the particular partners in the interaction is difficult to accept on purely conceptual grounds. Dunn (1979) reviews some of the evidence that continuity in infant interaction style is inextricably bound up with continuity in maternal behaviour, and concludes that it is more justified to think in terms of continuity in interactive style between mother and baby.

A specific aspect of the newborn which allows justice to be done to the role of the mother is the clarity with which the baby provides signals to the care-taker (Korner and Grobstein 1967; Thoman, 1975b). This characteristic has been called 'readability' by Goldberg (1977) and 'clarity' by Yang and Moss (1978). Whether it is a stable characteristic is yet to be determined but because its whole significance derives from the interaction it is not necessary that it should be independent of care-taker characteristics. Indeed the readability of mother by baby might also be worth exploring.

Higher-order characteristics are necessarily more difficult to define and quantify, but they may be a particularly rewarding area of individuality to pursue. For example the process of determining which aspects of a newborn result in increased readability is likely to provide illuminating insights about the whole process of interaction. Constructs at this level also have the advantage of being formulated to cope with an issue of clear significance and so avoid the problem of the piecemeal accumulation of examples of individual differences which in no way advance our understanding of the newborn.

CONCLUSION

During the past decade a number of reviews of individuality in the newborn have been published. They have usually taken the form of a listing of characteristics for which individual differences have been claimed, without evaluating the basis of the claim, nor discussing in any detail the significance of specific cases. The present survey is an attempt to evaluate the existing evidence in relation to clearly stated criteria which in turn specific what degree of stability must be demonstrated. The question of stability is a complex one, and not only because the requirement varies with the reason for being interested. Empirically demonstrated stability may be used as grounds for attributing a particular kind of significance, and as proof that more transient influences cannot be responsible. For example once it is demonstrated that some babies cry significantly more than others in the first days, it can be assumed with some confidence that the mother's behaviour will be influenced and so the crying is significant. However, rather greater stability must be demonstrated to ensure that the crying is not a reaction to perinatal influence or a difficulty in adjusting to feeding. A very different argument is involved when the discovery of a significant effect is used as evidence for stability. For example, the fact that mothers can learn to identify their own baby's cry means that some aspects of the cry must be stable over a number of days.

The relationship between stability and the criteria is quite comparable to the transactional relationship between infant and care-taker—no statement about one partner can be made without implications and assumptions concerning the other. The attempt to summarize findings about individual differences in Table 2 is therefore not entirely straightforward. Each class of characteristic is evaluated in terms of evidence for short term stability and significance under each of the criteria. The entries: E (established), F (feasible), G (grounds for), and blank, represent a crude scale of confidence. The entry in a particular location is a composite (and perhaps idiosyncratic) judgement based on empirical evidence for stability and inherent plausibility. So, taking the first case of food intake as an example, there is good evidence of short-term stability in individual differences so this is taken as established (E). There is a suggestion that differences in strength may be at least partly responsible so there are grounds for supposing a relationship with *fundamental* (G). Evidence of *Clustering* exists but it is not strong enough to raise this rating above G either. There is no particular reason to suppose that *research* or diagnostic findings would be directly influenced by food intake so this entry is left blank. Since food intake has been shown to be stable it can be assumed with considerable confidence that both the *adaptation* of the newborn, and the behaviour and attitudes of care-takers will be *influenced* by individual variation, so these criteria are regarded as established (E). There is no reliable evidence of a *prediction* to future significant function, and no compelling basis for expecting one from the short-term stability which is all that has been demonstrated so this entry is blank. Similar reasoning has been used to rate all of the characteristics reviewed with the exception of the two 'higher order' categories. The absence of a directly observable manifestation and the range of possible definition would make any summary statement concerning these misleading.

Although being less a definitive statement than a first attempt to coordinate the available information, the present survey as summarised in Table 2 generates some rather clear implications. The original interest in newborn individuality as a predictor of later pathology and personality assumed that differences between babies would index fundamental and enduring characteristics which would correlate with significant later functions. It is clear from the columns of

Table 2 Ratings of confidence claimed for the stability, and the significance of individual differences under six criteria

Characteristic	Criteria						
	Short-term stability	Fundamental	Clustering	Research	Adaptation	Influence	Predictive
Oral							
Food intake	E	G	G		E	E	
Non-nutritive	E		E			G	G
Vocalisation: quantity	E		F	E	E	E	F
Quality	E	E			E	E	G
Cognitive							
Sensory: visual	E		E		G	F	
tactile	E	F	E		G	F	E
auditory	E		E		G		
Perceptual							
Learning	G	G		G	G	G	
Psychophysiology							
Heart rate	E	G			G		
Respiration	E				F		F
Activation							
Activity	F				G		
Irritability	E	F	E	E	E	F	G
Soothability	F				G	G	
State	E		F	E	G	G	
Somatic							
Appearance	E	E			E	F	
Size	E				F		
Strength	E		F		F	G	
Maturity	E	E	E	E		G	G

E Established with reasonable confidence
F Feasible but evidence equivocal, interpretation obscure or requisite stability not demonstrated
G Grounds based only on weak evidence and/or plausibility

fundamental and predictive criteria that very few relevant characteristics fulfil even moderate requirements of this kind. The columns for which there are entries under most headings are those that relate to the capacity to adapt to the extrauterine environment, and influence on the care-taker. These two considerations have been emerging as the main themes in the study of the psychobiology of the newborn over the last decade and it is interesting that an overview of research which was largely undertaken with other objectives should show this effect so clearly.

The other major source of established significance comes under the criterion of clustering. Some caution may be necessary here as the relationships come from a small number of studies all but one of which is based on a single instrument, the Brazelton neonatal behavioural assessment. Further studies have been collected by Sameroff (1978), with the consistent finding that although the general pattern of clustering remained the same, the scores of individual babies were not at all stable from day to day. Furthermore, Brazelton scores consistently failed to predict any later characteristics. This could be due, as Sameroff (1978) claims, to the dynamic nature of neonatal development, and the sensitivity of BNBAS items. However, there remains the possibility that transient conditions may influence particular groups of items thereby generating reliable, but unimportant, correlations between them. The implication of the present survey is that individual differences between neonates need to be sought and evaluated in the context of a clear specification of the aspect of their significance which motivates the search. To expect useful measures of individuality to emerge from a scale which was constructed without such a specification would be over-optimistic. Even so the concordance between different studies with quite different samples is impressive and seems to justify confidence that the relationships have been established. The existing data may be regarded as a useful starting point. Many other relationships, possibly more fundamental and more powerful, must be waiting to be uncovered, but the search no longer has to be through a blind statistical analysis of arbitrarily juxtaposed measures. The clusterings so far identified should allow preliminary hypotheses to be formulated which would indicate which grouping of characteristics might be anticipated. Reliable findings of clustering of more widely sampled characteristics could then be expected to allow a meaningful interpretation perhaps leading to specification of higher forms of individuality.

The overall impression that emerges from this analysis of individual differences is that a concentration on continuity is inappropriate. Most of the significance of newborn individuality derives from the implications for the neonatal period itself. The determination of both the fundamental structural variation which may underlie manifestations of individuality, and the possible long-term consequences, should perhaps be a hope for the future. The present task is to chart, and hopefully to understand, the many aspects by which normal newborns are individually differentiated from each other. This enterprise has been shown to have its own justification, founded on the intrinsic value of the neonate as an object of scientific study and as a person.

REFERENCES

Ainsworth, M. D. S., Bell, S. M., and Stayton, D. J. (1972). Individual differences in the development of some attachment behaviour, *Merrill-Palmer Quarterly*, **18**, 123–143.

Aleksandrowicz, M. K. and Aleksandrowicz, D. R. (1974). Obstetrical pain relieving drugs as predictors of infant behaviour variability, *Child Development*, **45**, 935–945.

Als, H., Tronick, E., Adamson, L., and Brazelton, T. B. (1976). The behaviour of the full-term yet underweight newborn infant, *Developmental Medicine and Child Neurology*, **18**, 590–602.

Als, H., Tronick, E., Lester, B. M., and Brazelton, T. B. (1979). Specific neonatal measures: the Brazelton neonatal behavioural assessment scale in *Handbook of Infant Development* (Ed. J. D. Osofsky), Wiley, New York.

Anderson, R. B. and Rosenblith, J. F. (1964). Light sensitivity in the neonate: A preliminary report, *Biology of the Neonate*, **7**, 83–94.

Anokhin, P. K. (1964). Systemogenesis as a general regulator of brain development, in *Progress in Brain Research*, Vol. 9 (Eds W. A. Himwich and H. E. Himwich) Elsevier, London.

Ashton, R. (1973). The state variable in neonatal research, *Merrill Palmer Quarterly*, **19**, 3–20.

Balint, M. (1948). Individual differences of behaviour in early infancy, and an objective method for recording them, *Journal of Genetic Psychology*, **73**, 57–117.

Barten, S., Birns, B., and Ronch, J. (1971). Individual differences in the visual pursuit behaviour of neonates, *Child Development*, **42**, 313–319.

Bell, R. Q. (1966). Level of arousal in breast-fed and bottle-fed human newborns, *Psychosomatic Medicine*, **28**, 177–180.

Bell, R. Q. (1974). Contributions of human infants to care giving and social interaction, in *The Effect of the Infant on its Caregiver* (Eds M. Lewis and L. A. Rosenblum) Wiley, New York.

Bell, R. Q. and Costello, M. (1974). Three tests for sex differences in tactile sensitivity in the newborn, *Biology of the Neonate*, **7**, 335–347.

Bell, R. Q. and Darling, J. F. (1965). The prone head reaction in the human neonate: relationship with sex and tactile sensitivity, *Child Development*, **36**, 943–949.

Bell, R. W., Weller, G. M., and Waldrop, M. F. (1971). Newborn and preschooler: Organization of behaviour and relations between periods, *Monographs of the Society for Research in Child Development*, **36**, (Ser. 142), 1–2.

Bell, S. M. and Ainsworth, M. D. S. (1972). Infant crying and maternal responsiveness, *Child Development*, **43**, 1171–1190.

Bennett, S. (1971). Infant caretaker interactions, *Journal of the American Academy of Child Psychiatry*, **10**, 321–335.

Berg, W. K. and Berg, K. M. (1979). Psychophysiological development in infancy: state, sensory function and attention, in *Handbook of Infant Development* (Ed. J. D. Osofsky) Wiley, New York.

Bergman, P. and Escalona, S. (1949). Unusual sensitivities in very young children, *Psychoanalytic Study of the Child*, **3/4**, 332–352.

Birns, B. (1965). Individual differences in human neonates' responses to stimulation, *Child Development*, **36**, 249–256.

Birns, B., Blank, M., and Bridger, W. H. (1966). The effectiveness of various soothing techniques on human neonates, *Psychosomatic Medicine*, **28**, 316–322.

Brazelton, T. B. (1973). *Neonatal Behavioral Assessment Scale*, SIMP, London.

Bridger, W. H., Birns, B. M., and Blank, M. (1965). A comparison of behavioral ratings and heart rate measurements in human neonates, *Psychosomatic Medicine*, **27**, 123–133.

Bridger, W. H. and Reiser, M. F. (1959). Psychophysiologic studies of the neonate: An approach toward the methodological and theoretical problems involved. *Psychosomatic Medicine*, **21**, 265–276.

Broadbent, D. E. (1958). *Perception and Communication*, Pergamon, New York.

Bronshtein, A. I., Antonova, T. G., Kamenetskaya, A. F., Luppova, N. N., and Sytova, V. A. (1958). On the development of the functions of analyzers in infants and some animals at the early stage of ontogenesis, in *Problems of Evolution of Physiological Functions*, Academic Science, USSR.

Butler, B. V. and Engel, R. (1969). Mental and motor scores at 8 months in relation to neonatal photic responses, *Developmental Medicine and Child Neurology*, **11**, 77–82.

Campbell, D., Kuyek, J., Lang, E., and Partington, M. W. (1971). Motor activity in early life. II. Daily motor activity output in the neonatal period, *Biology of the Neonate*, **18**, 108–120.

Chisholm, J. S., Woodson, R. H., and Woodson, E. M. (1978). Maternal blood pressure in pregnancy and newborn irritability, *Early Human Development*, **2**, 171–178.

Clifton, R. K. and Graham, F. K. (1968). Stability of individual differences in heart rate activity during the newborn period, *Psychophysiology*, **5**, 37–50.

Crano, W. D. (1977). What do infant mental tests test? A cross lagged panel analysis of selected data from the Berkeley Growth Study, *Child Development*, **48**, 144–151

Crook, C. K. (1979). The organization and control of infant sucking, in *Advances in Child Development and Behaviour*, Vol. 14 (Eds H. W. Reese and L. P. Lipsitt) Academic Press, London.

Dubignon, J., Campbell, D., Curtis, M., and Partington, M. W. (1969). The relation between laboratory measures of sucking, food intake, and perinatal factors during the newborn period, *Child Development*, **40**, 1107–1120.

Dunn, J. F. (1975). Consistency and change in styles of mothering, in *CIBA Foundation Symposium No. 33—Parent–Infant Interaction*, Elsevier, Amsterdam.

Dunn, J. F. (1977). Patterns of early interaction: continuities and consequences, in *Studies in Mother–Infant Interaction* (Ed. H. R. Schaffer), Academic Press, London.

Dunn, J. F. (1979). The first year of life: continuities in individual differences, in *The First Year of Life* (Eds D. Schaffer and J. Dunn) Wiley, Chichester.

Dunn, J. F. and Richards, M. P. M. (1977). Observations in the developing relationship between mother and baby in the newborn, in *Studies in Mother–Infant Interaction* (Ed. H. R. Schaffer), Academic Press, London.

Eisenberg, R. B., Coursin, D. B., and Rupp, N. R. (1966). Habituation to an acoustic pattern as an index of differences among human neonates, *Journal of Auditory Research*, **6**, 239–248.

Engel, B. T. (1960). Stimulus-response and individual-response specificity, *Archives of General Psychiatry*, **2**, 305–313.

Escalona, S. K. (1968). *The Roots of Individuality*, Tavistock Publications, London.

Falender, C. A. and Mehrabian, A. (1978). Environmental effects on parent-infant interaction, *Genetic Psychology Monographs*, **97**, 3–41.

Field, T. M. (1977). Effects of early separation, interactive deficits, and experimental manipulations on infant–mother face-to-face interaction, *Child Development*, **48**, 763–771.

Friedman, S., Bruno, L., and Veitze, P. (1974). Newborn habituation to visual stimuli: A sex difference in novelty detection, *Journal of Experimental Child Psychology*, **18**, 242–251.

Fries, M. and Wolff, P. (1953). Some hypotheses on the role of the congenital activity type in personality and development, *Psychoanalytic Study of the Child*, **8**, 48–62.

Frodi, A. M., Lamb, M. E., Leavitt, L. A., Donovan, W. L., Neff, C., and Sherry, D. (1978). Fathers' and mothers' responses to the faces and cries of normal and premature infants, *Developmental Psychology*, **14**, 490–498.

Goldberg, S. (1977). Social competence in infancy: a model of parent-infant interaction, *Merrill Palmer Quarterly*, **23**, 163–177.

Graham, F. K. (1956). Behavioural differences between normal and traumatized newborns, *Psychological Monographs*, **427**, **428**, 1–33.

Graham, F. K., Clifton, R. K., and Hatton, H. M. (1968). Habituation of heart rate response to repeated auditory stimulation during the first five days of life, *Child Development*, **39**, 35–52.

Hanks, H. G. I. (1979). *Child Abuse and Infant Characteristics*. Unpublished thesis, University of Leeds.

Hess, E. H. (1970). Ethology and developmental psychology, in *Carmichael's Manual of Child Psychology*, Vol. 1 (Ed. P. H. Mussen) Wiley, New York.

Hirsch, J. (1963). Behavior genetics and individuality understood, *Science*, **142**, 1436–1442.

Hittelman, J. H. and Dickes, R. (1979). Sex differences in neonatal eye contact time, *Merrill Palmer Quarterly*, **25**, 171–184.

Kagan, J. (1971). *Change and Continuity in Infancy*, Wiley, New York.

Kagan, J. (1979). Overview: Perspectives on human infancy, in *Handbook of Infant Development* (Ed. J. D. Osofsky) Wiley, New York.

Karelitz, S., Fisichelli, V. R., Costa, J., Karelitz, R., and Rosenfeld. L. (1964). Relation of crying activity in early infancy to speech and intellectual development at age three years, *Child Development*, **35**, 769–777.

Kaye, K., (1977). Toward the origin of dialogue, in *Studies in Mother–Infant Interaction* (Ed. H. R. Schaffer), Academic Press, London.

Kennell, J. H., Trause, M. A., and Klaus, M. H. (1975). Evidence for a sensitive period in the human mother, in *Ciba Foundation Symposium No. 33 — Parent–Infant Relationship* (Eds R. Porter and M. O'Connor), Elsevier, Amsterdam.

Kessen, W., Williams, E. J., and Williams, J. P. (1961). Selection and test of response measures in the study of the human newborn, *Child Development*, **32**, 7–24.

Klein, R. P. and Jennings, K. D. (1979). Responses to social and inanimate stimuli in early infancy, *Journal of Genetic Psychology*, **135**, 3–9.

Kopp, C. B. and Parmelee, A. H. (1979). Prenatal and perinatal influences on infant behavior, in *Handbook of Infant Development* (Ed. J. D. Osofsky) Wiley, New York.

Korner, A. F. (1970). Visual alertness in neonates: Individual differences and their correlates, *Perceptual and Motor Skills*, **31**, 499–509.

Korner, A. F. (1971). Individual differences at birth: Implications for early experience and later development, *American Journal of Orthopsychiatry*, **41**, 608–619.

Korner, A. F. (1973). Early stimulation and maternal care as related to infant capabilities and individual differences, *Early Child Development and Care*, **2**, 307–327.

Korner, A. F. (1974). The effect of the infant's state, level of arousal, sex and autogenetic stage on the caretaker, in *The Effect of the Infant on its Caregiver* (Eds M. Lewis and L. A. Rosenblum) Wiley, New York.

Korner, A. F. (1979). Conceptual issues in infancy research, in *Handbook of Infant Development* (Ed. J. D. Osofsky), Wiley, New York.

Korner, A. F. and Grobstein, R. (1967). Individual differences at birth: Implications for mother–infant relationship and later development, *Journal of the American Academy of Child Psychiatry*, **6**, 676–690.

Korner, A. F. and Thoman, E. B. (1970). Visual alertness in neonates as evoked by maternal care, *Journal of Experimental Child Psychology*, **10**, 67–78.

Korner, A. F. and Thoman, E. B. (1972). The relative efficacy of contact and vestibular-proprioceptive stimulation in soothing neonates, *Child Development*, **43**, 443–453.

Kron, R. E., Ipsen, J., and Goddard, K. E. (1968). Consistent individual differences in the nutritive sucking behavior of the human newborn, *Psychosomatic Medicine*, **30**, 151–161.

Lacey, J. I. (1956). The evaluation of autonomic responses: Towards a general solution, *Annals of the New York Academy of Sciences*, **67**, 123–164.

Lacey, J. I. (1959). Psychophysiological approaches to the evaluation of psychotherapeutic process and outcome, in *Research in Psychotherapy* (Eds E. A. Rubenstein and M. B. Parloff), APA, Washington D. C.

Lacey, J. I. (1967). Somatic response patterning and stress: some revisions of activation theory, in *Psychological Stress: Issues in Research* (Eds M. H. Appley and R. Trumbull), Appleton-Century-Crofts, New York.

Lewis, M. and Goldberg, S. (1969). Perceptual-cognitive development in infancy: A generalized expectancy model as a function of the mother-infant interaction, *Merrill-Palmer Quarterly*, **15**, 81–100.

Lewis, M. and Rosenblum, L. A. (1974). *The Effect of the Infant on its Caregiver*, Wiley-Interscience, New York.

Lewis, M., Wilson, C. D., Ban, P., and Baumel, M. H. (1970). An exploratory study of resting cardiac rate and variability from the last trimester of prenatal life through the first year of postnatal life, *Child Development*, **41**, 799–811.

Lipsitt, L. P. (1978). Perinatal indicators and psychophysiological precursors of crib death, in *Early Developmental Hazards: Predictors and Precautions* (Ed. F. D. Horowitz) Westview Press, USA.

Lipsitt, L. P. and Jacklin, C. N. (1971). Cardiac deceleration and its stability in human newborns, *Developmental Psychology*, **5**, 535.

Lipsitt, L. P. and Levy, N. (1959). Electrotactual threshold in the neonate, *Child Development*, **30**, 547–554.

Lipton, E. L., Steinschneider, A., and Richmond, J. B. (1961). Autonomic function in the neonate: IV. Individual differences in cardiac reactivity, *Psychosomatic Medicine*, **23**, 472–484.

Lipton, E. L., Steinschneider, A. and Richmond, J. B. (1965). Swaddling, a child care practice: Historical, cultural and experimental observations, *Paediatrics* (Suppl.) **35**, 521–567.

Lipton, E. L., Steinschneider, A., and Richmond, J. B. (1966). Autonomic function in the neonate. VII. Maturational changes in cardiac control. *Child Development*, **37**, 1–16.

McCall, R. B. (1979). The development of intellectual functioning in infancy and the prediction of later I. Q., in *Handbook of Infant Development* (Ed. J. D. Osofsky) Wiley, New York.

McGrade, B. J. (1968). Newborn activity and emotional response at eight months, *Child Development*, **39**, 1247–1252.

McGrade, B. J., Kessen, W., and Leutzendorf, A. (1965). Activity in the human newborn related to delivery difficulty, *Child Development*, **36**, 73–79.

Mehrabian, A. (1977). Individual differences in stimulus screening and arousability, *Journal of Personality*, **45**, 237–250.

Michelsson, K., Sirviö, P., and Wasz-Höckert, O. (1977). Sound spectrographic cry analysis of infants with bacterial meningitis, *Developmental Medicine and Child Neurology*, **19**, 309–315.

Miller, D. J., Ryan, E., Short, E., Ries, P., McGuire, M., and Culler, M. (1977). Relationships between early habituation and later cognitive performance in infancy, *Child Development*, **48**, 658–661.

Morsbach, G. and Bunting, C. (1979). Maternal recognition of their neonates' cries, *Developmental Medicine and Child Neurology*, **21**, 178–185.

Neilon, P. (1948). Shirley's babies after 15 years: A personality study, *Journal of Genetic Psychology*, **73**, 175–186.

O'Gorman, J. C. (1977). Individual differences in habituation of human physiological responses: A review of theory, method, and findings in the study of personality correlates in non-clinical populations, *Biological Psychology*, **5**, 257–318.

Osofsky, J. D. (1976). Neonatal characteristics and mother–infant interaction in two observational situations, *Child Development*, **47**, 1138–1147.

Osofsky, J. D. (1979). *Handbook of Infant Development*, Wiley, New York.

Osofsky, J. D. and Connors, K. (1979). Mother–infant interaction: an integrative view of a complex system, in *Handbook of Infant Development* (Ed. J. D. Osofsky) Wiley, New York.

Osofsky, J. D. and O'Connell, E. J. (1977). Patterning of newborn behaviour in an urban population, *Child Development*, **48**, 532–536.

Ounsted, M. K. and Simons, C. D. (1976). Infant feeding, growth and development, *Current Medical Research and Opinion*, **4**, suppl. 1, 60–72.

Partington, M. W., Lang, E., and Campbell, D. (1971). Motor activity in early life. I. Fries' congenital activity types, *Biology of the Neonate*, **18**, 94–107.

Petrinovich, L. F. and Hardyck, C. D. (1969). Error rates for multiple comparison methods: Some evidence concerning the frequency of erroneous conclusions, *Psychological Bulletin*, **71**, 43–54.

Phillips, S., King, S., and Dubois, L. (1978). Spontaneous activities of female versus male newborns, *Child Development*, **49**, 590–597.

Pollitt, E., Gilmore, M., and Valcarcel, M. (1978). The stability of sucking behaviour and its relationship to intake during the first month of life, *Infant Behaviour and Development*, **1**, 347–357.

Prechtl, H. F. R. (1963). The mother–child interaction in babies with minimal brain damage, in *Determinants of Infant Behaviour*, Vol. II (Ed. B. M. Foss), Methuen, London.

Prechtl, H. F. R. (1974). The behavioural states of the newborn infant. *Brain Research*, **76**, 185–212.

Prechtl, H., Theorell, K., Gransbergen, A., and Lind, J. (1969). A statistical analysis of cry patterns in normal and abnormal newborn infants, *Developmental Medicine and Child Neurology*, **11**, 142–152.

Richmond, J. and Lustman, S. L. (1955). Autonomic Function in the Neonate (I): Implications for Psychosomatic Theory, *Psychosomatic Medicine*, **17**, 269–275.

Rosett, H. L. and Sander, L. W. (1979). Effects of maternal drinking on neonatal morphology and state regulation, in *Handbook of Infant Development* (Ed. J. D. Osofsky) Wiley, New York.

Salapatek, P. and Kessen, W. (1973). Prolonged investigation of a plane geometric triangle by the human newborn, *Journal of Experimental Child Psychology*, **15**, 22–29.

Sameroff, A. J. (1978). Organization and stability of newborn behaviour: A commentary on the Brazelton Neonatal Behaviour Assessment Scale. *Monograph of the Society for Research in Child Development*, **43**, (5–6, Serial No. 177).

Scanlon, J. W., Brown, W. U., Weiss, J. B., and Alper, M. H. (1974). Neurobehavioural responses of newborn infants after maternal epidural anaesthesia, *Anaesthesiology*, **40**, 121–128.

Schachter, J., Williams, T. A., Khachaturian, Z., Tobin, M., Kruger, R., and Kerr, J. (1971). Heart rate responses to auditory clicks in neonates, *Psychophysiology*, **8**, 163–179.

Schaffer, H. R. (1964). Patterns of response to physical contact in early human development, *Journal of Child Psychology and Psychiatry*, **5**, 1–13.

Schaffer, H. R. (1966). Activity level as a constitutional determinant of infantile reaction to deprivation, *Child Development*, **37**, 595–602.

Scheffé, H. (1959). *The Analysis of Variance*, Wiley, New York.

Shirley, M. M. (1933). *The First Two Years: A Study of 25 Babies*, Vol. 3, University of Minnesota Press, Minneapolis.

Smith, C. R. and Steinschneider, A. (1975). Differential effects of prenatal rhythmic stimulation on neonatal arousal states, *Child Development*, **46**, 574–578.

Sokolov, E. N. (1963). Higher nervous functions: The orienting reflex, *Annual Review of Physiology*, 545–580.

Sontag, L. W. (1941). The significance of fetal environmental differences, *American Journal of Obstetrics and Gynaecology*, **42**, 996–1003.

Sostek, A. M. and Anders, T. F. (1977). Relationships among the Brazelton neonatal scale, Bayley Infant Scales and early temperament, *Child Development*, **48**, 320–323.

Sostek, A. M. and Brackbill, Y. (1976). Stability of motor OR and heart rate habituation rates in infancy, *Developmental Psychobiology*, **9**, 353–358.

Standley, K., Swale, A. B., Copans, S. A., and Klein, R. P. (1978). Multidimensional sources of infant temperament, *Genetic Psychology Monographs*, **98**, 203–231.

Stratton, P. M. (1970). The use of heart rate for the study of habituation in the neonate, *Psychophysiology*, **7**, 44–56.

Stratton, P. M. (1977). Criteria for assessing the influence of obstetric circumstances on later development, in *Benefits and Hazards of the New Obstetrics* (Eds T. Chard and M. Richards), SIMP, London.

Stratton, P. M. (In Preparation). Attribution of qualities to the newborn by mothers and midwives.

Stratton, P. M. and Connolly, K. J. (1973). Discrimination by newborns of the intensity, frequency and temporal characteristics of auditory stimuli, *British Journal of Psychology*, **64**, 219–232.

Tanner, J. M. (1974). Variability of growth and maturity in newborn infants, in *The Effect of the Infant on its Caregiver* (Eds M. Lewis and L. Rosenblum). Wiley, New York.

Tanner, J. M. (1978). *Foetus into Man: Physical Growth from Conception to Maturity*, Open Books, London.

Thoman, E. B. (1975a). Sleep and wake behaviors in neonates: consistencies and consequences, *Merrill-Palmer Quarterly*, **21**, 295–314.

Thoman, E. B. (1975b).The role of the infant in early transfer of information, *Biological Psychiatry*, **10**, 161–169.

Thoman, E. B., Freese, M. P., Becker, P. T., Acebo, C., Morin, V. N., and Tynan, W. D. (1978). Sex differences in the ontogeny of sleep apnea during the first year of life, *Physiology and Behavior*, **20**, 699–707.

Thoman, E. B., Korner, A. F., and Beason-Williams, L. (1977). Modification of responsiveness to maternal vocalisation in the neonate, *Child Development*, **48**, 563–569.

Thoman, E. B., Miano, V. N., and Freese, M. P. (1977). The role of respiratory instability in SIDS, *Developmental Medicine and Child Neurology*, **19**, 729–738.

Thomas, A., Chess, S., Birch, H. G., Hertzig, M. R., and Korn, S. (1963). *Behavioral Individuality in Early Childhood*. University Press, New York.

Turkewitz, G. and Birch, M. (1971). Neurobehavioral organisation of the human newborn, in *Exceptional Infant*, Vol. 2, *Studies in Abnormalities* (Ed. J. Hellmuth), Brunner/Mazel Inc, New York.

Turkewitz, G., Moreau, T., Birch, H. G., and Davis, L. (1971). Relationships among responses in the human newborn: the non-association and non-equivalence among different indicators of responsiveness, *Psychophysiology*, 7, 233–247.

Vander Maelen, A. L., Strauss, M. E., and Starr, R. H. (1975). Influence of obstetric medication on auditory habituation in the newborn, *Developmental Psychology*, 11, 711–714.

Wasz-Höckert, O., Lind, J., Vuorenkoski, V., Partanen, T., and Valanne, E. (1968). *The Infant Cry*, Clinics in Developmental Medicine n. 29. Heinemann, London.

Wolff, P. (1969). The natural history of crying and other vocalizations in early infancy, in *Determinants of Infant Behaviour*, Vol. IV (Ed. B. M. Foss) Methuen, London.

Yang, R. K., Federman, E. J., and Douthitt, T. C. (1976). The characterization of neonatal behaviour: A dimensional analysis, *Developmental Psychology*, 12, 204–210.

Yang, R. K. and Halverson, C. F. (1976). A study of the 'inversion of intensity' between newborn and preschool-age behaviour, *Child Development*, 47, 350–359.

Yang, R. K. and Moss, H. A. (1978). Neonatal precursors of infant behavior, *Developmental Psychology*, 14, 607–613.

Yarrow, L. J. (1964). Personality consistency and change, *Vita Humana*, 7, 67–72.

Zeskind, P. S. and Lester, B. M. (1978). Acoustic features and auditory perceptions of the cries of newborns with prenatal and perinatal complications, *Child Development*, 49, 580–589.

Influences

The first two sections have surveyed the contribution that the newborn makes to his/her adaptation to extra-uterine life. However, complex though the relationships between structure, capacity, normative characteristic and individual variation may be, the transactional approach demands a further perspective. Neonatal adaptation can only be understood by combining what we know about newborns with an appreciation of the contexts in which they must function, and of the influences to which they may be subjected, whether arising from previous events, or from current social, care-taking and obstetric practices. All of these influences will be aggravated by unfavourable circumstances and the treatment of ill and premature babies, requires specific consideration. Furthermore, although a detailed consideration of infancy is beyond the scope of this book, it is important to remember that the significance of any adaptation can only be understood in relation to the future contexts in which its consequences will be worked out.

By birth the baby has already been subjected to a variety of influences and has adapted to them or perhaps has been unable to do so; Hagberg (1975) estimates that 85–90 per cent of severe intellectual and neurological problems stem from prenatal causes. From his preliminary survey of prenatal research John Barrett in Chapter 10 is led to a particularly clear statement of the need to conceptualize prenatal processes in terms of transactions within both current and future environments. From this perspective his analysis of adaptation in fetus and newborn generates important insights concerning the momentum of growth which tends towards adaptation and the fact that many forms of insult may impair the adaptive processes themselves. The consideration of underlying processes is complicated by the fact that many systems are 'being made while functioning' and so their development is affected by the consequences of their activity. A clear example of this has been provided by the discussions of the development of neonatal vision in Chapters 5 and 8. The fetus, just as much as the newborn, must be seen as a complete living organism, fully adapted to and viable within its own ecology. It is the cellular environment produced by the

263

transactions between the form and activities of the fetus and its environment, that trigger the successive genetic activities which result in maturation. Given the complexity of the interdependencies which ensure that this process optimally prepares each fetus for adaptation to the next stage of its changing environment, it is not surprising that interference in the process is almost invariably disruptive. Even the case of progesterone treatment, used in this chapter as an example of benign interference, has been the subject of considerable doubt and controversy (Lynch and Mychalkiw, 1978). Of much wider significance is the relationship of nutrition to other variables, which is the subject of a major analysis of interrelationships. The chapter concludes with a consideration of the evidence that the newborn is influenced by events occurring even before he/she is conceived.

The next two chapters consider rather different aspects of the treatment to which newborns may be subjected. Ann Oakley (Chapter 11) compares the obstetric and neonatal care of various cultures with that provided by Western medicine. It is important not only for the practitioner but also for the researcher, whether in trying to understand the reasons for and effects of specific practices, or in expecting research findings to modify these practices, to be aware of the extent to which they are determined by cultural attitudes and assumptions. Looking at other cultures not only makes it obvious that the treatment of the newborn is an expression of the values of the society as well as of beliefs about birth, it also gives a base against which to compare our own practices and perhaps to question procedures which might otherwise pass unnoticed.

It is always easier to view practices as being an expression of cultural values when the culture is different from our own, but having followed the examples given here it would be difficult to see the compulsory shaving of pubic hair and recumbent position during labour as being entirely attributable to medical necessity. Studying a wide variety of cultures should also give some indication of the range of environments to which newborns can successfully adapt. However, it will be clear from the review in this chapter that the information that we have available only allows us to begin to answer this question.

An alternative approach to determining the limits of neonatal adaptability is provided by Malcolm Chiswick's review of medical conditions and treatments in Chapter 12. This chapter is intended to provide an overview of the stresses and deficits under which viable newborns may be suffering and of the procedures to which they are likely to be subjected in Western hospital care. The demands of extra-uterine adaptation, and the hospital procedures for its facilitation are briefly described, then the major diseases are surveyed. The premature baby provides a particularly clear example of the process of balancing resources between growth and the demands imposed by the condition of the newborn and his environment. Each condition imposes its own demands and many of them (respiratory distress, temperature control, feeding difficulties) relate to the major physiological adaptations which are discussed elsewhere in this book. The problem for the premature and underweight babies is that, as for any disadvantaged group, the deficits are compounded. Not only is a baby with (say) respiratory problems more likely to be suffering from other difficulties in the neonatal period. There is also an increased probability that the fetal environment will have been inadequate, as will be the post-neonatal care. The task then, having reduced the damage from individual insults to a minimum, is to find ways to determine how competing adaptations interact. The review makes it clear that both disease and treatment must be regarded as imposed conditions to which the newborn must adapt. Many of the questions raised in this chapter concern the bias we can impose on the balance between adaptations which the newborn would naturally achieve.

Every aspect of the life of the newborn is affected by feeding and in his analyses of what is known about nutrition and feeding in early infancy, Peter Wright (Chapter 13) opens up all of the important themes of this book. Fundamental to many of the adaptations the newborn must make, is the ability to take in and retain adequate nutrition, and many competencies appear to have developed so as to achieve this with a minimum expenditure of energy. These competencies have, of course, been developed in the context of breast feeding and only a full understanding of the adaptive tendencies in this situation will enable us to predict the consequences of 'unnatural' practices such as bottle feeding or the tube feeding of premature babies. Although there are 'huge gaps' in our knowledge of very basic issues (Brans, 1976), the application in this chapter of recent advances in understanding of the mechanisms of hunger and satiety, could do more than just illuminate neonatal nutrition. It puts us well on the way to a detailed account of the signals and response tendencies which control this most fundamental transaction between mother and baby.

REFERENCES

Brans, Y. W. (1976). Neonatal nutrition: an overview, *Postgraduate Medicine*, **7**, 113–115.

Hagberg, B. (1975). Pre- Peri- and postnatal prevention of major neuropaediatric handicaps, *Neuropaediatrie*, **6**, 331–338.

Lynch, A. and Mychalkiw, W. (1978). Prenatal progesterone. II. Its role in the treatment of pre-eclamptic toxaemia and its effect on the offspring's intelligence: A reappraisal, *Early Human Development*, **2**, 323–339.

Psychobiology of the Human Newborn
Edited by P. Stratton
© 1982, John Wiley & Sons, Ltd.

CHAPTER 10

Prenatal Influences on Adaptation in the Newborn

JOHN H. W. BARRETT

A set of Russian dolls nested one inside the other. That is how Bronfenbrenner (1979), in his attempt to build a model of the ecology of development, pictures the relationships between the environments in which human development takes place. When we start thinking about the fetus in its environments, the metaphor begins to take on an almost literal meaning. A central concern of Bronfenbrenner's approach is with

the progressive, mutual accommodation between an active, growing human being and the changing properties of the immediate settings in which the developing person lives, as this process is affected . . . by the larger contexts in which the settings are embedded.

One of the aims of the present chapter is to discuss some of the ways in which 'the progressive, mutual accommodation' between the newborn and its environments may be influenced by what has happened before it is born, and particularly by the accommodation of the fetus to the uterine environment.

However, although many researchers into prenatal influences on the newborn (e.g. Brazelton *et al.*, 1977; Smith and Steinschneider, 1975; Zeskind and Lester, 1978) have suggested that the observed associations may have implications for mutual accommodation, usually between infant and mother, so far few studies appear to have addressed this issue directly. Further, much of the voluminous research on prenatal influences has studied associations with longer-term development, mainly over the period from 3 to 11 years, without making observations on the newborn. It has usually been assumed that when a longer-term association has been found, a related and often stronger change must have been present in some form in the newborn, although this is not necessarily the case as we shall see later. Consideration of the longer-term studies throws light on adaptive processes in general and is, of course, essential for evaluating the implications of neonatal effects for later development. So the discussion of influences on accommodation or adaptation in the newborn will be embedded in a wider but necessarily selective discussion of prenatal influences on behaviour throughout childhood and adolescence, and especially of some of the methodological and theoretical issues basic to their interpretation.

The behavioural problems associated with easily detectable physical conditions brought about by prenatal influences have been discussed frequently and comprehensively elsewhere. For example, Kopp and Parmelee (1979) review genetic and chromosomal conditions and congenital malformations. The present chapter will be mainly concerned with prenatal environmental influences which appear to have an effect on behaviour in the absence of any obvious effect on morphology. It will concentrate on the newborn delivered at term and will not specifically consider the premature infant. More detailed general reviews and evaluations of the methodology are to be found in Joffe (1969), Barrett (1971, 1981), and Sameroff and Chandler (1975).

AN OVERVIEW OF THE RESEARCH

What types of experience during pregnancy are likely to influence the newborn? To provide some background to the discussions that follow, let us first summarize the research findings. The groups of prenatal influences for which associations with postnatal behaviour have been reported in man include nutrition, infection, oxygen deprivation, hormones, emotions (especially anxiety), complications, sound, maternal heartrate, lead and other pollutants, smoking, alcohol, sedatives, narcotics, anaesthetics, and analgesics. Most of these influences, in dosages which do not produce obvious effects on morphology, have also been reported to have effects on postnatal behaviour in the much better controlled studies on rats. In addition, the rat research has found significant postnatal effects for radiation; magnetic fields; a wide range of drugs, herbicides and pesticides; and various types of stress, including overcrowding, heat and illumination. The animal studies have been reviewed in more detail by Barrett (1971, 1981), and comprehensively discussed by Joffe (1969).

The human studies have reported associations with a range of neonatal states and behaviours which includes activity and arousal level, irritability, crying, sleep patterns, orientation and sucking, as well as with performance on the Brazelton Neonatal Behavioural Assessment Scale. Changes in any of these behaviours may influence the mutual accommodation of newborn and parents.

Do these associations have long-term implications? When considering persisting outcomes it is important to bear in mind that much of the literature consists of reports either at a single relatively early age, or at a small number of early ages. There have been few systematic follow-ups, and very few which continue beyond 7 years or so. In favourable circumstances there appears to be a tendency for some effects to 'wash out' over time. However, some longer-term studies report associations with activity level, attention, motor co-ordination, and 'behaviour disturbance' which persist till at least 7 years, as well as associations with intelligence, ability, and school achievement (especially in reading) which persist till 11 years and beyond.

Most of the prenatal influences which have been studied are associated with disadvantages in subsequent development, but a few are associated with enhanced ability and achievement. The claims for antenatal abdominal decompression in normal pregnancies (Heyns *et al.*, 1962) have not been supported by a series of better controlled studies (Liddicoat, 1968; Murdoch, 1968; Murdoch *et al.*, 1976). The treatment with progesterone of mothers suffering from toxaemia of pregnancy is not only one of the few influences associated with positive outcomes, but the outcomes appear to be among the most persistent yet reported. As most of this chapter will be concerned with short-term disadvantageous influences on the newborn, we will here attempt to restore the balance by taking progesterone as an example to discuss at greater length.

Although toxaemia is associated in some studies with reductions in school achievement, Dalton (1968) reported that compared with both toxaemia and normal controls, children of progesterone-treated pregnancies walked earlier and achieved higher levels in a variety of school subjects at 9–10 years. A further report when the children had reached 18 years (Dalton, 1976) suggested the effect had persisted: the progesterone children performed better in public examinations (at both O and A levels) and secured many more university admissions. The enhancement showed considerable specificity: it was particularly strong in arithmetic, verbal reasoning, and science subjects. The interpretation of the study is inevitably complicated by a number of problems of design and control, including matching between experimental and control subjects. Lynch and Mychalkiw (1978) re-examined the data and found that many of the differences were not statistically significant, and their own two studies also found no significant differences. However, their studies traced only about 20% of the original subjects, from trials in which no progesterone had been administered before the 16th week. Dalton (1981) has suggested that the beneficial effect is limited to high doses administered during the first 16 weeks. Reinisch and Karow (1977) used different preparations (various combinations of synthetic progestin and oestrogen), a different design (including within family sib controls) and different outcome measures (Wechsler intelligence and Cattell personality assessment carried out at ages ranging from 5 to 17 years), so their study is not directly comparable with Dalton's. They obtained no association with intelligence (it was high in both subjects and controls), but subjects exposed to larger doses of progestin obtained high scores on personality factors found by Cattell to be predictive of school success, and this is consistent with Dalton's findings. High progestin/oestrogen ratios were associated with sensitivity, independence, individualism, self-assurance and self-sufficiency, while low ratios were associated with group orientation and group dependence. Both studies suggest that a prenatal treatment (more specifically, the side-effects of a prenatal maternal treatment) may have influenced adaptation in the postnatal environment.

SOME PROBLEMS OF INTERPRETATION

The progesterone studies present a mixture of suggestive trends and negative results—not surprising given the differing doses and timing, and the methodological problems. Further research is needed. The problems of interpretation are common to much of the area. Most of the studies of prenatal influences are of an epidemiological nature and were set up merely to detect associations between prenatal and postnatal observations. But in an area characterized by powerful interactions between large numbers of variables, including other pregnancy, pre-pregnancy, delivery and postnatal influences, any association found may reflect the operation of uncontrolled interacting variables and may thus be causally spurious, and failure to find an association may be just as spurious. Interpretation of the associations thus requires the evaluation of many methodological and theoretical issues and consideration of underlying processes. After reviewing some of the more physical risks, Kopp and Parmelee (1979) concluded:

We could not find a single group of behaviours or class of functioning that has been systematically explored across several age groups for any prenatal or perinatal diagnosis. There are, indeed, a number of excellent studies, but they are fragmented and isolated.

Not surprisingly, their conclusion also applies to the rather different range of influences under consideration here.

Many of the methodological problems arise directly from the adaptive processes on which we shall be focussing in later parts of this chapter, and will be discussed in more detail there. Interpretation would be greatly helped by more systematic exploration of such parameters of prenatal influences as intensity, timing and duration. This was a feature of the progesterone study already discussed (Dalton, 1968, 1976), but the practicality of controlling these para-meters varies greatly, and in many studies they are inevitably poorly controlled.

Another important issue concerns the nature, timing and stressfulness of outcome assessments. Only a limited range of outcomes has so far been investigated, and many studies have reported on just one type of outcome, most frequently IQ, at one time during development. Yet when the same subjects have been assessed on a number of outcomes or at a variety of times, assessment-specific differences have often been reported. For example, when assessed during the first week of life, newborns with a history of prenatal or perinatal hypoxia showed 'impairments' of visual responsiveness, pain threshold, irritability, muscle tension and maturation level (Graham et al., 1957). At 3 years the same hypoxic children scored lower than controls on all tests of cognitive functioning, but by 7 years differences in IQ assessments had 'washed out'. However, other assessments at 7 years still showed mild effects, and these included problems with conceptualizing and motor co-ordination as well as attention difficulties and distractibility (Corah *et al.*, 1965). Although some effects tend to 'wash out', 'sleeper' effects can also be found. For example, in a study of the relationship between obstetric medication and heart-rate responsiveness, Brackbill (1977) detected effects at 8 months but not at 1 month in one group of infants, and effects at 12 months but not at 4 months in another group.

The appropriateness of the theoretical models with which interpretations are underpinned, either explicitly or implicitly, and the problems of interpreting and predicting longer-term relationships have been discussed in detail by Sameroff and Chandler (1975), Stratton (1977) and Barrett (1981). Many studies, particularly the earlier ones, have tended to assume either a main-effect model, in which influences have independent additive effects on development and one-to-one relationships might be expected, or a simple interactional model, in which the effect of a particular variable is *statically* dependent on the contribution of other variables. Although it is an improvement on the main-effect model, the structure of the interactional model still matches rather poorly the reality it seeks to represent. A major reason for this is that other variables have often been assumed to be constant over time. But in the area of care-giver–infant relationships, for example, many studies (see Lewis and Rosenblum, 1974; Bell and Harper, 1977) have documented what Bronfenbrenner (1979) termed 'progressive mutual accommodation'. To put it another way, the simple interactional model is likely to be particularly inadequate where adaptive processes are common. A third model offers a better match with such phenomena: the transactional model mirrors a system of continually and *dynamically* developing reciprocal adaptations. The transactional model changes the nature of the research questions it is appropriate to ask: the emphasis shifts from influences on outcome behaviours to contributions to the facilitation or distortion of developing transactions. The latter emphasis has long been common in physical embryology where an insult to one developing system can result in a distortion of the inter-relationships between many systems as they develop (Dobbing, 1974). The change in emphasis has many implications for methodology, in particular greater use of systems methods. While recognizing the difficulties of operationalizing the transactional model, Stratton (1977) and Barrett (1981) have argued for its adoption on the grounds that by matching the real world more closely it can lead to improved understanding and prediction. Transactions between infant and care-giver in the first month of life may be particularly important for long-term outcome (Broussard 1977). Transactions can also occur on many levels within individuals. For example, maternal anxiety may give rise to complications of pregnancy which in their turn give rise to more anxiety and so on (see Interaction and Nutrition, below).

The methodological problems, especially the correlational nature of much of the data and the multifactorial and interactive nature of the phenomena, make it unrealistic to expect that any single existing study will permit confident attribution of postnatal characteristics to specific pregnancy influences. Indeed, the attempt is hardly compatible with a transactional model. However, if studies employing different methods and controls and carried out in different contexts cross-validate each other by implicating the same relationships, and if there are compatible animal data and physiological mechanisms, we can reach much more confident conclusions. The existing literature has great heuristic value for the generation of research hypotheses. And taken as a whole it already provides much support for the conclusion that in some circumstances environmental influences on the fetus play an important role in a team of interacting variables which together have a major effect on both short- and long-term development. The outcome depends on the rest of the team which includes genetic factors and variables operating before conception, during delivery and after birth. Postnatal experience appears to be particularly influential. As Barrett (1971) put it:

Provided damage to the brain is not too severe, the influences of an effective upbringing . . . can often swamp even serious obstetric problems. Where the postnatal environment is not so favourable, problems developed *in utero* may be exacerbated.

ADAPTATION IN FETUS AND NEWBORN

The child tries to grow toward adaptation, if the environment will permit him. The mistaken assumption made by the early investigators was that a node of pathology in infancy was like a blemish and, like Lady Macbeth's bloody hands, could not be wiped clean. The data do not support that pessimistic view. (Kagan 1979)

The notion of 'growth toward adaptation' covers a range of self-regulating and self-righting processes which include the pervasive homeostatic processes of physiology, classically discussed by Bernard and Cannon (see Cannon 1939), and the concept of canalization introduced into embryology by Waddington (1957). Particularly important examples of homeostatic processes likely to be impaired by pregnancy problems are those concerned in the efficient physiological and behavioural regulation of caloric intake, conservation and expenditure necessary for the vitally important early growth of the newborn. These are discussed in detail by Rovee-Collier and Lipsitt in Chapter 7. Self-regulatory processes confer a powerful resilience, but they operate only within certain limits and when these are passed self-correction breaks down (Selye, 1956). Prenatal influences of an intensity and duration which do not tax these adaptive processes beyond their limits are unlikely to have very strong postnatal implications. However, many of the adaptive systems, for example the immune response and many of the regulatory functions of the kidney, liver, and endocrine system, do not become fully effective until well after birth. To some extent the uterine environment may buffer the fetus against change and reduce the need for efficient adaptive processes, but 'the protection from external stimuli which the fetus is accorded by the womb is largely offset by its extreme sensitivity' (Joffe, 1969). Further, it is a common embryological finding that systems are most vulnerable when developing fastest, and this gives rise to a key question: Can some prenatal influences hinder the development of adaptive processes themselves, and thus impair the effectiveness of adaptation during neonatal and later life?

Many long-term cognitive deficiencies resulting from insults to the morphology of the brain or of the sensory or motor systems can be regarded as examples of the impairment of adaptive efficiency. But can such impairment occur in the absence of obvious morphological problems? Evidence that it can comes from a variety of physiological studies. For example, undernutrition in the human fetus during the second half of pregnancy is associated in early infancy with reduced immunocompetence, that is, with reduced ability to respond adaptively to infection by combating it (Chandra, 1975a), and this increases the likelihood of brain damage and impaired cognitive adaptability. In rat studies the reduced immunocompetence has been found to persist into adulthood (Chandra, 1975b). Similarly, perinatal hypoxia is associated with impaired ability to cope with psychological stress: children who had suffered hypoxia were indistinguishable from controls in routine situations but under stress showed significantly more behavioural disruption (Ucko, 1965). And after reviewing the effects of perinatal pharmacological insults, Brackbill (1975) concluded: 'It is the neonate's ability to cope effectively that is the most important predictor of later functioning and it is coping ability that most sensitively reflects the effects of perinatal medication.'

The possibility that the development of adaptive processes can be impaired at the fetal stage has profound implications for the methodology of research on prenatal influences: it provides an important further source of interaction with outcome measures. Most studies have employed outcome assessments which are relatively undemanding, unlikely to push the self-correcting systems to their limits and thus unlikely to be sensitive to deficiencies in them. The most frequently used outcome measure, namely IQ, does not call for such qualities as stamina, perseverance and vigilance, yet these not only feature strongly amongst the types of characteristics which are sensitive to stress, but are important determinants of life success. Consistent with this, many studies have found associations with school achievement in the absence of associations with IQ. Further, the standard form of one of the most commonly used neonatal outcome assessments, the Brazelton scale, records only the infant's best performance.

However, the probability of detecting impaired adaptive processes may depend on the stressfulness of the assessment conditions. Rather than assessment of best performance alone, a sensitive indication of impaired adaptability necessitates probing the limits of the system, for example by observing performance on more demanding, complex prolonged tasks and the extent to which it is disrupted in adverse or stressful situations. As Kopp and Parmelee (1979) point out: 'We have been inattentive to the *resources* infants mobilize to meet changing situations and tasks.' They define 'resources' to include the range, diversity, organization and adaptability of behaviour, and suggest that these major characteristics of development, largely neglected so far in studies of prenatal influences, should be exploited in monitoring outcomes. These methodological considerations, together with some of those discussed previously in Some Problems of Interpretation, support the speculation that conclusions based on the existing literature may underestimate the extent to which postnatal adaptive processes can be impaired during pregnancy.

We have already noted that the timing and duration of a prenatal influence are important parameters. A feature of some of the body's self-correcting systems is that deficits suffered during earlier parts of a *specific* phase of growth may be compensated for if conditions are more favourable during later parts of the *same* phase. An example of this type of adaptive process which has particular relevance for the newborn is the 'catch up' growth of the brain after a period of growth restriction. The growth spurt for the human brain as a whole takes off just before half-way through pregnancy, peaks around normal-term birth, and fades away during the second year of postnatal life. In terms of total weight gain, only one sixth of the brain growth spurt is fetal (Dobbing, 1974). Consequently deficits incurred during the later months of pregnancy can to some extent be rectified during the first year or so after birth, and especially during the early months.

'Catch-up' has important methodological and practical implications. It is necessary to distinguish between fetal and maternal undernutrition: maternal undernutrition does not necessarily imply fetal undernutrition, though it often does especially in the second half of pregnancy, and fetal undernutrition can occur in apparently well-nourished mothers (see Interaction and Nutrition, below). Maternal undernutrition during pregnancy accompanied by adequate neonatal and infant nutrition will produce relatively little long-term disadvantage, especially when, as in the Dutch famine study (Stein *et al.*, 1975), the health and nutrition of the mother has been adequate before conception. However, when growth is restricted during both the prenatal and the postnatal portions of the growth spurt, as often happens in areas of endemic food shortage, the prognosis is much poorer (Chase, 1976). Indeed, chronic mild undernutrition during much or all of the brain growth spurt is likely to have much more serious long-term effects than several months of acute severe undernutrition (Dobbing, 1974). The implications for the nutritional management of the newborn, particularly the already disadvantaged newborn, are obvious.

It must be recognized, however, that the concept of 'catch-up' has many limitations. Although rapid 'catch-up' is often observed, for example in the body growth of low-birth-weight infants born to mothers who smoked during pregnancy (Crosby *et al.*, 1977), it is rarely complete. Further, the concept is largely based on studies of somatic growth and growth in size and weight of the whole brain, and there is little information about its applicability to other aspects. The many different parts, systems and processes which make up the brain develop at different times and rates, and so the scope for 'catch-up', including its very existence, is likely to vary greatly. For example, the growth spurt starts later, proceeds faster and finishes earlier for the cerebellum than for other gross morphological features of the brain. This probably contributes to the greater vulnerability of the cerebellum, which may in turn contribute to the high incidence of some types of motor problem in 'at risk' infants (Dobbing, 1974). Further, the growth spurt for the whole brain reflects multiplication and growth of glial cells, together with growth in *size* and *connectivity* of neurones, but as far as *number* of neurones is concerned the spurt starts around the tenth week of pregnancy and finishes around the eighteenth week and there is thus no possibility of postnatal 'catch-up'. As Dobbing (1974) points out, 'the major general features of physical growth in the brain *cannot be delayed*, but must occur at pre-ordained ages even if environmental conditions are not good'. Where they are not good for a major part of the period of growth spurt, 'the ultimate result is gross deficit'.

Both stressors and the states of stress they induce can have cumulative effects, and adaptive responses can themselves become stressors (Selye, 1956). Can prenatal influences, or attempts to adapt to them, impair ability to cope with later demands, such as those of labour and of adaptation to extra-uterine life in the newborn? Perinatal hypoxia is an example of stress during labour that has often been associated with behavioural effects in both newborns (e.g. Als *et al.*, 1979) and older children, though some of the effects tend to 'wash out' (Corah *et al.*, 1965). Healthy term newborns have a greater ability to cope with oxygen deficiency without deleterious effects than have children or adults. However, this ability appears to be reduced in some newborns who have already suffered disadvantages. Indeed, although the earlier literature attributed much brain damage and many behavioural problems to perinatal hypoxia, it has been clear since the work of Knobloch and Pasamanick (1962) and of Drillien and Ellis (1964) that some of the damage originated long before birth and was itself responsible for difficulties in initiating respiration, which in turn sometimes exacerbated existing problems.

Another example of a potential stress during labour is provided by the use of pain-relieving drugs. Brackbill (1979) provides a detailed review and concludes that much obstetric medication is associated with dose-related degradations of behaviour in the newborn. Particularly strong degradations are associated with one of the most commonly used analgesics, namely pethidine (meperidine). Studies of anaesthetic drugs which include follow-up at 1 year typically find persisting effects, and in one long-term study (Muller *et al.*, 1971) a significant dose-related negative relationship was obtained with IQ at 9 years. Medication during labour is associated with degradations of a variety of behaviours in the newborn, including sleep, arousal, attention, motor competence, and sucking and feeding. Particularly when administered in higher doses and over longer periods to mothers whose fetuses are already at risk, pain-relieving drugs appear to increase the adaptive demands on newborns.

The histories of victims of cot death show a high incidence of such potential stressors as complications of pregnancy, prematurity, low birthweight and perinatal hypoxia. The research clearly indicates that cot death is multiply-determined and the outcome of complex interactions. Rovee-Collier and Lipsitt (Chapter 7) suggest that an important contribution may derive from pre- and perinatal hazards which bring about behavioural lethargy and impaired defensive responses in the newborn. This already maladaptive state of affairs may sometimes be exacerbated because, as a result of it, the infant may subject himself to fewer opportunities for learning the strategies, necessary after the period of reflexive transition, for coping with respiratory and other stresses.

As the newborn depends for his growth and survival on others, the social aspects of his adaptive status are amongst the most important. In addition to other ways in which they can operate, many prenatal events and conditions can influence newborn characteristics and behaviours which have social implications and which, in their turn, affect the reciprocal adaptation or 'progressive mutual accommodation' of the newborn and his care-givers. However, parent–newborn interaction is discussed in detail by Papousek elsewhere in this volume (Chapter 14), and so we shall here merely summarize the research by listing some of the relationships which have been found between pregnancy variables and factors which can affect the social adaptation of the newborn. Maternal blood pressure and heart rate, maternal alcohol and narcotic addiction, complications of pregnancy, medication during labour, perinatal hypoxia, and fetal under-nutrition even when mild and leading to only slightly depressed birthweight, are among the wide range of pregnancy influences for which associations have been reported with newborn characteristics which can have a strong effect on care-giver behaviour. These newborn characteristics include eye contact, sucking, activity and demand level, responsiveness to social stimuli, resistance to being cuddled, irritability, sleep patterns, and the quantity and acoustic quality of the cry (Als et al., 1979; Brazelton et al., 1977; Goggin et al., 1978; Lester, 1976; Ostwald et al., 1968; Richards, 1975; Smith and Steinschneider, 1975; Strauss et al., 1975). Some of the modifications of newborn behaviour associated with adverse pregnancy influences can induce severe stress in caregivers. The piercing, aversive cries of newborns with a history of high obstetric complications are a good example (Zeskind and Lester, 1978). And crying has been described as by far the most upsetting of the behaviours which trigger crises in battering (Kempe and Kempe, 1978).

Although many of the newborn characteristics associated with prenatal influences are likely to be relatively short-lived in themselves, they may still have long-term significance through their effect on the developing infant–care-giver transaction in the period before neonatal adaptive or catch-up processes have had time to modify them. The perceived characteristics of the newborn frequently affect how it is labelled:

Once a child is labelled as 'difficult' or 'deviant' or 'vulnerable', the label remains with the child throughout development. Eventually, the child incorporates these attributes into his developing self-image and, indeed actualizes the 'self-fulfilling prophesies' of his caretakers. (Sameroff, 1975)

SOME UNDERLYING PROCESSES

Up to this point we have discussed associations between prenatal influences and postnatal behaviour without much consideration of the mediating processes which may underly them. Is what we know about the biology and competence of the fetus compatible with the notion that intrauterine experience may have effects that can survive birth and influence the newborn? The sensory and motor competence of the fetus has recently been discussed in detail (Barrett, 1981) and will merely be summarized here, before considering at greater length some of the adaptive processes which may be involved.

The most relevant feature of fetal competence is the early age at which it appears to develop. The first behaviour, the perioral withdrawal reflex, appears about the seventh week from conception. By about 13 weeks sensitivity to touch has spread to most parts of the body, there are signs of EEG activity in the as yet far from complete cortex, and the fetus is becoming much more active. By 16 weeks, most of the tactile reflexes found in the normal neonate are present. And by about the same time morphological maturity of the olfactory, gustatory and vestibular receptors is virtually complete, and that of the auditory and visual receptory well under way. It is much more difficult to determine when functioning actually begins in the womb, but there is considerable evidence that morphology and some level of functioning develop together. Certainly, by about 24 weeks, when under current methods of intensive care some fetuses become viable, all the sensory systems are functional in some sense even though much development has still to occur in most of them.

Can the fetus learn? The question has generated much interest and speculation, but (not surprisingly) it has been little studied either in the fetus or in the premature infant. Aspects of the question have recently been discussed in Gottlieb (1976) and Barrett (1981), to which the reader is referred for more detailed treatment. The answer depends greatly on what is meant by learning. Sameroff and Cavanagh (1979) discuss some of the complexities involved in answering the question 'Can infants learn?', and conclude that traditional associationist concepts of learning permit only a limited perspective of the abilities of infants and are inadequate for understanding psychological change. On the other hand, as Rovee-Collier and Lipsitt (Chapter 7) point out, where task and situation parameters have been selected which exploit rather than interfere with normal neonatal regulatory and adaptive behaviours, learning including both classical and instrumental conditioning has often been shown in the newborn, especially in temporal tasks. However, many behavioural embryologists prefer to think in terms of biological and cognitive adaptation, and to employ such concepts as assimilation and accommodation, or the induction, facilitation and maintenance of behaviour (Gottlieb, 1976). In other words, they reformulate the issue and address themselves to specific aspects of the much more general question 'Can the fetus adapt?' which is considered throughout this chapter.

Why fetal competence should develop so early remains an intriguing subject for speculation. However, the early appearance of function is likely to provide many opportunities for adaptive processes to operate in a variety of systems that may be involved in the mediation of the effects of prenatal influences. As yet there is relatively little direct evidence about what happens *in utero*, but let us look at some of the suggestions which have been put forward.

Since the work of Krech *et al.* (1960), there has been extensive research on the influence of sensory stimulation on the chemistry and structure of the developing brain. As McIlwain (1966) pointed out: 'In a material sense much of the brain is made while its functioning is in progress . . . material growth of the brain progresses while it is receiving impulses from the rest of the body and the environment in which that body exists.' McIlwain (1970) discusses the influence of environmental factors on the metabolic adaptation of the brain during its development. Enzyme induction may 'play a part in the initial growth of the brain by favouring particular synaptic connections in a manner related to sensory input'. Changes in sensory input can alter cerebral functioning and thus bring about persisting changes in the enzyme composition of the brain. Even the availability of an amino acid at a critical time can alter permanently the expression of genetic potential. In sum, 'that the brain is capable of a multiplicity of enzymatically based adaptations is as significant as that it contains a multiplicity of cellular interconnexions' and enables it to respond with great sensitivity and sometimes persistence to environmental influences, especially during its early development (McIlwain, 1970).

The permanent alteration of the expression of genetic potential is exemplified by Tanner's 'brain tally' hypothesis. Tanner (1978) attempts to explain why children starved early *in utero*, perhaps through an imperfection of the placenta, usually fail to 'catch-up' completely in their growth. He hypothesizes that the genetically programmed growth curve is represented in the brain (probably in the hypothalamus) by a process or tally which can be affected by lack of the proper supply of molecules when the process is being constructed. In other words, 'recalibration' of the growth target has occurred in a manner which imposes constraints on later adaptability. This is yet another example of the way in which intrauterine experience may influence the development of the processes which make self-correction possible.

Other examples of possible early influences on the 'calibration' or 'tuning' of adaptive processes have been put forward. The endocrine system is an obvious candidate. The development of fetal endocrine function and regulation in relation to the transition from intra-to extrauterine life has been reviewed by

Challis *et al.* (1976). Levine and Mullins (1966) proposed that control of some hormonal functions is accomplished in part by means of a hypothesized 'hormonostat' whose range and sensitivity is determined by hormonal levels during development which in their turn vary according to levels of stimulation during early experience. Ader (1975) has criticized some specific features of this proposal, but there is clear evidence that some intrauterine adaptations in endocrine functioning persist into the neonatal period. For example, the fetal hypothalamic-pituitary-adrenal axis is active from about the third month of pregnancy and infants of mothers who suffered pre-eclamptic toxaemia with low urinary oestriol excretion show clear depression of function in the adrenal cortex, and this probably accounts in part for their poor adaptive response to stress (Forsyth, 1974).

The possibility of the 'calibration' or 'tuning' of the autonomic nervous system by stimulation levels *in utero* has been considered by a number of researchers, including Smith and Steinschneider (1975), who found that newborns of mothers with high heart rates in late pregnancy cried more, took much longer to fall asleep and slept less than those of mothers with normal heart rates. In electrocardiographic studies Sontag (1966) reported high correlations between fetal and maternal patterns of autonomic reactivity as well as between increased fetal activity and irritability or hyperactivity in the newborn, though in the absence of appropriate controls a variety of interpretations is possible (Copans, 1974). And Montagu (1962) discusses the hypothesis that when mothers are emotionally distressed and the fetal hypothalamus thus exposed to higher amounts of adrenergic hormones, increased levels will then be required to maintain normal operation after birth. However, direct research into such 'adaptation level' effects on the human fetal autonomic system remains a matter for the future.

A closely related problem is whether the hypothalamus of the human male fetus is organized or differentiated by testicular androgens, and if it is, whether this contributes to the development of sex differences in postnatal behaviour. Although it is clear that hypothalamic organization of this sort is responsible for some of the behavioural differences between male and female rats, it is equally clear that there are large variations between species even within the same zoological order, and that with regard to man the interpretation of the evidence remains uncertain and controversial (Friedman *et al.*, 1974; Lloyd and Archer, 1976; Tanner, 1978; Barrett, 1981). A main conclusion of Reinisch's detailed review (Reinisch, 1974) is that prenatal hormones are best understood as setting a bias on the neural substrate which in a limited and diffuse way predisposes sexual dimorphism in behaviour. Maccoby and Jacklin (1974) suggest this predisposition might take the form of a 'greater readiness to learn'. That is, an infant is slightly better adapted or 'prepared' (Seligman, 1970) to learn the behaviours linked with its biological sex, but can learn those of either. An interactionist position is also adopted by Archer in his (1976) review of the human hormonal evidence, and Singleton (1978) stresses its transactional implications: prenatal hormones may be responsible for subtle differences between male and female newborns which elicit differential parental behaviours which amplify the differences in the offspring, and so on.

Is neural development in general influenced by intrauterine experience? This question has recently been discussed at length by Gottlieb (1976) who concludes that 'sensory systems as well as motor systems become functional while they are still anatomically, physiologically, and behaviourally immature' and that there is much indirect evidence to support the view that 'genes give rise to structural maturation processes that are susceptible to (in some cases, possibly dependent upon) the influences of function'. Hamburger (1975) comes to similar conclusions, and both he and Gottlieb (1976) emphasize the importance of transactional feedback effects of the fetus' own activity not only for neural development, but also for general anatomical development. For example, normal fetal behaviour may be necessary for aspects of the normal development of skeleton, joints and musculature, and when it is inhibited such disorders as cleft palate, dislocated hip, and club foot may result. Gardner *et al.* (1977) conclude that uterine experience contributes to the marked tendency of the newborn to lie with its head turned to the right. They suggest that the resulting asymmetry of sensory input together with the asymmetry of muscle tonus may be responsible, at least in part, for the lateral differences often observed in the newborn's response to auditory, visual and somesthetic stimulation, which in turn may contribute to the development of adult hemispheric laterality.

The behaviour of the fetus itself may also play a part in its development in a variety of other ways. For example, the fetus actively sucks in and swallows amniotic fluid, which contains components which contribute significantly to its nutrition (Mistretta and Bradley, 1975). There are reports that 34-week fetuses swallow more amniotic fluid after intra-amniotic injections of a sweet-tasting substance, and less after the injection of an upleasant-tasting substance (Liley, 1972). The fetus actively makes use of its behavioural repertoire to achieve the vertex presentation and the safer, less complicated, more adaptive labour and delivery associated with it. Changes in the fetal pituitary-adrenal system may be responsible for the initiation of normal labour (Challis *et al.*, 1975), and may thus play a part in determining whether the child is born at an optimal stage in development. Schneirla (1957) proposed that an individual's own activity provides an important source of his own development, and regarded development as in part self-generated. Perhaps it is appropriate to extend the concept of the self-generation of development to the individual before birth. It seems likely that, together with many other aspects of uterine life, the fetus' own behaviour contributes to its adaptive status as a newborn.

INTERACTION AND NUTRITION

'The greater the number or severity of early risks, the greater the possibility that compensation will be ineffective in maintaining adaptive behaviour in the face of later stress' (Brackbil, 1979). Cumulative effects, and particularly inter-actions—the manner in which influences modify the operation of each other—are matters we have largely ignored in our discussions so far, but they are clearly of fundamental importance in the design and interpretation of studies of prenatal influences. Indeed, the 'main effects are interactions' (Bronfenbrenner, 1979).

Powerful two-way interactions have been found both within and between most of the main groups of influences studied. The interactions are often non-additive or non-linear—for example, two influences acting synergistically may have a much stronger effect than would be expected from merely adding their independent effects. Much evidence has accumulated on the influence of such classes of variables as nutrition, infection, and psychological stress on each other throughout life. To illustrate this, we will take a quick look at a few examples, concentrating on interactions with nutrition. (Other forms of interaction, particularly interaction with postnatal experience and long-term implications, are discussed in Barrett (1981).) The evidence casts grave doubts on the utility and validity of the general classifications themselves: 'The interactions between environment and nutrition are so complex in humans that they are inseparable, and the term "environutritional deprivation" should now be used' (Chase and Crnic 1977).

Knowledge of nutrition and its effects is extensive, complex, fragmented and controversial. Accurate assessment of dietary intake is in general notoriously difficult—how much deficiency of which nutrients, when and for how long?—and the problems are compounded when studying fetal intake, especially as the fetal brain actively extracts nutrients from the circulating pool.

If only one essential amino acid is missing in the total amino pool the production of all proteins which contain that amino acid is reduced . . . even though the overall amino acid pool may be very large, the entire protein production could be limited by deficiencies of one or a small number of amino acids, vitamins or trace elements. (Crosby *et al.*,1977)

Thus undernutrition can occur in apparently well-fed or over-fed subjects. The limiting factor varies according to the interactions involved: it differs, for example, between high and low socio-economic groups, and between developed and developing societies. In severe deficiency energy is often the limiting factor, but above a certain limit of calorie availability, lack of substrates especially amino acids gradually becomes the main limiting factor (Lechtig *et al.*, 1975). Interactions with genotype have been demonstrated in rodents, and it is thus likely that for genetic as well as for many other reasons the same undernutrition will affect some mothers and some fetuses more than others (Blizard and Randt, 1974). Undernutrition acts pervasively. For example it can affect DNA and RNA concentrations, enzyme activity, and neurotransmitters. It can distort neuronal development and the development of the hormonal regulation of later growth. It can bring about low birth weight and its many associated disadvantages, including impairment of many systems which assist adaptation in the newborn, for example reduced deposition of the lipid stores which buffer the newborn nutritionally while it adapts to extra-uterine life (Dobbing, 1974).

Undernutrition interacts with infection in a variety of ways: by reducing both antibody formation and cell-mediated immunity, it inhibits the immune response of mother, fetus and newborn, and thus increases susceptibility to infections, including the many which bring about brain damage and consequent intellectual impairment. As undernutrition and infection tend to co-exist, this increased vulnerability to infection is particularly common in those most likely to be exposed to it. On the other hand, many infections reduce nutrient availability by, for example, dulling appetite, decreasing absorption from the gastro-intestinal tract and increasing loss of essential nutrients through diarrhoea. Thus, in addition to the many other ways it may affect the fetus, maternal infection often leads to a nutritional deficit in both mother and fetus (Mata, 1974).

Interaction with placental transmission provides another route by which fetal undernutrition can occur even when the maternal diet is good. Placental transmission of nutrients and oxygen is influenced by a wide variety of factors, including the size and structure of the placenta, abnormal attachment and a variety of types of placental pathology, some of them the result of current or previous undernutrition or infection. More often, however, the maternal circulation sets the limit on placental transmission: fetal growth restriction is strongly related to maternal heart disease and anaemia, hypertensive disorders including kidney disease and toxaemia of pregnancy, smoking and pregnancy at high altitude. Incidentally, in all these conditions except the hypertensive disorders, the placenta is enlarged relative to the fetus, apparently as a compensatory mechanism, although even in normal pregnancies the fetus may outgrow placental transmission by term birth if not before (Gruenwald, 1974).

Smoking during pregnancy is associated with a wide variety of conditions which interact with nutrition. For example, it gives rise to vasoconstriction in the maternal intestine, the cord and the placenta, as well as to several types of placental pathology. As it also reduces the nutrients and oxygen available to the fetus in a number of other ways, it is not surprising that smoking is associated with greatly increased incidences of fetal distress, low birthweight. admission of the newborn to special care units, and fetal and perinatal mortality (Butler and Alberman, 1969; Meyer and Tonascia, 1977). The nutrient pool, including vitamins, available to the fetus is also reduced by maternal alcohol consumption, and both smoking and alcohol inhibit the immune response (Crosby et al., 1977; Wynn and Wynn, 1979). Even in relatively small quantities, smoking and alcohol can thus amplify existing disadvantages.

Maternal activity, fatigue and anxiety levels also interact with and often covary with undernutrition: in developing societies the undernourished pregnant mother anxiously searching for food from dawn to dusk is tragically common. As an example, the increase in maternal catecholamine secretion associated with anxiety brings about vasoconstriction both in the intestine, thus reducing maternal nutrient absorption, and in the placenta and umbilical cord, thus reducing nutrient and oxygen transmission to the fetus (Gruenwald, 1974). However, maternal catecholamines also have many other effects: for example, they increase uterine motility, and they pass into the fetus, thus increasing the activity of the fetus and consequently its nutritional requirements (Kelly, 1962). Maternal anxiety is also associated, though by no means in all studies, with the development of a wide range of complications of pregnancy (Sameroff and Chandler, 1975), and many of these not only contribute to fetal undernutrition but also operate transactionally to increase maternal anxiety.

The implications of these interactions in mother and fetus for the characteristics and behaviour of the newborn depend in part on labour and its management. We have already noted that the infant deprived *in utero* may be less able to cope with the stresses of labour, and of medication in particular. Maternal anxiety is associated with longer labours and more complications of labour, particularly in multigravida (Erickson, 1976a, 1976b). Maternal anxiety is also associated with higher levels of reported childbirth pain (Nettelbladt *et al.*, 1976), and with the administration of higher dosages of medication (Yang *et al.*, 1976). However, some of the medications employed themselves prolong labour (Kraemer *et al.*, 1972), thus sometimes further increasing stress on the infant. Another aspect of the management of labour with especially important interactive implications is maternal posture. Compared with the conventional recumbent and lateral posture, an upright and ambulant posture (that is, walking, standing or sitting at will during the first and second stage) is associated with very much shorter and less painful labours, less frequent contractions, greatly reduced administration of analgesics and need for forceps delivery, higher Apgar scores, and fewer difficulties in initiating breast feeding (Dunn 1978; Flynn *et al.*, 1978). Although some of the advantages of ambulation in labour no doubt derive from the effect of gravity, there is also likely to be an important contribution from the psychological and social effects on the mother, (see Oakley, Chapter 11).

Many studies have found interactions with the social environment of pregnancy and childbirth, especially with father, grandparents and professional staff. For example, participation of the father in antenatal classes and as 'Labour coach' throughout labour and delivery is associated with reduction in maternal anxiety, reported pain and likelihood of receiving medication (Henneborn and Cogan, 1975). Further, commenting on their path analysis of influences on Brazelton assessment of 3-day-old newborns, Standley *et al.* (1978) suggest that the fetus and newborn reflect the attitudes towards pregnancy and the emotional state of both parents during pregnancy. The birth of the family precedes the birth of the child.

The existence of interactions, and of variables which both co-vary and transact with each other, makes inappropriate most simple statements about the outcomes of prenatal influences. It signals a need for great caution in drawing conclusions, especially from negative or non-significant findings, and for the use of multivariate and systems forms of analysis (Denenberg, 1977). An optimistic implication is that appropriate combinations of other variables can often prevent or 'wash out' the effects of potentially disadvantageous experiences. The small sample of interactions which we have considered illustrates the fundamentally collective and dynamic way in which the newborn is influenced by its history and ecology from conception onwards. And it gives rise to a further question: Is the newborn influenced by the history of its mother and her environment before it is conceived?

PRE-CONCEPTION AND TRANSGENERATIONAL INFLUENCES

A quarter of a century ago, after a 20-year longitudinal study of 200 women and their pregnancies, Kirkwood (1955) concluded: 'Good obstetric care is a very broad type of care that must start with the birth of the future mother, or even before that, with her mother who is the grandmother of the baby we are discussing.' Associations with grandparents have been found in a number of large-scale longitudinal cohort studies, including the National Child Development Study cohort of 1958 births (Davie et al., 1972), and the second-generation follow-up of the National Survey cohort of 1946 births (Kiernan, in press). For example, even after allowing for such variables as family size, current social class, and duration of parental education, the reading attainment of 1958 cohort children at 7 years was associated with the social class of the maternal grandfather. Some of the physical variables likely to contribute to such transgenerational continuities have recently been discussed in detail by Wynn and Wynn (1979), and both physical and social variables by Rutter and Madge (1976). Our primary concern here will be the question: To what extent does a mother's history before conception influence the success of her physical and psychosocial adaptations to the requirements of her fetus and its delivery?

As the methodological problems we have already discussed become even more severe when we enlarge the time-scale, a brief look at studies of animals with much shorter intergenerational times might prove reassuring. In rats nutritional deficiencies over several generations are associated with size reduction and with behavioural changes such as decreased learning and increased activity and irritability which persist through at least one generation of nutritional re-habilitation. They do however tend to 'wash out' after two or three generations of rehabilitation, and this, together with the small number of generations involved, indicates that non-genetic processes are involved (Cowley and Griesel, 1966; Stewart, 1974). Despite normal nutrition for all three generations at all other times, impaired learning was found in the *grandpups* of female rats given a low protein diet for 1 month before conception and throughout pregnancy (Bresler et al., 1975). 'Granny effects' have also been reported for psychological stress. For example, 'handling' and conditioned anxiety either before conception or during pregnancy are associated with changes in the emotionality (open field test) of grandpups (Denenberg and Rosenberg, 1967; Wehmer *et al.*, 1970). Although many controls were used other interpretations are still not ruled out, but the findings are consistent with what Denenberg and Rosenberg (1967) described as the 'non-genetic transmission of information' across three generations.

In humans maternal nutrition and health before conception is strongly related to the birthweight and adaptive status of the newborn (e.g. Drillien 1957; Cravioto *et al.*, 1966; Birch and Gussow, 1970; Gruenwald, 1974; Brazelton *et al.*, 1977; Wynn and Wynn, 1977). The association between many aspects of the health of women and occupation of *husband* is particularly striking. For example, Wynn and Wynn (1979) discuss the very large differences in the illness rates of the wives of men across seventeen occupational groups and relate them to differences in nutrition. However, differences in stress and other aspects of 'life style' common to husband and wife are also likely to be involved (Fletcher, 1979). Birthweight is highly influenced by the mother's pre-pregnancy height and weight, and this in turn reflects her nutrition throughout her own development: a mother malnourished in her own childhood tends to have smaller offspring. Even when well-nourished during pregnancy, a mother may be unable to support a normal growth-rate in her fetus because her own growth was stunted during or before adolescence by undernutrition or infection (Ounsted and Ounsted, 1973). The anatomical and physiological efficiency of women can be permanently impaired by poor nutrition during growth and adolescence (Thomson, 1976). As Gruenwald (1975) puts it in his review of influences on placental transmission:

'It is inescapable to conclude from all information on nutritional and other socio-economic effects, that the mother's own past experience including her prenatal growth (as suggested by her birth-weight) influences her ability to provide for her fetus *in utero*, even while living under adequate conditions during her pregnancy.

Teenage pregnancy constitutes a special case of inadequate maternal growth before conception. Growth is often not yet complete—on average, for example, linear growth does not finish until 4 years after menarche—and the young mother, still subject to the high nutritional requirements of her own further growth, can have difficulty in adapting to the demands of the fetus as well (Siegel and Morris, 1970; Zlatnik and Burmeister, 1977). Even with such variables as socio-economic status and premarital conception controlled, increased rates of pre-eclampsia, low birthweight, neonatal mortality and morbidity and sensory and mental handicap are associated with deliveries to mothers under 20 years, and the rates increase with decreasing age (Chamberlain *et al.*, 1975; Zlatnik and Burmeister, 1977). No older age group has such a high overall rate of very low birthweight children. Children of young mothers typically also suffer from many postnatal disadvantages, both physical and social. Primiparity, grand multiparity, low birth spacing and a previous small infant are traditional predictors of low birthweight which reflect maternal experience before conception.

Many infections of the mother before she becomes pregnant can also lead to disadvantage in the fetus and newborn, some by reducing the mother's nutritional status, others more specifically by bringing about damage to the placenta or promoting premature rupture of the membranes. The latter is associated with a range of sexually transmitted infections, including trichomoniasis, chlamydia, hepatitis virus, herpes genitalis, gonorrhea and syphilis. Such infections, which can seriously prejudice subsequent childbearing, have their highest incidence in single women of 18–20 years and have recently been increasing at an average rate of 10 per cent per year (Wynn and Wynn, 1977). In addition to their overt forms which can have a variety of severe physical consequences for the fetus and newborn, some chronic maternal infections, which can chronically infect the infant either *in utero* or at delivery, can be asymptomatic or 'silent' in both mother and newborn and still induce a variety of defects in the developing sensory and nervous systems. Infections which commonly exist in 'silent' forms include rubella, toxoplasmosis (sometimes picked up from cats or by eating inadequately cooked meat), syphilis, herpes simplex virus and cytomegalovirus. The last two are most often initially acquired by the mother during her own childhood. Cytomegalovirus appears to be by far the commonest chronic 'silent' condition. It is particularly prevalent in disadvantaged populations, and is believed to be an important 'silent' contributor to impaired hearing and IQ (Alford, 1977).

The fetus can also be influenced by previous obstetric and birth-control practices. For example, previous induced abortion is associated with increased risk of cervical incompetence, infection and prematurity. The increased risks depend heavily on the operative techniques employed, adequacy of follow-up care and appropriate management of the early stages of the subsequent pregnancy, and are greatest among women who have not already delivered (Richardson and Dixon, 1976; Wynn and Wynn, 1977). Oral contraceptives can deplete the maternal pool of micronutrients and vitamins, depress immune competence and in the absence of a compensating diet can lead to residual nutritional deficiencies which can be exacerbated as pregnancy progresses (Hathcock, 1976; Wynn and Wynn, 1979). Because of their role in the early months of development, folic acid and pyridoxine are particularly important examples. Blood folate levels can remain depressed for many months after discontinuing the pill, and the low levels have been shown to persist into pregnancy (Martinez and Roe, 1977). Incidentally, seasonal differences in amounts of folic acid and other micronutrients in fresh fruit and vegetables may contribute to the commonly observed effects of season of birth on birthweight, neonate behaviour, and later intellectual and psychiatric status (Martinez and Roe, 1977; Salkind and Deaton, 1978).

Thus many aspects of the mother's physical health before pregnancy begins, and even in her own infant and fetal stage, appear to influence her capacity to adapt to the requirements of her fetus. However pregnancy, particularly a first pregnancy, entails not only physical but also psychosocial adaptations. We have already noted the influence of psychosocial experience on physical adaptation during pregnancy, especially on complications of pregnancy. It would be surprising if the mother's psychosocial adaptation were not influenced by her pre-conception experience and indeed there is a variety of research which supports this expectation. For example, using the Schedule of Recent Experience as an index of stress, Williams *et al.* (1975) found an association between magnitude of life change in the year prior to conception and number of medical problems during pregnancy. Baxter (1974) reported an association between ability to achieve intercourse and aspects of labour, including length of second stage and need for forceps, and suggested common learned psychological factors as well as common physiological mechanisms were involved. Wolkind *et al.* (1976) reported a relationship between separation from their own parents during childhood and the psychiatric status of mothers during their first pregnancy.

Further, in a series of studies Uddenberg and his colleagues have reported a range of 'granny effects'. These include similarities between the pregnancies and labours of mothers and daughters, and especially a higher incidence of obstetric problems and of very long or very short labours in the daughters of mothers classified as 'reproductively maladjusted'. From his analysis of the psychiatric status of pregnant women Uddenberg concluded that during pregnancy adaptations to motherhood take place which often involve much anxiety, that these adaptations put great demands on coping ability and that complications of pregnancy and labour occur primarily in those who have adaptive difficulties they are not coping with effectively. He found that a very high proportion of women who showed such 'reproductive maladaptation' and also showed poor adaptation to motherhood 4 months after the birth of their child had poor affective relationships with their own mothers (Uddenberg, 1974; Uddenberg and Fagerstrom, 1976; Uddenberg *et al.*, 1976). Many other studies (e.g. Melges, 1968; Nilsson and Almgren, 1970; Sherefsky and Yarrow, 1973; Breen, 1975; Lagercrantz and Lagercrantz, 1975) have also stressed the adaptive demands of pregnancy and early motherhood and suggested that difficulties in meeting them stem at least in part from the mother's earlier relationships with her own caregivers.

The studies which report psychosocial 'granny effects' must be treated with caution. Inevitably they have a variety of methodological problems: in particular most of them are retrospective and do not separate earlier from ongoing 'granny influences'. And they are mainly concerned with affective relationships. Uddenberg (1974) concluded that individuals may internalize some of the adaptational patterns of their parents and that these form part of their 'psychological heredity'. The concept of 'psychological heredity' can be widened to embrace cultural influences on cognition as a whole. As we have already seen, one of the commonest research conclusions is that psycho-socio-economic variables tend to swamp physical obstetric variables in predicting the long-term outcome of newborn status. But the physical variables are of course themselves frequently the outcome of cognitive decisions: there are psycho-somatic transactions. Nutrition is a potent physical variable for example, but food choice is very strongly influenced by the psychosocial environment, contemporary and transgenerational. Not only is the newborn's physical status highly influenced by nutritional variables operating before conception, but it is a common finding that many decisions about the rearing of the newborn, including diet and whether to breast feed or not, are made before it is conceived (Sacks et al., 1976; Peterson and Mehl, 1978).

In a detailed large-scale study of prematurity and fetal growth retardation, Miller et al. (1977) examined seven variables containing what they considered to be an element of maternal choice: smoking, indulging in certain drugs, restricting maternal weight gain in pregnancy, failing to obtain sufficient prenatal care, undertaking pregnancy at too early or too advanced an age, and being underweight for height at conception. The incidence of premature, short-for-dates and low birth-weight infants was remarkably low among mothers whose life style did not include any of the seven 'choice' variables, but increased dramatically, proportionately and significantly with each increase in the number of 'choice' variables from none to three or more. The 'choice' variables contributed much more to the absolute number of each group of 'at risk' infants than medical problems over which mothers had no immediate control. The incidences of the seven 'choice' variables, both singly and in combination, were inverse to the mother's socioeconomic status. However, the incidences of each group of 'at risk' infants were high among mothers with two or more 'choice' variables regardless of their socio-economic status. Miller et al.'s findings suggest that part, perhaps the greater part, of the 'social-class' variance observed in so many developmental indices may be accounted for by cognitive factors which influence choice. It is likely that the amount of variance accounted for would increase considerably if 'choice' variables over the previous two or three generations were to be brought into the analysis.

An element of choice is contained in a large number of the variables which appear to contribute to the life-long health of the mother, and to the status of the newborn and its later development. Wharton (1977) has stressed the role of chosen diet in the 'personal environment' of people in developed countries. Choices regarding contraceptive method or abortion policy and management have implications for subsequent pregnancies. Current pregnancies are influenced by decisions (often taken prior to conception) regarding life-style, whether and when to start attending ante-natal clinics, and the management of childbirth. And in their analysis of variables which influence the newborn's performance on the Brazelton Scale, Standley et al. (1978) emphasize the striking relationships between the ability of an expectant couple to cope with the adaptive demands of pregnancy and such characteristics as their age, educational level and financial security. Couples who cope effectively 'may well have entered the pregnancy with a more thoughtful decision which took cognizance of the responsibilities and other life changes a child would bring' (Standley *et al.*, 1978).

An element of choice contributes to the self-generation of development, both within and across generations. The degree of choice can of course be constrained, sometimes very severely, by knowledge, by attitudinal, situational and other variables, and particularly by previous choices. The nature of the choice is highly influenced by each of the layers of systems, micro-or immediate, meso-, exo-, and macro-or cultural, into which Bronfenbrenner (1979) dissects the ecology of development. Transgenerational influences on the fetus and newborn contribute to the historical dimension of the analysis: the characteristics of the newborn are in part a product of transactions between social history and personal cognition. 'Man has no nature, he has only a history' wrote Ortega y Gasset. But perhaps he went a little too far. The newborn is biologically constructed. But biology is itself shaped by psychosocial and historical variables: the newborn is socio-psychobiologically constructed.

The implications for disadvantaged populations are tragically clear. If knowledge, effort and resources are available at any points in the cycle, particularly pregnancy, infancy and the years immediately before pregnancy, dramatic improvements are possible. If they are available continuously over two or three generations, the cycle can be broken. Will they be available? And what about pregnancy in so called developed countries? There have recently been rapid changes in styles of feeding, working, travelling, entertainment, social and sexual relations, and particularly in attitudes towards pregnancy and child-rearing. Is it possible that successful adaptation before conception to some aspects of contemporary life styles is to some extent maladaptive for the fetus and newborn? Mothers pass on much more than some of their genes. The adaptive status of a mother's newborn girl determines in part the status of her grandchildren.

REFERENCES

Ader, R. (1975). Early experience and hormones: Emotional behavior and adrenocortical function, in *Hormonal Correlates of Behavior*, Vol. I (Eds B. E. Eleftheriou and R. L. Sprott), Plenum, New York.

Alford, C. A. (1977). Prenatal infections and psychosocial development in children born into lower socioeconomic settings, in *Research to Practice in Mental Retardation*, Vol. 3 *Biomedical Aspects*. (Ed. P. Mittler), University Park Press, Baltimore.

Als, H., Tronick, E., Lester, B. M., and Brazelton, T. B. (1979). Specific neonatal measures: The Brazelton Neonatal Behavioral Assessment Scale, in *Handbook of Infant Development* (Ed. J. D. Osofsky), Wiley, New York.

Archer, J. (1976). Biological explanations of psychological sex differences, in *Exploring Sex Differences*. (Eds B. Lloyd and J. Archer), Academic Press, London and New York.

Barrett, J. H. W. (1971). Pre-natal environmental influences on behaviour, in *A*

Handbook of Pre-Natal Paediatrics (Eds G. F. Batstone, A. W. Blair and J. M. Slater), MTP, Aylesbury.

Barrett, J. H. W. (1981) Intra-uterine experience and its long-term outcome, in *Foundations of Psychosomatics* (Eds M. Christie and P. Mellett), Wiley, London and New York.

Baxter, S. (1974). Orgasm and labour in primiparae, *J. Psychosom. Res.*, **18**, 357–360.

Bell, R. Q. and Harper, L. V. (1977). *Child Effects on Adults.* Lawrence Erlbaum, Hillsdale, N. J.

Birch, H. G. and Gussow, J. D. (1970). *Disadvantaged Children: Health, Nutrition and School Failure*, Grune and Stratton, New York.

Blizard, D. A. and Randt, C. T. (1974). Genotype interaction with undernutrition and external environment in early life, *Nature (Lond.)*, **251**, 705–707.

Brackbill, Y. (1975). Psychophysiological measures of pharmacological toxicity in infants: Perinatal and postnatal effects, in *Basic and Therapeutic Aspects of Perinatal Pharmacology* (Eds P. L. Morselli, S. Garattini and F. Sereni), Raven, New York.

Brackbill, Y. (1977). Long-term effects of obstetrical anesthesia on infant autonomic function, *Develop. Psychobiology*, **10**, 6, 529–535.

Brackbill, Y. (1979). Obstetric medication and infant behavior, in *Handbook of Infant Development* (Ed. J. D. Osofsky), Wiley, New York.

Brazelton, T. B., Tronick, E., Lechtig, A., Lasky, R. E., and Klein, R. E. (1977). The behavior of nutritionally deprived Guatemalan infants, *Develop. Med. Child Neurol.* **19**, 364–372.

Breen, D. (1975). *The Birth of a First Child*, Tavistock Publications, London.

Bresler, D. E., Ellison, G. and Zamenhof, S. (1975). Learning deficits in rats with malnourished grandmothers, *Devel. Psychobiol.*, **8**(4), 315–323.

Bronfenbrenner, U. (1979). *The Ecology of Human Development.* Harvard University Press, Cambridge, Mass.

Broussard, E. R. (1977). Neonatal prediction and outcome at 10/11 years, in *Child Psychiatry and Human Development.* Vol. 7, Academic Press, London and New York.

Butler, N. and Alberman, E. D. (Eds) (1969) *Perinatal Problems.* Livingstone, Edinburgh and London.

Cannon, W. B. (1939). *The Wisdom of the Body*, 2nd Edn, Norton, New York.

Challis, J., Robinson, J., Rurak, D. W. and Thorburn, G. D. (1975). The development of endocrine function in the human fetus, in *The Biology of Human Fetal Growth.* (Eds D. F. Roberts and A. M. Thomson), Taylor & Francis, London.

Chamberlain, R., Chamberlain, G. Howlett, B. and Claireaux, A. (1975). *British Births 1970*, Vol. 1, *The First Week of Life*, Heinemann, London.

Chandra, R. K. (1975a). Fetal malnutrition and postnatal immunocompetence, *Am. J. Dis. Child.*, **129**, 450–454.

Chandra, R. K. (1975b). Antibody formation in first and second generation offspring of nutritionally deprived rats, *Sci.*, **190**, 289.

Chase, H. P. (1976). Undernutrition and growth and development of human brain, in *Malnutrition and Intellectual Development.* (Ed. J. D. Lloyd-Still), MTP, Lancaster.

Chase, H. P. and Crnic, L. S. (1977). Undernutrition and human brain development, in *Research to Practice in Mental Retardation*, Vol. 3, *Biomedical Aspects*, (Ed. P. Mittler), University Park Press, Baltimore.

Copans, S. A. (1974). Human prenatal effects: Methodological problems and some suggested solutions, *Merrill-Palmer Quart.*, **20**(1), 43–52.

Corah, N. L., Anthony, E. J., Painter, P., Stern, J. A., and Thurston, D. (1965). Effects of perinatal anoxia after 7 years, *Psychol Monogr.*, **79**, 1–34.

Cowley, J. J. and Griesel, R. D. (1966). The effect on growth and behaviour of rehabilitating first and second generation low protein rats, *Anim. Behav.*, **14**, 506.

Cravioto, J., Delicardie, E. R., and Birch, H. G. (1966). Nutrition, growth and neurointegrative development: an experimental and ecologic study, *Pediatrics*, **38**, 319–373.

Crosby, W. M., Metcoff, J., Costiloe, J. P., Mameesh, M., Sandstead, H. H., Jacob, R. A., McClain, P. E., Jacobson, G., Reid, W., and Burns, G. (1977). Fetal malnutrition: An appraisal of correlated factors, *Am. J. Obstet. Gynec.* **128**, 1, 22–31.

Dalton, K. (1968). Antenatal progesterone and intelligence, *Brit. J. Psychiat.*, **114**, 1377–1383.

Dalton, K. (1976). Prenatal progesterone and educational attainment, *Brit. J. Psychiat.* **129**, 439–442.

Dalton, K. (1981). The effect of progesterone and progestens on the foetus. *Neuropharmacology*, **20**, 1267–1269.

Davie, R., Butler, N., and Goldstein, H. (1972). *From Birth to Seven*. Longman, London.

Denenberg, V. H. (1977). Interactional effects in early experience research, in *Genetics, Environment and Intelligence* (Ed. A. Oliverio), Elsevier/North Holland Biomedical Press, Amsterdam.

Denenberg, V. H. and Rosenberg, K. M. (1967). Nongenetic transmission of information, *Nature (Lond.)*, **216**, 549.

Dobbing, J. (1974). Prenatal nutrition and neurological development, in *Early Malnutrition and Mental Development* (Eds J. Cravioto, L. Hambraeus, and B. Valquist), Almqvist and Wiksell, Uppsala.

Drillien, C. M. (1957). Social and economic factors affecting the incidence of premature birth, *J. Obst, Gynec. Br. Commonw.*, **64**, 161.

Drillien, C. M. and Ellis, R. W. B. (1964). *The Growth and Development of the Prematurely Born Infant*, Williams and Wilkins, Baltimore.

Dunn, P. M. (1978). Posture in labour, *Lancet*, **1**, 496.

Erickson, M. T. (1976a). Influence of health factors on psychological variables predicting complications of pregnancy, labour and delivery, *J. Psychosom. Res.*, **20**, 1, 21–24.

Erickson, M. T. (1976b). Relationship between psychological variables and specific complications of pregnancy, labour and delivery, *J. Psychosom. Res.*, **20**, 3, 207–210.

Fletcher, B. (1979). Stress at work. Paper presented at the Conference of the British Psychological Society, London, Dec. 1979.

Flynn, A. M., Kelly, J., Hollins, G., and Lynch, P. F. (1978). Ambulation in labour, *Br. Med. J.* **2**, 591–593.

Forsyth, C. C. (1974). The growth and development of the endocrine glands—adrenal cortex, in *Scientific Foundations of Paediatrics* (Eds J. A. Davis and J. Dobbing), Heinemann Medical, London.

Friedman, R. C., Richart, R. M., Van De Wiele, R. L., and Stern, L. O. (Eds) (1974). *Sex Differences in Behavior*, Wiley, New York.

Gardner, J., Lewkowicz, D., and Turkewitz, G. (1977). Development of postural asymmetry in premature human infants, *Develop. Psychobiol.*, **10**, 5, 471–480.

Goggin, J. E., Holmes, G. E., Hassanein, K., and Lansky, S. B. (1978). Observations of postnatal developmental activity in infants with fetal malnutrition, *J. Genetic Psychol.*, **132**, 247–253.

Gottlieb, G. (1976). Conceptions of prenatal development: Behavioral embryology, *Psychol. Rev.*, **83**, 3, 215–234.

Graham, F. K., Caldwell, B. M., Ernhart, C. B., Pennoyer, M. M., and Hartman, A. F. (1957). Anoxia as a significant perinatal experience: A critique. *J. Pediat.*, **50**, 556–569.

Gruenwald, P. (1974). Pathology of the deprived fetus and its supply line, in *CIBA Foundation Symposium 27: Size at Birth*. Excerpta Medica, Amsterdam.

Gruenwald, P. (1975). Ill-defined maternal causes of deprivation. in *The Placenta and its Maternal Supply Line*, (Ed. P. Gruenwald), MTP, Aylesbury.

Hamburger, V. (1975). Fetal behavior, in *The Mammalian Fetus*, (Ed. E. S. E. Hafez), Charles Thomas, Springfield, Illinois.

Hathcock, J. N. (1976). Nutrition: toxicology and pharmacology, *Nutr. Rev.* **34**, 65–70.

Henneborn, W. J. and Cogan, R. (1975). The effect of husband participation on reported pain and probability of medication during labor and birth, *J. Psychosom. Res.* **19** (13), 215–222.

Heyns, O. S., Samson, J. M., and Roberts, W. A. B. (1962). An analysis of infants whose mothers had decompression during pregnancy, *Med. Proc.* **8**, 307–311.

Joffe, J. M. (1969). *Prenatal Determinants of Behaviour*, Pergamon, Oxford.

Kagan, J. (1979). Overview: Perspectives on human infancy, in *Handbook of Infant Development* (Ed. J. D. Osofsky), Wiley, New York.

Kelly, J. V. (1962). Effect of fear upon uterine motility, *Am. J. Obstet. Gynec.* **83**, 576.

Kempe, R. S. and Kempe, C. H. (1978). *Child Abuse*, Fontana/Open Books, London.

Kiernan, K. E. (in press) Teenage motherhood: associated factors and consequences—the experience of a British Birth cohort, *J. Biosocial Sci.*

Kirkwood, W. (1955). Aspects of fetal environment, in *Mechanisms of Congenital Malformation* (Ed. H. Wolff), Association for the Aid of Crippled Children, New York.

Knobloch, H. and Pasamanick, B. (1962). Mental subnormality, *New England J. of Medicine*, **266**, 1155–1161.

Kopp, C. B. and Parmelee, A. H. (1979). Prenatal and perinatal influences on infant behavior, in *Handbook of Infant Development* (Ed. J. D. Osofsky), Wiley, New York.

Kraemer, J. C., Korner, A. F., and Thoman, E. B. (1972). Methodological considerations in evaluating the influence of drugs used during labor and delivery on the behavior of the newborn, *Develop. Psychol.*, **6**, 128.

Krech, D., Rosenzweig, M. R., and Bennett, E. L. (1960). Effects of environmental complexity and training on brain chemistry, *J. Comp. Physiol. Psychol.* **53**, 509–519.

Lagercrantz, E. and Lagercrantz, R. (1975). The mother and her firstborn, in *Society, Stress and Disease*, Vol. 2 (Ed. L. Levi), Oxford University Press, London.

Lechtig, A., Habicht, J-P., Delgado, H. Klein, R. E., Yarbrough, C., and Martorell, R. (1975). Effect of food supplementation during pregnancy on birthweight, *Pediatrics*, **56**, 508–520.

Lester, B. M. (1976). Spectrum analysis of the cry sounds of well-nourished and malnourished infants, *Child Develop.*, **47**, 237–241.

Levine, S. and Mullins, R. F. (1966). Hormonal influences on brain organisation in infant rats, *Science*, **152**, 1585.

Lewis, M., Rosenblum, L. A. (Eds) (1974). *The Effect of the Infant on its Caregiver*, Wiley, New York.

Liddicoat, R. (1968). Effects of maternal antenatal decompression treatment on infant mental development, *S. Afr. Med. J.*, **42**, 203–211.

Liley, A. W. (1972). Disorders of amniotic fluid, in *Pathophysiology of Gestation*, Vol. II, *Fetal-Placental Disorders* (Eds N. S. Assali and C. R. Brinkman), Academic Press, New York.

Lloyd, B. and Archer, J. (1976). *Exploring Sex Differences*, Academic Press, London and New York.

Lynch, A. and Mychalkiw, W. (1978). Prenatal progesterone. II. Its role in the treatment of pre-eclamptic toxaemia and its effect on the offspring's intelligence: A reappraisal, *Early Human Development*, **2**, 323–339.

McIlwain, H. (1966). *Biochemistry and the Central Nervous System*. J. and A. Churchill, London.

McIlwain, H. (1970). Metabolic adaptation in the brain, *Nature (Lond.)*, **226**, 803.

Maccoby, E. E. and Jacklin, C. N. (1974). *The Psychology of Sex Differences*, Oxford University Press, London.

Martinez, O. and Roe, D. (1977). Effect of oral contraceptives on blood folate levels in pregnancy, *Am. J. Obstet. Gynecol.*, **128**, 255–261.

Mata, L. J. (1974). Relationship of maternal infection to fetal growth and development, in *Early Malnutrition and Mental Development* (Eds J. Cravioto, L. Hambraeus and B. Valquist) Almqvist and Wiksell, Uppsala.

Melges, F. T. (1968). Postpartum psychiatric syndromes, *Psychosom. Med.*, **30**, 95–108.

Meyer, M. B. and Tonascia, J. A. (1977). Maternal smoking, pregnancy complications, and perinatal mortality, *Am. J. Obstet. Gynec.*, **128**, 494–502.

Miller, J. C., Hassanein, K., and Hensleigh, P. (1977). Effects of behavioural and medical variables on fetal growth retardation, *Am. J. Obstet. Gynec.*, **127**, 643–648.

Mistretta, C. M. and Bradley, R. M. (1975). Taste and swallowing *in utero, Br. Med. Bull.* **31** (1), 80–84.

Montagu, A. (1962). *Prenatal Influences*, Blackwell Scientific Publications, Oxford.

Muller, P. F., Campbell, H. E., Graham, W. E., Brittain, H., Fitzgerald, J. A., Hogan, M. A., Muller, V. H., and Rittenhouse, A. M. (1971). Perinatal factors and their relationship to mental retardation and other parameters of development, *Am. J. Obstet. Gynec.*, **109**, 1205–1210.

Murdoch, B. D., Griesel, R. D., Burnett, L. S., and Bartel, P. R. (1968). Effects of pre-natal maternal decompression on EEG development of 3-year old children, *S. Afr. Med. J.*, **42**, 1067–1071.

Murdoch, B. D. *et al.* (1976). Antenatal maternal decompression and CNS function in the child: Cognitive, neurological and electrocortical investigation, *Psychologia Africana*, **16** (2), 117–123.

Nettelbladt, P., Fagerstrom, C-F., and Uddenberg, N. (1976). Significance of reported childbirth pain, *J. Psychosom. Res.*, **20**, 3, 215–221.

Nilsson, A. and Almgren, P. E. (1970). Paranatal emotional adjustment. A prospective investigation of 165 women. Part ii. The influence of background factors, psychiatric history, parental relationships and personality characteristics, *Acta psychiat Scand. Suppl.*, **220**.

Ostwald, P. F., Phibbs, R., and Fox, S. (1968). Diagnostic use of infant cry, *Biologia Neonatorum*, **13**, 68–82.

Ounsted, M. and Ounsted, C. (1973). *On Fetal Growth Rate*, Clinics in Developmental Medicine, no. 46. Heinemann, London.

Peterson, G. H. and Mehl, L. E. (1978). Some determinants of maternal attachment, *Am. J. Psychiat.*, **135**, 10, 1168–1173.

Reinisch, J. M. (1974). Fetal hormones, the brain and human sex differences: A heuristic, integrative review of the recent research, *Arch. Sexual Behav.*, **3**(1), 51–90.

Reinisch, J. M. and Karow, W. G. (1977). Prenatal exposure to synthetic progestins and estrogens: Effects on human development, *Arch. Sexual Behav.*, **6**(4), 257–288.

Richards, M. P. M. (1975). in Discussion of R. Q. Bell. A congenital contribution to emotional response in early infancy and the preschool period, *CIBA Foundation Symposium 33 (new series) Parent-Infant Interaction*, pp. 209–211, Associated Scientific Publishers, Amsterdam.

Richardson, J. A. and Dixon, G. (1976). Effects of legal termination on subsequent pregnancy, *Br. Med. J.*, **1**, 1303–1304.

Rutter, M. and Madge, N. (1976). *Cycles of Disadvantage*, Heinemann, London.

Sacks, S. H., Brada, M., Hill, A. M., Barton, P., and Harland, P. S. E. G. (1976). To breast feed or not to breast feed, *The Practitioner*, **216**, 183–191.

Salkind, N. J. and Deaton, W. (1978). Organization of infant behavior and season of birth, *J. Pediatric Psychol.*, **3**, 3, 110–112.

Sameroff, A. J. (1975). Early influences on development: fact or fancy? *Merrill-Palmer Quarterly*, **21** (4), 267–294.

Sameroff, A. J. and Cavanagh, P. J. (1979). Learning in infancy: a developmental perspective, in *Handbook of Infant Development* (Ed. J. D. Osofsky), Wiley, New York.

Sameroff, A. J. and Chandler, M. J. (1975). Reproductive risk and the continuum of caretaking casualty, in *Review of Child Development Research*, Vol. 4 (Ed. F. D. Horowitz), University of Chicago Press, Chicago.

Schneirla, T. C. (1957). The concept of development in comparative psychology, in *The Concept of Development* (Ed. D. B. Harris), University of Minnesota Press, Minneapolis.

Seligman, M. E. P. (1970). On the generality of the laws of learning, *Psychol. Rev.*, **77**, 406–418.

Selye, H. (1956). *The Stress of Life*, McGraw Hill, New York.

Sherefsky, P. M. and Yarrow, L. J. (1973). *Psychological Aspects of a First Pregnancy and Early Postnatal Adaptation*, Raven Press, New York.

Siegel, E. and Morris, N. (1970). The epidemiology of human reproductive casualties, in *Maternal Nutrition and the Course of Pregnancy*, pp. 5–40, National Academy of Science Washington DC.

Singleton, C. H. (1978). Sex differences, in *Psychology Survey No. 1.* (Ed. B. M. Foss) Allen and Uwin, London.

Smith, C. R. and Steinschneider, A. (1975). Differential effects of prenatal rhythmic stimulation on neonatal arousal states, *Child Develop.*, **46**, 574–578.

Sontag, L. W. (1966). Implications of fetal behavior and environment for adult personalities, *Annals NY Acad. Sci.*, **134**, 782–786.

Standley, K., Soule, A. B., Copans, S. A., and Klein, R. P. (1978). Multidimensional sources of infant temperament, *Genetic Psychol. Monog.*, **98**, 203–231.

Stein, Z., Susser, M., Saenger, G., and Marola, F. (1975). *Famine and Human Development: The Dutch Hunger Winter of 1944–1945*, Oxford University Press, New York.

Stewart, R. J. C. (1974). Experimental studies on nutrition and brain development, *Nutrition*, **28**, 151–162.

Stratton, P. M. (1977). Criteria for assessing the influence of obstetric circumstances on later development, in *Benefits and Hazards of the New Obstetrics* (Eds T. Chard and M. Richards), Heinemann, London.

Strauss, M. E., Lessen-Firestone, J. K., Starr, R. H., and Ostrea, E. M. (1975). Behavior of narcotics-addicted newborns, *Child Develop.*, **46**, 887–893.

Tanner, J. M. (1978). *Foetus into Man*, Open Books, London.

Thomson, A. M. (1976). Nutritional physiology during pregnancy, in *Early Nutrition and Later Development* (Ed. A. W. Wilkinson), Pitman Medical, London.

Ucko, L. E. (1965). A comparative study of asphyxiated and non-asphyxiated boys from birth to five years, *Develop. Med. Child Neurol.*, **7**, 643–657.

Uddenberg, N. (1974). Reproductive adaptation in mother and daughter: A study of personality development and adaptation to motherhood, *Acta Psychiatrica Scandinavica, Suppl*, **254**, 1–115.

Uddenberg, N. and Fagerstrom, C-F. (1976). The deliveries of daughters of reproductively maladjusted mothers, *J. Psychosomatic Res.*, **20**(3), 223–229.

Uddenberg, N., Fagerstrom, C-F., and Hakanson-Zaunders, M. (1976). Reproductive conflicts, mental symptoms during pregnancy and time in labour, *J. Psychosom. Res.*, **20**, 575–581.

Waddington, C. H. (1957). *The Strategy of the Genes*, Allen and Unwin, London.

Wehmer, F., Porter, R. H., and Scales, B. (1970). Pre-mating and pregnancy stress in rats affects behaviour of grandpups, *Nature (Lond.)*, **277**, 622.

Wharton, B. A. (1976). Genes, clocks and circumstances—the effects of over- and undernutrition, in *Early Nutrition and Later Development* (Ed. A. W. Wilkinson), Pitman Medical, London.

Williams, C. C., Williams, R. A., Griswold, M. J., and Holmes, T. H. (1975). Pregnancy and life change, *J. Psychosom. Res.*, **19**, 123–129.

Wolkind, S. N., Kruk, S., and Chaves, L. P. (1976). Childhood separation experiences and psychosocial status in primiparous women, *Br. J. Psychiat.*, **128**, 391–396.

Wynn, M. and Wynn, A. (1977). *Prevention of Preterm Birth*, Foundation for Education and Research in Child-Bearing, London.

Wynn, M. and Wynn, A. (1979). *Prevention of Handicap and the Health of Women*, Routledge and Kegan Paul, London.

Yang, R. K., Zweig, A. R., Douthitt, T. C., and Federman, E. J. (1976). Successive relationships between maternal attitudes during pregnancy, analgesic medication during labor and delivery, and newborn behavior, *Develop. Psychol.*, **12**, 6–14.

Zeskind, P. S. and Lester, B. M. (1978). Acoustic features and auditory perceptions of the cries of newborns with prenatal and perinatal complications, *Child Develop.*, **49**, 580–589.

Zlatnik, F. J. and Burmeister, L. F. (1977). Low 'gynecologic age': An obstetric risk factor, *Am. J. Obstet. Gynecol.* **128**, 183–186.

Psychobiology of the Human Newborn
Edited by P. Stratton
© 1982, John Wiley & Sons, Ltd.

CHAPTER 11

Obstetric Practice—Cross-Cultural Comparisons

ANN OAKLEY

There is a wide variation in the management of birth and of the newborn cross-culturally, and such variation is to be found not only between developed and undeveloped countries but within each of these types of society. Contrasts between such items as rates of caesarean section and instrumental delivery in different industrialized countries (Chalmers and Richards, 1977) are perhaps better known than parallel contrasts in the obstetric practices of non-industrialized cultures; yet the lesson conveyed by both sets of contrasts is the same—namely that nowhere in human society can childbirth be considered 'natural'. Attitudes to childbearing and the technical management of childbirth are interwoven with the general values of a culture. As the anthropologist Margaret Mead has said:

childbirth may be experienced according to the phrasing given it by the culture, as an experience that is dangerous and painful, interesting and engrossing, matter-of-fact and mildly hazardous, or accompanied by enormous supernatural hazards . . . Whether child-bed is seen as a situation in which one risks death, or one out of which one acquires a baby, or social status, or a right to Heaven, is not a matter of the actual statistics of . . . mortality, but of the view that a society takes of child-bearing (Mead, 1962; pp. 221–2).

Such a view embraces various areas of belief. First, what is the value of children to families and society in general? Secondly, how is human potential and personality seen and what strategies are espoused in the socialization of infants to render them acceptable members of society? Thirdly, what status does repro-duction have as an activity at the interface of the natural and cultural orders? Fourthly, what is the social position and ideological construction of women as the bearers of children? Beliefs in each of these areas underlie the means used to manage birth and the neonate in any and every society. However, those who provide maternity care may be relatively unaware of the philosophy underlying the type of care they provide and of its relationship to actual clinical practice, since to a large extent it will be shared and accepted by all members of the society. Thus, for example, in western society that childbirth is an emergency demanding attention, an essentially 'unnatural' activity, is a taken-for-granted 'fact'. Such a characterization of childbirth has to do both with the development of the professional ideology of medicine and with wider cultural attitudes to life and death, health and illness.

Examining our own society's obstetric practice and the values influencing it within a cross-cultural context is, thus, a valuable way of informing ourselves about our own society as well as about others. If we learn in the process something about the many different ways in which human biological potential shapes, and is shaped by, social factors, then we are surely learning a lesson that is relevant to the assessment and future development of our own obstetric practice.

There are clearly connections between different agendas of belief about reproduction, children and women on the one hand, and the techniques deployed in childbirth on the other. However, although a number of excellent ethnographic surveys of cross-cultural variation in childbirth management are available (e.g. Ford, 1945; Mead and Newton, 1967; Newton and Newton, 1972), the exact nature of the relationship between specific values and obstetric techniques has not been systematically evaluated. Similarly, although obstetric practice must be expected to have some influence on the condition and behaviour of the neonate and on her/his incipient relationship with mother, father and other family members, the area is not one in which definite conclusions can be drawn. All attempts to link specific items of obstetric practice with neonatal behaviour or with the quality of the mother–neonate relationship founder to some extent on the rock of the multiplicity of variables involved. If this is true of closely observed, intensively documented western practice, then it is likely to be even more true of the obstetric and relevant social data reproduced by anthropologists in their accounts of preliterate and other cultures. These accounts are very thinly endowed with the kind of information on obstetric practice we need to evaluate the effects of different techniques, chiefly because of the inability of most male ethnographers to witness childbirth, and their relative insensitivity to 'women's' issues such as maternal–infant bonding. Despite these problems, I shall make some suggestions about how the cross-cultural data on obstetric practice and the social destiny of the neonate might be interpreted at the end of this chapter. Before doing so, I discuss some examples of cross-cultural variation in particular aspects of obstetric management relevant to the social fate of the newborn baby. These aspects are: (a) the social context and location of childbirth; (b) delivery personnel; (c) the management of labour and delivery; (d) the immediate postbirth treatment of the baby; (e) conceptions of the status of the neonate and her/his physical and psychological requirements in the early weeks and months of life.

THE SOCIAL CONTEXT AND LOCATION OF CHILDBIRTH

Place of birth and the status of those who are present at it are aspects of obstetric practice that tend to be strikingly different in industrialized and non-industrialized cultures. Whereas institutional confinement rates in the former can approach 100 per cent, in the latter most births take place at home. For a first birth this may be the home of the mother's parents but for second and subsequent births it is more likely to be the mother's own home. Bronislaw Malinowski wrote of the Trobriand Islanders of the south pacific:

> The woman has to go to her father's house, for that is also her mother's home, and her mother is the proper person to look after her and the baby . . . when her time approaches, the parental house is made ready. The father and all the male inmates have to leave, while some female kinswomen come in to assist the mother (Malinowski, 1932; pp. 194).

Malinowski noted that the custom of removal to the mother's parental home was associated with a pronounced fear of the dangers which attach to a parturient women. A specific form of evil magic is feared; called vatula bam, it means the chilling or paralysing of the uterus. During the labour and delivery male relatives sit outside the house with spears to defend it against sorcerers who (specially at night) attempt to cast vatula bam magic. A well-known variation on this theme of the dangers of childbirth is the seclusion of the mother during birth and of the mother and baby afterwards. Either birth takes place in the open air or in a special dwelling provided for that purpose. Among the Arapesh of New Guinea birth is supposed to occur on the edge of the village in the 'bad place' reserved for excretion, menstrual guts, and foraging pigs (Mead, 1935). Many cultures have elaborate purification rituals after childbirth, as in the Hebrew–Christian religious tradition. The whole of Leviticus 12 is devoted to the ritual purification of the woman after childbirth: she was considered 'unclean' for a week after the birth of a boy and for 2 weeks after the birth of a girl (the lochia was supposed to last longer following a female birth) (Levin, 1960).

However, even birth in seclusion does not deprive the labouring women of attendants and support from female friends and relatives. 'In primitive culture by far the most usual arrangement' wrote Mead and Newton in their review of cultural patterns in perinatal behaviour, 'is for the labouring woman to have two or more attendants for labour and delivery'.

> Unattended birth does occur in many cultures, but it is a rare event to be gossiped about in the same manner as an American birth taking place in a taxi cab (Mead and Newton, 1967; pp. 169).

Among the Arande of Central Australia the usual practice described by a Government Medical Officer in 1947 was for the parturient woman and her attendants, all female blood relatives, to move away from the main camp to a place further than a baby's crying distance for the birth (de Vidas, 1947). For the Yoruba woman of West Africa birth takes place in her home in the presence of a herbalist, a female midwife and several elders of the family: the first person to hold the baby is its parental grandfather who ritually welcomes it before giving it to an attending woman for a herbal bath and massage with palm of coconut oil (Longo, 1964). Sometimes a formidable array of friends and relations may be present during birth. This was true of many births in western society before the advent of hospitalized childbirth. 'Far from being hidden, childbirth was frequently a communal event and undoubtedly many women learned about labour and delivery by assisting friends or family members' notes one commentator on the victorian scene (Miller, 1978; pp. 24). A woman would invite her mother and a number of friends called 'gossips'. One important role of such women was to act as official witnesses of the birth. Even Queen Victoria had to submit to this requirement, although her gossips were the extraordinary ones (at her first confinement) of the Archbishop of Canterbury, the Bishop of London, the Lord Steward of the Household and various Cabinet Ministers. (The Queen insisted on a minimum of decorum and the officials were made to stand in a room adjoining the lying-in chamber with the door open).

The important point about the setting of birth in a familiar social context is that it is not experienced by the mother as a narrowly clinical phenomenon separate from the routines and relationships of her ordinary life. Stacey (1975) has made the pertinent observation that modern hospitalization practices achieve this end much more effectively than seclusion rituals in primitive cultures. In western society, the mother may not be told that she is 'polluting' by her obstetrician, but the normal ritual of hospitalization for childbirth and the postpartum period effectively suggests the same message. Separation from home, family and friends, subjection to the authority and rules of hospital staff during delivery and afterwards, and treatment as a relatively powerless patient, are potential sources of strain for mothers that are likely to affect both satisfaction with childbirth and the initiation of the mother–child relationship. Allowing husbands to be present at the birth, decorating delivery rooms in a less antiseptic style, and similar modifications of hospital procedure, may make some difference to the mother's sense of alienation from ordinary social life, but it is doubtful whether they can altogether remove it. So far as the neonate is concerned, the different practices of industrialized and non-industrialized cultures mean either integration in or separation from family and community at the moment of birth. We do not know what effect the different experiences have on infant development, but it is difficult to believe that they have no influence at all.

DELIVERY PERSONNEL

A related consideration, and one of considerable psychological significance for the mother, is that the person who actually delivers the baby or who is regarded as in charge of the birth in non-industrialized cultures is virtually never a stranger. An elderly and experienced woman, whether a member of the mother's family or a friend, is the most usual birth attendant worldwide. In the Nigerian village of Ebiama described by Philip Leis in 1972 a woman on going into labour will call a village midwife who is assisted by the mother's female relatives. The village midwives consist of several elderly women who are qualified by age and experience and enjoy excellent reputations without being full time specialists in midwifery.

Among the Akwe-Shavante of Brazil a woman 'is attended by her close kinswomen, usually assisted by one or other of the older women of the community who are regarded as experienced midwives' (Maybury Lewis, 1967; p. 64). When the child is born it is the midwife who takes it outside the hut and nurses it in her lap for the crowd 'which always collects on these occasions' to see. C. S. Ford, (1945) found in his survey of sixty-four primitive cultures that elderly women were the birth attendants in 97 per cent of the cultures for which information was available. Continuity is further ensured in some cultures by the midwife also providing a form of antenatal care. Oscar Lewis found in Tepoztlan, a Mexican village, that antenatal care consisted principally of abdominal massages given by a midwife:

The patient lies down on her back with her knees slightly bent, and the midwife gently strokes the abdomen from right to left. No oils or unguents are used. It is thought that massage makes the birth easier and also allows the midwife to determine or even change the position of the fetus. Most women have great faith in the efficacy of massage and try to have it from two to four times a month. (Lewis, 1960; pp. 69–70)

Village midwives also give general advice on diet, exercise, and hygiene to pregnant women. They recommend not taking too much rest which would make the birth more difficult, avoiding urinating in places where an animal has just urinated (which might cause uterine inflammation) and watching out for the dangers of immersion in water, eclipses, rainbows and earthquakes, which are regarded as threatening the safety of the unborn child.

Although it may be difficult for obstetricians and their patients in industrialized cultures to see the value of such advice, one important point is that it is usually not at odds with the attitude of the pregnant woman towards reproduction. Childbirth has not been 'medicalized' and remains a social act integrated with the life and norms of the community. The status of the pregnancy adviser and delivery person as a member of the mother's everyday social network without a distinctive 'expert' training helps to ensure this continuity, and is another feature of obstetric practice rarely found in industrialized society today. In one sample of English primigravidae studied in the mid-1970s, three quarters had never actually seen the person who delivered their baby before. As one of these mothers said:

it was *horrific* that the midwife and the pupil midwife who were there I'd never seen in my life before and I've never seen them again since. And yet they were *the* people in about the most vital and powerful experience in my life so far. (Oakley, 1979; pp. 287)

Although it may be reassuring to know that the potential deliverer of one's baby (whoever he or she turns out to be) is going to be equipped with all the relevant clinical skills and resources, the act of giving birth is also an immensely personal one, and for the mother it is an inseparable part of her development as a person and the unfolding of her family life. Again, the psychological effect of a familiar deliverer on the mother's attitudes and behaviour during and after birth and on the neonate's reception as a member of society is likely to be considerable.

THE MANAGEMENT OF LABOUR AND DELIVERY

The active management of labour is not a prerogative of industrialized medicine. By this I mean that birth attendants and deliverers in most cultures are not prepared simply to wait for the biological process of labour and delivery to be completed on its own. They believe that certain interventions are required for the safe delivery of a healthy child.

Dietary regulation is one important way of influencing the biochemical status of women in labour. The African Hottentots gave soup to labouring women in order to strengthen them (Schultze, 1907); some North American Indian groups prohibit the drinking of water in labour (Dorsey and Murie, 1940; Spier, 1933); the Bahaya of Africa permit drinking during labour but not eating (Moller, 1961). Many cultures also feel the need for regulating activity in labour either by encouraging or restricting it. The not untypical custom of the Tuareg, a nomadic Saharan tribe, whereby the first labour pain is the signal for constant walking up and down small hills to encourage the most favourable presentation of the baby (Blanguernon, 1955) is at odds with the convention in most modern western hospitals whereby the supine position is recommended throughout labour. A recent study by Flynn *et al.* (1978) has shown the beneficial effect of ambulation in labour, but the opportunity for changing obstetric practice created by such studies is another question altogether. Fairly profound attitudes and values are challenged by research findings which suggest the superiority of practices that do not fit the paradigm of the mother (and the baby) as passive patients. Clearly, it may be 'easier' from the point of view of those caring for the mother during labour if she is horizontal, or at least sedentary. In a fixed position in which tests and procedures can be administered without difficulty the mother is 'under control': walking around the hospital or the labour ward she becomes an individual rather than a passive recipient of clinical procedures. That this may be 'easier' for her is, significantly, usually not a relevant consideration.

It is common to find in ethnographic accounts of birth the mention of medications and other substances used to hasten or ease labour pains and delivery. Ukrainian midwives gave whisky to ease the labouring woman's pains (Koenig, 1939); the Amhara of Ethiopia use mashed linseed for the dual purpose of relaxing the birth tract and reducing the pain (Messing, 1957). The Bahaya of Africa possess a drug of powdered bark and dried leaves which is said to be so powerful a labour stimulant that it sometimes causes uterine rupture (Moller, 1958). Herbs are used by the Sierra Tarcascans of Mexico to accelerate birth and cause abortion (Mead and Newton, 1967); physiological releasers of oxytocin such as breast stimulation and orgasm are employed by the Lepcha of Asia and the Siriouo of Bolivia (Mead and Newton, 1967). In Helen Gideon's moving account of a Punjabi birth (Gideon, 1962), the midwife gives the mother sips of milk and melted butter throughout labour. The woman's mother presses on the womb at every contraction and this stimulation is viewed as essential after the child's delivery to prevent the afterbirth rising to the heart and killing the mother. Abdominal stimulation in labour is commonly reported, but may be only for difficult deliveries. Thus in Tepoztlan it is said that an experienced widwife can alter the fetus's position in labour by massaging the mother's abdomen. When the pelvic bones are too narrow they are spread by digital manipulation. More aggressive interventions are also recorded, from external version among the Guatemalan Indians (Paul, 1974) to manual removal of the placenta by the Navaho Indians and episiotomy by the Chagga of Tanzania (Mead and Newton, 1967). Caesarean sections are reported too (Wright, 1921).

Having said that some pattern of active management of birth is most usual, it must be added that there are scattered references to cultures that adopt a more *laissez-faire* attitude. The Mundurucu mothers studied by Yolanda and Robert Murphy (1974) deliver their babies unaided on to the ground from a squatting position and cut the umbilical cord themselves with a sharpened sliver of arrow cane. Among the Australian Arande, there is apparently:

no interference whatever with the mechanism of childbirth. With the onset of pains following complete version and external rotation, the mother is lifted slightly by the posterior attendant, and the body of the child is received gently on to the surface of the ground or a shallow hole dug in the earth. Neither assistant touches the child or the vaginal outlet until the head and body are fully born. This 'no touch' attitude is strictly observed in normal labour. If the umbilical cord, however, is constricting the child's neck the front attendant slips the cord over the head or shoulder and then sits back again. Leaving the child untouched, all wait passively for it to cry. No measures are taken to hasten this. (de Vidas, 1947; p. 118)

Arande mothers may have the umbilical cord cut at this point or much later after the expulsion of the placenta. In general the treatment of the cord reflects different attitudes of passivity and intervention. However, the most common practice is to wait for the delivery of the placenta before severing the cord (Ford, 1945). In their survey of cross-cultural birth patterns Mead and Newton point out that the weight of the cross-cultural evidence and the research that has been done into the effects of cutting the cord at different times definitely indicate that the optimal time is 15–20 minutes after the arrival of the placenta (though the time depends on the relative heights of placenta and baby). This conflicts with much modern obstetric practice.

In most cultures vertical rather than horizontal positions are used for the actual delivery—82 per cent of societies in Ford's survey preferred the vertical position. According to Ford (1945; p. 58):

The woman usually assumes a sitting position; less commonly she either kneels or squats. In one society, the Tarahumara, the woman is reported to deliver her child in a standing position. In our modern hospitals the reclining position has been adopted since it facilitates antiseptic treatment. The evidence from our primitive societies indicates that this is a most unnatural position.

Sometimes cultural patterns require different positions for the different stages. Siriono women lie in their hammocks for the delivery of the baby but kneel for the placenta. As with other aspects of childbirth, the issue of delivery position has extensive implications for the fate of the mother and child. Obstetricians in many western countries appear to be quite resistant to the idea that the upright position is more effective and safer (Mengert and Murphy, 1933; see also Dunn, 1976). As with ambulation during labour, an upright delivery position contradicts certain key values about the role of the mother in the childbearing process. Lying down she can more easily 'be delivered of' her baby; that is, mechanical manipulations are more conveniently carried out (although they are also more likely to be needed). Rationales for a horizontal delivery position such as that it facilitates antiseptic treatment serve to beg the question—which is why antiseptic treatment is considered necessary in the first place. Associated rituals such as the shaving of pubic hair became a standard component of obstetric practice without any evidence that they contributed to health (which in fact, in the case of shaving they do not (Burchell, 1964)), and may be considered an item in the same agenda of reducing the mother to the status of a mechanical, or at least biological, object.

THE TREATMENT OF THE BABY AFTER BIRTH

The Manus of the Admiralty Islands place the crying neonate, cord uncut, facing the mother in the belief that the sight and sound of the baby will encourage the delivery of the placenta (Mead and Newton, 1967). This is not untypical of so called 'primitive' cultures' somewhat sophisticated recognition of a close relationship between emotional and biological state. Such a recognition has not been a prominent feature of obstetric practice in many industrialized countries, which has concerned itself much more specifically with physiological process and outcome. Hence the discovery in recent years of the measurable psychological effects imposed on newborn children and their mothers by separation after birth. As Richards (1978; p. 22) shows in his discussion of the evidence available, 'a *prima facie* case has been established that early separation has at least a short-term effect on patterns of mother–child relationships', and the possibility of long-term effects cannot by any means be ruled out.

Studies of birth in other cultures indicate that the pattern of close and unbroken contact between mother and child after birth is almost universal. This is perhaps one reason why cross-cultural surveys have not singled out the baby's handling after birth for special mention (another is that the fate of the placenta as an organ permanently capable of affecting the chances of neonatal survival is a much more colourful topic). Sheila Kitzinger has summarized much of the cross-cultural data on post-birth mother–child contact thus.

The general pattern in pre-industrial societies is for the baby to be with and close to the mother, and to remain with her, day and night, for the postpartum weeks. He is often fixed to her body in one way or another, bound by shawls, slung in a net or special carrier, or wound into a strip of cloth which may actually be her own dress, apart from the time when he is lying beside her, and frequently he is in flesh contact. Life outside the uterus is often thought of as a continuation of life inside it. The Ndembu of Zambia call the cloth which attaches the baby to the mother's back 'the placenta' (Kitzinger, 1978; p. 178).

By way of contrast, the neonate's destiny in many industrialized cultures is one of abrupt and persisting physical separation from the mother. Mead and Newton's description of the American cultural pattern in the late 1960s remains relevant today, although liberalism is creeping in in some quarters:

The crib, the play pen, the perambulator, and the car-bed all hold the baby some distance away from the mother's body and usually out of her sight. Most of the skin of both mother and baby is covered with clothing so that even during nursing often the only skin contact is the mouth against the nipple, rather than body against body. If the feeding is administered by bottle . . . still less skin-to-skin contact occurs. . . . Only 5 or 6 feedings a day are considered 'suitable' or 'ideal', and more than 8 are often regarded as indicating abnormality in the infant. Some American mothers boast about how quickly night feedings are eliminated, usually signifying that they have *no* contact with the baby whatsoever through the night hours. Sleeping with the baby is believed to be dangerous for the baby. (Mead and Newton, 1967; p. 182).

Attitudes to crying in babies are now more flexible than they used to be, but many parents and their professional advisers still do not advocate the immediate comforting (with breast feeding or other physical contact) of a crying baby. In contrast, most parents in primitive cultures respond instantly to a crying infant; consequently, 'Western observers record with amazement how quiet and 'good' many primitive babies appear to be' (Mead and Newton, 1967; p. 183).

In many such cultures, the baby may not be handed to the mother immediately after birth, and it seems that she does not always breastfeed it immediately (many people of Asia, Africa, North and South America and Oceania delay the first feeding for several days (Mead and Newton, 1967)). The baby is, nevertheless, born into a network of loving care and attention, and there is no question of physical separation from the mother or relegation to the clinical care of professionals as in the normative western practice.

The baby is quite often washed and anointed with various substances after delivery (see the Yoruba example on page 300). Gideon included the following description of post-birth behaviour in her account of a Punjabi delivery: the protagonists are Surjeeto, the mother, Mohindro, her mother, and Akki the midwife:

Akki cut the cord. She smeared the cut end with fresh cow dung ashes. She tied up the placenta in an old rag and put it aside. She cleaned and wiped Surjeeto, and used an old discarded shirt as a pad. Akki then got off the bed, and covering Surjeeto with the bed clothes she gave her attention to the child.

Meanwhile Mohindro had brought warm water in an iron bowl. As Akki sat beside the bed to bathe the child, Mohindro put a silver rupee in the water saying, 'Here is something for cutting the cord. Luck is your way. You would not have got this had the baby been a girl.' Akki gave the child a bath, dressed him, put black antimony powder in his eyes and a black spot on the temple to protect him from the evil eye. Then she put the child next to Surjeeto. (Gideon, 1962; p. 1226)

After birth, the Mundurucu mother washes herself and her baby in cold water, wraps it up and takes it into her hammock with her (Murphy and Murphy, 1974). Newborn babies are commonly given something to eat or drink other than breastmilk; among the Wachaga of Tanganjika this consists of a drink of water and a small amount of pre-chewed banana to 'clear its throat' (Moller, 1961; p. 75). Medications for the newborn, particularly laxatives to clear the meconium, are given in many parts of the world (e.g. Wellin, 1955).

Seclusion rituals following delivery which are common in many cultures have the effect of intensifying the mother–child bond, since others are not allowed to intrude on it. Mother and child therefore have a considerable amount of time together to get to know each other before the mother resumes her ordinary duties. Malinowski wrote of the Trobrianders:

Mother and baby spend the greater part of their time during the first month on one of the raised bedsteads with a small fire underneath. This is a matter of hygiene, as the natives consider such baking and smoking to be very beneficial for the health, and a sort of prophylactic against black magic. No men are allowed into the house, for, since the woman baked over the fire is usually naked, no male should enter . . . (Malinowski, 1932; pp. 196–197).

After a month a ritual magic is performed after which the mother is washed, and she is then able to go out into the village to visit her relatives. She then returns for another month in seclusion, before becoming an ordinary member of society again.

It is interesting—and paradoxical—to note that such separation of mother and child does not usually proceed from an articulated philosophy of motherhood in which mother and child are seen as instinctually dependent on one another. Conversely, a philosophy of motherhood which emphasizes the 'natural' maternalism of women and the child's need for its own biological mother, has been very influential in the West, despite the fact that the development of a relatively safe technology of artificial feeding has rendered the biological tie of mother and child much less total. Moreover, the delineation of motherhood as the ideal destiny of women which has been a feature of post-war western culture has also, paradoxically, been the condition under which obstetric practice has separated mother and child. To understand this, it may be necessary, as Lomas (1978) has suggested, to think in terms of hidden patterns in the psychology of men and women that influence the handling of childbirth in western society. Among the concealed conflicts identified by Lomas is that between creativity and sterility, between growth and stasis, Lomas writes:

The distrust and alarm with which manifestations of creativity in art, science or religion is met is impressive and adults do not take easily to the spontaneous creativity and innocent penetration of the child. Is it not then to be expected that the creative event of birth will be viewed with a similar degree of anxiety? A mother and baby are very appropriate symbols of growth, and for this reason a rigid and insecure society may see the necessity to control and restrict their spontaneous joy. (Lomas, 1978; p. 183)

A doctrine of women's instinctual fitness for motherhood and a practice of separating mother and baby in the postpartum period may both be forms of such a restriction. Further, it may not be out-of-place to suggest that men's envy of women's ability to bear children as manifested, for example, in the couvade syndrome of primitive cultures (Bettelheim, 1955), has other manifestations in our own. Certainly the historical male-domination of obstetrics and gynaecology, and to a lesser extent that of paediatrics, has been associated with a progressively more complete control of pregnancy, birth, and motherhood.

THE SOCIAL STATUS OF THE NEONATE

Even in a society where perinatal mortality is around 15 per 1000 live births a certain anxiety exists in relation to the dangers of childbearing. In non-industrialized cultures, where the perinatal mortality rate is many times greater than this, and where the percentage of maternal deaths is also relatively high, childbirth is even more obviously a time of personal peril and social threat. The inherent danger of childbirth is what lies behind the complex rituals developed by many cultures for the management of pregnancy, birth and the products of birth—both biological materials (cord, placenta, membranes) and social-biological product, the baby.

It is not simply, however, the risk of dying that is threatening, but the very fact of a biological process occurring in a social world which is potentially disturbing.

All cultures have their own idea of what constitutes an ordered social system. Within each such ideological frame-work there exist complex rules and classsifications, and certain conditions, processes and individuals are judged as especially threatening to the operation of these rules and classifications. Natural materials such as blood, excrement, milk and the products of birth, along with the individuals from which they emanate or in whom they are vested are especially liable to be viewed as contaminating and polluting (Douglas, 1966). From the point of view of the neonate, this means that its human status as a fully accredited member of society is often in doubt, or is in doubt at least until it has passed through a series of rituals establishing its human status (van Gennep, 1960).

Within Western culture the precise moment at which the unborn baby becomes properly 'human' has been a major moral preoccupation. Other cultures also debate this point. The Ojibwa of Perry Island, Ontario, Canada, believe that the baby from the moment pregnancy is recognized has a human soul (Jenness, 1935); elsewhere the social status of human beings is viewed as developing in stages. Most usually, however, even the infant for some time after birth is not accorded human status. The not uncommon practice of infanticide therefore does not automatically break a cultural taboo against murder, since what is disposed of is not regarded as a human being. This can be contrasted with the situation now obtaining in Western obstetric practice whereby parents who query the appropriateness of heroic efforts to save the life of an 800-g 24-week infant already damaged by intensive neonatal care are accused of rejection, negligence and callousness because they consider the quality of life such an infant is experiencing and is likely to experience in the future (Stinson and Stinson, 1979). An equation between, or rather disinclination to separate, quantity and quality of life is a habit of thought not found in all societies. In our own the measurement of the success of obstetric medicine by reference to the perinatal mortality rate has made it difficult to pursue the undoubtedly more complex, but nevertheless important, exercise of assessing morbidity in babies. Here there may be a clash between parental and professional perspectives, for it is the parents who have to rear a possibly damaged child, negotiate its impact on their own lives and the life of the family, and assess its probable destiny in a future without them. Conversely, those who deliver the child and manage its care in the post-partum period are quite understandably liable to accept a somewhat different view of the absolute value of preserving life.

The marginal status of the neonate—biological product and potential citizen of the social order—determines many cross-cultural practices obtaining in the period after birth. The seclusion of mother and baby falls under this heading. So does the fate of the placenta, often believed to be the 'twin' of the newborn baby. For example:

The Toba-bataks (of Queensland, Australia) call the placenta the younger brother of the child. They hold that every man has seven souls. One of these abides with the placenta which is buried, but can leave it to warn the child to whom it belongs or if he be acting rightly, to encourage him, and thus plays the part of conscience. (Gibson, 1929; p. 225).

Naming rituals reflect an initial uncertainty about the infant's chances of survival as a citizen of the community into which he or she has been born. The crucial period may be 3 days (among the Siamese; Wales, 1933), 7 days (the Bambara; Monteil, 1924) or several months (the African Fang; Trezenem, 1936). The bestowal of an individual name is a recognition of individual identity and in this respect modern Western practice is highly individualistic. Illick (1974) has pointed out that in the Middle Ages identical names were often given to siblings who were then distinguished by birth-order labels. By the early modern period this practice had ceased but a dead child's name was sometimes given to a sibling born later. Another practice, that of giving a parental forename to a child, is also much less common than it used to be (in one seventeenth century New England town nearly three quarters of first children bore a parental forename). These changes indicate a heightened sense of the value of each child's individuality and irreplaceability. It is in this context that contemporary Western practice operates, with its primary objective of preserving the life of each individual fetus and neonate.

CONCLUSION

Discussions of other cultures' obstetric practices should not be seen as attempts to recapture a 'golden age' of childbirth management in which nature took its course and everyone was happy. The survival of mothers and babies is crucial and the practices of those cultures lacking professional medical maternity care are associated with generally higher mortality. But, on the other hand, the value of cross-cultural data is not simply that they provide a quaint, esoteric and amusing backdrop to modern Western practice. In many ways, as I have suggested here, the same framework of analysis can be applied to childbirth in non-industrialized and industrialized cultures. For example, all cultures have developed and institutionalized rules for the management of pregnancy, delivery and the post-partum period and the treatment of the newborn which reflect human beings' desires to take control over the natural process of reproduction. There are also attempts, different in kind and efficacy in different places at different times, to obviate disaster by intervening in the natural process to correct nature's mistakes and salvage a mother or child whose life or normality is threatened.

Another respect in which the practices of other cultures are relevant to those of Western societies today derives from the absence of clearcut divisions between the normal and abnormal, the medical and the social, and the physiological and psychological parameters of maternal and infant welfare in societies which lack professionalized medical maternity care. Although this may be disadvantageous in some respects, it also has its advantages. For example, where obstetric analgesics are not routinely used because the necessary knowledge and technology is lacking, a few mothers and babies may suffer, but most will pass through childbirth without facing the iatrogenic risks of these drugs. It is therefore to be expected that the condition of the neonate will reflect his or her lack of exposure to agents which have been shown to have substantial short-term as well as possible long-term, effects (Richards, 1975; Richards and Bernal, 1971). The behavioural impact on the neonate of obstetric analgesia may affect the success with which breast-feeding is established, and this in turn may have profound implications for the mother–child relationship and the health of the neonate both in infancy and later (Jelliffe and Jelliffe, 1978).

Pain in labour, like all pain, is not a biological constant. Its expression varies according to the norms of the culture, a fact noted by obstetricians and midwives delivering ethnic minority mothers in Western society today (Shaw, 1974; Clark, 1978). Labour pain is also associated with the specific requirements of each culture pertaining to the role of women as mothers. Thus Clark and Howland (1978; p. 165) write of Samoan women: 'The process of labour is viewed . . . as a necessary part of their role and a part of the life experience . . . her culture tells her that she does not need medication.' It is a matter of pride among Samoan mothers that they do not have analgesia in childbirth. While some mothers in modern Britain or the United States may articulate a similar attitude, most have been effectively exposed to the dominant medical principle that it is a doctor's responsibility to abolish pain, and that in this respect the pain encountered while producing a baby is no different from the pain of any illness, a category in which it can be argued that modern obstetric care has unambiguously placed all childbirths, whether 'normal' or not (Graham and Oakley, 1981). However, chemical analgesics are not the only way to abolish or reduce pain. It is recognized in many cultures that companionship and support during labour is essential for the mother to find childbirth a bearable and satisfying experience. In other words, physical experience is affected by emotional state, a cross-cultural truism which modern research studies are now establishing—as in Henneborn and Logan's (1975) finding that the presence of husbands during labour and delivery reduces medication levels.

Other strategies for diluting labour pain include the burning of incense and the offering of prayers to ancestral gods (Gibson, 1929) and the chanting of ritual poems by the birth attendant. The herbalist doctor who attends Yoruba confinements incants the following poem of reassurance to his patients:

The goats have no midwives,
The sheep have no midwives.
When the goat is pregnant, she is safely delivered.
When the sheep is pregnant, she is safely delivered. You, in this state of pregnancy, will be safely delivered. (Longo, 1964; p. 471).

Once again, the suggestion of modern advocates of natural childbirth that music and singing be allowed in labour (e.g. Brook, 1976) makes a similar point. The pleas made by Frederick Leboyer (1975) on behalf of the newborn hark back to some of the neonatal practices I have described in this chapter, but the only randomized controlled trial of Leboyer delivery so far conducted came up with the interesting conclusion that the only difference between the Leboyer delivery group and the control group of women undergoing normal 'humane' childbirth was that the first group had a shorter first stage—presumably in anticipation of the delight of the Leboyer delivery in store for them (Nelson *et al.*, 1980).

Non-industrialized cultures' recognition of the close interplay between biological reproductivity and maternal emotions and their acceptance of childbirth as a normal part of life must, then, impinge on the fate of the neonate, although in ways that have not been precisely measured. Finally, what is perhaps most striking in accounts of childbirth in other cultures is that the mother is at the centre of the stage and is expected and aided by her attendants and her socialization for childbearing to have and retain control over the process of having a baby. The management of childbirth and the neonate in modern industrialized society, by contrast, offers women a very different experience, in which there is considerable disjunction between the behaviour ordinarily expected of them and the role allocated to them in the process of becoming a mother. The difficult transition from dependent patient to autonomous mother commented on by many women having babies is one important aspect of this disjunction. It is also one among various ways in which the management of childbirth in Western society may contribute to a significant incidence of puerperal depression in mothers (Oakley, 1980), a condition with, of course, considerable implications for the well-being of the neonate.

REFERENCES

Bettelheim, B. (1954). *Symbolic Wounds: Puberty Rites and the Envious Male*, Free Press, Glencoe.

Blanguernon, C. (1955). *Le Hoggar*, B. Arthaud, Paris.

Brook, D. (1976). *Naturebirth*, Penguin books, Harmondsworth.

Burchell, R. (1964). Predelivery removal of pubic hair, *Obstetrics and Gynecology*, **24**, 272–273.

Chalmers, I. and Richards M. (1977). Intervention and causal inference in obstetric practice, in *Benefits and Hazards of the New Obstetrics* (Eds T. Chard and M. Richards), Heinemann Medical Books, London.

Clark, A. L. (Ed.) (1978). *Culture, Childbearing and Health Professionals*, F. A. Davis, Philadelphia.

Clark, A. L. and Howland, R. I. (1978). The American Samoan, in *Culture, Childbearing and Health Professionals* (Ed. A. L. Clark), F. A. Davis, Philadelphia.

de Vidas, J. (1947). Childbirth among the Aranda, Central Australia, *Oceania*, **18**, 117–119.

Dorsey, G. A. and Murie J. R. (1940). Notes on Skidi Pawnee Society *Field Museum of Natural History, Anthropology Series*, **27**, 2, 65–119.

Douglas, M. (1966). *Purity and Danger*, Routledge and Kegan Paul, London.

Dunn, P. M. (1976). Obstetric delivery today, *Lancet*, **1**, 790–793.

Flynn, A. M., Kelly, J., Hollins, G., and Lynch, P. F. (1978). Ambulation in labour, *British Medical Journal*, **1978**, 591–593.

Ford, C. S. (1945). *A Comparative Study of Human Reproduction*, Yale University Publications in Anthropology, No. 32, New York.

Gibson, A. J. (1929). Obstetrical customs among savage and barbarous peoples, *The Medical Journal of Australia*, **1929**, 222–228.

Gideon, H. (1962). A baby is born in the Punjab, *American Anthropologist*, **64**, 1220–1234.

Graham, H. and Oakley, A. (1981). Competing ideologies of reproduction: Medical and maternal perspectives on pregnancy and childbirth, in *Women, Health and Reproduction* (Ed. H. Roberts), Routledge and Kegan Paul, London.

Henneborn, W. J. and Logan, R. (1975), The effect of husband participation on reported pain and probability of medication during labour and birth, *Journal of Psychosomatic Research*, **19**, 215–222.

Illick, J. E. (1974). Childrearing in Seventeenth Century England and America, in *The History of Childhood* (Ed. L. deMause), Harper and Row, New York.

Jelliffe, D. B. and Jelliffe, E. F. P. (1978). *Human Milk in the Modern World*, Oxford University Press, Oxford.

Jenness, D. (1935). *The Ojibwa Indians of Perry Island: Their Social and Religious Life*, Bulletin 78, Canada Department of Mines, Ottawa.

Kitzinger, S. (1978). *Women As Mothers*, Fontana, London.

Koenig, S. (1939). Beliefs and practices relating to birth and childhood among the Galician Ukranians, *Folk-lore*, **50**, 272–287.

Leyboyer, F. (1975). *Childbirth without Violence*, Wildwood House, London.

Leis, P. E. (1972). *Enculturation and Socialization in an Ijaw Village*, Holt, Rinehart and Winston, New York.

Levin, S. (1960). Obstetrics in the Bible *Journal of Obstetrics and Gynaecology of the British Empire*, **67**, 490–498.

Lewis, O. (1960). *Tepoztlan: Village in Mexico*, Holt, Reinehart and Winston, New York.

Lomas, P. (1978). An interpretation of modern obstetric practice, in *The Place of Birth* (Eds S. Kitzinger and J. A. Davies), Oxford University Press, Oxford.

Longo, L. D. (1964). Sociocultural practices relating to obstetrics and gynecology in a community of west africa, *American Journal of Obstetrics & Gynecology*, **89**, 470–475.

Malinowski, B. (1932). *The Sexual Life of Savages*, Routledge and Kegan Paul, London.

Maybury-Lewis, D. (1967). *Akwe Shavante Society*, Clarendon Press, Oxford.

Mead, M. (1935). *Sex and Temperament in Three Primitive Societies*, William Morrow, New York.

Mead, M. (1962). *Male and Female*, Penguin Books, Harmondsworth.

Mead, M. and Newton, N. (1967). Cultural patterning of perinatal behaviour, in *Childbearing—Its Social and Psychological Aspects* (Eds S. A. Richardson, and A. F. Guttmacher), Williams and Wilkins, Baltimore.

Mengert, W. F. and Murphy D. P. (1933). Intra-abdominal pressures created by voluntary muscular effort, *Surgery, Gynecology and Obstetrics*, **57**, 745–751.

Messing, S. D. (1957). The Highland Plateau Amhara of Ethiopia', Doctoral dissertation, University of Pennsylvania, Philadelphia.

Miller, J. H. (1978). 'Temple and sewer' childbirth, prudery and Victoria Regina, in *The Victorian Family* (Ed. A. S. Wohl) Croom Helm, London.

Moller, M. S. G. (1958). Bahaya customs and beliefs in connection with pregnancy and childbirth, *Tanganyika Notes and Records*, **50**, 112–117.

Moller, M. S. G. (1961). Custom, pregnancy and childrearing in Tanganyika, *Journal of Tropical Pediatrics and African Child Health*, **7**, 66–80.

Monteil, C. (1924). *Les Bambara du Segou et du Kaarta*, Emile Larose, Paris.

Murphy, Y. and Murphy, R. F. (1974). *Women of the Forest*, Columbia University Press, New York.

Nelson, N., Enkin, M. W., Saigal, S., Bennett, K. J., Milner, R., and Sackett D. L. (1980). A randomised clinical trial of the Leboyer approach to childbirth, *New England Journal of Medicine*, **302**, 655–660.

Newton, N. and Newton, M. (1972). Childbirth in cross-cultural perspective, in *Modern Perspectives in Psycho-Obstetrics* (Ed. J. G. Howells), Oliver and Boyd, London.

Oakley, A. (1979). *Becoming a Mother*, Martin Robertson, Oxford.

Oakley, A. (1980). *Women Confined: Towards a Sociology of Childbirth*, Martin Robertson, Oxford.

Paul, L. (1974). The mastery of work and the mystery of sex in a Guatemalan village, in *Women, Culture and Society* (Eds M. Z. Rosaldo and L. Lamphere), A. S. Barnes, New York.

Richards, M. P. M. (1975). Some recent research on the effects of obstetric anaesthetics and analgesics on mother and child: An annotated bibliography. Unpublished paper, Child Care and Development Group, University of Cambridge.

Richards, M. P. M. (1978). Possible effects of early separation on later development of children—A review, in *Separation and Special Care Baby Units* (Eds F. S. W. Brimblecombe, M. P. M. Richards, and N. K. C. Robertson), Heinemann Medical Publications, London.

Richards, M. P. M. and Bernal J. F. (1971). Effects of obstetric medication on mother–infant interaction and infant development, Paper presented to Third International Congress of Psychosomatic Medicine in Obstetrics and Gynaecology, London, April.

Schultze, L. (1907). *Aus Nanaland und Kalahari*, Gustave Fischer, Jena.

Shaw, N. S. (1974). *Forced Labour*, Pergamon Press, New York.

Spier, L. (1933). *Yuman Tribes of the Gila River*, University of Chicago Press, Chicago.

Stacey, M. (1975). Sociological and psychological implications of the new styles of childbirth, Paper given to Human Relations and Obstetric Practice Seminar, University of Warwick, 25th October.

Stinson, R. and Stinson, P. (1979). On the death of a baby, *Society for Obstetric Anesthesia and Perinatology Newsletter*, Fall, II, 2, 1–7.

Trezenem, E. (1936). *Notes Ethnographiques Sur les Tribus Fan du Moyen Ogoone (Garbon)*, Au Siege de la Societe, Paris.

Van Gennep, A. (1960). *The Rites of Passage*, Routlege and Kegan Paul, London.

Wales, H. G. Q. (1933), Siamese theory and ritual connection with pregnancy, birth and infancy, *Journal of the Royal Anthropological Institute of Great Britain and Ireland*, **63**, 441–451.

Wellin, E. (1955), Maternal and infant feeding practices in a Peruvian village, *Journal of American Dietetic Association*, **31**, 889–894.

Wright, J. (1921). Collective review—the view of primitive peoples concerning the process of labour, *American Journal of Obstetrics and Gynecology*, **2**, 206–210.

Psychobiology of the Human Newborn
Edited by P. Stratton
© 1982, John Wiley & Sons, Ltd.

CHAPTER 12

The Newborn Baby—Adaptation and Disease

MALCOLM L. CHISWICK

Recognition of the continuity between fetal and postnatal life is the basis for understanding physiology and pathology in the newborn. Birth is an incident—albeit an important one—in an individual's life-time.

BIRTH AND ADAPTATION

Adaptation to life outside the womb is not an event that occurs abruptly at birth. Although the onset of breathing normally occurs instantaneously, other changes take longer to complete. Cardiovascular adaptation takes several hours; modifications in the renal handling of water and electrolytes occur for several days after birth; changes involving the central nervous system take place so insidiously that they merge imperceptibly with continuous postnatal development.

The introduction of oxygen into the body and the excretion of carbon-dioxide are fundamental processes that permit oxidative metabolism; in fetal life the placenta is the organ of gaseous exchange. The fetal lungs are filled with liquid (Strang, 1977) which is continuous with the amniotic fluid (liquor amnii) that surrounds the outside of the fetus. As the fetus matures specialized lung cells produce increasing amounts of a complex phospholipid known as surfactant. This has the important property of reducing surface tension within the lungs, thereby facilitating their expansion after birth. Lack of surfactant is prone to occur in prematurely born babies and results in distressed breathing. Surfactant is detected in the amniotic fluid and its concentration may be measured during pregnancy to indicate whether the fetal lungs are yet mature enough for extra-uterine life—a test useful in the management of certain ill fetuses (Gluck et al., 1971; Gluck and Kulovich, 1973). From as early as 11 weeks gestation intermittent movements of the chest wall—fetal breathing movements—can be recognized by ultrasound examination (Boddy and Robinson, 1971). It is as though the fetus practises that activity which his life will soon become dependent upon. At present the measurement of fetal breathing movements is a research tool but it may have a place in clinical practice because some ill fetuses have a disturbed pattern (Boddy, and Dawes, 1975). Fluid is squeezed out of the lungs as the chest wall is compressed in the birth canal; it is usual to see a gush of liquid coming from the nose and mouth when the head is born. Lung fluid is also absorbed into the pulmonary lymphatics. The onset of breathing at birth is triggered by tactile stimuli, by exposure to a cooler environment and by a transient fall in blood oxygen and rise in carbon dioxide levels that occur when the umbilical cord is severed (Chernick, 1977).

The fetal blood circulation (Dawes, 1968a) is quite unlike that of the young baby. The umbilical vein carries oxygenated blood from the placenta to the fetus but even so, the oxygen content of fetal blood is much lower compared with that of newborn babies or adults. The fetal circulation is so designed that the head is supplied with blood of a higher oxygen saturation than that supplying the lower part of the body. Two umbilical arteries carry blood to the placenta from the fetus. Changes occur in the circulation at birth when, with the onset of breathing, a sudden increase in lung perfusion occurs, and when the placenta is excluded by severance of the umbilical cord. Functional closure of fetal channels precedes anatomical closure by several weeks or even months. Persistance of anatomical fetal channels between the venous and arterial sides of the circulation may lead to shunting of poorly oxygenated venous blood into the arterial circulation in some ill newborn babies (Gersony, 1973).

The central core temperature of the fetus is about 38.0°C which is 1°C higher than that of the mother; one function of the placenta is the dissipation of heat produced by the fetus. At birth the baby's temperature falls by 2–2.5°C as heat loss occurs via the skin. Drying and clothing the baby and preventing his exposure to draughts minimises heat loss so that a normal rectal temperature of 37°C may be achieved by 30–40 min. The baby is to a great extent dependent on his care-giver for successful thermal adaptation and it is likely that snuggling the dry but naked baby against his mother immediately after birth conserves heat satisfactorily providing that the room is not too cool. Subjected to cold stress, he cannot shiver to increase heat production but instead metabolizes brown fat (Dawkins and Hull, 1964), which is situated at the base of the neck, between the scapulae and surrounding the kidneys and adrenals. Brown fat, so called because its high vascularity gives a brown appearance, accounts for 2–6 per cent of the total body weight. Its metabolism in the face of cold stress is known as 'non-shivering thermogenesis' (Alexander, 1975). The cost of extra heat produced this way is the parallel increase in oxygen and calorie consumption which certain low birthweight babies can ill afford—(Adamson et al., 1965; Glass, et al., 1968).

The nutritional consequences of separating the baby from the placenta are no less important than the other sequelae. The neonate has an innate capacity to breathe, is largely dependent on his care-giver for the maintenance of a normal body temperature but is *wholly* dependent on his care-giver for adequate nutrition. Unlike the adult the baby also has to contend with growth. Fetal growth accelerates during the last 6 months of gestation and towards the end, weight gain is about 35 g per day (Usher, and McLean, 1974). The weight loss that normally occurs after birth mainly reflects loss of body water and does not normally exceed 10 per cent of the birthweight. By the tenth day the birth weight is usually regained and thereafter daily weight gain falls to 30 g by 2 months and declines throughout infancy. The nutritional advantages to the baby of breast milk compared with unmodified cows milk are well known but now many modified ('humanized') milks are commercially available. Unlike fresh human milk none of these commercial preparations contain factors that protect against infection and in a minority of babies they seem to precipitate allergic disorders (Butler, 1979). Breast feeding involves psychobiological feedback mechanisms that are not operative during bottle feeding. Transport of milk to the nipple ('let down') occurs when a mother interprets her baby's cry as being caused by hunger; milk production itself is stimulated by sucking. The concentration of certain constituents of breast milk changes progressively during a single feed—for example the fat concentration increases (Macy *et al.*, 1931; Wright, Chapter 13). One can only speculate about the significance of such changes; perhaps they are implicated in the feeling of satiation and are a signal to baby to terminate feeding (Hall, 1975). During a feed it is the baby who is likely to break contact with the breast by removing his mouth from the nipple; whereas in the bottle fed baby it is as likely to be the mother who decides when the teat should be removed from baby's mouth (Dunn, 1975). Nutritional adaptation in the normal baby need not be associated with the imposition of rigid constraints. Feeding, whether by breast or bottle, should be allowed on demand with the baby deciding how much to take and when to take it: *The Mechanical Baby* (Beekman, 1979) is an anachronism.

DISEASES OF THE NEWBORN

Virtually all disorders in the newborn have their origins with events that operate in the womb; just as there is continuity of physiology—so there is continuity of pathology. The expressions 'perinatal mortality' and 'perinatal morbidity' recognize this concept for they refer to death or disease occurring in the womb from the twenty-eighth week of gestation through to the end of the first week of life. Still births and early neonatal death make a roughly equal contribution to perinatal mortality.

Intrauterine hypoxia and malformation are the most common causes of still birth but perhaps up to 25 per cent of normally formed fetuses die without clinical or postmortem evidence of hypoxia and without definite evidence of the cause of death. Even when 'intrauterine hypoxia' is the label applied, there may be no clues to the underlying mechanism. Poorly growing fetuses are certainly vulnerable to hypoxia both before and after the onset of labour and the urge to use the term 'placental insufficiency' is understandable. However, this expression is certainly not justified on the basis of placental examination because significant placental lesions are hardly ever found. Most deaths in the neonatal period (i.e. birth–28 days) occur during the first week. Indeed, more babies die during the first week than in the whole of the succeeding four or five years. About 70 per cent of early neonatal deaths occur in babies who weigh less than 2500 g at birth—low birth-weight babies (LBW); lethal malformations account for most of the remainder of deaths. Of course mortality is only one side of the coin; the scars of some insults which occur in the womb or soon after birth may be manifest as handicaps such as cerebral palsy, blindness, deafness, epilepsy and mental subnormality in later infancy and childhood (Davies, & Stewart, 1975; Fitzhardinge *et al.*, 1978).

A full-term normally formed baby who suffers no complications before or during birth rarely develops significant problems after birth. Nevertheless, disorders that do not pose a threat to life such as transient feeding difficulty and physiological jaundice are common and may cause parental anxiety. When the onset of breathing is significantly delayed in a full-term normal baby there are usually precipitating factors associated with fetal hypoxia such as prolapse of the umbilical cord, or the baby's respiratory centre is depressed by maternally administered analgesic drugs. Although the full-term normal fetus is considered low risk his behaviour may be adversely influenced by current obstetric practices that are aimed at preventing complications. The balance between reduced fetal mortality and morbidity as a result of modern obstetric policies of monitoring and intervention in high-risk fetuses and their precipitation of undesirable effects in low-risk fetuses is a fine one.

LOW BIRTH-WEIGHT BABIES

About two-thirds of LBW babies are born prematurely before 37 weeks gestation yet have normal growth for their gestational age. The remainder are babies of different gestational ages, including those at term or beyond term, who have grown poorly in the womb—so called light-for-dates (LFD) babies. Of course a baby may weigh more than 2500 g and still be premature or LFD.

PREMATURITY

In general, perinatal and early neonatal mortality rates in a community reflect its incidence of prematurity; those countries with relatively low mortality rates enjoy a low incidence of prematurity. Much of the inter-regional variation in perinatal and neonatal mortality within a country parallels differences in premature birth rates. Numerous factors have been shown to be *associated* with

Table 1   Problems of premature babies

1   Respiratory distress syndrome
2   Recurrent apnoeic attacks
3   Impaired thermal homeostasis
4   Feeding problems
5   Jaundice
6   Infection
7   Intraventricular and subarachnoid haemorrhage
8   Necrotizing enterocolitis
9   Functional intestinal obstruction

premature birth but causative mechanisms are poorly understood. A prominent associated element is poverty and deprivation; premature birth is twice as common amongst social class 4 and 5 women in Britain compared with those of social class 1 (Chamberlain *et al.*, 1975). The explanation of this association is one of the most urgent needs in perinatal medicine. To cite inadequate nutrition, smoking, psychosocial stress and failure to take up antenatal care confuses association with cause. It also ignores the fact that numerous premature babies are born to women who appear to have a normal diet, do not smoke, suffer daily stress that is no worse than the average woman, and who avail themselves of regular antenatal care.

Gestational age may be assessed by the date of the last menstrual period (LMP), by antenatal investigation and by postnatal examination of the baby. The most reliable is the LMP but this may not be known with certainty. Gestational age of the baby is estimated by examination of the nervous system and certain physical characteristics (Dubowitz *et al.*, 1970). As gestation advances flexor muscle tone increases and certain reflexes appear in chronological order. There are also changes in the appearance of the skin, breast tissue, ears and genitalia.

The problems encountered in premature babies can usually be ascribed to maladaptation to extrauterine life because of immaturity of various organ systems (Table 1). Admission to a special care baby unit (SCBU) must never be based merely on birthweight because this might promote unnecessary separation of mothers and babies. Many premature babies have reached at least 35 weeks gestation; they can suck adequately or need only the occasional tube feed *(vide infra)* and they are preferably nursed with their mothers on the maternity ward. Those less than 35 weeks gestation require careful monitoring which is best carried out on the SCBU.

Respiratory Distress Syndrome (RDS)

This affects about 10 per cent of premature babies and is the single most common cause of death in the first week. There is a decreasing incidence from 28

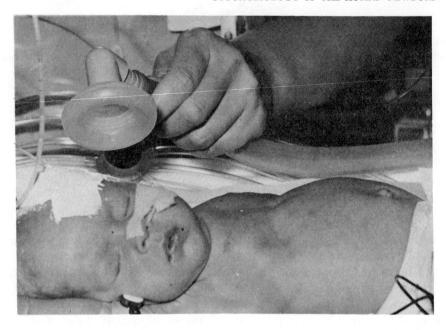

Figure 1   A premature baby with respiratory distress syndrome showing retraction of
the lower chest wall on inspiration

weeks gestation to term. A rapid respiratory rate, retraction of the thoracic cage
on inspiration, and grunting on expiration develop soon after birth (Figure 1).
The lungs are stiff, difficult to inflate and collapse readily on expiration. The
underlying abnormality is a high surface tension within the terminal air spaces
(alveoli) because of lack of surfactant (Avery and Mead, 1959) and at post
mortem the lungs usually appear solid because of the collapsed alveoli. The
histological hallmark of the disease is the presence within alveoli of hyaline
membranes that stain pink with eosin—hence the alternative name, 'hyaline
membrane disease'. The membranes consist of fibrin derived from the
circulation.

Surfactant is naturally replenished over the course of several days after birth.
During this time the baby must be kept safely oxygenated by adjusting the
ambient oxygen concentration to maintain the partial pressure of oxygen (PO_2)
in the blood between 50 and 90 mm Hg. The risk of hypoxic brain damage and
bleeding into the ventricles of the brain is increased at PO_2 levels below
40 mm Hg. On the other hand PO_2 levels maintained above 150 mm Hg for
several hours are associated with damage to the retina (retrolental fibroplasia)
and blindness (Kinsey et al., 1956; Committee on Fetus and Newborn, 1971). By
1950 this was the single most common cause of child blindness in the United
States. Careful monitoring of blood oxygen levels is a key part of a baby's care;
for this purpose small samples of arterial blood (less than 1.0 ml) are taken 4–6

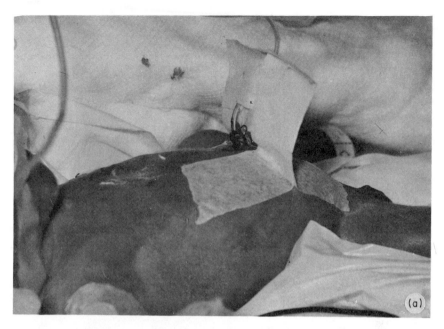

Figure 2a   A catheter for continuously monitoring the arterial PO_2 level is passed
into the umbilical artery and secured by adhesive tape

Figure 2b   A monitoring box to which the umbilical artery catheter is attached
continuously records the arterial PO_2 level (65 mm Hg)

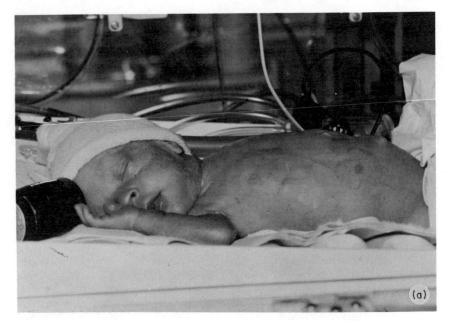

Figure 3a   An electrode is attached to the skin of the abdominal wall in this ill baby and continuously records the transcutaneous PO_2 level. The probe adjacent to the baby's forehead measures the ambient oxygen concentration

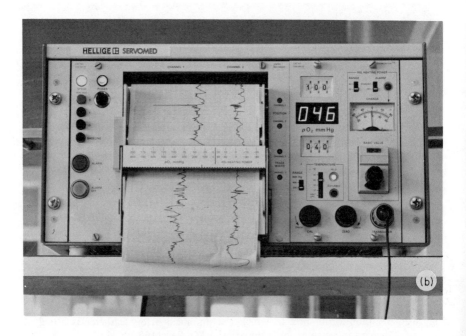

Figure 3b   A monitoring box to which the skin electrode is attached continuously records the transcutaneous PO_2 level (channel 1, 46 mm Hg)

hourly from an indwelling catheter that has been passed through an umbilical artery so that its tip lies within the aorta. The marked instability of PO_2 values in sick babies led to the development and widespread availability of an umbilical artery catheter with an electrode at its tip that continuously monitored PO_2 levels (Conway et al., 1976) (Figure 2). Another important finding was that PO_2 measured by a heated electrode placed on the baby's skin (transcutaneous PO_2 ($tcPO_2$)) correlated quite well with intra-arterial PO_2 (Le Souef et al., 1978). This non-invasive method of oxygen monitoring is a helpful adjunct to intra-arterial monitoring but does not entirely replace it (Figure 3). In 1971, Gregory et al. (1971) described the success of continuous positive airways pressure (CPAP) treatment for RDS. The baby is allowed to breathe spontaneously against a positive pressure of 5–10 cm H_2O applied by an endotracheal tube, face mask (Rhodes and Hall, 1973) or nasal prongs (Kattwinkel et al., 1973) or by enclosing the head in a small pressurized perspex cylinder.

In spite of CPAP and an oxygen enriched environment, progressive hypoxaemia or other signs of respiratory failure develop in a minority of babies and their breathing must be assisted by a mechanical ventilator or they will die. The facilities and skills needed for providing ventilatory assistance for several days or even weeks are such that the service is best concentrated in a limited number of neonatal intensive care units in each region. Regional organization of neonatal intensive care is already well developed in North America and in some European countries and it is a pattern that is emerging in Britain (Chiswick, 1980). Its success depends on the safe transportation of critically ill babies to the regional unit (Blake et al., 1975; Ferrara and Harin, 1980). Problems of maternal-infant separation have been raised but there are ways of minimizing these and they are of secondary importance to the immediate physical health of the baby.

Recurrent Apnoeic Attacks

During the first two weeks of life about one-third of babies less than 35 weeks gestation who are apparently healthy suffer recurrent episodes of cessation of breathing—apnoeic attacks. They range in frequency from one or two each day to numerous attacks in the space of an hour. Each may last several seconds before breathing spontaneously recommences, or more than a minute and resuscitation may be needed. When there is no apparent cause, as is common, the troublesome condition is labelled 'apnoea of prematurity'. It is as if the baby has reverted back to the fetal state of intermittent breathing movements. Unless attacks are anticipated and promptly treated severe hypoxaemia and circulatory failure may result. All babies less than 35 weeks gestation should have their breathing and heart rate continuously monitored during the first two weeks of life so that any abnormality can be at once detected by an audible alarm. At the beginning of an attack simple external stimulation such as stroking a limb is usually enough to restart breathing. The frequency of attacks can often be reduced by nursing the baby in 25 per cent oxygen instead of air, (Miller *et al.*, 1959), using CPAP (Kattwinkel *et al.*, 1975), maintaining the skin temperature at 36.1–36.2°C instead of 36.5°C (Daily *et al.*, 1969), repetitive tactile stimulation of the skin (Kattwinkel *et al.*, 1975), or by administering aminophylline (Kuzemko and Paala, 1973), theophylline (Shannon *et al.*, 1975), or caffeine citrate (Aranda *et al.*, 1977). In spite of these measures frequent or prolonged attacks threaten the lives of some babies and mechanical ventilation becomes necessary.

Thermal Homeostasis

The very premature baby is disadvantaged in a number of ways, not the least being that nursing observations are best made with him naked or semi-naked, particularly if there are respiratory symptoms. Unless the incubator temperature is accurately maintained and heat loss from the baby is minimized, significant brown fat metabolism is inevitable to maintain a normal central core temperature. Valuable calories are thus diverted away from growth and it is not surprising that premature babies subjected to cold stress grow poorly compared with appropriately nursed control babies (Glass *et al.*, 1969), and have a higher mortality (Silverman *et al.*, 1958).

Feeding Problems

The premature baby less than 35 weeks gestation cannot suck properly, has impaired swallowing, and has difficulty in protecting the airways from liquids that were intended for the stomach which itself has a small volume. With these handicaps and with milk as a food he strives to grow as well as he would have done in the womb where he received his nutrients directly into the blood. Babies who are extremely premature, say less than 30 weeks gestation, can be fed safely with milk through an indwelling tube that has been passed through the nose into the duodenum (Minoli *et al.*, 1978) or jejunum (Rhea *et al.*, 1973). This method of feeding extremely premature babies carries less risk of vomiting compared with nasogastric feeding—an important consideration because as much as 250 ml milk per kg body weight per day is required to sustain the growth of such small babies. Ill premature babies, particularly those with breathing problems, cannot be fed milk and require intravenous fluids and nutrients (Kerner and Sunshine, 1979). The vast majority of healthy premature babies more than 30 weeks gestation can be fed small volumes of milk at frequent intervals through a nasogastric tube, although the procedure is not without risk and fairly close nursing supervision is required. This is one reason why healthy cot-nursed premature babies remain on special-care baby units. What are the alternatives? Those babies could be cared for with their mothers on the maternity wards if the appropriate number of vigilant nursing staff were available there. They must recognize at an early stage those signs and symptoms which indicate that tube feeding should be stopped and the advice of a paediatrician sought. In trying to avoid separation of the mother from her premature baby the problem of the busy maternity ward containing high-risk antenatal women, and those recently delivered must be taken into account. Mothers are often ready to be discharged home when their babies are still requiring tube feeds but in most countries it is not feasible to provide domiciliary nursing services to safely supervise tube feeding in small babies.

Infection

Impaired defence mechanisms both at a cellular and circulating level render the premature baby vulnerable to infection (Larsen and Galask, 1977, Parkman 1977), Life-threatening conditions that may present with non-specific signs and symptoms include septicaemia, meningitis and pneumonia. Infection may be acquired from the maternal birth canal shortly before delivery. The organisms responsible are those that normally inhabit the vagina and ano-genital region, particularly *E scherichia* (*Coli* and Group B *haemolytic streptococcus*—the latter having become more prevalent during the past decade. Congenital haemolytic streptococcal infection is usually manifest as pneumonia and septicaemia in the first 48 h of life and carries a mortality of 50 per cent or more (Franciosi *et al.*, 1973). Infections acquired postnatally do not usually come to light until after the first week; they are liable to occur during exposure to 'invasive' treatment, e.g. indwelling endotracheal tubes, intravenous catheters or when organisms are transferred to the baby or his incubator by the unwashed hands of attendants. If antibiotics are to be effective they must be used early in the course of an infective illness. One problem is that infection in premature babies is difficult to diagnose in the early stages, presenting as it does with vague signs of ill health. A balance must be struck between on the one hand unnecessary exposure of babies to antibiotics and on the other hand delayed treatment.

Jaundice

Jaundice is very common in newborn babies, particularly in those born prematurely. 'Physiological jaundice' occurs between the third and sixth day and the vulnerability of premature babies is partly explained by their partial deficiency of a liver enzyme, glucuronyl transferase (*vide infra*). It is axiomatic that jaundice is also associated with a wide variety of serious disorders in the newborn including haemolytic disease, metabolic abnormalities, and infection. The decision to investigate a jaundiced baby is based on the history and clinical findings.

The pigment normally responsible for the yellow discolouration is fat-soluble bilirubin which is produced by the breakdown of the ageing population of red blood cells. Fat soluble bilirubin circulates in the blood bound to albumin; it is carried to the liver where it is changed to the water soluble form under the influence of the liver enzyme glucuronyl transferase. If the level of circulating bilirubin becomes very high it might exceed the binding capacity of plasma albumin and *free* fat-soluble bilirubin would be generated. This type of free bilirubin passes easily into certain brain cells and causes bilirubin encephalopathy or kernicterus, a condition with a high mortality and characterized by fits, arching of the back, downward deviation of the eyes and apnoeic attacks. The sequelae in survivors are cerebral palsy, deafness and mental retardation (Byers *et al.*, 1955; Odell *et al.*, 1970). The assay of free bilirubin in the blood is not generally available nor would it be helpful because by the time it is detectable the risk of kernicterus is substantial. Conventionally total serum bilirubin is measured which is normally all bound to albumin. In individual jaundiced babies an arbitrary bilirubin level is set above which there is thought to be a risk of kernicterus and treatment is aimed at preventing this level being exceeded (Table 2). The premature baby is at a disadvantage because he is prone to suffer kernicterus at lower levels of circulating bilirubin compared with a mature baby. Vulnerability to kernicterus is also increased in the presence of acidaemia, hypoxaemia and infection and these are all more likely to occur in premature babies.

Exchange transfusion was originally introduced as a method of removing sensitized red blood cells from the circulation in babies with rhesus haemolytic disease (Diamond 1947). It lowers the serum bilirubin concentration in jaundice from any cause. Small aliquots of blood (10–20 ml) are removed through an umbilical venous catheter and replaced by equal volumes of donor blood. The total volume of blood exchanged is generally 180–200 ml per kg body weight, which is about twice a baby's blood volume. Up until recently the main need for exchange transfusions was for babies suffering from Rhesus haemolytic disease, but the incidence of this condition has fallen abruptly since the use of Rhesus immune globulin (anti-D) in Rhesus negative mothers (Freda *et al.*, 1975). Now an increasing proportion of exchange transfusions are carried out on ill

Table 2 Serum bilirubin levels (μmol L^{-1}) above which it is considered the risk of kernicterus is increased and exchange transfusion is recommended in healthy and ill babies of different birthweights

Birthweight (g)	Serum bilirubin concentration (μmol L^{-1})	
	Healthy	Ill
< 1000	150	100
1001–1500	200	150
1501–2000	250	200
2001–2500	300	250
> 2500	350–400	300

premature babies who previously would not have survived long enough for jaundice to have become a problem.

Phototherapy is another method of lowering the serum bilirubin concentration. (Cremer et al., 1958; Lucey et al., 1968). When light at the blue end of the spectrum (450 nm) is shone onto the skin of jaundiced babies the bilirubin circulating in the capillaries is photo-oxidized to bilirubin metabolites which are thought to be harmless. Phototherapy is commonly used to slow down the rate of rise in bilirubin levels and to try and avert the need for exchange transfusion. There is much variation in policy regarding the indications for phototherapy in different maternity hospitals. There is no convincing evidence that a range of developmental abnormality occurs in response to a wide spectrum of serum bilirubin levels. It is therefore difficult to sanction the widespread use of phototherapy in otherwise healthy full-term jaundiced babies, particularly as the treatment itself is not conducive to mother–infant attachment.

Intracranial Haemorrhage

The ability to support the lives of critically ill premature babies, particularly those with respiratory failure has led to the emergence of intracranial haemorrhage as the most important factor limiting survival and the long-term prognosis. The cause of bleeding into the ventricles and subarachnoid space is not entirely known but it does appear to be associated with episodes of hypoxaemia and possibly transient rises in blood pressure (Pape and Wigglesworth, 1979). The use of the real-time ultrasound scanner has shown that small, symptom-free intraventricular haemorrhages are common in premature babies (Levine et al., 1981). It is too early to know how these small haemorrhages might influence long-term development. Certainly a significant proportion of premature babies who have survived acute symptoms of intracranial haemorrhage such as pallor, fits or apnoeic attacks develop post-haemorrhagic obstructive hydrocephalus in the ensuing weeks (Korobkin, 1975) (Figures 4 and 5). An increasingly common dilemma is the management of the baby who develops signs of intracranial haemorrhage whilst receiving mechanical ventilation. If there is a massive haemorrhage the baby generally dies promptly in spite of ventilatory support. A wide range of clinical abnormality accompanies lesser degrees of haemorrhage and the risk of long-term handicap in survivors is difficult to assess. The decision whether or not to terminate ventilatory support is rarely an easy one. It is clear that future developments in neonatal intensive care must be aimed at the prevention of intracranial haemorrhage in premature babies.

LIGHT-FOR-DATES BABIES

Many of the factors *associated* with premature birth are also *associated* with fetal growth retardation. Light-for-dates (LFD) babies are a heterogeneous group

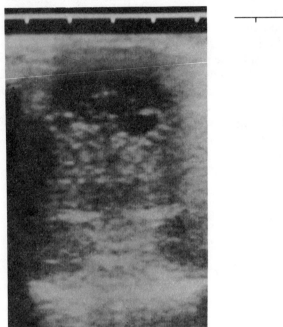
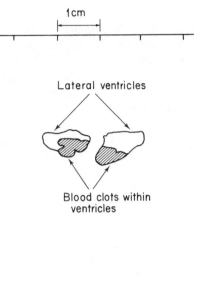

Figure 4a   Coronal plane ultrasound scan of the brain performed 2 days after birth in a
28-week gestation baby with respiratory distress syndrome. Both lateral ventricles contain
blood clots

with a varied aetiology. The term 'placental insufficiency' does little to explain the
cause of fetal growth retardation. Although the placentae of LFD babies are
small, the ratio of placental/fetal body weight is normal (Scott and Usher, 1966).
In about 10 per cent there are also one or more structural malformations and
here growth failure is just one part of an intrinsic fetal problem that was
determined early in gestation. The most commonly reported intrauterine
infections causing poor fetal growth are with cytomegalovirus and rubella virus.
The relationship between maternal nutrition and fetal growth is not a simple one;
there is certainly strong evidence that the mean birthweight of a population is
reduced by famine (Antonov, 1947). Although there appears to be some sparing of
the brain in fetal growth retardation, the weight of the brain is a crude reflection
of its growth. Dobbing showed that the human brain underwent two separate
growth spurts, from 15 to 20 weeks gestation and from 30 weeks gestation to 18
months postnatal age (Dobbing, 1974). The developing brain is most vulnerable
during times of rapid growth and the *timing* of fetal growth failure may be a
critical factor in determining the outcome in terms of intellectual function.

The continuum of mortality and morbidity between the fetus and the newborn

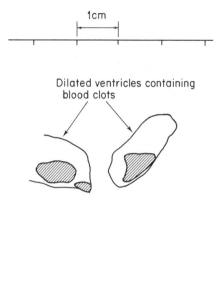

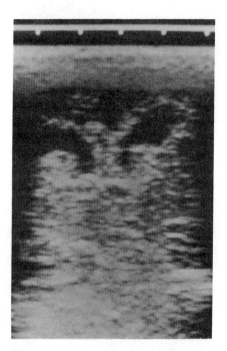

Figure 4b   The same patient scanned at 4 days. Both lateral ventricles have significantly enlarged and still contain blood clots. (Ultrasound scans by courtesy of Dr M Gowland, Department of Radiology, St Mary's Hospital, Marchester)

is illustrated *par excellence* by the LFD baby who is vulnerable during the last trimester of pregnancy, during labour and delivery, and in the neonatal period (Table 3). The increased risk of hypoxia in poorly growing fetuses is partly related to their low stores of liver and cardiac glycogen. One common dilemma is that to allow a fetus to remain inside a uterus that is not supporting growth exposes him to an increasing risk of hypoxia as gestation advances. On the other hand, to

Table 3   Vulnerability of light-for-dates fetuses

1   Congenital malformation
2   Antepartum hypoxia
3   Intrapartum hypoxia
4   Delayed onset of breathing
5   Meconium aspiration syndrome
6   Hypoglycaemia
7   Impaired thermal homeostasis
8   Pulmonary haemorrhage
9   Polycythaemia

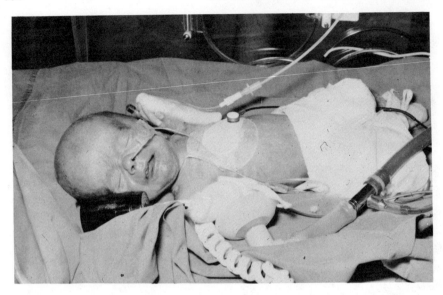

Figure 5   The patient whose ultrasound scans are shown in Figure 4 now seen at the age of 3 weeks. Enlargement at the head is caused by post-haemorrhagic obstructive hydrocephalus

expedite delivery before term leads to those hazards in the neonatal period associated with prematurity.

Fetal Hypoxia and Delayed Onset of Breathing

When there is clinical or some other evidence of fetal hypoxia a delay in the onset of breathing at birth can be anticipated and a paediatrician should be present at the delivery. If the hypoxia was relatively mild the baby's condition at birth is likely to be favourable with only moderate slowing of the heart rate and a normal blood pressure. An adaptive mechanism operates to preferentially direct blood to the brain, heart, and adrenal glands (Dawes, 1968b). In this stage of 'primary apnoea' various external stimuli such as a gentle pat on the soles of the feet usually induce a gasp followed by crying or normal breathing. Gasping also occurs in response to suctioning the pharynx with a soft catheter—a procedure that is performed routinely in many maternity hospitals. Oxygen is commonly given by face mask to babies with primary apnoea so that when breathing commences oxygen enriched air enters the lungs. Analgesics such as pethidine and morphine given in large doses to the mother during labour prolong primary apnoea and antagonists to these drugs may be given by injection to affected babies. When fetal asphyxia is severe the baby may be born in the stage of 'terminal apnoea'. The heart rate is slow, the blood pressure is low and circulatory failure causes the baby to appear very pale. Blood supply to the brain and heart are severely compromized. Death is certain unless artificial ventilation (positive pressure ventilation) is given—preferably through a tube passed into the trachea via the mouth. Cardiac massage is often necessary to improve the circulation and intravenous sodium bicarbonate is usually given to counteract the profound acidaemia.

Parents invariably question what the future will hold for their baby who has recovered from severe perinatal hypoxia. A poor prognosis should never be given unless there are compelling reasons for so doing. Parental–baby attachment during the first few weeks of life may become prejudiced by a few badly chosen words. It is far better to err on the side of optimism, to stress the need for regular developmental assessment and to allow the outlook to unfold gradually. Many affected babies are neurologically abnormal for several days after birth, but gradually improve thereafter and develop normally (D'Souza and Richards, 1978). As a general guide the features that adversely influence the long-term prognosis following perinatal hypoxia are the occurrence of terminal rather than primary apnoea, the presence of associated features such as LBW and hypoglycaemia (a low blood sugar concentration); frequent convulsions during the first week of life; the persistence of abnormal neurological signs; and lack of adequate stimulation at home.

Other Problems in LFD Babies

Hypoxia may cause the fetus to evacuate his bowels of meconium and to gasp whilst still in the womb. Aspiration of amniotic fluid contaminated with meconium may cause severe breathing difficulty after birth—meconium aspiration syndrome.

Babies who are LFD are prone to develop hypoglycaemia (blood glucose less than 1.1 mmol l^{-1}) during the first week of life; this is associated with poor liver stores of glycogen—a glucose precursor, and with impaired conversion of protein to carbohydrate by the liver. Hypoglycaemia can be rapidly detected by noting the colour change that occurs when a drop of capillary blood is placed on a paper test strip known as a Dextrostix (Ames Ltd). All LFD babies should be screened for hypoglycaemia at least 8 hourly during the first few days of life because it is commonly asymptomatic and easily treated by increasing the volume of the milk feeds. Symptomatic hypoglycaemia presents with diverse symptoms including fits, apnoeic attacks and lethargy; it was more common in the days when feeding of small babies was delayed and dilute milk feeds were given. A continuous intravenous infusion of 10 per cent glucose usually leads to a sustained increase in the blood glucose concentration. Nevertheless, symptomatic hypoglycaemia is a serious condition with a relatively high incidence of long term handicap in survivors (Koivisto et al., 1972), particularly if associated with perinatal hypoxia.

Finally LFD babies share with premature babies impaired thermal control. A large surface area relative to body weight and reduced amounts of subcutaneous fat make the LFD baby vulnerable to heat loss; poor stores of brown fat reduce his ability to compensate by increased heat production.

CONGENITAL ABNORMALITIES

Probably about a half of all conceptions are aborted—many at a very early stage of development, and 60 per cent of spontaneous abortions are associated with chromosome abnormalities (De Grouchy, 1976). It is clear that nature recognizes and deals appropriately with most of her imperfections. However, 3–4 per cent of newborn babies have a significant abnormality which is apparent on initial examination or is revealed during the first week. The incidence is about three times higher in infants of diabetic mothers (Simpson, 1978) and LFD babies (Ounsted and Ounsted, 1973). The most common sites involved are the central nervous system, limbs and heart; many affected babies have malformations involving more than one system. Furthermore, severe constraints may be put on metabolic function by genetic abnormalities. Although individual inborn errors of metabolism are rare, their importance is first that prompt diagnosis and dietary manipulation may control certain disorders; secondly there is the risk that further offspring of the parents will be affected.

The evolution of services for genetic counselling and antenatal diagnosis of certain abnormalities has been very rapid. There is no shortage of information available to the public through the popular media—and this at a time when the medical profession itself has much to learn about the most effective use of these newer services. Whereas in the past the birth of a malformed baby was inclined to be surrounded by taboo, even before conception today's mother-to-be might express her anxieties about the possibility of giving birth to abnormal offspring. The prevention of congenital abnormality is an irresistible concept but in the vast majority of cases the cause is unknown, a well-defined method of inheritance does not operate and antenatal diagnosis is not practical. Perhaps this simple and depressing message has become lost amidst our enthusiasm, and parents have been led to expect too much. There is the danger that those unfortunate enough to have abnormal babies become supercritical of themselves and their role in the abnormality and of the medical profession for letting them down.

True prevention might entail the avoidance of conception when the family history suggests a high risk of recurrence of an abnormality, or when a woman is of advancing years and has an increased risk of conceiving a child with a chromosome abnormality. Conditions that might be prevented this way make an extremely small contribution to the overall incidence of congenital abnormality. Another preventative measure is the avoidance of those insults early in pregnancy which are known to cause fetal abnormality. Probably the best publicized examples are infection with rubella virus (German measles)

(Hanshaw and Dudgeon, 1978) and ingestion of the drug thalidomide (McBride, 1977). Immunization against German measles is now widely practised and of course all drugs and exposure to X-rays should be avoided in early pregnancy. There is no evidence that such agents play a major role in the prevailing pattern of congenital abnormality. Poor nutrition (Naeye *et al.*, 1969), smoking (Witter and King, 1980), and excess drinking of alcohol (Smith, 1970) have each been implicated as possible causal agents; epidemiological research is bedevilled by the interdependance of these and other factors and by their possible adverse influence even before conception. The possibility of preventing neural tube defects (spina bifida, anencephaly) by maternal vitamin supplementation cannot be ignored (Smithells *et al.*, 1980).

Early antenatal diagnosis of fetal abnormality and termination of pregnancy is often cited as a method of 'preventing' congenital defects but of course it is not. Nor, with an increasing enthusiasm for antenatal diagnosis, must it be assumed that the technical wherewithal to make a diagnosis is a passport for termination of pregnancy. The extent to which an abnormality may be described as intolerably handicapping depends not only on the nature of the condition itself and its amenability to treatment, but also on the family ambience.

The largest *group* of disorders for which antenatal diagnosis is available is the inborn errors of metabolism (Bergsma, 1979). Diagnosis is generally based on biochemical analysis of the amniotic fluid, or of the fetal cells shed into the fluid. It is totally inpractical to offer all pregnant women amniocentesis for the diagnosis of inborn errors of metabolism because they are exceedingly rare and the biochemical tests are specific for individual disorders. Most are inherited as an autosomal recessive and the practical application of these tests is when the parents have already given birth to a baby with a known rare metabolic abnormality and there is a 1 in 4 risk of subsequent offspring being affected by the identical abnormality.

By far the most prevalent conditions for which antenatal diagnosis is performed is Down's syndrome (mongolism) and neural tube defects (spina bifida, anencephaly). Chromosome analysis of the fetal cells shed into the amniotic fluid allows those fetuses with an extra chromosome characteristic of Down's syndrome to be diagnosed and pregnancy terminated. Although there is an increased risk of this condition with advancing maternal age, even at 40 years the risk is only about 1 in 100, and at 35 years, 1 in 350 (Hook, and Chambers, 1977). In some hospitals all women older than 35 years are offered amniocentesis for Down's syndrome because beyond this age the diagnostic benefits are thought to outweigh the risks of amniocentesis. Even if all those women agreed to have amniocentesis, at least two-thirds of all babies with Down's syndrome would go unrecognized because they are born to women younger than 35 years.

An abnormally high concentration of the chemical alphafetoprotein (AFP) can be detected in the amniotic fluid early in pregnancy if the fetus has anencephaly or a severe form of spina bifida (Brock and Sutcliffe, 1972). Up until several years ago amniocentesis for the antenatal diagnosis of these conditions was reserved for women who had previously given birth to a baby with a neural-tube defect, which carries a recurrence risk of about 1 in 20, or when there was other evidence of familial predisposition. However, about 90 per cent of infants born with neural-tube defects result from pregnancies not known to be at risk in this way. It was subsequently shown that the measurement of maternal plasma AFP concentration in early pregnancy could be used as a useful screening test providing gestational age was known accurately because plasma AFP in early pregnancy is gestational age dependent (Brock et al., 1974). Many hospitals now offer plasma AFP screening to all pregnant women at 16–18 weeks gestation, and the need for amniocentesis is based on the result of the screening test.

A wide spectrum of congenital malformations ranging from isolated defects that pose no threat to life to multiple life-threatening abnormalities are amenable to surgical correction (Rickham et al., 1978). Improved methods of neonatal intensive care have led to better survival rates particularly in premature babies subjected to major surgery. The ethical dilemmas are well known. They are based on the enigma of the correct balance between on the one hand the emotional and physical pain babies and parents endure during a course of treatment that might involve not one but many operations and on the other hand the prospects of a normal or near normal life for babies born with an abnormality.

REFERENCES

Adamson, K., Gandy, G. M., and James, L. S. (1965). The influence of thermal factors upon oxygen consumption of the newborn human infant, J. Pediatr., 66, 495–508.

Alexander, G. (1975). Body temperature control in mammalian young, Brit. Med. Bull., 31, 62–68.

Antonov, A. N. (1947). Children born during the siege of Leningrad in 1942, J. Pediatr., 30, 250–259.

Aranda, J. V., Gorman, W. Bergsteinsson, H., and Gunn, T. (1977). Efficiency of caffeine in treatment of apnoea in low birthweight infant, J. Pediatr., 90, 467–472.

Avery, M. E. and Mead, J. (1959). Surface properties in relation to atelectasis and hyaline membrane disease, Am. J. Dis. Child., 97, 517–523.

Beekman, D. (1979). The Mechanical Baby, Dobson Books Ltd., London.

Bergsma, D. (Ed. 1979). Birth Defects Compendium, P. 1098, Macmillan, London.

Blake, A. M., McIntosh, N., Reynolds, E. O. R., and St. Andrew, D. (1975). Transport of newborn infants for intensive care, Lancet, 2, 13–17.

Boddy, K. and Dawes, G. S. (1975). Fetal breathing, Br. Med. Bull., 31, 3–7.

Boddy, K. and Robinson, J. S. (1971). External method for detection of fetal breathing in utero, Lancet, 2, 1231–1233.

Brock, D. J. H., Bolton, A. F., and Scrimgeour, J. B. (1974). Prenatal diagnosis of spina bifida and anencephaly through maternal plasma alpha-fetoprotein measurement, Lancet, 1, 767–769.

Brock, D. J. H. and Sutcliffe, R. G. (1972). Alpha-fetoprotein in the antenatal diagnosis of anencephaly and spina bifida, Lancet, 2, 197–199.

Butler, J. E. (1979). Immunological aspects of breast feeding, antiinfectious activity of breast milk, Sem. Perinat., 3, 255–270.

Byers, R. K., Paine, R. S., and Crothers, B. (1955). Extrapyramidal cerebral palsy with hearing loss following erythroblastosis, *Pediatrics*, **15**, 248–254.

Committee on Fetus and Newborn (1971). Standards and Recommendations for Hospital Care of Newborn Infants 5th. edition, Evanston, American Academy of Pediatrics.

Chamberlain, R., Chamberlain, G., Howlett, B., and Claireaux, A. (1975). *British Births 1970*, Vol. 1, *The First Week of Life*, Heinemann, London.

Chernick, V. (1977). Onset of breathing at birth, *Sem. Perinat.*, **1**, 343–346.

Chiswick, M. L. (1980). Regional organisation of neonatal intensive care, in *Topics in Perinatal Medicine* (Ed. B. A. Wharton), pp. 120–130, Pitman Medical, England.

Conway, M., Durbin, G. M., Ingram, D., McIntosh, N., Parker, D., Reynolds, E. O. R., and Soutter, L. P. (1976). Continuous monitoring of arterial oxygen tension using a catheter-tip polarographic electrode in infants, *Pediatrics*, **57**, 244–250.

Cremer, R., Perryman, P., and Richards, D. (1958). Influence of light on the hyperbilirubinaemia of infants, *Lancet*, **1**, 1094–1097.

Daily, W. J. R., Klaus, M., and Meyer, H. B. P. (1969). Apnoea in premature infants: Monitoring, incidence, and level of environmental temperature, *Pediatrics*, **43**, 510–518.

Davies, P. A. and Stewart, A. L. (1975). Low birthweight infants: neurological sequelae, *Brit. Med. Bull.* **31**, 85–91.

Dawes, G. (1968a). *Foetal and Neonatal Physiology*, Ch. 8, The foetal circulation, Year Book Medical Publishers, Chicago.

Dawes, G. (1968b) *Foetal and Neonatal Physiology*, Ch. 12, Birth asphyxia, resuscitation and brain damage, Year Book Medical Publishers, Chicago.

Dawkins, M. and Hull, D. (1964). Brown adipose tissue and the response of newborn rabbits to cold, *J. Physiol.*, **172**, 216–238.

De Grouchy, J. (1976). Human chromosomes and their anomalies, in *Aspects of Genetics in Paediatrics* (Ed. D. Barltrop), pp. 5–13, Unigate paediatric Workshops No. 3, Fellowship of Postgraduate Medicine, London.

Diamond, L. K. (1947). Erythroblastosis foetalis, *Proc. R. Soc. Med.*, **40**, 546–550.

Dobbing, J. (1974). The later development of the brain and its vulnerability, in *Scientific Foundations of Paediatrics* (Eds J. A. Davis and J. Dobbing), pp. 565–577, Heinemann, London.

D'Souza, S. W. and Richards, B. (1978). Neurological sequelae in newborn babies after perinatal asphyxia, *Arch. Dis. Child.*, **53**, 564–569.

Dubowitz, L., Dubowitz, V., and Goldberg, C. (1970). Clinical assessment of gestational age in the newborn infant, *J. Pediatr.*, **77**, 1–10.

Dunn, J. F. (1975). Consistency and change in styles of mothering, in *Parent-Infant Interaction*, pp. 155–176, Ciba Foundation Symposium 33 (new series), Elsevier, Excerpta Medica, North-Holland.

Ferrara, A. and Harin, A. (1980). *Emergency Transfer of the High-Risk Neonate*, C. V. Mosby, St. Louis, Toronto, London.

Fitzhardinge, P. M., Kalman, E., Ashby, S., and Pape, K. E. (1978). Present status of the infant of very low birthweight treated in a referral neonatal intensive care unit in 1974, in *Major Mental Handicap: Methods and Cost of Prevention*, pp. 139–144. Ciba Foundation Symposium 59 (new series); Elsevier, Excerpta Medica, North-Holland.

Franciosi, R. A., Knostman, J. D., and Zimmerman, R. A. (1973). Group B streptococcal neonatal and infant infections, *J. Pediatr.*, **82**, 707–718.

Freda, V. J., Gorman, J. G., Pollack, W., and Bowe, E. (1975). Prevention of Rh haemolytic disease—ten years clinical experience with Rh immune globulin, *N. Engl. J. Med.*, **292**, 1014–1016.

Gersony, W. M. (1973). Persistence of the fetal circulation, *Pediatrics*, **82**, 1103–1105.

Glass, L., Silverman, W., and Sinclair, J. (1968). Effects of the thermal environment on cold resistance and growth of small infants after the first week of life, *Pediatrics*, **41**, 1033–1046.

Glass, L. Silverman, W. A., and Sinclair, J. C. (1969). Relationship of thermal environment and calorie intake to growth and resting metabolism in the late neonatal period, *Biol. Neonat.*, **14**, 324–340.

Gluck, L., Kulovich, M. V., Borer, R. L., Brenner, P. H., Anderson, G. C., and Spellacy, W. N. (1971). Diagnosis of the respiratory distress syndrome by amniocentesis, *Am. J. Obstet. Gynecol.*, **109**, 440–445.

Gluck, L. and Kulovich, M. V. (1973). L/S ratios in amniotic fluid in normal and abnormal pregnancies, *Am. J. Obstet. Gynecol.*, **115**, 539–552.

Gregory, G. A., Kitterman, J. A., Phibbs, R. H., Tooley, W. H., and Hamilton, W. K. (1971). Treatment of idiopathic respiratory distress syndrome with continuous positive airway pressure, *N. Engl. J. Med.*, **284**, 1333–1340.

Hall, B. (1975). Changing composition of human milk and early development of an appetite control, *Lancet*, **1**, 779–781.

Hanshaw, J. B. and Dudgeon, J. A. (1978). *Viral Diseases of the Fetus and Newborn*, pp. 17–96, *Major Problems in Clinical Paediatrics*, Vol. XVII, W. B. Saunders, Philadelphia, London, Toronto.

Hook, E. B. and Chambers, G. M. (1977). Estimated rates of Down syndrome in live-births by one year maternal age intervals for mothers aged 20–49 in a New York state study—implications of the risk figures for genetic counseling and cost-benefit analysis of prenatal diagnosis programs, *Birth Defects*, **13**, 123–141.

Kattwinkel, J., Fleming, D., Cha, C. C., Fanaroff, A. A., and Klaus, M. H. (1973). A device for administration of continuous positive airway pressure by the nasal route, *Pediatrics*, **52**, 131–134.

Kattwinkel, J., Nearman, M. S., Fanaroff, A. A., Katona, P. G., and Klaus, M. H. (1975). Apnoea of prematurity: comparative therapeutic effects of cutaneous stimulation and nasal continuous positive airway pressure, *J. Pediatr.*, **86**, 588–592.

Kerner, J. A., Jr., and Sunshine, P. (1979). Parenteral alimentation, *Sem. Perinat*, **3**, 417–434.

Kinsey, V., Jacobus, J., and Hemphill, F. (1956). Retrolental fibroplasia: Cooperative study of retrolental fibroplasia and the use of oxygen, American Medical Association, *Arch. Ophthal.*, **56**, 481–543.

Koivisto, M., Blanco-Sequeiros, M., and Krause, U. (1972). Neonatal symptomatic and asymptomatic hypoglycaemia; a follow up study of 151 children, *Dev. Med. Child. Neurol.*, **14**, 603–614.

Korobkin, R. (1975). The relationship between head circumference and the development of communicating hydrocephalus in infants following intraventricular haemorrhage, *Pediatrics*, **56**, 74–77.

Kuzemko, J. A. and Paala, J. (1973). Apnoeic attacks in the newborn treated with aminophylline, *Arch. Dis. Child.*, **48**, 404–406.

Larsen, B. and Galask, R. P. (1977). Protection of the fetus against infection, *Sem. Perinat.*, **1**, 183–193.

Le Souëf, P. N., Morgan, A. K., Soutter, L. P., Reynolds, E. O. R., and Parker, D. (1978). Continuous comparison of transcutaneous and arterial oxygen tension in newborn infants with respiratory illnesses, *Acta Anesthiol. Scand. suppl.*, **68**, 91–97.

Levine, M. I., Wigglesworth, J. S., and Dubowitz, V. (1981). Cerebral structure and intraventricular haemorrhage in the neonate; a real-time ultrasound study, *Arch. Dis. Child.*, **56**, 416–424.

Lucey, J., Gerreiro, M., and Hewitt, J. (1968). Prevention of hyperbilirubinaemia of prematurity by phototherapy, *Pediatrics*, **41**, 1047–1054.

Macy, I. G., Nims, B., and Brown, M. (1931). Human milk studies. VIII. Chemical analysis of milk representative of the entire first and last halves of the nursing period, *Am. J. Dis. Child.*, **42**, 569–589.

McBride, W. G. (1977). Thalidomide embryopathy, *Teratology*, **16**, 79–82.

Miller, H. D., Behrle, F. C., and Smull, N. W. (1959). Severe apnoea and irregular respiratory rhythms among premature infants, *Pediatrics*, **23**, 676–685.

Minoli, I., Moro, G., and Ovadia, M. F. (1978). Nasoduodenal feeding in high risk newborns, *Acta Pediat. Scand.*, **67**, 161–168.

Naeye, R. L., Diener, M. M., and Dellinger, W. S. (1969). Urban poverty: effects on prenatal nutrition, *Science*, **166**, 1026.

Odell, G. B., Storey, B., and Rosenberg, L. A. (1970). Studies in kernicterus. III. The saturation of serum proteins with bilirubin during neonatal life and its relationship to brain damage at five years, *J. Pediatr.*, **76**, 12–21.

Ounsted, M. and Ounsted, C. (1973). *On Fetal Growth Rate*, Spastics International Medical Publications; Heinemann, London; J. B. Lippincott, Philadelphia.

Pape, K. E. and Wigglesworth, J. S. (1979). *Haemorrhage, Ischaemia, and the Perinatal Brain*, Ch. 9, The clinico-pathological relationships and aetiological aspects of intraventricular haemorrhage, Spastics International Medical Publications; Heinemann, London; J. B. Lippincott, Philadelphia.

Parkman, R. (1977). Immunology, in *Diseases of the Newborn* (Eds A. J. Schaffer and M. E. Avery), pp. 764–773, W. B. Saunders, Philadelphia, London, Toronto.

Rhea, J. W., Ghazzawi, O., and Weidman, W. (1973). Naso-jejunal feeding: An improved device and intubation technique, *J. Pediatr.*, **82**, 951–954.

Rhodes, P. G. and Hall, R. T. (1973). Continuous positive airway pressure delivered by face mask in infants with the idiopathic respiratory distress syndrome. A controlled study, *Pediatrics*, **52**, 1–5.

Rickham, P. P., Lister, J., and Irving, I. M. (Eds) (1978). *Neonatal Surgery,* Butterworths, London Boston.

Scott, K. E. and Usher, R. (1966). Fetal malnutrition, its incidence, causes and effects, *Am. J. Obstet. Gynecol.*, **94**, 951–963.

Shannon, D. C., Gotay, F. C., Stein, I. M., Rogers, M. C., Todres, D., and Moylan, F. M. B. (1975). Prevention of apnoea and bradycardia in low birthweight infants, *Pediatrics*, **55**, 584–594.

Silverman, W. A., Fertig, J. W., and Berger, A. P. (1958). The influence of the thermal environment upon the survival of newly-born premature infants, *Pediatrics*, **22**, 876–885.

Simpson, J. L. (1978). Genetics of diabetes mellitus and anomolies in offspring of diabetic mothers, *Sem. Perinat.*, **2**, 383–394.

Smith, D. W. (1970). Alcohol effects on the fetus, in *Drugs and Chemical Risks to the Fetus and Newborn* (Eds R. H. Schwarz and S. J. Yaffe), pp. 73–82, Alan R. Liss, New York.

Smithells, R. W., Sheppard, S., Schorah, C. J., Seller, M. J., Nevin, N. C., Harris, R., Read, A. P., and Fielding, D. W. (1980). Possible prevention of neural tube defects by periconceptional vitamin supplementation, *Lancet*, **1**, 339–340.

Strang, L. B. (1977). Fetal lung liquid, in *Neonatal Respiration*, pp. 20–46, Blackwell Scientific Publications, London.

Usher, R. H. and McLean, F. H. (1974). Normal fetal growth and the significance of fetal growth retardation, in *Scientific Foundations of Paediatrics* (Eds J. A. Davis and J. Dobbing), pp. 69–80, Heinemann, London.

Witter, F. and King, T. M. (1980). Cigarettes and pregnancy, in *Drug and Chemical Risks to the Fetus and Newborn* (Eds R. H. Schwarz and S. J. Yaffe), pp. 83–92, Alan R. Liss, New York.

Psychobiology of the Human Newborn
Edited by P. Stratton
© 1982, John Wiley & Sons, Ltd.

CHAPTER 13

Nutrition and Feeding

PETER WRIGHT and ROSEMARY CROW

Feeding and feeding difficulties are of prime concern to the mother when dealing with her newborn infant. The establishment of successful breast feeding is critically related to events in the first few days of life (Sosa *et al.*, 1976) and breast feeding is now considered to provide a wide range of benefits to the neonate in the form of increased protection against infection via specific antibodies derived from the mother, and by lactoferrin and lysozyme contained in human breast milk. In addition to such physiological benefits, it is widely held that breast feeding provides more unspecific psychological advantages, e.g. in the formation of mother-infant 'bonds'. With active encouragement from hospital staff a high proportion of mothers now breast-feed their infants while remaining in hospital for the first week after birth, but the proportion still breast-feeding at 3 weeks of age is much reduced. Here in Edinburgh, we have informally found (Crow, 1977) that mothers within the first three days post-partum, have fairly clear expectations of what it will be like to feed their infants, and some evidence that these expectations differ according to the technique of feeding. Breast-feeding mothers appeared more concerned with what could be called the psychological environment—they commented on the importance of both mother and baby enjoying the feed in a relaxed atmosphere. When mothers were asked what criteria they used to decide when the baby has had enough to eat, a wide variety of responses resulted including: baby stops sucking, baby is sleepy, baby looks content, baby spits out the teat/nipple, follow professional advice, etc. More breast-feeding mothers than bottle-feeding mother recognized falling asleep as a satiety cue (42 per cent as against 6 per cent) and more bottle-feeding mothers stopped feeding only when the baby spits out the teat/nipple (32 per cent as against 4 per cent). As there seem to be several stages in the process of terminating a feed—the baby's sucking decreases, it becomes drowsy, and if the mother still continues to feed, the baby will refuse to open its mouth and spit out the teat if forced into the mouth—it would appear that if these stages are indicative of satiety, then some bottle-feeding mothers are more likely to ignore early satiety signals and be in a greater danger of overfeeding their infants. If the reality of breast-feeding does not match the mother's expectations, then this may be a sufficient reason for her deciding to cease breast-feeding on the grounds of her own inability. Likewise if for some reason, bottle-feeding mothers have a different preparedness to accept baby behaviours as indicating satiety, there are environmental factors which could contribute to overfeeding and excessive weight gain.

In the past two decades, psychologists have paid increasing attention to observational studies of early social development, and as babies spend proportionately more time during the first 3 months in interaction with their mothers during the feeding situation than in any other context, feeding has been frequently investigated. Thus for Ainsworth and Bell (1969), the feeding situation is seen to be important because the baby's experience in influencing his mother's behaviour through his own actions is likely, they argue, to influence the nature of his attachment to her. Successful development, specified as normal weight, and ability to sustain separation from mother at 12 months, was found to be related to the sensitivity with which the mother responded to the baby's signals during feeding. Allowing the baby to regulate its own feeding schedule, to be an active participant during the feed, and to be appropriately responded to following various signals were used as measures of sensitivity. Twenty-six mother–infant pairs were studied and six became overweight because it was said that their mothers overfed them. Overfeeding was said to occur for two reasons, either through attempts to gratify the child, thus treating too broad a spectrum of cries as signals indicating hunger; or to make the children sleep for a long time. No consideration was given to the fact that the baby might be giving inappropriate signals.

In the UK a number of reports in recent years have emphasized the increasing proportion of babies who show rapid weight gains in the first year of life. The problem of infant obesity has been recognized as a potential health hazard because it produces ill health in the infant (Tracey et al., 1971) or, more problematically, because it may lead to adult obesity (Asher, 1966). Shukla et al. (1972), in a study of 300 normal infants, found that 16.7 per cent of babies were suffering from infantile obesity and a further 27.7 per cent were overweight. Eid (1970) had previously shown that babies with excessive weight gains in the first 3 months of life were likely to remain obese at 6–8 years of age. Although there is no agreement as to either incidence or cause, and indeed some more recent contradictory findings (De Swiet et al., 1977), it is widely held that the problem of obesity is more pronounced for the bottle-fed baby (Oates, 1973; Taitz, 1971, 1974).

Among the suggested explanations for this difference have been the earlier introduction of solids in the bottle-fed babies and the feeding of an over-concentrated formula on the part of mothers. Such explanations are essentially in terms of intake and output, and (as has been noted by Dwyer and Mayer, 1973) there is a noticeable lack of consideration that *feeding behaviour* is a possible contributory factor *per se*. Several potential sources are available. It could be through the mother's behaviour, the infant's behaviour or the resulting pattern of mother–infant interaction. Existing studies of infant feeding behaviour have mainly been concerned with the organization of sucking (Brazelton, 1956; Wolff, 1968), the infant's expressive responses associated with feeding (Korner *et al.*, 1968) and the pattern of social interaction involved (Ainsworth and Bell, 1969; Richards and Bernal, 1972). Apart from a few workers such as Richards and Bernal, there has been little interest in the study of the naturally occurring infant and mother feeding behaviours. Either various aspects of the infant's sucking behaviour during different stages of the feed are studied within a laboratory setting, or rating scales have been used to judge degrees of mother sensitivity during the feed. Perhaps even more surprisingly, rarely has a comparison been made between breast and bottle feeding beyond the first week of the infant's life, and certainly not to explore the potential precursors of obesity. This is particularly surprising since breast and bottle feeding are so different and therefore could provide very different (learning) experiences according to technique. This present chapter will review the behavioural studies concerning the expression of hunger and satiety in the neonate and describe some of our own findings on the development of feeding behaviour beyond the neonatal period to 6 months of age, and discuss the problem of overnutrition in relation to the technique of feeding.

DEVELOPMENT IN THE ABILITY TO RECOGNIZE HUNGER AND APPETITE

Mursell (1925) felt that hunger and appetite should not be considered as two independently motivated aspects of food consumption, rather the drive for food is a complex unit of behaviour that develops from an integration of a variety of learning experiences. Whilst, indeed, feeding behaviour has its origin in the learned connections between sucking and gastric hunger, it is also capable of functioning in the absence of gastric peristalsis. Learning is also said to occur through the tendency to suck, the general impulsions due to biochemical need and the incidence of the nipple on the mouth. Thus the time, place and circumstances of the meal, rather than gastric peristalsis, may well become the important motivating factors for feeding to occur. Mursell uses the process of conditioning to explain the establishment of adult feeding patterns, and calls this 'trophic education'. The innate components are the sucking reflex, peristalsis and a chemotrophic mechanism in combination with peristalsis. These chemotrophisms come to be linked behaviourally with taste, smell, texture, and temperature of food that restores the baby's biochemical balance; the learning occurs when the food elicits the secretary responses. Appetite as an experience is thus a combination of the reflex visceral responses with the acquired pleasure of the taste, and smell of food which may be present or imagined. The sucking reflex is said to start off as an undifferentiated activity. It then subsequently becomes integrated with hunger as a result of learning, (a) through positive chemotropism, and (b) through experiences provided by parents in their choice of the infant's food and in the regulation of meal times.

Hamburger (1960) takes as his starting point the physiological theories of Cannon (1932) and Carlson (1916), and similarly treats appetite and hunger separately but in a somewhat different sense from Mursell. For Hamburger, hunger refers to physiological regulations and processes at a cellular, hormonal or organ level, whilst appetite is a mental construct incorporating memory, symbolic representation, perception and affect. This latter cerebral cortical system is said to act as an integrator between the various physiological and psychological mechanisms involved in the regulation of food intake. Hamburger suggested that development essentially reflects a change from sub-cortical to cortical control. At birth the neonate is said to show no evidence of goal-directed, purposive appetite regulation; only instinctive hunger regulation operative at a sub-cortical level. The response of the newborn is an undifferentiated mass reaction so that whilst crying, motor restlessness, mouthing behaviours and autonomic changes may be interpreted as hunger, it cannot be assumed that the baby feels hungry. Hunger is simply one of the many stimuli that produce an unpleasant state. Acquisition of appetite and appetitive behaviour requires, (a) the ability to recognize food by sight, smell, and taste, (b) the ability to appreciate perceptually the feeding person, (c) the presumed memory of past feeding, and (d) the presumed anticipation of relief from the discomfort of hunger. Hamburger concludes that this ability is not present until about the fourth of fifth month of life and occurs as a consequence of repeated cycles of hunger-eating-satiety over many months. The early instinctive hunger regulatory behaviour is not seen as being a part of this developmental process. It is simply the result of conditioning or imprinting that survives as associations of strong feelings, (a) of displeasure with hunger, (b) of pleasure with appetite, and (c) of the self- and object-directed attitudes and expectations which become associated with the mother through the mother–child relationship, with eating and with oral gratification.

The development of motivation thus far is conceptualized either as a complex system incorporating hunger and appetite, or as two independent systems with different mechanisms; appetite as a cognitive system, and hunger as a sub-cortical system. Bruch (1974) offers a third possibility, and like Hamburger, distinguishes between the physiological state of nutritional depletion and the psychological processes involved in perceptual and conceptual awareness of the nutritional state. But unlike Hamburger, Bruch treats hunger and appetite as being on a *continuum*. Development within this theoretical construct is, therefore, the acquisition of the ability to perceive hunger and its associated necessary concept or 'engram'. Achievement of this ability rests on correct learning experiences and interaction with the environment. 'Correct' learning experiences are provided by the mother and are offers of food in response to signals indicating hunger (the only signal that Bruch actually specifies is the CRY). The necessary assumption for this theory is that right from birth there are clear signals that indicate biological needs, although no evidence is provided to support this view. Accordingly Bruch interprets the results of the Ainsworth and Bell (1969) study as indicating that overweight in these cases results from faulty learning experiences provided by the mother.

An alternative explanation to Bruch's comes from the results of a study by a group of workers who are also interested in the consequences of mother–infant interaction during feeding, but who focus on more specific aspects of behaviour (Sander, 1962; Sander and Julia, 1966; and Burns et al., 1972). They recorded whether feeding was on a fixed nursery schedule or by demand, and then observed to what degree an infant became distressed during a feed when the caretaker was changed. Distress was measured by the amount of grimacing, turning away from the nipple, spitting up, fussing and crying. This ability to show distress was considered as providing evidence of the ability of an infant to respond to change in the care-taking environment and it was suggested that this ability points to an establishment of expectations for key features in the environment. It was found that infants who were fed on demand in the first 10 days of life and thus received individualized and special care, were capable of responding in this way. Burns et al. (1972) consider that an important component of regulation in feeding may, therefore, be this capacity of the infant to signal that something is wrong. For the development of successful feeding what may matter is that the infant is allowed to use this signalling system, otherwise it will be 'turned off' or will drop out, and so lead to a failure to thrive. Not responding to infants rather than, as Bruch proposed, reinforcing incorrect behaviour is what really matters. Brody (1956) has also shown that satisfactory weight-gain was correlated with mothers who were 'sensitive, consistent and attentive . . . conspicuous for their ability to accommodate to the needs of their infants'. This also suggests that in feeding, what is important is to allow the *infants* to respond appropriately.

Signals for Hunger

Expressive behaviours that have been associated with feeding in infants are oral behaviours including mouthing, finger sucking, hand to face contacts, hand to mouth contacts and reflex sucking (Korner et al., 1968; Korner, 1973); fussing and crying (Wasz-Hockert et al., 1968; Bernal, 1972) and various actions used to indicate satiety such as refusal to open the mouth (Dubignon and Campbell, 1969). The assumption inherent in the use of the word expressive to describe feeding behaviours is that they indicate some feeling, state of need, associated with eating and that they in fact act as signals.

In one of the earliest systematic accounts Ripin (1930) compared bottle- and breast-fed infants with respect to specific feeding responses at different ages. Reflex sucking and finger sucking were observed in the breast-fed infants within 24 h of birth and were described as responses to accidental contacts of hands on the mouth, or as spontaneous movements without any previous stimulus. Only at 1 month were these said to be specific to the feeding situation. Ripin's bottle-fed infants were studied from 1 month of age and the oral behaviours of opening the mouth and sucking movements were found to be elicited by the bib at 1 month and by the sight of the bottle at 3 months. So although present from birth, Ripin did not consider that oral behaviours become part of the repertoire of feeding behaviour until the end of the neonatal period. Earlier, Mursell (1925) had pointed to the non-specificity of non-nutritive sucking in the very young infant and Piaget (1936) reported similar findings from observations of his own children.

Gesell and Ilg (1937) on the other hand, in their intensive naturalistic study of the feeding behaviour of ten infants, described mouthing and finger sucking as possible indicators of hunger throughout the first 4-weeks of life. Their interest lay in describing the morphology of behaviours at different ages and not in attempting to understand its causes, functions or developmental antecedents. No attempt was made to interpret the various behavioural patterns, so the fact that mouthing appears both before and after a feed to these workers does not appear to conflict with their statement that mouthing is an indicator of hunger. The relationship between hunger and mouthing must be studied carefully as mouthing could simply be a consequence of some accidental pressure on the neonate's hands. Peiper (1961) reports observations on a reflex named after Babkin (1956) that involves mouth–hand co-ordination in the young infant. During the first 3 months of life this co-ordination is reflected in an elicitation of reflex mouth opening and head turning to the midline through pressure of the palms on both hands when the infant is lying in the dorsal and lateral position. The mouthing described by Gesell and Ilg (1937) could, therefore, have included mouthing that is part of the Babkin reflex and which in no way represents a signal of hunger.

More recent studies of oral behaviour reflect the growing interest in each behaviour as a function of age, sex, time since feeding, and as a measure of individual differences. Kessen et al. (1961) examined mouthing and hand-mouth contacts of infants aged between $1\frac{1}{2}$ hours and 5-days, recording the behaviours once each day, for a 5-min interval. They found stable and significant individual differences in the frequency of hand–mouth contacts and reliable individual differences in the duration of mouthing. No regular increase or decrease in occurrence appeared over the 5-day period for either behaviour, so experience did not appear to influence their occurrence. More importantly for the question of their possible signal value, there appeared to be no correlation between feeding experience and the duration and frequency of the behaviours. In a later study using slightly different procedures, Hendry and Kessen (1964) showed that the oral responses are relatively low only in a second period of observation (i.e. about 30 min after the feed) and now found that mouthing was affected by age, being more frequent at 23 h than at 71 h of age. Although Kessen *et al.* (1961) did not specifically analyse the relationship of these oral behaviours to hunger, they suggested that hunger is only reduced some time after the feed when physiological processes are complete. It is therefore possible that the immediate satiating effects normally associated with the end of a meal may be learned and that oral behaviours in the early neonatal period are ambiguous signals because of this time between the physiological states of deprivation and satiety which psychological processes later come to bridge. Overall, the occurrence of hand to mouth contacting is more reliable as a measure of individual differences and this must be borne in mind when claiming it has possible value as a hunger signal.

Korner *et al.* (1968) did specifically examine the relationship between hunger and oral behaviours at ages 45-88 h, and included within their description of oral behaviours mouthing, hand-to-face contacts, hand-to-mouth contacts and finger sucking. They concluded that mouthing was indeed hunger related but that finger sucking, hand-to-mouth contacts, and hand-to-face contacts were related to high levels of arousal and not hunger. Subsequently Korner (1973) has reported sex differences in the frequency of hand-to-mouth contacts. Girls are significantly more likely to engage in hand-to-mouth approach behaviour where the mouth is dominant. The definition for this behaviour was that the mouth approached the hand and scoring only occurred if the mouth opened when the hand was at a distance of at least $1\frac{1}{2}$ inches or more from the face, the infant's head straining forward in an effort to meet the hand. When this particular behaviour was isolated and examined in terms of 'time since last feed' in both sexes it was found to be related to hunger. Korner's work does indicate that the neonate can use oral behaviours to signal hunger but oral means specifically mouth activities if it can be assumed that a mouth-dominated hand approach is mouth-directed. As Peiper's (1961) description of the Babkin response has shown, other hand to mouth activities may simply be reflexive behaviour elicited by environmental factors made more likely by the infant's level of arousal and activity (Kessen *et al.*, 1961, 1963). However, all these studies used bottle fed infants on what appears to be a strict 4-h schedule of feeding. Time since the last feed may not be a useful index for hunger under these conditions, nor should it be assumed that breast-fed babies behave in exactly the same way as bottle-fed babies (Richards and Bernal, 1972).

The validity of such sex differences in the behaviour of neonates has been recently questioned by Richards *et al.* (1976), who observed that most of these studies have been conducted in the USA where circumcision is widely practised. A recent study conducted in Sweden on breast-fed infants by Hwang (1978) in which circumcision did not occur, nevertheless observed that mothers showed more talking, smiling and '*en face*' responses to girls on day 2 and more skin-to-skin contact behaviour, and confirm the previous observations of Thoman *et al.*

(1972). But the differences reported by Hwang above had disappeared by day 4, and were replaced by alterations in the frequency and pattern of sucking which were not detectable on day 2. It is difficult to see what particular significance if any, can be attached to such transitory differences, especially when there is no evidence to suggest that the behavioural differences persist into later infancy.

Hunger and Crying

That crying in the newborn infant is sometimes indicative of hunger is obviously apparent. Gesell and Ilg (1937) assumed that because crying normally occurs before a feed and ceases after a feed, then crying signals hunger, a position that Peiper (1961) also presupposes in his study of the neurology of food intake. The problem with this interpretation is the lack of concern given to the possibility that crying is a feature of a certain level of arousal that can be reduced not only by feeding but also by contact, cuddling, rocking, and gentle human voices (Kessen and Mandler, 1961), continuous stimulation in a variety of modalities (Brackbill, 1971), vestibular-proprioceptive stimulation (Korner and Thoman, 1972), and non-nutritive sucking (Kessen and Leutzendorff, 1963). Crying may be a non-specific signal that acts as a distress call to be interpreted by the receiver according to certain external factors, and many early workers considered crying as non-expressive (Gesell, 1940), diffuse (Spitz, 1945), reflexive (Osgood, 1953) and conveying neither meaning nor intention (Sherman, 1927).

Two important studies demonstrate that crying is a complex behaviour. A spectographic and auditory analysis on 351 infants aged from birth to 7 months by Wasz-Höckert et al. (1968) differentiated four cries according to the situation in which they occurred. The birth cry has a flat falling melody, each signal lasting about 1 s, and is always tense. The pain cry has a falling melody with a high pitch and the signal is long, ranging from 1 to 1.5 s; the older the baby the shorter the cry. It is usually tense and there is a shift in pitch. The hunger cry has a characteristic rising-falling melody with little age changes or any noticeable alteration in pitch. Finally the pleasure cry is invariably flat in form with the most variable change in pitch. Wolff (1969) identified only three distinct patterns in the neonate—a rhythmical cry, a mad cry, and a pain cry. Like Wasz-Höckert and his workers, Wolff established that mothers could differentiate the cries, but found a lack of specificity in the mothers' response to the cry. Multiparous mothers would not necessarily respond immediately and would not always first try a feed. Primiparous mothers would respond immediately and would most frequently be prepared to feed the baby at once. This contrasts with a later study of Bernal (1972), who found that within the first 10 days of their baby's life, it was the second mothers who responded more quickly to crying and more often by feeding.

It appears that crying does have the potential to be a signal in that differences in structure are recognized not only in the laboratory but also in real life.

However, apart from the pain cry, receivers interpret the signal not according to the specific physical characteristics of the message, but according to the context in which the signal occurs, the events that have preceded it, and possibly by the age of the sender. The fact that Wolff (1969) and Bernal (1972) found such differences (even between mothers of similar parity) points to yet other possible sources that may affect practice—namely cultural practices and method of feeding—all of Wolff's sample of USA mothers were bottle-fed, whereas in Bernal's UK sample there were both bottle and breast feeders. Nevertheless, in 4-day-old infants, Wolff showed that babies do cry more before a feed than when satisfied, and importantly, do not stop crying until fed. During the second week of life, the crying is even more apparent for its signal value, since it occurs consistently with an interruption of feeding. The most vocal protest occurs when the feed is removed after the infant has taken the first ounce. The frequency of this protest continues to increase until the infant is 5 weeks of age when it declines.

Expression of Satiety

Peiper (1961) considers satiety essentially as a negation of those aspects concerned with hunger—an absence of the rooting reflex and a gradual increase in the pause length between sucks. Associated with this reduction in sucking is a motor restlessness when the infant may lose the nipple or push it out with his tongue. This particular expression of satiety according to Peiper is only suited to breast-fed babies. While satiety is a response both to food intake and to fatigue, Peiper argues the latter is a more efficient mechanism. When no effort is required, only very large food intakes will induce satiety and, therefore, because of the ease of bottle feeding, bottle-fed babies are in greater danger of the possibility of overfeeding.

Earlier, Gesell and Ilg (1937) had distinguished between satiety and 'final' satiety (refusal and rejection) with independent developmental histories. During the neonatal period the infant usually falls asleep when satiated, and if breast feeding, the head will drop from the breast. As the infant grows the head drop becomes a voluntary act, he is more likely to remain awake, and will then smile at his mother. By 16–20 weeks, satiety is reflected in an interest in his surroundings towards the end of the feed, and subsequently by playfulness at the breast or the bottle. Frank refusal and rejection, on the other hand, are not reported until after the fourth week when the infant will refuse to open his mouth or will push the nipple out with his tongue. The refusal then becomes more general and by 24 weeks will include arching the back, extending the neck to be followed by spitting out. Gesell and Ilg thus describe stages from a less to a more voluntary expression of satiety, the fundamental characteristic being that of head withdrawal.

In his attempt to offer an account of the causal mechanism, Peiper (1961) identifies two factors: food intake and fatigue. Gesell and Ilg (1937), on the other hand, offer no explanation. Throughout, their emphasis lies in the collection of normative data so that the richness of their behavioural categories rests on their systematic collection of data. This apparent paradox of data without explanation *vis-à-vis* explanation without data reflects the swing in the approaches to developmental questions during the two periods represented. Some of the early workers interested in children were painstaking in their data collection of behaviour in its natural setting (e.g. Shirley, 1931; McGraw, 1943) whilst those of a more theoretical persuasion engaged in speculation without a systematic study of possible hypotheses (Piaget, 1936; Mursell, 1925; Spitz, 1945; Freud, 1910). In fact this lack of concern for satiety as a signal seems to have arisen because it was lost in the primary consideration of that time—i.e. that of oral gratification of the need to suck. Hunger and the need to suck were studied and theorized about but satiety as a behaviour in its own right was given scant attention.

The various factors involved were finally separated out in experimental studies of Dubignon and Campbell (1969) from measurements of the different components of sucking in the 3–4-day-old bottle-fed infant. Fatigue and satiation do have separate effects, but not on sucking *per se*. The infants did not control their food intake by altering their sucking rate. Satiation was marked by less time spent sucking and a reduced amplitude of suction. In addition there appeared to be a change in the sucking mechanism with satiation as shown by an increase in the ratio of expression (the positive pressure created when the baby approximates his gums and elevates his tongue) to suction responses (the negative pressure produced when the baby lowers his tongue and bottom jaw) in the last quarter of the feed. After a burping period, the infants increased the time spent sucking, and recovery after such a rest was as great in the early part of the feed as towards the end of the feed. This, they argue, is recovery from fatigue. Satiation and fatigue are jointly responsible for the changes in sucking behaviour observed at the end of the feed, but refusal to accept the teat is due to satiation alone. They therefore suggest that if expression of satiety is to be used as an index, refusal to accept food and not sucking patterns is the more reliable measure to score. But this presumes that neonatal infants can regulate intake and that this regulation is independent of effort. Dubignon and Campbell (1969) found that regulation was by volume rather than calorific value, yet Peiper (1961) raises a doubt about the efficiency of volume as a regulatory mechanism. From Gesell and IIg's observations of behaviour in the natural setting, there is some support for Peiper. Frank refusal was not observed until after the fourth week of age. Satiation in the neonatal period was represented by the infant falling asleep and thus possibly by fatigue. The confounding factor in Dubignon and Campbell's (1969) study is the lack of data on intake other than at a single feed. One can only conclude with the suggestion that neonates do stop feeding of their own volition in the natural setting, but it is not clear whether this is anything more than cessation by falling asleep.

In the case of breast-fed infants, Hall (1975) has suggested that the changes in composition of human milk during the feed are associated with the development of an appetite-control mechanism, and in particular that changes in the composition and presumably the taste of the milk might act as a satiety cue for the breast-fed infant. She suggests that the baby ends feeding from the first breast with milk rich in fat and protein, then starts on the second breast with thin and watery milk and will therefore satisfy not only hunger but thirst as well. Such composition cues are clearly unavailable to the bottle-fed infant and Hall speculates that this might account for their increased risk of obesity and rapid weight gain (Asher, 1966; Eid, 1970; Shukla et al., 1972). This is an appealing hypothesis and information is clearly potentially available to the breast-feeding infant, and it remains to be demonstrated whether it is used as such. But, as Smart (1978) has pointed out, an alternative to Hall's notion of the high-fat milk taste inhibiting feeding and low-fat milk disinhibiting the feeding response, is simply that the baby stops feeding from the first breast when his sucking is insufficiently rewarded and resumes sucking on the second side because of the ready milk flow sustaining his feeding responses.

PATTERNS OF MILK INTAKE IN BREAST- AND BOTTLE-FEED INFANTS

In the first 10 days of life there is evidence (Gunther and Stanier, 1949) that the amount of breast milk taken at each meal is related to the composition of that

Table 1

Hospital procedure	
0–1 day	Select mother in hospital post-natal ward. Criteria for acceptance—first or second baby; male or female; normal delivery and apgar rating; home location; equal numbers of breast/bottle; weight range 2.5–4.3 kg Medical records.
2 days	Visit mother—explain aims of study, etc. Take details of family history; menstrual data; eating habits; knowledge of aspects of infant feeding.
3 days	Mother starts to keep activity diary. If breast-feeding test-weighs at each feed and record of meal size and intervals for 3 days. Diary for day 3, 4, 5, 6. Brazelton behavioural assessment and anthropometric measures (skinfold thickness, length, head circumference, etc.)
4 or 5 days	Videotape complete feed. Expressive behavioural signals observed approximately $\frac{1}{2}$ h before and $\frac{1}{2}$ h after feed.
Home visits	
1 month	Diaries. Anthropometric measures. Expressive behaviour before and after feeds. Videotape complete feed.
2–6 months	Home visits. Diaries. Anthropometric measures. Videotape complete feed.
1 year	Retrospective. Home visit. Anthropometric measures.

milk. In the course of a longitudinal study on the development of feeding in human infants (Wright *et al.*, 1980) we have collected meal pattern records which suggest that although the breast-fed infant may be responding passively to variation in milk composition at this stage, as they become older they learn to alter their intake patterns to predict and actively compensate for restrictions in the availability of milk. Details of recruitment and an outline of the study are shown in Table 1. Meal pattern records were recorded by the mothers for a three day period beginning on days 4, 5, and 6 within the hospital, then in the home at 1

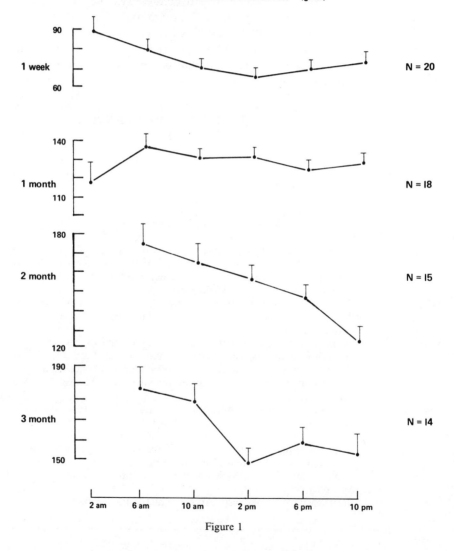

Figure 1

BREAST MILK INTAKE OVER 24 hrs. (gms.)

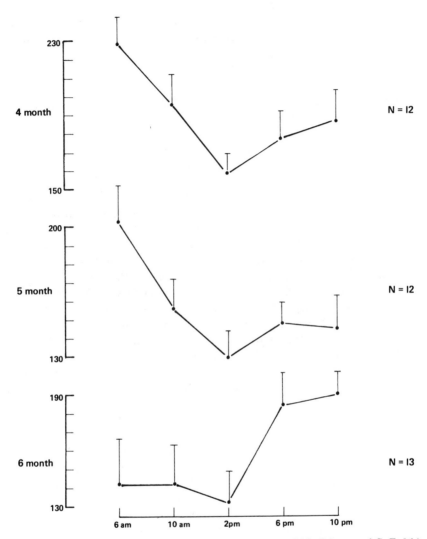

Figures 1 and 2   Milk intake in breast-fed infants over 24 h (Mean and S. E. M.)
N = 21; 12 male, 9 female, 10 first-born, 11 second-born. Thirteen babies were still
receiving at least two breast feeds a day at age 6 months

month of age, and thereafter at 4-weekly intervals until aged 6 months. bottle-feeding mothers recorded the nature of the formula used, the amount offered and taken, and breast-feeding mothers test-weighed their infants immediately before and after each meal. The data have been analysed by grouping feeds and plotting the mean meal size at the traditional feeding times of 2, 6, 10 am, and 2, 6, 10 pm. A feed initiated between midnight and 4 am contributes to the mean meal size plotted at 2 am, and so on through the 24-h period.

In breast-fed infants at week 1 (Figure 1), there is a clear diurnal pattern with the largest meals occurring early in the morning, and the smallest meals in the middle of the day. Although the breast milk supply is still increasing over the time our data were collected, they are in good agreement with those of Gunther and suggest the method of recording by mothers themselves to be satisfactory. Gunther found that expressed milk and milk obtained by emptying the breast following pitocin injection exhibits a definite and regular variation in the percentage of fat it contains. There is a continuous rise in the fat percentage of milk secreted between 4 am and 8 am. She suggested that the small volume of milk often taken at 2 pm (which we find) is a physiological response by the baby to the richness of the milk at that time, and similarly the large intake found by us at 2 am might be because the milk is most dilute at this time.

However, in our sample, the diurnal variations change markedly with age, and in the absence of any data (known to ourselves) of changes in the diurnal composition of breast milk with age of infant, we must look for other explanations. At 1 month diurnal variation is absent, but at 2 months a pronounced change in intake has developed, the largest meal appearing at 6 am and then decreasing throughout the day. At this age most of the infants in our sample are regularly sleeping through the early morning hours, and this first feed of the day follows a long night fast of 6–8 h. Between 3 and 5 months (Figure 2), although the largest meal continues to appear at the beginning of the day, the smallest meal taken now consistently appears in the middle of the day. At 6 months, this pattern again alters and becomes the reverse of that seen at 2 months, with the largest meal now appearing at the end of the day.

Figure 3 depicts the comparable data plotted for the bottle-fed infants and is remarkable for its complete contrast, and the absence of any changed diurnal pattern in meal size at any age, until possibly 6 months, when a tendency for smaller meals appears at midday. Invariably, at each age, meal size is constant across the day. A further difference between the two techniques is the more rapid progress towards a three-meal-a-day pattern in the bottle-fed infants, which is present in them all at 5 months, and in all but six infants at 4 months of age.

Interpretation of such data is not easy. As the infants become older, some mothers may offer only juice rather than milk at certain meals, and in addition the introduction of solids and whether these are offered before or after milk feeds would be expected to influence any intake patterns. However, if the data for breast-fed infants are reanalysed, separating out meals accompanied by solids

BOTTLE MILK INTAKE OVER 24hrs. (gms)

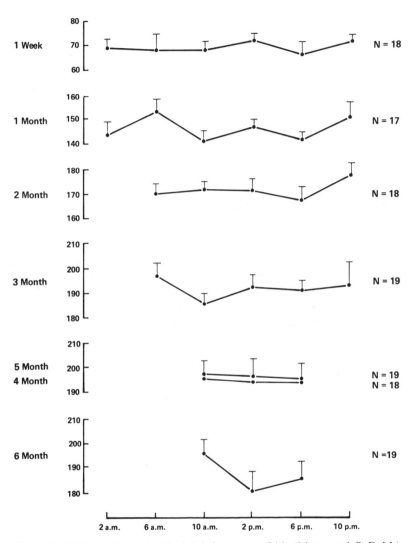

Figure 3   Milk intake in bottle-fed infants over 24 h (Mean and S. E. M.)
$N = 19$; 9 male, 10 female, 5 first-born, 14 second-born. All mothers had
decided definitely for various reasons to bottle-feed their infants from birth. At 1
month only eight infants were consistently fed at 2 a.m. and at 4 months only six
infants were receiving feeds at 10 p.m.

from those when only milk was offered, the meal-size patterns described above do not alter. If these changes seen in the breast-fed infants reflect some maturational change on the part of the infant, then their appearance is somehow prevented in the bottle-fed infant. It is tempting to speculate that the changes are adaptive for the breast-fed infant, and allow the baby to cope with the essentially continuous availability of milk in the neonatal period, and the transition to prolonged periods of absence of food. At 2 months, when most infants have abandoned the early morning feed, they consume a large meal following a long interval without food. This response we have earlier noted is more apparent in breast-fed than in bottle-fed infants, in response to a long intermeal interval in the first week of life (Wright et al., 1980). Infants at 2 months are essentially responding to a deficit signal and compensating for the long night interval without milk. At six months, however, there are clear signs of a shift in this mode of responding, infants now *anticipate* a forthcoming period of fasting by taking their largest meal at the end of the day. There is no evidence in our study that this represents a conscious strategy on the part of the mother.

Johnson and Salisbury (1975) found that the temporal pattern of sucking in babies aged 1–10 days differs when they are bottle-fed cow's milk as compared with expressed human milk. The babies were fed each milk for 1 min and the number of sucks and intervals between sucks counted. Although the total number of sucks was the same for breast milk and cow's milk, the frequency distribution was different. Whereas the pattern of sucking with cow's milk was the same in all the infants studied, the pattern of those feeding on breast milk showed considerable variation, and they conclude that it is the nature of the milk being sucked and not the feeding bottle which modifies the sucking behaviour. Examination of the fine structure of sucking in our own sample from 1 week to 2 months of age reveals clear differences in the distribution of the number of sucks in each burst of sucking and a far greater proportion of bursts in bottle-fed in-

Table 2   Percentage distribution of burst sizes within feeds

| | Burst Length (no. of sucks) | | | | | |
	2–9	10–19	20–29	30–39	40–49	> 50
Breast						
1 week (14)	55.9	31.5	5.9	2.3	1.9	2.3
1 month (10)	54.7	29.4	6.7	3.3	1.5	4.3
2 months (11)	58.3	23.5	7.2	3.7	—	5.5
Bottle						
1 week (11)	72.7	15.1	5.7	2.7	0.9	2.9
1 month (10)	72.4	14.5	5.3	2.3	2.6	2.8
2 months (10)	65.2	15.5	8.3	3.9	2.7	4.3

fants falling within the very short range of 2–9 sucks (Table 2). However, such differences are far more likely to be influenced by the mother than reflecting some response to the composition of the milk. From our videotaped feeds we have a continuous record of sucking and have calculated the true rate of sucking (as measured within bursts) for the first five and last five bursts on each breast (Table 3). Breast feeds are characterized by a reliable and significant change in the rate of sucking at all ages, i.e. babies suck faster towards the end of the feed at each breast. Dividing bottle feeds into two equal half-time periods, in agreement with Dubignon and Campbell (1969), we find no reliable differences in the true rate of sucking at the beginning and end of each half feed. The rate changes at the breast may reflect a decrease in the milk supply and together with changes in the state of the baby such as becoming more drowsy, bring about a switch to a 'non-nutritive' suck pattern and hence a faster rate. However, we do not find that the rate changes correlate with state, and such changes which also occur in the bottle-feeder are unaccompanied by alteration in the sucking rate. In breast feeders at 2

Table 3 A comparison of sucking rates during the first and last 5 min of each half of the feed

Breast	1st side			2nd side			
Start	1.23	*	1 week	1.32		NS	$n = 14$
Finish	1.64			1.35			
Start	1.39	**	1 month	1.45	**		$n = 10$
Finish	1.75			1.79			
Start	1.40	**	2 months	1.53	**		$n = 11$
Finish	1.72			1.88			
Bottle	1st half			2nd half			
Start	1.30	NS 1 week		1.28		NS	$n = 11$
Finish	1.35			1.35			
Start	1.28	*	1 month	1.56		NS	$n = 10$
Finish	1.51			1.56			
Start	1.72	NS 2 months		1.85		NS	$n = 10$
Finish	1.67			1.67			

$*p < 0.05$ $**p < 0.01$ (Wilcoxon Matched Pairs)

months, when the tendency to drowse towards the end of a feed is less apparent, the increased sucking rate in the breast feeder is maintained.

Introduction of Solids

A further example of how the technique of feeding permits a different pattern of feeding behaviour is seen from our sample when we examine the age at which mothers decide to introduce solids. The 1974 report *Present Day Practice in Infant Feeding* draws attention to the fact that 80–95 per cent of infants in the UK had solid foods introduced into their diets by 3 months of age. The report recommended that 'the early introduction of cereals or other solid foods to the diet of babies before about 4 months of age should be strongly discouraged'. The early introduction of solids has been suggested as a contributor to rapid weight gain during infancy (Taitz, 1971) and certainly tends to occur earlier in the bottle-fed than the breast-fed infant (Wilkinson and Davies, 1978).

In our Edinburgh study we have also found a difference in the age at which solids are introduced (see Figure 4) there being no preferred age in the case of the breast-fed infants and a peak for solid introduction in the bottle-fed infants at about 3 months of age. Given that our own study operated against a background of concern through both the media and the medical profession for too early an introduction, it is instructive to examine the reasons which mothers offered for their decision. Although the question was open-ended, the answers can be grouped into the few categories shown in Table 4. Erratic meal patterning included answers such as—'waking early before 4 since the last feed', and the re-emergence of demands for night feeds; erratic feeding behaviour included the baby being sick during the feed, suffering excessive wind and excessive crying. Independent decision by the mother included, 'consider the baby old enough to start solids', 'just to give the baby a try', 'must be bored with milk alone', to wean off the breast and following the clinic's advice. Again there is a different pattern of reasons according to technique, and of the sixteen bottle-feeding mothers who fall in the first category, in ten cases the reason was the re-emergence of a night feed.

We then independently examined the 3-day meal-pattern diaries kept by the mothers, and scored the instances of feeding occurring in what are arbitrarily designated 'unsocial' hours at night time, i.e. between 11 pm and 6 am. The results are given in Table 5, where meal frequency refers to the mean number of meals recorded in the 3-day period during these hours. At 1 month there is no difference in the incidence of night feeds for the two populations, but by 2 months the incidence of night feeds has dropped considerably in the bottle-fed infants, and disappeared at 3 months. In the breast-fed babies, although the number of babies waking at these ages decreases, the number of feeds barely alters, and it is not until 4 months that there occurs a decrease from 2.33 to 1.57 meals in this time period—a comparable drop to that shown by the bottle-feeders between 1

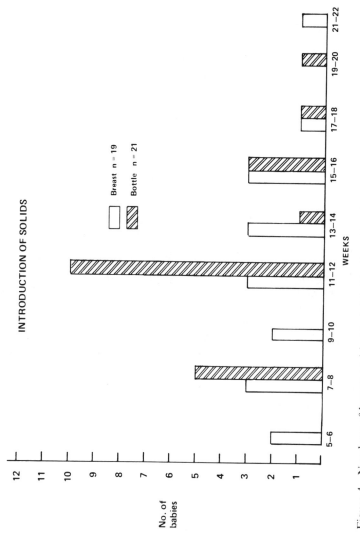

Figure 4   Numbers of breast- and bottle-fed babies introduced to solid foods at each 2-week interval

Table 4 Reasons given by mothers for introduction of solids

	Breast	Bottle
Erratic meal patterns	7	16
Underweight	1	—
Erratic feeding behaviour	2	1
Independent decision by mother	10	3

$\chi^2 = 8.6$, df 3 $p < 0.05$

Table 5 Feeding during 'unsocial' hours at night

	Breast		Bottle	
	No. of babies waking	Meal frequency	No. of babies waking	Meal frequency
1 month	21/21	2.86	16/17	2.88
2 months	11/20	2.36	13/18	1.85
3 months	9/15	2.33	3/19	—
4 months	7/14	1.57	1/20	—

and 2 months. At about 10–12 weeks of age, the bottle-feeding mother has therefore become accustomed to the changed night pattern of her infant to one of not-waking, whereas the breast-feeding mother has not experienced any change of feeding pattern. This suggests that the reason for introducing solids advanced by bottle-feeding mothers is indeed compatible with their experience of feeding their infants—by 2 months there *is* a noticeable decrease in night-waking but not so for the breast-fed babies. In the face of this difference in behaviour according to technique of feeding, it may well be far more difficult for the bottle-feeding mother to delay introducing solid foods until 4 months of age as recommended in the 1974 report.

Early Infant Feeding and Rapid Weight Gain

The relationship between excessive bodyweight in infancy and early childhood to that of obesity when adult remains a contentious issue. Within the last decade opinion has swung away from the reports of a continuity between obesity in childhood and rapid weight gain in infancy (Asher 1966; Eid 1970; Charney *et al.*, 1975) to recent findings that the majority of fat babies lose their excess fat during childhood (Poskitt and Cole, 1977, 1978). The speculation that early introduction of solids leads to excessive weight gain has not been confirmed (Davies *et al.*, 1977; De Swiet *et al.*, 1977). Nevertheless the relative success of behaviour therapy in the treatment of adult obesity by comparison with other treatments, supports the view that certain kinds of obesity are the result of incorrect learning. In addition, early-onset obesity with accompanying increase in adipose hypercellularity appears especially difficult to treat by comparison with adult-onset obesity. Bruch (1974) has suggested that obesity can result from faulty learning at an early age where the mother feeds for the wrong reasons—perhaps when the infant cries in discomfort rather than hunger. Consequently the infant does not learn to discriminate between discomfort and hunger. This approach implies that there are features in baby behaviour that must be detected by the mother and which demonstrate hunger and satiety and that if these are overruled for whatever reason, the infant is denied the potential to regulate intake according to requirements.

We examined the feeding patterns of neonates in the first week of life in an Edinburgh maternity hospital where the prevailing regime was one of 'demand feeding' (Crow and Wright, 1976; Wright et al., 1980). However, because of various constraints which operate in the wards, nurses advise mothers to approximate roughly to a 4-h rule, i.e. if the baby sleeps longer than 4 h he should be woken to feed and if he cries before this time, he is not necessarily hungry. We argued that the regulatory process might be more apparent in mothers who disregard such informal rules and allow their babies, for whatever reason, to go without food for a relatively long period of time—a kind of natural deprivation experiment. We accordingly selected from our meal-pattern records all instances of relatively long intervals between meals (range of 5.9–8.5 h) and found that bottle-fed infants tend to receive the same amount of milk either side of such long intervals, whereas breast-fed babies tend to receive larger meals following the long interval. In the first week of life, this suggests that the breast-fed infant experiences a matching between long intervals without food and large meal following the interval, a potential learning situation which is much rarer for the bottle-fed infant.

If, however, infants are fed in a more scheduled fashion, and are not free to choose how often they feed, the only possible way they have to control their intake is by being allowed to determine the amount taken at a particular meal. To study this aspect of feeding we need to discover how the expressive behaviours of the baby are responded to by the mother and the consequent learning experience this provides for the baby. Korner et al. (1968) have identified behaviours such as mouthing, which do indicate hunger and Dubignon and Campbell (1969) have described behaviours characteristic of satiety, but which are not necessarily recognized and responded to by the mother. If the bottle is unfinished or if the stipulated time on the breast is not achieved, the mother is far more likely to control the feed herself and overrule the baby's desire to terminate the feed. Thoman (1975) has emphasized the continuous feedback between mother and infant which has consequences for each and for the development of their interactive patterns of behaviour. She found that whether the mother bottle- or breast-feeds her 2-day-old infant, parity influences the feeding. Mothers with their first child spend more time feeding and in non-feeding activities within the meal, but the infants spent less time sucking, and consumed less than infants of experienced mothers.

Feeds are continuously interrupted by removal of the bottle or breast for a variety of reasons—choking, winding the baby, changing the breast etc. From the videotaped records of feeds in the Edinburgh study we have scored each interruption in terms of whether it is baby or mother determined, and such interruptions in the case of bottle-fed infants are almost entirely under the control of the mother at 1 week, 1 month, and 2 months of age. In the case of the breast-fed infants, the majority of such interruptions are baby-determined but the effect does not reach a statistically significant level and it would seem that some mothers are controllers and others are not. These results are very similar to observations of Dunn (1975) on 1-week-old infants and indicate that although inexperience on the part of the mother could in part account for such interruptions at 1 week, the behaviour becomes established and consistent across all three ages. Pollitt et al. (1978) recently examined whether selected behaviours of both mother and infant during feedings are predictors of growth velocity during the first month of life. They filmed a mother's first occasion on bottle feeding her infant at ages between 20 and 36 h. The mothers of heavy infants cleaned, inspected, talked to and adjusted the clothing of their babies more often than mothers of light infants, the latter spending more time encouraging their babies to suck and stimulating them by bouncing and rocking. A maternal variable which interrupted the feed, the frequency with which the nipple cover was replaced on the bottle, correlated significantly with weight gain in the first month.

The technique of bottle-feeding in itself therefore allows the infant far less control over the duration and pace of the feed compared to the breast-fed infant, and predisposes the mother to be less aware of the possible cues present in her infant's behaviour. It may also result in the appearance of other behaviours which are possibly more a response to this lack of control on the infant's part, than a reflection of its degree of hunger. One such behaviour is that of crying, which in the Edinburgh study we have found to be more pronounced in the breast-fed infants in the first week of life than in bottle-feeders, but which decreases with age, whereas in bottle-fed infants at age 4, 5, and 6 months crying has increased more than threefold by comparison with the ages 1 week and 1 month.

The emphasis in our own work on comparisons between bottle and breast feeding is certainly over-simplistic, and although we have chosen to characterize the two techniques as predominantly mother-controlled for bottle feeding and greater possibility of baby-controlled feeds at the breast, they should really be taken to represent the extreme ends of a single continuum. It is certainly possible for the baby to initiate and terminate actions at the bottle but, on balance perhaps, the situation prevents the mother from attending to cues from the infant which are more easily responded to at the breast. The dichotomy between external and internal controls on feeding behaviour which has been emphasized by Schachter and colleagues (Schachter, 1971; Rodin, 1978) could well originate from such early feeding experience. The infant that establishes control over the course of a feed and the frequency of meals across the day may become the adult whose feeding patterns and food intake are determined more by internal physiological signals in contrast to the adult whose food intake is controlled by external cues such as taste, appearance of food, quantity offered and the context in which eating occurs.

It is perhaps finally worth emphasizing that the variety of influences which undoubtedly affect infant feeding practice merge with the cultural norms characteristic of any particular society. As a first approach, we should perhaps accept that the kind of data collection which is possible cannot be rigidly controlled as in more conventional experimental situations. There is a virtual absence of well-documented accounts of meal patterns in infancy and the later and important transition to solid meals, together with the kinds of food preferences that are shown. They are highly likely to be dependent on familial eating patterns, and heavily culture-dependent (Rozin and Schiller 1980). The differences in diurnal patterns of feeding reported earlier in this chapter indicate how control over the course and frequency of feeds, which is more characteristic of the breast feeder, allows the infant to adapt to changing circumstances. We have chosen to interpret such changes in diurnal pattern as allowing for potential learning experiences but said nothing as to the underlying mechanisms. The advantages of such a psychobiological approach is that it emphasizes a natural feeding pattern which can then be examined in terms of its possible biological usefulness. It may well be that the developmental progression towards larger meals at the end of the day is some function of availability of the milk supply—possibly mothers who eat their main meal of the day in the evening will produce more milk at the end of the day. Alternatively if these changes are more infant initiated, they may well have appeared in bottle-fed infants if more emphasis was placed on the actual feeding experience by health professionals, with less concern about the amount and frequency of bottle feeds. Indeed, we do have some evidence that where true-demand feeding is practised for the bottle-fed infant, and where no constraints are placed on the upper limit of milk available at any one feed, then the indentical diurnal patterns to those of the breast-fed infant are seen. Only with such naturalistic studies can we accumulate sufficient data to test out such speculations and then provide a much firmer biological base for infant feeding practice.

REFERENCES

Ainsworth, M. D. and Bell S. M. (1969). Some contemporary patterns of mother-infant interaction in the feeding situation, in *Stimulation in Early Infancy* (Ed.) A. Ambrose, Academic Press, London.

Asher, P. (1966). Fat babies and fat children: the prognosis of obesity in the very young, *Arch. Dis. Childhood*, **41**, 672–673.

Babkin, P. S. (1956). The establishment of reflex activity in early postnatal life, in *Central Nervous System and Behaviour*, Vol 44 (Translated from the Russian by the American National Institute of Health and Josiah Macey, Jr Foundation).

Bernal, J. (1972). Crying during the first 10 days of life, and maternal responses, *Develop. Med. Child. Neurol.*, **14**, 362–372.

Brackbill, Y. (1971). The cumulative effect of continuous stimulation on arousal level in infants, *Child Develop.*, **42**, 17–26.

Brazelton, T. B. (1956). Sucking in infancy, *Paediatrics*, **17**, 400–404.

Brody, S. (1956). *Patterns of Mothering*, International Universities Press, New York.

Bruch, H. (1974). *Eating Disorders, Obesity, Anorexia Nervosa and the Person Within*, Routledge and Kegan Paul, London.

Burns, P., Sander, L. W., Stechler, G., and Julia, H. (1972). Distress in feeding: Short term effects of caretaker environment of the first ten days, *J. Am. Acad. Child. Psychiatry*, **11**, 427–439.

Cannon, W. B. (1932). *The Wisdom of the Body*, Norton, New York.

Carlson, A. J. (1916). *The Control of Hunger in Health and Disease*, University of Chicago Press, Chicago.

Charney, E., Goodman, H. C., and McBride, M. (1975). Childhood antecedents of adult obesity. Do chubby infants become obese adults? *New Eng. J. Med.*, **295**, 6–9.

Crow, R. A. (1977). An ethological study of the development of infant feeding, *J. of Adv. Nursing*, **2**, 99–109.

Crow, R. A. and Wright, P. (1976). The development of feeding behaviour in early infancy, *Nursing Mirror*, **142**, 57–59.

Davies, D. P., Gray, O. O., Elwood, P. C., Hopkinson, C., and Smith S. (1977). Effects of solid on growth of bottlefed infants in the first three months of life, *BMJ.*, **1977**, 7–8.

De Swiet, M., Fayers, P., and Cooper, L. (1977). Effect of feeding habit on weight in infancy, *Lancet*, **1**, 892–894.

Department of Health and Social Security (1974). *Present Day Practice in Infant Feeding*, HMSO, London.

Dubignon, J. and Campbell, D. (1969). Sucking in the newborn during a feed, *J. Exp. Child. Psychology*, **7**, 282–298.

Dunn, J. (1975). Consistency and change in styles of mothering, in *Ciba Foundation Symposium No. 33—Parent–Infant Interaction*, Elsevier, Amsterdam.

Dwyer, J. T. and Mayer, J. (1973). Overfeeding and obesity in infants and children, *Bibl. 'Nutri Diet'*, **18**, 123–152.

Eid, E. E. (1970). Follow-up study of physical growth of children who had excessive weight gain in first six months of life, *BMJ*, **2**, 74–76.

Freud, S. (1910). Three contributions to the sexual theory, *Nervous and mental Diseases Monograph Series, No. 7*.

Gesell, A. (1940). *The First Five Years of Life*, Harper, New York.

Gesell, A. and Ilg, E. L. (1937). *Feeding Behaviour of Infants*, Lippincott, London.

Gunther, M. and Stanier J. E. (1949). Diurnal variation in the fat content of breast milk *Lancet*, **2**, 235–237.

Hall, B. (1975). Changing composition of human milk and early development of an appetite control, *Lancet*, **1**, 779–781.

Hamburger, W. W. (1960). Appetite in Man, *Am. J. Clin. Nutr.*, **8**, 569–586.

Hendry, L. S. and Kessen, W. (1964). Oral behaviour of newborn infants as a function of age and time since feeding, *Child Development*, **35**, 201–208.

Hwang, C.-P. (1978). Mother-infant interaction; effects of sex of infant on feeding behaviour, *Early Human Development*, **2**, 341–349.

Kessen, W. and Leutzendorff, A. (1963). The effect of non-nutritive sucking on movement in the human newborn, *J. Comp. Physiol, Psychol.* **56**, 69–72.

Kessen. W. and Mandler, G. (1961). Anxiety, pain and inhibition of distress, *Psychol. Rev.*, **68**, 396–404.

Kessen, W., Williams, E. J., and Williams, J. P. (1961). Selection and test of response measures in the study of the human newborn, *Child Development*, **32**, 7–24.

Korner, A. F. (1973). Sex differences in newborns with special reference to differences in the organization of oral behaviour, *J. Child Psychol. Psychiatry*, **14**, 19–29.

Korner, A. F., Chuck, B., and Dontchos, S. (1968). Organismic determinants of spontaneous oral behaviour in neonates. *Child Development*, **39**, 1145–1157.

Korner, A. F., and Thoman, E. B. (1972). The relative efficacy of contact and vestibular-proprioceptive stimulation in soothing neonates, *Child Develop.*, **43**, 443–453.

Johnson, P. and Salisbury, D. M. (1975). Breathing and sucking during feeding in the newborn. *Parent-Infant Interaction: Ciba No. 33*. Elsevier, Amsterdam.

McGraw, M. B. (1943). *The Neuromuscular Maturation of the Human Infant*, Columbia University Press, New York.

Mursell, J. L. (1925). The psychology of nutrition, *Psychol. Rev.*, **32**, 317–333.

Oates, R. K. (1973). Infant-feeding practices, *BMJ*, **2**, 762–764.

Osgood, L. E. (1953). *Method and Theory in Experimental Psychology*, Oxford University Press, New York.

Peiper, A. (1961). *Cerebral Functions in Infancy and Childhood*, Pitman Medical, London.

Piaget, J. (1936). *The Origin of Intelligence in the Child* (1953 edition), Routledge and Kegan Paul, London.

Pollitt, E., Gilmore, M., and Valcarcel, M. (1978). Early mother–infant interaction and somatic growth, *Early Hum. Dev.*, **1**, 325–336.

Poskitt, E. M. E. and Cole, T. J. (1977). Do fat babies stay fat? *BMJ*, **1**, 7–9.

Poskitt, E. M. E. and Cole, T. J. (1978). Nature, nurture and childhood overweight, *BMJ*, **1**, 603–605.

Richards, M. P. M. and Bernal, J. (1972). Mother–infant interaction, in *Ethological Studies of Child Behaviour* (Ed. N. Blurton–Jones), Cambridge University Press, Cambridge.

Richards, M. P. M., Bernal, J. F., and Brackbill, Y. (1976). Early behavioural differences: Gender or circumcision. *Dev. Psychobiol.* **9**, 89–95.

Ripin, R. (1930). A study of the infant's feeding reactions during the first six months of life, *Arch. of Psychology*, **18**, 5–44.

Rodin, J. (1978). Has the distinction between internal versus external control of feeding outlived its usefulness, in *Recent Advances in Obesity Research II* (Ed. G. Bray), pp. 75–85, Newman, Oxford.

Rozin, P. and Schiller, D. (1980). The nature and aquisition of a preference for chili pepper by humans, *Motivation & Emotion*, **4**, 77–101.

Sander, L. W. (1962). Issues in early mother child interaction. *J. Am. Acad. Child. Psychiat.*, **1**, 141–166.

Sander, L. W. and Julia, H. L. (1966). Continuous interactional monitoring in the neonate, *Psychosom. Med.*, **28**, 822–835.

Schachter, S. (1971). Some extraordinary facts about obese humans and rats, *Am. Psychologist*, **26**, 129–144.

Sherman, M. (1977). The differentiation of emotional responses in infants. *J. Comp. Psychol.*, **7**, 335–531.

Shirley, M. M. (1931). The sequential method for the study of maturing behaviour patterns, *Psychol. Rev.*, **38**, 507–528.

Shukla, A., Forsyth, H. A., Anderson, C. M., and Marwah, S. M. (1972). Infantile overnutrition in the first year of life: a field study in Dubley, Worcestershire, *BMJ*, **4**, 507–515.

Smart, J. L. (1978). Human milk fat and satiety: an appealing idea revisited, *Early Human Development*, **2**, 395–397.

Sosa, R., Kennell, J. H., Klaus, M., and Urrutia, J. J. (1976). The effect of early mother–infant contact on breast feeding, infection and growth, in *Breast-Feeding and the Mother: Ciba Foundation Symposium, No. 45*. Elsevier, Amsterdam.

Spitz, R. A. (1945). Hospitalism, *Psychoanal. Stud. Child.*, **2**, 313–342.

Taitz, L. S. (1971). Infantile overnutrition among artificially fed infants, *BMJ*, **1**, 315–316.

Taitz, L. S. (1974). Overfeeding in infancy, *Proc. Nutr. Society*, **33**, 113–118.

Thoman, E. B. (1975). Development of synchrony in mother-infant interaction in feeding and other situations, *Fed. Proc.*, **34**, 1587–1592.

Thoman, E. B., Leiderman, P. H., and Olson, J. P. (1972). Neonate–mother interaction during breast feeding, *Dev. Psychol.*, **6**, 110–118.

Tracey, V. V., De, N. C., and Harper, R. J. (1971). Obesity and respiratory infection in infants and young children, *BMJ*, **1**, 16–18.

Wasz-Höckert, O., Lind, J., Vuorenkoski, V., Partanen, T., and Valanne, E. (1968). *The Infant Cry*, Clinics in Developmental Medicine No. 29, SIMP with Heinemann, London.

Wilkinson, P. W. and Davies, D. P. (1978). When and why are babies weaned? *BMJ*, **1**, 1682–1683.

Wolff, P. H. (1968). The serial organization of sucking in the young infant, *Paediatrics*, **42**, 943–956.

Wolff, P. H. (1969). The natural history of crying and other vocalisations in early infancy, in *Determinants of Infant Behaviour, Vol. 4* (Ed. B. Foss), 81–109.

Wright, P., Fawcett, J., and Crow, R. A. (1980). The development of differences in the feeding behaviour of bottle and breast-fed human infants, *Behavioral Processes*. **5**, 1–20.

SECTION IV

Implications

Each of the preceding chapters has reviewed a particular area in accordance with criteria which allowed clear decisions about which subject matter was significant. It is now time to draw out the immediate implications of our understanding of the psychobiology of the newborn, as portrayed in this book. This is a necessarily limited exercise for two reasons. First, an attempt at a comprehensive and fully coherent analysis would be a major theoretical undertaking well beyond the scope of this final section. Secondly it does not seem appropriate to make specific prescriptions concerning particular situations. Decisions over whether to intervene to modify the environment or adaptational processes of a newborn, or over the introduction of a different form of obstetric care, are usually complex and involve considerations in areas such as economics and administration which are not the province of this book. However, such decisions must be made, and usually under pressure of time and restrictions on available information. The task for this final section then, is to draw out the general principles in ways that make it easier for a wider perspective on neonatal psychobiology to be readily incorporated into such decision-making processes. This is tackled first by an analysis of what is probably the most complex and sophisticated of neonatal functions—social interaction, then by a summary of the major themes which have emerged from this review.

In Chapter 14, Hanuš and Mechthild Papoušek present a current view of how the psychobiology of the newborn predisposes towards the achievement of social integration within the normal caretaking environment. It is a complex story, but one in which we can use recent advances in our knowledge to get behind overgeneralized concepts like 'preference for the human face' to see some of the detail of the mechanisms which are involved. The high level of neonatal cognitive functioning demonstrated in Section 2 is here shown to be intrinsically involved in the social process. A concept discussed by the Papoušeks, which seems likely to play an increasingly important role in our theorizing of the next few years is that of contingency. It is a familiar aspect of current theories of attachment that the young infant is selectively sensitive to phenomena which occur as an apparent consequence of his or her own behaviour, and that in normal circumstances the motor abilities of the newborn are such that nearly all such contingent events will emanate from socially competent care-givers. While the empirical evidence for such a phenomenon is very strong, there are issues concerning its formulation which are far from trivial. Just what cognitive abilities of the newborn allow for this form of perception of causality, remains to be discovered, but the discovery may be delayed unless the question is appropriately formulated.

From the analysis of reciprocal interaction it becomes clear that a major obstacle to our understanding of neonatal social functioning is our ignorance of parental behaviour. As evidence begins to emerge showing that the behaviour of one parent is influenced by the presence and attitudes of the other, it would seem that we will have to extend our models from dyadic interaction to take account of transactions involving three or more participants. The Papoušeks also draw attention to the complex relationships between forms of parenting and the adaptational demands imposed by the particular ecology within which the family must function. However, they conclude that the major function of parenting in the neonatal period is to train the baby in forms of social interaction and that this will only be achieved in the context of a one-to-one interaction. The overall implication of this chapter would seem to be that our practical priority must be to provide the conditions which allow full expression to the predispositions of both mother and father to engage in didactically structured interchanges during dyadic interaction with their baby.

Although there is considerable diversity in the material and approaches of the different chapters, some very consistent common themes can be detected. In the final chapter I have attempted to draw out these themes and to illustrate them primarily by reference to material which is discussed in detail in earlier chapters. The themes that have been identified provide an interesting perspective and will hopefully function as useful summary statements for anyone who is planning for the care of, or for research with, human newborns. They are, however, a first attempt and no doubt reflect the personal biases of the author. Furthermore I would not claim that they encapsulate more than a proportion of the substance of the book. It is to be hoped that the inadequacy of this particular attempt will provoke others to refine and add to the themes described here. Many of the more important practical implications are indicated in the concluding review of the flow of influence and particularly of information between parents, institutional care-givers, and the newborn. While it becomes clear that there is considerable scope for using current knowledge to improve our practices, the limitations in both the factual and the theoretical background are even more apparent. Here too the hope is that these limitations will not be used as an excuse for disregarding the positive implications but rather, will inspire a determined attempt to add to our stock of reliable and significant information.

Psychobiology of the Human Newborn
Edited by P. Stratton

CHAPTER 14

Integration into the Social World: Survey of research

HANUŠ PAPOUŠEK and MECHTHILD PAPOUŠEK

The social integration of an individuum into the human society is a lifetime process; the first 28 days of it may seem to be a mere negligible part. The reader may seriously doubt whether any attributes of social integration or any forms of prosocial behaviour can be evident in the newborn at all. Parents do not doubt. Typically, they hold the newborn for a social being from the very beginning and start communicating with him as soon as a chance is given to them. An increasing amount of studies indicate as well that the neonatal period of social integration has become a topic of major research interest.

The main impulses for research have come from different directions, for instance from clinical reports on the consequences of early maternal deprivation (Lowrey, 1940; Goldfarb, 1944) or from biological studies on imprinting (Heinroth, 1910; Lorenz, 1935). Comparative biologists have drawn attention to the biological origins of human social behaviours (Blurton Jones, 1972; Hinde, 1974). A closer look at the first human social interchange revealed, however, how little had been known of either the manifestations or the underlying structure of the neonatal 'social integration'. Moreover, the behavioural rescue category of 'parental love' in the adult partner has appeared neither easy to define and operationalize for research nor reliable for guiding the infant's social integration. Parental neglect or maltreatment of infants have taken an unexpected position next to parental deprivation in the clinical pathology of social integration.

A re-evaluation of women's social roles, and changing attitudes towards the traditional Western family structure have nourished the public interest in early social experience and stressed the need for research. The present intensity of infancy research seems to indicate more than just a methodological and conceptual break-through in scientific approaches. It also constitutes a general correction to the trend of human efforts favouring technological progress beyond

367

the limits of natural resources, but neglecting the concern for a healthy individual development and the satisfaction of natural human rights.

These circumstances do not facilitate an attempt to synthesize the present state of knowledge. Even recent attempts to outline a general view of human social development (Cairns, 1979) reflect gaps in the knowledge of its very beginning and biological roots. Obviously, the present situation calls for successive attempts of syntheses even at the price of necessary successive corrections in the near future.

One of the most difficult problems is the attribution of social values to new achievements of research under the pressure of public interests. Although a scientist may bear in mind only the growth of knowledge, parents, teachers, social workers, and physicians usually expect him to be motivated by the practical social meaning of his discovery. They want to improve the outlooks of children and mankind not realizing that if it is difficult to prove correlations between early interventions and later human happiness, it is almost impossible to estimate how the prosperity of mankind could be influenced by interventions continued across many generations.

Some limited predictions can be derived from extrapolations of trends evident in comparisons between present and palaeontologic states of evolution. However, due to paucity of relicts related to parent-infant interchanges, this method has not helped significantly either. To a degree, a palaeontologic excursion can be substituted with a detailed analysis of the earliest ontogeny as an analogy for phylogeny. It is not necessary to do so on the recapitulationistic grounds of Haeckel (1866); such analogy may result from a mere lack of better alternatives (Koffka, 1928). For instance, Piaget (1969) draws parallels between the acquisition of logicomathematical knowledge in children and the history of Western science, although he denies recapitulation as a mechanism of such parallels. A close look at the initial parent–newborn interchange has been considered as one of the approaches to the biological roots of parenting (Papoušek and Papoušek, 1978). Hess (1970) gives Lorenz's (1943) 'babyishness' as an example of a biologically rooted releaser which may have promoted infant care in primitive man before societies were ever formed and thus may have had a high survival value for the species of man.

Within the framework of this book, the biological roots of social integration call for special attention. They should not be taken as separable equivalents of genetic determinants. The term 'biological roots' has been chosen for fundamental behaviours of major adaptive significance. Such behaviours, as generally acknowledged, depend more on genetic factors than on social prescriptions and conscious decisions, are rather universally distributed, and often develop early during ontogeny. Both aspects of early interchanges, the initial integrative capacities and behaviours relevant to social transaction, as well as both partners involved, the newborn and his adult care-taker, represent rather specific problems. Let us first consider what is known about the newborn's integration.

EARLY INTEGRATIVE CAPACITIES: TO KNOW MEANS
ALMOST EVERYTHING

Social interchanges, even the earliest ones, represent complex phenomena occurring in very dynamic situations the structure of which is dominated by the partners' behaviours. Both on stimulational and on responsive sides, large numbers of elementary units appear in constantly varying combinations. Their spatial and temporal patterns can be expressed only in probabilistic terms. Yet, they are not absolutely random; they are patterned under different influences such as seasonal and circadian regularities in environment or predictable inclinations in human response systems. Behavioural patterns are often ambiguous, and yet, situational contexts may give them quite specific meanings (Richards, 1974). Their perception and processing can hardly be explained without considering adequate complex operations such as the detection of cue signals and structural invariants, comparisons between present and past experience, categorization, concept formation, predictions, and decisions for optimal alternatives from a broad repertoire of potential responses.

Highly structured patterns appear already in the newborn's behaviour (Richards, 1974; Wolff, 1977), and parents as well as students of early interactions are eminently interested in their meanings. Parents may label neonatal behaviours naively and inadequately; however, they respond to them with consistencies of potential evolutionary significance, although perhaps being unaware of them. Observers may introduce elaborate systems for categorizing neonatal behaviours and yet end in traps of their own constructs perhaps due to zoomorphism, adultomorphism, restrictive methodology, disrespect to situational context, or dogmatic inability in appropriate cases to reopen concepts constructed *a priori*.

Similar fallacies have become evident under attacks on attachment and dependency concepts launched from social learning, psychobiological, and clinical positions (Gewirtz, 1972). Confrontations between behaviouristic, ethologic, cognitive, and psycholinguistic approaches have helped to point out further fallacies as exemplified in discussions on claims and limits of human ethology (von Cranach *et al.*, 1979). However, the lack of systematic research weakens the arguments of individual discussants. Even in the same book (Alloway *et al.*, 1977), help is being sought both in naturalistic observations (Marvin) and in the return from naturalistic observations to controlled conditioning procedures (Gewirtz).

Probably the most fruitful outcomes from such confrontations are acknowledgements of psychobiological aspects, systems for dyadic interactions, and psychological models including intrinsic integrative processes. The question of whether these individual outcomes call for differential approaches or share a common ground from which common fundamental phenomena could be pointed out and the confusing number of theories could be reasonably reduced at least in relation to the initial social integration, deserves some attention.

Let us consider the interrelation between emotional and social behaviours. Although both are difficult to define and to differentiate (Poirier, 1977; Sroufe, 1979), one or other has been explicitly or tacitly assumed to provide the primary basis for communicative or cognitive developments in most theories. For instance Vygotsky (1962) believes social activity to be the base for the development of psychological processes and affects to exist in a firm unity with intellect. As to early infancy, Trevarthen (1979) most radically stresses 'primary intersubjectivity' as the central motivator and regulator for human mental growth which, in embryonic form, is functional in the newborn. In theories on the evolution of mind, emotions together with intelligence and volition are considered as basic and not easily separable mental processes (Herrick, 1956). Piaget and Inhelder (1969) stress the interrelation of cognition and affect as of two inseparable and irreducible aspects of behaviour with particular explicitness. Lock (1978) holds emotions to be the initial basis of symbolic systems during the emergence of language.

Direct access to keys for better analyses of mental processes has remained sealed by nature. Perceptual psychology has no methods for the study of proprioceptive perception of muscle activities or for the perception of intrinsic invariants resulting from processes of thought comparable to the methods for exteroceptive reception. Labelled as 'black-box phenomena' both keys have been left aside for future discoveries in neurosciences, although hypothetical models including them allow interesting interpretations of early social integration (Papoušek, 1981).

In an attempt to conceptualize the infant's fundamental regulation of behaviour, Papoušek and Papoušek (1975; 1979a) attribute the primary significance to integrative nervous processes, i.e. to all those simple or complex processes involved in the analysis of situational stimulation and in the organization of the resulting adaptive responses. Their argument is that motor systems, autonomic or somatic, which are responsible for and common to all categories of behaviour observable during extrauterine life, are already integrated in complex adaptive patterns at birth, well before they may acquire new dimensions and meanings due to learning or situational contexts. The perfect coordination of sucking, swallowing, and breathing, eventually combined with grasping and postural reflexes, is a typical example. The structure of such patterns is hierarchical, involves immense numbers of units grouped in subsystems such as synergists and antagonists, can be adjusted to environmental and/or intrinsic requirements, and thus represents an analogy or even a precedent for the integration of experience in processes of thought.

The further argument is that the post-partum adaptive differentiation of motor patterns follows certain strategies which can be demonstrated soon after birth as well. It is relatively easy to demonstrate experimentally that a mere modification of the spatial and temporal structure of the same situation sets in operation different forms of adequate integrative processes in the infant as if triggering some preprogrammed inborn responses (Papoušek and Papoušek, 1975). Thus if exposed to a repetitive stimulation, the newborn will activate orienting responses and inhibit (habituate) them again if the stimulation appears to be irrelevant and independent of the newborn's behaviour. As soon as the newborn perceives a change in the repetitive stimulation, his orienting responses will increase (dishabituate) again (Bartoshuk, 1962; Bridger, 1961; Engen et al., 1963; Friedman, 1972; Graham et al., 1968; Keen, 1964). The same is true about aversive responses (eye-blink reflex) during the newborn's quiet, non-REM sleep (Martinius and Papoušek, 1970). If the same stimulation appears to be regularly associated with other relevant events, for instance elicitors of eye-blink responses, and thus to represent a conditioning signal, it will be answered with another adequate behaviour learned through associative conditioning (Janoš, 1959). Still another adjustment will be seen if the newborn is allowed to control the given stimulation by his own act. Orienting responses will then increase strikingly and remain resistant to habituation; the newborn will mobilize a lot of effort to learn how to control the stimulation through instrumental learning (Papoušek, 1964; 1967; Siqueland and Lipsitt, 1966).

In order to respond to any biologically relevant situation, the organism first has to activate the mechanisms controlling informational input and processing and all subsequent cognitive or learning processes up to the evaluation of the final outcome. Orienting, approach or exploratory activities parallel these processes in overt behaviour. The triggering structural invariants belong to relational intrinsic invariants resulting from the processing of information within the CNS. Thus 'novelty' or 'familiarity' can only result from some comparison between past and present experience, 'contingency' from some interaction between the exteroceptive perception of the environmental change and the interoceptive perception of behaviour eliciting that environmental change. It is difficult to imagine any type of integration of experience, for instance comparison, categorization, concept formation, or abstraction without taking intrinsic invariants into account.

Integrative processes of higher complexity, i.e. the fundamental cognitive operations, previously assumed to be analysable only at the verbal age, have been successfully demonstrated in preverbal infants not very far beyond the neonatal age. Categorical perception of certain phonetic distinctions of speech sound, for instance of voice-onset-time differences in stop consonants or their differences in place of articulation, has been shown in 1-month-old infants by Eimas and his collaborators (Cutting and Eimas, 1975; Eimas et al., 1971). Categorical perception of colour hues has been reported in 4-month-old infants (Bornstein, 1975; Bornstein et al., 1975). Innovative methods for the study of concept formation and rule detection have been introduced by Papoušek and Bernstein (1969) and Bower (1974).

It is difficult to say nowadays, whether categorical perception belongs to innate capacities of the human infant. If it is true that 1-day-old newborns precisely synchronize their movements to the articulation of adult speech (Condon and Sander, 1974) then a predominant biological origin is probable. Logically, however, the biological roots of the integrative processes mentioned above can be traced back to the neonatal or even prenatal age.

Other mechanisms obviously function in the opposite way enabling the organism to reduce the amount of informational input, to turn away or avoid sources of excessive stimulation or stimulation too difficult to process. Under everyday naturalistic conditions, the activation of mechanisms increasing or reducing informational input and processing fluctuate between orienting and its habituation. However, the activation may be overexaggerated in either direction in problematic situations if a solution is too difficult to find. Then it may be crucially important how effectively reduction mechanisms will protect the organisms against exhaustion and hardly tolerable frustration. In newborns and younger infants Papoušek (1969) has observed a protective 'biological fuse' in the form of a sudden change in the behavioural state resembling 'playing possum'. Infants above 2 months of age respond more frequently with a redistribution of attention in similar situations.

The Papoušeks' model of the fundamental adaptive response system necessarily mirrors contemporary ideas on the interrelation between actions and thoughts nourished by progress in neuropsychology, cognitive psychology, and epistemology (e.g. Bernstein, 1967; Bruner, 1974, 1975; Piaget and Inhelder, 1969; Pribram, 1971). However, their model has grown from a confrontation of those ideas with their own long-term studies of integrative capacities in human newborns and infants. In former studies, a convenient act was found in head-turns for modelling the development from a simple reflexive movement to a highly differentiated voluntary act and for analyses of integrative capacities reaching from orienting and instrumental conditioning to problem solving or detection and acquisition of rules (Papoušek, 1967; Papoušek and Bernstein, 1969).

Though analysed under non-social laboratory conditions, the integrative processes under study appeared to be closely related to communicative and affective behaviours as was made obvious by predictable changes of vocalizations, facial expressions, and autonomic parameters.

What deserves particular attention from the psychobiological point of view are the motivational aspects of the fundamental adaptive response system. Facial and vocal signs of displeasure may accompany the infant's confrontation with too much novelty and become strikingly strong in difficult learning or problem solving situations. On the other hand, various degrees of pleasure may be observed in connection with successful outcomes of the activation of integrative processes. An identification of a familiar object, a fulfilled prediction, successful learning or a mastery of control over a contingent event may elicit distinct signs of relaxation, pleasure or joy. In 4 to 5-month-olds, it was shown experimentally, that this sort of intrinsic motivation can exceed the gratification of other needs (Papoušek, 1967; Papoušek and Papoušek, 1975, 1979a). The infantile organism is strongly motivated for the acquisition of knowledge for which it can mobilize a lot of effort and overcome unpleasant difficulties, and which, in itself, is intrinsically rewarded with pleasant feelings, perhaps fundamental to all other pleasant categories of the gratification of needs.

The acquisition of knowledge can be viewed as a movement from 'known' to 'unknown', directed by the integrative processes so as to avoid the stress from novelty on one hand and the stress from boredom on the other (Papoušek and Papoušek, 1978). A high degree of novelty or incongruity compels the system to accumulate information and integrate it into a satisfactory concept and close this concept on the 'unknown'. As soon as this goal is reached, a high degree of familiarity may elicit an opposite tendency in the system, i.e. a tendency to open the seemingly complete concept, view the 'known' from non-traditional aspects, bring it into new relations and thus to make the 'known' more 'unknown' again. In this way a higher level of informational integration is reached in which more sophisticated concepts and higher degrees of knowledge can be achieved in playful or creative ways. According to this concept, play can only start at the point where a certain amount of integrated knowledge has already been accumulated, consequently not at the very beginning of postnatal life.

The human integration of experience enables the growth of a very complex cognitive competence including verbal communication, abstract symbolization, intentional action, and self-consciousness. Recently the question of their biological roots has been raised and rather speculative attempts have been made to trace the evidence of intentionality and consciousness back to the neonatal period of ontogeny (Trevarthen, 1979).

The development of intentional and conscious behaviours—two hardly distinguishable categories—may well have a common origin in some of the universal integrative capacities. Lewis and Brooks-Gunn (1979) assume that every knowledge of the 'other' reflects in some way in the knowledge of 'self'. Collecting experience with the world around, every organism potentially collects experience with its own 'self', however, this experience may be integrated in very different ways in individual species. For a neurophysiologist, it is obvious, that touching something else is perceived differently than touching oneself or being touched by something else. Similarly observing movements of one's own hand and of another hand, perceptions of own movements in a static environment versus movements of environment alone, hearing one's own voice or another voice are sources of differential information allowing the development of differential concepts of self and the rest of one's world.

The capability to detect consequences of one's behaviour is particularly relevant for self-awareness, intentionality, and causality. For this reason the interpretation of instrumental acts has played a major role in theories of cognitive development. Fundamental contingency awareness motivating the newborn for repeated trials to master contingent events can also be viewed as the earliest manifestation of causality awareness and self-awareness. The newborn's instrumental act is by principle the earliest form of purposeful, i.e. intentional act in spite of the newborn's incapability to preset a goal and look for ways of achievement consciously. The fundamental capacity of instrumental learning has obviously brought significant profits during evolution and, therefore, has become so universal and interconnected with a powerful system of intrinsic motivation. Its universality in the animal world has been stressed by Thorpe (1956), and its innate character demonstrated in human newborns by Papoušek (1964), Sameroff (1968) and Siqueland and Lipsitt (1966), in 1-day-old rats by Johanson and Hall (1979), and in human prematures by Solkoff and Cotton (1975). The affective signs of pleasure described by Papoušek (1967) correspond to Bühler's (1919) 'functional pleasure' or 'causality pleasure' studied in older children by Nuttin (1973) and Heckhausen (1974), Nuttin, for instance, has distinguished between 'stimulation pleasure' and 'causality pleasure' and demonstrated in 5-year-olds a much higher motivational effect in the 'causality pleasure'.

Though observed in non-social situations, the set of fundamental adaptive behaviours related to the course of integrative operations does include cues relevant for the analysis of early social integration. In fact, only in connection with social interchanges do these behaviours acquire their most significant dimensions, and the applicability of the Papoušeks' explanatory model reaches an encouraging level (Papoušek and Papoušek, 1975, 1978). The justification for the attention given to this model here is to be re-examined in the following sections.

SOCIAL INTEGRATION: THE NEGLECTED PARENT

Is the infant a social being, or is he formed to a social being from a non-social animal matter? The neighbouring chapters of Richards (1974) and Ainsworth *et al.* (1974) in the same book on the infant's social integration exemplify two opposing opinions of many other authors. Whereas Richards holds a newborn infant to be socially incompetent, totally dependent on the goodwill of adults, and therefore a non-social creature, Ainsworth and her co-workers view the newborn as genetically biased towards interactions with other people, pre-adapted to a social world, and in this sense social from the beginning.

It is difficult to bring convincing arguments and even more difficult to categorize behaviours as social or non-social for the purposes of exact evaluation without teleological interpretation or deliberate subjective predetermination. One can fall into the trap of the 'hen and egg' question when speculating; whether evolution has favoured the differentiation of facial movements because they belong to means of communication or vice versa preferential reading from facial movements during communication because they are most closely interrelated with integrative mechanisms and thus reflect processes of thought in a particularly fast, fine-grain manner.

Whereas in comparative sciences enough evidence has repeatedly been accumulated to justify the assumption of a pre-adaptation of social behaviour to the reciprocal behaviours of conspecifics, not enough is known about the human newborn. Let us consider the studies on the visual and auditory competence of infants, the two research areas with relatively exact methodologies and large collections of data.

The former assumption of Bowlby (1958) that there is an innate bias in human newborns to attend visually to human faces has attracted a lot of scientific attention, but has not been confirmed. The most careful analyses, reviewing this problem recently (Cohen et al., 1979; Haith, 1979), conclude that there is only very little evidence of an innate preference for human faces, and that the perception of faces seems to follow the general course of form and pattern perception.

An innate predisposition for the perception of the human voice in human infants has seemed to be documented even more reliably until recently. It has been supposed that the infant, although he has to learn to speak, does not have to learn to hear speech sounds; he discriminates all phonemically significant contrasts naturally from birth. Since language has been taken as a species-specific competence emerging with the human in the evolutionary process (Lenneberg, 1967), it has seemed only logical that the human would also have innate mechanisms for the perception of speech-sound categories (Liberman et al., 1967). Only the human has a supralaryngeal vocal tract capable of producing the full repertoire of speech sounds (Lieberman et al., 1972); thus categorical perception might evolve of phonetic categorization. Moreover, the newborn is influenced more by acoustic signals if their frequencies correspond to the carrier range for speech (Eisenberg, 1976), and infants—like adults—discriminate categorically and in linguistic mode continua such as voiced-voiceless (Eimas et al., 1971), place of articulation (Eimas, 1974), and ear to which presented (Eimas, 1975) as early as at the age of 1 month in some cases.

However, further studies, reviewed by Kuhl (1978), indicate that there are developmental trends in at least some discriminative capacities concerning speech sounds, and the categorical perception reflects more general, non-specific dimensions of acoustic signals so that it can be demonstrated even in the perception of non-speech sounds or in animals. This suggests that 'at least some of the perceptual discontinuities that underlie speech-sound contrasts are a natural result of the mammalian auditory system. Speech sound contrasts were selected to exploit these perceptual discontinuities' (Kuhl, 1978). Thus, language should rather be considered a result of a gradual evolution making use of specific combinations of underlying physiological, perceptual and integrative sub-systems functioning in non-human mammals in general, as suggested by Lieberman et al. (1972).

Interestingly enough, the present research into both the visual and auditory competence of human infants has led to a new view of the newborn as an active percipient with an integrative competence deserving much more attention than his perceptual sensitivity studied in most previous studies. Analysing the motivation of visual scanning in the newborn Haith (1979) stresses the newborn's need for being stimulated and for processing a stimulation, i.e. for maintaining visual cortical firing activity at a sufficiently high level. Next to the physical qualities of a stimulation, Haith draws attention to its meaning based on the infant's preceding experience with that particular stimulation. Haith suggests that scanning may be a very fine indicator of the course of integrative processes.

Wilson (1978) comes to similar conclusions on the infant's active responding to auditory signals and recommends improvements in the methodology of auditory assessment that would place certain integrative tasks in discriminative paradigms, thereby allowing direct assessment of higher order functions rather than of sensitivity alone.

Thus, from the disciplines in which the studies of the initial human competence have achieved relatively high standards, we can learn that the newborn is probably predisposed to respond to rather simple stimulus features, but at the same time able to integrate experience, to respond to intrinsic invariants resulting from such integrations with integrative processes of higher orders, and thus to develop intrinsic configurations of properties corresponding to the meaning of various situational contexts.

It is reasonable to keep this in mind if we are to turn attention to social stimuli and behaviours. There certainly exist social and non-social events in our world, and the difference between them is categorical in many dimensions. However, they can still be understood as structural differences in combinations of common invariants as long as we do not ignore intrinsic invariants resulting from the integration of accumulating experience with both categories of events. Let us for a moment compare the student of social behaviour with someone who tries to understand the meaning of telegrams written in the S. F. B. Morse alphabet. There would be little sense in a microscopic analysis of dots and dashes of this binary system to find the difference between social and non-social messages. Rather it would be necessary to learn the rules for combining the two elements into verbal, numeric, and other symbols allowing use of the same alphabet for giving messages either social or non-social meanings.

One crucial difference between social and non-social events becomes evident if the probabilities with which they fulfill assumptions for effective learning in the newborn are compared in naturalistic environments. As we explain in more detail later, an adequately responsive social partner produces optimal patterns of incentive stimulation in amounts unparalleled in non-social events. Vocalizations, facial expressions or hand movements elicited perhaps secondarily with integrative responsive operations may impose as social behaviours upon the observer mainly due to their highest occurrence in social interactions. From another side, Mason and Berkson (1975) provide a relevant argument in studies on maternal deprivation in monkeys. With one simple shift in the conditions of isolation — the installation of the non-living mother surrogate upon a pendulum swing — they significantly improved the infant's 'social' behaviour and reduced the incidence of 'irreparable social disturbances' reported in otherwise comparable experiments by Harlow and co-workers (Harlow and Harlow, 1969).

It is not difficult to imagine that the rich activation of integrative processes and gratification of 'cognitive needs' within social events soon tunes the newborn in to 'social stimuli' and points his integrative capacities in the proper direction of social integration. This hypothesis has still to be verified. It would allow an alternative interpretation for observations seemingly supporting the assumption of innate social predispositions. For instance Bowlby (1969) reports the newborn to orient to a 'mother figure' non-specifically and to be 'tuned in to stimuli coming from people' in general during the first few weeks. Kuhl (1978), otherwise sceptical about social predispositions, wonders why 6-month-olds imitate speech, but not doorslams, birdsongs, or the music made by mobiles. Marler (1973) does not see it as likely that the ontogeny of social integration could be left purely to chance by the grand design of evolution.

There are at least two more features to be considered in relation to the differences between social and non-social events: Plurimodality and reciprocity. It has been a wise (and inevitable) step of such outstanding experts in early visual perception and cognition as Haith and his collaborators to turn attention to the auditory–visual correspondence in the newborn's integration of environmental events (Haith, 1979; Mendelson, and Haith, 1976). The pilot observations that a human voice sharply reduces the amount of 'out-of-control eye movements' in newborns scanning a blank field indicates valuable potential profits of this orientation. The newborn capacity to process information across modalities has been proved in Papoušek's (1967) studies on neonatal learning in which the newborn learns that his head movement (interoceptive modality) leads to a milk delivery (gustatory modality) if a bell sounds (auditory modality). As Papoušek (1977) stresses, every operant learning, in effect, represents a cross-modal integration of kinaesthetic interoceptive and some exteroceptive modalities.

In naturalistic social interchanges, stimulations affecting the newborn are almost by definition plurimodal, not only visual and auditory, but also tactual, thermal, olfactory, vestibular, and kinaesthetic. Almost each of them has already been shown to be effective in the newborn's perception, integration, and eventually, identification of the mother. The features of cross-modal combinations are individually and culturally different. Macfarlane (1975) has been successful in demonstrating the newborn's ability to identify the mother according to olfactory cues. In the control of eye-to-eye distance between mothers and newborns interesting individual patterns of distance-fluctuations have been observed (Schoetzau, 1979) that should deserve more attention as potential identification features.

Cross-cultural comparisons have pointed out some universal patterns in parental behaviours (Lewis and Ban, 1977), but also differences, for instance in the proportions in which physical contact and contact through telereceptors are mixed in infant–care-taker interactions (Konner, 1977b). Having been observed in environments of evolutionary adaptedness these differences help to understand biological origins of cultural diversity (Wolff, 1977) and perhaps even disclose infant abilities otherwise heavily obscured by cultural practices in Western populations (Konner, 1977a; Papoušek and Papoušek, 1978).

The reciprocal, i.e. interactional character of social events may seem a trivial feature nowadays, however, its introduction into theoretical models has radically improved research in early socialization. At the same time, it has raised difficult methodological questions we still have to face.

Social events assume the participation of at least two persons to start with; thus analytic approaches should consequently work with models of dyadic interaction. This postulate is not a very new discovery; it goes back to James M. Baldwin as Cairns (1979) points out, and yet even after Sears' convincing argumentation (Sears, 1951) it still took years to accept them in developmental studies. Interactional models call for dialectic thinking which goes back to Hegelian philosophy and its antic origins in Socrates and Plato. Yet, its implication still causes difficulties, as is evident in static attempts to define, eventually 'standardize', interacting participants once and for ever, or in the necessity to re-introduce the term 'transactions' of Dewey and Bentley (1949) in order to stress dynamic concepts of interacting partners as if dynamic principles were not included in interactional processes *à priori*.

Individual members within an interacting system mutually influence each other, thus changing themselves. In communicative terms, they both are 'emitters' and 'receivers' simultaneously, even if they perhaps use turn-taking rules in some aspects of communication. Similarly, their responses and emitted signals represent a dialectic unity as much as every response is a potential stimulus for the other member. As living beings the individual members are also dynamic because they unite the features of both open and closed systems; they change with time not only due to the course of interaction but also due to their biological growth or aging (Bertalanffy, 1968).

Although the parent-infant interchange is a perfect example of a dynamic interacting system, it is also to be seen as a system *sui generis* because of a categorical heterogeneity of both members (Papoušek and Papoušek, 1981). They move in a similar direction but at a certain distance given by differences in age, in competence, and in sociocultural roles. This distance gives this dyadic system the character of a didactic system necessitating a specific psychobiological model. However, another gap in research makes this postulate difficult.

Whereas the biological roots of the newborn's behaviour have long been a matter of detailed studies, the biological roots of human parental behaviour have remained almost a *terra incognita*. It is difficult to expect relevant theoretical models for parent–infant interaction if nearly all of what we know about parental behaviour has to do with the physiology of reproduction, pregnancy, birth giving, and lactation. Why then, can maternal deprivation jeopardize the infant's mental health and social integration? And can a father–infant attachment reduce such a risk? Has the father been made an outsider in the infant's life by natural selection or by cultural deviations requiring a correction? Obviously, parenting calls for an increased attention and a more detailed discussion.

DIDACTIC PROGRAMS FOR THE NEWBORN: INTUITIVE PARENTING IN DYADIC INTERCHANGES

Analyses of parental behaviour in laboratory animals have clearly demonstrated that the parent–newborn interaction deserves our full attention. Only a few examples of the vast literature can be given here.

For instance the systematic studies at Rutgers University have elucidated the alternating roles of endocrinous and psychological factors in the regulation of maternal behaviour in rats (Rosenblatt, 1975). In virgin rats, a sensitization to newborn pups can occur on a non-hormonal base. During pregnancy, an effective sensitization develops under a complex hormonal influence, culminates shortly before parturition, but decreases sharply after parturition if not maintained by the psychological interaction with pups. During the transition from hormonal to non-hormonal regulation, maternal sensitization is labile and can be disrupted for instance by externally induced stress. Pup-killing in mice having a too large litter (Gandelman and Simon, 1978) might be a consequence of a similar lability and indicate its adaptive significance.

Animal male parents share parenting in manifold ways and different proportions including complete role-reversal with a female defending a harem of males in Jacanidae, the male emu incubating the eggs of one or several females and caring alone for the young, or the male fish (Osteoglossidae) mouthbrooding eggs (for a review see Ridley, 1978). The variety of behaviours such as nest building, territory defending, brooding, prosocial care for progeny etc., is rich, perhaps with the exception of behaviours supporting the development of integrative abilities.

The literature on human parenting is vast as well, but contrasts in the paucity of data on innate, instinctive forms of parental behaviours which can hardly be explained just in terms of the immense general plasticity of human behaviour. There are good reasons to believe that parenting necessitates reflexive, automated or ritualized behaviours as will be explained later. Moreover, instinctive behaviours are pointers to the biological roots and evolutionary past of parenting.

The first period of increased interest in parenting started with the earlier reports on maternal (Lowery, 1940; Goldfarb, 1944) and paternal deprivations (Bach, 1946; Lynn and Sawrey, 1959; Sears *et al.*, 1946; Stoltz, 1954). Retrospective approaches at that time did not yet include detailed analyses of parental behaviours. Later interest has been influenced by ethological concepts of attachment and experimental approaches. However, it has been directed toward later months of infancy. Thus even at present, it is not easy to construct a model of parenting that would fit the interactional counterpart in the newborn.

Logically, phylogeny might have favoured the following principles in the scenario of parental care for relatively immature human newborns:

1. be altruistic, the newborn's life is crucial for the future of your kin;
2. give the newborn necessary comfort and nourishment, do not leave it alone, and pay attention to signals indicating that you are doing something wrong;
3. protect the newborn against danger of any kind and do so in time, learn to anticipate danger;
4. show very distinctly what your offspring will need most to become socially integrated and similar to other members of your kin.

With respect to the significance of integrative processes in human evolution, the related principle should perhaps be specified in more detail. Studies of neonatal learning permit the definition of the following general assumptions (Papoušek and Papoušek, 1981):

1. optimal waking state and attention in the newborn;
2. optimal structure of stimulation provided by parents;
3. frequent repetitions of learning tasks;
4. gradual ordering of capacities to be trained according to their development in infancy;
5. facilitation with optimal rewarding mechanisms and respect to feedback signals indicating where the limits of tolerance are.

Basically, these assumptions of successful learning are similar to those used in educational programmes at school, but have not been consciously transformed in culturally determined programmes for the didactic care of newborns. In a recent attempt to trace documents back to the Mediterranean cradle of European civilization, Bell and Harper (1977) have not found a set of parental interventions of that kind. Thus, an impression might be generated that mental growth starts at a later age or is independent of parental efforts, unless both parents and their observers are unaware of interventions carried out under minimal conscious control.

The existence of a transitional lability of maternal sensitization in the rat immediately after parturition justifies to a degree the question whether something analogous exists in man and could perhaps help to explain some cases of child abuse or parental rejection. Here, even a trend with potential adaptive value would clearly violate ethical principles and laws in most present cultures. However, there seems to be evidence of a reversal in prosocial behaviour under extreme ecological pressure. Turnbull (1972) reports an interesting example in the Ik population of North Uganda. In concordance with the ecological theory which views the evolution of parenting as a process leading from primary environmental adaptations through alterations in the demographic parameters to changes in parenting (Wilson, 1975), altruism almost does not exist in the Ik population. A full stomach is the highest value, even defecation is more pleasurable than sexual intercourse, sickness or death of others elicit joy, the care for children is reduced to a minimum, and abuse of them does not lead to protests in the community.

It is questionable how far such behavioural aberrations are adaptive. However, they remind one of ecological differences that might easily be forgotten. If it is adaptive and culturally plausible to initiate vivid motor activities in Western newborns, it still may be maladaptive to do so under the circumstances of some Australian Aboriginals where any increase in loss of water may have fatal consequences.

The fact that parents provide the newborn with necessary care even under very unfavourable conditions indicates the existence of a reliable responsiveness to an attention-getting stimulus which is stable and thus probably morphological. Such a universal stimulus is known to exist in both animal and human infants in their 'babyishness' (Lorenz, 1943), i.e. in their relatively short and heavy limbs, large head with prominent, bulbous forehead, large eyes located below the middle of the face, and round, protruding cheeks. Hess (1967) measured the responsiveness to babyishness in terms of pupilary dilation which indicates a primary response to a biological releaser. This releaser might have promoted infant care in primitive man before societies were ever formed and might have proved of high survival value for the species of man, according to Hess.

Recent studies have confirmed the validity of responsiveness to babies across ages in both sexes, but with stage-related waxing and waning of sex differences as it corresponds to the notion of functionally based differences in sex roles rather than to sociobiological or trait theories (Berman *et al.*, 1979; Feldman and Nash, 1978, 1979a, b; Frodi and Lamb, 1978; Sternglanz *et al.*, 1977).

In the human, the typical behaviours providing the newborn with necessary comfort, protection, and nourishment have been taken over by cultural institutions to a degree reducing the rationale for further detailed studies of those behaviours. For instance, maternal behaviours facilitating nursing, such as massaging of the breast, stimulation of nipple erection before breast-feeding, and holding the newborn in an appropriate position have not attracted much attention, although deviations in those behaviours may cause practical difficulties including the newborn's rejection of breast feeding after a severe obstruction of nostrils once experienced by him during nursing (Gunther, 1961). Typical tendencies to touch the newborn with open palms, to give him maximum bodily proximity, and to direct breath toward him may be relics of necessary protection from our evolutionary past (Papoušek and Papoušk, 1979b). However, they may also be interpreted as emotional or communicative behaviours.

Unlike the newborn, the parent is undoubtedly capable of communicative skills and knows how to deliver, obtain or store information. In order to care for the newborn properly, the parent has to interpret the newborn's behaviour, i.e. to communicate (Richards, 1978). Moreover, he does communicate verbally and non-verbally toward the newborn as toward a competent dialogue partner immediately after birth. The earliest human social interchange starts with an urgent need for a dialogue on the adult's side and with a tacit readiness of the adult to accept any response in the newborn as a satisfactory share of dialogue.

During a few recent years, this dialogue has become a matter of increasing interest and application of modern methods enabling a real microanalysis of the vocal, facial, or other motor behaviours involved. Being aware of the early cognitive competence of human infants the students of human early interactions have paid more attention to the supportive role of parenting for the development of learning and cognitive capacities in the infants than their colleagues in animal research. Some of the assumptions for successful learning mentioned earlier have been found to be met within social interchanges to a surprising degree (Papoušek and Papoušek, 1978, 1979 b).

Several behaviours help the parent to evaluate the newborn's behavioural state or the level of arousal and thus to decide correctly whether to stimulate or not. They are interpretable as tests of muscle tone in the areas of mouth, chin, hands or legs. Attempts to open the newborn's mouth show not only the degree of resistance, but may also elicit a variety of oral responses corresponding to the degree of hunger or readiness to pay the parent increased attention. The position of hands and/or the resistance against opening the newborn's palm, and eventually the intensity of grasp provide similar information (Papoušek and Papoušek, 1977). In a waking newborn, arm and finger extension versus arm and finger flexion indicate approach or avoidance tendencies depending on the amount of stimulation (McGuire, and Turkewitz, 1978). The transition from waking states to sleep is characterized by a gradually decreasing muscle tone and dropping of fingers, hands, and finally arms, and thus gives the parent distinct visual cues for the interpretation of state. Moreover, the parent can intuitively manipulate ambiguous behavioural states in the newborn in order to attain optimal attention for interchange. Holding the newborn upright and talking to him is the most common pattern (Thoman et al., 1977).

One parameter of elicited attention and at the same time an important condition for the delivery of visual messages is the visual contact between the parent and the newborn. Its analysis is technically difficult, but rewarding, and has uncovered interesting parental behaviours facilitating the achievement and maintenance of visual contact.

Thus the parent tries to stay centred in the newborn's visual field in the face-to-face position whenever the newborn seems ready to pay attention to him. Independently of his own optimal observation distance (usually 40–50 cm) the parent chooses an eye-to-eye distance of 20–25 cm when talking to an attentive newborn (Papoušek and Papoušek, 1977; Schoetzau and Papoušek, 1977). And for every achieved visual contact the parent contingently carries out a 'greeting response' beginning with a slight retroflexion of the head, raised eyebrows, widely opened eyes, and slightly opened mouth, followed by a smile or verbal greeting. The relation between greeting response and visual contact has been shown with films of the mirror image of this response on the newborn's cornea (Papoušek and Papoušek, 1979b).

All behaviours controlling the visual contact are carried out even by parents who do not believe the newborn to be capable of seeing at all. The ranges within which the mean interactional eye-to-eye distance (22.5 cm) fluctuates show interesting individual differences (Schoetzau, 1979) the significance of which is not yet clear. They may help in maintaining the visual contact, since prior to 2 months of age infants respond to movement and rarely focus on internal features of a passive human face (Maurer and Salapatek, 1976). They may also represent a vestibular or proprioceptive stimulation allowing identification of the mother.

Still another aspect of visual contact concerns the cross-culturally universal (Richards and Finger, 1975) maternal tendency to hold their babies on the left shoulder. Salk (1973) has found this tendency to be independent of the maternal handedness and suggested that babies may be quieter on the left shoulder because they can perceive the mother's heartbeat there. Recently, however, Ginsburg *et al.* (1979) have shown that mothers hold babies on that arm which facilitates visual contact in relation to the infant's bias in head-turning. The majority of infants show right-head-turning preference and tend to be held on the mother's left arm whereas those with left-head-turning preference tend to be held on the right arm. The right-head-turning tendency had been reported before in different studies (Turkewitz *et al.*, 1965; Caron, 1967; Cohen, 1972; Papoušek, 1960; Siqueland, 1964), and occurs even in non-stimulated infants in supine position (Gesell, 1945). There it elicits an asymmetrical tonic neck reflex, which places one hand in the infant's visual field. As a result, the majority of infants have more visual experience with their right hands. Coryell and Michel (1978) hold this bias to be the origin of human handedness.

Parents tend to carry out simple and repetitive patterns in various behavioural categories when interacting with infants, and cope thus with another assumption of neonatal learning. The best example can be demonstrated in the adjustment of vocal performance, i.e. in babytalk (Papoušek and Papoušek, 1975). Infant-directed speech is slower and modified for intelligibility, its vocabulary is restricted and concrete, its pitch higher and more variable than in adult-to-adult dialogues (Newport, 1977). It is astonishing how quickly a mother may switch between two so strikingly different forms of speech when talking alternately to the newborn and to another adult (Papoušek and Papoušek, 1979b). This readiness develops early in 3–4-year-old children (Slobin, 1968), lasts to high age, and is used by non-parents as well (Snow, 1972).

Since imitation takes an important place among processes of social integration it is interesting that parents intuitively imitate some neonatal behaviours, facial expressions and vocalizations in particular, from the very beginning of interactions with the newborn. On one hand, they thus offer a 'biological mirror' or 'echo' which may help the newborn to associate observable correlates with the production of corresponding behaviours on his side. On the other, the matched behaviour of the parent represents a contingency which the newborn can control instrumentally as the first step leading to later imitation practicing. Another question is the age at which the infant can start imitating the parent. According to Meltzoff and Moore (1977), 12–21-day-old newborns can imitate tongue protrusion, lip protrusion, mouth opening, and sequential finger movements. Jacobson (1979) has tested and confirmed a competing hypothesis that seemingly imitative behaviour can be elicited non-specifically under a state of general arousal. Her data indicate that selective imitation develops gradually and is not present in very young infants. As in the case of 'pseudoconditioning' at the beginning of conditioning studies, a control procedure needs to be introduced in order to eliminate 'pseudoimitation' resulting either from a generalization of dominant behaviours or from an instrumental control of matching parental behaviour.

On the whole, those various examples show that in the intuitive parental behaviours there are tendencies initiating and supporting various fundamental integrative processes in the newborn during the early neonatal period. Due to them the parent may soon become familiar, predictable or controllable within the limits of the newborn's initial competence. The fundamental processes may only represent a modest beginning, however, it is the beginning of a very important development at the end of which the achieved social integration includes powerful means of communication and thought. Two particular aspects are relevant from the point of view of the conceptual frame of this chapter.

First is the intuitive character of observed behaviours. It should not be understood as a mere consequence of incidentally decreased conscious control, nor as a negligible relic of low-level responses. In fact, the amount of intuitively produced segments in the interlocked chain of social interchange could hardly be replaced with consciously controlled behaviours. It would disrupt the dialogue and exhaust the parent in a short time.

Secondly, it has become evident that a didactically structured interchange with a newborn is conceivable only in the dyadic form of interchange. A plurilateral interaction seems to come in question only much later during development. Thus Lamb (1978) observes that even 1- or 2-year-olds interact more with either parent when the other is absent than when both parents are simultaneously present. This should not mean that an infant cannot enjoy more than one care-taker, but rather that the infant can profit from the interchange with several care-takers only if he can interact with each of them consecutively.

ACKNOWLEDGEMENTS

The following foundations have kindly supported our research: Die Deutsche Forschungsgemeinschaft, Die Stiftung Volkswagenwerk, and Der Fund der Deutschen Bank beim Stifterverband für die Deutsche Wissenschaft.

REFERENCES

Ainsworth, M. D. S., Bell, S., and Stayton, D. J. (1974). Infant-mother attachment and social development: 'Socialisation' as a product of reciprocal responsiveness to signals, in *The Integration of a Child into a Social World* (Ed. M. P. M. Richards), pp. 99–135, Cambridge University Press, Cambridge.

Alloway, T., Pliner, P., and Krames, L. (1977). *Attachment Behaviour*, Plenum Press, New York.

Bach, G. R. (1946). Father-fantasies and father-typing in father-separated children, *Child Develop.*, **17**, 63–80.

Bartoshuk, A. K. (1962). Human neonatal cardiac acceleration to sound: Habituation and dishabituation, *Perceptual and Motor Skills*, **15**, 15–27.

Bell, R. A. and Harper, L. V. (1977). *Child Effects on Adults*, Erlbaum, Hillsdale, New Jersey.

Berman, P. W., Goodman, V., Sloan, V. L., and Fernander, F. (1979). Preference for infants among black and white children: Sex and age differences, *Child Develop.*, **49**, 917–919.

Bernstein, N. (1967). *The Co-ordination and Regulation of Movements*, Pergamon Press, New York.

Bertalanffy, L. von (1968). *Organismic Psychology Theory*, Clark University Press with Barre Publishers, Barre, Mass.

Blurton Jones, N. (Ed.), (1972). *Ethological Studies of Child Behaviour*, Cambridge University Press, Cambridge.

Bornstein, M. H. (1975). Qualities of color vision in infancy. *J. of Exp. Child Psychol.*, **19**, 401–419.

Bornstein, M. H., Kessen, W., and Weisskopf, S. (1975). Color vision and hue categorization in young human infants, *Science*, **191**, 201–202.

Bower, T. G. R. (1974). *Development in Infancy*, Freeman & Co., San Francisco.

Bowlby, J. (1958). The nature of the child's tie to his mother, *International J. of Psychoanalysis*, **39**, 350–373.

Bowlby, J. (1969). *Attachment and Loss*, Vol. 1, *Attachment*, Basic Books, New York.

Bridger, W. H. (1961). Sensory habituation and discrimination in the human neonate, *Am. J. of Psychiat.*, **117**, 991–996.

Bruner, J. S. (1974). The organisation of early skilled action, in *The Integration of a Child into a Social World* (Ed. M. P. M. Richards), pp. 167–184, Cambridge University Press, Cambridge.

Bruner, J. S. (1975). The ontogenesis of speech acts, *J. Child Lang.*, **2**, 1–19.

Bühler, K. (1919). *Abriß der geistigen Entwicklung des Kindes*, Quelle und Meyer, Leipzig.

Cairns, R. B. (1979). *Social Development. The Origins and Plasticity of Interchanges*, Freeman, San Francisco.

Caron, R. F. (1967). Visual reinforcement of head-turning in young infants, *J. of Experimental Child Psychol.*, **5**, 489–511.

Cohen, L. B. (1972). Attention-getting and attention-holding processes of infant visual preferences, *Child Develop.*, **43**, 869–879.

Cohen, L. B., DeLoache, J. S., and Strauss, M. S. (1979). Infant visual perception, in *Handbook of Infant Development* (Ed. J. D. Osofsky), pp. 393–438, Wiley, New York.

Condon, W. and Sander, L. (1974). Neonate movement is synchronized with adult speech: Interactional participation and language acquisition, *Science*, **183**, 99–101.

Coryell, J. F. and Michel, G. F. (1978). How supine postural preferences of infants can contribute toward the development of handedness, *Infant Behav. and Develop.*, **1**, 245–257.

Cranach, M. von, Foppa, K., Lepenies, W., and Ploog, D. (Eds) (1979). *Human Ethology. Claims and Limits of a New Discipline*, Cambridge University Press, Cambridge.

Cutting, J. E. and Eimas, P. D. (1975). Phonetic feature analyzers and the processing of speech in infants, in *The Role of Speech in Language* (Eds J. F. Kavanagh and J. E. Cutting), MIT Press, Cambridge.

Dewey, J. and Bentley, A. F. (1949). *Knowing and the Known*, Beacon Press, Boston.

Eimas, P. D. (1974). Auditory and linguistic processing of cues for place of articulation by infants, *Percept. Psychophys.*, **16**, 513–521.

Eimas, P. D. (1975). Auditory and phonetic coding of the cues for speech: Discrimination of the (r–1) distinction by young infants, *Percept. Psychophys.*, **18**, 341–347.

Eimas, P. D., Siqueland, E. R., Jusczyk, P., and Vigorito, J. (1971). Speech perception in infants, *Science*, **171**, 303–306.

Eisenberg, R. B. (1976). *Auditory Competence in Early Life: The Roots of Communicative Behaviour* University Park Press, Baltimore.

Engen, T., Lipsitt, L. P., and Kaye, H. (1963). Olfactory responses and adaptation in the human neonate, *J. Comp. Physiol Psychol.*, **56**, 73–77.

Feldman, S. S. and Nash, S. C. (1978). Interest in babies during young adulthood, *Child Develop.*, **49**, 617–622.

Feldman, S. S. and Nash, S. C. (1979a). Changes in responsiveness to babies during adolescence, *Child Develop.*, **50**, 942–949.

Feldman, S. S. and Nash, S. C. (1979b). Understanding sex differences in responsiveness to babies among mature adults, *Developmental Psychol.*, **15**, 430–435'

Friedman, S. (1972). Habituation and recovery of visual response in the alert human newborn, *J. of Exp. Child Psychol.*, **13**, 339–349.

Frodi, A. M. and Lamb, M. E. (1978). Sex differences in responsiveness to infants: A developmental study of psychophysiological and behavioural responses, *Child Develop.*, **49**, 1182–1188.

Gandelman, R. and Simon, N. G. (1978). Spontaneous pup-killing by mice in response to large litters, *Development. Psychobiology*, **11** (3), 235–241.

Gesell, A. (1945). *The Embryology of Behavior*, Harper, New York.

Gewirtz, J. L. (Ed.) (1972). *Attachment and Dependency*, Winston, New York.

Ginsburg, H. J., Fling, S., Hope, M. L., Musgrove, D., and Andrews, C. (1979). Maternal holding preferences: A consequence of newborn head-turning response, *Child Develop.*, **50**, 280–281.

Goldfarb, W. (1944). Infant-rearing as a factor in foster home placement, *Amer. J. Orthopsychiat.*, **14**, 162–167.

Graham, F. K., Clifton, R. K., and Hatton, H. M. (1968). Habituation of heart rate response to repeated auditory stimulation during the first five days of life, *Child Dev.*, **39**, 35–52.

Gunther, M. (1961). Infant behaviour at the breast, in *Determinants of Infant Behaviour* (Ed. B. M. Foss), pp. 37–39, Methuen, London.

Haeckel, E. (1866). *Generelle Morphologie der Organismen: Allegemeine Grundzüge der organischen Formen-Wissenschaft, mechanisch begründet durch die von Charles Darwin reformierte Descendenz-Theorie*, 2 vols, Georg Reimer, Berlin.

Haith, M. M. (1979). Visual cognition in early infancy, in *Infants at Risk: Assessment of Cognitive Functioning* (Eds R. B. Kearsley and I. E. Sigel), pp. 23–48, Erlbaum, Hillsdale, New Jersey.

Harlow, H. F. and Harlow, M. K. (1969). Effects of various mother-infant relationships on rhesus monkey behaviors, in *Determinants of Infant Behavior*, Vol. 4 (Ed. B. M. Foss), pp. 15–36, Methuen, London.

Heckhausen, H. (1974). *Leistung und Chancengleichheit*, Hogrefe, Göttingen.

Heinroth, O. (1910). Beiträge zur Biologie, namentlich Ethologie und Psychologie der Anatiden, *Verh. 5th Int. Ornith. Kongr. Berlin*, 589–702.

Herrick, C. J. (1956). *The Evolution of Human Nature*, University of Texas Press, Austin.

Hess, E. H. (1967). Ethology, in *Comprehensive Textbook of Psychiatry* (Eds A. M. Freedman and H. I. Kaplan), Williams and Wilkins, Baltimore.

Hess, E. H. (1970). Ethology and developmental psychology, in *Carmichael's Manual of Child Psychology* (Ed. P. H. Mussen), 3rd edn, pp. 1–38, Wiley, New York.

Hinde, R. A. (1974). *Biological Bases of Human Social Behaviour*, McGraw-Hill, New York.

Jacobson, S. W. (1979). Matching behavior in the young infant, *Child Development*, **50**, 425–430.

Janoš, O. (1959). Development of higher nervous activity in premature infants, *Pavlov J. of Higher Nervous Activity*, **9**, 760–767.

Johanson, I. B. and Hall, W. G. (1979). Appetitive learning in one-day-old rat pups, *Science*, **205**, 419–421.

Keen, R. (1964). Effects of auditory stimuli on sucking behavior in the human neonate, *J. of Exp. Child Psychol.*, **1**, 348–354.

Koffka, K. (1928). *The Growth of the Mind*, 2nd edn, Kegan Paul, Trench, Trubuer, London.

Konner, M. (1977a). Infancy among the Kalahari Desert San, in *Culture and Infancy* (Eds P. H. Leiderman, S. R. Tulkin, and A. Rosenfeld), pp. 329–355, Academic Press, New York.

Konner, M. (1977b). Evolution of human behavior development, in *Culture and Infancy* (Eds P. H. Leiderman, S. R. Tulkin, and A. Rosenfeld), pp. 69–109, Academic Press, New York.

Kuhl, P. K. (1978). Predispositions for the perception of speech-sound categories: A species-specific phenomenon? in *Communicative and Cognitive Abilities: Early Behavioral Assessment* (Eds F. D. Minifie and L. L. Loyd), pp. 259–255, University Park Press, Baltimore.

Lamb, M. E. (1978). Infant social cognition and 'Second-order' effects, *Infant Behavior and Develop.*, **11**, 1–10.

Lenneberg, E. H. (1967). *Biological Foundations of Language*, Wiley, New York.

Lewis, M. and Ban, P. (1977). Variance and invariance in the mother-infant interaction: A cross-cultural study, in *Culture and Infancy* (Eds P. H. Leiderman, S. R. Tulkin, and A. Rosenfeld), pp. 329–355, Academic Press, New York.

Lewis, M. and Brooks-Gunn, J. (1979). *Social Cognition and the Acquisition of Self*, Plenum Press, New York.

Liberman, A. M., Cooper, F. S., Shankweiler, D. P., and Studdert-Kennedy, M. (1967). Perception of the speech code, *Psychological Review*, **74**, 431–461.

Lieberman, P., Crelin, E. S., and Klatt, D. H. (1972). Phonetic ability and related anatomy of the newborn and adult human, Neanderthal man, and the chimpanzee, *Amer. Anthropology*, **74**, 287–307.

Lock, A. (1978). The emergence of language, in *Action, Gesture and Symbol. The Emergence of Language* (Ed. A. Lock), pp. 3–18, Academic Press, London.

Lorenz, K. (1935). Der Kumpan in der Umwelt des Vogels. Der Artgenosse als auslösendes Moment sozialer Verhaltensweisen, *J. Ornith.*, **83**, 137–213, 289–413.

Lorenz, J. (1943). Die angeborenen Formen möglicher Erfahrung, *Z. Tierpsychol.*, **5**, 235–409.

Lowrey, L. G. (1940). Personality distortion and early institutional care, *Amer. J. Orthopsychiat.*, **10**, 576–585.

Lynn, D. B. and Sawrey, W. L. (1959). The effects of father-absence on Norwegian boys and girls, *J. Abnorm. Soc. Psychol.*, **59**, 258–262.

Macfarlane, A. (1975). Olfaction in the development of social preferences in the human neonate, in *Parent-Infant Interaction*, A Ciba Foundation Symposium 33 (new series), pp. 103–117, Elsevier, Amsterdam and New York.

Marler, P. (1973). Constraints on learning: Development of bird song, in *The Clarence M. Hicks Memorial Lectures for 1970* (Ed. W. F. Norman), University of Toronto Press, Toronto.

Martinius, J. W. and Papoušek, H. (1970). Responses to optic and exteroceptive stimuli in relation to state in the human newborn: Habituation of the blink reflex, *Neuropädiatrie*, **1**, 452–460.

Mason, W. A. and Berkson, G. (1975). Effects of maternal mobility on the development of rocking and other behaviors in rhesus monkeys: A study with artificial mothers, *Develop. Psychobiol.*, **8**, 197–211.

Maurer, D. and Salapatek, P. (1976). Developmental changes in the scanning of faces by young infants, *Child Develop.*, **47**, 523–527.

McGuire, I. and Turkewitz, G. (1978). Visually elicited finger movements in infants, *Child Develop.*, **49**, 362–370.

Meltzoff, A. N. and Moore, M. K. (1977). Imitation of facial and manual gestures by human neonates, *Science*, **198**, 75–78.

Mendelson, M. J. and Haith, M. M. (1976). The relation between audition and vision in the human newborn, *Monographs of the Society for Research in Child Develop.*, **41**, (Whole No. 4).

Newport, E. L. (1977). Motherese: The speech to young children, in *Cognitive Theory*, Vol. 2 (Eds N. J. Castellan, Jr. D. B. Pisoni, and G. R. Potts), pp. 177–217, Erlbaum, Hillsdale, New Jersey.

Nuttin, J. (1973). Pleasure and reward in human motivation and learning, in *Pleasure, Reward, Preference* (Eds D. C. Berlyne and K. B. Madsen), pp. 243–274, Academic Press, New York.

Papoušek, H. (1960). Conditioned motor alimentary reflexes in infants. II. A new experimental method of investigation, *Československá Pediatrie*, **15**, 981–988. (In Czech).

Papoušek, H. (1961). Conditioned head rotation reflexes in infants in the first months of life, *Acta Paediatrica (Scan.)*, **50**, 565–576.

Papoušek, H. (1964). Conditioned reflectory movements of the head in the human newborn, *Activitas Nervosa Superior*, **6**, 83–84.

Papoušek, H. (1967). Experimental studies of appetitional behavior in human newborns and infants, in *Early Behavior: Comparative and Developmental Approaches* (Eds H. W. Stevenson, E. H. Hess, and H. L. Rheingold), pp. 249–277, Wiley London, New York.

Papoušek, H. (1969). Individual variability in learned responses in human infants, in *Brain and Early Behavior* (Ed. R. J. Robinson), pp. 251–266, Academic Press, London, New York.

Papoušek, H. (1977). Entwicklung der Lernfähigkeit im Säuglingsalter, in *Intelligenz, Lernen und Lernstörungen* (Ed. G. Nissen), pp. 75–93, Springer-Verlag, Berlin.

Papoušek, H. (1981). The common in the uncommon children: Comments on the child's integrative capacities and on the intuitive parenting, in *The Uncommon Child* (Eds M. Lewis and L. A. Rosenblum), Plenum Press, New York.

Papoušek, H. and Bernstein, P. (1969). The functions of conditioning stimulation in human neonates and infants, in *Stimulation in Early Infancy* (Ed. A. Ambrose), pp. 229–252, Academic Press, London, New York.

Papoušek, H. and Papoušek, M. (1975). Cognitive aspects of preverbal social interactions between human infants and adults, in *Parent-Infant Interaction* (Ed. O'Connor), pp. 241–269, Elsevier, Amsterdam.

Papoušek, H. and Papoušek, M. (1977). Mothering and the cognitive head-start: Psychobiological considerations, in *Studies in Mother-Infant Interaction* (Ed. H. R. Schaffer), pp. 63–85, Academic Press, London.

Papoušek, H. and Papoušek, M. (1978). Interdisciplinary parallels in studies of early human behavior: From physical to cognitive needs, from attachment to dyadic education, *Int. J. of Behavioral Dev.*, **1**, 37–49.

Papoušek, H. and Papoušek, M. (1979a). The infant's fundamental adaptive response system in social interaction, in *Origins of the Infant's Social Responsiveness* (Ed. E. Thoman), pp. 175–208, Erlbaum, Hillsdale, New Jersey.

Papoušek, H., and Papoušek, M. (1979b). Early ontogeny of human social interaction: Its biological roots and social dimensions, in *Human Ethology: Claims and Limits of a New Discipline* (Eds M. von Cranach, K. Foppa, W. Lepenies, and D. Ploog), pp. 456–480, Cambridge University Press, Cambridge.

Papoušek, H., and Papoušek, M. (1981). How human is the human newborn, and what else is to be done, in *Prospective Issues in Infant Research* (Ed. K. Bloom), Erlbaum, Hillsdale, New Jersey.

Piaget, J. and Inhelder, B. (1969). *The Psychology of the Child*, Basic Books, New York.

Poirier, F. E. (1977). Introduction, In *Primate Bio-social Development: Biological, Social, and Ecological Determinants* (Eds S. Chevalier-Skolnikoff and F. E. Poirier), pp. 1–39, Garland, New York.

Pribram, K. H. (1971). *Language of the Brain: Experimental Paradoxes and Principles in Neuropsychology*, Prentice-Hall, Englewood Cliffs, New Jersey.

Richards, J. L. and Finger, S. (1975). Mother-child holding patterns: A cross-cultural photographic survey, *Child Develop.*, **46**, 1001–1004.

Richards, M. P. M. (1974). First steps in becoming social, in *The Integration of a Child into a Social World* (Ed. M. P. M. Richards), pp. 83–97, Cambridge University Press, Cambridge.

Richards, M. P. M. (1978). The biological and social, in *Action, Gesture and Symbol. The Emergence of Language* (Ed. A. Lock), pp. 21–30, Academic Press, London.

Ridley, M. (1978). Paternal care, *Anim. Behav.*, **26**, 904–932.

Rosenblatt, J. S. (1975). Prepartum and postpartum regulation of maternal behavior in the rat, in *Parent–Infant-Interaction* (Ed. M. O'Connor), pp. 17–37, Elsevier, Amsterdam.

Salk, L. (1973). The role of the heartbeat in relations between mother and infant, *Scientific American*, **228**, 24–29.

Sameroff, A. J. (1968). The components of sucking in the human newborn, *J. of Experimental Child Psychol.*, **6**, 607–623.

Schoetzau, A. (1979). Effects of viewing distance on looking behavior in neonates, *International J. of Behavioral Develop.*, **2**, 121–131.

Schoetzau, A. and Papoušek H. (1977). Mütterliches Verhalten bei der Aufnahme von

Blickkontakt mit dem Neugeborenen, *Zeitschrift für Entwicklungspsychologie und Pädagogische Psychologie*, **9**, 231–239.

Sears, R. R. (1951). A theoretical framework for personality and social behavior, *Amer. Psychologist*, **6**, 476–483.

Sears, R. R., Pintler, M. H., and Sears, P. S. (1946). The effect of father separation on preschool children's doll play agression, *Child Develop.*, **17**, 219–243.

Siqueland, E. R. (1964). Operant conditioning of head-turning in four-month-old infants, *Psychonomic Science*, **1**, 223–224.

Siqueland, E. R. and Lipsitt, L. P. (1966). Conditioned head-turning in human newborns, *J. of Experimental Child Psychol.*, **3**, 356–376.

Slobin, D. I. (1968). *Question of Language Development in Cross-Cultural Perspective*, Reference in E. L. Newport (1977). *op cit.*

Snow, C. E. (1972). 'Mothers' speech to children learning language, *Child Develop.*, **43**, 549–565.

Solkoff, N. and Cotton, C. (1975). Contingency awareness in premature infants, *Perceptual and Motor Skills*, **41**, 709–710.

Sroufe, L. A. (1979). Socioemotional development, in *Handbook of Infant Development* (Ed. J. D. Osofsky), pp. 463–516, Wiley, New York.

Sternglanz, S. M., Gray, J. H., and Murakami, M. (1977). Adult preferences for infant facial features: An ethological approach, *Animal Behavior*, **25**, 108–115.

Stoltz, L. M. (1954). *Father Relations of War-Born Children*, Stanford University Press, Stanford.

Thoman, E. B., Korner, A. F., and Beason-Williams, L. (1977). Modification of responsiveness to maternal vocalization in the neonate, *Child Develop.*, **48**, 563–569.

Thorpe, W. H. (1956). *Learning and Instincts in Animals*, Harvard University Press, Cambridge.

Trevarthen, C. (1979). Instincts for human understanding and for cultural cooperation: Their development in infancy, in *Human Ethology, Claims and Limits of a New Discipline* (Eds M. von Cranach, K. Foppa, W. Lepenies, and D. Ploog), pp. 530–571, Cambridge University Press, Cambridge.

Turkewitz, G., Gordon, E. W., and Birch, H. G. (1965). Head-turning in the human neonate: Effect of prandial condition and lateral preference, *J. of Comparative and Physiological Psychol.*, **59**, 189–192.

Turnbull, C. M. (1972). *The Mountain People*, Touchstone Books, Simon & Schuster, New York.

Vygotsky, L. (1962). *Thought and Language*, MIT Press, Cambridge.

Wilson, E. O. (1975). *Sociobiology: The New Synthesis*, Harvard University Press, Cambridge.

Wilson, W. R. (1978). Behavioral assessment of auditory functions in infants, in *Communicative and Cognitive Abilities: Early Behavioral Assessment* (Eds F. D. Minifie and L. L. Loyd), pp. 37–59, University Park Press, Baltimore.

Wolff, P. H. (1977). Biological variations and cultural diversity: An exploratory study, in *Culture and Infancy* (Eds P. H. Liderman, S. R. Tulkin, and A. Rosenfeld), pp. 357–381, Academic Press, New York.

Psychobiology of the Human Newborn
Edited by P. Stratton
© 1982, John Wiley & Sons, Ltd.

CHAPTER 15

Emerging Themes of Neonatal Psychobiology

PETER STRATTON

This book began with a consideration of the general issues which make the psychobiology of the human newborn a particularly significant area of study and, arising from this consideration, a specification of adaptation and transaction as the major concepts in co-ordinating our knowledge. That discussion concluded that any influence on, or characteristic of, a newborn must be considered in relation to the widest possible range of both current and future circumstances. The content of the various chapters has shown, in each case, how the specific factors are interrelated and has pointed to their implications. One outcome of this general feature has been a considerable advance in the basis on which research findings and medical practice can be evaluated, and it is this theme of evaluation which has enabled the contributors to this book to select from the enormous mass of available material to present a coherent account of significant knowledge in each area. Many of the characteristics displayed by the newborn may be transient, having no lasting impact on either the baby or on his or her environment. Many variations in treatment may be trivial in that they either fail to provoke adaptations or the adaptation is transient and not of the kind that can initiate a transactional sequence. Within each area, the first concern has been to establish a basis for evaluating the facts so that research findings and medical practice, both existing and potential, have meaningful criteria against which their practical implications can be determined.

The present state of our understanding does not amount to a consolidation of reliable knowledge into conclusive answers. What this book has hopefully achieved is a co-ordination of significant recent advances which should facilitate a productive new era in neonatal psychobiology, while providing practitioners with information in a structure which allows specific concerns to be usefully conceptualized in relation to the necessary broader context. Accordingly this final chapter does not attempt to summarize existing knowledge nor to provide prescriptions for future research. What has seemed more useful is to explore a number of general themes which have emerged from the preceding chapters as being productive across different contexts in enhancing the basic concept of adaptation. In reviewing these themes the clearest implications are in terms of attachment or mother–infant bonding. This issue has come to dominate current considerations of the significance of early human psychobiology, which is why it forms the subject matter of the major chapter of this final section. It is, however, worth remembering that every science has in its history instances in which current cultural preoccupations have allowed one notion to dominate to the exclusion of other equally useful areas of research. This is not in any way to claim that the study of attachment does not justify a major sustained research effort, merely that we should be aware of the risk of being dazzled by this very significant and productive concept and so fail to see other areas of potential. Accordingly, while the principles to be described will most often be illuminated by reference to attachment, they are stated in a form that should facilitate their application in other, less well studied, areas.

REFLECTIONS FROM INFANCY

The productivity of the work on neonatal attachment is related to the fact that a considerable amount is known about the growth of sociability in infancy and later, and it was largely the neonatal research of the 1960s which allowed the productive formulations of the growth of attachment such as that by Schaffer (1971). There can be no doubt that many of the functions which develop in the neonatal period are employed in the process of attachment formation. It then becomes possible to attribute significance to particular capacities in terms of their contribution to this process. For example the structure of the perceptual system which ensures that the newborn will attend preferentially to the human face, the sensitivity to events contingent on the newborn's own actions, and the rapid learning of which stimuli are not worth orienting to, are some of the tendencies which ensure that the powerful cognitive capacities of young infants will be directed primarily to social stimuli. The availability of suitable stimuli (i.e. socially competent humans) is ensured by the signal characteristics and behaviours which mobilize adults to make contact in the forms required by the newborn. It is then easy to understand why certain perceptual and cognitive systems are relatively advanced at birth and why response systems such as crying and facial expression are so well differentiated at this time.

A similar awareness of other significant functions in infancy would allow a much wider basis for a specification of the criteria by which neonatal behaviours might be assessed. Prime candidates would be the basic functions of feeding and state control. There would seem to be considerable value in the proposal of Rovee-Collier and Lipsitt (Chapter 7) that the first consideration of any newborn adaptations must be in terms of the effect on weight gain. The importance of feeding is suggested by the fact that some aspect of it has been considered in almost every chapter. Despite this, it is clear (particularly from the discussions by Stratton in Chapter 9 and Wright in Chapter 13) that we have little reliable information about the consequences of variations in neonatal feeding for infancy or later. The extent to which prenatal nutritional variation is modified in its effects by interaction with other variables (Barrett, Chapter 10), warns us not to expect simple relationships here either.

The ability of the infant to maintain a state appropriate to the time of day, stage of feeding cycle, prospects for enjoyable social interaction or even to enforcing a suitable response from care-takers, will be a major factor in successful functioning. State has, however, been relatively little studied outside of the neonatal period and so attempts to determine the significance of state changes, as by Prechtl in Chapter 3 and Stratton in Chapter 6, have been forced to concentrate on evidence of internal structure. This would surely be one area in which knowledge from infancy could reflect back to discriminate the trivial or transient from the significant during the neonatal period.

It is interesting how the progress in a field of study can reflect the important principles which govern the target phenomena. The process of neonatal work inspiring an improved understanding of infancy which in turn provides a context from which neonatal work can be evaluated, looks very like the transactional processes described by Stratton in Chapter 1. It is to be hoped that the present exercise of extracting general principles from our current knowledge of the newborn will continue the transaction by offering a structure within which post-neonatal findings can be interpreted. In particular the possibility of understanding adaptations within their initial developmental context and then of exploring their implications for different future environments should supplant the unproductive notion of continuity. It was suggested in Chapter 1 that the search for correlations between functions at different ages has often served as a substitute for an understanding of the significance of the characteristic or influence at the time of its appearance, and of its contribution to the ensuing developmental progress. The attempt by each of the authors to establish criteria for significance within each of the areas covered adds up to a major attack on the first stage of developing a coherent understanding of the implications for neonatal adaptation of variations in viability, in competence, in structural and behavioural characteristics, and in the backgrounds, regimes, insults and care to which babies are subjected. The second stage of tracing the consequences of these variations as they are worked out during infancy was attempted where it was particularly appropriate, but in most cases our knowledge is so limited and the task so complex that it could not be contained within the framework of this book. Nevertheless infancy is the context in which neonatal adaptations must be worked out, so criteria for the significance of what we discover in our research and for the outcomes of the treatments we provide for newborns, cannot be specified by reference to the neonatal period alone. We need to develop a clear ept of what constitutes a satisfactory infancy so that the effects of neonatal ation can be assessed beyond the immediate confines of the period, but without requiring statistically reliable differences 20 years later. Even our present knowledge obliges anyone seriously concerned about newborns to consider certain rather obvious consequences. For example if it is suspected that a certain obstetric practice induces adaptations by either mother or baby which increase the probability of "non-accidental" injury being inflicted by the parents during the subsequent months, there can be no justification for excluding this consequence from an evaluation of the overall effect of the practice on morbidity or mortality.

EVOLUTION

Many aspects of newborn functioning considered in this book have been illuminated by a consideration of their evolutionary significance. Although much of the speculation about human behaviour which has appeared recently under the title 'sociobiology' has proved unproductive, there seem to be reasons why a consideration of evolutionarily determined genetic mechanisms is particularly useful in the case of the newborn. Much of neonatal adaptation is dependent on the physiological characteristics of newborn and care-taker, so it can be assumed that many aspects of their functioning have remained unchanged for a very long time. The fact that we have interfered with some aspects of the environment of evolutionary adaptedness merely provides an extra urgency to the task of establishing the determinants and consequences of normal neonatal adaptations.

In the process of rejecting operant conditioning accounts of early attachment, psychobiologists have often used imprinting as an alternative explanation (Bowlby, 1969). It is now clear that this amounts to explaining one unknown by another, possibly even more obscure, mystery. In fact it has been argued (Stratton, 1982a) that the situation has reversed and that we may now be in a position to explain animal imprinting in terms of what we have discovered about human bonding. An important general principle of early human adaptation is that genetic mechanisms have developed to exploit consistencies in the environment so as to ensure the necessary outcome with a minimum of predetermined structure. This not only ensures the most efficient use of the limited genetic information available, it also maintains the maximum degree of flexibility in the face of the need to guarantee certain kinds of outcome.

The perceptual and response tendencies of newborns, (mentioned above and described in more detail by Papoušek and Papoušek in Chapter 14) are examples of simple genetically determined characteristics which, in combination with a suitable environment, ensure that certain kinds of mother–baby interaction are likely to occur. There are likely to be many such instances waiting to be discovered but we should not restrict our attention to the social situation. The identification of any universal tendency justifies some effort to discover a biological significance. For example alerting and visually scanning the environment is the common response to being held at the mother's shoulder, and would appear to have just as much significance for cognitive development as do behaviours like making eye contact for social development. In fact, it seems that cognitive processes are so important at this age as to have become the subject of selection pressures which have resulted in an increased probability of attention and exploration in appropriate circumstances. The proposal by Bronson (Chapter 5) that the rapidly developing visual cortex requires suitable input in order to develop an optimal structure, suggests that the inherent tendencies may be concentrated on visual input during this period.

An acceptence of the significance of early cognitive functioning may allow a more fruitful interpretation of some neonatal tendencies. For example preferential turning to the right may guarantee eye-contact when the baby is held on mother's left arm as discussed in Chapter 14. It could be equally significant that, combined with a tendency of mothers to hold their baby at the left shoulder, turning the head to the right ensures an unobstructed field of view, rather than an out-of-focus close-up of mother's left ear. There should be no difficulty in accepting that the same behavioural tendency may have developed (or have come to be exploited) for both social and cognitive functions. It has already been pointed out that these functions are inseparable in early infancy:

the building-blocks of social and cognitive functioning seem to be so closely interdependent during infancy that it is no longer sensible to distinguish them. In practice, this means that anything which disrupts social interaction will also disrupt the motivations and expectancies which underlie cognitive growth, while anything which inhibits cognitive development will be depriving the infant of the capacities needed for early social development. (Stratton, 1977, p. 150)

It is easy to appreciate that other significant functions, which we may choose to study in relative isolation, are likely to be equally embedded in the newborn's total functioning. The virtual impossibility of studying something as basic as feeding and sucking rhythms, without becoming involved in social, let alone commercial, considerations (Chapter 6) indicates the necessity of eventually tackling the integration of every neonatal function.

The primary impetus for the current advances in developmental psychobiology has come from successfully combining our biological knowledge with a better understanding of social and cognitive functioning. The first major account of this integration in current terms was offered by Bowlby (1969), detail of the workings of the integration were added by Schaffer (1971) and a substantial restatement has been provided by Cairns (1979). It is notable that this synthesis has been dominated by the issue of attachment and in this respect, along with the secondary theme of cognitive development, reflects major current concerns of Western culture (one might add, particularly of the middle-class academic sub-culture). It is to be hoped that as we develop more successful ways of becoming aware of evolutionary influences, a wider range of functions may be brought into the synthesis.

TRANSITION

A perspective on the demands made on the newborn is provided by the concept of transition. Although most of the recent proliferation of research into transitions has been concerned with life crises during adulthood a general theme emerges that sudden changes in life circumstances or demands for significant changes in functioning, are stressors which in certain circumstances may provoke such disturbances as depression (Brown and Harris, 1978) or helplessness (Garber and Seligman, 1980). Quite how these findings, which tend to be discussed in terms of emotional responses and appraisal of the situation, can be usefully applied to the newborn is at present unclear. However, it seems very probable that during the next few years we will begin to acquire a clearer picture of the interrelated physiological and psychological changes provoked by abrupt demands. In the meantime we must take seriously the possible consequences of the many sudden changes in adaptation demanded of the newborn, and we might expect some interesting findings to emerge from a search for mechanisms which may exist to protect the newborn from such consequences.

Birth itself is an obvious environmental transition as discussed in Chapter 1, and many of the situations described in Section III suggest that newborns may quite frequently be subjected to substantial and abrupt changes in levels and quality of stimulation. Being moved into or out of intensive care is a clear example, and recent studies of the ecological characteristics of such units (Lawson et al., 1977) indicate how different from maternity ward or home such situations can be. The problem of premature babies adapting to a particular kind of hospital care and then having to cope with a totally different situation at home was discussed in Chapter 1, but all hospital born babies (and their mothers) must make this transition, though the more usual change may be from a high to a low level of stimulation.

During development, and particularly during the first year after conception, transitions are most likely to be provoked by maturational changes within the individual. The newborn must undergo many discontinuities in functioning which could be regarded as minor transitions, but several chapters have pointed to a major transition starting after the neonatal period as classically defined. Around two months, many functions shift from sub-cortical to cortical control (Bronson, Chapter 5). It is around this time also that reflex responses start to come under voluntary control (Rovee-Collier and Lipsitt, Chapter 7); a transition which carries considerable dangers for babies who have not success-fully completed the necessary preliminary adaptations. It is at this age that circadian rhythms first appear (Stratton, Chapter 6), diurnal variation in feeding emerges (Wright, Chapter 13) and there are advances in visual functioning (Atkinson and Braddick, Chapter 8).

There is enough convergence of evidence to suggest that it would be very profitable to focus on 2 months as a probable age of transition from neonatal modes of functioning. Indeed if, as seems likely, there is a wide range of functions which undergo qualitative change at this time (McCall *et al.*, 1978) it might be more meaningful to adopt 8 weeks as the neonatal period, and to abandon the traditional definition of 4 weeks which does not appear to correspond to any significant aspect of the psychobiology of infancy.

EARLY GENERALITY

Another theme is the progression from the general to the specific. An outcome of opposing orientations within psychology has been that behaviourists find it easier to conceive of behaviours being specific when first acquired, and then generalizing, while psychologists with their roots in biology (particularly embryology) are more likely to see behaviour, as well as morphology, undergoing progressive differentiation during development. It would seem that the latter perspective is implied by our present knowledge of the newborn. The review of rhythmic functions (Stratton, Chapter 6) was largely concerned with evidence that neonatal rhythms will be in the form best suited to entrainment by the widest possible range of environmental synchronizers; the analysis of learning (Rovee-Collier and Lipsitt, Chapter 7) concluded that it is the generality and not the specificity of early stimulus–response associations which facilitates early adaptation; and the subsequent chapter concludes with the suggestion that perceptual development involves the recognition of distinct modalities within a system in which they are initially undifferentiated (Atkinson and Braddick, Chapter 8). This tendency towards early generality may be responsible for the finding by Stratton (Chapter 9) that the significance of newborn individuality derives primarily from its implications for the neonatal period itself. The need for such generality emerges very clearly from Section III. The wide range of environmental circumstances to which newborns must be prepared to adapt, which is suggested by the substantial variations between different cultures described by Oakley (Chapter 11) is complemented by the evidence offered by Chiswick in Chapter 12 of the range of insults and the variations in treatment and care-taking which newborns have been found to be capable of surviving.

THE FAIL-SAFE NATURE OF NEONATAL ADAPTATION

Early generality of response can be seen as an effective means of ensuring adaptation to the widest possible range of circumstances. Associated with the tendency are the redundancies and fail-safe mechanisms examples of which range from the overproduction of brain cells, many of which will atrophy once their function has been achieved, (Oppenheim, 1981) to the appearance of essential functions well in advance of the stage of development in which they will be needed (Barrett, Chapter 10). The effect of all such tendencies is to maximize the likelihood of successful adaptation to a wide range of not always favourable circumstances. It is important that we should understand the nature and limitations of these protective processes and a helpful analogy may come from the 'Principle of least commitment' proposed by Marr (1976) as one of four general principles which have emerged from computer studies of the organization of complex symbolic processes. Neonatal adaptation may have many parallels with the early stages of such complex phenomena as perceptual processing, and the rule that 'one should never do something that may later have to be undone' (p. 485) seems likely to be particularly fruitful. It implies that we should expect to find newborns disposed towards those adaptations which maximize the range of future options, and so minimize the risk that the adaptation will have to be undone. There may also be a lesson in Marr's 'Principle of modular design', which states that any complex process should be broken down into sub-parts which are as independent of each other as possible, otherwise the system 'becomes extremely difficult to debug or to improve . . . in the course of natural evolution, because a small change to improve one part has to be accompanied by many simultaneous compensating changes elsewhere' (p. 485). Given the inevitability of at least some interdependence between aspects of neonatal functioning this warning is pertinent to any attempts we make to improve individual aspects of the system. Marr's final 'Principle of graceful degradation' is perhaps more productively applied to the mature psychobiologist than to the newborn.

The perspective of newborns being endowed with a variety of tendencies which will optimize adaptation in the widest possible range of environments seems to conflict with the idea that they are exceptionally vulnerable, and this conflict is central to the difficulty in making long-term prognoses from many neonatal conditions. While it is entirely appropriate to treat the newborn with special consideration and care, it is now clear that it is a mistake to assume that any departure from optimality necessarily causes permanent damage. Single indicators of risk cannot be expected to have predictive power, and neonatal assessments may not distinguish between a permanent deficit due to previous damage and the stress of current adaptations.

Even a completely successful adaptation or transition will impose a stress which is likely to lower performance during the period of adaptation itself. There is then a risk that a poor score on either a neurological or a behavioural assessment may be due to a successful current adaptation which will in fact enhance the future functioning of the newborn. Section I offers two possibilities for avoiding this problem. The first is an emphasis on understanding the causal factor which underlie a particular kind of performance. This understanding is approached in the successive chapters through considerations by Prechtl of the functioning of the nervous system (Chapter 2) and the influence of state (Chapter 3), and by Amiel-Tison of the forms and effects of neurological damage (Chapter 4). All of these issues are taken up in subsequent chapters and it is to be hoped that the progressive advances in our understanding of the newborn will assist the development of assessment techniques which are less affected by transient stressors.

The second suggestion for distinguishing between transient signs of stress and permanent deficit is derived from Prechtl's proposal (Chapter 2) of an optimality score. In a somewhat broader context than neurological assessment this can be seen as similar to Toffler's (1970) suggestion that successful coping with stress requires that the individual has other areas of stability in his or her life. It is now very clear that the effect of any insult must be evaluated in the whole context of the resources (internal and environmental) that the newborn has available. Assessment by counting deficits alone will be unable to predict the eventual outcome. The consequences for an individual of a particular insult or deficit can only be fully determined by taking account of previous relevant stressors and the adaptations they have provoked; of the individual strengths and vulnerabilities of the newborn; and of the pattern of support and challenge offered by the environment in which the baby will have to function.

THE NEED FOR CHALLENGE

It is a developmental principle dating back at least to Freud that healthy growth is achieved by surmounting challenges. Without problems to solve the individual is deprived of the incentive to expand existing capabilities, and it is the experience gained in successfully coping with challenges which equips the individual with the necessary expectations and skills to deal with future demands. The application of this principle requires a change in perspective from the main thrust of neonatal psychobiology which has tended to concentrate on the innate endowment of the newborn as the major resource for coping with challenges. The clearest example is provided by Rovee-Collier and Lipsitt in their discussion of crib death in Chapter 7. In its specific form their proposal is that newborns need the experience of difficulties in breathing in order to develop their capacity to cope with subsequent demands. More generally they make the intriguing suggestion that the significance of maturational transitions may derive more from the adaptations they provoke than from the new abilities which they confer directly.

In a sense the need for challenge is implied by any reference to the longer term significance of adaptations. Without challenge there is no need for adaptation and without adaptation there is no development beyond what is produced directly by maturation. In the initial discussion of adaptation in Chapter 1 it was suggested that the newborn may gain something by adapting to the demands of breast feeding. This suggestion can now be elaborated. If breast feeding presents babies with surmountable challenges, then it is likely that there are consequences arising from such experiences which will have value later on. Providing newborns with an easier method of feeding, for example by fistula or even by bottle, may deprive them of valuable opportunities to develop capabilities in a context which maximizes the chances of success, leaving them ill-equipped to cope with subsequent challenges when conditions might not be so favourable.

The general point being proposed here is that it is not necessarily always valuable to minimize the demands made on a newborn. The previous section suggests that there is some latitude available within the normal functioning of the newborn and this makes it possible to consider that particular challenges to a baby's functioning may have positive aspects. The newborn can then be brought within the application of a principle which has value throughout development: it is the responsibility of care-takers to prevent the damage done by failure by ensuring that challenges do not exceed the capacity of the individual, but they must also avoid the risk of forestalling development through succumbing to the temptation to remove the challenges completely.

DISMISSIVE LABELLING

As any physically handicapped person discovers, we have a strong tendency to assume that motor incompetence indicates cognitive incapacity. Much of the underestimating of the newborn, which is still quite widespread, must have derived from this tendency. While it would be difficult, in the face of the evidence amassed in Section II, to deny that neonates are well endowed with the basic cognitive competences, the treatment of newborns often suggests a failure to appreciate the full implications of our existing knowledge. A particular problem seems to have been in the inappropriate use of labelling which either undervalues the newborn or prematurely dismisses from consideration some function which could be usefully explored in its own right. A specific instance is the demonstration, discussed by Rovee-Collier and Lipsitt in Chapter 7, of the rapid acquisition by the newborn of stimulus-response relationships. It has been argued that the acquisition is too fast for the process to be properly described as learning, with the implication that if we are interested in learning, the phenomenon can be ignored. The answer would seem to be that this is a highly efficient (and essential) form of adaptation which deserves further investigation. If there is a problem about whether it is truly learning, this is a problem for learning theory and not something that need obstruct our study of the newborn.

Another limitation on our perception derives from the assumption that functions can only be achieved in the adult form. In his account of the nervous system at birth Bronson (Chapter 5) makes it quite clear that much of the newborn's performance is achieved using phylogenetically more primitive brain structures than are employed for similar purposes by the adult. A failure to appreciate this point leads to errors such as the acceptance by Korner (1979) of the claim that newborns cannot habituate because true habituation is a cortical phenomenon, or the opposite mistake of Stratton and Connolly (1973) who believed that their demonstration of temporal discrimination proved that the cortex must be functional at 3 days. A particularly interesting question arises concerning the widespread belief that newborns have no emotions (See Chapter 1). We now know that emotional experience is an outcome of cognitive and physiological processes in forms that are available to the newborn. 'The . . . feeling of emotion will be formed by a fusion between the initial evaluation of the event together with feedback from the limbic system and hypothalamus and from the peripheral physiological and behavioural consequences' (Blundell, 1975; p. 129). If this fusion can be achieved subcortically, or using the limited cortical capacity of the neonate, there would seem no reason to deny emotional feelings in the newborn. It would certainly be difficult to justify a claim that such feelings are impossible, even though we may wish to insist that they are different from the emotions of adults.

The more general view that much of the incapacity of the newborn is caused by immaturity can now be seen to be teleological. So far as we are able to analyse the adaptations made by newborns it seems that they have all of the capabilities needed for survival under the conditions that have applied in the environment of evolutionary adaptedness. Immaturity is not an arbitrary limitation imposed by the fact that the newborn is only part of the way towards becoming an adult. In a much more positive way the relative maturity of different systems is an expression of priorities which have emerged to ensure that particular adaptations will occur. We might also expect to identify cases in which newborns are protected by their immaturity from certain kinds of influence (for example the perception of certain stimuli) which would otherwise provoke adaptations with undesirable long-term consequences.

In reviewing biological rhythms (Chapter 6) and individual differences (Chapter 9) I was struck by a common characteristic of these rather different areas. In each case there had been a common tendency to state that particular phenomena fitted these headings without indicating what significance this classification might have. The result was that there were no clear criteria of what constituted a rhythm or an individual difference, respectively. Furthermore both areas were marked by reviews that listed examples but never seemed to proceed to make any productive use of the fact that so many instances could be classified in such a way. In these cases labelling based on inadequately specified criteria seems to have served the function of inhibiting rather than fostering further study.

The final category of dismissive labelling concerns the tendency to restrict ones concern to arbitrarily specified limits. If this book has a single objective it is to persuade researchers and practitioners that it is both futile and unproductive to attempt to deal with any aspect of the newborn in isolation. We are seeing a unique organism in which the various functions are richly and complexly adapted both to each other and to the natural environment. To designate any aspect as an overriding priority, to the exclusion of others with which it is likely to be intimately co-ordinated, is a mistake. It was argued in Chapter 1 that outcome measures must be appropriate, but it is now clear that any single measure is likely to be misleading. Too much concentration on perinatal mortality could lead to techniques which pointlessly prolong life in some instances and merely postpone problems until the baby is beyond the resources of the maternity hospital in others. Conversely, a total reliance on measures of long-term outcome can lead to ignoring the immediate stress of transient conditions. A fundamental disagreement over the range of factors which should be considered is the basis of the dispute between proponents of life at any price and those who would take account of the potential quality of all of the lives involved (Oakley, Chapter 12). Much less dramatic decisions, which would be simplified by prior consideration of which factors should be considered to be relevant, concern issues like the readiness to remove babies from their mothers, the amount of effort put into facilitating breast feeding, the imposition of feeding schedules, and allowing babies skin contact with their mothers. What factors, for example, should be taken into account when deciding whether mothers should be allowed to have their babies in bed with them? The honest attempt to list all of the potentially relevant effects is very different from the more common response of searching for reasons which would support existing practice.

TRANSACTIONAL ADAPTATION REVISITED

The basic theme which has been proposed for co-ordinating our knowledge of the psychobiology of the newborn is that of adaptation. In dealing directly with this topic Rovee-Collier and Lipsitt (Chapter 7) suggest that the first consideration in any adaptation is the gain and preservation of weight. It certainly seems that many of the capabilities of the newborn can be usefully interpreted in their relationship to this fundamental requirement. For example it is possible that the powerful learning capacities and dispositions towards interaction with adult caretakers developed largely in the service of eliciting, anticipating and responding appropriately to the availability of the breast. It is often enlightening to take such a principle, recognizing that it is over-simplified and incomplete, to see how much it is capable of explaining. In this instance there are two issues which should be incorporated to avoid overgeneralization: the tendency for capacities, once acquired, to be used for other purposes; and the probability that there are other fundamental demands which govern neonatal adaptation.

A feature of much neonatal behaviour is that it results in the maintenance of proximity to care-takers. In many species proximity serves to preserve heat and so this tendency can be viewed as primarily concerned with energy conservation, thereby maximizing the amount of nutrition available for weight gain. Proximity also ensures the availability of the food supply and of protection from predators. Any or all of these functions may have been responsible for the initial development of the proximity enhancing behaviours of the human newborn, but there can be no doubt that contact with care-takers has come to serve other purposes. It is unlikely that we will ever be certain of the path taken by the selection process that resulted in the present complex transactional relationship between mother and baby. It can however be assumed that it involved a long process in which fundamental requirements such as feeding were met in ways which enhanced the capacities of the newborn for eliciting and responding to maternal ministrations. These capacities must have been capitalized on for the aspects which facilitated bonding, as well as for other functions which improve the prospects of survival.

What we can see today is an extremely complex pattern of interrelated biological, cognitive, and social capabilities of the newborn which can only be meaningfully interpreted as a multifaceted adaptation to natural care-taking. As with any adaptation the particular form is determined by the characteristics of the current situation, but its success must be judged in terms of how well it prepares the baby for the tasks which lie ahead. What is particularly significant about neonatal adaptations is the extent to which they take the form labelled 'transactions', though they are not unique in this. As Barrett has shown in Chapter 10, the transactional model is needed for the interpretation of prenatal functioning as well. One implication of the newborn's incompetence in motor, as compared with cognitive, function, is the extent to which this will ensure that change in the environment depends on the mediation of care-takers. Adaptations may be achieved most easily by modifying the environment and the importance of many aspects of newborn functioning may derive from the effects on care-takers. For example the heightened alertness and responsiveness of babies during the first hour following birth (Desmond *et al.*, 1963) may facilitate learning to control functions such as respiration, though there seems little reason to posit prepared social learning of the kind involved in the imprinting of precocial birds. What does seem likely is that this alert state serves to provide caretakers with basic information about their new baby. Both mothers (Klaus *et al.*, 1970) and fathers (Rödholm and Larsson, 1979) will engage in a fairly standard sequence of exploration if they are given their undressed babies during this state.

At present we cannot always expect to be certain whether specific behaviours have developed primarily to adapt the newborn directly or through some modification to the environment. What does emerge from our current understanding of early mother-infant transaction is that the process demands quite a detailed knowledge by the mother of the characteristics of her baby. To ensure that this happens, many newborn behaviours may be specified in such a way as to educate any available and willing adult about the characteristics (both idiographic and nomothetic) of this particular baby.

It seems, then, that a major function of neonatal behaviour is to provide the mother with knowledge about her baby, and to establish an attitude towards him as towards an individual with whom she has a personal relationship. So far as the mother is concerned, the neonatal period is one of heightened receptivity in which a basis of knowledge and attitudes to her baby are rapidly acquired in a form which will be relatively resistent to modification, and which will form the basis of her transactions with the baby for some time to come. (Stratton, 1977; p. 152)

Although this passage refers only to the mother, it was not intended to imply that getting to know a baby should be or has to be restricted to the biological mother. From what is now known of attachment formation, the requirement is for a socially competent person who knows the baby well enough to interact contingently in ways that induce positive mood. The young infant is equipped with the requisite expressive behaviours to elicit such interaction from any adult who is willing to learn. This will normally include both parents but can be anyone who is charged with the individual care of a baby in circumstances that allow a relatively free expression of the baby's tendencies. It is convenient to speak of the mother as she is almost invariably one of the adults fulfilling the caregiving role, but it is important to recognize the concomitant risk of undervaluing the role of other care-givers, especially the father, who may be equally competent and effective in providing 'mothering'.

This section has, legitimately, emphasized the flow of information from baby to mother, father, or other committed adult (referred to hereinafter as the mother), but this would only be one aspect of the full story. We conclude with a consideration of the implications of our present understanding of neonatal psychobiology for the flow of information, and other forms of influence, in the tripartite system of mother, baby, and institutional care.

THE FLOW OF INFORMATION AND INFLUENCE

Each of the participants in the care of the newborn influence, and are influenced by, the newborn and each other. This section explores the flow between the major categories but there is also important communication among those who share the mothering functions and among those who provide different aspects of institutional care.

Newborn to Mother

I have suggested that a major function of the neonatal period is for the mother to get to know her baby. This conviction stems from a number of rather disparate sources. First is the evidence, surveyed by Papoušek and Papoušek in Chapter 14, that mothers are particularly prone to explore and find out about their babies. The availability of a rich supply of individual characteristics which are likely to influence the caregiver emerges clearly from Stratton's review in Chapter 9, and an indication of the strength of the tendency to build such characteristics into a coherent pattern is provided by Bennett (1971). In this study it was found that over the first few weeks of life, nurses constructed a 'personality' for babies in

The flow of information and influence

Figure 1   The six directions of flow of information.

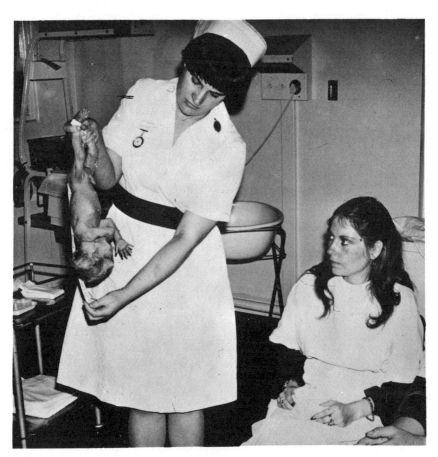

Figure 2   A specific instance of multi-directional flow of information between newborn, nurse, and parent.

their care, derived from tendencies which has been displayed in the first few days, and then based their treatment of the baby on this construct.

The importance of this early phase of learning about the newborn by the mother is indicated by recent studies of infancy. The detailed observational studies of mother–infant interaction by such researchers as Stern (1977) indicate that an essential aspect of successful sequences is that the mother should synchronize her behaviours so that they become (or appear to be) contingent on cues provided by the infant. Such sensitive timing and reciprocation can only be achieved when the controlling partner knows the other well enough to anticipate his or her likely responses. It seems entirely plausible that many aspects of the functioning of mother and baby during the neonatal period are specifically formulated to establish this knowledge. The need for mothers to learn about their babies seems to be recognized in many of the cultures described by Oakley (Chapter 11), in which mother and baby are secluded together throughout the first weeks after birth. A striking consequence of a study in which mothers were present while we filmed their babies, unclothed and without scheduled stimulation for 3 h periods, was the universal surprise at the variety of behaviours observed. Every mother (some were multiparous) made some comment to the effect that they had not realized how many interesting things their babies did. There would seem to be a risk that many of our attitudes about keeping babies well wrapped and lying undisturbed, may result in mothers being deprived of an early opportunity to elaborate their interest in and knowledge of their baby.

The other source of my belief that a natural function of the neonatal period is for the mother to learn about her baby, and that being natural the function will be facilitated by basic aspects of the psychobiology of the participants, comes from a consideration of the effect a baby has on its family. I have for a long time felt that young adults with less adequate capabilities for social relationships, are often resocialized through the experience of forming relationships with their own children. A number of growth points in developmental psychology are beginning to provide the necessary wider perspective. The influence that infants have on their parents has rapidly, if belatedly, become accepted (Bell and Harper, 1977); a large body of work is starting to emerge on the transition that couples must undergo to become parents (Kirkpatrick, 1978); there has been a remarkable boom in treating childhood disturbance within the context of the whole family (Framo, 1979); and this theme, along with the systems approach which has proved so productive in family therapy, is the basis of a recent attempt to extend the discussion of infant social interaction to all members of the family (Lewis and Rosenblum, 1979). All of this adds up to an excellent basis from which to begin to explore the processes whereby babies generate in their parents the attitudes, feelings and behaviours which ensure a suitable context for the future development of the infant. Meanwhile we should be giving very serious consideration to any practices and conventions which make it difficult for parents to know, and perhaps thereby to love, their babies.

Mother to Newborn

The major determinant of the environment to which the newborn must adapt is the mother. However much we stress the powers of the newborn to determine his or her own environment we must not lose sight of the fact that the mother is open to other, possibly competing influences, of which her memory of her own mother's attitudes may be among the most powerful (Cohler *et al.*, 1971). The surprisingly high level of cognitive functioning of the newborn is an indication of a substantial capacity to take in and be influenced by salient features of the environment. Much of Chapter 14 was concerned with the evidence that newborns are significantly affected by variations in their caretaking, and the Papoušeks make a very clear case that the control and processing of incoming information is a central feature of newborn adaptation. What is also clear is that we are particularly ignorant about both sides of this process: we have little solid data about the forms and variations of stimulation that mothers offer to their babies, and we have very little reliable knowledge about how the adaptations provoked by this influence affect future functioning, or even about how newborns monitor the information. Almost all of the findings that we have available concerning neonatal attention are suspect or open to a variety of interpretation, The selection of input, of which we know we newborn to be capable, is fundamental to all adaptations, but particularly those that involve discriminating significant from irrelevant stimuli. For the young infant 'significant' may be almost synonymous with 'involving the mother'. Selective attention may also be one of the most sophisticated functions of which the newborn is capable. Such considerations may help to explain the primitive state of our present understanding of these processes but they also indicate how important progress in this area is likely to be.

Newborn to Institution

Lipsitt (1979) has pointed out a number of ways in which newborns can be useful informants about their own developmental condition. The information is, however, only available to those who are receptive to the signs and are able to interpret them. Institutional care-givers are not usually in a mothering role (as were the nurses observed by Bennett, above) and are therefore more likely to be attuned to the normative features of babies than to their individual characteristics. This book has largely concentrated on putting together the existing knowledge about 'the newborn' in a usable form, but this section is concerned with the need to base treatment on the characteristics of the individual baby.

Stratton concluded in Chapter 9 that the newborn is richly endowed with an individuality which will exert a considerable influence on any care-giver. Much of this influence may operate without any particular awareness on the part of the recipient, but since the general effect of individual differences is to bring about a care-taking environment which is optimally suited to the needs of the particular individual, it must be advantageous if a special effort is made to learn which aspects of differences have significant implications for the care which is being provided, and to be alert for individual variation in these features. For example, a particular kind of cry may mean different things from different babies. If care is going to be related to the signals provided by the individual either the institutional care-givers must learn their meaning or else the responsibility for responding must be given to the mother, whose knowledge of her baby should be encouraged and facilitated as already discussed.

The necessity, which repeatedly emerges, to take a broad perspective on what is relevant in caring for the newborn, suggests that institutional care should attend to both previous and subsequent features. As Barrett points out in Chapter 10, prenatal, and even preconceptional influences, can have a major impact on the functioning of the newborn. Of particular significance are those factors which modify the adaptive processes themselves, and while there is much that we do not yet know about the operation of these, there is usually enough information available to the hospital concerning the previous experiences of the baby to identify individuals with particular vulnerabilities.

Apart from the need to relate some aspects of care to the characteristics of the individual baby, there is also a value in ensuring that the inevitably limited resources are allocated in the most effective ways. This will only be achieved by looking beyond the neonatal period to the influences and demands that will be imposed during and after the transitional period around 2 months. Newborns who are destined for an environment which will be optimally adjusted to their needs seem to be able to accept considerable insult without long-term deficit. For most babies however, warning signs in the postnatal period should raise concern about the stress that will be imposed on the care-taking environment, while for some the resources available for coping with stress will be so limited that any difficulty presented by the baby, even if it falls within the range regarded as normal, must be a cue for mobilizing extra help. So any baby with a particularly disturbing cry (see Stratton, Chapter 9 and Barrett, Chapter 10) should be a target for extra attention while in the case of babies who will be in a high-risk environment, even a moderate disposition towards more frequent crying should be cause for concern.

As we learn more about newborns, both the scope and the responsibility to attend to their characteristics increases. We may, for example, come to question our belief that distress such as that shown by the baby in Figure 2 does not matter. Once we accept the claim made under 'dismissive labelling' above that the potential for emotion exists, and that the expressions of newborns must be treated as legitimate and meaningful even if they do not correspond to adult forms, the ability to ignore the objections of newborns to unnecessarily stressful procedures may come to look like the convenient belief of some gourmets that lobsters do not mind being put into boiling water. As we come to understand the function of various features shown by all newborns we can, and should, increase our ability to recognize in the pattern shown by a particular individual the effects of previous and current influences, and an early indication of future special needs.

Institution to Newborn

Our recently acquired understanding of the extent of neonatal cognitive capacities, and of the readiness with which these capacities will be used to adapt to particular aspects of the postnatal environment, demands that we should pay much more attention to the situations in which our babies start their lives. Most Western newborns make their first adaptations to the noise, smell, fluorescent lighting and other characteristics of a hospital medical ward. They are superbly equipped and disposed to learn what kind of world they have come into, and we should be very careful not to mislead them.

Some influences are rather obvious. We know how readily newborns adapt to particular types of feeding so there can rarely be any justification for giving a bottle to a breast-feeding baby. But given the ready adaptation to the style of a single care-giver, what are the effects of care being provided by a sequence of different individuals? Does it matter if the newborn is transported in a wheeled crib so that the changes in light and sound are associated with vibration rather than the rhythmical vestibular stimulation provided by a walking adult? Since babies are very quick to learn to ignore regularly repeated noises and to attend only to sounds which relate to biologically significant aspects of the environment, do we need to reduce the quantity and variety of noise, particularly of different human voices, to which newborns are exposed? Is there any risk of maladaptive adaptation to a relatively high ambient temperature which remains constant over the 24-h period, for babies who will go home to much less stable (but more natural) conditions?

The issue of adaptation to particular hospital environments, and the possible consequences when the baby is moved to a different environment, were discussed in Chapter 1. The insights and information contained in the intervening chapters indicate that questions such as those above must be taken much more seriously than would have seemed necessary only 10 years ago, but they do not provide definite answers. If we are to move beyond speculation we will need to conduct research specifically designed to discriminate possibilities that might until recently have seemed too fanciful to justify effort in exploring them.

Mother to Institution

Just as adequate care of the newborn requires attention to be paid to both prior and subsequent factors, a similarly broad perspective is desirable when considering the information available from the mother. Amiel-Tison (Chapter 4) has surveyed the wide range of influences which may operate during pregnancy to put the newborn at risk, and Barrett (Chapter 10) has discussed the fact that the strongest associations are with variables such as nutrition and drug intake over which the mother has a certain amount of choice. However, as Chiswick (Chapter 12) points out, simple causal relationships are difficult to establish because of the interdependence of the different kinds of influence. A knowledge of the mother's life style and habits and of complications during pregnancy can give general indications of particular needs that the newborn is likely to have, as well as in some cases predicting future disadvantages.

In discussing what prognosis is implied by the outcome of neurological assessments both Prechtl (Chapter 2), and Amiel-Tison (Chapter 4) conclude that outcome is highly related to subsequent home conditions, a point made more generally by Stratton in Chapter 1. If extra resources are to be made available to cases of special need, the assessment must include not only the condition of the newborn, but also certain information about the mother. Furthermore we need to look beyond measures such as social class and related factors like income and housing. Some idea of the kinds of information that would be valuable is provided by the work of Kempe and Kempe (1978) who claim to predict 76 per cent of cases of non-accidental injury from measures taken around the time of birth. If, as seems reasonable, overt abuse can be regarded as the extreme of a continuum of breakdown in parenting then similar measures should identify a larger group in which any initial handicap of the baby is likely to be amplified rather than compensated. Although the possibilities of prediction from the Kempes' measures cannot yet be fully evaluated, their combination of observation of the way the mother handles the baby, with assessment of familial relationships, attitudes to the pregnancy etc., looks promising.

As well as being open to information from the mother which may have implications for future care, there is a need for institutions to make special efforts if their procedures are to be influenced by the needs and wishes of their clients. The complex dependence of neonatal adaptation on particular forms of interaction with the mother demands that we should be very careful not to unnecessarily disrupt the natural processes of mothering. In our present state of knowledge we cannot claim to be able to comprehensively specify the forms and functions of all important aspects of the process. We therefore have to accept that it is the mother who is the expert, and so should be allowed an environment in which she can exercise her expertise. This will not happen easily. The inhibiting and deskilling effects of entering an institution with established and fixed routines are well known, and these effects can only be exaggerated by the current proliferation of technology. It requires an effort even to be fully aware of our own routines, and much greater commitment to be able to perceive their consequences and question their necessity. To ask what needs (and whose needs) are being met by keeping newborns tightly wrapped and laid out in neat rows of cribs requires courage. To find out whether mothers would prefer to have their babies in bed with them at all times might require a radical change in outlook for ward staff. Such changes will not occur unless they are made a priority at all levels, and they will only be fruitful if we can develop and display greater confidence in the ability of mother and baby in normal circumstances, to negotiate the mutual adaptation which best meets their needs.

Institution to Mother

One of the dilemmas of providing care is that it almost inevitably involves removing autonomy and competence from the recipient. The professional ideology of medicine, as discussed by Oakley in Chapter 11, has at its core the taking of responsibility and, therefore, needing complete control of the situation, including the patient. A more or less unique aspect of maternity care is that in most cases neither the mother nor the newborn can be said to be ill. It is the fact that our system requires large numbers of healthy people to be treated within a medical framework which is a major source of the present conflict between the professional care-givers and pressure groups like the National Childbirth Trust and the Association for Improvements in the Maternity Services, as well as provoking considerable discussion within the professions themselves. There is however another aspect of maternal control which is more directly relevant to our present concern.

A major theme at present in developmental psychobiology is the experience of contingencies (events over which the individual has control) in the acquisition of competence (Stratton, 1982b). The natural process of interactions with infants providing parents with contingency experiences which produce feelings of efficacy and self-confidence has been described by Goldberg (1977), who suggests that these feelings are essential for effective parent–infant interactions. If feelings of efficacy are so crucial then the experience of parents, particularly mothers, in maternity units might be expected to have a substantial effect on future trans-actions. There is now considerable evidence that this is indeed so. For example the Vancouver study (Bradley and Ross, 1978), which was originally set up to investigate factors such as type of birth, found that the strongest effects on the quality of the subsequent mother–infant relationship derived from the amount of control mothers were allowed before going home. The best relationships were found when mothers had actively participated in the care of their babies and been 'allowed' some autonomy in deciding how they should be treated.

The argument for being particularly concerned about the control that mothers are allowed has three branches: institutions have powerful tendencies to deprive their inmates of autonomy and to render them helpless; helplessness, the obverse of effectance, is widely believed to be associated with depression (Garber and Seligman, 1980); and the post-partum mother is particularly vulnerable to depression. We might therefore expect to find that regimes or patterns of events which deprive the mother of feeling and being in control, put her at risk of depression. This is precisely what Oakley (1980) found in her study of 'Transition to Motherhood'. Depression during the 5 months following birth was significantly correlated with the level of technology used during the birth and with feelings of lack of control in labour. Once again we return to the need for an open, even an imaginative, attitude to the wider implications of specific care-giving practices, particularly in the calculation of the overall benefit or cost of particular patterns of care.

The difficulty of making reliable prognostications (Prechtl, Chapter 2; Amiel-Tison, Chapter 4) makes us justifiably cautious in what we tell parents about possible negative outcomes, for example from hypoxia (Chiswick, Chapter 12). However, other kinds of information may be transmitted inadvertently through the priorities displayed in our institutional practices and, being inadvertent, will not be subject to the same caution. I would suggest that parents' future transactions with their babies may be affected not only by practices which have a direct effect of rendering then helpless but also by the whole ethos apparent in the institutional care provided. A narrow concentration on immediate physiological needs or an undue reverence for technological aids can easily be generalized by parents into a belief that their feelings or their relationship with the newborn have been judged to be irrelevant by the experts. By the power and the consistency of their influence, our institutions can provoke adaptations and induce expectations which may have an enduring effect on the mother's treatment of her baby. I would suggest that we need to examine the implicit assumptions on which our institutional practice is founded, not least because these assumptions are being adopted by parents with consequences that are not always in the best interests of their babies.

CONCLUSION

While there is an enormous amount waiting to be discovered, the contents of this book provide a secure foundation for a much more usable understanding of the newborn than has been possible in the past. The hope that the present synthesis will be used by those who are in any way concerned with the care of the newborn derives from more than just the fact that we have significantly advanced our knowledge of neonatal psychobiology. The overview that we are working towards is no longer one that deskills the care-taker. On the contrary the psychobiologist has come to accept that all of the participants—parents, baby, and institutional care-givers must be viewed as fully competent contributors to the construction of the total system. From this perspective we can first learn to appreciate the complex of finely balanced adaptations in the naturally functioning situation, and then identify ways of enhancing the competencies of one or more of the participants when the balance of a particular adaptation is in danger of leading to deleterious consequences.

REFERENCES

Bell, R. Q. and Harper, L. V. (1977). *Child Effects on Adults*. Erlbaum, Hillsdale, N. J.

Bennett, S. (1971). Infant caretaker interactions, *J. Amer. Acad. Child Psychiat.*, **10**, 321–335.

Blundell, J. (1975). *Physiological Psychology*, Methuen, London.

Bowlby, J. (1969). *Attachment and Loss*, Vol. I *Attachment*, Hogarth Press, London.

Bradley, C. F. and Ross, S. E. (1978). *Perinatal Health Care for the City*. Report of the Vancouver Perinatal Health Project.

Brown, G. W. and Harris, T. (1978). *Social Origins of Depression*, Tavistock Publications, London.

Cairns, R. B. (1979). *Social Development: The Origins and Plasticity of Interchanges*, W. H. Freeman, San Francisco.

Cohler, B. J., Grunebaum, H. U., Weiss, J. L., and Moran, D. L. (1971). The childcare attitudes of two generations of mothers, *Merril-Palmer Quarterly*, **17**, 1.

Desmond, M. M., Franklin, R. R., Vallbona, C., Hill, R., Plumb, R. and Watts, J. (1963). The clinical behaviour of the newly born. I. The term baby, *Journal of Pediatrics*, **62**, 307–325.

Framo, J. L. (1979). Family theory and therapy, *American Psychologist*, **34**, 988–992.

Garber, J. and Seligman, M. E. P. (1980). *Human Helplessness: Theory and Applications*, Academic Press, New York.

Goldberg, S. (1977). Social competence in infancy: a model of parent–infant interaction, *Merril-Palmer Quarterly*, **23**, 163–177.

Kempe, R. S. and Kempe, C. H. (1978). *Child Abuse*, Fontana, London.

Kirkpatrick, S. W. (1978). Adjustment to parenthood: A structural model, *Genetic Psychology Monographs*, **98**, 51–82.

Klaus, M. H., Kennell, J. H., Plumb, N., and Zuehlke, S., (1970). Human maternal behaviour at the first contact with her young, *Pediatrics*, **46**, 187–92.

Korner, A. F. (1979). Conceptual issues in infancy research. in *Handbook of Infant Development* (Ed. J. D. Osofsky), Wiley, New York.

Lawson, K., Daum, C., and Turkewitz, G. (1977). Environmental characteristics of a neonatal intensive-care unit. *Child Development*, **48**, 1633–1639.

Lewis, M. and Rosenblum, L. A. (1979). *The Child and its Family*, Plenum, New York.

Lipsitt, L. P. (1979). The newborn as informant, in *Infants at Risk—Assessment of Cognitive Functioning* (Eds R. B. Kearsley and I. E. Sigel), Erlbaum, Hillsdale, N. J.

Marr, D. (1976). Early processing of visual information, *Philosophical Transactions of the Royal Society of London*, Series B, **275**, 483–519.

McCall, R. B., Eichorn, D. H., and Hogarty, P. S. (1977). Transitions in early mental development. *Monographs of the Society for Research in Child Development*, **42**, (3, Serial No. 171).

Oakley, A. (1980). *Women Confined: Towards a Sociology of Childbirth*. Martin Robertson, Oxford.

Oppenheim, R. W. (1981). Ontogenetic adaptations and retrogressive processes in the development of the nervous system and behaviour: A neuroembryological perspective, in *Maturation and Development: Biological and Psychological Perspectives* (Eds K. J. Connolly and H. R. Prechtl), Heinemann, London.

Rödholm, M. and Larsson, K. (1979). Father-infant interaction at the first contact after delivery, *Early Human Devel.*, **3**, 21–27.

Schaffer, H. R. (1971). *The Growth of sociability*, Middlesex Penguin Books,

Stern, D. (1977). *The First Relationship: Infant and Mother*, Fontana/Open Books, London.

Stratton, P. M. (1977). Criteria for assessing the influence of obstetric circumstances on later development, in *Benefits and Hazards of the New Obstetrics* (Eds T. Chard and M. Richards), SIMP, London.

Stratton, P. M. (1982a). Biological pre-programming of infant behaviour, *Journal of Child Psychology and Psychiatry* (In Press.)

Stratton, P. M. (1982b). Contingency, control and competence, *Developmental Medicine and Child Neurology*. (In Press.)

Stratton, P. M. and Connolly, K. J. (1973). Discrimination by newborns of the intensity, frequency and temporal characteristics of auditory stimuli, *Brit. J. Psychol.*, **64**, 291–232.

Toffler, A. (1970). *Future Shock*, Random House, New York.

Author Index

Abe, K. 139, 142
Abraham, W. 218
Abramson, M. D. 48
Acebo, C. 260
Adams, G. 142
Adams, J. 5, 15
Adamson, K. 316, 334
Adamson, L. 47, 52, 255
Adamsons, K. J. 94
Ader, R. 279, 289
Adolph, E. F. 148, 177, 180
Ahlstrom, M. 143
Ainsworth, M. D. S. 230, 251, 255, 340, 343, 361, 374, 385
Aiu, P. 216
Akiyama, Y. 50, 71, 72
Albano, J. E. 212, 219
Alberman, E. D. 282, 290
Alberts, J. R. 148, 163, 178, 180, 185
Aleksandrowicz, D. R. 234, 255
Aleksandrowicz, M. K. 234, 255
Alexander, G. 316, 334
Alford, C. A. 286, 289
Allen, J. L. 195, 196, 214
Alloway, T. 369, 385
Almgren, P. E. 287, 293
Alper, M. H. 259
Als, H. 41, 42, 45, 47–48, 51, 52, 232, 255, 275, 276, 289
Altman, J. 102, 116
Amatruda, C. S. 55, 70
Ambrose, A. 140, 142, 153, 185
Amiel-Tison, C. 18, 35, 36, 48, 75, 78, 81, 82, 85, 88, 90, 92, 93, 94, 399, 409, 410, 412

Amlie, R. 79, 94
Anders, T. F. 58, 59, 60, 67, 69, 70, 133, 142, 260
Anderson, C. M. 363
Anderson, C. O. 190
Anderson, G. C. 336
Anderson, R. B. 175, 177, 180, 231, 255
André-Thomas, A. 34, 48
Andrews, C. 386
Anokhin, P. K. 29, 48, 139, 142, 224, 227, 249, 255
Anthony, E. J. 290
Antonov, A. N. 328, 334
Antonova, T. G. 256
Appel, M. A. 201, 214
Aranda, J. V. 324, 334
Arbib, M. A. 63, 70
Archer, J. 279, 289, 292
Aron, M. 187
Aserinsky, E. 55, 59, 70, 134, 142
Ashby, S. 335
Ashby, W. R. 55, 70
Asher, P. 340, 349, 358, 362
Ashton, R. 64, 70, 132, 133, 142, 244, 255
Aslin, R. N. 116, 199, 200, 214, 215, 216
Atkinson, J. 97, 191, 195, 196, 200, 201, 203, 214, 215, 397
Aubry, R. H. 22, 49
Avery, M. E. 320, 334

Babkin, P. S. 344, 362
Bach, G. R. 380, 385
Baker, P. 143
Bakker, H. H. 72
Baldwin, J. M. 378

Baldwin, R. B. 118
Balint, M. 128, 129, 142, 228, 255
Ball, W. 202, 215
Ban, P. 144, 258, 378, 387
Banker, B. Q. 84, 93
Banks, M. S. 113, 116, 183, 195, 196, 198,
    199, 201, 204, 215, 200n
Barnes, I. 185
Barrera, M. 205, 206, 218
Barrett, J. H. W. 263, 267, 268, 271, 272,
    277, 279, 281, 289, 290, 393, 398,
    403, 408, 410
Bartel, P. R. 293
Barten, S. 232, 255
Barton, L. L. 93
Bartoshuk, A. K. 371, 385
Bauer, C. 79, 93
Baum, D. 7, 15
Baumel, M. H. 144, 258
Baxter, S. 287, 290
Beard, R. 94
Beason-Williams, L. 260, 390
Becker, P. T. 73, 260
Beckman, D. 317, 334
Behrle, F. C. 337
Beintema, D. J. 34, 35, 36, 37, 38, 39, 41,
    42, 43, 47, 48, 50, 59, 68, 72
Bell, R. A. 380, 385
Bell, R. Q. 68, 73, 222, 228, 229, 231, 232,
    233, 234, 240, 241, 247, 255, 270,
    290, 406, 413
Bell, S. M. 230, 255, 340, 343, 361, 385
Bennett, E. L. 112, 118, 292
Bennett, K. J. 313
Bennett, M. 208, 215
Bennett, S. 225, 255, 404, 407, 413
Bentley, A. F. 378, 386
Berg, K. M. 126, 142, 234, 236, 244, 255
Berg, W. K. 126, 142, 234, 236, 244, 255
Berger, A. P. 337
Bergman, P. 232, 255
Bergsma, D. 333, 334
Bergsteinsson, H. 334
Berkson, G. 377, 388
Berman, P. W. 381, 385
Bernal, J. F. 149, 180, 310, 313, 341, 343,
    345, 346, 347, 362, 363
Bernard, C. 272
Bernstein, N. 372, 385
Bernstein, P. 372, 389
Bernuth, H. von 49, 62, 70, 71, 73, 217

Berry, R. C. 216
Bertalanffy, L. von 378, 385
Bertoncini, J. 210, 218
Bertucci, M. 184
Bethmann, O. de 93
Bettelheim, B. 307, 311
Bierman-Van Endenburg, M. 51
Bindra, D. 170, 181
Birch, H. G. 260, 261, 285, 290, 291, 390
Birch, M. 238, 261
Birns, B. 140, 142, 232, 233, *233*, 243,
    255, 256
Bishop, P. D. 151, 181
Blain, A. W. 72, 73, 145
Blake, A. M. 323, 334
Blakemore, C. 113, 116, 197, 201, 215
Blanco-Sequiros, M. 336
Blanguernon, C. 302, 311
Blank, M. 142, 256
Blizard, D. A. 281, 290
Blundell, J. 401, 413
Blurton Jones, N. 367, 385
Boddy, K. 316, 334
Bodian, D. 112, 116
Bodis-Wollner, J. 215
Bolles, R. C. 150, 170, 181
Bolton, A. F. 334
Borer, R. L. 336
Bornstein, M. H. 371, 385
Bosack, T. N. 185
Bowe, E. 335
Bowen, W. 186
Bower, T. G. R. 202, 213, 215, 371, 385
Bowlby, J. 375, 377, 385, 394, 395, 413
Brackbill, Y. 41, 48, 140, 142, 148, 152,
    153, 154, 168, 181, 183, 237, 260,
    271, 273, 275, 281, 290, 346, 362,
    363
Braddick, O. 97, 191, 195, 196, 198, 200,
    201, 214, 215, 397
Bradley, A. 199, 217
Bradley, C. F. 411, 413
Bradley, R. M. 280, 293
Brady, J. 121, 137, 142
Brans, Y. W. 265
Braun, H. W. 155, 181
Brazelton, T. B. 13, 15, 18, 35, 40, 41, 42,
    43, 46, 47–48, 51, 52, 64, 70, 149,
    176, 181, 234, 236, 242, 243, 255,
    256, 267, 276, 285, 289, 290, 341,
    362

Breen, D. 287, 290
Brenner, P. H. 336
Bresky, P. A. 93
Bresler, D. E. 284, 290
Bresson, F. 216
Bridger, W. H. 4, 15, 142, 222, 238, 239,
    256, 371, 385
Brittain, H. 293
Broadbent, D. E. 235, 256
Brock, D. J. H. 333, 334
Brodal, A. 112, 117
Brody, L. R. 189
Brody, S. 343, 362
Bonfenbrenner, U. 267, 271, 281, 289, 290
Bronshtein, A. I. 229, 256
Bronson, G. W. 95, 99, 101, 110, 111, 112,
    117, 176, 207, 215, 226, 395, 396,
    400
Brook, D. 311
Brookman, K. E. 198, 215
Brooks-Gunn, J. 373, 387
Broughton, J. M. 215
Broussard, E. R. 271, 290
Brown, G. W. 396, 413
Brown, J. L. 68, 70
Brown, M. 336
Brown, S. B. 78, 94
Brown, W. V. 259
Bruch, H. 342, 343, 359, 362
Bruner, J. S. 372, 385
Brunner, E. 51
Bruno, L. A. 183, 257
Brunswick, E. 150, 181
Bühler, C. 55, 70, 374, 385
Bull, D. 219
Bunting, C. 231, 259
Burchell, R. 304
Burgoyne, K. 93
Burke, P. M. 131, 142, 185
Burmeister, L. F. 285, 295
Burnett, L. S. 293
Burns, G. 291
Burns, P. 343, 362
Bushnell, I. W. R. 206, 211, 215
Butcher, M. J. 144
Butler, B. V. 238, 248, 256
Butler, J. E. 317, 334
Butler, N. 282, 290, 291
Butterfield, E. C. 169, 179, 181
Butterworth, G. 210, 215
Byers, R. K. 326, 335

Cadilhac, J. 70
Cairns, G. F. 169, 179, 181
Cairns, R. B. 368, 378, 385, 395, 413
Caldwell, D. F. 155, 181
Campbell, B. A. 171, 172, 181
Campbell, D. 241, 256, 259, 343, 348, 355,
    359, 362
Campbell, H. E. 293
Campos, J. J. 111, 117, 201, 214
Cannon, W. B. 163, 175, 177, 181, 272,
    290, 342, 362
Carlson, A. J. 342, 362
Carmichael, L. 54, 70
Caron, R. F. 383, 386
Carpenter, G. C. 152, 183, 206, 211, 215
Carpenter, R. 187
Casaer, P. 45, 48
Cass, L. K. 6, 15
Castan, P. 70
Castillo, M. 210, 215
Castiloe, J. P. 291
Cattell, P. 147, 181
Cavanagh, P. J. 153, 178, 188, 277, 294
Cekan, P. 70
Cha, C. C. 336
Challis, J. 279, 280, 290
Chalmers, I. 297, 311
Chamberlain, G. 290, 335
Chamberlain, R. 285, 290, 319, 335
Chambers, G. M. 333, 336
Chandler, M. J. 11, 16, 268, 270, 283, 294
Chandra, R. K. 273, 290
Chaplin, E. R. 93
Chard, T. 9, 15
Charney, E. 358, 362
Chase, H. 184
Chase, H. P. 274, 281, 290
Chase, R. A. 143
Chaves, L. P. 295
Cheatle, M. D. 163, 164, 172, 187
Chernick, V. 316, 335
Chesni, Y. 48
Chess, G. F. 143
Chess, S. 260
Chisholm, J. S. 234, 242, 256
Chiswick, M. L. 9, 264, 315, 323, 335,
    397, 410, 412
Chow, K. L. 113, 117
Chuck, B. 363
Claireaux, A. 290, 335
Clark, A. L. 310, 311

Clarke, A. D. B. 6, 15
Clarke, A. M. 6, 15
Clifton, R. K. 151, 153, 154, 178, 181,
    182, 183, 235, 238, 239, 256, 257,
    386
Coates, L. 184
Cochran, W. D. 48, 143
Cogan, D. G. 216, 217
Cogan, R. 283, 292
Cohen, L. B. 151, 170, 182, 184, 189, 375,
    383, 386
Cohler, B. J. 407, 413
Cole, T. J. 358, 363
Collis, G. M. 144
Commey, J. O. O. 89, 93
Condon, W. S. 140, 141, 142, 372, 386
Conel, J. L. 104, 117, 197, 215
Connolly, K. J. 64, 70, 140, 145, 153, 182,
    237, 260, 401, 414
Connors, K. 221
Conway, M. 323, 335
Cooper, F. S. 387
Cooper, L. 362
Cooper, Z. K. 139, 142
Copans, S. A. 51, 260, 279, 290, 294
Corah, N. L. 271, 275, 290
Cornwell, A. C. 155, 182
Coryell, J. F. 383, 386
Costa, J. 257
Costello, M. 232, 233, 255
Cotton, C. 169, 374, 390
Coulter, X. 171, 181
Coursin, D. B. 256
Cowley, J. J. 284, 290
Cranach, M. von 369, 386
Crano, W. D. 250, 256
Cravioto, J. 285, 291
Crawley, J. N. 62, 72
Crelin, E. S. 387
Cremer, R. 327, 335
Crnic, L. S. 281, 290
Crook, C. K. 128, 130, 131, 142, 170, 182,
    211, 215, 228, 256
Crosby, W. M. 274, 281, 282, 291
Croskerry, P. G. 185
Cross, E. E. 143
Crothers, B. 335
Crow, R. A. 339, 359, 362
Crowell, D. H. 68, 70, 142, 209, 215
Cukier, F. 89, 93
Cullen, J. K. 128, 143
Culler, M. 259

Curio, V. E. 152, 182
Curtis, B. A. 109, 110, 117
Curtis, M. 256
Curzi-Dascalova, L. 66, 71
Cusik, G. 94
Cutting, J. E. 217, 371, 386
Czerny, A. 55, 70

Daily, W. J. R. 335
Dalton, K. 269, 270, 291
Daniels, J. D. 113, 117, 207, 215
Darling, J. F. 247, 255
Davie, R. 284, 291
Davies, D. P. 14, 15, 356, 358, 362, 364
Davies, P. A. 318, 335
Davis, G. D. 117, 216
Davis, J. 170, 171, 172, 182
Davis, L. 261
Davis, M. 51, 151, 157, 182
Dawes, G. S. 127, 143, 316, 330, 334,
    335
Dawkins, M. 316, 335
Day, R. H. 199, 202, 217, 218
Dayton, G. O. 195, 200, 216
De, N. C. 364
Deaton, F. K. 217
Deaton, W. 286, 293
DeCasper, A. J. 169, 182
DeGrouchy, J. 332, 335
De Haan, R. 126, 142
Delange, M. 58, 68, 70
De Lee, C. 71
Delgado, H. 292
Delicardie, E. R. 291
Dellinger, W. S. 337
DeLucia, C. A. 193, 219
Dement, W. C. 144
Denenberg, V. H. 73, 190, 284, 285, 291
Dennis, W. A. 147, 182
Department of Health and Social Security
    356, 362
De Schonen, S. 202, 216
Desmedt, J. E. 106, 117
Desmond, M. M. 403, 413
Desor, J. A. 211, 216, 218
De Swiet, M. 340, 358, 362
de Vidas, J. 300, 303, 311
DeVido, C. J. 184
Dewey, J. 378, 386
Diamond, L. K. 326, 335
Dickes, R. 232, 257
Diener, M. M. 337

Dijkstra, J. 37, 50
Dittrichova, J. 51, 68, 70
Dixon, G. 286, 293
Dobbing, J. 176, 182, 271, 274, 275, 282, 291, 328, 335
Dobson, M. V. 203, 219
Dobson, V. 195, 196, 216
Donovan, W. L. 257
Dontchos, S. 363
Dopfer, R. 49
Dopfer-Feller, P. 49
Dorsen, M. M. 117, 216
Dorsey, G. A. 302, 311
Douglas, M. 308, 312
Douthitt, T. C. 261, 295
Drage, J. S. 186
Dräger, U. C. 213, 216
Dreher, B. 219
Dreier, T. 45, 48, 129, 143
Dreyfus-Brisac, C. 58, 64, 71, 78, 93
Drillien, C. M. 85, 86, 93, 275, 285, 291
D'Souza, S. W. 331, 335
Dubignon, J. 228, 229, 256, 343, 348, 355, 359, 362
Dubois, L. 259
Dubowitz, L. 319, 335
Dubowitz, V. 40, 48, 78, 93, 335, 336
Duchowny, M. S. 51
Dudgeon, J. A. 333, 336
Duke-Elder, W. S. 198, 216
Dumais, S. T. 216
Dunn, J. F. 4, 16, 221, 229, 230, 251, 256, 317, 335, 360, 362
Dunn, P. M. 283, 291, 304, 312
Durbin, G. M. 335
Dwyer, J. T. 340, 362

Eager Cross, E. 48
Easler, C. A. 183
Ebel, H. C. 159, 182
Eichorn, D. H. 126, 143, 413
Eichorn, W. 118
Eid, E. E. 340, 349, 358, 362
Eimas, P. D. 168, 182, 210, 216, 371, 375, 386
Eisele, W. A. 209, 216
Eisenberg, R. B. 236, 256, 386
Eliet-Flescher, J. 58, 64, 70, 71
Ellingson, R. J. 107, 117
Ellis, R. W. B. 275
Ellison, G. 290
Elwood, P. C. 362

Emde, R. N. 46, 48, 57, 58, 70, 121, 134, 143, 153, 176, 182
Emery, J. 187
Engel, B. T. 233, 238, 256
Engel, R. 248, 256
Engelmann, T. G. 138, 143
Engen, T. 152, 182, 211, 216, 371, 386
Enkin, M. W. 313
Enright, M. 187
Erickson, M. T. 283, 291
Escalona, S. K. 55, 70, 232, 233, 241, 255, 256
Escobedo, M. 79, 93
Esque-Vaucouloux, M. T. 92
Estes, W. K. 134, 143
Estevez, O. 118
Ewer, R. F. 148, 154
Eykern, L. A. van 72

Fagan, J. F. 170, 183, 216
Fagen, J. W. 170, 187
Fagerstrom, C.-F. 287, 293, 294
Falender, C. A. 221, 232, 235, 256
Fanaroff, A. A. 93, 336
Fantz, R. L. 195, 196, 201, 205, 207, 216
Fargo, N. 143
Fawcett, W. 118
Fayers, P. 362
Federman, E. J. 261, 295
Feldman, S. S. 381, 386
Fernander, F. 385
Ferrara, A. 323, 335
Ferriss, G. S. 107, 117, 196, 216
Fertig, J. W. 337
Field, T. M. 251, 256
Fielding, D. W. 337
Fifer, W. P. 169, 182
Findlay, J. M. 200, 219
Finger, S. 383, 389
Finnegan, L. P. 49
Fisher, C. 135, 143
Fisichelli, V. R. 257
Fitz, C. R. 79, 93
Fitzgerald, H. E. 148, 153, 154, 169, 181, 183
Fitzgerald, J. A. 293
Fitzhardinge, P. M. 89, 90, 93, 94, 318, 335
Fleming, D. 336
Fletcher, B. 285, 291
Fling, S. 386
Flynn, A. M. 283, 291. 302, 312

Foard, C. F. 217
Foppa, K. 386
Forbes, B. 218
Ford, C. S. 298, 301, 303, 304, 312
Forfar, J. O. 26, 48
Forsyth, C. C. 279, 291
Forsyth, H. A. 363
Forsythe, A. 48
Fox, R. 201, 216
Fox, S. 293
Fragel, J. W. 72
Framo, J. L. 406, 413
Franciosi, R. A. 325, 335
Franklin, R. R. 413
Frauenrath, C. 51
Freda, V. J. 326, 335
Freedman, D. G. 6, 16
Freeman, D. N. 218
Freeman, R. D. 113, 117
Freese, M. P. 145, 189, 260
French, J. 214, 215
Freud, S. 348, 362, 399
Friedman, E. A. 86, 93
Friedman, R. C. 279, 291
Friedman, S. 135, 143, 152, 183, 235, 236,
    237, 257, 371, 386
Fries, M. 242, 257
Frodi, A. M. 231, 257, 381, 386
Fuller, J. L. 155, 182, 183

Gaensbauer, T. 58, 70
Galask, R. P. 325, 336
Gandelman, R. 379, 386
Gandy, G. M. 334
Garber, J. 396, 411, 413
Gardner, J. 280, 291
Garey, L. J. 215
Gassett, O. Y. 289
Geiselhart, R. 155, 181
Gekoski, M. J. 157, 165, 168, 169, 172,
    179, 183, 187
Gelber, E. R. 170, 182
Gellis, S. S. 216, 217
Georgeson, M. A. 199, 216
Gerbig, W. 49
Gerreiro, M. 336
Gersony, W. M. 316, 335
Gesell, A. L. 1, 16, 55, 70, 134, 147, 183,
    344, 346, 347, 348, 362, 383, 386
Gewirtz, J. L. 369, 386
Ghazzawi, O. 337

Gibson, A. J. 309, 310, 312
Gibson, K. R. 102, 117
Gideon, H. 303, 306, 312
Gilmore, M. 259, 363
Ginsburg, H. J. 383, 386
Glass, L. 316, 324, 335
Gluck, L. 315, 336
Goddard, K. E. 258
Goggin, J. E. 276, 291
Golambos, R. 106, 118
Goldberg, C. 335
Goldberg, S. 235, 236, 251, 257, 258, 411,
    413
Goldfarb, W. 175, 183, 367, 380, 386
Goldstein, A. J. 151, 184
Goldstein, G. W. 81, 93
Goldstein, H. 291
Goldstein, P. J. 218
Goodman, H. C. 362
Goodman, V. 385
Gorden, E. W. 390
Goren, G. C. 205, 206, 216
Gorman, J. G. 335
Gorman, J. J. 195, 216, 217
Gorman, W. 334
Gotay, F. C. 337
Gottlieb, G. 102, 113, 117, 277, 278, 280,
    291
Graham, F. K. 40, 48, 151, 176, 183, 184,
    234, 235, 238, 239, 256, 257, 270,
    291, 371, 386
Graham, H. 310, 312
Graham, W. E. 293
Gransbergen, A. 144, 259
Gray, J. H. 390
Gray, M. L. 142
Gray, O. O. 362
Gray, P. H. 155, 183
Greenberg, N. 68, 70
Greenwood, M. H. 144
Gregory, G. A. 323, 336
Gregory, S. 94
Griesel, R. D. 284, 290, 293
Griswold, M. J. 295
Grobstein, P. 113, 117
Grobstein, R. 251, 258
Groves, P. M. 151, 183
Gruenwald, P. 282, 283, 285, 291
Grunebaum, H. U. 413
Guidasci, S. 65, 71
Guilleminault, C. 118

Gunn, T. 334
Gunther, M. 9, 16, 176, 183, 349, 352, 362, 381, 386
Gussow, J. D. 285, 290
Gustavson, K. H. 89, 93

Haber, A. 49
Habicht, J. P. 292
Hack, M. 90, 93
Hackett, E. R. 117, 216
Haeckel, E. 368, 387
Hagberg, B. 93, 263, 265
Hagberg, G. 93
Hainline, L. D. 207, 217
Haith, M. M. 16, 49, 111, 117, 203, 204, 205, 217, 375, 376, 377, 387, 388
Hakanson-Zaunders, M. 294
Halberg, F. 186
Hall, B. 317, 336, 348, 349, 362
Hall, D. 40, 48
Hall, R. T. 323, 337
Hall, V. 144, 186
Hall, W. G. 166, *166*, *167*, 167, 184, 374, 387
Halverson, C. F. 229, 232, 240, 261
Hamburg, J. M. 172, 183
Hamburger, V. 280, 292
Hamburger, W. W. 342, 362
Hamilton, W. K. 336
Hanks, H. G. I. 231, 257
Hanshaw, J. B. 333, 336
Hardyck, C. D. 238, 259
Harin, A. 323, 335
Harlow, H. F. 148, 183, 377, 387
Harlow, M. K. 377, 387
Harper, L. V. 271, 290, 380, 385, 406, 413
Harper, R. J. 364
Harper, R. M. 126, 143
Harris, L. 218
Harris, M. A. 71, 78, 145
Harris, P. 185, 202, 217
Harris, R. 93
Harris, S. 337
Harris, T. 396, 413
Hart, S. 94
Harter, M. R. 196, 217
Hasher, L. 150, 183
Haskims, R. 149, 183
Hassanein, K. 291, 293
Hathcock, J. N. 286, 292
Hathorn, M. K. S. 127, 143

Hatton, H. M. 183, 257, 386
Haxby, V. 15
Hayes, J. 15
Haynes, H. 198, 217
Heckhausen, H. 374, 387
Hecox, K. 106, 117, 208, 209, 217
Heinroth, O. 367, 387
Held, R. 217
Hellbrügge, T. 138, 139, 143, 154, 183
Hellwig, U. 144, 186
Hemphill, F. 336
Hendersen, R. 148, 188
Hendry, L. S. 344, 362
Henneborn, W. J. 283, 292, 310, 312
Hensleigh, P. 293
Herbert, T. S. 15
Herbkova, M. 117, 118
Herrick, C. J. 370, 387
Hertzig, M. R. 260
Herz, J. J. 150, 151, 187
Herz, M. J. 190
Hess, E. H. 246, 257, 368, 381, 387
Hess, R. F. 199, 217
Hetzer, H. 55, 70
Hewitt, J. 336
Heyns, O. S. 269, 292
Hill, R. 413
Hillyard, S. A. 118
Himwich, W. 102, 117
Hinde, R. A. 148, 164, 183, 367, 387
Hirsch, J. 241, 257
Hittelman, J. H. 232, 257
Hobel, C. J. 22, 48
Hodgman, J. E. 143
Hofer, M. A. 149, 183
Hoffman, H. S. 157, 184
Hoffman, K. P. 200, 217
Hogan, M. A. 293
Hogarty, P. S. 413
Hollins, G. 291, 312
Holmes, G. E. 291
Holmes, T. H. 295
Hook, E. B. 333, 336
Hope, M. L. 386
Hopkinson, C. 362
Hoppenbrouwers, T. 134, 143, 145
Hopson, B. 15
Horne, J. A. 148, 152, 184
Horowitz, F. D. 31, 45, 48, 51
Houang, M. T. W. 94
Hoving, K. L. 172, 183

Howland, H. C. 215
Howland, R. I. 310, 311
Howlett, B. 290, 335
Hrbek, A. 72, 106, 107, 114, 118
Hubel, D. H. 205, 213, 216, 217
Hughes-Davies, T. H. 14, 16
Huisjes, H. J. 26, 49, 51
Hull, D. 149, 154, 177, 184, 316, 335
Hulsebus, R. C. 169, 184
Humphrey, N. K. 207, 217
Hutchison, D. 206
Hutt, C. 43, 49, 70, 217
Hutt, S. J. 49, 62, 70, 209, 217
Hwang, C. P. 345, 362
Hyvarinen, M. A. 48

Ikeda, H. 197, 217
Ilg, F. L. 147, 183, 344, 346, 347, 348, 362
Illick, J. E. 309, 312
Ingram, D. 335
Inhelder, B. 370, 372, 389
Ipsen, J. 258
Irving, I. M. 337
Irwin, O. C. 53, 70, 137, 143

Jacklin, C. N. 239, 258, 279, 292
Jaco, N. T. 143
Jacob, R. A. 291
Jacobson, G. 291
Jacobson, S. W. 384, 387
Jacobus, J. 336
James, L. S. 334
Janoš, O. 153, 184, 371, 387
Jaynes, J. 172, 181
Jeddi, E. 148, 184
Jeffrey, W. E. 51, 151, 178, 184
Jelliffe, D. B. 310, 312
Jelliffe, E. F. P. 310, 312
Jenness, D. 308, 312
Jennings, K. D. 226, 257
Jerison, H. J. 150, 184
Joffe, J. M. 268, 272, 292
Johanson, I. B. 166, *166*, 167, *167*, 184, 374, 387
Johnson, P. 130, 143, 354, 363
Jones, M. H. 200, 216
Jones, R. H. 215
Jonson, B. 143
Joppich, G. 34, 36, 49
Julesz, B. 215
Julia, H. L. 343, 362, 363

Jurgens-Van der Zee, A. 51
Jusczyk, P. W. 182, 210, 217

Kagan, J. 227, 239, 248, 257, 272, 292
Kalman, E. 335
Kamenetskaya, A. F. 256
Kane, J. 48
Kaplan, M. G. 170, 171, 184
Kaplan, S. L. 41, 49
Kapuniai, L. E. 215
Karelitz, R. 257
Karelitz, S. 230, 257
Karlberg, P. 118
Karmel, B. Z. 204, 217
Karow, W. G. 269
Kasatkin, N. L. 153, 184
Katona, P. G. 336
Kattwinkel, J. 323, 324, 336
Kavanau, J. L. 174, 184
Kaye, H. 153, 169, 170, 182, 184, 185, 386
Kaye, K. 120, 128, 143, 229, 257
Keen, R. 151, 152, 170, 171, 184, 371, 387
Keiser, E. F. 186
Kelly, J. V. 283, 291, 292, 312
Kempe, C. H. 276, 292, 410, 413
Kempe, R. S. 276, 292, 410, 413
Kennedy, G. C. 148, 184
Kennell, J. H. 222, 257, 364, 413
Kerner, J. A., Jr. 324, 336
Kerr, J. 260
Kerr Grant, D. 50, 72
Kessen, W. 1, 16, 30, 49, 229, 232, 240, 241, 257, 258, 259, 344, 345, 346, 362, 363
Kestermann, G. 52
Khachaturian, Z. 260
Kiernan, K. E. 284, 292
Kimmel, H. D. 151, 152, 181, 184
King, S. 259
King, T. M. 333, 337
Kinsey, V. 320, 336
Kirkpatrick, S. W. 406, 413
Kirkwood, W. 284, 292
Kitterman, J. A. 336
Kittner, S. 26, 49
Kitzinger, S. 305, 312
Klatt, D. H. 387
Klaus, M. H. 257, 335, 336, 364, 403, 413
Klein, R. E. 290, 292

Klein, R. P. 226, 257, 260, 294
Kleitman, N. 53, 55, 56, 59, 70, 71, 121,
    133, 134, 135, 136, 138, 142, 143
Kling, J. W. 152, 184
Knoblock, H. 275, 292
Knostman, J. D. 335
Kobre, K. R. 169, 170, 184
Koch, J. 154, 168, 185
Koenig, K. L. 70
Keonig, S. 303, 312
Koffka, K. 368, 387
Koivisto, E. 189
Koivisto, M. 331, 336
Kolb, S. 190
Koltsova, M. M. 153, 181
Komisaruk, B. R. 126, 143
Konner, M. 174, 185, 378, 387
Kopp, C. B. 5, 16, 51, 250, 257, 268, 270,
    273, 292
Korn, G. 94
Korn, S. 260
Korner, A. F. 57, 58, 71, 114, 118, 221,
    225, 229, 230, 232, 233, 236, 241,
    242, 243, 251, 257, 258, 260, 292,
    341, 343, 345, 346, 359, 363, 390,
    400, 413
Korobkin, R. 78, 81, 92, 93, 327, 336
Koslowski, B. 181
Kott, G. 144, 186
Kraemer, J. C. 283, 292
Krames, L. 385
Krasnogorskii, N. I. 153, 185
Krause, U. 336
Krausz, H. I. 118
Krech, D. 278, 292
Kron, R. E. 49, 169, 185, 228, 258
Kropfl, W. 215
Kruger, R. 260
Kruk, S. 295
Kuhl, P. K. 210, 217, 375, 377, 387
Kulikowski, J. J. 203, 217
Kulovich, M. V. 315, 336
Kupersmidt, J. 187
Kuzemko, J. A. 324, 336

Lacey, J. I. 238, 241, 249, 258
Ladis, B. 186
Lagercrantz, E. 287, 292
Lagercrantz, H. 127, 143
Lagercrantz, R. 287, 292
Lamb, L. 218

Lamb, M. E. 179, 185, 257, 381, 384, 386,
    387
Lang, E. 256, 259
Lange, J. E. 143
Lansky, S. B. 291
Larroche, J. Cl. 80, 81, 84, 93, 94
Larrson, K. 403, 413
Larsen, B. 325, 336
Lashley, K. S. 119, 144
Lasky, R. E. 290
Lawson, K. 396, 413
Leach, P. 4, 16
Leaton, R. N. 151, 189
Leavitt, L. A. 257
Leboyer, F. 7, 16, 311, 312
Lechtig, A. 281, 290, 292
Lecours, A. 102, 118
Lee, C. P. 216
Lehrman, D. S. 149, 185
Leiderman, P. H. 364
Leis, P. E. 301, 312
Lenard, H. G. 49, 59, 62, 65, 70, 71, 72,
    118, 217
Lenneberg, E. H. 375, 387
Lennie, P. 207, 217
Leon, M. 148, 163, 185, 190
Lepenies, W. 386
Le Souef, P. N. 323, 336
Lessen-Firestone, J. K. 294
Lester, B. M. 41, 47, 49, 255, 261, 267,
    276, 289, 292, 295
Letson, R. D. 116, 215
Leutzendorf, A. 258, 346, 363
Leventhal, A. 219
Levine, M. I. 327, 336
Levine, S. 189, 279, 292, 299, 312
Levy, N. 232, 258
Lewis, M. 6, 11, 16, 126, 144, 220n, 225,
    235, 236, 239, 258, 271, 292, 373,
    378, 387, 406, 413
Lewis, O. 301, 312
Lewis, T. L. 207, 218
Lewkowicz, D. 291
Liberman, A. M. 375, 387
Liddicoat, R. 269, 292
Lieberman, P. 375, 387
Liley, A. W. 280, 292
Lind, J. 73, 128, 144, 145, 189, 259, 261,
    364
Lindroth, M. 143
Lindsley, D. B. 58, 71, 107, 118

Linn, P. 48
Lintz, L. M. 181
Lipsitt, L. P. 26, 49, 96, 127, 129, 130,
　　142, 144, 147, 152, 153, 164, 165,
　　165, 168, 169, 170, 173, 174, 175,
　　176, 177, 178, 182, 184, 185, 186,
　　188, 211, 216, 224, 225, 232, 235,
　　237, 239, 240, 258, 272, 276, 277,
　　371, 374, 386, 390, 392, 396, 397,
　　399, 400, 402, 407, 413
Lipton, E. L. 238, 239, 258
Lister, J. 337
Litt, M. 49
Little, A. H. 153, 155, *156*, 157, 158, 159,
　　159, 160, *160*, *161*, 162, *162*, 164,
　　165, 170, 171, 172, 185
Littman, B. 26, 49
Lloyd, B. 279, 292
Lobban, M. C. 139, 144
Lock, A. 370, 388
Lockman, J. J. 219
Loesch, J. 70
Logan, R. 310, 312
Lomas, P. 307, 312
Lombroso, C. T. 78, 94
Longo, L. D. 300, 310, 312
Lorenz, J. 368, 381, 388
Lorenz, K. Z. 151, 152, 185, 246, 367, 388
Loring, C. B. 16
Lowenberg, M. E. 147
Lowrey, L. G. 367, 380, 388
Lucas, D. 187
Lucey, J. 327, 336
Lund, R. D. 113, 118
Luppova, N. N. 256
Lustman, S. L. 222, 239, 259
Lynch, A. 264, 265, 269, 292
Lynch, P. F. 291, 312
Lynn, D. B. 380, 388

McBride, M. 362
McBride, W. G. 333, 337
McCall, R. B. 238, 258, 413
McClain, P. E. 291
McDonnell, P. M. 213, 217
McFarland, D. J. 155, 186
McGinty, D. J. 143
McGrade, B. J. 241, 258
McGraw, M. B. 108, 109, 118, 173, *173*,
　　176, 186, 348, 363
McGuire, M. 259, 382, 388

McIlwain, H. 278, 292
McIntosh, N. 334, 335
McKenzie, B. 199, 202, 216, 217, 218,
　　220n
McLean, F. H. 317, 337
McNeal, K. 183
McNeish, A. S. 15
McWeeny, P. 187
Maccoby, E. E. 279, 292
Macfarlane, A. 15, 157, 185, 202, 211,
　　217, 377, 388
Macy, I. G. 317, 336
Madge, N. 284, 293
Magoun, H. W. 55, 71
Main, M. 181
Maisel, E. B. 204, 217
Maitland, J. 93
Malinowski, B. 299, 306, 312
Maller, O. 211, 216, 218
Mameesh, M. 291
Mandler, G. 346, 363
Manil, J. 106, 117
Mann, I. C. 197, 218
Manniello, R. L. 48
Marg, E. 196, 218
Marler, P. 377, 388
Marola, F. 294
Marquis, D. P. 153, 186
Marr, D. 398, 413
Martin, L. T. 163, 178, 185
Martin, R. D. 155, 185
Martin, R. M. 16
Martinez, O. 286, 292
Martinius, J. W. 43, 49, 371, 388
Martorell, R. 292
Marvin, R. S. 369
Marwah, S. M. 363
Masi, W. 23, 51
Mason, W. A. 377, 388
Mata, L. J. 282, 293
Maurer, D. 203, 205, 206, 207, 218, 383,
　　388
Maury, L. 216
Maybury-Lewis, D. 301, 312
Mayer, D. L. 216
Mayer, J. 340, 362
Mayers, K. S. 189
Mead, J. 320, 334
Mead, M. 297, 298, 299, 303, 304, 305,
　　312
Mehl, L. E. 288, 293

Mehler, J. 210, 218
Mehrabian, A. 221, 232, 235, 256, 258
Meier-Koll, A. 124, 136, 144, 186
Meier-Koll, V. 144, 154, 186
Melges, F. T. 287, 293
Melhuish, E. 169, 186, 210, 211, 218
Meltzoff, A. N. 213, 214, 218, 384, 388
Mendelson, M. J. 212, 218, 377, 388
Mengert, W. F. 304, 312
Merkatz, I. R. 93
Merritt, T. A. 186
Messing, S. D. 303, 312
Messmer, J. 186
Metcoff, J. 291
Meyer, H. B. P. 335
Meyer, M. B. 282, 293
Meyers, W. J. 178, 181
Miano, V. N. 145, 189, 260
Michaelis, R. 25, 27, 30, 31, 36, 40, 45, 49
Michel, G. F. 383, 386
Michelsson, K. 231, 258
Milewski, A. E. 168, 186, 206, 218
Miller, D. J. 236, 259
Miller, H. D. 324, 337
Miller, J. 93
Miller, J. C. 288, 293
Miller, J. H. 300, 312
Miller Sostek, A. 58, 70
Millodot, M. 117
Mills, J. N. 137, 138, 144
Mills, M. 169, 186, 210, 218
Milner, R. 313
Minkowski, A. 93
Minoli, I. 324, 337
Miranda, S. 195, 205, 216, 218
Misanin, J. R. 172, 186
Mistretta, C. M. 280, 293
Mitchell, D. E. 117
Moar, K. 214, 215
Moller, M. S. G. 302, 303, 306, 312, 313
Monod, N. 58, 59, 65, 66, 68, 71, 78, 93
Montagu, A. 279, 293
Monteil, C. 309, 313
Moore, M. K. 213, 214, 215, 218, 384, 388
Moran, D. L. 413
Morath, M. A. 136, 144, 153, 154, 186
Moreau, T. 261
Morgan, A. K. 336
Morgan, J. J. B. 153, 186
Morgan, S. S. 153, 186
Moriette, G. 93

Morin, V. N. 260
Moro, G. 337
Morris, N. 285, 294
Morrongiello, B. A. 187
Morsbach, G. 231, 259
Moruzzi, G. 55, 71
Moss, H. A. 229, 230, 248, 251, 261
Moylan, F. M. B. 337
Muir, D. 210, 218
Muller, P. F. 275, 293
Muller, V. H. 293
Mullins, R. F. 279, 292
Muntjewerff, W. J. 70, 217
Murakami, M. 390
Murdock, B. D. 269, 293
Murie, J. R. 302, 311
Murphy, D. P. 304, 312
Murphy, J. M. 172, 186
Murphy, R. F. 303, 306, 313
Murphy, Y. 303, 306, 313
Mursell, J. L. 341, 342, 344, 348, 363
Musgrove, D. 386
Mussen, P. H. 54, 71
Muzio, J. N. 144
Mychalkiw, W. 264, 265, 269, 292
Myers, A. 132, 133, 144
Myers, R. E. 77, 81, 94

Naeye, R. L. 175, 186, 333, 337
Nagy, Z. M. 172, 186
Naito, T. 153, 186
Nakgawa, J. K. 215
Nash, S. C. 381, 386
Nearman, M. S. 336
Neff, C. 257
Neilon, P. 222, 259
Nelhaus, G. 78, 94
Nelson, M. N. 182, 186
Nelson, W. 151, 154
Nesbitt, R. E. L. 22, 49
Netsky, M. G. 100, 111, 118
Nettelbladt, P. 283, 293
Nevin, N. C. 337
New, M. 93
Newport, E. L. 383, 388
Newson, J. 140, 144
Newton, M. 298, 313
Newton, N. 298, 299, 303, 304, 305, 311, 312, 313
Nilsson, A. 287, 292
Nims, B. 336

Nolte, R. 49
Norman, D. 93
Norman, J. L. 215
Nuttin, J. 374, 388

Oakley, A. 264, 283, 297, 302, 310, 311, 312, 313, 397, 402, 406, 411, 412, 413
Oates, R. K. 340, 363
O'Brien, M. J. 18, 48, 53, 72
O'Connell, E. J. 224, 234, 236, 242, 247, 248, 259
Odell, G. B. 326, 337
O'Doherty, N. 35, 36, 49
Odom, J. V. 217
O'Gorman, J. C. 236, 259
Oh, W. 48
Ohlrich, E. S. 155, 186
Okada, D. M. 48
Oken, A. 49
Olimga, A. A. 51
Olson, J. P. 364
Olsson, T. 118
Oppenheim, R. W. 7, 16, 398, 413
Ordy, J. M. 216
Osgood, L. E. 346, 363
Osofsky, J. D. 4, 5, 16, 54, 71, 221, 224, 234, 236, 242, 247, 248, 250, 259
Ostrea, E. M. 294
Ostwald, P. F. 276, 293
Ounsted, C. 284, 293, 332, 337
Ounsted, M. K. 228, 247, 249, 259, 285, 293, 332, 337
Ovadia, M. F. 337

Paala, J. 324, 336
Paine, R. S. 176, 186, 335
Painter, P. 290
Pajot, N. 58, 68, 71
Palmer, J. D. 121, 144
Pape, K. E. 79, 89, 93, 94, 327, 335, 337
Papoušek, H. 43, 49, 61, 71, 152, 165 168, 169, 170, 186, 276, 365, 366, 367, 368, 370, 371, 372, 373, 374, 377, 378, 380, 382, 383, 384, 388, 389, 394, 404, 407
Papoušek, M. 365, 366, 367, 368, 370, 371, 373, 378, 380, 382, 383, 384, 389, 394, 404, 407
Parker, D. 335, 336
Parkman, R. 325, 337

Parmelee, A. H. 5, 16, 26, 30, 31, 34, 35, 36, 40, 49, 51, 55, 58, 59, 70, 71, 114, 118, 127, 138, 144, 145, 250, 257, 268, 270, 273, 292
Parsons, G. 144
Parsons, P. 172, 188
Partanen, T. 261, 364
Partington, M. W. 242, 256, 259
Pasaminick, B. 275, 292
Passquant, P. 70
Patrick, J. 143
Patterson, C. J. 189
Paul, L. 303, 313
Peeke, H. V. S. 150, 151, 187, 190
Peiper, A. 30, 39, 49, 129, 144, 147, 153, 164, 187, 344, 345, 346, 347, 348, 363
Pelchat, R. 190
Perryman, P. 355
Peterson, G. H. 288, 293
Peterson, J. 218, 219
Petre-Quadens, O. 59, 71
Petrinovich, L. 151, 187, 238, 259
Pettigrew, J. D. 113, 117, 215
Pettzman, P. 218
Phibbs, R. 293, 336
Philip, A. G. S. 79, 94
Phillips, S. 242, 259
Phoenix, M. D. 49
Piaget, J. 57, 119, 144, 344, 348, 363, 368, 370, 372, 389
Pick, H. 202, 219
Picton, T. W. 107, 118
Pintler, M. H. 390
Pittendrigh, C. S. 138, 144
Pliner, P. 385
Ploug, D. 386
Plumb, N. 413
Plumb, R. 413
Poirier, F. E. 370
Pollack, W. 335
Pollitt, E. 228, 259, 360, 363
Porges, S. W. 153, 154, 169, 183, 189
Porter, R. H. 295
Poskitt, E. M. E. 358, 363
Pratt, J. 189
Pratt, K. C. 30, 50
Prechtl, H. F. R. 17, 18, 21, 24, 25, 30, 31, 32, 33, 34, 35, 36, 37, 38, 39, 41, 42, 43, 44, 48, 49, 50, 53, 55, 58, 59, 60, 61, 62, 64, 65, 66, 67, 68, 69, 70, 71,

72, 73, 125, 128, 133, 144, 145, 224,
231, 243, 244, 247, 259, 393, 398,
399, 410, 412
Preyer, W. 55, 72
Pribram, K. H. 372, 389
Prokasy, W. F. 159, 182
Protestos, C. 175, 187
Purpura, D. P. 104, 118, 176, 187
Purves, M. J. 125, 144, 177, 187

Raab, E. 215
Rakic, P. 197, 218
Ramey, C. T. 11, 16
Randt, C. T. 281, 290
Rashbass, C. 201, 218
Rawlings, G. 94
Rawson, R. A. 216
Rayner, R. 147, 189
Read, A. P. 337
Reaser, G. P. 104, 118
Regal, D. M. 203, 218
Reid, W. 291
Reilly, B. M. 144
Reinisch, J. M. 269, 279, 293
Reiser, M. F. 222, 238, 239, 256
Reits, D. 118
Relier, J. P. 93, 94
Remy, M. 71
Rendle-Short, J. 153, 187
Rescorla, R. A. 157, 168, 187
Reynold, J. 94
Reynolds, E. O. R. 88, 89, 94, 334, 335,
336
Rhea, J. W. 324, 337
Rhodes, P. G. 323, 337
Riccio, D. C. 184
Richards, B. 331, 335
Richards, D. 335
Richards, J. L. 383, 389
Richards, M. P. M. 229, 256, 276, 293,
297, 304, 310, 311, 313, 341, 345,
363, 369, 374, 382, 389
Richardson, J. A. 286, 293
Richart, R. M. 291
Richmond, J. B. 222, 239, 258, 259
Richter, C. P. 122, 124, 144, 175, 187
Rickham, P. P. 334, 337
Ridley, M. 379, 389
Ries, P. 259
Rieser, J. 210, 218
Ripin, R. 343, 344, 363

Ritterhouse, A. M. 293
Roberts, W. A. B. 292
Robertson, E. 208, 218
Robertson, R. T. 189
Robinson, J. 176, 182
Robinson, J. S. 290, 316, 334
Rödholm, M. 403, 413
Rodin, J. 361, 363
Roe, D. 286, 292
Roffwarg, H. P. 59, 72, 134, 144
Rogers, M. C. 337
Rogers, M. G. H. 23, 50
Rohr, M. 49
Ronch, J. 255
Rose, A. L. 78, 94
Rose, M. 216
Rosenberg, K. M. 285, 291
Rosenberg, L. A. 337
Rosenblatt, J. S. 379, 389
Rosenblith, J. F. 40, 51, 175, 177, 180,
231, 255
Rosenblum, L. A. 11, 16, 164, 187, 225,
258, 271, 292, 406, 413
Rosenfeld, L. 257
Rosenweig, M. R. 112, 118, 292
Rosett, H. L. 246, 259
Rosner, B. S. 217
Ross, L. E. 155, 186
Ross, S. E. 411, 413
Rovee, C. K. 170, 187
Rovee-Collier, C. K. 96, 127, 147, 168,
169, 170, 171, 172, 179, 182, 187,
189, 224, 235, 237, 240, 272, 276,
277, 392, 396, 397, 399, 400,
402
Rozin, P. 361, 363
Rudy, J. W. 163, 164, 172, 187
Rupp, N. R. 256
Rurak, D. W. 290
Rusoff, A. C. 197, 207, 218
Rutenfranz, J. 143
Rutter, M. 284, 293
Ryan, E. 259

Sachtleben, M. S. 93
Sackett, D. L. 313
Sackett, G. P. 141, 144
Sacks, S. H. 288, 293
Saenger, G. 294
Saigal, S. 313
St. Andrew, D. 334

Saint-Anne Dargassies, S. 30, 34, 36, 48, 51
St. Clair, K. L. 31, 48
Salapatek, P. H. 16, 49, 195, 196, 199, 204, 205, 207, 214, 215, 218, 232, 259, 383, 388
Salisbury, D. M. 130, 143, 354, 363
Salk, L. 140, 144, 383, 389
Salkind, N. J. 286, 293
Sameroff, A. J. 11, 16, 43, 45, 46, 51, 153, 158, 164, 169, 170, 178, 187, 188, 254, 259, 268, 271, 277, 283, 294, 374, 389
Samson, J. M. 292
Sander, L. W. 140, 141, 142, 246, 259, 343, 362, 363, 372, 386
Sandstead, H. H. 291
Sarnat, H. B. 82, 94, 100, 111, 118
Sarnat, M. S. 82, 94
Sars, K. 93
Sarty, M. 216
Satinoff, E. 148, 188
Sawrey, W. L. 380, 388
Scales, B. 295
Scanlon, J. W. 52, 247, 259
Scarr, S. 41, 51
Schachter, J. 240, 260
Schachter, S. 361, 363
Schaffer, H. R. 140, 144, 145, 225, 232, 242, 250, 260, 392, 413
Scheffé, H. 238, 260
Scheving, L. 186
Schiller, D. 361, 363
Schleidt, W. M. 62, 72
Schloon, H. 64, 72
Schneider, B. A. 208, 219
Schneirla, T. C. 280, 294
Schoetzau, A. 378, 383, 389
Scholten, C. A. 60, 72
Schorah, C. J. 337
Schulman-Golambos, C. 106, 118
Schulte, F. J. 34, 36, 44, 49, 51, 71, 106, 107, 110, 114, 118
Schultz, M. A. 71
Schultze, L. 302, 313
Schwenzel, W. 44, 51
Scott, K. E. 328, 337
Scott, K. G. 23, 51
Scrimgeour, J. B. 334
Sears, P. S. 390
Sears, R. R. 378, 380, 390
Self, P. A. 31, 51

Seligman, M. E. P. 175, 176, 178, 188, 279, 294, 396, 411, 413
Seller, M. J. 337
Selye, H. 272, 275, 294
Shaak, M. E. 184
Shaffer, D. 4, 16
Shair, H. 149, 183
Shankweiler, D. P. 387
Shannon, D. C. 324, 337
Shaw, N. S. 310, 313
Shea, S. L. 216
Sheppard, S. 337
Sher, P. K. 78, 94
Sherefsky, P. M. 287, 294
Sherman, M. 346, 363
Sherry, D. 257
Shirataki, S. 66, 72
Shirley, M. M. 222, 260, 348, 363
Short, E. 259
Shriner, T. H. 216
Shukla, A. 340, 349, 363
Siegel, E. 285, 294
Sievel, J. 73
Sigman, M. 37, 51, 114, 118
Silverman, W. A. 324, 335, 336, 337
Simon, N. G. 379, 386
Simons, C. D. 228, 247, 249, 257
Simpson, J. L. 332, 337
Sinclair, J. 335, 336
Singleton, C. H. 279, 294
Siqueland, E. R. 153, 165, *165*, 168, 169, 171, 178, 179, 182, 186, 188, 189, 193, 219, 371, 374, 383, 390
Sirvio, P. 258
Skinner, B. F. 150, 169, 188
Slater, A. M. 200, 219
Sloan, V. L. 385
Slobin, D. I. 384, 390
Sluckin, W. 180, 188
Smart, J. L. 349, 364
Smith, C. A. 53, 73
Smith, C. R. 140, 145, 244, 260, 267, 276, 279, 294
Smith, D. W. 333, 337
Smith, G. J. 163, 164, 172, 178, 188
Smith, G. K. 185
Smith, L. B. 217
Smith, S. 362
Smithells, R. W. 333, 337
Smrkovsky, M. 51
Smull, N. W. 337
Snow, C. E. 384, 390

Snyder, D. 51
Socks, J. 118
Sokolov, E. N. 151, 170, 188, 234, 260
Solkoff, N. 169, 374, 390
Sollberger, A. 119, 124, 126, 145
Solomon, G. 178, 181
Sontag, L. W. 243, 260, 279, 294
Sosa, R. 339, 364
Sostek, A. M. 237, 260
Soule, A. B. 41, 51, 294
Soutter, L. P. 335, 336
Spear, N. E. 163, 164, 171, 172, 178, 179,
    181, 183, 188
Specht, T. 186
Spekreijse, H. 105, 118
Spelke, E. S. 212, 219
Spellacy, W. N. 336
Spencer, W. A. 150, 189
Spier, L. 302, 313
Spitz, R. A. 175, 188, 346, 348, 364
Spock, B. 147, 188
Sroufe, L. A. 8, 16, 116, 118, 370, 390
Stacey, M. 300, 313
Stamps, L. E. 153, 154, 189
Standley, K. 41, 51, 234, 242, 248, 249,
    260, 283, 288, 289, 294
Stanier, J. E. 349, 362
Starr, A. 79, 94
Starr, M. D. 6, 16
Starr, R. H. 261, 294
Stayton, D. J. 255, 385
Stechler, G. 362
Steele, B. 216
Stehr, K. 143
Stein, I. M. 337
Stein, L. 151, 189
Stein, Z. 274, 294
Steiner, J. E. 210, 211, 219
Steinschneider, A. 127, 140, 145, 175, 177,
    189, 244, 258, 260, 267, 276, 279,
    294
Stembera, Z. K. 22, 51
Stennert, E. 26, 51, 118
Sterman, M. B. 133, 134, 143, 145
Stern, D. 127, 134, 140, 145, 406, 414
Stern, E. 49, 58, 71, 127, 134, 140, 144,
    145
Stern, J. A. 152, 189, 290
Stern, L. O. 291
Sternglanz, S. M. 381, 390
Steven, E. M. 90, 93
Stewart, A. 89, 94

Stewart, A. L. 318, 335
Stewart, R. J. C. 284, 294
Stinson, P. 308, 313
Stinson, R. 308, 313
Stoltz, L. M. 380, 390
Stone, J. 207, 219
Storey, B. 337
Strang, L. B. 125, 145, 315, 337
Stratton, P. M. 1, 5, 8, 11, 16, 119, 140,
    145, 153, 182, 221, 229, 236, 237,
    249, 260, 271, 294, 391, 393, 394,
    395, 396, 397, 401, 404, 407, 408,
    410, 411, 414
Strauss, M. E. 261, 276, 294
Studdert-Kennedy, M. 387
Sturner, W. Q. 185
Sullivan, G. D. 199, 216
Sullivan, J. W. 48
Sullivan, M. W. 170, 187, 189
Sunshine, P. 336
Susser, M. 294
Sutcliffe, R. G. 333, 334
Suzuki, B. 143, 182
Svenningsen, N. 143
Swale, A. B. 260
Swedberg, J. 143, 182
Sytova, V. A. 256

Taitz, L. S. 340, 356, 364
Tanner, J. M. 246, 247, 248, 249, 260, 278,
    279, 294
Teller, D. Y. 195, 196, 216, 219
Telzrow, R. 41, 51
Tharp, B. R. 79, 94
Theorell, K. 60, 65, 72, 73, 134, 144, 145, 259
Thoman, E. B. 7, 16, 57, 73, 127, 145, 168,
    175, 177, 178, 179, 189, 232, 240,
    243, 244, 245, 251, 258, 260, 292,
    345, 346, 359, 363, 364, 382, 390
Thomas, A. 242, 260
Thomas, C. B. 6, 15
Thompson, R. F. 150, 151, 183, 189
Thompson, T. 89, 94
Thomson, A. J. M. 93
Thomson, A. M. 285, 294
Thorburn, G. D. 290
Thorpe, W. H. 151, 189, 374, 390
Thurston, D. 290
Tighe, T. J. 151, 189
Tinbergen, N. 149, 189
Tizard, P. P. M. 15, 78, 93
Tobin, M. 260

Todres, D. 337
Toffler, A. 399, 414
Tolhurst, D. J. 203, 217
Tonascia, J. A. 282, 293
Tooley, W. H. 336
Touwen, B. C. L. 25, 38, 42, 49, 51, 110, 118
Towbin, A. 84, 94
Tracy, V. V. 340, 364
Trause, M. A. 257
Trehub, S. E. 219
Tremain, K. E. 197, 217
Trevarthen, C. 214, 370, 373, 390
Trezenem, E. 309, 313
Tronick, E. 41, 46, 47–48, 51, 52, 202, 215, 255, 289, 290
Truby, H. M. 128, 145
Turcan, D. 94
Turkewitz, G. 233, 238, 261, 291, 382, 383, 388, 390
Turnbull, C. M. 381, 390
Turner, R. E. 216
Tynan, W. D. 57, 73, 260
Tynes, D. M. 189

Ucko, L. E. 273, 294
Uddenberg, N. 287, 293, 294
Udelf, M. C. 216
Ungerer, J. A. 150, 171, 189
Urrutia, J. J. 364
Usher, R. H. 317, 328, 337

Valanne, E. 261, 364
Valcarcel, M. 259, 363
Valdes-Dapena, M. A. 175, 189
Vallbona, C. 413
Van den Hoed, J. 118
Vander Maelen, A. L. 236, 260
VanDeWiele, R. L. 291
Van Gennep, A. 308, 313
Venge, O. 154, 189
Vietze, P. 183, 257
Vital-Durand, F. 197, 215
Vlach, V. 62, 72, 73
Volkmann, F. C. 203, 219
Vollrath, M. 51
Volpe, J. J. 38, 52, 77, 93
Von Uexküll, J. 149, 189
Vos, J. E. A. 60, 72, 73
Vuorenskoski, V. 149, 189, 261, 364

Vygotsky, L. 370, 390

Waddington, C. H. 272, 294
Waldrop, M. F. 255
Wales, H. G. Q. 309, 313
Wallace, S. J. 86, 94
Wasz-Höckert, O. 189, 231, 258, 261, 343, 346, 364
Waters, E. 116, 118
Watson, J. B. 147, 189
Watts, J. 413
Wehmer, F. 285, 295
Weidman, W. 337
Weinmann, H. 50, 72
Weir, C. 208, 209, 219
Weiss, A. P. 147, 189
Weiss, J. B. 259
Weiss, J. L. 413
Weizmann, F. 170, 189
Weller, G. M. 68, 73, 255
Wellin, E. 306, 313
Wenger, M. A. 153, 189
Wenner, W. H. 71
Werboff, J. 155, 181
Werner, J. S. 168, 171, 189, 203, 219
Wertheimer, M. 210, 219
Westheimer, G. 201, 218
Wetzel, A. 189
Wever, R. 122, *123*, 124, 139, 145
Wharton, B. A. 288, 295
White, B. L. 217
White, C. L. 118
White, C. T. 107, 118
Wiesel, T. N. 205, 217
Wigglesworth, J. S. 327, 336, 337
Wikner, K. 218
Wilkinson, P. W. 356, 364
Williams, C. C. 287, 295
Williams, E. J. 257, 363
Williams, J. P. 257, 363
Williams, M. L. 41, 51
Williams, R. A. 295
Williams, T. A. 260
Williemsen, E. 169, 189
Wilson, C. D. 144, 258
Wilson, E. O. 150, 190, 390
Wilson, W. R. 376, 381, 390
Winfree, A. T. 119, 121, 139, 145
Wise, S. 52
Witter, F. 333, 337

Wolff, P. H. 48, 56, 57, 61, 63, 64, 68, 73, 119, 120, 121, 128, 129, 130, 131, 132, 133, 141, 143, 145, 230, 242, 257, 261, 341, 346, 347, 364, 369, 378, 390
Wolkind, S. N. 287, 295
Woodside, B. 148, 190
Woodson, E. M. 256
Woodson, R. H. 256
Wooten, B. R. 203, 219
Wright, J. 303, 313
Wright, P. 128, 130, 137, 229, 265, 317, 339, 350, 354, 359, 362, 364, 393, 397
Wu, P. Y. K. 216
Wulbrand, H. 118
Wurtz, R. H. 212, 219
Wyers, E. M. 150, 190
Wynn, A. 282, 284, 285, 286, 295
Wynn, M. 282, 284, 285, 295

Yakovlev, P. I. 102, 118
Yang, R. K. 229, 230, 232, 240, 242, 247, 248, 251, 261, 283, 294

Yarbrough, C. 292
Yarrow, L. J. 242, 261, 287, 294
Yates, A. E. 183
Yonas, A. 202, 218, 219
Youkeles, L. 48
Youngstein, K. P. 164, 187

Zacks, R. T. 150, 183
Zamenhof, S. 290
Zapella, M. 109, 118
Zarrow, M. X. 154, 190
Zeidner, L. P. 73
Zelazo, N. 190
Zelazo, P. R. 174, 189, 190
Zeskind, P. S. 11, 16, 41, 49, 231, 261, 267, 295
Zezulakova, J. 51
Zimmerman, R. A. 335
Zinkin, P. 50, 72
Zipperling, W. 55, 73
Zlatnik, F. J. 285, 295
Znamenacek, K. 51
Zuehlke, S. 413
Zweig, A. R. 295

Subject Index

Acoustic impedance, measurement of, 208
Acoustic reflex, 193, 208
Activity level
   and behavioural state, 53–54, 241–242
   and subsequent adaptation, 241
   individual differences in, 240–245
Activity, spontaneous
   in neurological assessment, 35
Adaptation, 8–11, 147–180
   and activity levels, 241
   and fetal competence, 277–278
   and obstetric medication, 275–276
   and social integration, 370–371
   and transaction revisited, 402–404
   as a criterion for significance of
      individual differences, 223,
      224–225, 253
   biological specification of, 178–179,
      370
   consequences of, 11, 14, 394
   consequences of interference with,
      263–265, 394
   cost–benefit interpretation of, 9–10, 13,
      265
   detection of impaired processes of,
      272–277
   during neonatal period, 8–11, 96,
      315–317, 397
   evaluation of, 11
   fail-safe nature of neonatal, 397–399
   future implication and continuity, 393
   growth facilitated by, 399–400
   growth towards, 272
   in feeding, 265, 317
   in fetus and newborn, 272–277
   in intrauterine endocrine functioning,
      279
   in the uterine environment, 272–273
   model of fundamental responses, 372
   nutritional, 317, 402
   of mother to her fetus, 286–287
   of premature newborns, 264–265
   possible consequences of sudden
      changes in, 396–397
   prenatal influences on, 263–265,
      267–289
   prenatal impairment of processes of,
      273
   rhythmic functioning contributing to, 96
   significant *versus* trivial aspects of, 391
   stress during transition or, 396,
      398–399
   the concept of challenge as a facilitator
      in, 399–400
   thermal, at birth, 316
   to extra-uterine environment, 5, 31, 149,
      264, 315–317
   to motherhood/parenthood, 283, 287
   transactions as a general form of, 12
Adaptive significance of newborn
      behaviour
   biological origins of, 147–149, 394–395
   see also Energy conservation
Akive-Shavante of Brazil
   childbirth attendants in, 301
Alcohol in pregnancy, 333
Alphafetoprotein (AFP)
   in antenatal diagnosis of neural tube
      defects, 333–334
   screening of, 334

Ambulatory behaviour, 174
Amhara of Ethiopia
  use of mashed linseed in labour, 303
Amniocentesis, limitations of, 333–334
Amniotic fluid
  a source of nutrition for the fetus, 280
  contaminated with meconium, 331
  in fetal lungs, 315–316
  used for antenatal diagnosis of abnor-
      mality, 333
Anencephaly
  see Neural tube defects
Anoxia
  and neonatal risk scores, 22
  incidence of lesions caused by, 81
  long-term consequences, 5–6, 275
  perinatal, 75, 84, 275
  research into, 77
  see also Hypoxia
Antenatal diagnosis of abnormality,
      333–334
  ethical issues raised by, 333–334
Apgar scale, 76
  limitations, 47
Apnoea
  as clinical feature of CNS dysfunction,
      77
  link with sudden infant death syndrome,
      127, 175, 240
  primary, 330
  prolonged by obstetric analgesics, 330
  recurrent attacks, 319, 323–324
  stable individual frequency and length,
      240
  terminal, 330–331
Appetite
  acquisition of appetite behaviour, 342
  as a cognitive function, 342
  a learnt response, 343
  behaviour associated with, 341–343
  control mechanisms, 349
Appetitive conditioning in newborn rat
      pups, 166–169, 166, 167
Arande of Central Australia
  childbirth practices of, 299–300
  passive treatment of birth, 303
Arapesh of New Guinea, childbirth
      practices of, 299
Arousal, level of
  as an obsolete concept, 55, 60–61, 241,
      244

Asphyxia
  see Anoxia
Assessment, 12–13, 17–19, 21–47
  comparison between different methods,
      34–9, 46–47
  limitations of, 12–13, 46–47
  morphological, 21
  of low birth-weight infants, 85–86, 86
  physiological, 21
  potential usefulness of, 17–18, 21, 46–47
  see also Behavioural assessment,
      Neurological assessment
Association for Improvements in the
      Maternity Services (AIMS), 411
Attachment, 340, 394
  conceptual and research issues, 369–370
  consequences of disruption, 10
  endangered by labelling newborn as
      defective, 331
  evolutionary influences on, 394–395
  importance of contingency, 404, 411
  necessity of mother's detailed
      knowledge of neonate, 404–406
  neonatal behaviour, 392
  quality related to mother's earlier
      relationships, 287
  role of learning in, 13
  see also Mother–infant interaction
Auditory functioning
  competence in newborn, 375–376
  coordinated with visual input, 212
  development of, 115
  during behavioural states, 62
  neocortical mediation of, 111
Auditory localization, 210
Auditory sensitivity, 208–210
  diagnostic of stress, 234
  discrimination of speech sounds,
      209–210
  functional significance of, 209–210
  individual differences in, 233–234
  prognosis from, 233–234
  thresholds, 208–209, 233–234
  to frequency (pitch), 209
Auditory system
  development of, 104–105, 108
  myelinization of, 103
Autonomic Nervous System (ANS)
  individual differences in functioning of,
      238–240
  in utero 'calibration' of, 279

Babinski reflex, 62
Bahaya of Africa
　chemical induction of labour, 302
　management of labour, 302
Basic-Rest-Activity cycle (BRAC)
　and behavioural states, 59
　defined, 133–137
　evidence for rhythm in, 135–136, *135*
　rhythmicity questioned, 121
Behavioural assessment, 18, 39–46
　age specificity of, 47
　distinguished from neurological assess-
　　ment, 22, 40
　Graham/Rosenblith scale, 40
　Graham scale, 40
　selection of items for, 39
　see also Assessment, Brazelton
　　Neonatal Behavioural Assess-
　　ment Scale
Behavioural states, 18, 53–69
　ability of infant to maintain, 393
　arousal levels in, 60
　as diagnostic tool, 58
　Basic-rest-activity cycle in, 59
　choice of variables as indicators of,
　　62–66
　classification of, 62–63, 66–69
　computer processing techniques, 60
　consecutive epoch analysis, 60
　continuous moving window analysis,
　　60, 65, *66*
　criteria, 18, 56–57, 62–69
　criteria for individual differences in, 244
　cyclic organization, 56–57, 62,
　　133–137
　defined, 54–56
　differences in response intensity, 61–62
　discrete rather than continuous, 60–61
　EEG as state criterion, 64–65
　EEG studies of, 53–60
　heart rate as poor indicator of, 64–65
　history of the concept of, 53–54, 68
　in babies with neurological problems, 59
　individual and sex differences in, 57,
　　244–245
　manipulated by parents, 382
　manual of a standardized assessment of,
　　69
　'noise' in state sequences, 65–66
　observational studies of, 57–58
　of drowsiness, 64
　of REM sleep, 59, 62, 68
　of sleep, 63, 64, 67, 69
　optimal during neurological examina-
　　tion, 33–34, 36
　organization of, 245
　parents' evaluation of newborn's, 382
　polygraphic investigations of, 53–60,
　　68, 69
　respiratory rate as poor indicator of,
　　64–65
　sleep states not rhythmic, 133
　state profile, *66*
　studies on input–output-state relation,
　　60–62
　unstable sequences in, 59
　validity of classification of, 60–61
　vectors defined as, 67–68, *67, 68*
　vestibulo-ocular response, 62
　wakefulness as, 67, 69
　Wolff's original classification, 57, 61,
　　63, 68
Behaviour, spontaneous
　see Spontaneous behaviour
Bilirubin encephalopathy, 326
Bilirubin levels, 325–327, *326*
　lowered by exchange transfusion, 326
　see also Jaundice
Binocular functioning, 200–201
　possible critical period for, 201
Biological requirements for neonatal sur-
　　vival, 148–149
　see also Energy conservation
Biological response systems, role in early
　　learning, 178–179
Biological rhythms
　see Rhythmic functions, Rhythms
Birth
　alertness of neonate immediately after,
　　403
　and adaptation, 315–317
　and fetal distress during, 76
　as a social act in non-industrialized
　　cultures, 301
　as illness, 310
　attendants at, 299–332
　fetal contribution to, 280
　hypoxia at, 330–331
　induction of, 9, 303
　official witnesses in Victorian times, 300
　practices reflecting cultural assump-
　　tions, 309–311

Birth (*contd.*)
  purification rituals following, 299
  seclusion rituals following, 306–307
  social context and location, 299–300
  surveys of cross-cultural variation, 297,
      298, 299
  timing of, 9
  treatment of baby following, 304–307
  viewed as a transition, 396–397
Birth control practices, risks to fetus from,
      286
Blood oxygen level, monitoring of,
      320–323, *321, 322*
Body image
  requiring intermodal and sensory-motor
      integration, 212
  role of proprioceptive senses in, 192
Bottle feeding
  absence of diurnal variation in meal
      size, 352–354
  adjustment to drop in feeds, 137
  and overfeeding (obesity), 340, 349,
      352, 356–358
  and recognition of satiety, 340
  behavioural pattern determined by
      baby, 360–361
  comparisons between breast and,
      130–131, 317, 339–341,
      343–344, 354, 360–361
  distribution of burst size in, 354–355,
      354
  expression of satiety in, 347–348
  hazards of, 10
  introduction of solid foods and,
      356–358, *357, 358*
  lack of genetic predispositions for, 13
  patterns of milk intake during, 349–356,
      359
  patterns of sucking, 354–355, 355, *355*
  process of terminating feed, 339
  sucking pattern and commercial
      formula in, 130–131
  sucking patterns compared with breast
      feeding, 130–131
  see also Feeding
Brain
  concept of 'catch up', 274–275
  consequences of delay in growth, 275
  coronal plate ultrasound scan, *328,* 329
  effects of fetal growth retardation, 328
  growth of evoked potentials in, 105–108

growth spurts, 274, 328
hierarchical view of, 115
histological development within the
    neocortex, 104–105
indices of developmental status,
    101–108
patterns of myelinization in, 102–104
patterns of neural growth, 108, 275
rhythms in, 125–126
role of sensory input in development of,
    112–114, 278, 280, 395
'sensitive period' in neural development,
    113
sequence of neural maturation, 115
sub- and neocortical system at birth,
    100, 101
subcortical mediation of neonatal
    behaviour, 108–112
transitional status of the neocortex at
    birth, 114–115
transition from subcortical to cortical
    control, 207, 396–397
weight of at birth, 102
see also Central Nervous System
Brain damage
  aetiology and implications, 75–92
  and fetal distress during labour, 76
  and neurological assessment, 30
  and perinatal injuries, 75–92, *91*
  and perinatal risk factors, 89–90, 92
  anoxia, 5–6, 8, 81
  assessment of perinatal injury, 75–90
  caused by fetal undernutrition, 273
  clinical features implying, *77*
  diminishing incidence of severe, 75,
      89–90
  effect of on non-nutritive sucking, 129
  effects minimized by good environment,
      11–12, 272
  follow-up studies of babies with, 84–90
  follow-up studies for children of school
      age with, *87,* 87–90
  haemorrhage, 79, *80,* 81
  hypoxia, 81–82, 270–271, 320, 331
  identification of, 75–76
  incidence of during last decade, 82
  in small-for-date term infants, 90
  oedema, 79, 81–82
  patterns of transitory abnormalities and
      examination, 87–88, *87*
  prenatal causes of, 263–267

recognition of cerebral symptoms, 77–78
related to birth process, 82
related to degree of maturation, 76
specific types of, 80–84
Brain lesions
see Brain damage
Brazelton Neonatal Behavioural Assessment Scale, 18
association with prenatal influences, 268–269
behavioural state during, 42–43, 44
critical evaluation of, 40–46
effect of ambient temperature on items, 43
habituation items questioned, 43, 236
individual differences in, 44–45
individual differences in irritability, 242–243
individual differences in perceptual items, 234
neurological reflex items, 41–42
omission of significant behaviours from, 45
sensitivity to change versus stability of scores, 45–46
test items discussed, 43–45
Breast feeding
adaptive consequences of, 9–10
adjustment to drop in feeds, 137
behavioural pattern determined by baby, 360–361
changes in concentration during a feed, 317
comparisons between bottle and, 130–131, 317, 339–341, 343–344, 354, 360–361
composition of human milk, 349–356
developing characteristics of pendulum oscillations, 137
distribution of burst sizes in, 354–355, *354*
diurnal variation in food intake, 352–354
expressions of satiety in, 347–349
introduced to solid foods and, 356–358, *357, 358*
patterns of milk intake during, 349–356, *350, 351*, 359
protection against infections, 339
sucking pattern compared with bottle feeding, 130–131

sucking patterns in, 128–131, 354–355, 355, *355*
transactions in, 11
unspecific psychological advantages, 339, 399–400
weight gain in, 349, 352, 356–358
see also Feeding
Breathing
assisted by ventilator, 323
coordinated by theta rhythms, 126
coping with difficulties in, 399
delayed onset of, 330–331
movements in fetus, 315–316
need for monitoring below 35 weeks gestation, 323
onset at birth, 316
rhythmic characteristics of, 126–127
see also Respiration
Brown fat metabolism, 9, 12, 316
effects on growth, 324

Caesarean section, 82
Cardiac and resporatory functions, 126–127
Caretakers, effects of treatment regimes on, 15
see also Mother–infant interaction, Parenting
Central Nervous System
abnormalities indicated by cry, 231
clinical features leading to dysfunction of, 77
crying reflecting structural aspects of, 231
dysfunction of, 77
feedback loops for sensory input, 113
innate specification controlling neonatal adaptation, 370
integration of processes between different levels, 112–113
main causes of malfunction of, *83*, 84
multiple feedback processes in, 116
sequence of neural maturation in, 115
see also Brain, Nervous system functioning
Cerebellum, myelinization of pathways to and from, 103
Cerebral necrosis, 81–82
characteristics of, *82*
cortical areas involved in, 81
EEG data as prognostic tool, 82

Cerebral necrosis (*contd.*)
  three-grades classification of, 82
Cerebral oedema, 79, 81–82
Cerebral palsy, 84
  and leucomalacia, 84
  and neonatal jaundice, 326
  incidence in small-for-date term infants,
    90
Cerebral symptoms
  in full-term newborns, 90–92
  recognition of, 77–78
  seizure discharge during neonatal
    period, 77
Cerebrospinal Fluid (CSF)
  blood in, 81
  checking of, 78–79
  protein in, 79
  red cells in, 78
Chagga of Tanzania, use of episiotomy,
    303
Chemical senses, 210–211
  innate preferences, similar to adult, 211
  marked preferences in, 211
Cheyne-Stokes breathing, 127
Chromosome abnormalities, 332–334
Classical conditioning, 152–164
  comparison of trace and delay proce-
    dures, 158–162, *159, 160, 162*
  demonstrated in the newborn, 153
  facilitated by longer interstimulus
    intervals, 155–157, *156*
  see also Conditioning, Trace condition-
    ing, Temporal conditioning
Clustering of measures
  as a criterion for significance of
    individual differences, 223, 224,
    253
  interpretation of, 254
Circadian rhythms, 136, 137–139
  advantages of delayed onset in sleep,
    139
  and pendulum oscillation, 137, 139
  development of in constant environ-
    ment, 138–139
  differentiation of internal and external
    control, 137–138
  fetal, 137
  in more mature functions, 138, 139
  in urinary flow, 138
  mitosis in preputial skin, 139
  of sleep, 138, 139

  potentially available from birth, 139
  timing of onset of, 139
  see also Rhythms
Cognitive competence
  contrasted with poor motor functions,
    13, 191
  in the neonatal period, 370, 371, 372,
    392, 407
  leading to study of parental behaviour,
    382
  relationship to social and emotional
    capabilities, 370, 395, 400
  underestimation of newborn's,
    400–401
Colour vision, 203
Coma, clinical features of, *77*
  see also Brain damage
Computed Axial Tomography scan (CAT
    scan)
  as diagnostic tool, 79, 81
  evaluating ventricular size, 79
Conditionability, 151–152
  relation to habituation, 151–152,
    157–164
  see also Habituation
Conditioning
  distinction between classical and
    operant, 164
  obscured by orienting responses, 154,
    157, 160–162, 164
  of eyeblinks, 157
  role of environmental familiarity in,
    163–164, 178
  theory of, 151–152
  see also Appetitive conditioning,
    Classical conditioning, Hybrid
    conditioning, Operant
    conditioning, Temporal
    conditioning, Trace conditioning
Congenital abnormalities, 332–333
  chromosome abnormalities, 332
  higher incidence in diabetic mothers,
    332
  limited possibility of prevention,
    332–333
Congenital haemolytic streptococcal
    infection, 325
Consecutive epoch analysis
  used in research of behavioural states, 60
Continuity in development
  deficiencies of 'main effect' model, 271

importance of, 5–6
limitations of concept, 5–6
not a basic criterion of significance of
    individual differences, 222–223,
    254
unproductiveness of notion, 393
Continuous moving window analysis
used in research of behavioural states,
    60
Continuous Positive Airway Pressure
    (CPAP), 89, 323–324
Contrast sensitivity, 194–196
defined, 194
functional implications of, 199
methods of assessing, 195–196
more informative than visual acuity,
    194–195
qualitative changes at 1–2 months,
    196–197
Corneal reflex method, systematic error in,
    200
Crib death
see Sudden infant death syndrome
Critical periods
for learning in first two months, 176
in binocular functioning, 201
Cross-cultural comparisons
and childbirth, 297, 298, 299
and crying, 305
of obstetric practices, 297–311
of parenting practices, 381
see also Birth
Cross-species comparisons
on prenatal influence, 268
rationale of, 147–148
similarity of human to other newborn
    mammals, 164, 166–168
Crying
adaptive consequences of, 9
advantages of persistence, 163
as a signal of hunger, 346–347
as relaxation oscillations, 125
causes of persistence, 226, 230
comparison between breast- and bottle-
    fed babies, 360–361
cultural variations in attitude to, 305
distinction between different forms of,
    346–347
effect on caretakers, 128
individual differences in, 230–231, 252
mother's response to, 346

reflecting structural aspects of the CNS,
    231
rhythmic properties of, 128
Cuddliness
and avoidance of tactile stimulation,
    232
assessed in Brazelton Neonatal
    Behavioural Assessment, 43
Cytomegalovirus, 286, 328

Deafness, following jaundice, 326
Defensive reflex
adaptive utility of, 162–163
conditionability of, 162–163
limited to emergencies, 163
Delivery personnel, 300–302
see also Labour
Depth perception, 201–202
criteria for demonstration of, 201–202
evidence for neonatal, 202
Diabetes, maternal
and congenital abnormalities, 332
Diseases of the newborn, 317–318
see also Infections
Dismissive labelling
of newborn characteristics, 275–276
of newborn learning, 178–179
reviewed, 400–402
Distance perception
see Depth perception
Down's syndrome, occurrence of, 333
Drugs
see Obstetric medication

Ebiama (Nigerian village)
childbirth attendants in, 301
Electroencephalogram (EEG)
and status epilepticus, 77
as diagnostic tool, 77–78
as state criterion, 64–65
data in cerebral necrosis, 82
indicating rhythmic brain activity,
    125–126
in differentiating sleep states, 53, 55–56,
    58
in pre-term newborns, 58–59
interpreted as rhythms, 125–126
maturation of pattern, 58–59
onset in fetus, 277
seizure recognition, 77–78
studies during wakefulness, 58

Electroencephalogram (EEG) (*contd.*)
   synchronizing function of theta rhythm,
      126
   systematic studies in infants, 58
   see also Epilepsy
Electroretinogram, indicating maturity of
   sensory pathways, 194
Emotions, neonatal, 8, 408
   relationship to cognitive development,
      370, 395, 400
   relationship to social behaviours,
      370–371
Electromyogram (EMG) activity, poor
   indicator for sleep, 64
Endocrine function, fetal, 278–279
Energy conservation
   advantages of persistence, 163
   characteristic of newborns of all species,
      169
   determining the effectiveness of
      conditioning paradigms, 169
   irrelevance of defensive reflex, 162–163
   obscuring the effects of learning, 172
   role of habituation in, 152
   through inactivity during sleep, 148
   through thermal homeostasis, 148
   see also Temperature
Environment
   and adaptation, 268–272
   comprehensive adaptation to, at all
      stages, 149
   interaction with nutrition, 280–284
   mediating consequences of birth
      trauma, 11–12, 272
   newborn's attempt to cope with,
      391–411
   newborn's competence in controlling,
      169
   role of familiarity of, in conditioning,
      163–164, 178
Epilepsy, clinical features of, 77
   see also Status epilepticus, Seizure
      discharges, EEG
Ethological studies
   see Observational studies
Evoked potentials (EP)
   auditory, 106–107
   elicited by somatosensory stimulation,
      106
   growth of, 105–108
   in pre-term newborns, 106, 114

in the study of sensory function, 193
   long latency components in, 106–107
   medium latency components of, 105,
      106, 107
   positive and negative peaks of, 105, 106
   pre-term and full-term responses, 107,
      113
   research data on, 105–106
   sensory processing indicated by, 106
   short latency components in, 106
   visual, (VEP) a test of visual
      functioning, 196
   visual mode in pre-term and full-term
      infants, 107
Evolution
   consequences modified by current
      neonatal care, 150
   illuminating attachment and cognitive
      competence, 394–396
Evolutionary perspective of the brain,
   100–101
   and development of sensory system,111
Exchange transfusion
   for treatment of jaundice, 326–328
   for treatment of rhesus haemolytic
      disease, 326
Expectancy, effects of violating, 168
Experimental control, stultifying effects of,
   180
Externality effect, visual, 205, 206–207
Eye
   functioning of neonatal, 197–198
   see also Retina, Visual system
Eye movements, 199–200
   neonatal differentiated from adult,
      199–200
   optokinetic nystagmus, 195, 200
   saccadic, 199
   tendency to fixate outer boundaries,
      206–207
   see also Visual system
Eye-to-eye contact, 383, 394
   see also Mother–infant interaction,
      Social interaction

Face
   innate preference questioned, 375
   visual preference for, 205–206,
      382–383, 392
Facial grimaces coordinated by theta
   rhythms 126

Familiarity
  in testing memory, 170–171
  of parent established through
        interaction, 384
  with environment, role in conditioning,
        163–164, 178
Febrile convulsion, as indicator of perinatal
        abnormality, 86
Feeding 339–361
  and compositional changes in human
        milk, 348–356
  and mother–infant interactions, 341,
        343, 359–360
  and weight gain, 317, 340, 352,
        356–358
  breast and bottle compared, 130–131,
        317, 339–341, 343–344, 354,
        360–361
  by tube, and maternal separation,
        324–325
  core phenomenon in neonatal
        adaptation, 392–393
  correlation with crying, 228
  cultural variations in time of starting,
        305
  dextrose solution as a reinforcer,
        165–166
  distribution of 'burst sizes' within,
        354–355, 354
  diurnal variation in food intake,
        352–354
  during unsocial hours, 356, 358
  expressions of satiety, 339, 340,
        347–349
  expressive behaviours during, 359–360
  external and internal control in,
        360–361
  individual differences in intake,
        228–229
  intravenous, 324
  introduction of solid foods, 356–358,
        357
  learned behaviours relating to hunger,
        341
  maternal behaviour facilitating nursing
        and, 381–382
  mother–infant interaction during,
        359–360
  need to let the newborn control, 317
  need to regulate, 192
  on demand, 343, 358–361

patterns of milk intake during, 349–356
  problems of premature babies, 324–325
  rapid weight gain, 358–361
  reasons for introducing solid foods,
        356–357, 358
  schedules, 317
  see also Breast feeding, Bottle feeding
Feeding cycle, 134
  pendulum characteristics of, 137
  relationship with ultradian rhythms,
        136–137
  subject to external and internal signals,
        137
  see also Sleep-wakefulness cycle
Fetal blood circulation, 316
  different from that of young baby, 316
  low oxygen content, 316
  postnatal closure of fetal channels, 316
Fetal breathing movements, 127, 315
Fetal competence, 277
  development of, 277–278
Fetal distress
  acute and subacute, 77
  and neonatal risk scores, 22
  brain damage resulting from, 76, 81
  importance of history of labour, 76
Fetal growth retardation, 327–332
  effects on brain growth, 328
  significance of timing, 328
Fetal hypotrophy
  see Hypotrophy, fetal
Fetal undernutrition
  and mental development, 11–12
  consequences of, 273
  distinguished from maternal
        undernutrition, 274
  effects of alcohol, 282
  effects of smoking, 274, 282
  interaction with genotype, 281–282
  interaction with infection, 282
  through limited placental transmission,
        282
  through specific amino acid deficits, 281
Fetus
  core temperature, 316
  circadian rhythms in, 137
  see also Prenatal influences
Floppy infant
  see Hypotonia
Focusing
  see Visual accommodation

Formula feeding
    see Bottle feeding

Generality of early adaptations, 397
    in learning 179
    lack of differentiation between sensory
        modalities, 213–214
Genetic counselling, 332–333
Genetic potential for growth, 278
Genetic predispositions
    capitalizing on environmental
        regularities, 179, 394–395
    of nervous system maturation, 29–30
    to parenting behaviour, 378–380
    to social behaviour, 368, 378
    to vulnerability, 27
Geniculo-striate pathway, cell development
        in, 207
Gestational age
    assessment of, 319
    of pre-term newborn defined, 76, 78
Group differences, implications for
        individual differences, 226–227
Growth
    competing demands of fetus and young
        mother, 285–286
    concept of 'catch-up', 274–275
    fetal, 317
    genetic potential 'recalibrated', 278
    postnatal, related to birth weight,
        246–247
    retardation in fetus, 327–332
    the primary task for the newborn,
        148–149
    towards adaptation, 272
    see also Weight
Growth retardation
    see Hypotrophy, fetal
Guatemalan Indians, obstetric practices of,
        303

Habituation, 150–151, 371
    a prerequisite for neonatal conditioning,
        157
    and behavioural state, 152
    criteria for demonstrating, 236
    function of, 150–151
    in demonstration of externality effect,
        206
    lack of information on individual
        differences, 235–237

not obtained in Brazelton Assessment,
        43, 236
    relation to conditionability, 151–152,
        157–164
    retention of, 151
    role in energy conservation during sleep,
        152
    theories of, 151, 235
    used to investigate perception, 193
Haemorrhage
    intracranial, 79, 327
    intraventricular, 79, 80
    retinal, 79
    subarachnoid, 79, 81
    subdural, 79
Hand to mouth contact, 343–344
    individual differences in, 345
Head turning
    and feeding, 164–165
    and visual contact with caretaker, 383
    conditioning of, 165–166, 165
    to sound, 210
    see also Rooting reflex
Heart beat used as rhythmic stimulus, 140
Heart rate
    and non-nutritive sucking, 129–130
    as poor indicator for behavioural state,
        64–65
    changes from fetus to infant, 126
    individual differences in, 235–236,
        238–239
    need for monitoring below 35 weeks
        gestation, 323
    of mother, related to soothability of
        newborn, 244
    rhythmic characteristics of, 126–127
    temporal conditioning of, 153–154
Helplessness
    of mothers in childbirth, 311, 411–412
    possible fatal consequences of, 175–176
Homeostatic processes
    in adaptation, 272
    see also Physiological regulation
Hormonal levels
    during fetal development, 279–280
    fetal, predisposing to sexual dimorphism
        in behaviour, 279–280
Hottentots of Africa, management of
        labour, 302
Hunger
    crying behaviour and, 346–347

effects of conditioning on, 342–343
in the absence of gastric peritalsis, 341
oral behaviours associated with,
341–343
physiological regulation of, 341–343
relationship between mouthing and, 344
relationship between oral behaviour
and, 345
signals for, 343–346
Hyaline membrane disease
see Respiratory distress syndrome
Hybrid conditioning procedures, 164–170
Hydrocephalus 81, *330*
diagnostic procedures, 78
following intracranial haemorrhage, 327
Hyperexcitability
as a clinical feature of CNS
dysfunction, 77
Hyperglycaemia
in light for dates babies, 331
poor prognosis following, 331
Hypertension, maternal
and infant neurological abnormalities,26
Hypertonia
clinical feature of CNS dysfunction, 77
generalized, 78
in neck extensors, 78
Hyporeactivity, as clinical finding in brain
oedema, 81
Hyporeflectivity, as clinical finding in brain
oedema, 81
Hypotonia, as clinical finding in brain
oedema, 81
Hypotrophy, fetal
as perinatal risk factor, 89
causes of, 288
defined, 76
detection of, 76
Hypoxia 77
and impaired ability to cope with stress,
272
causes of, 318
causing meconium aspiration
syndrome, 331
effects of, 270–271
fetal, 330–331
increased risk in poorly growing fetuses,
329
intrauterine, 317–318
perinatal, 81–82, 270–271, 320
see also Anoxia

Ideopathic respiratory distress syndrome
(IRDS)
see Respiratory distress syndrome
Imitation, 213–214, 384
as a prototype of social behaviour, 214
Immaturity of newborn
a misleading concept, 30, 139, 401
an artefact of experimental procedures,
164
possible advantages of, 248
see also Maturity
Incapacity of the newborn
an artefact of conditioning procedures,
164
a self-fulfilling belief, 157–158
Individual differences, 221–255, 401
and Brazelton Neonatal Behavioural
Assessment Scale, 44, 254
and optimally suited environments for
neonate, 407–489
as a precursor of personality, 222
as predicting future psychopathology,
222
criteria described, 223–226
criteria of significance of, 221–226
early studies, 222
in activity, 240–245
in adaptation, 235–236
in apnoea, 240
in appearance, 246
in auditory sensitivity, 233–234
in autonomic nervous system
functioning, 238–240
in cognitive functioning, 231–237
in crying, 230–231
in cuddliness, 232, 250–251
in food intake, 228–229, 252
information on stability but not
magnitude, 227
in habituation, 235–237
in hand to mouth contact, 345
in heart rate responses, 235–236,
238–239
in higher order functions, 250–251
in interaction style, 250–251
in learning, 235–237
in maturation, 226
in maturity, 115–116, 248–250
in mouthing, 344
in non-nutritive sucking, 229–230
in oral functioning, 227–230

Individual differences (*contd.*)
  in orienting, 234
  in perceptual functioning, 234–235
  in psychobiological integrity, 250
  in respiration, 240
  insensitivity of neurological examination
    to, 39, 46
  in sensory function, 231–234
  in size, 246–247
  in somatic characteristics, 245–250
  in soothability, 221, 243–244
  in state, 57, 244–245
  in strength, 247
  in sucking, 228
  in tactile sensitivity, 232–233
  in visual functioning, 195–196,
    231–234
  in vocalization, 230–231
  in weight, 246–247
  irrelevance of continuity as a criterion,
    222–223
  significance of, 97, 221–223, 252–255
  summary of findings, 252–255, *253*
Infanticide
  and belief in human status of
    newborn, 308
  and quality of life, 308
Infections
  breast feeding as protection against,
    339
  chronic maternal, 286
  diagnosis and treatment of, 325
  intrauterine, 328
  of premature babies, *319*, 325
  preconceptual, 286
  sexually transmitted, 286
Intensive care
  ethical problems relating to, 88, 308,
    334
  evaluating new methods, 87
  evaluation of Units, 84–85, 396
  follow-up studies of newborns in, 84
  increasing centralization of, 323
  repeated neurological assessment in,
    92
  therapy for neonates, 89
  see also Special care baby unit
Interactional models discussed, 379
Intersensory integration, 212–214
Intracranial haemorrhage, 79, 327
  need to prevent, 327

Intrauterine growth, 76
Intraventricular haemorrhage (IVH),
  80–81
  as perinatal risk factor, 89
  characteristics of, 80
  symptoms of, 81
Irritability
  derived from Brazelton Neonatal
    Assessment, 242–243
  individual differences in, 242–243
  prenatal factors in, 242
  relation to state, 245
Ischaemia, 77

Jaundice, 318
  bilirubin levels in, 325–326
  exchange transfusion and, 326–327
  in premature babies, 325–327
  sequelae of, 326
  treatment by phototherapy, 327
Joint senses
  lack of reliable knowledge of, 192

Kernicterus, an example of multiple
  determination, 27, 326, *326*

Labour
  abdominal stimulation in, 303
  acid base sampling during, 82
  ambulation in, 283, 302
  cultural variation in management of,
    302–304
  cultural variation in restriction of
    activity, 302
  effects of complications on newborn,
    87
  effects of father's presence, 283
  fetal contribution to initiation of, 280
  fetal distress during, 76
  fetal heart-rate monitoring during, 82
  importance of history of, 76
  maternal anxiety in, 283
  position of mother in, 302, 303, 304
  see also Birth, Obstetric practice
Labour pains, cultural differences in
  managing, 302–303, 310
Laterality, attributed to fetal position, 280
Learning, 147–180, 397
  capacity to process information across
    modalities, 370–377
  defined, 150

development of intentional and conscious behaviours, 373
facilitated by degrees of novelty, 372–373
fetal, 277–278
in establishing hunger and appetite behaviours, 343–345
in feeding behaviour, 341
mediational processes underlying neonatal, 110–112
process in social integration, 371
rapidity of neonatal, 178
relationship of laboratory to natural, 180
role of biological response systems in, 178–179
significance in first days of life, 45, 177
states in newborn, 380
to detect consequences of one's behaviour, 373–374
used to investigate auditory and visual responsiveness, 193
Leboyer delivery, effects of, 311
Lepcha of Asia, use of physiological releasers of oxytocin, 303
Leucocytes, 78
Leucomalacia
characteristics of, *83*, 84
periventricular, *83*, 84
Light for dates (LFD) babies, 90, 327–332
impaired thermal control, 332
incidence of congenital abnormalities, 332
intrauterine infections in, 328
vulnerability of, 329–330, *329*
see also Low birth weight babies, Prematurity
Low birth weight babies
and fetal growth retardation, 327–329
assessment of, 85–86, *86*
care of, 14–15
categories of perinatal risk and, 89–90
cold stress in, 316, 324
feeding of, 10
neurological deficits in, 85–86
outcome of follow-up studies, *86*, 90
perinatal mortality of, 318
sequellae, 85–86, 90
summary of lesions and outcome, *91*

see also Light for dates babies, Prematurity
Lumbar punctures, in hydrocephaly, 81
Lungs
adaptation of during fetal stage, 315
condition in respiratory distress syndrome, 320
surfactant in fetal, 315
surfactant in neonatal, 320

Malnutrition
maternal, interacting with anxiety, 282–283
transgenerational effects, 284–289
see also Fetal undernutrition
Manus of the Admiralty Islands, treatment of baby following birth, 304
Maternal anxiety
and labour, 283
interaction with malnutrition, 282–283
transgenerational effects, 284–285
Maternal deprivation, 10–11
cultural variations in mother–newborn separation, 304–307
Maturation
accounting for sex differences, 226, 232
individual differences in, 226
of brain, 176
process more important than achievement, 174
Maturity
assessment from neurological items, 47
effects on adaptation, 249
individual differences in, 115–116, 248–250
measurement of, 248–250
of flicker sensitivity at birth, 203
of middle ear structures, 208
of sensory pathways, 194
possible dangers of, 248
Meconium aspiration syndrome, 331
Memory, 170–172
evidence of long-term retention, 171
implicit in learning, 112, 170
methods of assessing, 170
ontogenetic changes in, 171–172
probability of in newborn, 112
prolonged by reinstatement experiences, 172

Metabolism, inborn errors of, 332
Middle ear, structures mature at birth, 208
Midwives, role in other cultures, 300–302
Milk
    changes in composition of human, 348–356
    intake of bottle fed infant, 349–356, *353*, 359
    intake of breast fed infants, *350, 351*
    patterns of intake in breast fed babies, 349–356, *350, 351*
Milk let-down reflex, 131
    effect of newborn cry, 149, 317
Moro reflex, 61
    absence of in CNS dysfunction, *77*
    in Brazelton Neonatal assessment, 44
Mother–infant interaction, 340
    and feeding behaviours, 339–340, 343, 359–360
    and mother's knowledge of her baby, 404–406
    and neonatal care in institutions, 404–412
    asymmetry of competence of partners, 382
    comparison between institution and home, 404–412
    continuity of style in, 251
    contributing to newborn physiological regulation, 149
    dynamic concept of partners in, 377–379
    effect of sex differences in eye contact, 232
    facilitated by seclusion rituals, 306, 406
    following birth, cultural variations, 305–307
    imitative behaviour in, 384
    neonates adaptation to mothers, 407
    proximity enhancing behaviours in, 402–403
    rhythmic nature of, 140–141
    sucking pattern as basis for, 229
    see also Attachment
Motor areas
    development of, 104–105
    myelinization of pathways in, 102
    neural development in primal, 110
Motor development
    silent period of at 1 year of age, 87

studies of subcortical mediation of, 109–110
Motor function
    and skills, 85
    contrasted with cognitive competence, 13, 191
    in utero, 280
    maturity correlated with parental characteristics, 249
Motor patterns
    post-partum adaptive differentiation of, 370–371
Mouthing
    age differences in, 345
    as part of feeding behaviour, 343–344
    individual differences in, 344
Mundurucu tribe
    laissez-faire attitude to birth, 303
    postnatal treatment, 306
Muscle senses
    lack of reliable knowledge of, 192
Myelinization
    afferent pathways, 102, 103, 107
    auditory system, 103
    motor pathways, 102
    neocortex, 103
    optic nerve, 197
    patterns of in the brain, 102–104
    sensory pathways, 102
    somatosensory system, 103
    vestibular system, 102

Naming rituals, 309
Nasal occlusion reflex, 176–177
    adaptive consequences of, 9
    deficiency in SIDS babies, 177
National Childbirth Trust, (NCT), 411
National Child Development Study
    cohort of 1958 births, 284
National Survey cohort of 1946 births, 284
Navaho Indians, manual removal of placenta, 303
Neocortex
    at birth 100, 101, 110
    histological development of, 104–105
    limitations of assessment at birth, 115–116
    myelinization of, 103
    onset of involvement in vision, 207
    postnatal growth in cell size, 197
    see also Brain, Central nervous system

Neonatal Behavioural Assessment Scale
  see Brazelton Neonatal Behavioural
    Assessment Scale
Nervous system
  heterochronic maturation of, 29–30
  indices of developmental status,
    101–108
  schematic representation of, *101*
  structure, status and characteristics at
    birth, 99–116
  unique form of newborn, 29–30
Nervous system functioning
  as active information processing, 29
  capacities and characteristics of at
    birth, 95–96
  complexity of newborn, 32
  concepts of, 28–29
  dependency on behavioural state, 33
  inadequate models underlying
    assessment of, 28–30
  unique form of newborn, 29–30, 31
  see also Brain, Central nervous system
Nervous system structure
  heterochronic maturation of, 29–30
  unique form of newborn, 29–30
Neural dysfunction
  abnormal behavioural states as signs
    of, 59
  clinical features of, *77*
  see also Brain damage
Neural tube defects
  detection from AFP concentration in
    early pregnancy, 333–334
  ethical dilemmas in treatment, 334
  prevention by vitamin supplementa-
    tion, 333
Neurological assessment, 17–18, 28–39
  age specificity of, 31, 34, 37
  comparison of methods, 34–35
  design methodology, 31–34
  distinguished from behavioural assess-
    ment, 22, 40
  evaluation of obstetric care and, 92
  in low birth-weight infants, 85–86
  objectives of, 30–31
  of neurologic development, 85
  of perinatal injury, 75–90
  reliability of, 37
  role of reflexes in, 28
  scales for, 33, 36
  screening test versus comprehensive
    method, 38

theoretical background, 28–30
validity of, 34, 37–38
see also Assessment, Neurological
  examination
Neurological conditions, 18–19
  aetiology and implication of, 75–92
  and maternal hypertension, 26
  major causative factors and perinatal
    risk, 89
Neurological diagnostic procedures,
    78–79
  cerebrospinal fluid (CSF) in, 78–79
  evaluation of head measurements, 78
Neurological evaluation and consequences
    of damage in early infancy, 84–85
Neurological examination
  and acute gross pathology, 35
  and behavioural states, 61
  and patterns of transitory abnor-
    malities, 87–88, *87*
  behavioural items in, 39
  comparison of methods, 34–35
  importance of state during, 33–34, 36,
    53
  objectives, 30–31
  predictions from, 37–38
  sequence of items in, 33–34
  standardization of procedure, 32–33,
    35–36
  technique of, 31–34, *32*
  see also Neurological assessment
Nociceptive responses, and behavioural
    states, 62
Non-nutritive sucking, 344
  and mother–infant dialogue, 229
  arising in primitive brain, 129
  burst-pause pattern in, 129–130, 131,
    229
  individual differences in, 229–230
  optimally suited to stimulate breast
    milk flow, 131
  rhythmic properties of, 121, 129–131
  significance of, 229
  see also Sucking
Non-shivering thermogenesis, 316
Novelty
  as a test of memory, 170–171
  effect in maintaining responding, 168
  facilitating conditioned taste aversions,
    178
Nutrition 339–361
  breast milk and formula compared, 317

Nutrition (*contd.*)
   dependence on care-giver, 316–317
   fetal and maternal, 273, 274
   inseparable from environment, 281
   interaction with other factors,
      280–284
   maternal, 282–283, 328, 333
   preconceptual effects, 274

Obesity
   as a result of faulty learning, 343
   relationship between infant and adult,
      358–359
   risk of in bottle fed babies, 340, 349,
      352, 356–358
   see also Weight
Observational studies
   difficulties of, 369
   of behavioural states, 57–58
   of parenting behaviours, 380
Obstetric complications, 22–24
   and sudden infant death syndrome,
      276
   cumulative effects in, 23
   effects modified by subsequent
      environment, 5–6, 11, 85, 288
   effects on newborn, 87
   follow-up care and subsequent preg-
      nancies, 286
   measures combined with optimality
      scores, 25–26
   measures compared with optimality
      scores, 25
   risk factors in the term newborn, 90
   vulnerability derived from prenatal
      problems, 275
Obstetric medication
   and brain impairment, 275–276
   and delayed onset of breathing, 318
   effects on neonatal behaviour, 275,
      310
   in non-industrial cultures, 303
   prolonging labour, 283
   prolonging primary apnoea, 330
Obstetric practice
   criteria for evaluating, 14–15,
      393–394, 394–396
   cultural differences in, 264–265,
      297–311
   demonstrating cultural assumptions,
      302, 304, 309–311

   depriving mothers of normal
      relationships, 300
   maternal autonomy versus depression,
      311, 411–412
   related to demands of future environ-
      ment, 393
   taking account of individual
      differences, 407–409
Ojibwa of Perry Island (Canada), belief
      in human status of fetus, 308
Olfactory discrimination, 210–211
   an essential early capacity, 192
   by newborn rat pups, 167, *167*
   preferences in, 211
Operant conditioning, 164–170
   and reflex responses, 173–174, *173*,
      176
   competence of newborn, 69–70
   effectiveness related to energy cost,
      169
   of head turning, 165–167, 168
   of sucking, 168–169
   reviews of, 169
   see also Appetitive conditioning
Optic fundus, as a diagnostic indicator,
      79
Optic nerve, myelination of, 197
Optimality scores, neurological, 36–37
Optimality scores, obstetrical, 24–27, *24*
   applications of, 26–27
   combination with complication scores,
      25–26
   compared with complication scores, 25
   distributions of, *24*, 27
   misuse of, 26
Optokinetic nystagmus (OKN)
   and newborn visual pursuit, 200
   a test of visual functioning, 195
   subcortical control in newborn, 200
Oral functioning
   individual differences in, 227–230
   rhythms in, 127–131
   stability of measures of, 229–230
   see also Non-nutritive sucking,
      Sucking
Orienting response
   a positive feedback reflex, 151
   depending on intrinsic invariants, 371
   indicating auditory sensitivity, 193
   indicating central representation of
      space, 212–214

individual differences in, 234
in social learning, 371, 392
obscuring conditioning, 154, 157,
    160–162, 164
optimal testing conditions for, 210
recorded in Brazelton Assessment, 43,
    234
to sound sources, 210

Papilloedema, 79
Parental characteristics
determining norms for the newborn,
    224, 410
influencing newborn characteristics,
    285–289
Parent–infant interactions, 374–385
imitative behaviour in, 384
research into animal behaviours of,
    379
see also Mother–infant interaction
Parenting, 1
and assessment of newborn's
    behavioural state, 382
cultural differences in, 381
ethological concepts of, 380
in dyadic interchanges, 379–385
relationship between forms of, 366,
    368, 381, 382, 410
research into behaviour of animal, 379
Pattern perception, 204–206
measures of availability of informa-
    tion, 194–196
see also Visual functioning
Pavlovian state of optimal excitability of
    the CNS, 61
Pendulum oscillations, 119, 122–125
and circadian rhythms, 137, 139
as a characteristic in breast feeding,
    137
characteristic of lower frequencies,
    122–125
characteristics of, 123
defined, 122
predominance in mature functions,
    123–125
Perceptual functioning, 191–214
and neonatal adaptation, 397, 398
facilitated by theta rhythms, 126
intersensory integration, 212–214
see also Depth perception, Sensory
    processing

Perinatal brain damage, 75–92
and subsequent development of infant,
    85, 318
summary of lesions and outcome, 91
Perinatal complications
see Obstetric complications
Perinatal hypoxic brain damage, 81–82,
    270–271, 320
prognosis following, 331
Perinatal morbidity, 89, 318
Perinatal mortality
and attitudes to childbirth, 307–309
caused by respiratory distress syn-
    drome, 319–323
causes of neonatal death, 318
causes of still birth, 317–318
correlated with prematurity, 318–319
incidence of, 77, 317–318
in low birth weight babies, 318
Perinatal risks
and prevention of major mental
    handicap, 88–90
and small-for-date term infants, 90
major causative factors of, 89
obstetrical risk factors in the term
    infant, 90
of low birth-weight babies, 89–90
Periodic breathing
see Cheyne-Stokes, Breathing
Phacoma, optic fundus as diagnostic
    indicator of, 79
Phototherapy, 7, 327
Physiological regulation, 148–149
homeostatic processes in, 272
imposing constraints on forms of
    learning, 149
through mother–infant interaction, 149
Placental insufficiency, an unjustified term,
    318, 328
Poisson distribution, 59
Polygraphic recordings
assessment of long, 59–60
manual for a standardized assessment
    of states, 69
of behavioural states, 58–60, 68
Preferences in looking, 204–206
alternative explanations of, 204–205
as test of visual functioning, 195–196
at faces, 205–206
attempts to quantify, 204
Prefrontal lobes, development of, 104

Preconceptual influences, 284–289
   birth control practices, 286
   health of mother, 274, 285
   infections, 286
   life events, 287
   maternal nutrition, 274, 286
Pregnancy
   and 'granny effects', 287
   and mother's nutritional status,
      284–286
   importance of history of, 76
   problems related to life events, 287
   see also Prenatal influences, Teenage
      pregnancy
Prematurity
   and social class, 11, 319
   bilirubin levels in, 325–327
   causes of, 288, 319
   compounding of deficits, 264–265
   defined, 76
   feeding problems, 324–325
   infection in, 325
   intracranial haemorrhage in, 327
   jaundice in, 325–327
   monitoring of blood oxygen levels in,
      320–323, 321, 322
   monitoring of breathing and heart rate,
      323
   problems arising from, 319
   recurrent apnoeic attacks in, 323–326
   respiratory distress syndrome in,
      319–323, 320
   thermal regulation, 324
   transition from hospital to home,
      396–397
   treatment in, 14–15
   see also Light for dates babies, Low
      birth weight babies, Pre-term
      birth
Prenatal functioning, continuity to
   postnatal life, 45
Prenatal influences, 267–289
   and homeostatic processes, 272
   and neural development, 280
   and postnatal behaviour, 267–277
   associated with later disadvantage, 268,
      269
   causing perinatal hypoxia, 275
   chronic maternal infections, 286
   effect on social adaptation of newborn,
      276–277

from earlier birth control practices, 286
   hypoxia, 270–271
   impairing adaptive processes, 273
   infections, 282, 286, 328
   interactions between, 280–284
   life-style of mother, 288
   maternal consumption of alcohol, 333
   maternal smoking, 274, 282, 288, 333
   newborn characteristics associated with,
      276–277
   on ability to cope with stress, 273
   on adaptation, 263–265, 267–289
   on longer-term development, 267–268
   on the newborn, 267
   outcome studies, 270–271
   overview of research, 268–273
   placental transmission, 282
   preconceptual influences, 284–289
   problems of interpretation, 270–272
   seasonal effects, 286
   sexually transmitted infections, 286
   transactional model applied to,
      271–272, 276–277
   transgenerational influences,
      284–289
   see also Fetal undernutrition
Pre-term birth
   defined, 76
   long-term consequences, 5–6
   see also Prematurity
Pre-term newborn
   care of, 14
   evoked potentials in, 106, 114
   EEG patterns in, 58–59
   neural functions of, 31
   neurological assessment of, 47
   major causes of death in, 80–81, 80
   summary of lesions and outcome, 91
Primary intersubjectivity, 214
Progesterone treatment
   controversy over, 264, 269–270
   of toxaemia, 269–270
   possible beneficial effects on newborn,
      269–270
Proprioceptive senses, role in developing
   body representation, 192
Puerperal depression, and lack of control
   over birth by mother, 311, 411–412
Punjab
   childbirth practices in, 303
   postnatal treatment, 306

Purification rituals following childbirth, 299

Rapid eye movements (REM)
  age related changes in, 59
  and behavioural states, 58, 62, 68
  lack of evidence for rhythmic
      properties, 133, 134
Reactivity
  see Irritability
Reflex responses, 17
  abdominal, 62
  as clinical feature of CNS dysfunction,
      77
  Babinski, 62
  conditionability of defensive, 162–163
  in Brazelton Assessment Scale, 41–42
  mediated by subcortical mechanisms,
      109
  Moro-reaction, 61
  role in adjustment of the sensory
      system, 192–193
  role in neurological assessment, 28
  rooting, 164
  transition to operant responding,
      173–174, 173, 176
Relaxation oscillations, 119, 122–125
  characteristic of higher frequencies,
      122–124
  characteristics of, 123
  crying and, 125
  defined, 122
  predominance in early ontogenesis,
      123–125, 123
  spontaneous behaviours as, 132–133
  see also Rhythmic function
Research
  applications of, 14–15
  effects of excluding irritable babies, 243
  prerequisites for neonatal, 12
  see also Observational studies
Respiration
  and non-nutritive sucking, 129–130
  as example of varied functioning in
      rhythms, 124–125, 126
  cyclic variability in, 127
  role in sudden infant death syndrome,
      175–176, 240
  temporal conditioning of, 153–154
  varied functions of, 124–125
  see also Breathing

Respiratory Distress Syndrome (RDS), 89,
    319, 319–323, 320, 321
  association with intraventricular
      haemorrhage, 80–81
  treatment by continuous positive
      airways pressure, 323
  treatment by oxygenation, 320–323
Respiratory failure, 323
Respiratory rate
  as poor indicator for behavioural state,
      64–65
  individual differences in, 240
Rest-activity cycle
  see Basic rest activity cycle
Retina
  cell types at birth, 197
  quality of image, 197–198
  see also Eye, Eye movements
Retinal haemorrhage, 79
Rhesus haemolytic disease, 326
Rhesus immune globulin (anti-D), 326
Rhythms, 119–149
  absence of low frequency in early
      gestation, 124
  and cyclic variability in breathing, 127
  and heart rate, 126–127
  and startles, 132
  biological advantages of, 119
  characteristics and functioning of, 123
  criteria discussed, 120–122, 141, 397,
      401
  decrease in frequency with maturation,
      124–125
  different manifestations of, 121, 122
  EEG studies of, 125–126
  hormonal, 7
  in crying, 128
  in mother–infant interactions, 140–141
  in sleep, 124, 133, 138, 139
  in sucking, 128–129
  in the brain, 125–126
  in vocalization, 127–128
  non-nutritive sucking as, 121
  not evident in REM sleep, 133, 134
  respiration as example of varied
      functioning in, 124–125,
      126–127
  role of in adaptation, 96
  significance of, 119
  significance of variation under load,
      121, 122, 141

Rhythms (*contd.*)
    state cycles and, 133–137
    urinary, 138
    variation under load, 129
    see also Circadian rhythms, Pendulum
        oscillations, Relaxation
        oscillations
Rhythmic stimuli, 140–141
    effectiveness related to spontaneous
        neonatal rhythms, 140
    for soothing, 140
    heart beat used as, 140
    rocking as, 140
Risk factors
    criteria for identification, 28
    for brain disorder, 22–27
Risk registers
    criteria for inclusion in follow-up
        studies, 90
    limitations of, 23–24, 27–30
Rocking, as a rhythmic stimulus, 140
Rooting reflex, 164
    see also Head turning
Rubella virus, 332–333

Samoa, attitudes to labour pains in, 310
Satiety
    expressions of, 347–349
    in bottle-fed babies, 340
    mothers recognizing cues of, 339
    sucking mechanisms and, 348
Schedule of Recent Experience (stress
    index), 287
Seclusion rituals following delivery,
    306–307, 308
Seizure discharges
    during neonatal period, 77
    identification through EEG recordings,
        77–78
    see also Epilepsy
Sensory areas
    development of, 104, 115
    evolutionary development of systems in,
        111
    functional at 24 weeks gestation, 277
    maturity of, 194
    myelinization of pathways, 102–104
    neocortical mediation in, 111
    neural development in primal, 110
Sensory-motor correspondences,
    212

Sensory processing, 191–214
    contribution of early, 112–114
    dominance of vision and hearing in
        study of, 191–192
    feedback loops linking cortical systems,
        113
    indicated by evoked potentials, 106, 114
    individual differences in, 231–234
    in utero, 280
    lack of neocortical information
        processing at birth, 110
    methods of studying, 192–194
    role of early sensory stimulation, 114
    subcortical mediation of motor and,
        109–110
Separation of mother and newborn
    cultural variations, in, 304–307
    from need for tube feeding, 324–325
    in intensive care units, 323
    in phototherapy, 7, 327
    in special care baby units, 319
    in Western obstetric practice, 307
Septicaemia, 325
Sex differences
    and prenatal hormones, 279–280
    in neonatal behaviour, 345–346
    in vocalization, 226
    limiting explanations of individual
        differences, 226
Sierra Tarcascans of Mexico, herbs used to
    accelerate birth, 303
Siriouo of Bolivia, use of physiological
    releasers of oxytocin, 303
Skin responses, exteroceptive, and
    behavioural states, 62
Skin senses
    individual differences in tactile
        sensitivity, 232–233
    lack of reliable information on, 192
Skull
    fractures of, 79
    periventricular calcification, 79
    X-ray of the, 79
Sleep
    as energy conservation, 148
    circadian rhythms and, 138, 139
    distribution over 24h, 55
    EMG activity in, 64
    endogeneous determination of rhythms
        in, 138
    lack of rhythmic variation in, 133

non-rapid eye movement (NREM),
58–59
rapid eye movement (REM), 58–59, 62
states, 55–56, 63, 64, 68, 69
Sleep–wakefulness cycle
and temporal conditioning of feeding,
153
cycle defined, 133–134
effect on orienting responses of
4-month-olds, 154
evidence for, 136–137
identification with feeding cycle,
136–137
see also Sleep
Smoking during pregnancy, 274, 282, 288,
333
Social class
and prematurity, 11, 319
uninformative about individual
differences, 227
Social interaction, 367–385
and imitation, 213–214, 384
and parenting behaviour, 379–385
development of intentional and
conscious behaviours in, 373
dyadic relationship in, 377–379
early integrative capacities, 369–374
experience and behaviour as part of,
373, 395
extending to all members of family,
406
fundamental cognitive operations, 371
gratification of needs, 372–373
innate predisposition, 368, 374,
376–377
interrelation between emotional and
social behaviour, 370
interrelationship between motor and
cognitive behaviour, 370–372,
395
perception and, 370–371
recognition of facial and vocal signs,
372, 382–383, 395
training the baby in forms of, 365–366
see also Mother–infant interaction
Social interaction, newborn capabilities for
giving contingent cues to caretakers,
406
imitation as a precursor of, 214
implications for behavioural
assessment, 39

Solid foods
introduction of, 356–358
reasons for introducing, 356–358, 358
Somatic characteristics
individual differences in, 245–250
Somatosensory afferents
evoked potentials elicited by stimulation
of, 106
myelinization of, 103
Soothability
individual differences in, 243–244
possible influence on caretaker, 221
problems of measurement, 243–244
Space, central representation of, 212–214
Special care baby unit (SCBU)
and separation from mother, 319
criteria for admission, 319
see also Intensive care
Speech sounds, discrimination of, 209–219
Spina bifida
see Neural tube defects
Spontaneous activity in neurological
assessment, 35
Spontaneous behaviours, 131–133
as relaxation oscillations, 132–133
lack of evidence for rhythmic
properties, 133, 134
Stapedial response
see Acoustic reflex
Startles, spontaneous, 131–132
in deep sleep, 132
rhythmic nature discussed, 132
State
see Behavioural state
State cycles, 56–57, 62
rhythmic properties of, 133–137
Status epilepticus
definition, 77, 77
hypotonia and lethargy in, 88
in cerebral necrosis, 81
see also Epilepsy
Stimulation
counteracting mental retardation,
11–12
reduced in care of low birth-weight
newborns, 14
Stimulus discrimination, use of satiation of
reinforcers to test, 168–169
Strength
individual differences in, 247
related to food intake, 228–229

Subarachnoid haemorrhage, 79, 81
Subcortical system
    at birth, 100, 101
    mediation of behavioural capacities,
        108–112
    myelinization of, 102–103
    see also Brain, Central nervous system
Subdural haemorrhage, 79
Sucking
    as relaxation oscillations, 125
    behaviours during feeding, 341
    causing contraction of the visual field,
        202
    conditioning of, 168–169
    coordinated by theta rhythm, 126
    correlation with later maternal
        behaviour, 229–230
    deficient in premature babies, 324
    individual differences in, 228–229
    mechanisms and satiation, 348
    rates of breast and bottle fed babies,
        355, 355
    reflex, 341–342, 344
    related to individual differences in food
        intake, 228
    relationship between swallowing and,
        131
    rhythmic properties of, 128
    taste affecting patterns of, 130, 131, 211
    see also Non-nutritive sucking
Sudden infant death syndrome (SIDS),
    172–177
    apnoea in, 127, 175
    as a learning deficit, 175–177
    behavioural contribution to, 175–177
    characteristics of, 174–175
    frequency and time of occurrence, 174
    hypothesis of converging behavioural
        deficits, 177
    precursors, 175
    respiratory anomalies in, 175–177
    stressors in, 276
Superior colliculus, multimodal representa-
    tion of space, 212–213
Surfactant
    in fetal lungs, 315
    in neonatal lungs, 320
Swallowing
    coordinated by theta rhythms, 126
    coordinated with respiration, 125
    relationship between sucking and, 131

Systemogenesis, 29, 139
    and maturity, 249
    conferring significance on clusters of
        characteristics, 224
Systems theory
    applied to social interactions, 378
    definition of state in, 54–55

Tactile threshold
    individual differences in, 232–233
    related to later characteristics, 232
Taste
    an essential early capacity, 192
    discrimination, 211
    effect on sucking patterns, 130, 131,
        211
Teenage pregnancy
    competing nutritional demands of
        mother and fetus, 285
    unfavourable outcome from, 285
Temperature
    and skin contact with mother, 148, 316
    behavioural control of, 148
    changes at birth, 316
    maintenance by brown fat metabolism,
        9, 12, 316, 324
    need for sensing of, 192
    of fetus, 316
    physiological control achieved, 169
    regulation of body, 148–149
    see also Energy conservation, Thermal
        homeostasis

Temporal conditioning, 153–155
    advantage of individual variation in,
        155
    functional utility of, 154–155
    proclivity of newborn for, 153–154
Temporal morphology of rhythmic
        phenomena, 121
Theta rhythms
    speculation of function of, 126
    synchronizing function of, 126
tepoztlan (Mexican village)
    altering fetal position by massage, 303
    antenatal care in, 301
Thermal homeostasis
    and energy conservation, 148
    in light for dates babies, 332
    in premature babies, 324
    see also Temperature

Toba-bataks of Australia, treatment of
placenta, 308–309
Tonus
effect of epidural block, 247
relationship to strength, 247
see also Hypotonia
Taxaemia
and neonatal risk scores, 22
and social class, 11
progesterone treatment, 269–270
Toxoplasmosis, optic fundus as diagnostic
indicator of, 79
Trace conditioning, 157–162
compared with delay procedures,
158–162, 159, 160, 164
obscured by responses to CS offset,
159–162
operant task in, 160–161
Transactional model, 11–12, 276–277,
402–404
and adaptation, 12, 402–404
applied to the fetus and its environment,
263–264
defined, 11
discussed, 271
illustrated by flow of influence between
newborn, mother, and institution,
404–412, 405
of breast feeding, 11
of prenatal influences, 271, 403
Transgenerational influences, 284–289
animal studies, 284–285
'granny effects' in nutrition and stress,
284–285
in affective relationships, 287
Transillumination, as diagnostic indicator, 79
Transitions
and cortical control, 396–397
consequences and effects of sudden
change, 396–397
defined, 5
for premature babies, 396
from reflex to voluntary responding:
2–4 months, 172–174, 173, 176
stress during, 396, 398–399
to extra-uterine environment, 5,
177–178
Trobriand Islanders, childbirth practices of,
299
Tympanogram
see Acoustic impedance

Ultradian sleep rhythms
relationship with feeding cycle, 136–137
Umbilical artery catheter, 321, 323
Umbilical cord
breathing triggered by cutting, 316
optimal time for cutting, 303–304
Urinary rhythms, 138

Vascular malformation, optic fundus as
diagnostic indicator of, 79
Vectors
defining behavioural states, 67–68
defining state concomitants, 68
Ventilation
breathing assisted by, 323
in cases of terminal apnoea, 331
risk of intracranial haemorrhage during,
327
Ventricular dilatation, 81
Ventricular intracranial haemorrhage
CAT scan as a diagnostic tool of, 79
Vertex position, actively achieved by fetus,
280
Vestibular system
lack of reliable knowledge of, 192
myelinization of, 102
Vestibulo-ocular response and behavioural
states, 62
Visual accommodation, 197–198
accuracy of adjustment in newborn,
198
functional implications of, 199
limited by poor acuity, 198
major determinant of quality of infant
vision, 198
rapid postnatal improvement, 198
Visual acuity, 194–196
defined, 194
functional implications of, 199
limiting factor in accommodation, 198
methods of assessing, 195–196
Visual evoked potentials
a test of visual functioning, 196
see also Evoked potentials
Visual functioning
accommodation as a major determinant
of quality, 198
and neural development after visual
deprivation, 113
colour discrimination, 203
competence in newborn, 375–376

Visual functioning (*contd.*)
  contraction of visual field during
      sucking, 202
  coordinated with auditory input, 212
  early process of, 102–103
  effects of angle and distance on
      attention, 202–203
  externality effect, 205, 206–207
  functional implications of, 199
  individual differences in, 231–234
  individual differences in attention, 233
  major research area in neonatal period,
      97, 191–192
  measures of, 195–196
  onset of cortical, 207
  perception in newborns, 371, 372
  post-neonatal development, 207–208
  predisposition of newborn, 375
  preference for faces, 205–206
  preferences in looking, 204–206
  preferentially attending to face,
      382–383, 392
  qualitative changes around 2 months,
      207
  restricted visual field in newborn, 202
  sensitivity to flicker, 203
  sensitivity to motion, 203
  sex differences in, 232
  social interactions, 382–383
  visually directed reaching, 213
Visual system
  colour specific visual activity, 107
  development of, 104–105
  development of visual pathway at birth,
      196–197
  externality effect, 205, 206–207
  level of functioning at birth, 207–208
  myelinization of optic nerve, 197
  myelinization of subcortical, 102
  neural development of other mammals,
      197
  rapid postnatal development, 103,
      107–108, 111
  refraction hypermetropic in newborn,
      197–198
  retarded structural development in
      newborn, 107

types of visual reactions, 110–111
  see also Eye, Retina
Vocal
  perception of phonetic distinctions, 371,
      372, 375
  predisposition to voice, 375
  see also Auditory functioning
Vocalization
  rhythms during sleep, 135, *135*
  rhythms in, 127–128
  sex difference in, 226
  see also Crying
Vulnerability
  as a consequence of adaptation, 10–11,
      398
  increase in, following trauma, 8
  individual differences in, 224–225
  of light for dates babies, 328–330

Wakefulness
  as a behavioural state, 67, 69
  EEG studies during, 58
  neglect in EEG studies, 56
Weight
  breast feeding and gaining, 349, 352,
      356–358
  comparison between bottle and breast
      fed babies, 340, 349, 352,
      356–358
  gain indicating quality of adaptation,
      247
  gain of fetus, 317
  gain of newborn, 317
  individual differences in, 246–247
  intrauterine influences on, 246
  loss following birth, 317
  of neonatal brain at birth, 102
  postnatal growth related to birth,
      246–247
  rapid gain of, 358–361
  see also Growth
Weaning, 356

Yoruba of West Africa
  childbirth practices of, 300